THE MOZART FAMILY

THE MOZART FAMILY

Four Lives in a Social Context

Ruth Halliwell

CLARENDON PRESS · OXFORD

1998

Oxford University Press, Great Clarendon Street, Oxford OX2 6DP
Oxford New York
Athens Auckland Bangkok Bogota Bombay Buenos Aires
Calcutta Cape Town Dar es Salaam Delhi Florence Hong Kong
Istanbul Karachi Kuala Lumpur Madras Madrid Melbourne
Mexico City Nairobi Paris Singapore Taipei Tokyo Toronto Warsaw
and associated companies in
Berlin Ibadan

Oxford is a trade mark of Oxford University Press

Published in the United States
by Oxford University Press Inc., New York

British Library Cataloguing in Publication Data
Data available

Library of Congress Cataloging in Publication Data
Halliwell, Ruth.
The Mozart family : four lives in a social context /
Ruth Halliwell.
p.   cm.
Includes bibliographical references and index.
1. Mozart family.   2. Mozart, Wolfgang Amadeus, 1756–1791.
3. Salzburg (Austria)—History.   I. Title.
ML410.M91H35   1998   780′.92′2—dc21   [B]   97–9676
ISBN 0–19–816371–1

1 3 5 7 9 10 8 6 4 2

Typeset by Graphicraft Typesetters Ltd., Hong Kong
Printed in Great Britain
on acid-free paper by
Biddles Ltd
Guildford & Kings Lynn

This book is dedicated
to my parents
JACK AND RENA GAINFORD
with gratitude and love

PREFACE

꧁꧂

I T is a pleasure to thank all those who have helped this project along in various ways. Generous grants from The British Academy and from the Alice Horsman fund of Somerville College, Oxford, enabled me to make research trips to Salzburg and to Brno; I would like to express my gratitude to both institutions.

The Universitätsverlag Anton Pustet in Salzburg kindly allowed me to use and adapt the map from H. Dopsch and H. Spatzenegger (eds.), *Geschichte Salzburgs: Stadt und Land*, vol. ii, pt. 1, p. 355, as a basis for Map 2. The *MBA* letter texts in Appendix 3 are from *Mozart: Briefe und Aufzeichnungen* (published by the Internationale Stiftung Mozarteum), with kind permission of the publishers Bärenreiter of Kassel. The material reproduced in Appendix 1 is from pp. 340–3 of Neal Zaslaw's *Mozart's Symphonies* by kind permission of Oxford University Press. A&C Black kindly gave permission to reproduce material from O. E. Deutsch, *Mozart: A Documentary Biography*, in Ch. 31.

Many librarians and academics not only arranged with promptitude and courtesy for me to work in 'their' libraries, but showed friendliness beyond the call of duty in helping me find my way around the material. I would particularly like to thank Dr Rudolph Angermüller, Frau Geneviève Geffray, Dr Johanna Senigl, Dr Gabriele Ramsauer, and Frl Therese Muxeneder of the Internationale Stiftung Mozarteum in Salzburg; Frau Christiane Gärtner of the Salzburg Landesarchiv; Dr Ernst Hintermaier of the Erzbischöfliches Konsistorialarchiv in Salzburg (who also helped with several enquiries unconnected with the archive for which he is responsible); Dr Andrea Lindmayr-Brandl of the Institut für Musikwissenschaft of Salzburg University; Professor Heinz Dopsch of Salzburg University; Dr Augustin Kloiber of the Heimatkundliches Museum der Gemeinde St Gilgen; Dr Blažek of the Moravský Zemský Archiv in Brno; and the staff of the Staatsbibliothek in Munich and the Universitätsbibliothek in Salzburg. Here is also the appropriate place to thank Frau Karin Greinz of the Fremdenverkehrsverband in St Gilgen, who kindly hunted out a copy of the out-of-print history of the village school in St Gilgen by Leopold Ziller, and sent it to me when there seemed no other easy way of getting hold of it.

Professor Peter Branscombe, Professor Cliff Eisen, and Dr Edward Olleson read the book in their capacity as advisers to the publishers. All gave generous encouragement and constructive suggestions for its improvement, and saved me from taking some embarrassing mistakes into print. (Needless to say, any that remain are mine alone.) At several points when the going was difficult it was their belief in the value of the work that helped me to keep up the momentum. I am very grateful to them all.

Several people helped by answering specific queries or allowing me to use their work. Professor Leopold Ziller gave me useful information about the musical situation in St Gilgen in the eighteenth century. Professor Neal Zaslaw allowed me to use material from his book on Mozart's symphonies in Appendix 1. Dr Heinz Schuler sent a copy of his article 'Mozart und Mailand', which would otherwise have been difficult to obtain. Dr Josef Mančal answered several questions about Leopold Mozart, and sent me a copy of his article '"... durch beyhülff hoher Recommandation"', which would also not have been easy to obtain from England. (It is a curious feeling to return home after a research trip abroad: one moment all the local bookshops, libraries, and museums are at one's disposal and everything seems possible; a few hours later they all seem remote, and one is again dependent on the kindness of correspondents such as these for the desired information and material.) Cliff Eisen and Peter Branscombe answered many queries on disparate topics, always promptly, and several times alerted me to relevant pieces of bibliography; Peter Branscombe also offered guidance on various points of translation. Professor Manfred Heim not only transcribed Nannerl Mozart's marriage contract, but also added explanatory notes about certain abbreviations and phrases in it; I am very grateful to him. Dr John Arthur gave me useful general advice about the autographs of the letters, and about some of the styles in which passages in them were later crossed out. Professor John Hatcher provided reassurance when I wrote to outline the way in which I proposed to tackle the question of income and expenditure. Bruce Cooper Clarke read Chapter 33 and made several detailed suggestions for its improvement.

Many other people helped in miscellaneous ways. Before my research trip to Brno, Dr Jan Smaczny and Dr Stephen Roe both gave me introductions to people who would have helped me there if necessary. Some debts of gratitude are to personal friends; Stephen and Mary Roe gave me warm hospitality in London, while Emily Kearns, Nicholas Purcell, Catherine Whistler, and Richard Rutherford did the same in Oxford on several occasions. Heidi and Reinhard Hübner, of Eichstätt, Bavaria, undertook all kinds of commission on request—photocopying, sending books, helping with translations, and passing some of my queries on to others for advice. They also opened their house to our whole family, enabling us to combine holiday with work, and putting themselves completely at our disposal in ways that would be difficult to repay. Some of their children also enlisted, and I would like to thank Anne Spanhel for help with translations, and Johannes Hübner and Beate Meierfrankenfeld for making me welcome in Munich during one of my visits.

By comparison with most authors of academic books, I had few relevant credentials when I submitted the proposal for this work to various publishers. It is fitting, therefore, that I should thank Bruce Phillips of Oxford University Press for giving me the chance to write some sample chapters for professional judgement. The initial idea was to write a book focusing specifically on Nannerl Mozart, but it later became clear that it would be better to write about the whole Mozart family. In the course of this expansion the work grew to twice its original planned length, and I am very grateful to Bruce for his enlightened understanding and steady encouragement. I hope that the finished product will justify his confidence in the project. Here is also the appropriate place to thank Helen Foster, Janet Moth, and Mary Worthington for smoothing the book's passage through the production processes, and the designers in the Graphics Department for redrawing the figures and maps.

Lastly, I would like to thank members of my family. When I began work on the book five years ago, our younger son was being educated at home rather than at school. My parents, Jack and Rena Gainford, helped out educationally, domestically, and in other practical ways on countless occasions. With consistent generosity and selflessness, they cancelled plans of their own to fit in with ours, and never arrived without a contribution to the week's meals. Our elder son Luke drew Map 3 and Figs. 1, 3, 4, and 5; he also checked my arithmetical calculations on many occasions. Our younger son Edmund checked the arithmetic needed for the compilation of Table 2, the *Licitations-Protocoll* table. My husband Stephen gave advice on Latin translations, and read parts of the book for me, making many helpful comments. He also undertook several menial but important tasks for me. Above all, however, he gave strong encouragement from the beginning to the end: not only did he keep up my morale on occasions when it was flagging, but also made it a matter of course to rearrange his own work schedules so that everything at home ran smoothly on the occasions when I was away. His generous support is acknowledged here with thanks and love.

CONTENTS

Contents

Contents

ILLUSTRATIONS, MAPS, AND TABLES

❧

Acknowledgements

The author and publisher would like to thank the following for kind permission to reproduce the illustrations:

Internationale Stiftung Mozarteum, Salzburg, Plates 2, 7, 11, 12, 13, 15, 16, and 18.
Museum Carolino Augusteum, Salzburg, Plates 1, 4, 5, 6, 9, and 10.
British Library, Plate 3.
Deutsches Medizinhistorisches Museum, Ingolstadt, Plate 8.
Archiv für Ortsgeschichte, St Gilgen, Plate 14.
Moravský Zemský Archiv, Brno, Plate 17.

LIST OF MAPS

LIST OF FIGURES

LIST OF TABLES

ABBREVIATIONS

AM | *Acta Mozartiana*

AmZ | *Allgemeine musikalische Zeitung*

Deutsch, *Documents* | O. E. Deutsch, *Mozart: Die Dokumente seines Lebens* (*Neue Mozart-Ausgabe*, X/34) (Kassel, 1961). Eng. trans. E. Blom, P. Branscombe, and J. Noble as *Mozart: A Documentary Biography* (London, 1965; 2nd edn. 1966; 3rd edn. 1990). The third English edn. is cited

Eisen, *Documents* | C. Eisen (ed.), *New Mozart Documents: A Supplement to O. E. Deutsch's Documentary Biography* (London, 1991). Unless otherwise stated, references are to the document numbers rather than the page numbers

JRMA | *Journal of the Royal Musical Association*

K. | L. von Köchel, *Chronologisch-thematisches Verzeichnis der Werke W. A. Mozarts* (Leipzig, 1862)

Letters | E. Anderson (ed. and trans.), *The Letters of Mozart and his Family* (London, 1938; rev. 2nd edn. 1966 ed. A. H. King and M. Carolan; rev. 3rd edn. 1985, eds. S. Sadie and F. Smart). The 1st edn. also contains extracts from Constanze's letters to André. Unless otherwise indicated, the 3rd edn. is cited, and references are to letter numbers rather than page numbers

MBA | W. A. Bauer, O. E. Deutsch, and J. H. Eibl (eds.), *Mozart: Briefe und Aufzeichnungen* (Kassel, 1962–75). Unless otherwise stated, references are to letter numbers followed by line numbers (e.g. *MBA* 32/10–15 means letter 32, lines 10–15)

MGSL | *Mitteilungen der Gesellschaft für Salzburger Landeskunde*

MJb | *Mozart-Jahrbuch*

MM | *Mitteilungen der Internationalen Stiftung Mozarteum*

MT | *Musical Times*

MZA | Moravský Zemský Archiv (Moravian Provincial Archives, Brno)

Abbreviations

NAMB	*Neues Augsburger Mozart Buch (= Zeitschrift des historischen Vereins für Schwaben 62/3, Augsburg, 1962)*
Neues MJb	*Neues Mozart-Jahrbuch*
NMA	*Wolfgang Amadeus Mozart: Neue Ausgabe sämtlicher Werke* (Kassel, 1955–)
ÖMz	*Österreichische Musikzeitschrift*
SLA	Salzburger Landesarchiv

INTRODUCTION

❧

A T 11.55 a.m. on St Pantaleon's Day (27 July) 1785, Mozart's sister Nannerl gave birth to her first baby, a son, in the Dancing-Master's House in Salzburg. This was the home of Nannerl's father Leopold, who took the baby to the nearby church of St Andrä at 5.00 p.m. on the same day to have him christened. He was given the names Leopold Alois Pantaleon, and became known as Leopoldl, meaning 'little Leopold'. Just over five weeks later, on the same day that Mozart was writing the Italian dedication to Haydn of his six 'Haydn' string quartets, Nannerl left Leopoldl in Salzburg with her father and travelled the thirty kilometres to her home in the village of St Gilgen, where her husband and five stepchildren awaited her. The arrangement was made primarily for the baby's welfare, childcare conditions in St Gilgen being poor. Leopold used persuasive tactics to win round Nannerl and her husband to his offer to look after Leopoldl, and promised to bear all the costs himself. Just over a year later, Mozart learnt about the matter, though Leopold had tried to keep it secret from him, and asked Leopold to take charge of his two children while he and and his wife Constanze went to England. Leopold refused, suggesting to Nannerl that the travel plans were not well conceived, the responsibility on him would be too great, and the financial recompense offered was in some way unsatisfactory.

Most biographers who have commented on these two incidents have done so mainly to highlight perceived negative aspects of Leopold's character. On the one hand, a typical interpretation goes, he was displaying harshness towards his son Wolfgang that must have been hurtful, probably as vengeance for unforgiven offences. On the other hand, his behaviour to Nannerl has not been seen any more favourably; one author claims that in taking charge of Leopoldl, Leopold was asserting his authoritarian position over Nannerl, who is assumed to have wanted to keep her child, but to have been overruled.[1] And, in perhaps the only attempt to explain the mystery of why Leopoldl's living with his grandfather should have been concealed from Mozart, another author

---

[1] E. Rieger, *Nannerl Mozart: Leben einer Künstlerin im 18. Jahrhundert* (Frankfurt am Main, 2nd edn. 1991), 206–8.

suggests that Leopold had deep, dark secrets: the request by Wolfgang was nothing so simple as a desire to make practical arrangements for the care of his children, but was really the offer of a gift to Leopold, made to regain Leopold's affection; Leopold, on the other hand, saw Leopoldl as a surrogate son, whom he would bring up to be another miraculous prodigy, supplanting Wolfgang; keeping Leopoldl formed part of a barely veiled incest scenario between Leopold and Nannerl; and these pathological manifestations had to be kept secret because of what they might reveal about Leopold's disturbed personality.[2]

Though criticisms of Leopold do not often take such fanciful forms as the one last mentioned, it is nevertheless the case that attempts to portray the relationship between father and son (and father and daughter, though there is not much literature about this) very seldom engage with the question by applying stringent historical procedures to the evidence. In every case such as the one mentioned above, where the relationship comes under the spotlight, Leopold's point of view is apt to be misrepresented through inadequate use of the source material; and the same thing tends to happen in assessing Mozart's relationship with the other members of his family. The reasons for this are discussed below. All in all, therefore, although so many biographical works about Mozart have been written, the view of him in the context of familial assumptions and expectations is seriously and consistently distorted.

The fundamental premises of this book are first that a rigorous contextual study of Mozart's family addresses a subject whose interest and importance have been routinely neglected for two hundred years, and second that such a study necessarily sheds new light on the biography of Mozart himself; the two topics of enquiry cannot be divorced. The book tries to do several things, but its foundation is an account of the course of the lives of Leopold and Maria Anna, Mozart's parents, and Nannerl, his sister, in the context of social conditions then prevailing in Salzburg. As such, it naturally also contains a great deal of material about Mozart himself, but the events of his life are shown primarily in the light of the effects they had on the lives of the others. This gives them a new significance by setting them against the background of family expectations, a context which many biographers have tried to deny because of a passionate feeling that Mozart had to escape from his family before he could write his greatest music. Nevertheless, although this context is one of several ways in which I hope the book will make a substantial contribution to

---

[2] M. Solomon, *Mozart: A Life* (London, 1995), 394–8.

Mozartian biography (these are discussed further below), the heart of the work is the presentation and discussion of the material as it offers insight into the family into which Mozart was born. In order that the case for the value of this material can be presented, a sketch of the shape of the book follows first.

The work is divided into six parts, the divisions being suggested by naturally occurring demarcations in the lives of the people concerned. Part I begins with Leopold Mozart's long struggle for a salary as violinist at the archiepiscopal court of Salzburg, before he could marry the impoverished woman of his choice. It traces his ambition and promising career, which had to be modified when the extraordinary musical talents of the couple's last-born child, Wolfgang, were thrust insistently on the parents' notice. Because Nannerl, four and a half years older, was also musically gifted, Leopold decided first to educate both children himself, and then to travel with them in order to broaden their education and show the fruits of his work through their performances. At the beginning he believed that this would enhance his own career, but he later learnt, to his mortification, that he was given insufficient credit for the educational achievements, while his long absences were recorded by the Salzburg court as debits. From 1762 to 1769 the family was frequently away together, during which absences Leopold almost always drew his Salzburg salary. Because of the high costs of living away from home, however, the chief income was from freelance sources. The experiences of living on an uncertain income, especially during the ordeals of life-threatening illnesses which the family endured several times, gradually strengthened Leopold's belief that a salary was the essential, the only responsible, foundation of family life. Though he wanted both children to be capable of earning a living from music as adults, the educational paths of Nannerl and Wolfgang were not identical, and by the time Nannerl was 18 the demands of Wolfgang's compositional development were causing a situation in which Leopold no longer thought it worth taking her on further tours; she and Maria Anna therefore reluctantly stayed at home. At the same time Leopold was becoming increasingly dissatisfied with his own career progress in Salzburg, but he continued to believe that Wolfgang's development took precedence over everything else. The core material on which this part is based is Leopold's letters to the family's landlords, Lorenz and Maria Theresia Hagenauer; their responses are lost.

Between 1769 and 1777, Leopold and Wolfgang went together three times to Italy and once to Vienna, leaving the women at home. During their carnival visit to Munich in 1774–5, when Wolfgang composed his opera *La finta giardiniera*, Nannerl was permitted to join them for a few weeks, but Maria Anna stayed at home even for this. The events of these years are related in Part II. The first visit to Italy was primarily educational, but Leopold's hope of each subsequent absence was that Wolfgang would gain an honourable appointment. He had been given a salary in Salzburg soon after the accession of the new archbishop, Hieronymus Colloredo, in 1772, but it was very small. Nannerl was being neglected, Leopold's career was causing him humiliations, and he was beginning to worry about getting his children settled before he died. Because he could not yet afford to burn his boats with Salzburg, however, he had simultaneously to try to give the impression that his commitment to his employment there was undiminished. One effect of this attempt was that the women were used as hostages during the visits to Vienna and Munich; they (or at least one of them) had to stay in Salzburg in order to counter suspicion that the whole family intended to take flight. During the summer of 1777, after a protracted period of ignominy for Leopold, dissatisfaction with Salzburg service came to a head, and Wolfgang resigned in order to seek work elsewhere. The core material on which this part is based is Leopold's and Wolfgang's letters home; the replies of Maria Anna and Nannerl from Salzburg are lost.

The years 1777–80 saw the first major family crises. Part III chronicles these events, telling how Wolfgang and Maria Anna travelled as far as Paris in search of a better job for Wolfgang, and Wolfgang returned alone to work in Salzburg again. Debts were incurred to find the starting capital, Wolfgang's salary was lost to the family, and the responsibility on him was heavy: he had to gain a post commanding a salary which could form the foundation of an income for the whole family, or if he was not successful in this, he had to try to earn a handsome sum of money. He failed on both counts, and angered Leopold by his attitude to the enterprise. When he fell in love with the singer Aloysia Weber in Mannheim, dedication to his mission decreased dramatically, and at several critical points his deeds belied his words of devoted affection for his parents and sister. After Maria Anna had died in Paris, Leopold's displeasure with Wolfgang was so severe that he blamed him for the death. Having meanwhile negotiated a new post for Wolfgang in Salzburg, at a greatly enhanced salary, he insisted that Wolfgang return to clear the debt, which had risen to a sum approximately equal to two years' worth of Leopold's salary. During this period, Leopold was separated from Wolfgang for the first time, and was able to devote more attention to Nannerl's musical development. He became much closer to her, and was by now seriously worried about her future financial security. By the time Wolfgang returned, with the utmost reluctance, Leopold was close to breaking point, and the stresses had caused the relationships within the family to change. The core material for this part is letters from Leopold and Nannerl to the travellers, and from the travellers home: the first surviving two-way correspondence.

Wolfgang's next hope of escaping Salzburg, which he now loathed, cropped up in the autumn of 1780, when he was commissioned to write the opera *Idomeneo* for the Munich Carnival of 1780–1. Part IV narrates how the family's situation changed further from 1780 to 1784. Wolfgang wanted to be offered a post in Munich, but was not. However, Colloredo summoned him to Vienna directly afterwards, and there Wolfgang resigned again. Having no appointment in Vienna, he had to earn a living from freelance sources; he hoped he would win a salaried post in time. Leopold was furious at the decision, which left him and Nannerl tied as firmly as ever to Salzburg, but without Wolfgang. During this period, Nannerl herself wanted to marry, but there were hindrances, probably of a financial nature. When Wolfgang married Constanze Weber in 1782, Leopold and Nannerl finally realized that they had nothing more to expect from him. On returning home from the carnival visit to Munich in 1781, they had taken with them the 11-year-old Heinrich Marchand, son of a theatrical family, who was to be their resident pupil. The following year Heinrich was joined by his older sister Margarethe ('Gretl'), and later still by their cousin Johanna ('Hanchen') Brochard. These children came to mean a great deal to Leopold, but the arrangement came to an end in 1784, when Nannerl finally married, aged 33. Her husband was a 47-year-old widower with five surviving children from his previous two marriages. He occupied the administrative post of Pfleger in the village of St Gilgen, some thirty kilometres east of Salzburg, and Nannerl moved there to join him. The core material for this part is the letters from Wolfgang to Leopold and Nannerl, and theirs to him, while he was in Munich; and Wolfgang's letters to them from Vienna. All Leopold's and Nannerl's letters to Wolfgang from March 1781 onwards are lost.

The correspondence between Leopold and Nannerl after she married bears out Leopold's often-repeated claim that he would strive to his dying day for the welfare of his children. Part V covers the years 1784–7, from the wedding until Leopold's death. It describes the circumstances of Nannerl's marriage: the situation of St Gilgen, the difficulties of village life and of her attempts to bring order into her husband's household, the problems of hiring servants and educating the children, and the adjustment to her husband's demands. Because she had an insatiable appetite for new keyboard music, she became involved in a three-way concerto traffic with Wolfgang and Leopold. Wolfgang would send concerto scores to Leopold, who would have the parts copied and send them to Nannerl. The main lines of communication between Salzburg and St Gilgen were a weekly official messenger service, and a more irregular service offered by a woman carrying glassware between the two places. Whichever service was used, Wolfgang's concertos travelled rolled up in a backpack with candles, lard, and anything else ordered by other people on the route. Despite chronic problems in keeping her fortepiano usable in the damp lakeshore house through bitter village winters when no one from Salzburg could get out to service it, Nannerl persisted in playing everything she could lay her hands on, and probably gathered sundry friends, relations, and neighbours to play even the concertos in vastly scaled-down arrangements, in informal domestic circumstances. Leopold's loneliness was at first severe, but it was eased after the birth of Nannerl's son Leopoldl in 1785. The baby stayed with Leopold in Salzburg, because Nannerl was still struggling to master the situation in St Gilgen. Later still, Heinrich returned to Salzburg to work, lived with Leopold again, and helped entertain Leopoldl, whose development was faithfully reported to Nannerl at every opportunity. Leopold became very pessimistic during the last few months of his life; he was ailing, and was worried both about Wolfgang's financial situation and about the education and health of Nannerl's oldest stepson (also called Wolfgang). However, he continued to help and encourage Nannerl in every possible way until his final illness in the spring of 1787. This part ends with a reappraisal of the settlement of Leopold's estate, about which new information has recently become available. The core material consists of Leopold's letters to Nannerl; Nannerl's to Leopold, Leopold's to Wolfgang, all but one of Wolfgang's to Leopold, Nannerl's to Wolfgang, and almost all of Wolfgang's to Nannerl, are lost.

Despite the fact that the correspondence became much more sporadic after Leopold's death, the period from 1787 to 1842 (the year of the death of Mozart's widow Constanze) offers a wealth of documentation relevant to Mozartian biography. Part VI begins by sketching the development of Wolfgang's family life in Vienna and Nannerl's in St Gilgen until Wolfgang's death in 1791. After this, both Nannerl and Constanze had material which soon became sought after; Constanze had Mozart's musical estate in the form of his scores and other important material, and Nannerl the bulk of the surviving correspondence. This part continues by examining how each woman controlled the material in her possession.

Nannerl first used the letters to furnish in 1792 an account of Mozart's childhood for the first biography of Mozart, Schlichtegroll's *Nekrolog*, while Constanze provided another biographer, Niemetschek, with material for his work about Mozart, which appeared in 1798. After Constanze had also become involved in selling Mozart's music to the publishers Breitkopf & Härtel, they too wanted biographical material in order to promote public interest in the edition they were preparing. Gathering anecdotes about Mozart from various sources, they published these under the editorship of Rochlitz in the house journal, the *Allgemeine musikalische Zeitung*. Though it now seems that the exercise was a cynical marketing activity, of which biographical truth was the least important consideration, these anecdotes have taken tenacious hold; like weeds, however many times they appear to have been killed, they sprout up somewhere else. Constanze remarried in 1809, and on the retirement of her second husband Nissen the pair moved to Salzburg. Here Nissen was the first person to be granted access to most of the letters held by Nannerl, and he used them to write his biography, published posthumously in 1828. Though Nissen had a significant advantage over Schlichtegroll and Niemetschek, this work too was idealized; material which might have damaged Mozart's posthumous reputation was suppressed, and some passages in the letters themselves were even deleted. However, though it was not possible for a comprehensive biography to be written while either of the women was still alive, Constanze and Nannerl did not destroy even offending letters, but handed on the bulk of the correspondence intact. This part finishes with an overview of the ways in which this happened, and mentions losses in the correspondence after it had left their hands. The core material consists of Wolfgang's letters to Constanze, his letters begging the fellow Freemason Puchberg for money, Nannerl's and Constanze's letters to Breitkopf & Härtel, Constanze's to the rival publisher André, and the miscellaneous correspondence of Constanze's family after she had married Nissen.

At the centre of the book is a detailed examination of the family correspondence, in so far as it informs the biographical events outlined above. The correspondence covers a period of just over a hundred years, from Leopold's first surviving letters of 1755 to letters written by Mozart's sons in the mid-nineteenth century. The complete German edition, published between 1962 and 1975, numbers almost fifteen hundred items (though a small number are not letters or diary entries). Furthermore, some of Leopold's letters are the length of short pamphlets; the text of this edition occupies more than two thousand pages in four volumes, without the commentary and indexes, to which a further three volumes are devoted.[3] A complete English translation has never yet been made. Emily Anderson's edition, first published in 1938, prints only the letters of Mozart complete, and includes almost nothing after his death in 1791;[4] the letters of other members of his family are given in extract form and many, especially Leopold's to Nannerl from 1784 to 1787, are omitted completely. In the most recent edition of Anderson, the material occupies almost one thousand pages. Despite the quantity of subject-matter, the range of topics covered by it, and the difficult questions it often throws up, the way in which the correspondence is used in biographies of Mozart suggests a widely held view that the material is sufficiently well known for quick, confident, and uncomplicated judgements to be made about the characters of the people concerned in it, and the relationships within the family. This view, I believe, is seriously misguided, and involves fundamental problems in the usage of the letters.

The root of these problems is the persistent and almost universal belief that the chief value of the letters is what they reveal about Mozart himself, for this has meant that about half of the correspondence has been treated as if it did not much matter. When Anderson prepared her edition, for example, she had to omit large parts of the letters not written by Mozart himself, because of space constraints. Although in many cases she found this regrettable, the principles of exclusion reveal her view that the omissions would not damage the depiction of Mozart. Believing that 'tiresome descriptions of illnesses', gossip, and long lists of greetings had little bearing on him,[5] she cut huge parts of the correspondence if it treated of such topics—unless he himself was the writer. In doing so she subscribed to an attitude which has dogged Mozartian biography to its detriment from the beginning—that everything (no matter how trivial) written by Mozart is worth printing, while material written by members of his family (no matter how interesting) is worth printing only if it immediately concerns him. Sixty years on in the third edition, under different editors, Anderson's original sentiments are repeated, albeit with altered wording.[6] This is despite the fact that the letters reveal vastly more about Leopold Mozart than they do about Wolfgang; and since every biography of Mozart discusses the relationship between the two men, valuable contributory material is being routinely ignored. Determined engagement

---

[3] *MBA.*   [4] *Letters.*

[5] *Letters*, Introduction to the 1st edn. (but cited here from its reproduction in the 3rd edn.), p. xvii, inc. n. 3.

[6] *Letters*, Publisher's Preface to the 3rd edn., p. v.

with the whole corpus, on the other hand, not only provides illumination into the lives of the other family members (which in turn adds contexts to Mozart's life), but also imposes a discipline on the interpretation of evidence which could profitably be used to improve future biographical writing about Mozart. I shall return to this point shortly.

The detailed examination of the correspondence on which this book is based starts from the recognition that it was once dialogue, and from the assumptions both that it was coherent and that it mattered to the people who wrote it.[7] The topics discussed in the letters range from music, politics, religious matters, and education to medicine, child care, gossip, marital relationships, and other domestic concerns. Using the whole of such a voluminous correspondence to chronicle the lives of four people who often had separate concerns is a challenging undertaking, but the nature of the central source means that this is not enough. For one thing, there are cases where the veracity of the letter-writer might be suspect, and searches have to be made elsewhere (as well as back and forth in the correspondence) to try to check this. Secondly, the letters throw up problems and questions, which likewise have to be tackled by examining other sources of information. Thirdly, the people who wrote the letters shared certain assumptions, hopes, expectations, and fears about their lives which did not then need to be voiced. These remain hidden from the modern reader unless they can be recovered by a combination of sensitive reading and recourse to other evidence. When this attempt is made, it becomes clear that the society in which Mozart lived was in many respects quite alien to ours.[8] A good illustration of how remote it was is offered by the area of medical practice.

There has not yet been any systematic attempt in Mozartian biography to account for the way in which contemporary medical beliefs influenced the larger outlook of the people who held them. The broader picture has suffered neglect because of the tendency to address attention to concerns of Mozart alone. Thus there is a vast literature, which has been described as an inverted pyramid resting on a small corpus of primary documentation,[9] on Mozart's illnesses and death. While argument rages about these diagnoses, an enormous quantity of more revealing information in

---

[7] The obviousness of these points is a reflection of the extent of the continuing damage to Mozartian biography resulting from the attitudes mentioned.

[8] Conversely, when this is not attempted, psychological anachronisms are sure to be made. This is particularly true of underlying assumptions about death, which are rarely given enough significance by biographers, many of whom apparently continue to believe (in the teeth of all evidence to the contrary) that young men and women should not die.

[9] W. Stafford, *Mozart's Death: A Corrective Survey of the Legends* (London, 1991), 56.

the letters about medicine is ignored because it concerns 'only' the members of his family. Even a cursory acquaintance with the passages concerned shows that the medical assumptions of the Mozarts were linked with diet, morality, superstition, and religion in a complex web of relationships difficult to conceive from a present-day standpoint. What is to be made of Wolfgang's advice to Leopold (so preposterous at first sight as to suggest he must be joking) that he should cure his dizziness by wrapping wagon-grease in paper and wearing it next to his chest, and by wrapping up a particular veal bone (*kayserbeinl*) with a herb thought to cure dizziness and carrying it in his pocket?[10] How was a 'rising womb' thought to settle itself when a castor-oil gland was sewn into a bandage and wrapped round the knees?[11] Was the same principle at work when spirit of hartshorn was applied to the soles of baby Leopoldl's feet in order to draw his intestinal spasms from his body?[12] And what view of anatomy is suggested by the fact that when the 3-month-old baby was turning blue from a choking fit, his grandfather Leopold apparently believed that he could be resuscitated by blowing not only into his mouth but also into his anus?[13] How should beloved but exceptionally vulnerable beings such as babies be regarded? How could the belief that a sick person was in principle curable be reconciled with the simultaneous conviction that recovery or death were in the hands of God? What were the factors involved in deciding whether or not to inoculate against smallpox, and did some parents really believe that the inoculator was the devil? Why was menstruation crucially important to a woman's health? How could an ulcerated foot necessitate fantastically expensive cures at a spa? And how could people die of a cold?

In the burgeoning speciality of the history of medicine, there is a good deal of excellent and stimulating literature discussing the ways in which medical beliefs interacted with other factors in different types of society in times past (and sometimes also present). In particular, patient-centred studies are flourishing; instead of examining the subject from the point of view of the healers, many authors now study what the patients thought about their ailments, how they tried to ward off illness, how they treated themselves, what kind of practitioners they consulted, and how they came to terms with chronic suffering and the fear of death.[14] The central

---

[10] *MBA* 631/60–4 (not in *Letters*).   [11] *MBA* 885/93–100 (not in *Letters*).
[12] *MBA* 881/31–2 (not in *Letters*).   [13] *MBA* 895/4–13 (not in *Letters*).
[14] A good introduction to the themes is in R. Porter, 'The Patient's View: Doing Medical History from Below', *Theory and Society* 14/2 (Mar. 1985), 175–98. For more specific accounts of the interdependency of medical and other assumptions, see the essays in R. Porter (ed.), *Patients*

idea which emerges from such studies is that the interaction of the factors mentioned above formed the very basis of beliefs about how a life should be lived, so that (for example) a north German Protestant would not merely worship differently from a south German Catholic, but would follow different medical, dietary, behavioural, and moral codes too, and there were necessary connections between the beliefs about each of these aspects of life. The medical material in the Mozart letters lends itself admirably to a study of this kind, and without attempting to understand these situations little progress can be made in comprehending the outlook of the characters in the correspondence, and correspondingly little in assessing their relationships with each other. Furthermore, to continue to ignore the significance of this topic is to perpetuate the isolation of Mozart studies from other branches of history, thereby depriving the area of valuable insights, expertise, and the example of rigorous procedural methods.

The case of medicine is a salient example of how distant earlier societies can be from our own, but broader social context would also allow insight into every other aspect of the lives lived by the Mozarts and their contemporaries. Thus Leopold's profound dissatisfaction with the working conditions in Salzburg is clarified when his career progression is set in the context of the court music as a whole. When all the conditions of his employment (rank, salary, extra allowances, and entitlement to leave) are compared with those of his colleagues, it becomes clear that his sour remarks about these people stem from more subtle considerations than he is usually given credit for. This is not necessarily because he was hard-done-by, though he sometimes was, but because the full picture shows a court music structure which did not consistently apply firm principles to the careers of the employees; the arbitrariness of preferment bred seething discontent throughout the band. In a similar manner, to go behind the gossip by seeking further information about the stories told about acquaintances is to gain insight into the most basic concerns of the people in the Mozarts' circle. Many of the stories are about marriage, sickness, death, and financial provision for dependants, and many of the subjects were people in a fundamentally comparable situation to that of the Mozarts. The accounts in the letters give the writer's (usually Leopold's)

and Practitioners: Lay Perceptions of Medicine in Pre-Industrial Society (Cambridge, 1985). Perhaps the most intriguing of these for readers new to the subject is that by G. Karmi, 'The Colonization of Traditional Arabic Medicine', which, because it discusses the continuing use of classical Arabic medical practices (including cautery, cupping, and venesection) in 20th-c. rural medical practice in Syria and Jordan, vividly shows how such a contemporary study can illuminate aspects of past societies.

presentation of the particular case as it stood at the time of writing the letter, but it is not always possible to profit much from these accounts alone. For one thing, sequels to the stories are often not given; and for another, the shared knowledge and cultural assumptions which at that time completed the significance of the stories were not articulated. Enquiring into the previous and further history of the people concerned, which is usually possible through searches in court records, both supplies the factual information necessary to check and enrich the stories,[15] and (if enough enquiries of this kind are made) helps overcome the disadvantage of culture difference.

The necessary consequence of the desire for broader social context is that more attention should be paid to local history. This might seem odd when local history is by its nature fairly narrow, but 'broader' in a biographical context means first of all simply widening the circle of enquiry beyond the immediate family under investigation. Too broad an enquiry is not appropriate; generalizations about eighteenth-century German life as a whole are no use here. What is needed rather is greater knowledge of the local issues and situations that were of immediate concern to the members of Mozart's family. Nor should it be forgotten that artefacts in local museums play their part in illuminating aspects of daily life, especially in the sphere of folk beliefs and practices, which do not usually generate extensive written records. It should not automatically be assumed that such practices have nothing to do with educated families such as the Mozarts; there are hints in the letters, for example, that Leopold Mozart, occasionally at least, took medical advice from his female servants.

It should now be clear that a second important aim of this book is to add an awareness of the types of context mentioned above to the material of the Mozart correspondence, in order to enrich the account of the lives of the family members by recreating some of their 'silent history'. The salient word in the previous sentence is 'awareness'; the work makes no claim to elucidate with systematic thoroughness all or even most of the topics mentioned in the letters which add significance to the course of the lives of the people concerned. That goal will not be attainable until certain prior tasks have been done; for some of the topics more archival groundwork is needed, for others more synthesis of discrete studies. What I try to do here is to direct attention to a fascinating piece of micro-history which could profit from further development.

---

[15] Death, especially the death of a father of under-age children, generated copious documents —pension appeals and the responses to them, guardianship reports, inventories, and estate settlement papers are some examples.

Having presented a justification for writing about Mozart's family, it remains to explain how the work adds something useful to knowledge about Mozart. In fact, the two initial premisses presented on p. xx above are inextricably linked, because the working procedures adopted to write about his family necessarily affect the way in which the source material is used to write about him. In order to illustrate this point, it is necessary to repeat that the book depends essentially on a reading of the letters which remembers that they were once dialogue, and assumes that they were coherent and that they mattered to the people who wrote them.

First, the fact that the letters were once written in two directions necessitates a crucial point of procedure—the missing letters must systematically be taken into account. The survival, for the most part, of only one side of the correspondence has given rise to a tendency to distort its meaning by ignoring its original status as dialogue. The problem has been exacerbated by the failure of the German edition of the correspondence to tackle methodically the question of missing letters. In this work, the letters were numbered and placed in order, according to the date on which they were written; and the decision was taken to assign numbers even to missing letters if their original existence could be demonstrated or inferred from evidence in surviving ones.[16] The intention was to give an overview of the total shape of the correspondence. However, the policy was not implemented consistently, and large numbers of missing letters which certainly once existed have not been given numbers.[17] Because of the authority of the edition, however, there is a tendency to depend uncritically on the information it gives. Essential requirements of any future edition of the correspondence are not only that every missing letter should be numbered, but also that information should be given showing which letter it answers, which answers it, and (where possible) what its contents were. This is not as easy as it might seem: it involves showing alertness to the clues in each existing letter which indicate the possible existence of another letter, now lost; and a sensitivity to earlier and later letters in the sequence, some of which will also be lost. Furthermore, the travelling time of the post has to be taken into account, because a letter frequently answers not the one immediately preceding it when the letters are ordered according to the date on which they were written, but an earlier letter still. The procedure, however, is not a luxury; only by this

[16] *MBA*, vol. v, Foreword, pp. xii–xiii.

[17] Though this is true for all periods of the correspondence, it is particularly damaging in the cases discussed in Ch. 21 and Appendix 2, and in the correspondence between Leopold and Nannerl after her marriage.

means, for example, can the correspondence chronicling discord be discussed accurately and concisely. Serious misrepresentations of some of the family disputes have been made through failure to take adequate account of missing letters.[18]

Secondly, the premisses that the correspondence was coherent and of importance to the people concerned mean that even when it appears utterly garbled, confusing, and perhaps trivial to boot, the will must exist to tease out its meaning. Often, of course, there is simply not enough information to do so, but on a significant number of occasions the effort is rewarded by a realization of something noteworthy. This might concern the dating of a letter or other document, the identification of a person referred to only by an incomplete form of the name, the identification of one of Mozart's works, or something significant about the words themselves which has been overlooked. With respect to this last case, it should be noted that there are very many inaccuracies in the Anderson translations, a substantial number of which obscure the meaning of passages in serious ways.[19]

Following the above-mentioned procedures also imposes a more general discipline on the reading of the letters which is beneficial to all questions of interpretation. It is difficult to ignore the point of view of one of the correspondents when the effort has been made, slowly and painstakingly, to reconstruct what (s)he wrote in a letter now lost, and to ponder why (s)he wrote it. Nor is it so likely that the chronology of the correspondence will be disregarded, that assertions unsupported by any evidence will be made, or that too much will be read into small amounts of information. Furthermore, close involvement with the primary documents discourages excessive dependence on secondary literature, and a fuller knowledge of the letters fosters a sensitivity to the complexity of characters—in particular, perhaps, the recognition that the things people write to and about each other do not necessarily represent their immutable opinion.

In his thought-provoking book about books about Mozart, William Stafford studies different ways in which Mozart's life has been portrayed by biographers, especially in relation to his death. Tackling successively six major ideas about how Mozart's character and the course of his life have been perceived, and surveying the evidence assembled by authors in support of each of these ideas, Stafford notes objections to each in turn.

---

[18] See Ch. 21, pp. 351–2, for one example.
[19] Examples of all these new findings are noted in the book, but are too numerous to list here.

These invariably address the question of the selection and interpretation of evidence in order to present the desired case. In the conclusion to the book, Stafford presents two opposing views about whether it is possible to cleanse the biographical portrait of Mozart and depict him more accurately. The first view is negative, and argues that even if all the myths based on dubious foundations could be stripped away, there would still be formidable problems concerned with the interpretation of the information conveyed by the family correspondence, and it would be naïve to suppose that future writers would be less fettered by their own outlook than past ones have been. The second view is more positive, and argues that if stringent historical standards are applied to biographical writing about Mozart, a truer picture will emerge, and that the letters, if read carefully, remain a wonderful and trustworthy source. He invites the reader to choose the preferred conclusion.[20] Stafford earlier makes the point that major new finds of material relating to Mozartian biography are now unlikely to be made, so that future work will hinge increasingly on better interpretation and evaluation of evidence already available.[21] That is precisely the third major aim of this book. Moreover, in trying to show how the methods used here to write about Mozart's family can contribute to a more accurate picture of him, it becomes clear that any attempt to study him without sufficiently considering the expectations of his family is a futile undertaking; if the attitudes of his closest relations to his actions and decisions are not taken sufficiently into account, his own assumptions and thought processes about those actions and decisions are necessarily also being devalued. This is true even when he appears to be trying to escape the claims of his family. It is also why the two opening premises of this introduction are linked.

The key to everything the book tries to do is context. First, there is the internal context of the letters themselves, with the implications detailed above. The most urgent need of English-language Mozart scholarship is a complete translation of the correspondence with a critical apparatus which addresses these. Secondly, there is the context of official documents in the category that would now be called public records, especially the marriage contracts, and the wills, inventories, guardianship reports, and other documents of death. Although a number of such documents relating to Mozart and some members of his family have been printed and are easily accessible, it is very rare indeed to find even a partial explanation of their meaning in the context of the circumstances of their creation. This

---

[20] Stafford, *Mozart's Death*, 263–70.   [21] Ibid. 28.

inevitably means that they are unlikely to be well understood. Until the necessary background information about the function of the documents, and the ways in which they related to each other, percolates through into the literature on Mozart, the information they offer needs to be used with the utmost caution.[22] Thirdly, there is the broader social context. Although this has already been discussed, the remarks above need to be qualified by reference to the work on 'applied' types of context which has been and is being done.

The most fruitful studies of Mozart's life in the last twenty years or so have surely been those which add something new by exploring the conditions of certain aspects of the society in which he lived and worked. For the ten Viennese years, stimulating works have resulted: some examples are the biographies set in the social context by Robbins Landon and Braunbehrens; studies of Mozart's links with Freemasonry; much research into financial matters, including Moore's recognition of the usefulness of studying Mozart's estate in the context of other Viennese estates; Bär's work on the illnesses, death, and burial; and Morrow's and Edge's studies of Viennese concert life. There are also distinguished contextual studies of aspects of Mozart's work which are not confined to the Viennese years, such as Zaslaw's work on the symphonies, and Branscombe's examinations of the literary and theatrical background. And despite continuing resistance in some quarters to the study of Mozart's music in relation to that of his contemporaries,[23] it seems certain that this type of investigation too will thrive, to the enhancement of the subject. As far as the Salzburg contexts are concerned, the situation in some respects is not as advanced, though this emphatically does not mean that little is being done. With respect to musical matters, Eisen and M. H. Schmid have studied Mozart against the background of the Salzburg compositional tradition, and have made outstanding contributions to the study of performance practice (including the Mozarts' many domestic performances) by examining the relationship between Mozart's autograph scores and the authentic performance parts derived from them; and Eisen has also worked extensively on Leopold Mozart. Hintermaier has drawn on local archival documents to produce a study of the structure

---

[22] See Ch. 35, pp. 615–16, for an example of the complicated connections between some of these documents.

[23] Zaslaw describes an occasion when he encountered intense hostility at a conference for presenting a paper in which he mentioned his view that this was a reasonable thing to attempt. See N. Zaslaw, 'Mozart as a Working Stiff', in J. M. Morris (ed.), *On Mozart* (Woodrow Wilson Center Press and Cambridge, 1994), 102–12.

and the personnel of the court music in Salzburg, enabling the careers of Leopold and Wolfgang to be compared with those of their colleagues. Outside musical matters, Schuler and others have published genealogical studies of many of the families with whom the Mozarts were acquainted. The best of these enable the comments about the families in the Mozart correspondence to be more fully and sensitively understood, by drawing on further information to supplement the stories told in the letters. There is also an illustrious tradition of local history in Salzburg. The city's local archives and museums contain a wealth of source material, which is used with impressive scholarship to publish works on every aspect of its history, from studies of the noblest institutions to examinations of popular beliefs. To repeat the view mentioned above, however, what could still profitably be done is to apply more of this research to a sustained study of Mozart and his family in Salzburg; much of it is discrete, and needs synthesis before the local contexts will reveal the full extent to which they can serve Mozart studies. Given that the Mozart correspondence is itself often drawn on as a rich source of information about life in Salzburg in the mid-eighteenth century, the potentially reciprocal nature of this undertaking is clear. There is ample scope to weave Mozart studies further into the web of other historical pursuits if this is thought a desirable goal.

A number of miscellaneous points should here be addressed, to explain the principles behind my handling of certain aspects and details of the subject-matter. Perhaps the most necessary caution to be given is a statement of what the book is not. Mozart scholarship has become increasingly technical and detailed, and the number of sub-specialities within it (all with implications for the writing of biographical works) means that it is difficult for one person to master the evidence sufficiently to write a comprehensive biography which is equally strong in all desirable respects. Moreover, the form of this particular book was dictated by the neglected material in the Mozart family correspondence, which I believe provided of itself very coherent structural threads: from the beginning of the project, the shape of the work I wanted to write was in all essentials perfectly clear to me. Lastly, the material I chose to use to present the story of the Mozart family is copious. Because of all these considerations (personal deficiencies in expertise, the desire to keep the threads untrammelled, and the need to avoid excessive length), there are certain topics it was never my aim to address. I do not write systematically about Mozart's music: the few discussions of it that do appear usually serve a purpose such as illustrating the role of music in the Mozarts' domestic life. Nor do I discuss Leopold Mozart's compositions in any sustained way. Mozart's life after his father's death is handled with brevity, and many aspects of his ten Viennese years are not treated in detail unless they can be shown to be relevant to one of the central themes. No doubt many readers will be disappointed by some of these omissions, but to have covered more ground would have been to increase the length further and to risk losing sight of the threads which give the book its structure.

A related consideration is responsible for the fact that though the letters are referred to almost constantly, they are not quoted as extensively as many readers might wish. Though this is particularly regrettable in view of the lack of a complete English edition, the peculiar ways in which the correspondence has been used in biographies of Mozart made it necessary to devote substantial space to questions concerning its meaning and interpretation. It gives me no satisfaction to have replaced so much of the colourful and vigorous language of the letter-writers with my own inevitably duller abridged summaries, but ultimately and reluctantly I decided that it would be better for the focus of the book to restrict the quantity of translated quotations. A few practical points to be noted about the use of the letters in this book follow. First, *MBA* includes not only letters but also diary entries, Mozart's thematic catalogue entries, and sundry other items, while *Letters* includes only letters. When I refer to a letter (or part of one) not included in *Letters*, this is indicated by a footnote giving the *MBA* reference and followed by a phrase such as 'not in *Letters*'; in references to diary entries or other items which *Letters* never purported to include, however, the *MBA* reference is given with no mention of *Letters*. Secondly, though I always give a reference to *Letters* when a passage under discussion is included there, the translations are all my own. Thirdly, in the translated quotations, I have followed the orthography and punctuation of the original as far as possible. This is a potentially confusing practice, since the Mozarts often spelt the names of particular acquaintances in several different ways, but I prefer to preserve as much of the character of the originals as possible; where any real doubt as to identification results, I indicate my own view. Outside the quotations, however, I adopt the spelling and the form of people's names used by the *MBA* index. This again is potentially confusing, not least because the *MBA* commentaries sometimes give a name in a different form from that used in the index; but since my book depends so heavily on the letters texts as rendered by *MBA*, it seemed better to adopt a system already in use than to introduce further complexities. Some families making their appearance in the book were so large, and contained so many 'Johann's or 'Maria Anna's (most, fortunately, with at least one additional name allowing a distinction to be made) that it would have been unwise (and very unfriendly to *MBA* users) to do otherwise than accord with this index. The only occasions when I depart from the principle are those when the *MBA* index has Germanicized a well-known English or semi-English name; this happens, for example, with the composer Stephen Storace, whom *MBA* calls 'Stephan', and whom I change back to 'Stephen'. Characters in the book but not in *MBA* have their names rendered according to the forms used in the documents which are most likely to give the 'authentic' version (although even the owner of a name could adopt a number of different variations). Because the cast of characters is large, and many appear several times in different narratives throughout the book, cross-references are provided for easier orientation, and the index is partially biographical. A glossary is provided both to give help with terms that may be unfamiliar to some readers, and because many terms are virtually untranslatable. Place-names are anglicized where appropriate, and in cases where the name has changed since the eighteenth century, both names are given (this applies particularly to places formerly in the Habsburg Empire and now in states such as the Czech Republic).

An important aspect of the book is money—what people earned, how much was needed for the support of a family, the expenses of travelling, the value of a deceased person's estate, the level of pensions, and so forth. The main question facing the author becoming involved with these matters is how the sums of money mentioned are to be made meaningful to the modern reader. In this book, the method adopted is to indicate salary and other income levels where known, and to allow the cost of items bought to be compared with these. Thus, for example, the cost of the dress Nannerl Mozart had made for her visit to Munich in the winter of 1780/1 was 70 gulden (the abbreviation 'fl.' is henceforth used for gulden) at a time when her father was earning 454 fl. annually. Had his salary been the family's only income, the dress would have accounted for about two months' worth of it. In fact, both Wolfgang and Nannerl were also earning during this period, and the family was still living together, so the financial situation was presumably fairly comfortable; nevertheless, the purchase seems quite startling when modern income and clothes expenditure relationships are considered. In order that comparisons of this kind can be made easily, I convert all sums of money mentioned to gulden (there were 60 kreuzer per gulden). This, however, is not a straightforward procedure. More than sixty different types of coin make their appearance in the family correspondence, and the relationships between them all changed during the Mozarts' lifetimes. Many coins (the ducat is one example) existed in different types, giving differing gulden values, and often the type of ducat or other coin mentioned in the letters is not specified. Another problem is that when coins were being exchanged at frontiers while travelling, the rate could differ from that offered by merchants acting as bankers. And though the letters often themselves indicate a gulden conversion, it is not always accurate. For example, Leopold Mozart sometimes gave a conversion based on the hypothetical assumption that a particular small-denomination foreign coin was equivalent to a particular small-denomination coin in Salzburg currency. Usually it was not (he was aware of this), and by the time the error in his conversion had been multiplied several times so that the larger-denomination coins in the same currencies could be compared, the discrepancy could be considerable.[24] He nevertheless found his system useful as a gauge in comparing the cost abroad with that at home of cheap items such as food. Difficulties such as these mean that to give precise gulden equivalents for all the sums of money mentioned in the correspondence is an unrealistic aim, but in most of the more common cases it is possible to give conversions accurate enough for the exercise to be profitable. Until recently, biographies of Mozart tended to iron out many of the intricacies of currency conversion (giving, for example, a flat and unchanging rate of $4\frac{1}{2}$ fl. per ducat, despite the existence of the several types of ducat and the fluctuations in their values during different periods).[25] Increasingly, however, this is now seen as unsatisfactory. Scholars studying eighteenth-century Viennese musical life have begun to draw attention to the importance of the complex world of finance, and to the desirability of giving clearer and more accurate accounts of it. In this book, therefore, although imperfectly, I try to give a conversion to gulden, accurate

---

[24] An example of this is in his letter to Hagenauer from Paris of 8 Dec. 1763—*MBA* 73/70–87 (not in *Letters*). Here, because Leopold's approximate conversion was based on the equivalence of the French sols and the Salzburg kreuzer, he finished with 8 Salzburg fl. per French louis d'or. Yet he was actually receiving 11 fl. (sometimes even slightly more) per louis d'or as an exchange rate while in Paris, as his letters of 1 Apr. and 8 June 1764 show—*MBA* 83/143–51 and 89/59–65 (neither passage in *Letters*).

[25] Here it should be noted that the *MBA* commentaries do not give consistently accurate conversion information.

for the date, of each sum mentioned. Much of the time the necessary information is given in the correspondence and is satisfactory; sometimes the value of one denomination in relation to another is given in a different but contemporary reliable document; as regards the ducats circulating in Vienna, I have relied on the work of Dexter Edge for the conversions; and on the occasions where the conversion is doubtful I have indicated this. Nevertheless, a major desideratum is a comprehensive survey addressing this complex topic and making easily accessible the necessary conversion tables for a wider range of coins.

The least known material used in the book is that from the Berchtold family archive held in Brno. Hardly any of it has yet appeared in works about Mozart, and though a good deal of information from it is incorporated here, there is also a considerable amount which awaits further study and publication. I particularly regret that time and resources did not permit me to attempt to trace the paths by which the several documents found their way to the castle of Buchlov, the family seat of one branch of the Berchtold family, and the place from which the archive was removed to Brno at the end of the Second World War. For there are important documents pertaining to Leopold Mozart's estate (the will and the *Sperrrelation* inventory) which are still missing; and the fact that the *Licitations-Protocoll* (the record of Leopold's personal belongings which were sold at auction after his death) is in the Berchtold archive suggests that the transmission history of the Berchtold papers might shed light on the fate of the missing documents. A further task relating to the Berchtold archive concerns the Family Chronicle, which was apparently compiled by a number of different people at different dates; handwriting and paper analyses would no doubt bring to light useful evidence about which members of the Berchtold family handled the chronicle, and when it passed through their hands.

There are many descriptions of illness in the book, and I nearly always present the diagnosis as it was given in the correspondence or other contemporary documentation. This is because I find it more interesting to try to understand the thought processes of the people concerned about their ailments than to try to speculate (belatedly and often futilely) what might 'really' have been wrong with them. Occasionally, however, I suggest a modern diagnosis for a given set of symptoms if there is sufficient reason to do so: for example, when Nannerl's baby Leopoldl had *Mehlhund* (which literally means 'flour dog', which caused his mouth to become white and sore, and which later spread to his genital area, also causing internal discomfort), it would have been excessively cautious and clumsy to avoid the use of the word 'thrush', considering that there is no adequate phrase for the translation of *Mehlhund*.

Two final points: the German term *clavier*, a generic one for several types of keyboard instrument, is translated throughout as 'keyboard' or 'keyboard instrument'; and Mozart's works are referred to by the original and most familiar Köchel numbers.

PART I

The United Family
(1747–1769)

1

'The Order of Patched Trousers':
The Marriage of Leopold and Maria Anna

WHEN Mozart's parents married on 21 November 1747, the event marked the end of several years of struggle to establish the necessary financial foundations. Their union was a love match, and when the love began Maria Anna was well-nigh destitute while Leopold was eking out a living which could support only himself. One of their feelings on marriage, therefore, was perhaps satisfaction that they had had the tenacity to win the fight for their love. But what they could not then have imagined was that one of the children to be born to them would not only determine the future course of the lives of everyone in the family, but would even cause the marriage itself to be built into theories of God's purpose for man on earth. Since there does not survive one all-embracing, coherent, and unambiguous statement by anyone in the Mozart family about these matters, it is necessary to study clues throughout the Mozart correspondence and from the early lives of Leopold and Maria Anna in order to try to understand how and why their lives and outlooks were shaped by the experience of being the parents of Mozart.

The difficulties in comprehension begin in Leopold Mozart's youth, for it is not known what ideas he initially had about a career, nor why he abandoned what ought to have been a promising education. His father Johann Georg Mozart was a bookbinder and citizen of the imperial free city of Augsburg. Johann Georg's road to marriage had been the traditional one for craftsmen—he had first married the widow of his master, thus obtaining the business, and on her death he had promptly married a younger woman. The first marriage took place in 1708 when he was 29 years old, and it remained childless. His wife died after ten years of marriage, enabling Johann Georg in 1718, at the age of 39, to marry a woman who could bear children. The interlocking of marriage with the establishment of a business was the accepted norm.[1]

---

[1] J. Mančal, 'Vom "Orden der geflickten hosen": Leopold Mozarts Heirat und Bürgerrecht', in Mozartgemeinde Augsburg (ed.), *Leopold Mozart und Augsburg* (Augsburg, 1987), 31–2.

The first child to be born to the couple, on 14 November 1719, was Johann Georg Leopold, the future father of Mozart. He was followed into the world by eight siblings. His father evidently attached importance to education, for Leopold was sent as young as 4 to the Jesuit school of St Salvator. The Jesuits educated him, there and in their Lyceum, until 1736, the year in which his father died. By this time he was 17, and he left school in August with a glowing report a few months after his father's death.[2] His school years were devoted to a scholastic education based on Classical languages, literature, and philosophy (which embraced mathematics and various branches of science). Music was also an important part of the curriculum, and Leopold learnt to play the violin and organ, and to sing. As well as appearing on the school stage, he was a choirboy at the Church of St Ulrich and St Afra, and at the monastery of Heilig Kreuz. It is not known what his relations with his father had been like, how he felt about the death, nor what he did for the first sixteen months after leaving school. But the pride and independence he had inherited as the first son of a citizen who was his own master could only have been reinforced by the education provided by the Jesuits. One aim of their schools was to train the mind and heart in order to make self-advancement possible.

Details about how the family fared after the death of Leopold's father are lacking, but in December 1737 Leopold matriculated at Salzburg's Benedictine university.[3] Salzburg was an important metropolitan centre, and its university drew students from all over south Germany and Austria. But the thoughts both of Leopold and of his mother about this step, the purpose of the education, and how it was paid for, are all unknown. There is some suggestion that Leopold had let it be believed in Augsburg that he intended to become a priest, but it is not known for certain whether this was ever a serious inclination of his, or whether it was simply in his interests at one stage to pretend that it was.[4] It is possible, for example, that a declaration of an intention to enter the Church enabled him in one way or another to study at university. Nor is it known whether his decision to go to university implied determination at that point to become

---

[2] J. Mančal, 'Leopold Mozart (1719–1787): Zum 200. Todestag eines Augsburgers', in W. Baer (ed.), *Leopold Mozart zum 200. Todestag* (Augsburg exhibition catalogue, 1987), 9.

[3] Ibid. 12.

[4] The documentation for this suggestion comes from Wolfgang's letter to Leopold of 11 Oct. 1777—*MBA* 347/156–65 (*Letters* 219b). Wolfgang had met Franziskus Erasmus Freysinger, who had known Leopold during his youth, and who told Wolfgang about the young Leopold's masterful organ playing, and about how he had 'led the holy men down the garden path about becoming a priest'.

entirely self-reliant, rather than to take over his father's business; though he never in fact returned to live in Augsburg, he may initially have intended to after the completion of his degree.

Meanwhile another family story was unfolding in St Gilgen, a village some thirty kilometres east of Salzburg. This was the home for most of their married life of Mozart's maternal grandparents, the Pertls. Wolfgang Nikolaus Pertl, like Leopold Mozart, was also from a craftsman's family. He too had a good education, which began at the Gymnasium of St Peter's Benedictine Abbey in Salzburg and culminated in the study of law at Salzburg University. Like Leopold Mozart, Wolfgang Pertl was active in music and drama throughout his school career. Graduating around 1697, he undertook further legal training before being taken on by the Salzburg court in one of its administration departments.[5] The court needed numerous administrators with legal backgrounds, because apart from central departments requiring legal expertise, each outlying *Pfleg* (an administrative area outside the city but within the *Land* or province of Salzburg) was manned by a Pfleger (administrator) with the help of one or more clerks, and the Pfleger had to be able to administer justice in simple cases, as well as collect taxes and perform a host of other duties. There were some thirty-six Pfleger in the archbishopric of Salzburg, and since the clerks too were often aspiring Pfleger, a steady stream of lawyers was needed.

Pertl did not marry until 1712, by which time he was almost 45 and his wife (the widow Eva Rosina Barbara Puxbaum) almost 31. At first they lived in the Bergstrasse in Salzburg, on the east side of the River Salzach, but moved to St Andrä in the Lavanttal in 1714, when Pertl obtained the post there of Pflegeamtsmitverwalter (co- or deputy Pfleger).[6] Here, things started to go badly wrong for them. Pertl succumbed to a serious five-month illness of *Frais* (a term embracing cramp-like symptoms of all kinds) accompanied by mental disturbances. He almost lost his life, and he failed to remain in control of the finances of the *Pfleg*.[7] Despite leaving St Andrä with a question mark over his competence at balancing the books, however, he obtained an interim appointment as clerk in Maria Saal, until on 21 June 1716 he was sworn in as Pfleger of Hüttenstein and St Gilgen.[8]

---

[5] R. Angermüller and H. P. Kaserer, 'St Gilgen und die Mozarts', *MM* 32 (1984), 5–6.

[6] Ibid. 7.

[7] L. Ziller, *Vom Fischerdorf zum Fremdenverkehrsort: Geschichte St Gilgens und des Aberseelandes* 3 vols. (St Gilgen, 1988–90), i. 38–9.

[8] Angermüller and Kaserer, 'St Gilgen und die Mozarts', 7.

Whether Pertl was poor at handling money, or whether the situations he was in were really too difficult to manage, will only emerge from a more thorough study of the court records, but in St Gilgen too he ran into financial problems. The duties of the Pfleger of St Gilgen are discussed more fully later in this book[9] (for Nannerl Mozart's husband was to hold the same post), but broadly speaking he had to manage every aspect of the *Pfleg*, acting as magistrate, tax collector, customs officer, and peacekeeper. He also had to liaise with other court officers (hunting and fishing officials, for example) with business in the area, and supervise the many industries carried on around the Abersee, the lake on which St Gilgen stood (now called the Wolfgangsee). One big job, for example, was the supervision of the iron industry, which used the Abersee as an important link in the transport of iron from the mines near Leoben in the east to Salzburg and beyond. And he had to settle accounts with and report to the court in Salzburg. The *Pfleg* was supposed to be self-financing, which is to say that the expenses of the Pfleger and his assistants were meant to be met by income from customs duties, other taxes, fines for misconduct levied by the Pfleger himself, and so forth. Pertl and his family (together with the three clerks) were provided with accommodation, and Pertl was supposed to be able to pay himself a basic salary of 250 fl. annually. In addition he was entitled to benefits in kind, such as fish and game.[10]

Unfortunately for his family, Pertl was wholly unable to make ends meet in St Gilgen. He complained that it was quite impossible to do the work with fewer than three clerks, since the workload was constantly increasing. Already by 1722 the *Pfleg* was showing a negative balance of around four years' worth of Pertl's salary; his wife's fortune had disappeared, and he was struggling for his very existence. Many accounts of Pertl describe him as a conscientious, hard-working, honest, sober, and kind man, and one author suggests that he lacked the harshness to levy fines for the common offences of fornication and adultery, so that one of his sources of income was not rich enough.[11] A detailed contextual study of his management of the *Pfleg*'s finances, however, is lacking.

When Pertl first went to work in St Gilgen the accommodation both for the offices of the *Pfleg* and for his family and staff was completely

[9] See Ch. 25.

[10] H. Schuler, 'Mozarts Grossvater Pertl in St Gilgen', *MM* 23 (1975), 30.

[11] Ibid. 30–1, esp. n. 22, which explains how the Pfleger was entitled to keep a proportion of all the fines he levied. Other contemporary accounts bearing on Pertl's character are quoted in Ziller, *Geschichte St Gilgens*, i. 37–40, but though Ziller usually appears to be transmitting exactly the wording of official documents, he often does not cite the source precisely. This is a pity, because the work is a mine of information about the area, and it is clear that Ziller's knowledge of his subject is both broad and deep.

inadequate. Pertl's major achievement was that he persuaded the current archbishop, Prince Franz Anton von Harrach, to authorize the building of a large new house on the lakeshore. It was to consist of offices on the ground floor and living accommodation above. By the time the house was finished in 1720, Pertl and Eva Rosina had had two daughters, one of whom had died. On Christmas Day 1720 their third was born. This was Maria Anna Walburga, the future mother of Mozart. Her sister, Maria Rosina Gertrud, was sixteen months older.[12]

Pertl's financial situation became increasingly hopeless, and it is even possible that it affected his health. In January 1724 he made a desperate appeal to the court, insisting that it was impossible to make the *Pfleg* pay. Two months later he was dead, and the authorities moved into action. His estate, in accordance with the normal procedures, was frozen or 'barred' until investigations had revealed the state of his finances. Only when all the debts had been paid could any of it be left to his family. Because his finances were intertwined with those of the *Pfleg*, a thorough investigation had to be carried out into the bookkeeping as soon as it became apparent that there were financial problems. In the course of the investigations it emerged that the offices and the books of the *Pfleg* were in chaos. Many records were damaged by mildew, having been kept in damp conditions with inadequate ventilation (the building apparently suffered from damp from the beginning, and this was still a problem when Nannerl later lived there in the 1780s and 1790s). Whether this situation had developed through Pertl's incompetence, or whether it was rather a reflection of his poor physical and mental health, is not clear. Worse still, there was now a deficit of 1,141 fl. 58 kr. Pertl's furniture and library were confiscated to repay the money, and when this was not enough three Salzburg traders who had been Pertl's financial guarantors were required to make good the deficit.[13] The house, of course, was needed for the next Pfleger. This left Eva Rosina with no roof over her head, no money, no property of any kind, and two little girls of 3 and 4 to bring up on her own. She returned to Salzburg, and was granted a widow's pension of 8 fl. per month, which was later raised to 9 fl.[14] How she managed on it is not known, but she must have belonged to the poorest class of respectable people, and was perhaps in a similar position to that of the 'poor cap-mender' Sandl Auer, whom Leopold's charity was to help in 1777.[15] Eva Rosina's elder daughter Maria Rosina Gertrud died in 1728, a month before her ninth

---

[12] Schuler, 'Mozarts Grossvater Pertl in St Gilgen', 32–3.
[13] Ziller, *Geschichte St Gilgens*, i. 39.   [14] Mančal, 'Vom "Orden der geflickten hosen"', 36.
[15] Sandl Auer's story is told in Ch. 17.

birthday. In 1734, when the younger daughter Maria Anna was 14, Eva
Rosina successfully appealed for the continuation of her pension. The
appeal mentioned that Maria Anna was continually unwell.[16] It is not
known whether Maria Anna was ever able to work to support herself and
her mother before her marriage. The only field open to her would have
been some kind of domestic work. Since the portrait in oils of Maria Anna
shows her holding a piece of lace (lace-making was a cottage industry
in the Abersee area),[17] it is possible that she and her mother undertook
needlework of various kinds to supplement the pension. This was at least
work that could be done seated at home, and put down at times of illness.

Leopold Mozart had arrived in Salzburg in 1737, and he married
Maria Anna Pertl in 1747. From a later reference by him to the fact that
they had thought of marrying 'many years' before their desire was realized, it has been suggested that the two might have met almost as soon
as Leopold arrived.[18] If they did so, the fact might have had some bearing on the abandonment of Leopold's studies at the university. At first
he did well in Salzburg. At the end of his first year his report was satisfactory. But things started to go wrong soon afterwards, and in 1739 he
was required to leave for want of application. Leopold did not contest the
decision, so he needed abruptly some means of earning his livelihood.[19]
What could have induced him to do something apparently so foolhardy?
A number of factors might have influenced him, but there are too many
missing links in the evidence to construct anything but hypotheses.

The most banal is a mere lack of motivation—a disinclination to continue to apply himself to the work required in the absence of paternal discipline. Much later in life, he wrote a letter to Wolfgang in which he
commented on the fact that as a young man he had lacked a father's advice
and had had to accustom himself to thinking out for himself the best course
to take.[20] This may have been a hint that he felt he had suffered from the
lack of paternal stimulus, but it is equally possible that he mentioned the
fact simply to impress on Wolfgang his good fortune in having a father
to advise him.

A second possibility is that he had been destined (either by adults
who might have advised him in Augsburg or by his own inclination) to

[16] Angermüller and Kaserer, 'St Gilgen und die Mozarts', 8.

[17] This picture is thought to have been painted around 1775 by Rosa Hagenauer-Barducci.

[18] Mančal, 'Vom "Orden der geflickten hosen"', 32. Leopold's reference to their having
wanted to marry 'many years before' the event is in a letter to Maria Anna of 21 Nov. 1772—*MBA*
267/17–19 (*Letters* 162).

[19] Mančal, 'Leopold Mozart (1719–1787)', 12.

[20] Leopold to the 22-year-old Wolfgang, 6 Apr. 1778—*MBA* 444/71–81 (*Letters* 301).

enter the Church, but had decided in Salzburg not to do so after all. If this was so, there are various conceivable reasons for the change of mind. He might have decided that he did not want to remain celibate, that he did not feel a strong enough commitment to the priesthood, or that there was something else he had a strong desire to do. Since he later showed enormous dedication both to marriage and to a completely different discipline (music) from the one in which he was being trained at the university, it is tempting to believe that one or both of these were goals he had in mind when he abandoned his studies.

There are two passages in the Mozart correspondence which might have a bearing on this stage of Leopold's life. Both were written to the Mozarts' landlord Lorenz Hagenauer from the longest journey made by the Mozarts, the tour of Europe from 1763 to 1766. In the first passage, Leopold was responding to Hagenauer's news that his 18-year-old son Kajetan had decided to enter St Peter's monastery as a novice. Leopold's reaction was cautious, and he stressed the importance of the novitiate year, during which the novice had the opportunity to change his mind. He also likened Kajetan's step to his own decision to enter the 'Order of Patched Trousers' (a jocular reference to marriage).[21] In the second passage, Leopold was describing to Hagenauer the meeting in 1766 of an old Salzburg acquaintance who had entered the Church but had subsequently discovered he had no vocation for it. He was now wandering round Europe, his life an aimless wreck. This time, Leopold used strong language, stating explicitly that young people should not be allowed to take such important decisions under the age of 25, since they could not yet know their own abilities and desires. Many would find that they could serve God in a more appropriate way (the two examples Leopold gave were through wealth and through an 'intelligent head') if they would only wait a little longer.[22]

When Leopold wrote both these passages, his own life had assumed a direction impossible to foresee from his early educational path. He was Vice-Kapellmeister at the Salzburg court and was educating his own children,

---

[21] Leopold to Hagenauer, 27 Nov. 1764—*MBA* 93/184–206 (*Letters* 32).

[22] Leopold to Hagenauer on 16 May 1766—*MBA* 108/83–120 (*Letters* 41, but most of the passage is omitted). Leopold was not alone in his proposal to delay the taking of monastic vows. In the 1770s the Austrian chancellor Wenzel Kaunitz drew up a series of regulations intended to reduce the influence of monastic houses, one of them being a prohibition on the taking of vows under the age of 24. Both Leopold and Kaunitz gave as their reasons usefulness to the state (well-educated young men were too valuable to society to be allowed to live out their lives in celibate seclusion), but Leopold also alluded to the importance of individual fulfilment. See T. C. W. Blanning, *Joseph II and Enlightened Despotism* (London, 1970), 34.

two musical prodigies, through whom he had visited some of the most illustrious courts of Europe. In almost every letter he wrote from 1762, when he first began to travel with them, his sense of the purpose of his life strikes the reader with considerable force. This being so, it is tempting to read the two above-mentioned passages with the strong possibility in mind that Leopold was indirectly expressing his gratitude that he himself, after thinking of entering the Church, had found that there was a much better way in which he could serve God. Through the marriage which brought him his children, and through his pursuit of music (which fitted him better than anything else to educate his children when they turned out to have outstanding musical abilities), he was able to find a high degree of self-fulfilment.[23] If this hypothesis is right, it can be extended by suggesting that Leopold, who had taken a big risk in dropping out of university, later felt that the children (particularly, of course, Wolfgang) were a sign from God that Leopold had not been wrong to abandon his studies, and that his work on earth was to be accomplished through music and his children. This might account for Leopold's description of Wolfgang as 'a miracle, which God caused to be born in Salzburg',[24] and whom it was Leopold's duty to show to the world, in gratitude for the joy the child had brought him. On the other hand, it should be borne in mind that Leopold might have been motivated to parade his children largely from parental pride, and that the miracle theory was not so much the driving force behind the tours as a construction of Leopold's to justify his prior desire. Whichever way round is correct (and it is also possible that the two motives were intertwined to such an extent that Leopold himself, even if confronting the question with complete honesty, could not have untangled them), there was certainly scope in the theological thinking of the Mozarts' acquaintances in Salzburg for the idea that God had a purpose for everyone on earth, that the purpose was sometimes hidden from the person in question (at least for a time), but that signs might be sent to show what it was. Quite specific individual acts and decisions could be built into these theories.

Having left university prematurely, Leopold needed work. He was still a citizen of Augsburg, but he did not return there—perhaps he would have lost too much face, or perhaps he calculated that his prospects were better in Salzburg, or both. What kind of place was Salzburg, and what employment could he hope to get?

---

[23] It was only later than this in his life that Leopold began to feel dissatisfied with the course his career had taken.

[24] Leopold to Hagenauer, 30 July 1768—*MBA* 135/70–89 (*Letters* 62).

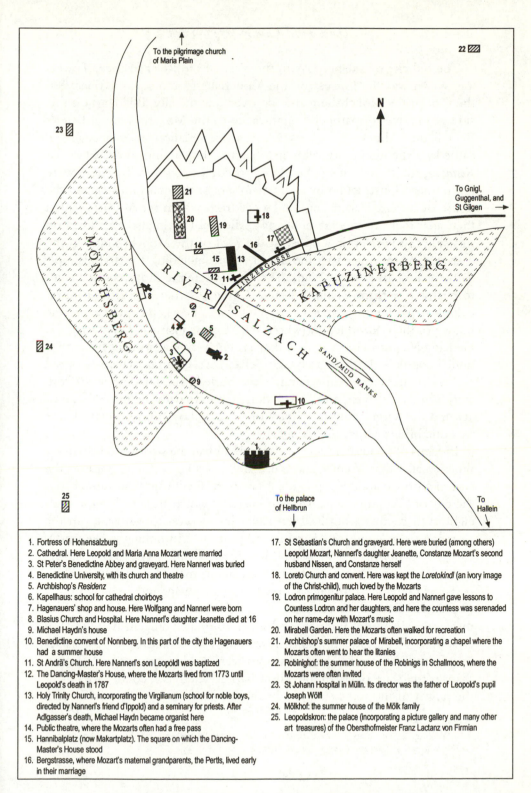

1. Fortress of Hohensalzburg
2. Cathedral. Here Leopold and Maria Anna Mozart were married
3. St Peter's Benedictine Abbey and graveyard. Here Nannerl was buried
4. Benedictine University, with its church and theatre
5. Archbishop's *Residenz*
6. Kapellhaus: school for cathedral choirboys
7. Hagenauers' shop and house. Here Wolfgang and Nannerl were born
8. Blasius Church and Hospital. Here Nannerl's daughter Jeanette died at 16
9. Michael Haydn's house
10. Benedictine convent of Nonnberg. In this part of the city the Hagenauers had a summer house
11. St Andrä's Church. Here Nannerl's son Leopoldl was baptized
12. The Dancing-Master's House, where the Mozarts lived from 1773 until Leopold's death in 1787
13. Holy Trinity Church, incorporating the Virgilianum (school for noble boys, directed by Nannerl's friend d'Ippold) and a seminary for priests. After Adlgasser's death, Michael Haydn became organist here
14. Public theatre, where the Mozarts often had a free pass
15. Hannibalplatz (now Makartplatz). The square on which the Dancing-Master's House stood
16. Bergstrasse, where Mozart's maternal grandparents, the Pertls, lived early in their marriage

17. St Sebastian's Church and graveyard. Here were buried (among others) Leopold Mozart, Nannerl's daughter Jeanette, Constanze Mozart's second husband Nissen, and Constanze herself
18. Loreto Church and convent. Here was kept the *Loretokindl* (an ivory image of the Christ-child), much loved by the Mozarts
19. Lodron primogenitur palace. Here Leopold and Nannerl gave lessons to Countess Lodron and her daughters, and here the countess was serenaded on her name-day with Mozart's music
20. Mirabell Garden. Here the Mozarts often walked for recreation
21. Archbishop's summer palace of Mirabell, incorporating a chapel where the Mozarts often went to hear the litanies
22. Robinighof: the summer house of the Robinigs in Schallmoos, where the Mozarts were often invited
23. St Johann Hospital in Mülln. Its director was the father of Leopold's pupil Joseph Wölfl
24. Mölkhof: the summer house of the Mölk family
25. Leopoldskron: the palace (incorporating a picture gallery and many other art treasures) of the Obersthofmeister Franz Lactanz von Firmian

MAP 1. The City of Salzburg, showing sites significant to the book

The old city of Salzburg lay to the west of the River Salzach. Towering over it was the fortress on the Mönchsberg, and squashed between the foot of the Mönchsberg and the river was the city. Buildings on this side of the river of particular significance to the Mozarts were St Peter's Benedictine Abbey (the oldest Christian foundation in Salzburg), the cathedral, the university with its theatre, the archbishop's palace or *Residenz*, the Kapellhaus (where the cathedral choirboys lived and were given musical instruction by many members of the court music), and the house of Lorenz Hagenauer, the grocer from whom the Mozarts rented their apartment from 1747 until 1773. Michael Haydn also later lived on this side of the river, in a house at the foot of the Mönchsberg. On the east side of the river was the newer town, including the archbishop's garden palace of Mirabell (with the chapel where the Mozarts often went to hear and perform litanies), Loreto Convent (where the famous miraculous ivory figure of the Christ child was kept), the palace of one branch of the Lodron family (whom the Mozarts instructed in music), the Dancing-Master's House (where they rented a large apartment from 1773 until Leopold's death in 1787), St Sebastian's Church (where Leopold and other members of the family were buried), the building used from 1775 as a civic theatre, and Holy Trinity Church, with the priests' seminary and the Virgilianum (a school for wealthy boys) in its wings. There was one bridge across the river.[25]

In terms of population, Salzburg was about half the size of Munich, many times smaller than Vienna, and the same size as Linz. But its status as the seat of a prince-archbishop made it far more significant than Linz. From the city of Salzburg a state was administered which stretched in the mid-eighteenth century from Zell am Ziller in the west to Moosham in the east, and from Windisch Matrei in the south to Tittmoning in the north, with more northerly and southerly enclaves still.[26] The fact that the prince was a cleric, and therefore a bachelor, made Salzburg special, in so far as there was no ruling family to inherit power and give continuity to policies. Nor was there (apart from a few notable exceptions, such as the families Lodron, Firmian, and Kuenburg) a significant nobility long established in the city. Instead there was the Cathedral Chapter, consisting of twenty-four canons, most of whom were nobles with lands elsewhere than in the state of Salzburg. The Chapter acted as a counterweight to the power of the archbishop, and relations between the two could often

---

[25] See Map 1.

[26] See Map 2. The map is based largely on that in H. Dopsch and H. Spatzenegger (eds.), *Geschichte Salzburgs: Stadt und Land*, vol. ii, pt. 1 (Salzburg, 1988), 355.

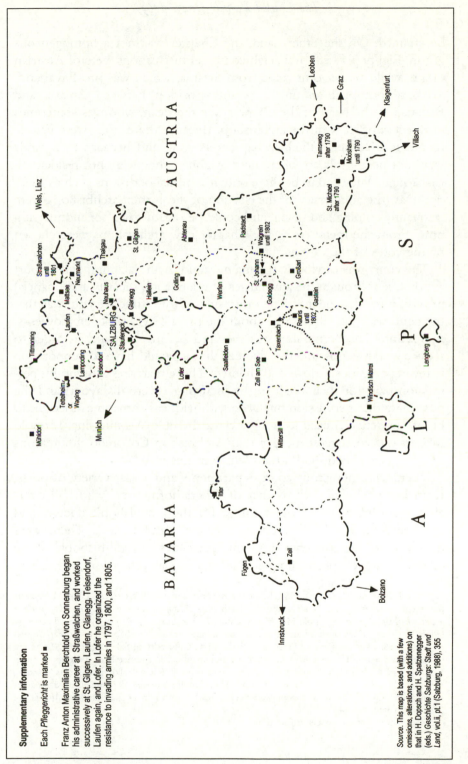

Supplementary information

Each *Pfleggericht* is marked ■

Franz Anton Maximilian Berchtold von Sonnenburg began his administrative career at Straßwalchen, and worked successively at St. Gilgen, Laufen, Glanegg, Teisendorf, Laufen again, and Lofer. In Lofer he organized the resistance to invading armies in 1797, 1800, and 1805.

Source. This map is based (with a few omissions, alterations, and additions) on that in H. Dopsch and H. Spatzenegger (eds.) *Geschichte Salzburgs: Stadt und Land*, vol.ii, pt.1 (Salzburg, 1988), 355

MAP 2. *Salzburg Land* in 1803

BAVARIA

AUSTRIA

S

A L P

Mühldorf

Münich

Tittmoning

Tettelheim, or Waging

Lampoding

Teisendorf

Straßwalchen until 1801

Neumarkt

Mattsee

Laufen

Thalgau

St. Gilgen

Neuhaus

SALZBURG

Staufeneck

Glanegg

Hallein

Gölling

Abtenau

Werfen

Radstadt

Wagrein until 1802

St. Johann

Goldegg

Großarl

Taxenbach

Rauris until 1802

Gastein

Wels, Linz

Leoben

Graz

Klagenfurt

Tamsweg after 1790

Mooshäm until 1790

St. Michael after 1790

Villach

Lofer

Saalfelden

Zell am See

Windisch Matrei

Mittersill

Lengberg

Itter

Fügen

Zell

Innsbruck

Bolzano

be strained. On the other hand, the Chapter was not a homogeneous group. Eighty per cent of its eighteenth-century canons were of Austrian origin, while 10 per cent came from Swabia, which was pro-Bavarian.[27] Salzburg occupied an uncomfortable position between Austria and Bavaria. At the head of the Chapter was the dean, who was sometimes in direct conflict with the archbishop. Because the canons were usually members of other cathedral chapters as well, and because their lands were not necessarily anywhere near Salzburg, they were not resident all year round. They had to be there only for special occasions such as Election Day (the anniversary of the election of the current archbishop), were frequently coming and going, and could be out of town for months at a time. From the members of the Chapter new archbishops were chosen by the votes of the canons.[28]

The court was obviously the main employer in Salzburg, and a court appointment brought the advantages of relative job security and financial provision for dependants. The other side of this attractive coin was that the court was quite inquisitive about the private lives of its employees— for example, its permission was required before marriage, in order to reduce as far as possible the chances that it would have to support too many impecunious widows and children. Those marrying without this permission paid for their boldness by incurring severe disfavour, and the possibility that permission might be withheld was sometimes thought to be (if not actually) used to bring awkward employees into line. Leopold Mozart was to suggest in 1777 that Archbishop Colloredo, for reasons of spite, persecuted the Barisani family in this way.[29]

There were numerous court departments and a vast variety of posts, from key positions such as that of Obersthofmeister (who had overall responsibility among other things for the archbishop's doctors and musicians) to the lowliest ones of runners and lackeys. There were dozens of councillors with different specialities, several bishops, all the canons, many chaplains, umpteen secretaries, lawyers galore, officials in

[27] See J. Mančal, ' "... durch beyhülff hoher Recommandation": Neues zu Leopold Mozarts beruflichem Anfang', in J. Mančal and W. Plath (eds.), *Leopold Mozart: Auf dem Weg zu einem Verständnis*, Beiträge zur Leopold-Mozart-Forschung I (Augsburg, 1994), 158–9. Mančal acknowledges that some of his work is indebted to that of E. Hintermaier, 'Die Salzburger Hofkapelle von 1700 bis 1806. Organisation und Personal' (Ph. D. diss., University of Salzburg, 1972). There are occasional differences between them, however, in emolument details for members of the court music.

[28] Most of the information in this paragraph comes from H. Klein, 'Salzburg zur Zeit Mozarts', *MJb* (1964), 55–61, and from J. Graf von Moÿ, 'Die Hintergründe der Fürstungen im Salzburger Domkapitel: ein Beitrag zur Verfassungsgeschichte des Erzstiftes im 18. Jahrhundert', *MGSL* 119 (Salzburg, 1979), 231–59.

[29] See Ch. 16 for the details of this affair.

departments as diverse as forestry, brewing, salt, and wardrobes, the thirty-six Pfleger and their clerks, all the military personnel, and the army of maids, valets, and grooms. In many types of position there were employees who were 'actually serving' and ones who were on the books but in dormant categories.

The court attracted the young people of noble families hoping to settle their sons in sinecures. Many of these young counts came first to be educated in Salzburg, as *Edelknaben* ('noble boys'). There were twelve of these (though the numbers were reduced under Archbishop Colloredo, the last employer of the Mozarts), and they had their own quarters, tutors, and costume. On special occasions they served as pages. In time most of them attended the university and many stayed after that, having been given court posts. Originally the *Edelknaben* lived in the *Residenz*, on the west side of the Salzach, close to the cathedral, but in 1775 their quarters were moved and their institution merged with that of the Virgilianum, which offered a similar education (without the page duties) to other well-to-do boys, and was based in a wing of Holy Trinity Church, on the east side of the river.[30] (Franz Armand d'Ippold, the man whom Nannerl Mozart wanted to marry, headed the Virgilianum for years.) Thus the court and university in Salzburg attracted members of the German Catholic aristocracy from far and wide.

In addition to the grand aristocracy, there was the *wilde Adel*, or minor aristocracy. Members of this group of nobles also occupied key court posts, though not such high-ranking ones. A huge gulf separated it socially from the higher aristocracy. Musicians mixed with both types of aristocracy, but only to a certain extent, namely when music was being made together. In general, society was extraordinarily hierarchical, and while most musicians probably accepted this, the Mozarts, who liked to think they were the moral and intellectual equals of the 'best' people in Salzburg, often found their position uncomfortable. However, they seem to have been on genuinely friendly terms with some members of the lower aristocracy, playing cards and going for walks with them as well as making music together.[31]

Leopold found his first employment in 1740 with one of the cathedral canons, the Swabian President of the Consistory, Count Johann Baptist

---

[30] Klein, 'Salzburg zur Zeit Mozarts', 58.

[31] A well-known example is the Mozarts' friendship with the Schiedenhofen family, documented in the Mozart correspondence and in the diaries of Nannerl Mozart and of Johann Baptist Joseph Joachim Ferdinand von Schiedenhofen. See O. E. Deutsch, 'Aus Schiedenhofens Tagebuch', *MJb* (1957), 15–24.

Thurn-Valsassina and Taxis, as valet and musician. This was hardly the kind of work one might expect would appeal to the proud and intelligent son of a self-employed craftsman and citizen of Augsburg, but when Leopold composed and published his first work, a set of six church sonatas for two violins and bass (which he engraved himself), he wrote a grateful dedication to his master, in which he thanked Taxis for having rescued him from 'the harsh darkness of need'.[32] Leopold remained with Taxis for several years, but on 4 October 1743 he was granted an *Anwartschaft* for a post in the court musical establishment. This was a post-in-waiting—it meant that he had court musical duties with no remuneration, on the understanding that he would be considered for a salaried post when one became available. The unpaid position was offered him because of a larger reshuffle—the Kapellmeister, Matthias Siegmund Biechteler von Greiffenthal, had died, and Karl Heinrich Biber von Bibern had advanced to Kapellmeister. Giuseppe Lolli (using a sly trick)[33] had moved up to Vice-Kapellmeister ahead of Johann Ernst Eberlin, who had expected the promotion himself, and space was then created down the line at the depths of the violins for Leopold's unpaid post. The archbishop at the time was Baron Leopold Anton von Firmian.[34]

By this time it seems highly likely that Leopold and Maria Anna knew each other and had formed the intention of marrying. Leopold, however, probably knew from others in the court music that he might have to wait years for his position to attract a salary, since the vagaries in the system of promotion were notorious.[35] When Firmian died on 22 October 1744, therefore, Leopold seized his chance. After the death of an archbishop there was a period of *Sedisvacanz* or interregnum while a new one was elected by the Chapter. During this period the Chapter governed the archbishopric, and since it did not carry overall responsibility for very long, it was often persuaded to give indulgent decisions to those presenting petitions. Time and again court employees exploited the situation to press for better conditions which the archbishop himself would have been more cautious in granting. Leopold was always to be aware of the need to cultivate the goodwill of the canons in the Chapter, not for

---

[32] K. Schumann, 'Ein Genie der Rechtschaffenheit: Leopold Mozarts Weg durch das 18. Jahrhundert', in W. Baer (ed.), *Leopold Mozart zum 200. Todestag* (Augsburg exhibition catalogue, 1987), 2.

[33] See Ch. 10 for details of this and of other bones of contention among the musicians.

[34] Most of the information in this paragraph is from Mančal, ' "... durch beyhülff hoher Recommandation" ', 162–3.

[35] The most extreme case was that of Johann Judas Thaddäus Wessenauer, who waited sixteen years for a salary. See ibid. 162.

this reason alone, but also because future archbishops were chosen from their ranks.[36]

On this occasion, Leopold's petition of 7 November 1744 noted that two members of the court music (Anton Heinrich Biber von Bibern and Johann Franz Biarelle) had died and not yet been replaced. Their salaries, therefore, had not been reassigned, and Leopold asked that one of them should be given to him. One of the 'vacated' salaries was 8 fl. per month, while the other was 25 fl. per month plus a bread and wine allowance. The higher salary represented a sum on which it was possible for a man to support a family, while the lower one was too small for this purpose—many widows' pensions (including that of Maria Anna's mother) were set at this level. Leopold was in luck—the Chapter compromised and granted him 20 fl. per month plus the bread and wine allowance.[37]

If Leopold and Maria Anna had expected to be able to marry now, however, they were to be disappointed, for when the new archbishop, Count Jakob Ernst von Liechtenstein, was installed, he cancelled all the *Sedisvacanz* awards, and Leopold was back where he had started, though he was now named as court Kammerportier, a post which gave him chamber duties as well as musical ones. He was still waiting for a salary.[38] By 1 May 1746 he had been granted 5 fl. per month, and this was increased to 11 fl. five months later, but the sum still represented a mere retainer. A full salary eluded him until after the death of Liechtenstein on 12 June 1747. Now, in the autumn of 1747, he was finally granted a salary of 20 fl. per month, or 240 fl. annually. Later a bread and wine allowance of 54 fl. annually was added.[39]

With the salary secured, Leopold and Maria Anna could think of marrying. Their wedding took place in Salzburg Cathedral on 21 November 1747. Nothing is known of their courtship except Leopold's later remark that it had lasted many years, and that they had apparently entered into a formal betrothal at Aigen, just outside Salzburg, a few weeks before the wedding.[40] Forty-five years later, after the deaths of Maria Anna,

[36] See Ch. 10 for a case in 1771 where Leopold used the intercession of one of the canons, Count Joseph Gottfried Saurau, to obtain payment of his salary, which had been withheld by Archbishop Schrattenbach because of Leopold's absence with Wolfgang in Milan. It was the Chapter, during a period of *Sedisvacanz* in December following Schrattenbach's death, that granted him his appeal.

[37] The information in this paragraph is from Mančal, ' "... durch beyhülff hoher Recommandation" ', 163–6.

[38] Ibid. 166–7.   [39] Ibid. 168, inc. n. 102.

[40] Probably on 19 Oct. 1747. See H. Schuler, 'Die Hochzeit der Eltern Mozarts. Eine Quellenstudie', *AM* 28 (1981), 5.

Leopold, and Mozart himself, in an essay about Mozart's childhood, a family friend described the youthful Leopold and Maria Anna as 'the handsomest married couple in Salzburg'.[41] They had now entered the Order of Patched Trousers.

For the next fifteen years Leopold was to strive energetically and successfully to improve his personal standing at the Salzburg court, but he apparently did not want immediately to burn his boats with Augsburg. Since he was no longer resident there, however, he had formally to renew his citizenship from time to time, and he needed the permission of the civil authorities there to marry. Failure to obtain this permission could lead to the cancellation of the citizenship. Leopold did not seek permission until after his marriage, leaving it until 12 December 1747 to appeal for it. Contained in the petition was a purportedly incidental reference to his desire to marry. Leopold got his way, obtaining permission to marry, to live outside Augsburg, and to keep his citizenship, but his appeal is full of puzzling lies, some of which make it difficult to understand the way his mind was working. He claimed that his father, a bookbinder, was still alive, though he had been dead more than ten years; that he had been in Salzburg only for a short time, though he had been there nearly ten years; that he had pursued his studies diligently in Salzburg, though he had been sent down from the university; that he had the opportunity to marry a woman of fortune, though Maria Anna was entirely without means and he had already married her; and that he was currently a valet in Salzburg, though this had ceased to be the case in September when his salary had been raised to 20 fl. per month. The point of some of these lies is easy enough to see, since he was trying to persuade the authorities that he was an upright man who with his wife was not likely to become a burden on the city's resources. But why he should have claimed that his father was still alive is mysterious, not only because there were people in the relevant offices in Augsburg who must have known that he was not, but also because Leopold's citizenship in no way depended on the fact.[42]

Whatever Leopold's motives for making the false statements in his petition, a number of points about his marriage and character seem clear. His desire to marry Maria Anna almost certainly stemmed from love

---

[41] Albert von Mölk, in a postscript to the essay on Mozart written by Nannerl in the spring of 1792 for Schlichtegroll's *Nekrolog*, the first biography of Mozart. See *MBA* 1212/408–9 (Deutsch, *Documents*, 462). For a discussion of the trouble caused by this postscript, see Ch. 33.

[42] The information in this paragraph comes from Mančal, 'Vom "Orden der geflickten hosen"', 38–46.

of her, since she brought no means to the union. The decision seems to have been a mature one, since they had apparently known each other for several years before their marriage, and Leopold had had to struggle for an adequate salary before they could realize their intention. His motive for wanting to keep his Augsburg citizenship was almost certainly not so much that he expected to need any of its benefits (for, after all, he applied to keep it *after* he had gained relative security in Salzburg), but rather that he might appear with more pride and independence in Salzburg. Pride and independence were very much features of the character of the young Leopold Mozart. Finally, he was quite prepared to lie to achieve his end, so that his later frequent descriptions of himself as an 'honest' man clearly had a meaning different from the literal one. Since he also taught his son Wolfgang to lie in certain circumstances (especially where employment preferment was concerned), yet expected absolute truthfulness from him as son to father, there was clearly a code of honour at work which would now have to be reconstructed from contextual comparisons.[43] Leopold's route to marriage thus reveals aspects of his character as a young man which may profitably be borne in mind when considering later relationships within the family.

[43] See ibid. 44–5. For an example of Leopold suggesting that Wolfgang lie (in order to obtain the salary he wanted), see Leopold's letter of 3 Sept. 1778—*MBA* 482/51–8 (*Letters* 329).

2

The Early Years of the Children:
Building a Career

HAVING got his own way with regard to his marriage and his Augsburg citizenship, Leopold could now apply himself to the advancement of his career. He rose steadily up the ranks of the violinists in the court orchestra, took on private teaching, and composed, finding outlets for his compositions not only at the Salzburg court but also at the Benedictine abbey of Lambach, the court of Count Philipp Karl Oettingen-Wallerstein, and the Collegium Musicum (a concert-giving society composed of professional and amateur musicians) in Augsburg. The teaching and composition not only earned him welcome extra income, but rounded his musical abilities, giving him the opportunity to be promoted beyond the scope of a mere instrumentalist. But his interests were not confined to music alone, and he was clearly keen to develop other intellectual pursuits, particularly literature, economics, politics, and theology. Nor was he content to be one of many; he sought to promote himself by being superior to run-of-the-mill musicians. This trait apparently sometimes got him into trouble, as in 1753, when he circulated a pamphlet attacking the canon, Count Thurn und Taxis, and a priest, Egglstainer, and was compelled publicly to apologize;[1] but although he was to become more circumspect with maturity, he was never to lose his pride in the superiority of his opinions, nor energy to promote his views.[2]

---

[1] See E. Schenk, *Mozart: Eine Biographie* (Vienna, 1955; 2nd edn. 1975: here cited from the Goldmann Sachbuch paperback edn. with no place or date), 45. The scanty information about this affair comes from a document in the SLA, Domkapitel Protokoll (*Sedisvacanz*), 27 Feb. 1753, fo. 636–7. I am grateful to Frau Christiane Gärtner of the SLA for this information.

[2] Several of Leopold's petitions to the Salzburg court contained miniature moral lectures. The most famous is that of 1 Aug. 1777, in which he (writing as if he were Wolfgang) asked for Wolfgang's discharge for the purposes of travelling to earn his bread and support his parents—*MBA* 328 (*Letters* 206). A less well-known one dates from 1759, when Leopold asked for the wherewithal to buy wine prescribed for his sciatica. After stating various figures, he complained that salaried employees should be compensated for the effects of inflation, since otherwise their position was unfair by comparison with farmers and shopkeepers, who could raise their prices. See H. Klein, 'Ein unbekanntes Gesuch Leopold Mozarts von 1759', *Neues MJb* (1943), 95–101.

In 1757 a report was published by Marpurg about the musical establishment at the Salzburg court.[3] It has long been accepted that Leopold
Mozart was the author, since the entry on him is far longer and more
detailed than on any other musician named in it. The report described
in brief the structure of the court music and the way the forces were disposed in the cathedral, and listed the personnel. It is a valuable document for a number of reasons, one being that it indicated the full range
of abilities of each member, thus showing the versatility of the band. It
claimed, for example, that almost every trumpeter could play at least the
violin as well. It also revealed to a certain extent whom Leopold Mozart
admired in the band, and whom he felt only lukewarm about. His warm-
est comments were made about the Kapellmeister Johann Ernst Eberlin
(a fellow Swabian who had, like Leopold, been attracted to Salzburg
initially by the university), the cellist and composer Caspar Cristelli, the
organists Anton Cajetan Adlgasser and Franz Ignaz Lipp (whose tenor
voice Leopold picked out for praise), the horn players Wenzel Sadlo and
Franz Drasil, the bass singer Joseph Meissner—and himself. By contrast,
the Italian Vice-Kapellmeister Giuseppe Lolli received an entry as cool
as it was brief. Finally, the report mentioned one of the advantages of
being named as a composer within the band, since the Kapellmeister
and the three other court composers took it in turns to organize the
music on a weekly basis. For the week when he was in charge, the composer could choose what music was performed, and thus had an excellent means to promote his own compositions if that was what he wished.
At the time of the Marpurg report, the three named composers other than
the Kapellmeister Eberlin were Caspar Cristelli, Leopold Mozart, and
Ferdinand Seidl.

The Marpurg report, taken together with other information (such as
the court calendars), allows in outline the routines of the court musicians
to be reconstructed, although the timetable of any one man depended to
a large extent on which instrument he played, whether his supplementary
instruments were in demand, whether he was also a composer, and
whether he was a teacher at the Kapellhaus. The court calendars listed
the days on which special events were celebrated, and sometimes prescribed
the form taken by the celebrations. For Corpus Christi, for example, the
calendar set out in lengthy detail which members of the court should attend

---

[3] 'Nachricht von dem gegenwärtigen Zustande der Musik Sr. Hochfürstl. Gnaden des
Erzbischoffs zu Salzburg im Jahr 1757', in F. W. Marpurg (ed.), *Historisch-Kritische Beyträge zur
Aufnahme der Musik* (Berlin, 1757), iii. 183–98. The report is translated into English and included
as Appendix C in N. Zaslaw, *Mozart's Symphonies: Context, Performance Practice, Reception* (Oxford,
1989), 550–7. Refs. to the work in this book are to the translation.

at what time, what they should wear, and what route would be followed in the processions.[4] Since Salzburg was a Catholic ecclesiastical court, the number of church feast-days requiring the forces of the court music was considerable, and the Kapellmeister and the three named composers must have had to be well organized to have suitable music written and rehearsed for all these events. But the music in the cathedral was only one part of it, for (depending on the inclination of the current archbishop) there were regular evening concerts at court requiring a steady supply of secular music as well.[5] And when the court had important visitors, the musicians might be required for extra duties in or out of the town.[6] They could even be lent to neighbouring monasteries for special occasions.[7] It is easy broadly to envisage, therefore, the working day of one of the composers, which would have been punctuated by frequent interruptions for rehearsals, services, teaching, and concerts. Court duties alone would have necessitated frequent travelling between home, cathedral, *Residenz*, and Kapellhaus, quite apart from further trips to the homes of private pupils, or to other churches in the town where many of the musicians had additional duties, and where the court band was required to play on certain church feast-days. Composing had to be fitted in to the time between these events.

Although the period between his marriage in 1747 and Wolfgang's birth in 1756 was one which also brought Leopold domestic burdens in the form of Maria Anna's seven pregnancies and confinements, and the illnesses and deaths of five babies, he was extremely prolific. The Marpurg report stressed that he composed in every branch of music (in contrast, for example, to Lolli, who was said to have composed virtually nothing for the chamber), and had written 'numerous' contrapuntal and church pieces, many symphonies, more than thirty grand serenades, a good number of concertos for diverse instruments, 'countless' trios and divertimentos, twelve oratorios and other theatre pieces, martial music and other music for special occasions, and hundreds of smaller pieces such

---

[4] See SLA, Hochfürstlichen Salzburgischen Kirchen- und Hofkalender, Historische Bibliothek, B00192.

[5] Under Colloredo, who was elected in 1772, these took place on Tues., Thurs., and Sun.; but I have not been able to confirm this pattern during Leopold's early career.

[6] See the *Hofdiarium* for 12 Aug. 1762, which mentioned that the musicians had to go to the palace Hellbrun outside Salzburg—F. Martin, 'Vom Salzburger Fürstenhof um die Mitte des 18. Jahrhunderts', *MGSL* 80 (1940), 168; hereafter 'Fürstenhof 80'.

[7] Cf. Beda Hübner's diary for 23 Jan. and 11 Feb. 1765, which mentioned four of the best musicians being sent to the abbey of Lambach to help entertain the bride of Joseph II—H. Klein, 'Nachrichten zum Musikleben Salzburgs in den Jahren 1764–1766', in *Festschrift Alfred Orel zum 70. Geburtstag 1959* (Vienna, 1960), 94–5.

as minuets. Though the Marpurg report has to be treated with some caution because of Leopold's evident desire to blow his own trumpet (the entry on him, for example, claims that he had completed his studies at university), it is clear from other sources of information that Leopold Mozart was very active as a composer during the early part of his career.[8] Furthermore, he was concerned to sell what he had written outside Salzburg as well as within it, and this involved him in forging contacts with possible buyers, with all the effort implied by such active marketing of his compositions.

But the work mentioned in Marpurg's report which brought him most fame during his lifetime was his *Violinschule*, a pedagogical work for aspiring violinists.[9] From it can be learnt a good deal not only about playing the violin, contemporary performance practice, aesthetics, ideas of musical history, and so forth, but also about the character of the young Leopold Mozart. Leopold took on himself the publishing of the work, asking the printer Johann Jakob Lotter of Augsburg to print it for him, but bearing all the expenses and organizing all the sales himself; and by great good fortune his letters to Lotter about preparing the first edition have largely survived.

It is well-nigh impossible to separate discussion of Leopold's comments about the technicalities of playing the violin from those about taste, sensitivity, and general culture, for everything in his book tended to the one end of producing violinists capable of reflecting seriously on the purpose of their art, at the level of every single performance. It was this which differentiated Leopold's essay most markedly from previous treatises on violin playing. Thus, for example, Leopold gave detailed instructions for alternative ways of bowing triplets, while insisting that the performer pay attention to the *Affekt* (approximately, emotion) intended by the composer,[10] so that the most appropriate bowing could be chosen.[11] Leopold envisaged that the performer should be capable of studying a piece for clues about the intended *Affekt*, and should be prepared to do so, for

---

[8] For more information about Leopold as a composer, see C. Eisen, 'The Symphonies of Leopold Mozart and their Relationship to the Early Symphonies of Wolfgang Amadeus Mozart: A Bibliographical and Stylistic Study' (Ph. D. diss., Cornell University, 1986); D. M. Carlson, 'The Vocal Music of Leopold Mozart (1719–1787): Authenticity, Chronology and Thematic Catalogue' (Ph. D. diss., University of Michigan, 1976); and M. H. Schmid, 'Zu den Klaviersonaten von Leopold Mozart', *MJb* (1989–90), 23–30.

[9] L. Mozart, *Versuch einer gründlichen Violinschule* (Augsburg, 1756). For an edn. with introduction and commentary, see that edn. by H. R. Jung (Wiesbaden, 1983). English trans. E. Knocker, as *A Treatise on the Fundamental Principles of Violin Playing* (Oxford, 1948, 2nd edn. 1951). Henceforth the German work (ed. Jung) is called *Violinschule* and the English trans. (2nd edn.) *Treatise*.

[10] See Glossary for an explanation of *Affekt*.   [11] *Treatise*, 104.

although the composer ought to have made it clear, many would not have done so.[12] One element in the business of finding the right *Affekt* was an education broad enough to encompass the study of literature and especially poetry, for a cantabile style should be the aim of every instrumentalist, and poetry was the key to good phrasing in music.[13] Leopold clearly believed that some composers did not know their business—he complained about the poor metre in many Italian arias, and about the fact that the *Affekt* was often not indicated by the composer. The performer had therefore to be able to compensate for these defects by studying the most effective way of playing the piece.[14]

Although it is clear from Leopold's essay that he knew much Italian violin music and that he had even seen a copy of Tartini's treatise on ornamentation,[15] he was by no means overawed by the work of anyone else. On the contrary, his work displayed a sureness of purpose and the confidence of someone who knew exactly what he wanted to say. Since he was exposed to many Italian musicians in Salzburg, either as part of the court music or passing through on their way to and from Italy, it is possible that some of his scornful remarks about superficial brilliance resting on unsure foundations were directed at Italian instrumentalists and composers. Later remarks in the correspondence fairly consistently reveal a belief that Italians tended to be full of unmerited braggadocio. On the other hand, Leopold did not always find it easy to train even his own pupils (most of whom were German) in the way he wanted them to play. The one about whose education in violin playing most is known, Heinrich Marchand, was apparently very competent technically, but was inclined both to be lazy and to want to show off.[16] No doubt this was a common fault among talented younger men (Heinrich was still a teenager when Leopold made these complaints), but Leopold obviously found it difficult in some respects to educate Heinrich, despite having him as a captive resident pupil for more than three years. Although there are too few surviving examples of Leopold indicating satisfaction with violin playing to make general inferences about the attributes he admired, there are hints both in the correspondence and in the *Violinschule* that humility and a desire to serve the music were of paramount importance to him.

---

[12] *Treatise*, 124, inc. n. 1.   [13] Ibid. 101–2, esp. n. 2.   [14] Ibid. 216–17, inc. footnotes.

[15] The treatise was not yet published, but it has been suggested that it circulated in manuscript before publication, and that a copy could have found its way to Salzburg. See editor's introduction to *Violinschule*, 15–16. The Marpurg report on music at Salzburg mentioned that the violinist Franz Schwarzmann was currently in Padua studying at Tartini's school, so this suggestion seems very plausible. See L. Mozart, 'Report', Appendix C in Zaslaw, *Mozart's Symphonies*, 551.

[16] See Leopold's letter to Nannerl of 9 Mar. 1787—*MBA* 1038/6–26 and 33–47 (not in *Letters*).

When he praised the playing of Regina Strinasacchi in 1785, for example, he was impressed by her attention to expression both in solo adagio movements and in orchestral playing. He wrote to Nannerl that in general he found that women played better than men because they were more sensitive to the needs of the music.[17] In 1787, when Heinrich was his star pupil, he taught his lesser pupil Anton Breymann to play the slow movement of a concerto more beautifully by introducing rubato and other sensitive effects, so that Breymann's performance impressed even Heinrich's 'wild, turbulent head'.[18] And he stated in the *Violinschule* both that the greatest tests of a violinist were the adagio movements, and that the greatest skills were required in orchestral playing rather than solo performance.[19]

At the level of practical comments on improving aspects of violin technique, Leopold showed himself to be full of common sense, and to be capable of expressing his explanations in robust and clear language. The letters to Lotter reveal what the *Violinschule* by itself could not do so fully —the meticulous care about details of spelling, grammar, style, length, layout, balance, and cost.[20] The work, together with the correspondence about it, shows that Leopold knew exactly what he wanted to do, that he had strong opinions on how pupils should be taught to play the violin, that he had thought out how to present his material in the clearest possible way, that he wanted even impoverished pupils to be able to afford his book, and that he was prepared to put in all the necessary work to get the details just right. The only material in the work that does not seem completely integrated into the purposeful thrust of the whole is the outline of musical history in the Introduction. Leopold had in fact complained of the lack of an adequate history of music, but tried to provide his own sketch anyway. His attempt, which cited numerous works from the Bible through Classical, medieval, and renaissance texts to contemporary treatises, gives the impression not quite that he was out of his depth (for he had clearly read the works he referred to), but that he was not convinced that the theories contained in many of the works were of much practical help.[21] His comments on the ideas expressed in the works he cited

---

[17] Leopold to Nannerl, 7 Dec. 1785—*MBA* 907/33–51 (not in *Letters*).

[18] Leopold to Nannerl, 9 Mar. 1787—*MBA* 1038/33–47 (not in *Letters*).

[19] *Treatise*, 215–17.

[20] The letters are *MBA* 1–30, with the exception of 21 (not in *Letters*).

[21] For a full list of the historical and theoretical works cited by Leopold, see P. Petrobelli, 'La cultura di Leopold Mozart e la sua "Violinschule"', *MJb* (1989–90), 9–16. C. P. E. Bach also expressed scorn for theory in his treatise on keyboard playing—see C. P. E. Bach, *Versuch über die wahre Art das Clavier zu Spielen* (Berlin, 1753–62); English trans. W. J. Mitchell as *Essay on the True Art of Playing Keyboard Instruments* (London, 1949, 2nd edn. 1951). Cited from the 2nd English edn., here at 151–2.

ranged from the naïve to the critical, suggesting that his intellectual sympathy was not quite engaged with the topic.[22] Where issues of immediate practical application were concerned, however, he was eloquent about what was needed, expressing the wish, for example, that scientists would use their knowledge to improve the making of musical instruments rather than to explain abstractions such as why consecutive octaves and fifths sounded awkward.[23] It may be that the material on the history of music was included for the sake of completeness (since the work was conceived as far more than merely a set of technical tips and drills), and to demonstrate the learnedness of the author. For the overall impression given by both the text of the book and the letters to Lotter is of a man very sure of his own abilities, and keen to be accepted for his cultural merits in a class-ridden society.[24]

Leopold had indicated in the *Violinschule* that he was conscious of the need for his book to be affordable even by impoverished students who might not have the money for lessons.[25] For this reason he tried to keep the length down, and because he was publishing it himself he had much greater autonomy over the setting of the price. Though this concern benefited him, too, by increasing the number of possible purchasers, the later correspondence reveals that he did indeed feel a strong sense of responsibility to his pupils, and was extremely generous with his time. He tried only to take pupils he thought would reward his efforts, and lavished attention on them with a concentrated will, inviting them round (sometimes almost daily) for long sessions of ensemble playing in addition to their regular lesson slots, extending the lesson time considerably, and giving them extra help when they had concerts to play in. Talented and industrious pupils could hardly fail to thrive under Leopold's tuition.[26]

The *Violinschule* was published in July 1756, later by several months than Leopold had hoped. There were a number of strategic dates in the spring of 1756 by which it would have been profitable to have the work out. One was 28 February, the birthday of Archbishop Schrattenbach (to

---

[22] Though the conjunction of the traits of naïvety and scepticism stems in part from Leopold's orthodox belief in the literal truth of events recounted in the Bible. For although he was able to allow the possibility of scepticism about whether Orpheus had really existed, and of forming an opinion about the question by reasoning, having read without prejudice ancient accounts of him, no such possibility with respect to biblical characters was admitted. See *Treatise*, 19–20.

[23] Ibid. 15.

[24] See e.g. ibid. 20 n. 12, in which Leopold wrote of a time when 'learned people were idolized'.

[25] Ibid. 8.

[26] Some non-resident pupils helped at various times by Leopold in these ways were Francesco Ceccarelli, Anton Breymann, and Joseph Wölffl. It can be assumed that the resident ones (Heinrich and Margarethe Marchand, and their cousin Johanna ('Hanchen') Brochard) received even closer attention.

whom it was dedicated), when all the canons would be in town and there was an important fair or market. Another was 5 April, Schrattenbach's Election Day, when the canons would be around to collect their annual 'election money' (a present of money for having chosen Schrattenbach as archbishop). And a third was 1 May, Schrattenbach's name-day. After these dates the canons dispersed to their estates until the autumn.[27] But the work progressed with frustrating slowness, Leopold sending Lotter instalments which then often had to be discussed before being set. Lotter did not always respond as quickly as Leopold wanted him to, and Leopold, who was on very friendly terms with him and his wife, Christina Sabina, occasionally appealed to Frau Lotter to deny her husband all 'special nocturnal entertainment' until the latest piece of his work had been dealt with.[28] In January 1756 Leopold expressed concern because there was a hold-up caused by a feverish illness of Lotter's; since the Lotters had recently had a baby son, Leopold hoped that the cause of the fever was merely sexual abstinence caused by the lying-in period, and that it would soon disappear once Lotter's wife returned to her conjugal duties.[29] Perhaps it did, but if so there were further delays, and by April Leopold was complaining that it was clearly not going to be ready even for the name-day, and that Lotter was going to make him into a liar.[30] What does not seem to have impeded the work much, however, was Leopold's own family life, despite the fact that the Mozarts, too, had a new baby son in the house from 27 January.

During all the time since his marriage, while Leopold had been building his career, he and Maria Anna had experienced seven times the birth of an infant. Their first child, a boy, was born in August 1748 but died in February 1749. By this time, Maria Anna was pregnant with the second, a girl, who was born in June 1749 but died only six days later. In May 1750 another girl was born, and again died young, this time at eleven weeks.[31] Immediately following this event, in August 1750, Maria Anna went for a four-day cure at Bad Gastein, some seventy kilometres south of Salzburg. It was a favourite destination for the sick, weary, and sorrowful of Salzburg, and an acquaintance of the Mozarts, Maria Kunigunde Niderl (wife of the doctor whose grisly end Leopold was to be involved with in

---

[27] See letters from Leopold to Lotter of 27 Oct. 1755, 26 Jan. 1756 (the day before Wolfgang was born), 9 Feb. 1756 (in which Wolfgang's birth was reported), 12 Feb. 1756, and 1 Apr. 1756— *MBA* 11/10–23, 20/16–20, 22/15–28, 23/25–48, and 30/5–15 (none in *Letters*).

[28] Leopold to Lotter, 4 Oct. 1755—*MBA* 10/34–8 (not in *Letters*).

[29] Leopold to Lotter, 26 Jan. 1756—*MBA* 20/20–2 (not in *Letters*).

[30] Leopold to Lotter, 1 Apr. 1756—*MBA* 30/5–15 (not in *Letters*).

[31] Deutsch, *Documents*, 5–6.

Vienna in 1773),[32] was there at the same time as Maria Anna.[33] Leopold later reported to Nannerl that the cure had cost him 12 ducats (60 fl.),[34] at a time when his salary had been only 29 fl. 30 kr. per month.[35] It had clearly been difficult to afford, but perhaps the Mozarts later came to feel that the expense had been justified, for on 30/1 July of the following year, 1751, Maria Anna Walburga Ignatia was born. This was 'Nannerl', the first of their children to survive infancy and childhood. After Nannerl came another son in November 1752, who died in February 1753, and another daughter in May 1754, who died in June of the same year. Finally, on 27 January 1756, came Joannes Chrysostomus Wolfgang Theophilus, the second child to survive to adulthood, and the one who became the composer Mozart and 'Wolfgang' within the family.[36] Because Leopold was corresponding with Lotter during the period of this pregnancy and birth, there is slightly more information about the event than about the others— Maria Anna was 'incredibly weak' following delivery, because the afterbirth had had to be removed by intervention.[37]

By the time the *Violinschule* was published, therefore, Leopold and Maria Anna were well settled into the routines of married life. In the 5-year-old Nannerl they were perhaps able to feel a cautious optimism that they might keep her with them on earth, but it must still have been too soon to have the same thought about Wolfgang. Virtually nothing about the earliest days of their childhood is known, but Leopold's later letters to Nannerl about her infant son (who lived with his grandfather Leopold until he was nearly 2) suggest that the children were cherished as a joy to their parents, whilst being regarded as a 'borrowed blessing'.[38]

---

[32] See Ch. 12.

[33] See H.Z. (initials only given), 'Mozarts Mutter, Gattin und Freunde als Gasteiner Kurgäste', in *Bad Gasteiner Badeblatt*, 16/22, 15 July 1956. Niderl wrote on bathing cures—see H. Schuler, 'Dr. med. Franz Joseph Niderl, Hausarzt der Familie Mozart: Ein Beitrag zu seiner Familiengeschichte', *MM* 26 (1978), 6 n. 15.

[34] I have not been able to check that the ducat/florin conversion in Salzburg was 5 fl. per ducat for this early date; however, it could be confirmed as 5 on almost all the occasions from the 1760s to the 1780s which were relevant to this book.

[35] Leopold to Nannerl, 12 Aug. 1786—*MBA* 976/20–31 (not in *Letters*). Leopold's memory of his salary at that date appears to be faulty—the official records show that in 1750 it was actually only 20 fl. per month, not including the customary bread and wine allowance of 4 fl. 30 kr. per month. In 1756 it increased to 25 fl. per month, still without the bread and wine allowance. Cf. Hintermaier, 'Hofkapelle', 290; and Mančal, '"... durch beyhülff hoher Recommandation"', 168 n. 102. Mančal believes that Leopold did not receive this allowance of 54 fl. annually until 1761, but Hintermaier does not mention this. If Mančal is right, 1761 was the earliest date when the salary was 29 fl. 30 kr. per month, and 12 ducats represented around 3 months' worth of the 1750 salary.

[36] Deutsch, *Documents*, 7–9.

[37] Leopold to Lotter, 9 Feb. 1756—*MBA* 22/22–4 (not in *Letters*).

[38] Leopold to Nannerl, 22 Sept. 1785—*MBA* 881/40–5 (not in *Letters*).

Financially, things improved after the publication of the *Violinschule*. The early married years must have brought heavy medical expenses connected with the pregnancies, confinements, illnesses, and deaths, and Leopold apparently supported Maria Anna's mother Eva Rosina too.[39] Relations with his own family in Augsburg were not satisfactory (although the details are not known), and he seems to have had some difficulty in gaining his share of his father's estate.[40] The dedication of the *Violinschule* to Archbishop Schrattenbach was presumably rewarded by a gift of money, however, and his salary rose in the year of publication to 25 fl. per month (300 fl. annually). Furthermore, he was appointed violin teacher at the Kapellhaus from 13 November 1756, and this brought him another 18 fl. annually.[41] Finally, the sales of the work brought Leopold a fairly steady extra income for the rest of his life. Later he was to estimate that he earned 50 fl. annually from the *Violinschule* alone.[42] At the time he made this remark, 50 fl. represented either about 14 per cent or 11 per cent of his annual income,[43] but if he was earning 50 fl. from the work earlier in his career it would have been a far higher proportion.[44] The book received very good reviews,[45] and was priced low at 2 fl. 15 kr.[46] For German students it was thus ideal, though its fame and sales were to spread far beyond German-speaking Europe. Leopold handled all the marketing himself. He kept piles of the product in chests at home, and sent a number of copies to booksellers elsewhere in Germany at regular intervals. It was particularly important to top up the booksellers' supplies just before the big markets, because these were the main sales opportunities. Leopold therefore had constantly to think ahead in order to transport the piles of books to the right places at the right times in the cheapest possible way— he usually negotiated with Salzburg merchants who were themselves sending goods at the same time. Reckoning up was also complicated because of the different currencies involved and the mechanisms for remitting cash.

[39] Leopold to Wolfgang, 5 Feb. 1778—*MBA* 417/28–38 (*Letters* 282).

[40] Leopold to Lotter, 21 July 1755, 11 Sept. 1755, and 15 Dec. 1755—*MBA* 6/5–19, 9/8–22, and 14/2–9 (none in *Letters*).

[41] See Hintermaier, 'Hofkapelle', 290.

[42] Leopold to Wolfgang, 27 Aug. 1778—*MBA* 478/163–9 (not in *Letters*).

[43] In Aug. 1778 Leopold was earning 354 fl. annually, but his salary rose to 454 fl. from 1 Sept. 1778 (both figures include the bread and wine allowance). Hence the two alternative percentage figures. See Hintermaier, 'Hofkapelle', 290.

[44] From 1747 to 1756, Leopold's salary was 240 fl. annually (not including the customary bread and wine allowance—cf. n. 35 above), so the *Violinschule* earnings could have represented about 21 per cent of this.

[45] Cf. Deutsch, *Documents*, 10; and C. Eisen, 'Leopold Mozart Discoveries', *MM* 35 (1987), 6–9.

[46] Leopold to Maria Anna, 7 Jan. 1770—*MBA* 152/113–9 (not in *Letters*). This passage also makes it clear that of the 2 fl. 15 kr., the bookseller kept 30 kr. and Leopold received 1 fl. 45 kr.

The Mozarts were renting an apartment on the third floor of the house of Johann Lorenz and Maria Theresia Hagenauer. The Hagenauers had a thriving grocery business and traded over an extensive area, with connections as far as Hamburg, Rotterdam, Marseilles, and Venice.[47] They acted as bankers to the Mozarts, and must have made much of the *Violinschule* sales business easier for Leopold by making their credit network available to him. Like the Mozarts, they had a young family, and since most of their children survived infancy, the house was full of playmates for Nannerl and Wolfgang. The Mozarts seem to have been extremely sociable, inviting round friends for music-making, card-playing, and chat. If the routines followed when the children were small were similar to those recorded in the later correspondence and in Nannerl's diary, there would have been visitors in the house almost every day, and some would have stayed several hours to make music. The essay Nannerl was to write in 1792 for Schlichtegroll's biography of Mozart drew on her own memories and those of Andreas Schachtner, a court music colleague of Leopold's. These accounts suggest that there was easy familiarity between the adult friends of Leopold and Maria Anna and the children. Schachtner described yielding to the young Wolfgang's demands regarding play and music, and was able to intercede for Wolfgang when Leopold would not allow the child to join in some ensemble music-making.[48] All the sociability notwithstanding, however, as Nannerl and Wolfgang grew older, the main business of the day seems to have been work.

Nothing is known of Nannerl's education before the age of 8, but on her eighth name-day, 26 July 1759, she received as a present a music book written by Leopold, and began to learn to play the keyboard.[49] Wolfgang, at $3\frac{1}{2}$, was still barely more than a toddler. The book's cover bore a grave and formal greeting from Leopold to Nannerl in French. Inside were minuets and other short pieces, many written by Leopold himself. It is not known how Nannerl progressed in her early lessons, but the younger Wolfgang evidently began to demand to play too, and only a few months after Nannerl had been given the book, Leopold was recording in it the remarkable achievements of his son, noting the time taken for him to learn to play the pieces in it.[50] The fact that Leopold had not done

---

[47] G. Barth, 'Die Hagenauers. Ein Salzburger Bürgergeschlecht aus Ainring: Die Einbindung einer Handelsfamilie in Wirtschaft, Politik und Kultur Salzburgs im späten 17. und 18. Jahrhundert', in *Ainring: Ein Heimatbuch* (Ainring, 1990), 313.

[48] See Deutsch, *Documents*, 451–4.

[49] In her essay for Schlichtegroll of 1792, Nannerl stated that she had begun to play the keyboard at the age of 7—Deutsch, *Documents*, 455.

[50] Ibid. 12.

this for Nannerl suggests that there was nothing exceptional about her own progress, good though it presumably was. Wolfgang also later used blank pages at the end of the book to write his earliest compositions. It is tempting to see the taking over by Wolfgang of this special gift from her father as a symbol of the way in which Wolfgang both overshadowed Nannerl and usurped their father's attention, but without further knowledge of the musical relationship between Leopold and Nannerl during the period when Wolfgang was using Nannerl's book, it would be unwise to make too much of this. Nevertheless, there is one small piece of evidence to suggest that Nannerl did suffer psychologically from the precociousness of her brother, who was after all considerably younger.[51] How Leopold and Maria Anna handled this situation is not well documented, but Nannerl was clearly encouraged to continue to play and to strive for excellence, and she and Wolfgang were able to work together affectionately throughout their childhood and teens, and were supportive of each other's achievements.

Leopold now had the education of two children to supervise in addition to all his other duties. Since later documentation suggests that the whole family typically rose early (around six) and went to bed late (around midnight), it may be that some of the children's work was fitted into the early morning hours before Leopold's court and teaching duties began, and that long evenings were devoted to domestic music-making, often involving Leopold's colleagues.[52] The education was by no means only a musical one, but encompassed mathematics, reading, writing, literature, languages, and dancing. Above all it had a moral and religious foundation. Maria Anna's role in it is unfortunately not known, although there is some evidence to suggest that she was involved at least in moral training.[53] As the children grew older, their educational paths were to diverge. Nannerl was to spend time, in addition to playing the keyboard, learning from her mother all the arts of housekeeping, while Wolfgang was to concentrate on musical composition and other skills which would

---

[51] Leopold specifically suggested as much in a letter to Hagenauer of 20 Aug. 1763—*MBA* 63/74–6 (*Letters* 16). The passage is discussed in Ch. 4.

[52] In a draft letter to Albert von Mölk in 1792, Nannerl gave details of Wolfgang's childhood routine, for use in Schlichtegroll's *Nekrolog*: she stated that he frequently sat at the keyboard at nine in the evening and would have extemporized all night if he had not been forced to stop at midnight; he also composed from six or seven until nine or ten in the morning, in bed, after which he composed nothing more all day long. See *MBA* 1213/45–55 and 92–101 (not in *Letters* or Deutsch, *Documents*).

[53] She asked Hagenauer, through Leopold, on 30 Mar. 1768, to send her a children's magazine which in all probability included material for moral development—*MBA* 128/43–4 (not in *Letters*).

be needed by a Kapellmeister. A likely schedule would seem to be that Leopold set work for the children each morning, and that Maria Anna supervised it while he was out. Leopold then probably spent most of his spare time checking it, listening to music learnt, and so forth. It also seems very probable that he arranged for the children to play some part in the informal ensemble music sessions to which he invited his colleagues, and possible that certain colleagues gave one or both of the children some of their musical instruction.[54] The importance to the formation of good taste of listening to good ensemble playing should not be underestimated. Had Wolfgang not shown such precocity, the obvious alternative form of education for him would have been the Kapellhaus, which would have educated, fed, clothed, and housed him free of charge in return for his services as a choirboy. Nannerl would probably have received a more basic education at home, which would have included keyboard playing and housekeeping. But long before Wolfgang had reached the age at which he could be admitted to the choir school it was clear that the ideal for him was a more individually tailored education.

Once the education of the children was under way in earnest, therefore, there was a substantial extra demand on Leopold's time. And given that he had formerly fitted composition (which was an important component of his work, assuming he wanted further promotion) into the spare time between court duties, there were clearly implications for his own career. Nannerl later claimed that he had given up all his spare time for his children, so that he could no longer take private pupils or compose.[55] Leopold also told Wolfgang that he had sacrificed all his time to the education of his children.[56] One well-entrenched version of Leopold's biography, however, has suggested that he was an indifferent composer who gave up his efforts when he began to realize, from Wolfgang's compositions, his own mediocrity.[57] This view of Leopold has for some

---

[54] See Eisen, *Documents*, 1.

[55] See Nannerl's essay of 1792 for Schlichtegroll's biography—Deutsch, *Documents*, 454.

[56] Leopold to Wolfgang, 5 Feb. 1778—*MBA* 417/38–43 (*Letters* 282).

[57] For a summary of opinions about Leopold as a composer, see Carlson, 'The Vocal Music of Leopold Mozart', 9–60. Among the opinions collated by Carlson are those that Leopold was worthless as a composer even without the disadvantage of being compared with his son; that he was a correct composer but nothing more; that his youthful works show affinities to those of Joseph Haydn, but that (unlike Haydn) he failed to develop; and that his active compositional period fell between two musical styles, so that he had no persuasive style of his own. Carlson enumerates the faults underlying these opinions—they range from poor sampling, through copying of earlier authors' opinions, to failure to recognize the impossibility of an assessment of Leopold while his exact *œuvre* remains unknown.

time now been challenged on several fronts,[58] but it is still not possible to determine when he stopped composing, or just how extensive his role in Wolfgang's compositional education was. Without basic factual information about his *œuvre*, ideas about his reasons for giving up composition can only be tentative; but it seems likely that several interconnecting factors were at work. First, those who have combined the home education of children with other work are likely to feel instinctively that something of Leopold's former activities would have to lapse in order to fit in the unremitting daily attention to two children with different needs in several areas of work. Individual attention tends to foster more rapid progress, which means that new work is needed much more frequently than for children in a school. Furthermore, the investment of parental love and pride, together with a deeper knowledge than a teacher usually has of a child's character and needs, tends to mean that far greater effort is lavished on one's own children than on others. From this perspective, the statement by Nannerl about Leopold's declining attention to composition seems entirely comprehensible. Secondly, it is quite possible that there was an element of a feeling of inferiority to Wolfgang at work, though this can be believed without detriment to Leopold's compositional standing in comparison with his other Salzburg colleagues. Thirdly, Leopold's confidence in his teaching ability can only have increased as he watched the development of his children, so that he may in later years have derived more satisfaction from the idea of writing pedagogical and theoretical works than from composing.[59] Fourthly, Leopold became increasingly disenchanted with the Salzburg court, not only because of the

[58] For example, Wolfgang Plath first distinguished Leopold's handwriting from Wolfgang's, enabling much confusion of attribution to be avoided and (by establishing that Leopold was correcting Wolfgang's compositions at least until Wolfgang was 16) challenging the views that Leopold lost interest in composition and that Wolfgang rapidly outstripped him as a composer. See W. Plath, 'Beiträge zur Mozart-Autographie I. Die Handschrift Leopold Mozarts', *MJb* (1960–1), 82–117; id., 'Zur Echtheitsfrage bei Mozart', *MJb* (1971–2), 19–36. Cliff Eisen has done essential groundwork on the authenticity, chronology, and style of Leopold Mozart's symphonies, enabling more secure assessments to be made of the relationship between Leopold's work and Wolfgang's. See Eisen, 'The Symphonies of Leopold Mozart' (diss.); id., 'The Symphonies of Leopold Mozart: Their Chronology, Style and Importance for the Study of Mozart's Early Symphonies', *MJb* (1987–8), 181–93. David Carlson has done similar groundwork on Leopold's vocal music—see previous note. And Manfred Hermann Schmid has placed some of Leopold's work in the context of composition at the Salzburg court, identifying local traditions common to all composers working there. See M. H. Schmid, *Mozart und die Salzburger Tradition* (Tutzing, 1976).

[59] In the last paragraph of the *Violinschule*, Leopold suggested that he might write a further theoretical work. When the 3rd edn. appeared in 1787 (the year of his death), he had not given up the idea, despite his claim that his travels had hindered him. See *Treatise*, 225.

way his own career was to stagnate after 1763, but because he felt that the policies did not encourage the development of an excellent band. Poor morale may therefore have helped sap his creative energy.[60] Whatever combination of factors may have been at work, Leopold was to be slow to realize that the education of his children, brilliant though the results were, was not necessarily a complement to his own career.

By the time Wolfgang was 6 and Nannerl 10, early in 1762, the achievements of both children were remarkable enough for Leopold to think that they could be shown to people outside Salzburg. He therefore took them to Munich for a visit of three weeks, where they played to the elector. There is no documented detail about this trip,[61] but it must have been successful, for Leopold decided to follow it up by a similar but more ambitious one to Vienna. On 18 September 1762 they set off all together for the imperial capital. Leopold was 42, Maria Anna 41, Nannerl 11, and Wolfgang 6. Behind them in Salzburg was the vacant position of Kapellmeister—Eberlin had died on 19 June, and though Lolli was Vice-Kapellmeister, he had not been promoted.

[60] In a letter to Padre Martini of 4 Sept. 1776, signed by Wolfgang but written by Leopold, Leopold complained of the lack of opportunities for rewarding music-making in Salzburg, and of the neglect of older, long-serving musicians, and used these grievances to explain why he intended to devote his energy to literary interests rather than music—*MBA* 323 (*Letters* 205).

[61] The only account of it is given by Nannerl in her essay of 1792 for Schlichtegroll's *Nekrolog*. She does not make it clear whether Maria Anna went too. See Deutsch, *Documents*, 455.

3

Wolfgang as Linchpin:
The Visit to Vienna in 1762

T HE first well-documented absence of the Mozart family from Salzburg is of interest for its introduction of some of the themes which were to prove so important in the lives of all the members of the family—the beguiling but risky nature of the freelance way of life, and the economic importance of Wolfgang to the family. Corollaries of this economic factor were to be the dependence on him of everyone else, and the way in which almost every aspect of family life was to be made subservient to his development: Leopold's own ambitions, for example, had to be modified and eventually abandoned, Maria Anna died away from home on Wolfgang's account, and Nannerl's adult life was lived for nearly fifteen years in suspension while she waited for her brother to provide her with a more stimulating environment. Tracing these and other themes through the lives of the various members of the family, it is possible to see how, in ways which may seem obscure at first, the relationships between the people concerned altered because of their different attitudes to the events which they all experienced.

During their visit to Vienna in 1762, Leopold sent all their news regularly in letters to Lorenz Hagenauer. On 3 October 1762, therefore, Leopold opened the correspondence with Hagenauer which was to continue intermittently until the end of 1768 and chronicle everything on their travels around Europe which Leopold considered newsworthy. The letters were usually open ones, which Hagenauer was encouraged to pass round the circle of the Mozarts' acquaintances. Leopold was especially keen for news of the children's triumphs to reach the ears of the archbishop and other influential people in Salzburg, but he also prided himself on his ability to write lucid and lively reports on aspects of life in the places they visited. In this way he tried to give people at home the impression that he was effectively an ambassador of the Salzburg court. If he had news that he did not want circulated, he marked it for Hagenauer's eyes alone. But even Hagenauer probably did not know everything, for he was the banker on all the Mozarts' travels, and Leopold's letters were thus not motivated by friendship alone. Hagenauer provided the letters of credit to his business contacts which enabled Leopold to draw cash in distant places. The debts then bounced back to Hagenauer in Salzburg along the mercantile credit network, and had eventually to be repaid by Leopold. Though the correspondence suggests that all this was done extremely amicably, it nevertheless has to be borne in mind that the relationship between the two men was not an equal one. This means that the letters need to be read with an alertness to the possibility that Leopold did not always tell Hagenauer the whole truth when things were going badly. His financial credit depended on Hagenauer's continuing confidence in his success.

The first letter was written from Linz, where the Mozarts had stopped to give a concert on the way to Vienna. Leopold complained that they had been delayed five days by the prince-bishop of Passau, who had kept them waiting before summoning them to play, and had then only listened to Wolfgang, and had only given him one ducat (4 fl. 10 kr.).[1] Since travelling (with its many overnight stops) was so expensive, it was essential to earn as much as possible by giving concerts as they went, but also to move on promptly if there was no opportunity to do this. Leopold was aggrieved because he thought they could have earned more in Linz if they had arrived earlier.[2] This was only the first occasion of very many when the Mozarts could only chafe at the unnecessary expense they were put to through what they considered the inconsiderate behaviour of a patron.

When Leopold next wrote to Hagenauer, on 16 October 1762, the family had been in Vienna a week and had appeared at Maria Theresia's court and at a host of other musical functions. Leopold did not mention Nannerl except to indicate that she had been fully involved in the concerts so far; instead his talk was all of Wolfgang. Wolfgang had played the organ at Ybbs so well that people had left a meal they were eating to wonder at him, Wolfgang had eased their passage through Viennese customs by playing a minuet on his violin for the customs officer, all the ladies in Vienna had fallen in love with Wolfgang, Archduke Leopold had been

---

[1] This conversion was given by Leopold himself in the course of his letter. I have not been able to check whether this was the Salzburg value of a ducat in 1762; from 1766 at latest the conversion in Salzburg was 5 fl. The sum does not correspond to any of the three types of Austrian ducat (Kremnitz, imperial, and ordinary) at this date; according to Dexter Edge, from 1753 to 1783 the Kremnitz ducat was worth 4 fl. 18 kr., the imperial ducat 4 fl. 16 kr., and the ordinary ducat 4 fl. 14 kr. See D. Edge, 'Mozart's Fee for *Così fan tutte*', *JRMA* 116/2 (1991), 218.

[2] *MBA* 32 (*Letters* 1).

overheard in the theatre praising Wolfgang, and everyone who heard him agreed that his talents were inconceivable.

Maria Theresia had sent a court costume for each child to wear at the next imperial reception, and Leopold claimed that they had been treated by the royal family with extraordinary graciousness.[3] This might well have been more because of the charm of the children than because of admiration for Leopold's enterprise as a whole,[4] but Leopold appears generally to have believed that a civil reception indicated esteem for him beyond that normally accorded to musicians, from whom he always tried to distance himself. It is probable that he read too much into the friendly behaviour of patrons, and exaggerated to himself both his standing with them and his prospects of employment outside Salzburg.

At this juncture, however, they appeared to be in the empress's favour. She sent them 100 ducats (426 fl. 40 kr.), and requested them to prolong their stay in Vienna. Leopold remitted the cash to an account of Hagenauer's in Vienna, and mentioned the possibility of buying his own carriage to make the return journey more comfortable for the children.[5] The money was riches to Leopold, whose annual salary by now was 354 fl.[6] Yet in his next letter, of 30 October 1762, came the acknowledgement of the fragility of their good fortune. Wolfgang was ill with a fever and painful rash, and was to be indoors for a fortnight.[7] As bad luck would have it, his name-day occurred while he was unable to go out, and Leopold lamented that he would otherwise have been given some handsome presents by their Viennese patrons, who had been booking them for private concerts.[8] The fact that Nannerl did not appear in concerts while Wolfgang was ill, though perfectly healthy herself, may be taken to mean that she was not considered sufficiently interesting on her own —when she was to be ill in The Hague in 1765, Wolfgang gave concerts without her. This is the first indication that Wolfgang, for all his tender years, was chiefly responsible for the family's income when they were away from home. Nannerl might contribute to it by joining her brother on the concert platform, and Leopold might make the whole business possible by his formidable powers of organization, but if Wolfgang could not appear, everything collapsed.

---

[3] *MBA* 34 (*Letters* 2).

[4] See Chs. 8 and 10 for material suggesting that Maria Theresia, later if not as early as this, held the Mozarts in contempt for their itinerant life-style.

[5] Leopold to Hagenauer, 19 Oct. 1762—*MBA* 35 (*Letters* 3).

[6] This figure includes the bread and wine allowance, but not the small fee for teaching in the Kapellhaus. See Hintermaier, 'Hofkapelle', 290.

[7] *MBA* 36 (*Letters* 4).   [8] Leopold to Hagenauer, 6 Nov. 1762—*MBA* 40 (*Letters* 5).

At the end of the letter describing Wolfgang's illness, which Leopold estimated had cost them 50 ducats (213 fl. 20 kr.) in lost revenue, Leopold asked Hagenauer to report to him on his chances of promotion to Vice-Kapellmeister in Salzburg. He seems to have been presuming that Lolli would advance to Eberlin's Kapellmeister post:

I beg you, do everything possible to find out for me what His Grace is eventually going to do, and what hopes I'll eventually have of the Vice-Kapellmeister appointment. I'm not asking idly. You are my friend. Who knows what I'll do: if I only knew what the eventual outcome will be., one thing is certain, that I find myself in circumstances which enable me to earn my bread here too.

I still prefer Salzburg to any other advantage: but at the same time I must not be kept back. I repeat my request: because otherwise I don't even know myself what I might be persuaded to do.[9]

And Leopold tackled the same question again in his next letter, stating that it would be greatly to his advantage if he could receive the appointment while he was in Vienna, and adding that people in Vienna already thought him Kapellmeister in Salzburg.[10] It is clear from these letters that he held himself in high regard, and that his personal ambition had been strengthened by his favourable reception in Vienna. It is also quite likely that he thought the advantage that would accrue to him of being appointed Salzburg's Vice-Kapellmeister while in Vienna was that his chance of obtaining a good appointment at Maria Theresia's court would thereby be increased. In fact, he was to be promoted on this occasion to Vice-Kapellmeister; but it was to be promotion for the last time—the post of full Kapellmeister was always to elude him. All the energy he might have used to drive on his own career was to be poured into promoting Wolfgang's. Evidently at this stage in his life he believed that the two things could be combined, and that his own career could only benefit from showing to the world the children he had taught. Unfortunately, this was not to be the case.

❧

The Hagenauer family performed many favours for the Mozarts when the latter were absent from Salzburg, and without their help the journeys could never have proceeded as smoothly as they did. Taken for granted was that the Hagenauers would look after the Mozarts' apartment, and

---

[9] Leopold to Hagenauer, 30 Oct. 1762—*MBA* 36/59–67 (*Letters* 4).
[10] Leopold to Hagenauer, 6 Nov. 1762—*MBA* 40/58–70 (*Letters* 5).

prepare it for their return. In addition, Hagenauer had evidently placed his network of mercantile credit at Leopold's disposal, because Leopold was able to use an account of Hagenauer's in Vienna. Leopold also asked Hagenauer to exert himself in the matter of the appointment of a Vice-Kapellmeister, by speaking to influential people in Salzburg and relaying the news of the Mozarts' triumphant reception in Vienna. It was Hagenauer too who acted as intermediary when Leopold needed to extend his leave of absence. It may be thought that when the Mozarts were away from home, the excitement of their activities would leave them little interest in news of Salzburg, but this was never the case. Hagenauer in his letters to Leopold chronicled illnesses, births, deaths, marriages, gossip of all sorts, and political news—all of which was devoured avidly by the Mozarts and commented upon by Leopold in his replies.[11] On his side, Leopold could report not only on the activities of his family, but also on Viennese life and politics, the imperial family and the Habsburg court, shopping, and trade—all of which was of great interest to the Hagenauers. Frequently Leopold found that he lacked the time to describe something as fully as he would like to, so he simply alluded to it, intending to discuss it in more detail with the Hagenauers when they met again. It seems clear that when they were at home, the Mozarts and the Hagenauers spent a good deal of their leisure time together, and each family took a friendly interest in the children of the other, and offered moral support, comfort, and condolence when a misfortune occurred. When the Mozarts had left home for this particular trip, Lorenz Hagenauer the younger, aged 18, was ill, and Maria Theresia Hagenauer had charged Nannerl with praying for him at the pilgrimage church of Maria Hilf above Passau.[12] Nannerl had done so, but he did not recover, and while they were in Vienna, Hagenauer reported the worsening of his condition. On 10 December 1762 Leopold replied, 'I am disturbed by Herr Lorenz's circumstances and I share your sadness. Such is life; God will do what is necessary for the cure of his soul. by all appearances, little good was to be hoped for: and yet I do still hope for it.'[13] This apparently laconic remark was fairly typical for the circumstances. Deaths occurred commonly in all age-groups—Leopold and Maria Anna had watched five of their own children die in infancy, and all their acquaintances suffered bereavements from time to time. Leopold's comment should therefore be seen

---

[11] Hagenauer's letters to Leopold are lost, and their contents can only be inferred from Leopold's replies.

[12] Leopold to Hagenauer, 3 Oct. 1762—*MBA* 32/40–2 (*Letters* 1).

[13] *MBA* 45/24–7 (not in *Letters*).

against the background of a resigned acceptance of God's will where death was inevitable, the acknowledgement that life had to go on, and the consciousness that there was nothing shocking about it. On the other hand, this attitude did not prevent enormous distress being felt, especially on the part of bereaved parents. Nannerl's future brother-in-law Franz Anton Maximilian Berchtold von Sonnenburg was to express his sorrow in the family chronicle about his newborn son, Ubald August Kaspar, who died on the day of his birth, 17 May 1794, 'to the greatest heartache of his father'.[14] Similarly sorrowful entries were to be made for Nannerl's daughter Maria Babette on 24 April 1791—she 'had not even reached the age of half a year'.[15]

Arranging for Masses to be said at specific altars in specific churches was a reciprocal favour usually carried out by the women of each family. Maria Theresia Hagenauer was frequently requested to have Masses said for the Mozarts at the various churches in and around Salzburg, especially when someone was, or had been, ill or there was a particularly difficult time ahead. In return Nannerl and Maria Anna Mozart did the same for her at churches they visited. The fact that this appears to have been one area of daily life arranged largely by the women perhaps reflected the situation of most women—deprived of active influence and power over their lives, they could at any rate pray with great fervour to try to affect the course of events. Nannerl was to do this when she and Leopold were helplessly waiting at home in 1778 for Wolfgang to improve the circumstances of the family by obtaining well-paid employment away from Salzburg.[16]

❧

Leopold's leave of absence had been extended, but when it was time to return to Salzburg he was still reluctant to leave Vienna. Later in his letter of 10 December 1762 he wrote to Hagenauer:

now there are still many things which could keep us here at least another month: Because, just think, count Durazzo the music director of this court hasn't been able to let us appear at his academy or public concert yet. if we agreed to do that; we could stay on here until Lent and easter, and take in a fine sum

---

[14] Brno, MZA, Rodinný archiv Berchtoldů (hereafter Berchtold Family Archive), Kronika rodu (hereafter Family Chronicle), unpaginated, but p. 73 on my count.

[15] Ibid., pp. 45 and 107 on my count.

[16] Leopold to Wolfgang, 25/26 Feb. 1778—*MBA* 430/119–21 (*Letters* 291).

each week. You'll be thinking: Vienna makes a fool of everyone. Well yes, it's true, if I compare certain aspects of Salzburg and Vienna: I could soon become bewildered.[17]

Resisting these temptations, however, the Mozarts contented themselves with a fortnight's visit to Pressburg (Bratislava), and then returned briefly to Vienna before travelling home, where they arrived on 5 January 1763. The atmosphere in the house they entered after their four-month absence must have been first anxious and then sad. Lorenz Hagenauer the younger, whose serious illness had been mentioned by Leopold in his letter of 10 December 1762, died only two weeks after their return and one week before Wolfgang's seventh birthday—as far as is known, he was only the second of the Hagenauers' eleven children to die.[18]

Leopold brought home with them from Vienna contact addresses for France and Holland, and was obviously thinking in terms of travelling further afield if permission to do so were forthcoming. On 17 February 1763, he wrote to his old Augsburg friend and printer Lotter to tell him about the success of the Viennese trip, on which they had been showered with presents by the top nobility. Towards the end of the letter he wrote, 'God willing, we'll soon see each other, because I've promised the French ambassador in Vienna that I'll go to Paris as soon as practicable. We're just waiting for the arrival of the swallows; so that we can begin our journey.'[19] On 28 February 1763, shortly after writing this letter, Leopold received the promotion to Vice-Kapellmeister which he had coveted, and Lolli became Kapellmeister. Neither man received a salary increase, however—the two things did not necessarily go hand in hand.[20]

Some three months later Leopold had the satisfaction of seeing, in the *Augsburgischer Intelligenz-Zettel* of 19 May 1763, a report on his children's success in Vienna. The report makes it clear that the two children were already displaying, in public at any rate, quite different musical skills. Later reports consistently confirm the information given in this one—that Nannerl was remarkable for her masterly performance of the most difficult pieces available, and played them not only with exceptional accuracy and brilliance but also in the best of taste, but that Wolfgang demonstrated a far wider range of musical abilities, and in particular an astonishing capacity for creative invention. As well as playing sonatas, trios, and concertos 'in a manly way', he could accompany symphonies, arias, and

---

[17] *MBA* 45/52–60 (*Letters* 8).   [18] See Barth, 'Die Hagenauers', 310.
[19] *MBA* 47/13–16 (not in *Letters*).   [20] See Hintermaier, 'Hofkapelle', 232 and 290.

recitatives at sight, improvise, add a bass to a melody without preparation, and so forth. He had also started to play the violin.[21]

It may be asked why Nannerl did not display some of these other
abilities in public. Did she lack the talent for them, was her musical
imagination constrained by her father's and society's idea of the kind
of musician a girl should be, was she inhibited by Wolfgang's precociousness, or was Leopold too absorbed in Wolfgang to encourage her
development beyond that of set-piece performance? Questions about
Nannerl's musical abilities suggest themselves periodically as her biography unfolds, but the evidence to answer them satisfactorily is tantaliz-
ingly thin. With respect to those arising from the reports of the children's
abilities during their European travels, it has been asserted by Nannerl's
biographer Eva Rieger that it occurred to no one to allow Nannerl to play
the organ or violin, which were outside the sphere of a woman, and that
Leopold only taught her the skills she needed to become a proficient
keyboard player. Hence she was not encouraged to compose. Improvisation, score-reading, and sight-reading were requisites for Kapellmeisters,
and since she was not destined to be one, her creative potential was
never awoken.[22]

The position, however, was almost certainly more complicated than
this. In the first place, Rieger tacitly assumes that what might have been
true of Nannerl's childhood remained valid throughout her life, but what
little evidence there is suggests rather that she was encouraged at different points to concentrate on different skills, according to diverse factors
such as how much time Leopold could spare for her (this was naturally
bound up with what Wolfgang was doing at the time), what the outlook
for the future of the family seemed currently to be, and even what the
emotional relationships were like. Of the skills mentioned in this report
as having been displayed by Wolfgang, for example, most (despite Rieger's
claim to the contrary) were also taught by Leopold to Nannerl at some
point in her life, though it is not known from how young an age.[23] There

[21] See Deutsch, *Documents*, 20–1.

[22] E. Rieger, *Nannerl Mozart: Leben einer Künstlerin im 18. Jahrhundert* (Frankfurt am Main, 2nd edn.
1991), 67–73.

[23] Rieger is right to observe that Nannerl might have, but did not, learn to play the violin and
organ, as Wolfgang did. But her suggestion that Nannerl's sex was the factor deciding that she should
not is probably an over-simplification (ibid. 70). Women could function as violinists, not only as
virtuosi such as Regina Strinasacchi, but also more modestly, for example in convents. While not
suggesting that Leopold would have considered either of these possibilities suitable for Nannerl,
it seems unwise to make sweeping judgements until more groundwork has been done on the multiplicity of ways in which women could function musically in (and out of) society. This involves research
into local conditions. For example, the convent for noble women on the Nonnberg, just outside

are surviving exercises, as well as references in the correspondence, to show that she learnt to vary a melody, accompany other instruments or voices at sight, compose a bass to a given melody and figure it (probably at sight), and improvise.[24] It should not be assumed, therefore, that because she did not display these skills publicly as a child she was not being taught them.

Secondly, Rieger appears to underestimate the creative nature of keyboard playing in the eighteenth century. To be able to play a fully-written-out piece accurately and in good taste was only one part of it. Most keyboard players, even amateur ones, also needed to be able to accompany solos and ensembles, and the accompaniments were not written out—only the bass-line was provided, and the harmony notated below it in shorthand by figures. Because figured bass accompaniment is no longer practised by most keyboard players, it is difficult to recapture the spirit of the time and appreciate just what this meant in terms of skill and creative imagination. Insight can be obtained, however, from reading contemporary didactic works for keyboard players, such as that by C. P. E. Bach.[25]

Bach enumerated the capabilities required of a keyboard player. He had to be able to improvise fantasias in all styles, work out extemporaneously any requested setting following the strictest rules of harmony and melody, be able to transpose anything instantly and faultlessly, play everything at sight, and have a complete knowledge of thorough-bass (the art of constructing an accompaniment from the shorthand figures). The study of thorough-bass alone involved a host of challenging skills. Its aim was a correct performance of the harmony of the piece, at the proper volume, with a suitable distribution of notes. To do this often involved departing from the notation (because it was faulty or inadequate), and sometimes deriving the bass-line from large scores with unfigured basses. When the bass-line paused, the player had to supply something suitable by extracting the correct harmony from one of the other voices. He had

Salzburg, had close links with St Peter's Abbey, which itself had a strong musical tradition. The nuns there played the instrumental parts necessary to accompany the Mass (including violins, double bass, timpani, and a special 'trumpet violin' which imitated the sound of a trumpet), and court composers wrote music for them. They might be lent to the court for a special occasion, and daughters of court musicians sometimes performed with them in the convent church. See F. Martin, 'Vom Salzburger Fürstenhof um die Mitte des 18. Jahrhunderts', *MGSL* 77 (1937), 14 and 35 (hereafter 'Fürstenhof 77'); and Klein, 'Nachrichten', 99, inc. n. 40.

[24] See W. Plath, 'Leopold Mozart und Nannerl: Lehrer und Schülerin', in W. Plath, *Mozart-Schriften: Ausgewählte Aufsätze*, ed. M. Danckwardt (Schriftenreihe der Internationalen Stiftung Mozarteum Salzburg, 9; Kassel, 1991), 375–8. See also Leopold's letter to Wolfgang of 25–6 Feb. 1778—*MBA* 430/89–110 (*Letters* 291).

[25] C. P. E. Bach, *Keyboard Instruments*.

to be able to provide an accompaniment in many voices or few, in strict or *galant* style, and to know which was appropriate for the piece in question. Taken for granted was complete familiarity with the intervals of every key, since many pieces modulated chromatically without the accidentals being noted in the figurings. Extensive practice was needed to provide middle parts with satisfactory voice-leading and a singing upper part, and to this end composition, melody, and singing were ideally also studied. Since Bach, like Leopold Mozart, believed that the aim of every performer was to ascertain and recreate the *Affekt* of the piece, he urged that a large part of the keyboard player's education should consist of listening as much as possible to good music, in order to develop the necessary good taste. All kinds of refinements (including the imitation in the accompaniment of the material of the solo part) were desirable if the accompaniment was to be (as Bach thought it should be) an essential part of the composition. Finally, the keyboard player had to show initiative in a crisis, coping with inept basses, the demands and faults of the soloist, the lack of preparation time, and much more. Bach wrote of the nobility of a good accompaniment, and questioned whether the soloist or the accompanist deserved greater credit, for although the soloist would have lavished time and care on the practising of the piece (which he might also have composed), the accompanist had to be able to enhance it extemporaneously.

Bach stated that his book was intended as a fundamental course for aspiring professional musicians, but he acknowledged that amateurs would also want to learn at least something of the material in it. He did not really cater for them, but tried nevertheless to be encouraging, suggesting, for example, that they could still learn to provide a limited but adequate accompaniment even if they could not master all the skills covered by his book.[26] Since it is known that Nannerl was not a mere player of written-out keyboard pieces, but also accompanied soloists, singers, small ensembles, and symphonies, it seems doubtful whether Rieger's claim that she was not encouraged to be creative can be an adequate description of the case. Indeed, Rieger's black-and-white distinction between amateur and professional keyboard requirements is surely questionable, and it seems more likely that there was a sliding scale of creative abilities among amateur keyboard players. The question that is difficult to answer is what Nannerl's position on this scale was.

[26] The information in this and the preceding paragraph is from C. P. E. Bach, *Keyboard Instruments*, at places too numerous to list separately.

There is also evidence that Leopold allowed Nannerl to sing, and that he wanted her to be capable of earning money from music when she grew up.[27] These pieces of evidence suggest that caution should be applied before assuming that Leopold did not give her the chance to broaden her musical horizons, though there is nevertheless also reason to believe that she was neglected by him during some periods, especially from the end of 1769 until the autumn of 1777, when he was travelling much of the time alone with Wolfgang.

❧

The Mozarts had been away about three and a half months, a short interval in comparison with the length of some of their later travels. Brief and to some extent experimental though the visit to Vienna had been, however, it nevertheless introduced some of the factors which were later to be of such importance to the decisions made for the future of the different family members, and to their attitudes to these decisions. In deciding to travel to Paris to exhibit his children to a wider audience, Leopold took the next step along the road which he thought held such exciting prospects for them all.

---

[27] Nannerl is depicted singing in the Parisian water-colour of her, Wolfgang, and Leopold by Louis Carrogis de Carmontelle (plate 3), and Leopold mentioned her singing in his letter to Maria Anna of 24 Mar. 1770—*MBA* 170/66–8 (*Letters* 84). References to his wish that she should be capable of earning money from music include Wolfgang's petition to Colloredo of 1 Aug. 1777, which was actually written by Leopold (*MBA* 328; *Letters* 206), and Leopold's letters to Wolfgang of 25–6 Feb. 1778 (*MBA* 430/89–110; *Letters* 291) and 6 Apr. 1778 (*MBA* 441/49–55; *Letters* 301).

4

The Grand European Tour (I):
Petty Setbacks on the Journey to Paris

T HE most valuable perk of being a court musician in Salzburg was that occasional foreign travel was not only allowed but encouraged—it was seen as ultimately beneficial to the court. It was usual for the salary to continue to be paid in full during an absence of this kind, and not uncommon for a gift of money to be made by the archbishop at the outset as well.[1] Musicians therefore, unlike most other court employees, had the opportunity for combining a refreshing break from their usual duties with the chance to earn extra money while they were away. The Mozarts left home on 9 June 1763 on the first stage of the most ambitious journey they were ever to make—one which was to last almost three and a half years, and take them as far as England, which Leopold claimed had never been visited by any of their contemporaries in Salzburg.[2] Despite the great length of the absence, it seems that Leopold's salary continued to be paid, but there is no record that he received any other help towards the expenses.[3] Whatever financial resources Leopold took with him at the outset, however, they did not represent the whole of the family's wealth, for he later told Hagenauer of another 200 fl. left in their apartment in Salzburg.[4] This was probably money saved from the visit to Vienna.

Planning such a journey was a considerable enterprise, because travel and accommodation expenses were so high that it was necessary to earn

---

[1] A valuable source of information for such payments under Archbishop Schrattenbach are Schrattenbach's *Schatullegelder* records. The *Schatulle* was a privy purse—a sum of money over which the archbishop had free disposition, without reference to the Chapter or anyone else. Every archbishop enjoyed the privilege, but only for the period 1756–71, under Schrattenbach, have records of the expenditure survived. It was from the *Schatulle* that gifts of money for musicians' journeys tended to be made. See the list of *Schatullegelder* outgoings in Martin, 'Fürstenhof 80', 180–7.

[2] Leopold to Hagenauer, 13 Sept. 1764—*MBA* 92/247–9 (*Letters* 31).

[3] No such payment is documented, at any rate, by the *Schatullegelder* records—see Martin, 'Fürstenhof 80', 180–7.

[4] Leopold to Hagenauer, 4 Nov. 1763—*MBA* 68/41–2 (not in *Letters*).

money as they went. On leaving home they had to have with them music, medicines, money, suitable clothing for all occasions, and letters of introduction and credit for their first destination at least. The letters of introduction would be addressed to anyone who might be able to help further their cause (for example, by arranging for a concert to be given). The letters of credit were to merchants. Leopold knew which Salzburg merchants had business with which other European towns, and acted accordingly. Typically, the procedure would be that one of the Salzburg merchants would give Leopold a letter which could be presented to a specified business contact elsewhere, and the letter would authorize the recipient to provide a specified sum of money. When moving on again, if no Salzburg merchants had direct contact with anyone at the next destination, the initial credit could be extended by a letter from the first contact to a business acquaintance of his own, and any money drawn from such a third party would be reimbursed in stages along the merchant network, the debt eventually finding its way back to Salzburg. The process was strictly formal, and any attempt to draw money without observing the correct procedure was likely to be unsuccessful.

On arrival at any new centre, Leopold had to establish as quickly as possible the chances of being invited to play at court (if there was one) or giving a profitable concert, which would help finance the next stage of the journey. He therefore had to visit influential people even before unpacking, and present any letters he might have. If the prospects seemed poor, they had to travel on immediately, to avoid pointless accommodation costs. If they were told that a court appearance might be possible, however, they had to wait until summoned and, having played, had to wait again until a present was forthcoming. Alternatively, if a public concert seemed feasible, music was chosen, rehearsals held, advertisements placed in the press, and so on. Meanwhile, preparations had to be made for the next stage of the journey, because it was imperative to move on as quickly as possible once there was nothing more to be earned.

This involved knowing the next promising place for concert-giving along the route, establishing (if it was a court) whether the ruler was in residence, and ensuring that the letters of introduction and credit for the next stage were collected together. In particular, Leopold had to keep in mind special days of celebration at all the courts he thought of visiting, since the prospects of handsome presents were increased on occasions such as the name-days of rulers. In the absence of good earning prospects, the most economical route to the next musical centre had to be chosen instead. Leopold and Maria Anna had with them maps showing how many post stages there were between one town and the next—travellers were charged by the stage.

In addition, of course, suitable music had to be at hand for every opportunity, and the children had to keep up their practice as they went. There had to be a broad idea of where to spend winter (since it was almost impossible to travel then) and how to survive the summer (when wealthy people left the towns and dispersed to their country estates, to the detriment of concert life). On this particular journey, Leopold had in mind that their first winter would be spent in Paris, where there was plenty to be earned, and had therefore to pace their journey to arrive in time for them to be slotted in to any concerts arranged.

One problem frequently encountered was that nobles often paid with trinkets rather than cash, and Leopold then had to decide whether or not to part with them. When times were hard, valuable objects had to be sold. There also had to be contingency plans in case of illness or other hindrances, and spare money was ideally always at hand for emergencies. Thus the undertaking as a whole involved ceaseless work, forethought, chasing of useful acquaintances, and an ability to spot opportunities and grasp them.[5]

Leopold kept a record of points he considered important about their journey. This included the names of people they met on the way (especially the influential acquaintances), the inns they stayed in, and the sights they saw. He also kept a note of their income and expenditure, and the many complicated currency conversions they had to make as they left one region and entered another.[6] For the reasons given above, he planned a route to Paris via towns and courts which he calculated would afford the best opportunities for the children to perform. A calendar noting the progress of their journey is given below:

1763

9 June	Left Salzburg and arrived in Wasserburg just after midnight, after suffering a broken carriage wheel.
11 June	Wolfgang played the organ in Wasserburg while they waited for the wheel to be mended.

[5] The material about the organization of the journeys is derived from many references in the family correspondence, in particular from that of 1777–9, when Wolfgang and Maria Anna travelled to Paris without Leopold, and he wrote a stream of letters offering advice.

[6] Leopold's travel diary entries are given in *MBA* but not in *Letters*. But his financial records are lost, and their original existence only known from his letters to Hagenauer (e.g. *MBA* 67/58–71; not in *Letters*), and those to Wolfgang of 1777–9 (e.g. *MBA* 433/68–72; not in *Letters*).

12 June	Travelled on to Munich.
13 June	Wolfgang played to Elector Maximilian from 8.00 p.m. until late in the evening, but there was no time for Nannerl to perform.
14 June	Both children played to Duke Clemens of Bavaria.
15 June	They again played to Duke Clemens.
18 June	The family was present at a gala dinner given by the elector.
19 June	Nannerl played at court.
22 June	Travelled on to Augsburg.
28 June	Gave public concert in Augsburg.
30 June	Another public concert in Augsburg.
4 July	Final public concert in Augsburg.
6 July	On to Ulm, taking with them a small keyboard instrument made by Stein of Augsburg, to facilitate practice while travelling.
7 July	Wolfgang played the Minster organ in the morning, and then they travelled on, probably to Cannstatt.
9 July	Arrived in Ludwigsburg.
12 July	Left Ludwigsburg for Bruchsal, having failed to play to the duke of Württemberg, Karl Eugen.
14 July	Arrived in Schwetzingen, the country seat of the elector Palatine.
18 July	Played for Karl Theodor, the elector Palatine and founder of the famous Mannheim orchestra.
after 19 July	Visited Heidelberg.
19 July–2 Aug.	Itinerary uncertain.
3 Aug.	Arrived at Mainz, via Mannheim and Worms.
after 3 Aug.	Public concert in Mainz, but no performance for Elector Emmerich Joseph because he was ill.
c.10 Aug.	By boat to Frankfurt, leaving heavy luggage in Mainz for later collection.
18 Aug.	Public concert in Frankfurt.
22 Aug.	Second public concert in Frankfurt.
25 Aug.	Third public concert in Frankfurt.
26 Aug.	Fourth public concert in Frankfurt.
30 Aug.	Fifth public concert in Frankfurt.
31 Aug.	Returned to Mainz, remaining until mid-September.
Early Sept.	Another concert in Mainz.
13 Sept.	Left Mainz for Koblenz—a trying journey; see below, p. 53.
17 Sept.	Arrived in Koblenz.
18 Sept.	The children played to the elector, Johann Philipp.
21 Sept.	Gave concert in Koblenz.
27 Sept.	Arrived in Bonn.
28 Sept.	Via Brühl to Cologne.

30 Sept.	Cologne to Aachen (where they were delayed by Leopold's attack of sciatica).
2 Oct.	Aachen to Liège.
3 Oct.	Arrived in Tirlemont.
4 Oct.	Arrived in Louvain.
5 Oct.	Arrived in Brussels.
4 Nov.	Attended a free ball in the theatre.
7 Nov.	Were eventually asked to play to Prince Karl Alexander of Lorraine, Governor of the Austrian Netherlands and brother of Emperor Francis 1.
15 Nov.	Arrived in Mons.
16 Nov.	Arrived in Bonavis.
17 Nov.	Arrived in Gournay.
18 Nov.	Arrived in Paris, where they were able to stay in a private lodging rather than an inn.[7]

When they had stayed in Vienna in 1762, Leopold and Maria Anna had gained some limited experience not only of the possibility of acquiring great wealth through their children's performances, but also of the perilous nature of such an enterprise. On this, their grand tour, they were to experience the same thing again, but with the added major complication of all the travelling. The journey to Paris was accomplished without a serious illness affecting any member of the family, and yet the petty setbacks would have been daunting enough to anyone less well organized, confident, and courageous than Leopold. It is worth paying some attention to the things which could go wrong on journeys, in order to gain a clearer understanding of Leopold's state of mind when Wolfgang travelled without him from 1777 to 1779. That journey was to go about as wrong as anything could, and Leopold was well aware of all the risks which Wolfgang faced on it, and the action that he should be taking at each stage to prepare for them. The experience he drew on then was experience hard gained by journeys such as this one beginning in 1763, and fifteen years later, Leopold had forgotten very little of it. What he could not remember, his travel notebooks reminded him of.

---

[7] The calendar is derived from the chronology in Deutsch, *Documents*, and from J. H. Eibl, *Wolfgang Amadeus Mozart: Chronik eines Lebens* (2nd paperback edn., Kassel, 1977). The two sources do not always quite agree, and sometimes both seem questionable, but the information is accurate enough for this purpose, which is to provide quick orientation while reading this chapter. The second concert in Mainz is mentioned neither by Eibl nor Deutsch, but is known from Leopold's letter to Hagenauer of 26 Sept. 1763 (*MBA* 64/6–7; *Letters* 17) and Nannerl's 1792 essay for Schlichtegroll (*MBA* 1212/72; Deutsch, *Documents*, 455). In a letter to Wolfgang of 4 Dec. 1777, Leopold in fact stated that they had given three concerts in Mainz, and earned 200 fl. from them—*MBA* 385/43–5 (*Letters* 255).

The first mishap occurred on only the second day, just outside Wasserburg, when a carriage wheel broke. Leopold reported that they had waited on the open road for an hour while a temporary repair was effected. Then the iron hoop of the old wheel was strapped to the carriage so that it could be reused when the full repair was carried out. In this way the carriage limped into Wasserburg, Leopold and their servant Sebastian Winter accompanying it on foot in order not to strain it further. They arrived after midnight, and the following two days were taken up with repairing the wheel, so they had to stay three nights in the Golden Star, spending money which could have been saved. On 11 June 1763 Leopold wrote to Hagenauer:

What was to be done now? — — it meant being patient, reluctantly! and as I write this nothing's changed. because the job won't be finished before nightfall. So it means: sit here and stay tonight as well. The main thing about the business is the expense. because at the very least I have the honour of feeding the horses and coachman. In God's name: It's better to lose ten wheels than a foot or a couple of fingers. We are well, thank God.[8]

Leopold's philosophical attitude to hindrances of this kind rarely deserted him, partly no doubt because he saw to it that he was rarely without the means to cope with them.

The next irritation occurred in Munich and was caused by the elector, Maximilian, who indicated his desire to hear both children play, but who had the reputation of being slow to give a present. On 21 June Leopold wrote to Hagenauer, 'Now the question is how we're going to get along here: since the charming custom here is to keep people waiting a long time for presents; so that you have to be content if you take in what you've spent. Herr Tomasini has already been here three weeks. Now at last he's got away.'[9] The Mozarts were more fortunate than the violinist Tomasini. Wolfgang had played to the elector on the day after their arrival, 13 June; but there had not been time for Nannerl to perform too, and so they faced the prospect of staying on in Munich waiting for the elector to summon her. Leopold hit upon the idea of getting the artless Wolfgang to let slip to the elector the fact that they wanted to be away, and Nannerl then played to him on 19 June. Meanwhile the children had played twice for Duke Clemens, and could therefore hope for a present from him too. When Leopold wrote the above lines to Hagenauer, therefore, the only thing preventing their departure was the fact that

---

[8] *MBA* 49/28–34 (*Letters* 10).   [9] *MBA* 50/18–21 (*Letters* 11).

they had received no present from the elector. This was forthcoming very soon afterwards, however, and they were able to leave on 22 June. They took with them 100 fl. from the elector and 75 fl. from Duke Clemens, after a sojourn of ten days, so they did better than Tomasini who, according to Leopold, received only 10 Maximilian d'or (about 70 fl.) after playing twice and staying there three weeks.[10] On the other hand, Tomasini's travelling expenses would have been lighter—when Leopold wrote to Hagenauer, he still did not know what his bill at the inn would be. He later reported, on 26 September 1763, that it had been 47 fl. 58 kreutzer.[11]

In Augsburg, according to Leopold's report to Hagenauer of 11 July 1763, though they gave three concerts they only just covered their expenses.[12] They also made there a major purchase—from the organ and keyboard instrument maker Johann Andreas Stein they bought a miniature keyboard designed for use while travelling. This then became the children's practice instrument when nothing better was available.[13] From Augsburg, Leopold had intended to travel via Ulm to Stuttgart, in order to play to Karl Eugen, the duke of Württemberg. However, they learned that the duke had decided on the spur of the moment to go to his hunting lodge at Grafeneck, near Ludwigsburg. Leopold promptly changed his plans and travelled to Ludwigsburg instead of Stuttgart, hoping to catch the duke there. But it was not to be. Nothing was forthcoming in Ludwigsburg and, to compound the nuisance, the duke had commandeered most of the horses there for his hunting expedition, so that the Mozarts had to stay even longer while Leopold combed the town for horses in order to continue their journey. Coming as it did on top of the disappointing income from Augsburg, the Ludwigsburg episode clearly riled Leopold, and he gave vent to one of his periodical malicious outbursts against Italian musicians, accusing the duke's Italian Kapellmeister Jommelli of blocking the appearance at Karl Eugen's court of all German musicians.[14]

Fortunately the Mozarts were able to give a number of concerts in reasonably quick succession following the Ludwigsburg annoyance. They had reached the part of the journey offering the greatest earnings potential.

---

[10] Leopold to Hagenauer, 21 June 1763—*MBA* 50 (*Letters* 11). *MBA* gives Tomasini's present as 10 Maximilian d'or, *Letters*, however, as 8. My conversion here is an approximation for rough guidance only.

[11] *MBA* 64/115–20 (not in *Letters*).

[12] *MBA* 53/5–8 (*Letters* 12). On 26 Sept. Leopold reported to Hagenauer that the inn bill in Augsburg had been 95 fl. (*MBA* 64/115–20; not in *Letters*).

[13] Leopold to Hagenauer, 20 Aug. 1763—*MBA* 63/76–8 (*Letters* 16).

[14] Leopold to Hagenauer, 11 July 1763—*MBA* 53/16–42 (*Letters* 12).

After playing to the elector Palatine, Karl Theodor, in Schwetzingen, they had before them the prospect of three more electors in close concentration (in Mainz, Koblenz, and Bonn) and public concerts in Frankfurt. The electors had particularly thriving courts, partly because, as they were ecclesiastical electors and hence single, the succession did not run in the families concerned. As a result, nobles were attracted to the several courts by the possibility of ascendancy to the position of elector.[15]

In fact the Mozarts could not play to Elector Emmerich Joseph (Count von Breidbach-Bürresheim) in Mainz, because he was ill, nor to Elector Maximilian Friedrich (Count von Königsegg-Rothenfels) in Bonn, because he was away in Westphalia. Even so, they gave two or three concerts in Mainz (which had a blooming musical life and favoured German artists), and five in Frankfurt. They also played to Elector Johann Philipp (Baron von Walderdorff) in Koblenz, and the money they took in was to enable them to continue their journey from Mainz. But Leopold's letter to Hagenauer of 26 September 1763 demonstrated vividly how wearisome and expensive travelling could be when conditions were poor. They had decided to go from Mainz to Koblenz by boat along the Rhine. The distance was about eighty kilometres, and when conditions were good it could be accomplished in one day by starting very early in the morning. The passengers were packed in, their carriages were loaded on to the roof, and merchants' goods were stowed on to covered fore and aft decks. Skiffs were also carried, for landing. The voyage along this most impressive stretch of the Rhine should have been one of the highlights of the Mozarts' journey, but unfortunately the weather was atrocious, and Leopold described their painfully slow progress to Hagenauer at length.[16] It took four days, and involved making sorties from the boat to struggle through the weather on foot to the nearest inn, to secure beds for the nights and food, in competition with everyone else on the boat. Leopold claimed, however, that going overland would have been even worse. This one journey alone cost them, according to his account, 4 louis d'or (44 fl.), which was about an eighth of his annual salary.[17]

In Aachen they were delayed because Leopold had sciatica and, as he wrote to Hagenauer in a letter begun on 17 October and finished on

---

[15] See H. Schuler, ' "Nun kömt eine merkwürdige Reise!": Mozarts herbstliche Rhein-Fahrt des Jahres 1763 in zeitgenössischen Schilderungen', *MM* 42 (1994), 50–1.

[16] For other contemporary accounts of this journey, cf. ibid. 63–9. Despite the drastically reduced visibility for the Mozarts because of the rain, however, no other account is as dramatic as Leopold's.

[17] *MBA* 64/7–55 (not in *Letters*). The louis d'or/florin conversion derives from Leopold's letter to Hagenauer of 20 Aug. 1763—*MBA* 63/2–9 (not in *Letters*).

4 November 1763, this cost them 75 fl. because the inn was so expensive.[18] But this was nothing compared with the frustration they suffered in Brussels, and the experience there drew from Leopold, in the same letter, remarks which indicated some concern about whether they could reach Paris without falling into debt. This letter is of interest because Leopold evidently felt it necessary that Hagenauer should maintain confidentiality about the second part of it. Leopold had expected that in Brussels the children would play for Prince Karl Alexander of Lorraine, Governor of the Austrian Netherlands and brother of Maria Theresia's consort, Emperor Francis I. Prince Karl showed a willingness to hear them, but neglected to summon them. As their inn bill mounted, Leopold suspected that the prince had in any case little money with which to pay them:

We've already been held up for nearly three weeks now in Brussels, and Prince Carl has spoken to me himself and said that he'd like to hear my children in a few days, and yet nothing has happened so far. in fact, it looks as if nothing at all will come of it, because the good Prince does nothing but hunt, guzzle and swill, and at last it's emerged that he has no money.[19]

But, for the sake of their reputation in Salzburg, appearances had to be kept up, and so the first part of his letter to Hagenauer contained news which Leopold was happy for all their Salzburg acquaintances to know. The second part, containing the news just quoted, was begun on 4 November, and Leopold marked it 'Something for you alone'. After a complicated account of the way in which he had used his various letters of financial credit, Leopold asked Hagenauer to arrange for him to draw more cash in Paris. He wanted this facility in case his eventual expenses in Brussels would leave him in debt there; if that happened, he wanted to be able to send money from Paris to Brussels immediately to settle such a debt.[20]

The Mozarts in fact stayed more than a month in a Brussels inn and apparently only appeared once before Prince Karl. Perhaps the best thing they had to show for their ordeal of nerves was a written composition by Wolfgang, notated in Nannerl's *Notenbuch*.[21] In 1777, when Wolfgang and Maria Anna travelled without Leopold and were uncertain how long they would stay in Mannheim, and therefore whether it was worth their while to rent a private lodging, Leopold's emphatic advice was: if in

---

[18] *MBA* 67/71–83 (*Letters* 18, though the reference to sciatica is omitted).
[19] *MBA* 68/6–11 (*Letters* 18).
[20] *MBA* 68/24–32 (*Letters* 18, but the passage is not given complete).   [21] *MBA* 71.

doubt, stay in a private lodging rather than an inn. This was what he had learnt in Brussels.[22]

Luckily for the Mozarts, they had a very favourable accommodation arrangement when they arrived in Paris on 18 November 1763. They had secured an invitation to stay with a Salzburg acquaintance, the Countess Maria Anna Felicitas van Eyck. She was married to the Bavarian ambassador in Paris; and the Mozarts' close friend in Salzburg, Maria Anna Rosalia Joly, was maid in the household of the countess's father, Count Georg Anton Felix Arco. So, through their network of friends, the Mozarts obtained what was presumably free accommodation in Paris, and Leopold must have breathed more easily. They probably intended to repay the countess by giving concerts for her. As for the costs of the journey so far, some idea can be gained from Leopold's letter to Hagenauer of 26 September 1763 (which was written before the Brussels fiasco). In brief, Leopold was not too dissatisfied (despite the miserable boat journey) with the situation at that point, for though the expenses totalled the fantastic sum of 1,068 fl., or approximately three times his annual salary, other people had paid for it all—in other words they had earned that sum from their concerts.[23] Leopold justified the heavy expenditure by reference to the necessity of having had fine clothes made for public appearances, and the obligation to travel in style for the sake of the reputation of the Salzburg court:

and apart from what we had made for ourselves, and a few knick-knacks, there was nothing to be saved, because we have to travel in a noble or courtly style for the preservation of our health and the reputation of my court. On the other hand, we also have no society except for the nobility or other distinguished people: and even if I shouldn't say it myself; the truth is nevertheless that through such behaviour I'm doing our court great honour, and encounter exceptional civility and special attention everywhere.[24]

❧

That the Mozarts had managed to complete the first stage of their long journey successfully, earning the money for the travel as they went along, may be seen as a considerable achievement in the light of the difficulties they met with and the fact that in order to give all their concerts each child's practice had to be fitted into a demanding travel schedule.

---

[22] They did not take his advice, however—see Ch. 17, pp. 262–72.
[23] *MBA* 64/113–32 (*Letters* 17, but most of the information is omitted).
[24] *MBA* 64/132–40 (*Letters* 17, but some of the passage is omitted).

It is only necessary to look at the calendar provided to appreciate something of the fatigue which must have been involved in long days' travel, settling into new quarters, almost constant packing and unpacking, the care of fine costumes for public appearances, keyboard and (for Wolfgang) violin practice, and the irregular sleeping patterns necessitated by concert performances. Yet Nannerl and Wolfgang appear to have thrived through all this, and to have developed their musical abilities further during the course of the journey. Looking at contemporary reports of their appearances, the same pattern appears that was noted in the account of their Viennese appearances in 1762—Nannerl was praised in the highest terms, but only for her keyboard playing, whereas Wolfgang was actually increasing his already wide range of accomplishments by adding to them public performances on the violin and organ. Leopold had mentioned Wolfgang's organ playing in his letter to Hagenauer of 11 June 1763. He had allowed Wolfgang to play the organ in Wasserburg while they were waiting for their carriage wheel to be mended:

The latest is that to amuse ourselves we went up to the organ and I explained the pedal to Wolferl. At which he immediately started to experiment standing up with the bench pushed back, and improvised standing and working the pedal, and all this as if he'd already been practising for many months. everyone was amazed, and it's a new grace of God, which many a one only receives after great labour.[25]

Wolfgang's organ playing developed further, to the point at which he could include an organ performance in the programme of the Frankfurt concerts, and the same must have been true of his violin playing. On 30 August 1763 a Frankfurt newspaper announced that the Mozarts' concert on that date would involve Nannerl playing the greatest and most difficult pieces on the keyboard, and Wolfgang playing a violin concerto, accompanying symphonies at the keyboard, and improvising both at the keyboard and at the organ in any key that might be named.[26] It was also from Frankfurt that Leopold wrote the letter to Hagenauer containing the only known piece of evidence that Nannerl did (as might be expected) find her brother's precociousness problematic. On 20 August 1763, Leopold wrote, 'Nannerl doesn't suffer at all through the boy any more, because her playing is such that everybody talks about her and admires her accomplishment.'[27] If comparisons with Wolfgang had made life

[25] *MBA* 49/50–6 (*Letters* 10).
[26] *Ordentliche Wochentliche Franckfurter Frag- und Anzeigungs-Nachrichten*, in Deutsch, *Documents*, 24–5.
[27] *MBA* 63/74–6 (*Letters* 16).

difficult for Nannerl, this might partly account for the fact that she apparently only played set pieces in public during this period. It may even be that Nannerl would not have become so fine a keyboard player if her brother had been closer to her in age. The difference of four and a half years in their ages meant that she already had a good grounding in keyboard playing before he began to overshadow her (for at the time of Wolfgang's earliest recorded interest in music, his hands would still have been too small to give such accomplished performances as she was capable of), and this head start may have been a critical psychological factor enabling her to continue to improve. Even so, it is hard to see how she could have done so without great determination on her part, and encouragement on the part of her parents. This comment of Leopold's is therefore interesting for its suggestion that, though the period of Wolfgang's childhood was one in which Leopold gradually became more and more absorbed in his son, he also understood and sympathized with Nannerl's position.

❧

Music practice and concert-giving were not the only things to be fitted into the time on the European tour. A good deal of sightseeing was also done, and it seems to have constituted a substantial part of the children's education. Its importance should not be underestimated, for it was no casual or everyday experience for the Mozart family. Rather, under Leopold's guidance, it was a fairly systematic attempt (in the circumstances) to observe and make sense of the religion, politics, art, history, morals, and customs of the widely different lands, cities, and towns they passed through. Since both Leopold and Nannerl kept travel diaries or notebooks, since the entries in Nannerl's book often accord fairly precisely with those in Leopold's, and since Maria Anna wrote one or two of the entries in Nannerl's book, it seems likely that her travel diary was written with her parents' encouragement and under their supervision.[28]

As is the case with the diaries she kept in later life, Nannerl's travel notebooks consist of notes or jottings, and were presumably intended as an *aide-mémoire*. Leopold sometimes followed the same practice in his letters to Hagenauer—if he found that he lacked the time or space to describe something as fully as he wished, he simply noted it and told Hagenauer that he would give a full verbal account on his return. So at first sight Nannerl's travel diary may look disappointing, for though it is clear what

---

[28] The entries are given in *MBA*, but are not yet available complete in English.

she saw, it is impossible to know from this alone what she made of the experiences. The evidence for the suggestion that the sight-seeing formed a significant part of the children's education comes from Leopold's letters to Hagenauer, which often described in some detail the things noted only briefly in the diaries.

In these letters, Leopold did not confine himself to description alone. Never shy of giving his opinion of everything and everyone in the world about him, he often expressed his views in strong terms to Hagenauer, and it is this fact that suggests that he used some of the opportunities of sight-seeing to give moral lessons to his children. The evidence of later moralizing letters to each child supports this argument. Yet it should not automatically be assumed that Leopold always displayed exactly the same opinions to his children as he did to Hagenauer, for there are suggestions in some of the letters to the Hagenauers from the European tour that Leopold liked to flatter their conservative Catholic views.[29]

The journey to Paris afforded Leopold relatively little scope for comment on the customs of the people they encountered, for they were at least still on German soil for most of the way. It was to be from Paris and London that he was to make his most critical remarks about unfamiliar ways of life. Nevertheless, he found time to express scorn for the military apparatus at Ludwigsburg, which involved lavish attention to the dress and drill of a body of men too small to be any use in a crisis,[30] and reserved his most acerbic remarks for a description of Cologne Cathedral, with its drunken guide, its decrepit pulpit and lack of ornamentation (Leopold likened it to a stable), and its pitiful attempts at choral music.[31]

Nannerl had merely noted the military sights at Ludwigsburg and the visit to Cologne Cathedral. What little expression there is in her diary suggests, however, that she had a child's engaging enthusiasm for the grandeur of many of the palaces they visited. At Nymphenburg, the Bavarian elector's palace just outside Munich, she described a 'lovely bed' and the kitchen 'where the elector's wife did her own cooking', and also mentioned a mirrored room, a marble bath, and walls of majolica.[32]

[29] This was particularly true of his letters to Maria Theresia Hagenauer—see Ch. 5.
[30] Nannerl's diary, 9–12 July 1763 (*MBA* 55) and Leopold to Hagenauer, 11 and 19 July 1763 (*MBA* 53/62–80 and 56/4–9; *Letters* 12 and 13).
[31] Nannerl's diary, 12 Aug.–3 Oct. 1763 (*MBA* 66) and Leopold to Hagenauer on 17 Oct. 1763 (*MBA* 67/22–56; *Letters* 18, but nearly all the passage is omitted). Other contemporary reports of Cologne (including Goethe's) were much more favourable than Leopold's—cf. Schuler, 'Rhein-Fahrt', 76—Leopold was clearly more at home with Baroque than Gothic architecture.
[32] Nannerl's diary, 12 June–7 July 1763—*MBA* 52.

At Schwetzingen she mentioned the French theatre and 'the most beautiful ballet', and in Mannheim she noted the opera-house, picture gallery, library, and treasury.[33] Though she did not note it in her diary, they also made the acquaintance in Mannheim of a French officer who showed them all sorts of curious treasures he had collected during his career in the Indies, including dresses made of paper, wood, and stucco. This man gave Nannerl a little ring and Wolfgang a toothpick box.[34] At the palace of Falkenlust, between Bonn and Cologne, Nannerl mentioned the Indian house, the Chinese house, and the 'snail shell house', Leopold elaborating on these sights and mentioning a work of art there by the Obersthofmeister in Salzburg, Count Franz Lactanz von Firmian, a gifted artist.[35] And in Brussels they went to the market, which had its best stalls indoors and could therefore stay open in the evenings. Leopold commented on the beauty of silver, gold, mirrors, and rich cloth glinting in the generous illumination.[36] Not recorded by Nannerl, but mentioned by Leopold in his diary and in his letters to Hagenauer, were the Netherlands paintings they started to encounter from Louvain onwards. These made a deep impression on Leopold, as also did the black and white marble in the churches.[37]

Already by the time they reached Paris, therefore, the family had enjoyed experiences which to many of their friends at home in Salzburg were the stuff of fairy-tales and dreams. In addition they had met countless travelling companions from many walks of life, sharing conversations with them during mealtimes at inns, sometimes for weeks at a time. To Leopold and Maria Anna the experiences were no doubt an interlude in the normal, more humdrum, routines of their lives. But to the children they surely appeared quite differently. For one thing, it was their achievements which were making it all possible, and for another the travelling constituted a far higher proportion of their lives so far. The further adventures in Paris and London, and those of the long journey home, meant that when they eventually arrived back in Salzburg, they had developed in such a way as might have set them apart from their old friends

---

[33] Nannerl's diary, 13 July–2 Aug. 1763—*MBA* 58.

[34] Leopold to Hagenauer, 3 Aug. 1763—*MBA* 59/17–25 (*Letters* 14, but most of the passage is omitted).

[35] Nannerl's diary, 12 Aug.–3 Oct. 1763 (*MBA* 66) and Leopold to Hagenauer, 17 Oct. 1763—*MBA* 67/6–22 (not in *Letters*).

[36] Nannerl's diary, 4 Oct.–15 Nov. (*MBA* 70) and Leopold to Hagenauer, 17 Oct. 1763—*MBA* 67/151–8 (not in *Letters*).

[37] Leopold's diary, 12 Aug.–3 Oct. 1763 (*MBA* 65/158–62) and his letter to Hagenauer of 17 Oct. 1763 (*MBA* 67/122–31 and 158–73; *Letters* 18, but the passage is not complete).

for ever. This did not happen, but in all their later dealings with people in Salzburg, their position was to be awkward because of the gulf between their early exposure to a wide range of experiences in diverse European cultural centres, and their later return to the narrower and more repressive atmosphere of their home town. Wolfgang was eventually to solve the problem by escaping to Vienna, but Nannerl was to be left to fit in as best she could.

5

The Grand European Tour (II): Triumphs in Paris

AFTER an expensive journey from Brussels, the Mozarts arrived in Paris on 18 November 1763 with little money. They stayed for about five months, and when they left for London, on 10 April 1764, Leopold was delighted with the income they had earned there, despite a precarious start. Below is a calendar of the main events affecting them in Paris:

1763

18 Nov.   Arrived at 3.30 p.m. in Paris and went to lodge with Count van Eyck and his wife as their guests.

24 Dec.   Went to Versailles for two weeks to be presented at court.

1764

1 Jan.   Attended a court dinner. Wolfgang played the organ in the chapel and they were given presents.

8 Jan.   Returned to Paris at 8.30 p.m.

Feb.   Received a present of 1,200 livres (550 fl.) from the court at Versailles.[1]

Feb.   Wolfgang ill with a severe inflammation of the throat and a very high fever.

6 Feb.   Death of their hostess, Countess van Eyck.

Mar.   Wolfgang's dedication (written, however, by the Mozarts' new friend Grimm) of his keyboard and violin sonatas K. 6 and K. 7 to Princess Victoire, the second daughter of the king of France.

c.4 Mar.   Moved from Count van Eyck's house.

10 Mar.   Gave their first public concert in Paris, taking 112 louis d'or (1,232 fl.).

Apr.   Wolfgang's dedication (again written by Grimm) of his keyboard and violin sonatas K. 8 and K. 9 to the lady-in-waiting of the dauphine, Comtesse de Tessé.

---

[1] This conversion is based on the information in Leopold's letter to Hagenauer of 8 Dec. 1763—*MBA* 73/76 (not in *Letters*). Here Leopold explained that there were 24 livres in each louis d'or. Since he had already reckoned the louis d'or to be 11 fl. (cf. Ch. 4, n. 17), 1,200 livres represented 50 louis d'or or 550 fl.

9 Apr.   Second public concert in Paris.
10 Apr.   Departed from Paris, leaving some luggage with the banker Hummel.
23 Apr.   Arrived in London, via Dover, having left their carriage in Calais.

Leopold had always intended to remain some time in Paris; on leaving Salzburg, this had been his goal. On arrival he had to exert himself and cultivate possible patrons, in order that they might appear at court and give some public concerts too. Yet despite his efforts their progress in Paris was very slow at first. In a letter to Hagenauer of 8 December 1763, he mentioned that they were being hindered from appearing at court by the mourning for the infanta, which also involved Leopold in the expense of a mourning outfit for each of them. In addition, everything in Paris was very expensive. Food and transport were heavy items, and Leopold even found it necessary to ask Hagenauer to use his letter paper more economically when writing to the Mozarts, since the recipient as well as the sender had to pay for letters according to the weight.

On the positive side, however, Leopold was delighted with their lodging at the house of van Eyck and his wife. This almost certainly cost them nothing, and they had the use of the countess's two-manual harpsichord. Also of great benefit to them was the *Petite Poste*, a city-wide letter service with deliveries four times daily. It enabled them to establish in advance whether the people they wanted to call on were at home, and thus saved them the expense of many wasted carriage rides as they tried to make some acquaintance in the city.

Towards the end of this letter, Leopold expressed the hope that he would soon receive a letter of credit from Hagenauer's mercantile acquaintance in Augsburg, Caligari. He knew it was advisable to have a good sum of money in hand on arrival at a new place, precisely because it took time to start earning. In addition, a reserve fund was desirable in case of illness. His concerned request shows that three weeks after their arrival in Paris, they had taken in no money and were still living on the little they had arrived with and on letters of credit.[2] In fact, it was at least another nine weeks after Leopold wrote this letter before they had played before the court at Versailles and received a present of money for doing so.[3]

Fortunately, the appearances at Versailles took place before Wolfgang became ill with a virulent inflammation of the throat in February 1764, and although Leopold estimated that this illness cost them 12 louis d'or

---

[2] The information in these three paragraphs comes from Leopold's letter to Hagenauer of 8 Dec. 1763—*MBA* 73 (*Letters* 19, but virtually everything is omitted).

[3] Deutsch, *Documents*, 29.

(132 fl.) in lost income,[4] this was around the time that they received their present of 1,200 livres (550 fl.) from the court. Even so, the constant uncertainty of their position forced Leopold to have contingency plans always at the ready. There is no record of what these plans might have been in Paris, but they were invariably a feature of Leopold's organization. On 22 February 1764, after three months in Paris, Leopold wrote to Hagenauer, 'Anyone who hasn't made these journeys can't imagine everything that's required for them. You need your hands constantly in your purse, and your wits about you all the time, and a plan for many months ahead continually before your eyes; but at the same time a plan that can immediately be changed according to changes in circumstances.'[5] When Wolfgang travelled without his father in 1777–9, Leopold was to remind him more than once that he should always have several alternative plans in case something went wrong.[6] That Wolfgang so signally failed to follow this advice was to be one reason for Leopold's later firm belief that his son was not sufficiently worldly-wise to attempt any career which did not bring with it an assured salary.

After their return to Paris from Versailles on 8 January 1764, Leopold put his mind to giving some public concerts. This was not achieved without difficulty. In a letter to Hagenauer of 1 April 1764, Leopold reported on the success of the first of the two concerts which had been given, including information about how it was all managed. The number of public concerts was controlled, and special permission had to be sought to mount anything which did not fit into the usual pattern of musical life. Influential acquaintance was needed to arrange this, and though Leopold had brought with him from Germany 'a whole litany' of letters of introduction to Parisian nobles, he claimed that they had not advanced him very far. It was a letter to Friedrich Melchior Grimm from the wife of a merchant in Frankfurt that paved the way for the Mozarts' successful appearances in Paris. Grimm belonged to the same generation as Leopold. He was a native of Regensburg, and his father had been a Protestant pastor. Grimm had lived in Paris for most of his adult life, having arrived as escort to a young German prince, and stayed on as secretary to various expatriate Germans. Gradually becoming established in Parisian society, he was an important figure in the French Enlightenment long before the Mozarts visited Paris. He was friendly with Rousseau, Voltaire, Diderot, d'Alembert, and other radical reformers. As well as helping Diderot with

---

[4] Leopold to Hagenauer on 22 Feb. 1764—*MBA* 81/61–3 (*Letters* 23).
[5] *MBA* 81/78–83 (not in *Letters*).   [6] See Pt. III.

his work on the *Encyclopédie*, he edited a twice-monthly newsletter, the *Correspondance littéraire, philosophique et critique*. This contained uncensored reports about every aspect of cultural life in France, and was sent in manuscript copies to about twenty European subscribers, most of whom were heads of state. His acquaintance in Paris was enormous, and having befriended the Mozarts he set to work to promote their public appearances. On 1 April 1764, writing to Hagenauer after the first concert but before the second, Leopold claimed that it was Grimm who had arranged for them to play at court, and he had also organized their two public concerts. Having obtained permission for these from the police, he had done the lion's share of ticket distribution. Tickets had to be bought in advance, but not from a box office. Instead, Leopold and Grimm distributed them among all the people they knew, many of whom in turn (especially the ladies) took a dozen or more to sell to their friends. Four tickets cost 1 louis d'or, making them almost 3 fl. each. For the first concert, Grimm alone distributed 320 tickets, and paid for the lighting too. Leopold was astounded and delighted when the receipts totalled 112 louis d'or (1,232 fl.), especially as he knew that a hundred tickets had already been sold for the forthcoming second concert. He calculated that this ought to bring them at least a further 50 or 60 louis d'or (550 or 660 fl.), and that he would shortly be able to deposit 200 louis d'or (2,200 fl.) with the bankers Turton et Baur.[7]

Despite the eventual triumphant outcome, the memory of the labour involved in presenting themselves to the Parisian public remained with Leopold. It had, after all, taken about three months to receive the first substantial income from playing at court, and another one before the first public concert was successfully accomplished, and until then there had been complete uncertainty about the possible outcome of his efforts. More than fourteen years later, when Wolfgang and Maria Anna returned to Paris without him, he had not forgotten the uncomfortable feeling of having arrived with nothing but credit to live on.[8] He also commended Wolfgang to Grimm, who Leopold was sure could arrange everything for Wolfgang just as he had in 1764. But on that ill-fated trip Grimm could or would not.[9]

˙ঌ৵ৎ˙

[7] *MBA* 83/37–65 and 112–38 (*Letters* 25).

[8] On 23 Feb. 1778 Leopold wrote to Wolfgang as Wolfgang was preparing to leave Mannheim for Paris, and told him that he had had to borrow 100 fl. in Frankfurt in 1763, and another 300 fl. on arrival in Paris—*MBA* 429/81–101 (*Letters* 290).

[9] See Chs. 18 and 19.

Contemporary reports of the children's appearances in Paris again testify to the quite different talents of each child. The main difference between the Parisian reports and the earlier ones from other European musical centres is that Wolfgang had now started to compose and to have his compositions printed. He wrote two sets of keyboard and violin sonatas, each containing two sonatas. One set (K. 6 and K. 7) was dedicated to Princess Victoire, the second daughter of the king, and the other (K. 8 and K. 9) to the Comtesse de Tessé, lady-in-waiting to the dauphine. Grimm wrote the saccharine dedications to both sets.[10] He also wrote about the Mozarts in the *Correspondance littéraire* on 1 December 1763. After giving examples of what the children could do, he commented that it was difficult to guard against madness when confronted by true prodigies, and went so far as to say that he was no longer surprised that St Paul should have lost his head after seeing his strange vision.[11]

Leopold too continued to be astonished by the progress of his children, which had advanced by leaps and bounds in the nine months since they had left Salzburg. Grimm's report had mentioned that Wolfgang's mastery of accompaniment (which involved a thorough knowledge of composition) equalled that of any Kapellmeister, and Leopold made the same claim in his letter to Maria Theresia Hagenauer of 1 February 1764. Introducing the subject by telling her about Wolfgang's sonatas, which were currently at the engraver's, he said that Wolfgang would be capable of court music duties by the time they returned. Nannerl's progress was also remarkable, and Leopold was convinced that as a keyboard player she could hold her own with the finest European performers:

Now four sonatas by Mr: Wolfgang Mozart are at the engraver's. picture to yourself the furore which these sonatas will make in the world when it says on the title-page that they are the work of a child of 7 ... And I can tell you, dearest Frau Hagenauer, that God daily works new wonders through this child ... My little girl plays the most difficult pieces we have at present by Schoberth and Eckard etc., of which Eckard's are still the more difficult, with unbelievable precision, so much so that this *low Schoberth* cannot conceal his *jealousy* and envy, and makes himself a laughing stock with Mr Eckard, who is an honest man, and with many others. I shall tell you many things in more detail which would be too long to explain here. Mr: Schoberth is not at all the man he's supposed to be. He flatters you to your face and is the falsest person; But his religion is the fashion. God convert him![12]

---

[10] Deutsch, *Documents*, 29 and 31–2. [11] Ibid. 26–7.
[12] *MBA* 80/155–76 (*Letters* 22).

Schobert and Eckard were German professional musicians living in Paris. Leopold had reported in the same letter that they and other composers had presented the children with copies of their sonatas. Nannerl and Wolfgang presumably profited from the works, because Wolfgang was later to choose music by both men for arrangement purposes when he made his first attempts at writing keyboard concertos. Yet in this letter, for the first time, are suggestions that Leopold had become so dazzled by his children's musical progress that his pride in them had taken on an unlovely competitive character with respect to the other musicians with whom they came into contact. Despite all his later exhortations to his children that they should study themselves thoroughly in order to guard against moral failings, it is quite likely that his own unhealthy attitude was one reason for the resistance which was to be shown by musicians towards the Mozarts on their next visit to Vienna from 1767 to 1769. It is also very probable that the attitude rubbed off on Wolfgang, who as an adult was not to lack conceit.

～✲～

Considering that the Mozarts were five months in Paris, it is surprising that there is little record of sightseeing there. Nannerl's travel diary consists of one entry, covering the period 24 December 1763–8 January 1764, and concerning Versailles: 'How latona changed the farmers into frogs, how neptune stopped the horse, diana in the bath the rape of broserpina, very beautiful vase of white marble and alabaster.'[13] The entry refers to a sculpted group on the fountain of the goddess Latona at Versailles. The sculpture depicts scenes from Ovid's *Metamorphoses*, and Nannerl's entry suggests that she had had the stories explained to her. Leopold wrote in his Parisian diaries only the names and addresses of acquaintances made there, and his letters home to the Hagenauers hardly mentioned sightseeing either. One reason for this was that to describe Paris would have been too large an undertaking. In his letter of 8 December 1763, after commenting that the skin of a rhinoceros would not afford enough space to do so, he recommended Hagenauer to buy a particular guidebook and read everything for himself.[14] It may be, too, that the sheer size of Paris meant that his time was largely taken up in cultivating the people who might be useful to them, and that there was rather little time left for family outings and letter-writing. This was also the period in which Wolfgang had his first compositions printed, and Leopold had to supervise their

[13] *MBA* 77.   [14] *MBA* 73/61–5 (*Letters* 19).

composition and arrange for them to be engraved in addition to all his other duties.

But what Leopold did write about at length to the Hagenauers was religious practice and the way of life of the French leisured classes. His comments, however, are problematic, because of the difficult position of the Mozarts in Paris, and the kind of people the Hagenauers were.

Salzburg was a religiously conservative state until the accession of Archbishop Colloredo in 1772. Protestants had been expelled in 1731–2, so there was restricted scope for debate about broad theological questions.[15] On the other hand, enormous attention was devoted to outward forms of piety. And it was the women in Salzburg who were particularly pious. They had Masses said at particular altars in particular churches, according to the nature of their prayer, they adhered scrupulously to the prescriptions for fast days, they searched for divine clues to the outcome of situations such as illness, they had their rosaries always at hand, they believed in miracles, and they made regular excursions to pilgrimage churches and bought relics there. The Virgin Mary was the main object of their devotion, but a host of other saints was called on according to the situation. In short, they expended enormous amounts of time on Church-related activities. The magical aspects of their belief which were sanctioned by the Church were often supplemented by older pagan magical tenets. Rosaries, for example, might include objects deriving from pagan folklore as well as the Christian prayer beads. These objects were thought to have healing properties of all kinds—a piece of malachite promised fruitfulness and easier births, a mole's paw (preferably bitten from the living animal) helped ease children's teething difficulties, and haematite warded off anaemia and other blood-related problems. Rosaries were also sometimes made from seeds or nuts from the Holy Land, because it was thought that they must have absorbed special powers from the soil near Christ's tomb. If, in addition, the rosaries were bought at a pilgrimage church, where they had come into contact with the relics of a saint with miraculous powers, their potency increased further.[16]

[15] There was, however, a small group of progressive young courtiers and officials that became involved in sometimes acrimonious theological debates with Salzburg conservatives. Ironically, in the 1740s this group even included three nephews of Count Leopold Anton Eleutherius von Firmian, the archbishop who had expelled the Protestants. See H. Wagner, 'Die Aufklärung im Erzstift Salzburg', in *Salzburg und Österreich: Aufsätze und Vorträge von Hans Wagner* (ed. *MGSL* as *Festschrift für Hans Wagner zum 60. Geburtstag*) (Salzburg, 1982), 99–115. But popular feeling was conservative, and under Archbishop Schrattenbach larger theological debate stagnated.

[16] These practices were still thriving in Salzburg during the lifetime of the Mozarts. Many people bequeathed their rosaries to the Loreto Convent, intending that the charms might be sold whenever the nuns needed money. When the convent was turned over to the use of the Post Office

No doubt some of these characteristics were displayed by Parisian Catholics too, but the Mozarts were also exposed there to vigorous criticism, which they would not so often have encountered in Salzburg, of many of the fundamental tenets of their Church. Their main friend, Grimm, was closely involved in the debates about man's place in the world and his relation to God. The idea of an all-powerful, all-loving God was scathingly attacked (most famously by Voltaire), and Catholic intolerance was seen as an obstacle to the progress of man as a humane being. Superstitious practices were denounced along with miracles, and a plea was made for man to fashion a new order based on knowledge, reason, and humanity.

The contrast for the Mozarts between these two worlds must have been acute. To complicate matters, they wanted to maintain good relations both with the Hagenauers and with Grimm. Close reading of Leopold's letters to the Hagenauers suggests both that their religious thinking was conservative and that Leopold liked to flatter their views. Of the six letters written to them from Paris, one and a half very long ones were addressed specifically to Maria Theresia, and it is precisely in these letters that Leopold's views appear most reactionary. This could well be explained by the suggestions that women tended to attach more importance to the daily rituals of faith, and that Leopold wanted to say the right things to his landlady. For both suggestions there is other evidence in the correspondence, and this is what makes the interpretation of the letters written from Paris difficult.

On the journey to Paris, Leopold had mentioned aspects of the travel which tended to make devout Catholics uneasy. From Wasserburg to Schwetzingen the inn rooms no longer contained crucifixes or holy water stoups, and it was difficult to get food suitable for fast days.[17] In Brussels, rosaries were not used in church.[18] Nor were they in Paris, and Leopold told Maria Theresia Hagenauer that they had to use theirs secretly, hidden in their muffs.[19] But from Paris he also mixed more shocking reports with those of mere lapses in piety. Sexual morality was so lax that it was difficult to tell who was the lady of the house; men spent all their money on their Lucretias (who did not stab themselves); babies

---

in 1941, chest upon chest of these donated rosaries was placed in the convent garden, and it was noted that most dated from the 18th c. See J. Bartelt, 'Anhänger und Amulette in Volksglauben und Volksmedizin', *MGSL* 100 (1960), 569–77.

[17] Leopold to Hagenauer, 19 July 1763—*MBA* 56/38–56 (*Letters* 13).
[18] Leopold to Hagenauer, 17 Oct. 1763—*MBA* 67/178–82 (*Letters* 18).
[19] Leopold to Maria Theresia Hagenauer, 4 Mar. 1764—*MBA* 82/113–25 (not in *Letters*).

and young children were sent out to the country to be brought up in gross neglect by peasants, because their parents could not be bothered with them; corpses were rushed out of the house so that the reminder of mortality should interfere as little as possible with daily pleasures; hardly any one observed fast days, so that he wished he had a special dispensation from their observance; the Parisians could even find excuses for attending balls during periods of fasting; carriages were decorated with the utmost refinement while churches were neglected; and, in short, everything tended towards sensual comfort.[20]

The problem of gauging Leopold's feelings about his Parisian experiences is compounded by the almost total lack of evidence, other than the letters to the Hagenauers, for his relations with the people he met there. Clearly he got on very well with Grimm, but there is no documented evidence for what they discussed. The only expression of admiration for non-Catholics was made by Leopold of two barons whom the Mozarts had first met in Munich and who had travelled much of the same route to Paris with them. Their names were respectively Bose and Hopfgarten, and they were Protestants from Saxony. From Paris they intended to go south to Italy, and then north again, possibly via Salzburg. Leopold therefore gave them a letter of introduction to Hagenauer, and wrote to Hagenauer separately to ask him to ensure that the men were treated with respect at court, since they had enjoyed great honours at all the other courts they had attended. He described them as good, cultured men, from whose conversation he had profited much, 'even though they were both Lutherans'.[21] If the demeanour of the barons had caused him to reconsider the relationship between religion and moral worth, therefore, he was clearly not prepared to admit as much in any detail to the Hagenauers; and when he had been describing Schobert's jealousy of Nannerl, he had obliquely linked Schobert's faults with his 'fashionable' religion.

Given this almost complete lack of other documentation for Leopold's relations with his Parisian acquaintances, the letters to the Hagenauers remain the best evidence for his beliefs during this period. One approach to their interpretation is to examine the views they contain in the light both of comments to others later in the correspondence, and of Leopold's actions in matters of theological importance. Such examination suggests that though the Parisian encounters gave Leopold matter for serious reflection on the state of his Church, aspects of which he was

---

[20] Leopold to Maria Theresia Hagenauer, 1 Feb. and 4 Mar. 1764—*MBA* 80 (*Letters* 22) and 82 (these passages not in *Letters*).

[21] Leopold to Hagenauer, 1 Apr. 1764—*MBA* 83/76–104 (*Letters* 25).

certainly to criticize, ultimately he believed that particular reforms would suffice, leaving the essential foundation untouched.[22] This stance was doubtless bolstered by his knowledge of the proposals of the Italian-led Catholic Enlightenment movement, proposals which were well known in Salzburg.[23]

On 22 February 1764, just after Wolfgang had recovered from his sore throat and fever, Leopold wrote to the Hagenauers to say that people in Paris had been trying to persuade him to have the child (Nannerl was not mentioned) inoculated against smallpox. Leopold claimed that he had refused, because it was God's decision whether the child He had placed on earth should live or die. To examine the background of this orthodox contemporary Catholic opinion is to approach a deeper understanding of a position which can now seem fairly clichéd, but behind which was a complex and fraught issue.

There had been a centuries-long stagnation in the treatment of smallpox until the idea of inoculation spread to Western Europe from the East in the second decade of the eighteenth century. So accustomed had people become to the inevitability of smallpox that many (certainly most Catholics in the province of Salzburg) believed it as necessary as original sin. They tried to ward it off by prayer and amulets, but otherwise felt helpless. Their only comfort was that they were taught that the souls of children dying from it were automatically saved, and since this salvation was the goal of every Catholic, its importance as a means of solace should not be underestimated. A further factor hindering acceptance of inoculation was the nature of medical practice. Most people in Salzburg, including the Mozarts, still held to humoral concepts of disease, believing that by regulating (according to the nature of their personal fundamental constitution) the various elements such as air, diet, evacuation, sleep, exercise, and passions of the mind, they would be able to maintain their health. Harmful matter which if not controlled might lead to disease had to be encouraged to make its exit from the body. Hence the importance, for example, of regular menstruation for women, of being bled and purged, of sweating out a cold, and of inducing blisters on the skin

---

[22] The individual remarks and actions supporting this view are too numerous to review here, and the most important will be mentioned at appropriate points.

[23] Leopold read books by Lodovico Muratori, one of the chief figures in the movement, and also sent them to Nannerl to read, when she was living in St Gilgen after her marriage (Leopold to Nannerl, 1 Mar. 1787—*MBA* 1036/4–6; not in *Letters*). Muratori pleaded, among other things, for excesses such as the exaggerated reverence of saints (which had flourished since the Counter-Reformation) to be curbed. Muratori's works were also read and discussed by many other progressives in Salzburg—see Wagner, 'Aufklärung', 100.

through which matter could escape. The visible surface aspect of any disease, therefore, was usually not in itself feared, because it might be the key to recovery. One of the things that happened with smallpox was that many people did not believe it to be transmitted solely by contact with other cases—there were deeper factors too, tied up with personal constitution and regimen. They were very suspicious of inoculation, therefore, because they feared that the disease could still occur but might present itself without the pox, so that the matter would be hindered from escaping, and cause worse problems by being pent up.

The bringing of inoculation to the West has been credited to Lady Mary Wortley Montagu, who had her own child inoculated according to Eastern practice when she was living with her ambassador husband in Constantinople from 1716 to 1718. In 1734 Voltaire praised her courage in resisting the arguments of her chaplain, who had tried to tell her that the practice only worked on infidels. This kind of argument reveals another element in resistance to inoculation in the West. People were already instinctively doubtful about making the enormous leap from helplessness to self-help. It involved overturning the old order, and since they were taught that this was precisely the aim of the anti-Christ, the fact that the idea came from Islamic parts formed an insurmountable barrier to early popular acceptance in the West.

But the instinctive mistrust of the morality of inoculation was not the only factor. If religious scruples had not existed there would still have been a problem. For despite the alleged improved outlook *vis-à-vis* smallpox for the population as a whole, it was of course impossible to persuade many parents that the practice was safe for their particular child. Before Jenner discovered empirically the safer method of vaccination from the relatively harmless cowpox in 1796, inoculation was done by a series of 'removes' of the smallpox matter itself. This involved obtaining the mildest possible strain of the disease and using it to inoculate a batch of about a dozen people. They would develop (it was hoped) a mild form of the disease, and were observed while they recovered. More inoculation matter was taken from the pustules of the mildest cases in the batch, and used to inoculate another batch, and so on. In theory, the more removes the milder the strain. But some people nevertheless suffered a catastrophic reaction to inoculation, and died. Furthermore, there was the risk that far more smallpox was circulating. Isolation hospitals were set up to combat this problem, but it remained a big popular fear.

When children died as a result of inoculation, the parents were understandably inconsolable, for to make the grave decision only to lose a perfectly healthy child was far more traumatic than losing children to smallpox naturally caught. Even Kant, who championed the idea that people should use their reason to take control of their lives, had doubts about whether it was morally right to expose healthy children to the risk. And religious opponents of inoculation made the most of such tragedies by stressing their inevitability when God's will was challenged. In fact, in Salzburg it was not to be until the Church and State worked together to combat smallpox that significant progress was made. This was not until the early years of the nineteenth century, by which time vaccination from cowpox was used instead of inoculation from the smallpox virus. It was thus to take many decades to overcome the deepest fears of the population, and the fact that Leopold did not allow Wolfgang to be inoculated in Paris in 1764 was not necessarily a reflection simply of die-hard Catholic beliefs.[24] As for the fact that Leopold did not mention the possibility of Nannerl's being inoculated, this raises the question of whether it was a family assumption that Wolfgang might receive preferential medical treatment. When the Mozarts were in Vienna in 1767–9 and both children contracted smallpox, greater steps were to be taken in advance to protect Wolfgang from the disease than Nannerl, but this seems to have been an isolated incident born of Leopold's panic.[25] Whenever Nannerl was actually ill, she was always to receive devoted medical and nursing care. The fact that she was not mentioned with Wolfgang in connection with inoculation in Paris may have been because the people who had suggested the procedure to Leopold had played on the argument that Wolfgang was a special child because of his genius, and hence deserved special protection. It does not necessarily imply that Wolfgang might have been inoculated, but Nannerl not.

⁓✲⁓

Leopold maintained a lively interest in the state of music in Salzburg, and when Hagenauer wrote to tell him that his colleague Anton Cajetan Adlgasser had been granted permission by Archbishop Schrattenbach to travel to Italy, Leopold wrote an enthusiastic response on 4 March 1764:

[24] The information about smallpox is from F. F. Cartwright, *A Social History of Medicine* (London, 1977), 75–92; and S. Falk and A. S. Weiss, ' "Hier sind die Blattern": Der Kampf von Staat und Kirche für die Durchsetzung der (Kinder-) Schutzpockenimpfung in Stadt und Land Salzburg (Ende des 18. Jahrhunderts bis ca. 1820)', *MGSL* 131 (1991), 163–86.

[25] See Ch. 8.

I received your letter on the 3rd inst. Above all I must tell you that the news of Herr Adlgasser's journey has given me the greatest pleasure. *Long live our most gracious Prince!* God be praised and thanked! nothing can move me more than when I see a great prince, in whose hands God has placed the power and the means to do so, help along those talents which God by special grace has vested in many honest souls. Now I just wish that Madlle: Fesemayer, or the so-called Hofstaller Nannerl, might yet also stay a year in Venice, if I had *one single wish* that I could see fulfilled in the course of time, it would be to see Salzburg become a court which made a tremendous sensation in Germany with its own local people.[26]

Adlgasser had been appointed court organist in Salzburg in 1750, after Eberlin had advanced to the post of Kapellmeister at the end of 1749.[27] On 22 January 1764 Schrattenbach granted Adlgasser 500 fl. from his *Schatulle* for Italian travel. The woman mentioned by Leopold was Maria Anna Fesemayr, the daughter of the court stablemaster. She was a promising young singer, and was, as Leopold hoped she would be, sent to Italy for two years at Schrattenbach's expense. Two more young female singers from Salzburg, Maria Anna Braunhofer and Maria Magdalena Lipp, were already in Venice, their education also being funded by Schrattenbach.[28]

This passage suggests that Leopold was still full of zest for his court work. Salzburg had had a tendency to favour Italian musicians by appointing them rather than German ones and paying them more. Naturally the Germans resented this, and Leopold's fervent gratitude to Schrattenbach stemmed from his optimism that Schrattenbach had the will to change the position. Building up the Salzburg court orchestra using German musicians under a sympathetic archbishop was an undertaking Leopold would have relished, but it would have been necessary for him to be Kapellmeister first, and he was never to rise quite so high. Schrattenbach permitted Leopold to take extremely generous amounts of leave, most of it paid, no doubt partly with a view to increasing his use to the Salzburg court. But though Leopold appeared to believe that the European activities of himself and his children could work together to the same end of serving Salzburg, the reality was to prove very different. Leopold was simply not at home for long enough to repay the indulgence he had been shown. As Wolfgang grew older, Leopold's absorption in him did not diminish one whit. By the time Schrattenbach died in 1771, his patience with the Mozarts had been severely strained.

※

[26] *MBA* 82/7–17 (not in *Letters*). [27] Hintermaier, 'Hofkapelle', 3–4.
[28] See Martin, 'Fürstenhof 80', 183–4.

Little is known of Maria Anna's activities in Paris, or her feelings about the city. Leopold hardly mentioned her in his letters home, and she apparently wrote not a single letter to Maria Theresia Hagenauer, although there was much that she wanted to tell her. Instead, Leopold passed on some of his wife's news. She had enjoyed the journey, but found many aspects of life in Paris distasteful and trying. The drinking water, which came from the Seine, disgusted her, and she had to boil it and let it stand before it was fit to use.[29] The Mozarts had no cooking facilities while staying with Countess van Eyck, so they had to order their meals from a cookshop. Maria Anna found it almost impossible to eat well and satisfy her conscience on fast days, because of the inadequate choice. In reporting this snippet of information to the Hagenauers, Leopold specifically said that the fast day problems were ones that affected her and the children. He did not mention himself.[30] Since he too certainly observed the fast days whenever possible, this might mean that Maria Anna was often at home eating the food from the cookshop while he was invited out to dine. Both she and Leopold mistrusted French doctors, and when Wolfgang was ill in February 1764 they made sure they found a German doctor to attend him.[31] Perhaps it was Countess van Eyck's experience that put them off the French ones.

Right at the end of January, the countess fell suddenly ill in the middle of the night, spitting blood. Next day she was bled three times, but was still bringing up blood in the evening, and was bled again. The blood continued to be 'very bad indeed'. After a few days of worsening illness, she died on 6 February, aged 23. When Leopold reported the illness and death to the Hagenauers on 1 February and 22 February 1764, he hinted that her case had been mishandled by her doctors, probably by excessive bloodletting. He also revealed the deep unease felt by himself and Maria Anna at the thought of dying on foreign soil. 'Nowhere does one die willingly,' he wrote, 'only here it appears doubly sad for an honest German when he falls ill or even dies.'[32] The Mozarts must have known the countess from her childhood, and were anxious about the effect her death would have on the Arco family back at home, and on their friend Rosalia Joly. After her death, though they stayed on for a while in her house, they moved out on 4 March 1764 to different lodgings. It had been with

---

[29] Leopold to Hagenauer, 8 Dec. 1763—*MBA* 73/34–9 and 88–95 (not in *Letters*).
[30] Leopold to Maria Theresia Hagenauer, 4 Mar. 1764—*MBA* 82/64–80 (not in *Letters*).
[31] Leopold to Hagenauer, 22 Feb. 1764—*MBA* 81/17–31 (*Letters* 23).
[32] *MBA* 80/177–210 and 81/3–13 and 41–3 (*Letters* 22 and 23, but the passages are not complete).

the countess rather than her husband that they were particularly friendly, and Leopold felt uncomfortable at not being able to ease the count's grief.[33]

Maria Anna must have become quite friendly in Paris with Grimm's lover, the author Mme Louise d'Épinay, who collaborated with him on many of his literary projects. Perhaps the two women spent time together when Leopold was busy or was invited elsewhere. At any rate, Mme d'Épinay gave her a red satin dress, a fan, and a small amethyst ring, and when Maria Anna returned to Paris with Wolfgang in 1778, she was to take all three gifts with her.[34] She had initially had no intention of accompanying Wolfgang so far, and only changed her mind with reluctance because she was far from happy with the arrangement he had made. When she learned that Grimm would take them under his wing again as he had in 1764, however, her relief was profound. Yet if the first Parisian stay had been in some respects unsatisfactory for her, the second proved disastrous. From the beginning she was neglected by Wolfgang, whose life she could not share, and she had no occupation of her own. She put off being bled because she wanted to find a German doctor. Then she fell ill and her treatment was mismanaged. Finally she died, like Countess van Eyck, away from home, friends, and family, and Mme d'Épinay's amethyst ring had to be given to the nurse in lieu of payment.[35] Leopold certainly had cause then to remember the two women who had befriended his wife in Paris in 1764.

❧

On 1 April 1764, Leopold wrote to the Hagenauers:

I beg you to have Holy Mass said for us daily beginning on the *12th April*, and then on the *13th*, *14th*, *15th*, *16th*, *17th*, *18th* and *19th*, namely eight days one after the other. You may share them out as you like, in any church and at any altar. As long as *4* of them are read at the Holy Child in Loreto and *4* at an altar of our dear Lady, It could be in the *Pfarr* or anywhere else; wherever it's convenient for Frau Hagenauer, who will perhaps contribute to it by her devout presence. But please be sure to have them read on those eight days, from the 12th to the 19th April inclusive. If this letter should unexpectedly only arrive

---

[33] Leopold to Hagenauer on 4 Mar. 1764—*MBA* 82/41–7 (not in *Letters*).
[34] Leopold to Wolfgang and Maria Anna on 6 Apr. 1778 (*MBA* 444/127–9; *Letters* 301), and Leopold to Wolfgang on 10 Dec. 1778 (*MBA* 509/57–60; *Letters* 344).
[35] Cf. Chs. 18 and 19.

after the 12th April, however, please get them started immediately on the next day: There are important reasons for it.[36]

The important reasons were almost certainly a reference to the forthcoming journey to England, which was going to necessitate the first sea journey ever made by the Mozarts. In the event, they did not leave France until after 19 April, the last day on which they had requested Masses to be said, but Leopold probably expected to make the crossing earlier than that. The Holy Child at Loreto was a famous ivory statue of the Christ-child in the Capuchin Loreto Convent. It was bedecked with rich cloth and jewels by the nuns, and had miraculous powers. At difficult deaths it was some-times sent for, and was prized for its ability either to ensure recovery or to put the sufferer out of his misery.[37] Maria Anna Mozart was particu-larly attached to it, and placed enormous reliance on it.

Nannerl's diary entry for April 1764 forms a succinct and appropriate coda to this chapter and the five months the Mozarts had spent in France: 'In Calais I saw how the sea runs away and advances again.'[38] On 10 April, the day after their second public concert in Paris, they had left for Calais. Some of their luggage remained in Paris with the banker Hummel, for collection on the way back. The carriage stayed in Calais, and the Mozarts crossed the Channel in a chartered boat, for a sojourn in London of more than a year.

[36] *MBA* 83/66–76 (*Letters* 25, but the passage is truncated).
[37] Archbishop Liechtenstein had the Loreto figure (see Plate 10) carried to him on his death-bed in 1747, and died only half an hour later, after previously having lingered painfully for weeks. See Martin, 'Fürstenhof 77', 41–2.
[38] *MBA* 85.

6

The Grand European Tour (III):
Triumphs in London?

LEOPOLD was later to regret having left luggage in Paris, because while in England he changed his mind about their return route, and it proved inconvenient to have to go back through France. There was little else to be done, however, because their belongings had grown considerably in number. They had acquired new clothes and presents in the ten months since leaving Salzburg, and were also taking to England sets of Wolfgang's sonatas and prints of the family portrait which had been painted in Paris by Carmontelle and then engraved. Leopold intended to sell these at every opportunity. Below is a calendar detailing the most important events of their stay in London.

1764

23 Apr.	Arrived in London and stayed one night at The White Bear, Piccadilly.
24 Apr.	Arranged lodgings with the barber John Cousins in Cecil Court (now No. 19), St Martin's Lane.
27 Apr.	Appeared before King George III and Queen Sophie Charlotte and received a present of 24 guineas (264 fl.).[1]
19 May	Appeared at court again, Wolfgang playing the organ. Again given 24 guineas (264 fl.).
22 May	Wolfgang was ill and could not appear in a concert for Graziani's benefit in Hickford's Great Room, Brewer Street.
5 June	Both children gave a concert at the Great Room, Spring Garden (near St James's Park) at 12.00 p.m. Tickets cost

---

[1] The guinea/florin conversion given here of 11 florins to the guinea derives from Leopold's letter to Hagenauer of 28 May 1764, in which he stated that a guinea was worth the same as a French louis d'or—*MBA* 88/8–12 (*Letters* 27). This in turn he had already converted at 11 fl.—cf. Ch. 4, n. 17.

	half a guinea (5 fl. 30 kr.) each, expenses were 20 guineas (220 fl.), and receipts 100 guineas (1,100 fl.).
29 June	Wolfgang performed in the concert room in Ranelagh Gardens (on the Thames at Chelsea) for the benefit of the new Lying-In Hospital.
8 July	Leopold's dangerous illness began, after a private evening performance at Lord Thanet's house.
5 Aug.	Leopold was carried to Chelsea to rent a house in a healthier part of London.
6 Aug.	The Mozarts moved into the house at Five Fields Row, Chelsea (now 180 Ebury Street).
*c.*25 Sept.	Moved back into town, to Thrift Street, Soho (now 20 Frith Street).
25 Oct.	Third appearance at court.

1765

18 Jan.	Wolfgang's dedication of six sonatas for harpsichord with violin or flute, K. 10–15, to Queen Charlotte. They were written almost entirely in London. His present was 50 guineas (550 fl.).
21 Feb.	Both children gave a concert at 6.00 p.m. in the Little Theatre, Haymarket. The concert had had to be postponed twice because of competing attractions. Programme contained symphonies by Wolfgang, and the net takings were about 100 guineas (1,100 fl.).
Mar. and Apr.	The Mozarts advertised that they would receive people daily at their lodgings in order to demonstrate the skills of the children.
13 May	Concert in Hickford's Great Room, Brewer Street. Tickets cost 5 shillings (about 2 fl. 30 kr.). The sonata for 4 hands, K. 19*d*, was played.
8 July	Advertisement for daily performances from 9 July in the Great Room of the Swan and Harp Tavern in Cornhill. Tickets—2*s.* 6*d.* (about 1 fl. 15 kr.).
*c.*19 July	Wolfgang presented to the British Museum his motet *God is our Refuge* (K. 20), 3 sets of sonatas, and a copy of the family portrait.
24 July	Left London for Canterbury.
25–30 July	Stayed at Bourn Place near Canterbury, the seat of Sir Horace Mann.
25 July	Advertisement for a concert in Canterbury, but no evidence that it took place.

Night of 30/31 July   In Canterbury, where they watched a horse race.
1 Aug.   Left Dover for Calais at 10.00 a.m.[2]

On arrival in Paris, the Mozarts had had the van Eycks to go to, and were able to live with fellow Germans without paying rent. In London it was quite different. They had letters of introduction with them, but had to fend for themselves as far as accommodation was concerned. In addition, while they had arrived in Paris at just the right time of year for the beginning of the winter concert season, their arrival in London occurred in April—quite the wrong time, since everyone had gone into the country. Leopold had taken this into account, and was prepared for the Parisian profits to be a cushion until they started to earn money in London. Having survived the crossing, they made their way to London, enjoying the sight of fine horses and rich farmland on the way. They spent their first night in London at the White Bear in Piccadilly, and then found lodgings in the premises of a barber in Cecil Court. In gratitude for their safe arrival, Leopold asked the Hagenauers to have twelve Masses said for them—three at the Holy Child in the Loreto Convent, three at the pilgrimage church of Maria Plain just outside Salzburg, two at the altar of Francisco de Paula in the Church of Maria am Bergl, two at any convenient altar of Johann von Nepomuk, and two at the altar of St Antonio in the Pfarrkirche. In the same letter, Leopold revealed that from Paris they had been urged to go to Hamburg, Copenhagen, and even Russia, and that Holland would also have been a possibility. However, he considered England quite daring enough, because he did not want to go too far north or travel any further from home. As it was, the climate in England was dangerous to non-natives, because of its constant oscillation between hot and cold. He said emphatically that they would not be going to Holland.[3]

The first few days after their arrival in London were exceedingly busy. First they had to find convenient accommodation, suitable for receiving genteel visitors, at a moderate price. Their first lodgings, in Cecil Court, cost 12*s.* (about 6 fl.) per week, but Leopold later accepted that they were too small, and that he really had to be prepared to pay 18*s.* or a guinea (9–11 fl.) per week.[4] Then they had to get to grips with English coinage

---

[2] The calendar is derived from Deutsch, *Documents*; Eibl, *Chronik*; and Eisen, *Documents*. The works do not always quite agree on details, and Eisen's finds are more recent than those of Deutsch and Eibl.

[3] Leopold to the Hagenauers, 28 May 1764—*MBA* 88 (*Letters* 27, but much is omitted).

[4] Leopold to Hagenauer, 28 June 1764—*MBA* 90/35–46 (not in *Letters*).

and food prices, to find a Catholic church (they attended the chapel of the French embassy),[5] and to deliver their letters of introduction so that they could make good progress in London's musical circles. And all this had to be done without much familiarity with the English language. That they had appeared at court within four days of their arrival testifies both to Leopold's usual competence, but also probably to luck.

At first, their affairs in London looked reasonably promising, despite the fact that it was the quiet season. When Leopold wrote to Hagenauer on 28 May 1764, it was to report on two successful appearances at court, at each of which they had been given 24 guineas (264 fl.).[6] And having discovered that the king's birthday was on 4 June, and would attract some of the nobility back into town, Leopold decided to risk arranging a benefit concert for the following day, 5 June:

Now we're going to give a so-called Benefit, or a concert for our own profit, on the 5th June. It's really too late now to give a concert of this kind, and we can't bank on its being much use to us, because it's out of season and the costs of a concert like this will be getting on for 40 guineas: Only since the 4th is the King's birthday, and consequently many of the nobility will come back into town for it from the country; we have to chance it and use the opportunity to make ourselves known. Each person pays half a guinea, and if it took place in winter, I could certainly count on 600 people, consequently on 300 guineas: but at the moment they've all gone to their gardens and into the country. *Basta!* It will turn out fine, if only with God's help we can stay healthy, and if only God keeps our invincible Wolfgang well.[7]

Leopold's optimistic assertion that the benefit concert would be fine was more than borne out by the event. In his next letter to Hagenauer, on 8 June 1764, he was able to give a favourable report of it. Despite the fact that there had been less than a week in which to sell the tickets, they attracted 'a couple of hundred' people from the highest classes—all the ambassadors, and members of the leading noble families. Moreover, the expenses only came to about 20 guineas (220 fl.), because most of the musicians gave their services for nothing. Leopold calculated that the profit when all the ticket money was in would not be less than 90 guineas (990 fl.). At the end of the letter, he remarked that Nannerl, although only 12 years old, was one of the most skilful players in Europe, and that Wolfgang, in his eighth year, had the abilities of a 40-year-old man. His

[5] Leopold to Hagenauer, 8 June 1764—*MBA* 89/32–5 (not in *Letters*).
[6] *MBA* 88/88–103 and 158–64 (*Letters* 27).   [7] *MBA* 88/164–75 (*Letters* 27).

progress since leaving Salzburg was quite incredible. As he signed off, Leopold referred to 'our all-powerful Wolfgang'.[8]

The final receipts from the concert on 5 June must have been eminently satisfactory, because on 28 June 1764 Leopold was able to inform Hagenauer that he was entrusting another 100 guineas (1,100 fl.) to his London bankers Loubier et Teissier. This sum of money could be made available to anyone at home who would find it useful for trading purposes, perhaps Hagenauer himself; and Leopold went on to say that if a larger sum were needed, he could add 30, 40, or even 50 guineas (330–550 fl.) to it without leaving himself short of cash.[9] Hagenauer had in fact taken over for his own purposes the sum of 200 louis d'or that Leopold had deposited with Turton et Baur in Paris, and had offered him 2,250 fl. for it, plus 3 per cent interest annually.[10] This had been in response to Leopold's hope that he might be able to get a better conversion rate on the sum than 11 fl. per louis d'or.[11] Leopold had been delighted with the terms Hagenauer had offered, and was presumably hoping for a similarly favourable arrangement for his London guineas. The spectacular earnings evidently did not prevent him from exercising his usual careful husbanding of resources.

Twice in two letters Leopold had revealed his awareness of the economic importance of the 8-year-old Wolfgang to the family—he was invincible and all-powerful, and everything would be fine if only they all (but especially Wolfgang) stayed healthy. When he made the comments, Wolfgang had recently had to withdraw through illness from playing in a benefit concert for the cellist Carlo Graziani, and this incident no doubt reminded Leopold of the fragile nature of their good fortune.

Leopold decided to consolidate their promising start to becoming known and admired in London by allowing Wolfgang to take part in a concert for a charity—the Lying-In Hospital. The concert was to take place in the Rotunda, the round hall in the pleasure gardens of Ranelagh. Leopold's idea was that by allowing Wolfgang to donate his services and play an organ concerto, they would win the hearts of this 'quite exceptional nation'. Having attracted favourable attention to themselves in this way, Leopold obviously hoped to capitalize on the event immediately afterwards. In the same letter, he announced his other intention—it was to go to Royal Tunbridge Wells after the concert, in the hope of earning

---

[8] *MBA* 89/35–59 and 73–85 (*Letters* 28).
[9] *MBA* 90/11–20 (*Letters* 29, but the passage is not complete).
[10] Leopold to Hagenauer, 8 June 1764—*MBA* 89/59–65 (not in *Letters*).
[11] Leopold to Hagenauer, 1 Apr. 1764—*MBA* 83/143–51 (not in *Letters*).

money from the wealthy and fashionable people who flocked there during the summer.[12] Leopold must have hoped that, by performing several times in Tunbridge, they would be able to boost their income further, and support themselves comfortably until the winter concert season recommenced in London. But before they could leave for Tunbridge, Leopold was struck down with an illness so severe that he was out of circulation for more than two months—and during that time, not a penny was earned. This blow to their plans, in conjunction with other unfavourable circumstances, was to mean that they had barely recovered their financial equilibrium by the time they left England a year later.

After his letter of 28 June 1764, Leopold's next letter home to Hagenauer was started on 3 August:

Sir,
Don't be frightened! only prepare your heart to hear about one of the most unhappy events. Perhaps you can already tell from my writing the sort of state I'm in. Almighty God has visited me with a sudden and grave illness, which I'm too weak to describe. enough! I've been clystered, purged, and even bled because of a fierce inflammation of the throat. Now that all this is over, and according to the pronouncement of the doctors I have no fever; they say I'm supposed to be eating, only I'm like a child. I don't fancy anything and I'm so weak that I can hardly think straight. For several days already now I've

Here the letter broke off, and was continued on 9 August—without, however, finishing the interrupted sentence.[13] In the meanwhile the Mozarts had moved from central London to Chelsea on 6 August. Leopold explained how they had moved out for the sake of the fresh air and a lodging with a garden, and asked the Hagenauers to have twenty-two Masses said for them. Seven were to be at Maria Plain, seven at the altar of the Holy Child in Loreto Convent, two at the altar of St Walburgis in the convent on the Nonnberg, two at the altar of St Wolfgang in the monastery of St Peter, and four at Maria Hilf in Passau. At the time of writing, Leopold was still not sure that he would recover.[14] The fact that he was asking for so many Masses to be read in five different carefully selected churches is an indication of the gravity of the situation. It seems clear from Leopold's choice of altars that he was desperately worried that he might die and leave his family unprovided for, and in a strange

---

[12] Leopold to Hagenauer, 28 June 1764—*MBA* 90/25–30 and 138–45 (*Letters* 29).

[13] This letter, however, is known only from a copy, so that neither the state of Leopold's handwriting nor any definite inference from the interruption can be established. See *MBA* 91, commentary.

[14] *MBA* 91 (*Letters* 30, but the passage is not complete).

land with a difficult and expensive journey home.[15] Walburgis was the third name of both his wife and his daughter, and with the Masses to be read at her altar, together with those to be read at the altar of St Wolfgang, he had appealed on behalf of every member of his family. Had Leopold died at this point, the outlook for his family would have been grim. The pension which Maria Anna could have expected from the Salzburg court would have been a pittance, and she would have faced a future of grinding poverty such as her own mother had endured.

Leopold's next letter was written on 13 September 1764, and judging by its length alone he was clearly considerably better. He described his illness and its treatment in detail, gave encoded pharmaceutical recipes for Hagenauer to have written out in full, recounted aspects of the English diet, and announced his intentions for the winter concert season in London. The experience of the treatment he had received had reinforced his mistrust of unknown doctors and his determination to take as much responsibility as possible for the health of himself and his family.

On 8 July, an extremely hot day, he and the children had been engaged by Lord Thanet to appear at a private concert. Because it was a Sunday, the usual hired vehicles were in great demand, and he could not get one. He therefore took a sedan chair for the children, and walked behind it himself. But the chair-carriers walked too fast for him, and this, together with the distance and the heat, meant that the exertion was too much. He felt ill before the end of the evening and succumbed to a heavy cold. He tried to treat it with homely measures, but on 14 July had to take to his bed, and a doctor was called in. By this time he had a dreadful inflammation of the throat. But what seems clear from the subsequent description of his treatment is that he was poisoned by some of the medicine he was prescribed, one element of which was opium. For whereas previously he had had the symptoms of a severe throat infection, after the doctor's intervention his stomach and nerves were wrecked too. The doctor himself seemed surprised at the worsening of Leopold's condition and shamefacedly announced, on 25 July, that Leopold was no fit subject to take much medicine. With these cheering words, he left him to get better as he might. At this point, a family friend, a Jewish cellist called Sipruntini, asked his cousin to visit Leopold. This second doctor presided over Leopold's successful recovery, while, in return, Leopold tried to convert him to Christianity. By 29 July Leopold was well enough to

---

[15] Leopold later alluded, in a letter to Wolfgang of 8 Dec. 1777, to having had to think out a way to get his family into safe hands if he had died in London, but he did not say what his idea had been. See *MBA* 387/29–32 (*Letters* 257).

be carried into St James's Park for some fresh air, and the subsequent move to Chelsea helped further. In Chelsea, Maria Anna took firm control of the family's diet by doing her own cooking, and Leopold reported that they were all much the better for it.

The Mozarts had brought with them from Salzburg several of their household recipes for the treatment of the more common minor complaints such as constipation, catarrh, and so forth, but these gave the ingredients in abbreviated Latin form, and used the symbols of measurement from the system of apothecaries' weight. English pharmacists did not understand them, except for the weights. Leopold, clearly alerted by his terrible experience to the possibility that they might need one of their home remedies and not be able to get it dispensed, asked Hagenauer to have five of these recipes written out in full for him, so that he could get them made up in London and treat his family himself with the medicines he trusted:

You'll easily appreciate for yourself that we've got to have the kinds of medicine that we're already accustomed to in case of need: because the doctors here treat their patients in their own way, even when they're faced with Germans, who have a different nature and temperament. and who wants to run to the doctor at every little ailment? — — the whole way of life of the English is as different from ours as night is from day.[16]

The vexed question of medical treatment abroad was to be raised again in The Hague in 1765, when Nannerl lay desperately ill and Leopold successfully intervened in the diagnosis and treatment because he thought her doctor was incompetent;[17] and also in Paris in 1778, when Maria Anna fell ill and died. On this latter occasion Leopold, who was not with his wife and could exercise no control over what happened, strongly believed that her treatment had been at fault. Maria Anna had run out of 'black powders', one of the household remedies most commonly used by the Mozarts for reducing fever; and because she would only be treated by a German doctor, she delayed being bled and was inadequately prepared for bloodletting when she did eventually get round to it. Leopold, in his agonized frustration at not having been there to look after her

---

[16] *MBA* 92/12–150 (*Letters* 31, but the passages describing the gravity of Leopold's condition and the pharmaceutical recipes are omitted). It is the truncated version in *Letters* that is responsible for the frequently encountered assumption in books relying solely on *Letters* that Leopold's illness in London was 'only' a cold. The five recipes Leopold asked Hagenauer to have written out in full are interpreted in J. Dalchow, 'Leopold Mozarts Haus- und Reiseapotheke', *AM* 25 (1955), 3–6. But Leopold also gave Hagenauer the details of four recipes with which he had been treated by his first English doctor, and these are not discussed by Dalchow.

[17] See Ch. 7.

himself, blamed Wolfgang for not taking firm control of the situation at an early stage. He ascribed her death to the will of God; but this had operated in such a way as to prevent Leopold, *who would not have allowed her to die*, from being with her.[18]

At the end of the long letter of 13 September 1764, Leopold gave Hagenauer some information about his plans for the approaching winter. He intended them to stay for the whole of it, and hoped to earn several thousand guineas. Having dared to travel to a country never before visited by anyone in Salzburg, he wanted to make the most of the opportunities it offered. He regretted that his illness had forced him to draw on money that might have been saved, but was preparing to 'gallop round' visiting all the people who could help them recover from their financial misfortune by promoting their winter concerts.[19]

In preparation for the winter season, the Mozarts moved back into central London around 25 September 1764, this time lodging in Thrift Street, Soho. On 25 October they were at court for the third time, but Leopold, when he mentioned this to Hagenauer in his letter of 3 December 1764, gave him no details of their reception.[20] They were presumably given a present of money for this, and if it followed the pattern of their two previous court appearances, this would have been 24 guineas (264 fl.). But an occasional sum of this sort did not go far in a city in which Leopold later estimated it cost £300 (about 3,143 fl.) annually to live;[21] and when he wrote to Hagenauer on 27 November 1764, he betrayed some anxiety about the prospect of filling his purse again. One problem was that Parliament was not going to reassemble until 10 January 1765, later than usual. This meant that the nobility would not be in town before then. Another was that Leopold had had a heavy outlay of money on the engraving and printing of six sonatas for keyboard and violin or flute (K. 10–15) by Wolfgang. They were to be dedicated to Queen Charlotte, and it was hoped that the expenses would be more than recovered, but meanwhile they were simply yet another drain on Leopold's finances. He said that they had spent 170 guineas (1,870 fl.) since July.[22]

A third problem was that London was swarming with musicians jostling for concert-giving opportunities, and it was by no means easy to be slotted into series arranged by others, or to find a free date to give a concert organized by oneself. Despite all Leopold's efforts to pursue influential acquaintance, he seems to have found it uphill work to squeeze

---

[18] See Ch. 18. [19] *MBA* 92/244–59 (*Letters* 31). [20] *MBA* 94/28–30 (*Letters* 33).
[21] Leopold to Hagenauer, 19 Mar. 1765—*MBA* 96/166–70 (*Letters* 35).
[22] *MBA* 93/2–14 (*Letters* 32).

performances by the children into the 1764/5 season. He must have expressed his anxieties to his friend Grimm, with whom they were still in touch, because on 13 December 1764 Grimm wrote from Paris to Ernst Ludwig, the duke of Saxe-Gotha, asking him to use his influence with the duke of York, in order that the Mozarts might be involved in the concert series run by Mrs Teresa Cornelys at Carlisle House in Soho Square. Grimm mentioned that the Mozarts had done well at first, but that the summer had been a dead season, and Leopold had been very ill, so that they now needed to make good their losses.[23] Mrs Cornelys was an opera singer turned society hostess, and her concerts (of which twenty-one were planned for the 1764/5 season) were effectively very exclusive large-scale soirées.[24]

There is no record of the Mozarts appearing at any of Mrs Cornelys' subscription concerts, so this plan of Leopold's was presumably unsuccessful. On 18 January 1765, Wolfgang's six newly engraved sonatas were dedicated to the queen, and Leopold later reported (on 19 March 1765) that she had presented Wolfgang with 50 guineas (550 fl.) for them;[25] but there is no record of what they had to pay to have them engraved. On 8 February 1765 Leopold wrote to Hagenauer that they were preparing for a concert on the 15th (in fact, it was postponed twice and eventually took place on the 21st), at which he hoped to take in 150 guineas (1,650 fl.). But even in this letter are hints that they were not doing as well as they would have liked: Leopold expressed doubts about whether they would manage to earn anything more after this concert, and reported despondently that in delaying the return of Parliament for two months the king had dealt a heavy blow to the arts; and then he launched into an account of the fantastically high earnings of the Italian castrato Manzuoli in London during this same season. According to Leopold, Manzuoli was going to earn 20,000 fl. for the season.[26]

The reason for the two postponements of the Mozarts' concert was that there was too much going on. Many of the instrumentalists needed for it were engaged for Arne's oratorio *Judith*. Even when the second new date of 21 February was arranged, the advertisement took pains to point out that the Mozarts' concert would start at 6.00 p.m., and would not therefore prevent anyone from attending other assemblies later the same evening.[27]

[23] Deutsch, *Documents*, 37–8.
[24] See S. McVeigh, *Concert Life in London from Mozart to Haydn* (Cambridge, 1993), 14–15.
[25] *MBA* 96/145–6 (*Letters* 35).   [26] *MBA* 95/5–16 (*Letters* 34).
[27] Deutsch, *Documents*, 40–1.

But a final factor in the Mozarts' struggles to earn as much as they would have liked may have been a personal one—that they had lost some of their popularity with the nobility. In Leopold's letter to Hagenauer of 19 March 1765, he reported that the concert on 21 February had not been as well attended as he had hoped. He first blamed the wearisome number of entertainments, and seemed dissatisfied with his profit of 100 guineas (1,100 fl.). But he went on to hint that he had given offence by refusing to agree to a proposal which had been made to him. He did not say what it had been, but claimed that it had caused him sleepless nights, and that he had arrived at his eventual decision by the consideration that England was too dangerous a place to bring up his children—most people had no religion, and the children would see nothing but bad examples. He also said that he wanted to be away from London by the beginning of May.[28]

Whatever the reasons for their lack of progress during the winter season in London of 1764/5, by mid-March the situation could not be described as satisfactory. On 11 March 1765 appeared the first of the advertisements which invited members of the public to visit the Mozarts at their lodgings in Thrift Street between 12.00 and 3.00 p.m. every day except Tuesday and Friday, to put Wolfgang's musical powers to the test. To be admitted on one of these occasions, each person had to buy a ticket costing half a guinea (5 fl. 30 kr.) for what was advertised to be the Mozarts' last concert before leaving England—a concert which would take place at the end of March or the beginning of April. The advertisement also mentioned that they would be leaving England in six weeks' time.[29] This is broadly consistent with Leopold's remark to Hagenauer that they wanted to leave London by the beginning of May. Yet even this effort to revive interest in the prodigies of nature appears not to have been very successful. Leopold was frustrated in his intentions, presumably through lack of public interest, and the remaining documents pertaining to the Mozarts' stay in London chart a sorry decline in their status and fortunes.

In the advertisement of 11 March 1765, the public had been offered, in return for its half-guinea, the ticket for the forthcoming concert, and the opportunity both to listen to the children play in private, and to test

[28] *MBA* 96/5–18 and 105–7 (*Letters* 35). Other contemporary reports concur with Leopold's that there was an embarrassment of entertainments in London—cf. McVeigh, *Concert Life in London*, 65. Curiously, although the Mozarts were by this date planning to leave England, a notice in *Lloyd's Evening Post* on 22 Feb. 1765 announced their presence in London as if they had just arrived—see Eisen, *Documents*, 6. Perhaps the placing of this notice formed part of Leopold's campaign to revive interest in the children.

[29] Deutsch, *Documents*, 43.

the musical powers of Wolfgang. A particular feature of the Mozarts' music-making in London, and one which was apparently quite a novelty, was the performance by Nannerl and Wolfgang of duets, using four hands sometimes on one keyboard and sometimes on two.[30] On 9 April a similar advertisement appeared, but the concert tickets were now priced at only 5*s*. (about 2 fl. 30 kr.) and the public was invited to call on any day of the week. The concert eventually took place on 13 May 1765 in Hickford's Great Room, Brewer Street.[31] Since Leopold had originally planned to give it at the end of March or the beginning of April, all this suggests that the tickets sold very sluggishly. It is not known what the income from the concert was, but there are good grounds for believing that it was disappointing. Leopold had apparently only been waiting for this concert to be behind them before leaving England. Yet they did not depart from London until 24 July, and on 30 May 1765 there appeared yet another advertisement inviting members of the public to call on the Mozarts at their lodgings to hear the children play in private. This time the terms were either to pay 5*s*. (about 2 fl. 30 kr.) for admission, or else to buy the six sonatas dedicated to the queen, which were priced at half a guinea.[32] Leopold was also offering for sale, on all these occasions, copies of the sonatas which had been printed in Paris, and the portrait which had been engraved there. A probable reason for the delay in their departure, therefore, is that Leopold could not contemplate the journey before them with the funds he had at this point, and was determined to boost them by all the means at his disposal before they left England. His intention was to return via Paris, but he knew that he could not count on earning much there before the winter season began, and would therefore need a good sum of money in hand to support them until then.

The final indignity for the Mozarts in London was the taking of a room in a tavern in Cornhill, the Swan and Harp, and performing there daily from 12.00–3.00 p.m. during their last few weeks in England.[33] The admission price had now sunk to 2*s.6d*. (about 1 fl. 15 kr.). The financial

---

[30] See Eisen, *Documents*, 7, for a report testifying to the rarity of four hands playing at one keyboard in England in 1765. Eisen notes that Nissen mentioned a claim by Leopold in his letter to Hagenauer of 9 July 1765 that no one had written a sonata for four hands until Wolfgang did so in London. See G. N. von Nissen, *Biographie W. A. Mozarts* (Leipzig, 1828), cited here from the unaltered reprint by Georg Olms Verlag (Hildesheim, 1991), 102. (Though Eisen states that the passage by Nissen appeared only in his draft biography and not in the published version, this is not so.) The passage quoted by Nissen does not form part of the letter of 9 July 1765, however—see *MBA* 98. Nissen often paraphrased letters in his biography, and a number of letters used by him have since disappeared. It may be that the passage in question came from a different letter, now lost.

[31] Deutsch, *Documents*, 44–5.   [32] Ibid. 45.   [33] Ibid. 45–6.

outcome of this enterprise is unknown, but if the letters to Hagenauer that now survive are all the ones that were written, it is surely not without significance that Leopold gave Hagenauer no inkling of these occasions, nor even of the slightly more respectable private ones which had taken place in their own lodgings.[34] Daytime concerts in London at this date had a completely different status from evening ones. Special permission was needed for them, and was rarely given. Events such as those arranged in the Swan and Harp, a tavern whose City of London address was less than august, came into the category of public exhibitions rather than concerts. They would not have attracted the nobility, as the evening concerts at the more dignified locations in the West End had. In 1762 the glass harmonica player Marianne Davis had appeared in events of 'exhibition' status, and had found herself on one occasion sharing the platform with three Cherokee chiefs.[35] For someone who prided himself on setting his family apart from the despised class of travelling musicians by living and performing in style, Leopold's experience of their last three months in London must have been perilously close to degradation. When he, on a later occasion, warned Wolfgang in strong terms that he would become an object of contempt unless he always had the means to move on when travelling,[36] it may well have been that the final phase of their stay in London was in his mind.

❧

Disappointing in some respects though the stay in London was, Leopold was fascinated by English life, and in the fifteen months that they were there, the Mozarts did not neglect the opportunity to see as much as possible. Leopold evidently felt proud that he had taken his family to a country that seemed quite exotic to their acquaintances in Salzburg, and he wanted to be able to give people at home full accounts of it. In contrast to the time spent in Paris, Nannerl made a fairly long list in her diary of what she had seen, and some of Leopold's letters to Hagenauer were the length of pamphlets, as he described in detail aspects of London life. Nannerl's diary entry ran:

London
I saw the park and a young elephant, a donkey that has white and coffee-brown stripes, and so even that no one could paint them better. chelsea, the invalid house,

---

[34] It is possible, however, that there are missing letters in this series, since nothing survives between that of 18 Apr. 1765 (*MBA* 97; *Letters* 36) and 9 July 1765 (*MBA* 98; *Letters* 37).
[35] See McVeigh, *Concert Life in London*, 38–9.
[36] Leopold to Wolfgang, 8 Dec. 1777—*MBA* 387/70–7 (*Letters* 257).

westminster bridge, Westminsterkirch, fauxhall, ranelagh, Tower, Richmond, where there is a very beautiful view, and the royal garden, kiw and Fulhambridge; the waterworks and a camel; westminster hall, lord perong trial, marlebon; Kensington, where I saw the royal garden, british mauseum, where I saw the library, antiquities, all sorts of birds, fish, insects and fruits; a special bird called a basson, a rattlesnake, a film of bark and hair from the fibre of a bark; a Chinese shoe, a model of the tomb in Jerusalem; all sorts of things that grow in the sea, stones, indian balsam, the globe of the world and the globe of the heavens and all sorts of other things; I saw greenwich, the invalid house, the Queen's ship, the park, in which I saw a very beautiful view, London bridge, St. Paulkirch, Soudwark, Monument, foundling hospital. enchange, Lincolsin fielsgarten, Templebar, Soumerset hauss.[37]

Leopold commented on some of the sights mentioned by Nannerl, and in addition bought prints showing London scenes. Though he wrote at considerable length about their English experiences, he indicated that he had much more to say, and he wanted to be able to bring the additional promised verbal accounts to life through the illustrations.[38] Perhaps the most striking aspect of his London reports is the sense of his being overwhelmed by the sheer size of the place, the magnitude of the organization of institutions, and the multiplicity of experiences. In describing the Royal Exchange (noted by Nannerl as 'enchange'), for example, he explained that its courtyard was bigger than the one at Mirabell, and that traders from all nations were to be found in its arcade. It was almost impossible to push one's way through the crowd in the courtyard, and the trade directory was 'the thickness of two fingers', and had to be arranged alphabetically. The number of ships and sailors was staggering, and to look down at the Thames from London Bridge was to see a forest of masts.[39] Similarly, when describing the pleasure gardens of Ranelagh and Vauxhall by the Thames, Leopold said that he and Maria Anna were overcome by the scale of the arrangements designed for the visitors' comfort, especially the illuminations at Vauxhall. He compared Vauxhall with the Elysian Fields, and after a vivid account of the avenues lit with

[37] Nannerl's diary from 23 Apr. 1764 to 4 Sept. 1765—*MBA* 100.

[38] Fifteen prints of England (as well as twenty-four from Italy) from Leopold's collection survive in the Salzburger Museum Carolino Augusteum, Salzburg's museum of local history. See R. Angermüller and G. Ramsauer, ' "du wirst, wenn uns Gott gesund zurückkommen läst, schöne Sachen sehen": Veduten aus dem Nachlass Leopold Mozarts in der Graphiksammlung des Salzburger Museums Carolino Augusteum', *MM* 42 (1994), 1–48.

[39] Leopold to Hagenauer, 27 Nov. 1764—*MBA* 93/23–47 (not in *Letters*). This letter continued with other London statistics, such as the numbers of churches and other major institutions. The figures (e.g. 1,318 nightwatchmen, 166 public paupers' schools, 50 squares) must have been almost impossible for most of the Mozarts' Salzburg acquaintances to grasp.

many thousands of lamps in beautiful glass casings, the refreshment alcoves, and the summerhouse where music was played, he claimed that nowhere other than in England could one find such bright lamplight on so large a scale, since the expense would normally be too great for any one class of society. In England, however, the greater unification of the nobility with the common man enabled the expense to be shared.[40]

Leopold was keenly alert to large issues in politics, economics, religion and morality, and the administration of justice. He described in detail a riot of silk weavers, angry because their livelihoods were threatened by French goods, and he said that he was impressed by the ability of the common man 'earning his bread by the sweat of his brow' to obtain accurate information about the issues relevant to him, and by his freedom to lodge complaints when he had a just claim.[41] He also mentioned the trial of Lord Byron (the 'lord perong trial' of Nannerl's diary) for duelling and fatally wounding his opponent.[42] And he described a christening at which Maria Anna had been persuaded to be a reluctant godmother to the baby. Leopold enumerated the faiths of the various parties concerned, not forgetting to mention that the father had no denominated faith at all, and commented that the only person lacking was a Jew.[43]

Details of domestic life were just as interesting to Leopold as larger matters, and he wrote at length about English food and drink, and the routines of daily life. He admired the fine, large, healthy cattle and sheep, and the abundance of good produce, and was impressed by the changing seasonal foods, especially the fish. He praised the high quality of the different types of beer, but was too cautious to drink it regularly. Cider was said to be 'not unhealthy', and rum and punch were other alcoholic novelties to him. Plum pudding he found wretched, and was disgusted by the English practice of 'guzzling solidified fat' (this was probably dripping). Though his comments about food occasionally seem narrow, maintainance of the accustomed diet was then an important element of health care, and some of Leopold's remarks were made directly following the description of his illness, in which he had complained that English doctors treated everyone alike, even though the way of life of the English was completely different from that of Germans.[44]

---

[40] Leopold to Hagenauer, 28 June 1764—*MBA* 90/97–184 (not in *Letters*).
[41] Leopold to Hagenauer, 9 July 1765—*MBA* 98/8–84 (not in *Letters*).
[42] Leopold to Hagenauer, 8 Feb. 1765 and 18 Apr. 1765—*MBA* 95/47–52 and 97/3–7 (not in *Letters*).
[43] Leopold to Hagenauer, 19 Mar. 1765—*MBA* 96/19–46 (not in *Letters*).
[44] Leopold to Hagenauer, 28 May 1764, 13 Sept. 1764, and 19 Mar. 1765—*MBA* 88/40–7, 92/150–212, and 96/74–8 (none in *Letters*).

Hagenauer had at least once commented that Leopold's long letters from London were much appreciated. Writing on 19 March 1765, Leopold listed a number of topics which he would like to have written about in more detail, but feared that they would make the letter turn into another one that took half an hour to read. He simply listed them, therefore, and indicated that they would discuss them at length when he returned. One of these topics was costume and hair style. He said that students at Oxford had their hair cut short so that the growth of hair did not hinder the growth of their intellects, and he compared this with the equally English practice of docking horses' tails to improve their strength. Other topics were the orphanage hospitals, the burying of the dead, various items of machinery, and aspects of low life, for example cock-fighting and street brawls. In particular, he seems to have wanted to note the conjunction of an exceptionally fortunate land in terms of agricultural fertility, and the horrifyingly brutal behaviour of many of its inhabitants.[45]

When it is considered that, in addition to all the experiences described by Leopold in his letters home, the family must have met on their travels hundreds of people from many different classes of society, an inkling is obtained of the way in which they might have been growing away from many of their compatriots. Although some of Leopold's court music colleagues also travelled abroad, it was unusual for a family with young children to do so together, and the childhood of Nannerl and Wolfgang was something quite exceptional by Salzburg standards.

❧

As usual when the Mozarts were away, the Hagenauers were actively promoting their interests at home. Hagenauer saw to the distribution in Germany of the music published by Wolfgang in Paris and London, and of the family portrait which had been engraved in Paris. He also arranged for colleagues of Leopold to perform Wolfgang's published sonatas before the archbishop's court, thus helping to keep Schrattenbach's goodwill.[46] In addition, his son Johannes evidently wrote at great length to the Mozarts on Salzburg matters, and his letters, which Leopold jocularly called newspapers, were much appreciated.

Leopold was particularly interested in developments in the court music, and was keen to know if the two female singers recently returned from

---

[45] *MBA* 96/58–104 (not in *Letters*).

[46] Leopold to Hagenauer, 3 Dec. 1764—*MBA* 94/18–21 (*Letters* 33). And according to the court diary, music of Wolfgang's was indeed played at court, on 3 Jan. 1765—see Martin, 'Fürstenhof 80', 173.

Italy had been taken into salaried employment.[47] The women he meant were Maria Anna Braunhofer and Maria Magdalena Lipp, who had been in Italy at Schrattenbach's expense. They had in fact gained court appointments, and their subsequent careers were identical in terms of emoluments until 1783, after which time Lipp (by that time married to Michael Haydn) gained an increase ahead of Braunhofer. On 8 January 1765 they each got a contract offering an annual salary of 100 fl. and a daily wine allowance—at this date, neither woman was aged more than 20. Their salaries were to increase to 120 fl. annually on 23 January 1766, following the death of their colleague Maria Franziska Strasser, daughter of the deceased Kapellmeister Eberlin. It was to be suggested that their spiteful treatment of Strasser had contributed to her untimely death.[48]

On their side, the Mozarts were reciprocally generous to their friends while they were away, sending news and collecting together specialities which did not normally find their way to Salzburg. On 27 November 1764 Leopold sent greetings through Hagenauer to the Dancing Master, Franz Speckner. Speckner gave dancing lessons in the large room of the Dancing-Master's House, in which the Mozarts were to rent a handsome suite of rooms from 1773, turning the dancing room into a music room. Leopold indicated that he was going to bring home a book of *contredanses* for Speckner's use, but warned him that though this dance was native to England, it was not an impressive sight. In the same letter, he answered a query from a violinist called Vogt, who appears to have wanted Leopold to make enquiries about sending home violins bought in London.[49] Above all, however, he was trying to choose English watches for a number of people, including their wealthy friend Frau Robinig von Rottenfeld. This involved him in extensive enquiries, since the choices and prices were so variable. Moreover, since the English watches were so advanced in design, he was concerned that Salzburg watchmakers might be unable to repair them if they ever broke.[50] In March 1765, while he was busy investigating watches, he also made enquiries about the most economical way to send Hagenauer a length of scarlet cloth that had been requested. It could not be carried as part of their luggage, because they were returning through France, where the customs checks were very stringent.[51]

[47] Leopold to Hagenauer, 13 Sept. 1764—*MBA* 92/236–8 (not in *Letters*).

[48] The salary figures are from Hintermaier, 'Hofkapelle', 45 and 227. For details of Strasser's death, see Ch. 7.

[49] *MBA* 93/233–49 (not in *Letters*).

[50] Leopold to Hagenauer, 3 Dec. 1764 and 19 Mar. 1765—*MBA* 94/22–8 and 96/123–36 and 148–65 (not in *Letters*).

[51] Leopold to Hagenauer, 19 Mar. 1765—*MBA* 96/107–15 (not in *Letters*).

The passages about shopping for friends show that Leopold spent considerable time and trouble seeking out the things he thought would interest and please them. He evidently did not buy trinkets casually, for the sake of good form, but on the contrary tried to ensure that people at home knew what was available, so that they could make an informed choice. Taken in conjunction with the fact that he must have spent long hours writing at generous length about London life, and all this in addition to the arduous business of promoting his family's prosperity, it is clear that Leopold was a staunch friend and neighbour. The later correspondence confirms the view that no matter how busy he was, or how great his own worries were, he could always find time to help or please other people.

❧

When the time arrived for the Mozarts to leave London on the first stage of their long journey back to Salzburg, the prospect was daunting. In the first place, the financial arrangements had to be thought out, and on 19 March 1765, Leopold explained that he would have bought many more curiosities if they had earned as much as it first seemed that they would. What he had to do now, rather, was to conserve his money for the journey. He had to think out a route which would ensure that other people would pay the costs.[52] Since they were obliged to return via Paris, he must have had to calculate how they would live there until the winter concert season began. Secondly, the packing up of all their belongings was an enormous undertaking, involving calculations of how to get everything safely back to Salzburg as cheaply as possible, and bearing in mind that they had already left a stack of acquisitions in Paris to be collected on the return journey. On 18 April 1765 Leopold told Hagenauer that the mere thought of the luggage made him sweat. They could not possibly take everything with them, but nor could they leave anything behind.[53] And despite the fact that he had wanted to buy more souvenirs in London, they must in any case have bought a good many, for when Leopold's possessions were auctioned after his death in 1787, valuable English optical equipment was listed in the advertisement.[54] Leopold most probably sold some of their belongings before leaving London, to ease the packing problems and realize some cash for the journey.

[52] *MBA* 96/136–42 (not in *Letters*).
[53] *MBA* 97/12–19 (*Letters* 36, but the passage is not quite complete).
[54] See ad in the *Salzburger Intelligenzblatt* on 15 Sept. 1787—Deutsch, *Documents*, 296–7.

But in addition to these practical considerations, there appears to have been an undercurrent of unease about returning home—one which suggests for the first time that Leopold saw a difficulty in realizing his twin desires of promoting Wolfgang as a child prodigy and at the same time advancing his own career in Salzburg. In his last letter to Hagenauer from London, written on 9 July 1765, he referred to Frau Hagenauer's hints that they might be intending to stay in London for ever. He claimed that they were certainly planning to return, but that the journey home was to be dictated by any opportunities that presented themselves to be grasped. He then begged to be left in peace to finish the work which, with God's help, he had begun.[55] The misgivings hinted at here were to surface again more strongly in the following year as the Mozart family approached nearer and nearer to Salzburg (for the return journey from London was to take sixteen months). It was to become clear then that Leopold had received news from home which made him question whether he would be warmly welcomed back at his court post after his exceptionally long absence, and when he then spent a further year in Vienna with his children only ten months after his return from the long European tour, the damage done to his personal prospects and the irreconcilable nature of his dual aim—that of promoting the careers both of his son and of himself—could no longer be doubted.

On 24 July 1765 the Mozarts left London for Canterbury, and spent a few days on Sir Horace Mann's estate at Bourn Place. Nannerl's last diary entries before leaving England read:

In Canterbury
The Hauptkirch, and from Canterbury we went 4 miles into the country to Mtr: Man at burn plas, this was a very beautiful estate. The horse-racing.
Dover
the port.[56]

Their intention on leaving England had been to return home through France and Italy. But chasing them out of London rode the Dutch ambassador, with urgent requests that they travel first to The Hague to appear before Princess Caroline of Nassau-Weilburg. The ambassador must have made a favourable financial proposition, because Leopold accepted the suggestion, contradicting his assertion to Frau Hagenauer of fifteen months previously that they would not go to Holland. On 1 August 1765, therefore, they set sail from Dover for Calais.[57]

---

[55] *MBA* 98/141–56 (not in *Letters*).   [56] *MBA* 100/19–24.
[57] Leopold to Hagenauer on 19 Sept. 1765—*MBA* 102/12–34 (*Letters* 38).

7

The Grand European Tour (IV):
Near-Disaster on the Journey Home

THE outward journey from Salzburg to London had lasted ten months; the return took sixteen, and they had to make radical changes to all their plans. The acceptance of the offer to go to The Hague meant that they were travelling in a completely different direction from a large part of their belongings, which had already been sent on to Paris, but Leopold did not expect the detour to detain them very long. Once they were on their way, however, matters were taken out of their hands by a succession of illnesses. They had to stay four weeks against their will in Lille, while first Wolfgang and then Leopold recovered from severe head colds; and then, no sooner had they arrived in The Hague than first Nannerl and then Wolfgang succumbed to illnesses which nearly cost them their lives, and which required intensive nursing on the part of Leopold and Maria Anna for more than three months. Here is the calendar, as far as their movements are known, for the return journey:

1765

1 Aug.	Left Dover for Calais. Collected their carriage, which had been left there.
3(?) Aug.	Arrived in Dunkirk.
5(?) Aug.	Arrived in Lille, where the illnesses of Wolfgang and Leopold kept them a month.
18 Aug.	Emperor Francis of Austria, consort of Maria Theresia, died at Innsbruck.
4 Sept.	Travelled from Lille to Ghent.
5 Sept.	Wolfgang played the organ at the Cistercian monastery in Ghent.
6 Sept.	Left Ghent.
7 and 8 Sept.	In Antwerp, where Wolfgang played the organ in the cathedral.

9 Sept.	Leaving their carriage in Antwerp, they travelled to Rotterdam via Moerdijk.
10 Sept.	Arrived at The Hague, staying first at an inn, and then in private lodgings.
12 Sept.	Nannerl fell ill with chest catarrh. Wolfgang played at court to Princess Caroline, without Nannerl.
18–27 Sept.	Wolfgang played several times before Prince William V of Orange, still without Nannerl.
27 Sept.	Advertisement for a concert to be given by both children on 30 September 1765, but Nannerl cannot have appeared on this date.
21 Oct.	Nannerl was given extreme unction, and on the same day a second medical opinion was sought, after which she began to recover.
15 Nov.	Wolfgang became ill, a week after Nannerl had left her bed for the first time.
12 Dec.	Wolfgang was just beginning to recover.

1766

22 Jan.	The children gave a concert in The Hague.
*c.*26 Jan.	The family travelled to Amsterdam.
29 Jan.	Concert in Amsterdam, by both children.
26 Feb.	Second concert in Amsterdam.
Early Mar.	Returned to The Hague.
7 Mar.	Music of Wolfgang's offered for sale—the two sets of variations, K. 24 and K. 25.
11 Mar.	The children performed at court. Both sets of variations were played, and possibly also Wolfgang's Quodlibet K. 32. Leopold's *Violinschule*, in Dutch, was presented to the prince.
Mar.	Dedication of Wolfgang's sonatas for keyboard and violin K. 26–31 (written in The Hague) to Princess Caroline.
End Mar.	Left The Hague.
Early Apr.	In Haarlem, where Leopold was presented with the Dutch edition of his *Violinschule*. Wolfgang played the famous organ.
Apr.	In Amsterdam again.
16 Apr.	Third concert in Amsterdam. Wolfgang's six sonatas for violin and keyboard, K. 26–31, offered for sale.
18 Apr.	Left Amsterdam for Utrecht, picking up their own carriage again.
21 Apr.	Concert in Utrecht.

End Apr.	Left Utrecht for Brussels, via Moerdijk, Antwerp, and Malines.
30 Apr.	Concert in Antwerp.
8 May	Arrived in Brussels.
9 May	Left Brussels for Valenciennes.
10 May	To Paris, via Cambrai. Took lodgings in Paris.
28 May–1 June	In Versailles.
9 July	Left Paris at 8.00 p.m.
12 July	Arrived in Dijon, where they stayed two weeks.
18 July	Concert in Dijon.
26(?) July	Arrived in Lyons, and stayed four weeks.
13 Aug.	Concert in Lyons.
20 Aug.	Arrived in Geneva.
After 20 Aug.	Gave two concerts in Geneva.
14(?) Sept.	Arrived in Lausanne.
15 Sept.	Concert in Lausanne.
18 Sept.	Second concert in Lausanne.
19(?) Sept.	On to Berne for a week.
28(?) Sept.	Arrived in Zurich, via Baden in Aargau.
7 Oct.	Concert in Zurich.
9 Oct.	Second concert in Zurich.
10–16 Oct.	From Zurich to Donaueschingen, via Winterthur and Schaffhausen.
17–28 Oct.	Daily concerts at the court of Prince Joseph Wenzel von Fürstenberg in Donaueschingen (where their former servant, Sebastian Winter, now worked).
Late Oct./early Nov.	Left Donaueschingen.
3 Nov.	Reached Dillingen, via Messkirch, Ulm, and Günzburg.
4 or 5 Nov.	Concert in Dillingen.
6 Nov.	To Augsburg, via Biberach, where the Fugger family had its pilgrimage church.
8 Nov.	Arrived in Munich.
9 Nov.	Wolfgang played and improvised for the elector, Maximilian III Joseph.
12–21 Nov.	Wolfgang was ill.
22 Nov.	Wolfgang played for the Bavarian court again, this time with Nannerl.
29 Nov.	Arrived back in Salzburg, after an absence of nearly three and a half years.[1]

---

[1] The calendar is derived from Deutsch, *Documents*; Eibl, *Chronik*; and Eisen, *Documents*. There are several minor uncertainties as to date. In particular, Eisen (*Documents*, 11–26 inc.) offers new details about the journey. Also to be noted is that though Deutsch calls Nannerl's illness 'intestinal typhoid', Leopold described it as 'chest catarrh'.

The Hagenauers had already expressed some impatience, while the Mozarts were still in London, to see their friends and tenants back in Salzburg; and Leopold's last letter to them from London, dated 9 July 1765, had been written before the itinerary was changed. It must have been with considerable surprise, therefore, that they read the opening lines of his next letter, of 19 September 1765, and discovered that the Mozarts were in The Hague, even further away from Salzburg than they had been in England. Leopold explained that his initial plan had been to return first to Paris, and then travel to northern Italy before making their way home. After writing about the offer to go to The Hague, he said that they had revised their plans, and now intended to spend August in Holland, to return to Paris at the end of September, and from there to make their way home. In Lille, however, Wolfgang had suffered a bad attack of catarrh, and Leopold had followed him down with it. He had been too dizzy to sit up, and they had been delayed four weeks while he recovered sufficiently to travel on. They had now been a week in The Hague, and Wolfgang had played to the princess and the prince, but Nannerl had been unable to do so, because she now had heavy catarrh on her chest, which was only just beginning to loosen. The rest of the letter contained brief descriptions of some of the things they had seen in Holland so far, but Leopold's thoughts were chiefly fixed on the journey home, and on living arrangements at home when they arrived. He was clearly not very worried about Nannerl's chest, and was planning soon to be able to progress with the journey. The last line of the letter was typically laconic: 'It makes me think a bit when I reflect on our journey. *ma foi*, It's quite a walk.'[2]

But when Leopold wrote his next letter to Hagenauer, on 5 November 1765, any thoughts of travelling on had been temporarily banished by Nannerl's illness, which, far from continuing to improve, had worsened to such an extent that she had had to be given extreme unction on 21 October. Leopold described minutely Nannerl's decline and subsequent improvement to the Hagenauers, including the details of three medical recipes prescribed for her, the diet that formed an essential accompaniment to the medicines, the first doctor's diagnosis, Leopold's doubts about its accuracy and the man's competence, and his last-ditch efforts to get a second opinion before she died.

Leopold began by saying that at first they made nothing of her indisposition, and she did not even have to stay in bed. But on 26 September,

---

[2] *MBA* 102 (*Letters* 38, but it is not complete).

two weeks after she first had the catarrh, she began to run a fever, and developed an inflammation of the throat. Next day she was no better and Dr Hayman, who attended many of the foreign ambassadors in The Hague, was called in. Nannerl was bled on 28 September, and the blood was 'very bad'—it was inflamed, and half of it was 'white slime or grease'. She still had a catarrhal expectoration, and the doctor, in the belief that an abscess was forming in one of her lungs, embarked on what Leopold described as a 'milk cure', whose effect he perceived as stopping up the cough and driving the 'matter' of the disease down into her lower body. To combat this problem, the steadily weakening Nannerl was then prescribed medicines intended to stimulate the urinary tract and bowel to expel the injurious material. At this point, however, Leopold seems to have had a terrible fear that she would develop diarrhoea, which would be the last straw for her weakened frame. The doctor had given up hope, and Leopold lost patience with him, deciding that he had misdiagnosed the case from the beginning. On 21 October, though he and Maria Anna had been preparing Nannerl (who could by now hardly speak) to accept death, Leopold arranged for Professor Thomas Schwenke, the virtually retired physician of Princess Caroline, to join Dr Hayman and himself for a consultation at Nannerl's bedside. Hayman was forced to justify his treatment in Schwenke's hearing, while Leopold contradicted much of his evidence. Then Schwenke examined Nannerl thoroughly, announced that the problem was 'nothing more than extraordinarily thick mucus', and changed the dietary and medical prescription completely. Later the same day, Leopold and Maria Anna called in a priest to give Nannerl Holy Communion. He was so shocked by her poor condition that he also administered the sacrament of extreme unction. But Nannerl then began to turn the corner. Though she raved in several languages about topics connected with their travels (her bizarre ramblings were the only things that could distract Wolfgang from his sadness), the fever started to subside. Schwenke continued to visit, and she slowly regained her strength.

All this time, Leopold and Maria Anna had been nursing her themselves, having decided that they did not want to entrust their child to strangers. Maria Anna took the night watch from midnight to 6.00 a.m., and Leopold then took over, so that Maria Anna could sleep till noon. During the most anxious period of about six weeks, they prayed, and searched the Bible for clues to the outcome of her illness. Leopold mentioned in particular two Gospel passages from which they drew cautious comfort; his brief allusions allow them to be identified as the

Gospels for the twentieth and the twenty third Sunday after Whitsun respectively.[3] In addition to all this, Leopold and Maria Anna might even, in their desperation, have consulted a quack doctor.[4] All thought of travelling on, or of earning and saving money, was abandoned. Their winter furs were waiting in Paris, their money disappearing fast,[5] and it was going to be almost impossible to travel because of the season, but these worries had to be set aside as they tried to keep calm for Nannerl's sake. When her condition was improving, the Hagenauers were asked to have five Masses said for her at specified altars, and to enquire whether Nannerl could be allowed her wish to have a Mass read in honour of 'the pious Crescentia', who had not been canonized.[6]

Nannerl had needed continuous nursing care for six weeks before she rose from her bed around 7 November, nothing but skin and bone, and started to learn to walk again. Hardly had this point been reached when Wolfgang underwent an equally perilous experience, and Leopold and Maria Anna had to endure the same torment all over again for another four weeks.[7] By the time Leopold was able to report to Hagenauer that Wolfgang was recovering, it was mid-December, the month when Leopold

[3] The 20th Sunday after Whit in 1765 was 13 Oct., and the Gospel was John 4: 46–53, about Jesus healing a nobleman's sick son. The 23rd Sunday was 3 Nov., and the Gospel was Matthew 9: 18–26, about the daughter who was thought to be dead, but who was reawakened by Jesus. These refs. are supplied by the commentary to *MBA* 103/105–9. On 13 Oct. Nannerl was still declining; by 3 Nov. she was recovering.

[4] Leopold's travel notes for 11 Sept. 1765–10 May 1766 contain a one-line entry, 'Aly the cunt', a few lines down from the names of Dr Hayman, Professor Schwenke, and an apothecary. 'Aly' was a known itinerant quack doctor. See *MBA* 105/40, inc. commentary. My translation of the German *Hundsfott* as 'cunt' is not satisfactory, but perhaps the closest idiomatic translation possible. *Hundsfott* means literally 'the cunt of a bitch', and was an epithet sometimes implying cowardice on the part of the person being thus insulted. The Mozarts also used the word in its adjectival and adverbial forms. I am grateful to Professor Peter Branscombe for guidance with this translation.

[5] On 8 Dec. 1777, when Wolfgang was in Mannheim in his attempt to gain a post elsewhere than in Salzburg, Leopold wrote complaining about Wolfgang's casual attitude to preparing for the possibility of adverse circumstances. He stated that when the children had been ill in The Hague he had had to withdraw 600 fl. in order to meet expenses, at least one of which was the bill at the inn. This sum was not far short of twice his annual salary in Salzburg. See *MBA* 387/25–41 (*Letters* 257, but the reference to the sum of money is omitted).

[6] *MBA* 103 (*Letters* 39, but not complete). The three pharmaceutical recipes given in this letter are interpreted in J. Dalchow, *Drei Rezepte für Nannerl Mozart* (Berlin, 1952). Dalchow uses pharmaceutical reference works stretching back into the 18th c. to make the terms of the recipes comprehensible and explain their intended efficacy.

[7] Although Nannerl and Wolfgang are usually both said to have suffered from typhus in The Hague, their symptoms as described by Leopold do not sound the same, and the treatment was also different. Under Schwenke, Nannerl was prescribed chiefly expectorants, the other medicines she took serving to guard against unwelcome secondary effects. Wolfgang, however, was treated by Schwenke not with expectorants but with fever-reducing medicines and, later, mixtures to restore his strength. See Dalchow, *Drei Rezepte*, and the commentary to *MBA* 103 and 104.

had counted on being home in Salzburg again.[8] In fact, they were not to arrive home until November of the following year. On 12 December 1765, Leopold wrote to Hagenauer to describe Wolfgang's illness. It had struck him down on 15 November and rendered him completely unrecognizable in the space of four weeks. Like Nannerl, he became mere skin and bones. Leopold described his illness as a raging fever. On 23 November he was given an enema, and was critically ill on the 30th. The fever then subsided, but he lay in a stupor for a week, unable to speak. After that, he raved day and night, but started to regain his strength. The night vigils were carried on as they had been through Nannerl's illness. Again, Leopold gave the Hagenauers details of the treatment, again he said that the cost was absolutely not to be thought of, and again he asked for Masses to be read. He also said that had it not been for God's exceptional blessing, they could never have pulled through such a difficult period as the last three months had been.

Leopold asked for nine Masses to be read for Wolfgang. Because he had only asked for five for Nannerl, and because when he had been ill in England he had asked for twenty-two, he has been accused by Nannerl's biographer Eva Rieger of valuing Nannerl's life less highly than his own and that of Wolfgang. But the altars chosen for the Masses after Wolfgang's recovery included those of St Anne and St Walburgis, both of which were the names of Maria Anna and Nannerl. Taken together with the fact that the request for Masses directly followed Leopold's remark that the whole family had successfully come through a dreadful ordeal lasting three months, this suggests that the nine Masses were not desired for Wolfgang's sake alone, any more than the twenty-two in London had been for Leopold alone.[9]

Of the nineteen weeks which had passed since the family had left England, weeks in which Leopold had expected to travel all the way home, about seventeen had been wasted by the illnesses described above. In

---

[8] Leopold to Hagenauer, 5 Nov. 1765—*MBA* 103/123–6 (*Letters* 39).

[9] *MBA* 104 (*Letters* 40, but not complete). Rieger also sees Leopold's attempts to prepare Nannerl for death, and his search for divine clues to the outcome of her illness, as evidence of his passive, undespairing, attitude to Nannerl's situation. Rieger's characterization of the discussions about death held among Leopold, Maria Anna, and Nannerl gives the impression that Leopold was crudely fatalistic about Nannerl's illness. See Rieger, *Nannerl Mozart*, 62–4. Close reading of the relevant letter, however, suggests that Leopold's attitude was more complex, and that the relationship between the duty to act to preserve health and the duty to trust in God for the outcome of illness was a subtle one. Leopold was to be more explicit on the relationship between the duty to act and the belief that events were divinely predetermined when Wolfgang travelled without him from 1777 to 1779—see Chs. 17 and 18. And Leopold's behaviour during the Viennese smallpox epidemic of 1767–8 also sheds light on his attitude to this issue—see Ch. 8.

his relief at having both children restored to health, Leopold was naturally reticent about the financial damage that had been done, but it must have been considerable. The fact that the rest of their journey home from Holland was frequently interrupted by concert-giving, although they were already far behind their projected travel schedule, suggests that Leopold was anxious to replenish his purse. Of all the financial setbacks they encountered on their grand tour, those experienced on the return journey probably did more than anything else to instil in Leopold grave doubts about whether it was wise for the whole family to travel together. When Nannerl and Maria Anna were to be disappointed at not being able to accompany Leopold and Wolfgang to Italy at a later date, Leopold's partial justification was that accommodation costs could be cut considerably by leaving the women behind. One reason for this was that he and Wolfgang could often stay in monasteries, an option not so often available to mixed parties.

❧

Yet the return journey was not entirely taken up with worries and woes. During Nannerl's illness and after his own, Wolfgang was busy composing. Among other items he was able to publish, in April 1766, six sonatas for violin and keyboard (K. 26–31), which he dedicated to Princess Caroline. In addition, as the calendar shows, they were able to give a number of public concerts in The Hague, Amsterdam, Utrecht, and Antwerp, before travelling on to Paris. As in London, an attractive feature of these concerts was the performance by both children together, sometimes on one keyboard, sometimes on two. And in Haarlem, Leopold was delighted to be presented with a fine Dutch edition of his *Violinschule*, a copy of which was also presented to Prince William V of Orange in Leopold's presence.[10]

By the time Leopold wrote the letter telling Hagenauer about this, they had arrived in Paris, where Grimm found them lodgings, and where they were reunited with all their luggage—some of which had been there since April 1764, when they had left for England. Little is known about this second stay in Paris, because Leopold had evidently tired to some extent of writing long travel reports to Hagenauer. In his letter of 16 May 1766, he explained that the illnesses of the children had forced him to give up writing home at length; and no doubt he was also looking forward to giving the Hagenauers verbal accounts before long of their activities on

---

[10] Leopold to Hagenauer, 16 May 1766—*MBA* 108/30–8 (*Letters* 41).

the return journey. One small piece of information not contained in the correspondence, however, is that Leopold subscribed to an appeal for the Calas family by buying a print of the family's portrait. The father, Jean Calas, had been a Protestant cloth merchant in Toulouse, and the victim of brutal religious persecution. His eldest son had committed suicide and Jean was accused of murdering him in order to prevent his conversion to Catholicism. After Jean Calas had been cruelly executed, Voltaire led a campaign to have him declared posthumously innocent. The case became a *cause célèbre*, the campaign succeeded, and in March and April 1765 Grimm's *Correspondance littéraire* reported news of it and gave advance notice of the subscription sales of the portrait.[11] Unfortunately, however, no safe inferences about Leopold's views on this case can be drawn from his subscription, since he might have signed up at least in part in order not to offend Grimm.

On 15 July 1766 Grimm wrote again about the Mozart children in the *Correspondance littéraire*. Again Nannerl, now almost 15, but described in the report as 13, was praised for her beautiful and brilliant execution at the keyboard, and she was also said to have 'grown much prettier'. Wolfgang's age was given as 9, though he was 10. His printed compositions were mentioned, and the fact that he had started to compose arias. His acquaintance with the castrato Manzuoli in London, and the latter's influence on his singing, was commented upon, and Grimm predicted that he would write an opera and have it performed by the age of 12. His gaiety and wit were mentioned with approval, and the report finished with another prediction—that if the children lived, they would not long remain in Salzburg, because monarchs would vie for their possession. Leopold was praised for uniting fine musicianship with sense, good nature, and merit.[12]

A number of points of interest are raised by Grimm's report. First, as in all the reports on the children, the keyboard brilliance shown by Nannerl was still almost completely overshadowed by the astonishing range of her brother's talents; and since their last visit to Paris two years previously, Wolfgang had been concentrating increasingly on composition. This was a natural development from the manifold keyboard skills he had shown as a younger child, and from this point on, the way in which the paths of the two children were diverging becomes ever clearer.

---

[11] See F. Steegmuller, *A Woman, a Man, and Two Kingdoms: The Story of Madame d'Épinay and the Abbé Galiani* (London, 1992), 96–100. Leopold described himself as Kapellmeister on the subscription list.

[12] See Deutsch, *Documents*, 56–7.

Leopold was soon to suggest, in his letter to Hagenauer of 10 November 1766, that the children would have different working patterns on their return to Salzburg.[13] That Nannerl (who could hardly any longer be described as a child prodigy) was to be left behind, when Leopold took Wolfgang to Italy to learn more about composition in 1769 and the 1770s, was a logical step along the road which was already being mapped out.

A second point of interest is the reference to Wolfgang's singing, and the way in which Leopold allowed him to profit from Manzuoli's instruction in London, while Nannerl is not mentioned as a singer at all during the period of her childhood. Yet it is unlikely that Leopold objected in principle to her practising this branch of music. Given that the one well-paid musical career open to her as an adult female musician would have been that of singing, it might be thought that Leopold had every motive for encouraging her in this endeavour.[14] While they were on their grand tour, he took a great interest in the careers of three female singers in Salzburg at the time (Braunhofer, Fesermayr, and Lipp), hoping that after they had returned from educational tours to Italy, they would be engaged by the Salzburg court and do it honour. He must therefore have been alert to the possibility that Nannerl might later be able to follow this course. It is possible that Leopold would have had reservations about a career of this kind for her, on account of the aura of dubious respectability surrounding the singing profession; yet there were situations in which she could conceivably have practised as a singer without risking her moral reputation. The most obvious one was precisely that offered by Salzburg—working at a small ecclesiastical court under the guidance of her parents. Two main possibilities therefore exist for the fact that singing does not appear to have loomed large in her musical career—she may have had little interest in or aptitude for it, or Leopold may have been too preoccupied with Wolfgang's compositional education from around 1766 to arrange a comprehensive singer's education for her. It is difficult to decide which is more likely to be right. Other evidence about Leopold suggests that in general he warmly encouraged all musical talent, regardless of sex, and since there is one instance of Wolfgang teasing Nannerl about her 'unbearable' voice,[15] it may be that she did not have any great

---

[13] *MBA* 112/80–92 (*Letters* 44).

[14] See Ch. 3, n. 27, for references to Nannerl singing and to Leopold's wish that she should be able to earn money from music when she grew up.

[15] Wolfgang to Nannerl, 4 Aug. 1770—*MBA* 202/58–60 (*Letters* 106a). The letter was written while Wolfgang was touring in Italy with Leopold; the contents of Wolfgang's letters to Nannerl from this first visit to Italy are discussed in Ch. 9.

gift for singing. On the other hand, the period 1767–77 was one when Leopold does appear rather markedly to have neglected Nannerl.[16]

Grimm's prediction that Wolfgang would write an opera before he was 12 years old was proved accurate. This was precisely what Leopold was to strive to enable him to do during the family's next absence from Salzburg, in 1767–9, when they went to Vienna.[17] The opera was *La finta semplice*, but it was not performed on the occasion for which it had been intended. The enormous trouble caused by this commission notwithstanding, it is still the case that, by the age of 10, Wolfgang was well initiated into the world of the theatre. This world was to become increasingly important to him, and was one in which his sister could participate only as a spectator.

On the other hand, Grimm's second prediction—that the children would not remain at Salzburg, and that monarchs would vie for their possession—proved completely wrong. Who could have guessed, during this period of universal acclaim and triumph, that Maria Anna would sacrifice her life in Paris in the family's attempt to establish Wolfgang in a good post; that Wolfgang would eventually be able to tear himself away from Salzburg only by the most drastic means; that Leopold would remain there alone until his death; and that Nannerl would have to give up what little society and entertainment existed in her home town, to live isolated from family and friends in a tiny village?

As the Mozarts made their way slowly south from Paris through Switzerland back to Salzburg, other first-hand reports of the children's abilities corroborated Grimm's. Wolfgang's compositions, the way in which he could compete with adults, and his merriness and high spirits in particular were singled out for comment. In addition, Maria Anna and Leopold were accorded praise for the upbringing and education of their charming and talented children, Leopold receiving tributes for the sensible and unforced way in which he had fostered Wolfgang's genius, and for the attention he had paid to moral education. At the end of one of these accounts, a long essay on genius, the author admired the way in which the children clearly loved their father so much that his approval meant more to them than any other type of praise.[18]

Leopold Mozart has often been characterized as an authoritarian father who, by treating Wolfgang as a child long after he had grown up, and insisting on remaining in control of everything, prepared his son

---

[16] See Part II.   [17] See Ch. 8.

[18] In the periodical *Aristide ou le Citoyen* on 11 Oct. 1766—given in Deutsch, *Documents*, 61–5.

inadequately for the management of his own affairs. Reports from the childhood years, however, suggest that if Leopold was autocratic within the family it had not yet caused serious problems. The children were consistently described as charming, uniting liveliness with good natural manners and an obvious love of their parents. These reports corroborate what the correspondence suggests—that the Mozart family was very close, and that Leopold enjoyed a relationship of tenderness and intimacy with his children.

⁓✳⁓

Leopold did not report very fully to Hagenauer on the towns they visited during their return journey. He was more preoccupied with sending home the luggage and planning how their lives would proceed once they were home again. What does stand out from his travel notes and the letters to Hagenauer, however, is that he was again deeply moved by the paintings they saw in the Netherlands.[19] Nor was the family tired of travelling. On 16 August 1766 Leopold wrote to Hagenauer from Lyons to say that they were being pestered to go to Bordeaux and Marseilles. From there they could continue to Venice, where they might experience the festival of the Ascension the following spring, and then wend their way home through the Tyrol. They were tempted to do so by the facts that they were in demand everywhere, the children were still young enough to draw profitable audiences, and their zest for travelling was undiminished. Leopold claimed that they were acting nobly in keeping their promise to return.[20]

The plan to visit Italy was thus reluctantly shelved for the time being, and in fact Maria Anna and Nannerl were never to go there. Unknown to them, the days of their most ambitious journeys undertaken all together were at an end. After returning from their grand tour, the farthest Nannerl was to travel from Salzburg was to Vienna; and though Maria Anna later accompanied Wolfgang to Paris, her second visit there was to lack the vibrancy of the first and to be characterized by loneliness, anxiety, illness, and ultimately death.

One big problem that Leopold and Maria Anna anticipated on arriving home was lack of space in their old apartment in the Hagenauers' house. During the three and a half years that they had been away, the children had grown. Their working patterns were going to be quite different from

---

[19] Leopold to Hagenauer, 19 Sept. 1765—*MBA* 102/72–81 (*Letters* 38); and Leopold's travel notes, 23 Apr. 1764–4 Sept. 1765—*MBA* 99/199–209.
[20] *MBA* 111/45–55 (*Letters* 43).

earlier ones, and each person needed space in which to work without distracting other members of the family. In addition, they were bringing trunks and chests back with them, which were full of objects acquired on their travels. All these things necessitated the purchase of extra cupboards and other furniture, so that they could be housed adequately. Already by 19 September 1765, when Leopold wrote to Hagenauer on arrival in The Hague, this was on his mind. He told Hagenauer to look out for a very large chest which he had dispatched from London, and also asked him to get a writing desk made, with big drawers for storing all the 'junk'.[21] And on 12 December 1765, also from The Hague, he mentioned the same subject again. After going into some detail about the style of desk or cupboard he wanted (which was to be made according to English taste), and also about what would have to be moved to make room for it, he wondered where Nannerl was now to sleep, and how they would find room for separate work places, especially since Wolfgang would have so many different types of work. Hagenauer had by this time received the chest sent from London, and Leopold warned him to look out for another one coming from Holland, and a pair of trunks which he would be sending from Paris.[22] On 16 May 1766, Leopold wrote from Paris to say that the chest sent from Holland was now on its way, and that when it arrived, Hagenauer should remove the music from it and present it to the archbishop with the compliments of the Mozarts. The music consisted of the sonatas and two sets of variations published by Wolfgang in Holland, and Leopold probably had it in mind to placate the archbishop by this means, in case he was impatient for their return. In addition, the two trunks which Leopold had told Hagenauer he would send from Paris had now grown to three, and even so the carriage would be packed with a large and a small packing case, a big bag of coats, and two chest seats, to say nothing of the luggage stowed in the normal storage area.[23]

In his letter from Lyons of 16 August 1766, Leopold asked Hagenauer to have a glass cabinet made for him, and to have good locks fitted to one of the chests of drawers in their apartment. The cabinet was presumably intended for displaying some of the treasures they were bringing back, and the lock on the chest to secure valuables from the servant they would engage on their return. In addition, Leopold asked Hagenauer to have a bed made for Nannerl.[24] But it was one thing to plan how to dispose all the new possessions, and quite another to contemplate in detail how they were

---

[21] *MBA* 102/119–32 (not in *Letters*).   [22] *MBA* 104/71–96 and 104–9 (not in *Letters*).
[23] *MBA* 108/16–30 and 75–81 (*Letters* 41, but not complete).
[24] *MBA* 111/55–66 (not in *Letters*).

all going to find space to work. By the time Leopold wrote to Hagenauer from Munich on 10 November 1766, he had decided not to keep the servant who had been travelling with them, but to dismiss him before they reached Salzburg. In this way, they were at least spared the problem of how to accommodate him. On the other hand, Frau Hagenauer was asked to engage a maid for them, and Leopold was wondering how they would all fit in:

The necessary disposal of ourselves in our apartment is troubling my heart; which you'll partly appreciate yourselves, and which you'll see with your own eyes on our (God grant) happy arrival. God (who has been all too gracious to me, poor sinner) has given my children such talents as, without thinking of my duty as a father, would spur me to sacrifice everything for their good education. every moment that I lose is lost forever. and if I ever knew how precious time is for young people, I know it now. You know that my children are used to working: if they were to get used to idling the hours away, with the excuse that the one was hindering the other, my whole plan would collapse in a heap; habit is an iron shirt. and you know yourselves how much my children, especially Wolfgangerl, has to learn. — — —[25]

Hagenauer must have realized from the luggage that was arriving, from the furniture that he was asked to procure, and from Leopold's remarks about space for work, that the small apartment was now simply inadequate; and he probably suggested to Leopold the idea of moving house completely, because Leopold's next letter from Munich, on 15 November 1766, discussed various possible alternative dwellings.[26] Nothing was done, however, and Leopold and Maria Anna continued to live with the closest friends of their early married years until 1773.

❧

Leopold was returning to the same court position that he had left, but it should not be assumed that his homecoming would be straightforward, and that his career could be taken up again as if he had never been away. For meanwhile the jostling for favour so characteristic of Salzburg's musical establishment had been carrying on constantly during his absence, and he could not be sure that there would not be new favourites. The nub of the problem of seething discontent seems to have been the lack of a consistently fair emoluments structure. Leopold, as Vice-Kapellmeister, was earning 354 fl. annually (including the bread and wine allowance)

---

[25] *MBA* 112/80–92 (*Letters* 44, but not complete).   [26] *MBA* 113/33–44 (not in *Letters*).

when he returned in November 1766; but his subordinate Michael Haydn, who had been appointed Konzertmeister on 14 August 1763, during the Mozarts' absence, was immediately offered 300 fl. plus the *Hoftafel* (dining rights), which was worth 100 fl. annually.[27] The organist Anton Cajetan Adlgasser was also probably earning more than Leopold by 1766, and in addition he had received substantial sums of money from Schrattenbach's *Schatulle* towards his one-year tour of Italy.[28] The *Schatulle* payments were a bone of contention because some employees seemed to do so well from them, while others were ignored. The celebrated bass singer Joseph Nikolaus Meissner was to complain bitterly in 1769 that, among other things, he had never received anything from the *Schatulle* for any of his journeys.[29]

Schrattenbach was a great lover of the opera and theatre. He apparently disliked castrati, and therefore sent local young women with promising voices for a thorough singing education in Italy, probably at the Pietá, one of the four famous charitable institutions in Venice which gave girls a complete musical education.[30] The first woman known to be educated in this way was Maria Franziska Eberlin, daughter of the Kapellmeister Eberlin and future wife of Johann Nikolaus Paul Strasser. She was probably sent to Italy in the mid-1750s, and was given a court singing appointment in 1758.[31] Next to go was Meissner's sister, Maria Elisabeth Sabina, who went to Italy in 1758 and won a court appointment in 1759.[32] In October 1761 two of the three girls in whom Leopold had already expressed interest in his letters from Paris and London were sent together. One was Maria Magdalena Lipp, daughter of one of the organists and the future wife of Michael Haydn, and the other was Maria Anna Braunhofer. These two, who were only in their mid-teens when they left, were apparently friends during this period, and Braunhofer lodged with the Lipp family. They were absent almost three years and were appointed to court posts together in January 1765. Finally, Maria Anna Fesemayr (the third of the trio mentioned by Leopold) was sent for two years from January

[27] Hintermaier, 'Hofkapelle', 166–9.

[28] For Adlgasser's salary, see W. Rainer, 'Anton Cajetan Adlgasser: Ein biographischer Beitrag zur Musikgeschichte Salzburgs um die Mitte des 18. Jahrhunderts', *MGSL* 105 (1965), 212–13. Rainer suggests that by the time Adlgasser returned from Italy in Jan. 1765 he was earning 448 fl. annually, including the *Hoftafel* and a supplement for teaching at the Kapellhaus and playing the organ at Holy Trinity. Adlgasser received 100 ducats (500 fl.) from the *Schatulle* on leaving for Italy, and an unknown proportion of a later payment of 242 ducats (1,210 fl.)—ibid. 221.

[29] His long petition is given in full in Hintermaier, 'Hofkapelle', 263–73.

[30] The Benedictine monk and diarist Beda Hübner mentioned on 4 Jan. 1766 that the deceased court singer Maria Franziska Strasser had been sent to the Pietá—see Klein, 'Nachrichten', 97.

[31] Hintermaier, 'Hofkapelle', 81–3.   [32] Ibid. 274–6.

1764. She travelled out with Adlgasser, who was beginning his Italian tour at the same time. Later, after the death of Adlgasser's second wife, he and Fesemayr were to marry. Fesemayr received her court appointment on her return in December 1765.[33]

Once all five women had appointments in Salzburg, there was trouble among them. Braunhofer and Lipp in particular were accused of knowing how to keep on the right side of Schrattenbach and how to make their colleagues feel uncomfortable. On 13 January 1766, when the Mozart children were regaining strength after their severe illnesses in The Hague, Maria Franziska Strasser died, and a Requiem was held for her in St Peter's the following day. The Benedictine monk Beda Hübner claimed in his diary that she had been pregnant, and had died from the after-effects of a miscarriage brought on by the spite and envy of her female colleagues. He further claimed that Fesemayr, who had just returned from Italy, was also suffering from malicious treatment.[34]

Apart from favouritism (real or imagined) in the form of emoluments and *Schatulle* payments, there was enormous scope for ill feeling over occasional extra payments. While the Mozarts had been away, some of the other court musicians had had a number of opportunities to earn supplementary sums. In January 1765, four of the finest musicians, including Meissner, had been lent to the abbot of Lambach to help entertain the bride-to-be of the empress's son Joseph.[35] Adlgasser was paid 35 ducats (175 fl.) in April 1766 for the composition of his opera *La Nitteti*.[36] And the relative newcomer Michael Haydn wrote a cantata for the consecration of the abbess of Nonnberg in April 1766.[37] During the Mozarts' absence other court musicians, especially if (like Adlgasser and Haydn) they were composers, had had a better opportunity to promote their own compositions and thereby earn extra cash. The return of the Mozarts spelt fiercer competition.

Leopold was already uneasy about his reception at court long before they arrived home. On the one hand, the tour had increased his self-esteem enormously by showing him how the talents and charm of his children had impressed well-to-do people throughout Europe; and how he himself was admired not only for the way in which he was educating his

---

[33] Ibid. 109–11. See Fig. 1 for clarification of some of the relationships mentioned in this paragraph.

[34] Klein, 'Nachrichten', 97–8.   [35] Ibid. 94.

[36] Rainer, 'Adlgasser', 219. The conversion of ducats to florins here (5 fl. to the ducat) derives from the Salzburg *Schatulle* records for 1766, which often give sums of money in both forms. See Martin, 'Fürstenhof 80', 184.

[37] G. Croll and K. Vössing, *Johann Michael Haydn: sein Leben, sein Schaffen, seine Zeit* (Salzburg, 1987), 60.

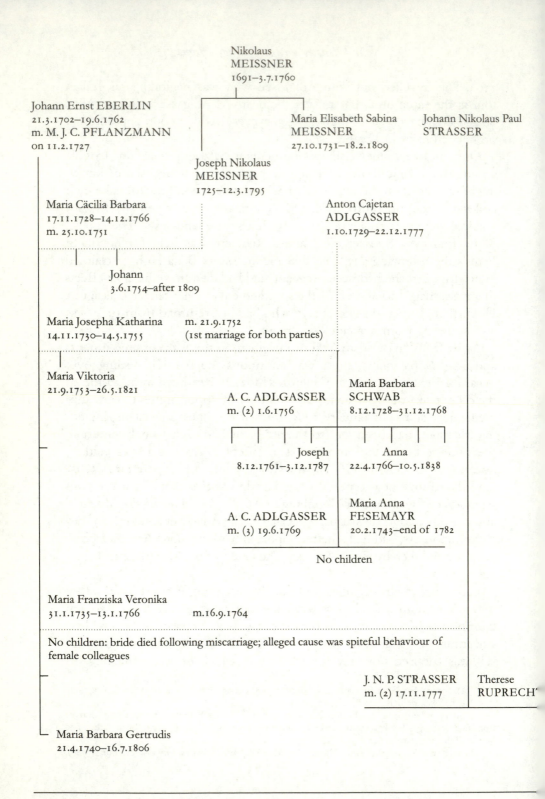

Nikolaus
MEISSNER
1691–3.7.1760

Johann Ernst EBERLIN
21.3.1702–19.6.1762
m. M. J. C. PFLANZMANN
on 11.2.1727

Maria Elisabeth Sabina
MEISSNER
27.10.1731–18.2.1809

Johann Nikolaus Paul
STRASSER

Joseph Nikolaus
MEISSNER
1725–12.3.1795

Maria Cäcilia Barbara
17.11.1728–14.12.1766
m. 25.10.1751

Anton Cajetan
ADLGASSER
1.10.1729–22.12.1777

Johann
3.6.1754–after 1809

Maria Josepha Katharina
14.11.1730–14.5.1755

m. 21.9.1752
(1st marriage for both parties)

Maria Viktoria
21.9.1753–26.5.1821

A. C. ADLGASSER
m. (2) 1.6.1756

Maria Barbara
SCHWAB
8.12.1728–31.12.1768

Joseph
8.12.1761–3.12.1787

Anna
22.4.1766–10.5.1838

A. C. ADLGASSER
m. (3) 19.6.1769

Maria Anna
FESEMAYR
20.2.1743–end of 1782

No children

Maria Franziska Veronika
31.1.1735–13.1.1766

m.16.9.1764

No children: bride died following miscarriage; alleged cause was spiteful behaviour of
female colleagues

J. N. P. STRASSER
m. (2) 17.11.1777

Therese
RUPRECH'

Maria Barbara Gertrudis
21.4.1740–16.7.1806

FIG. 1. Some interrelationships among the court music personnel in Salzburg

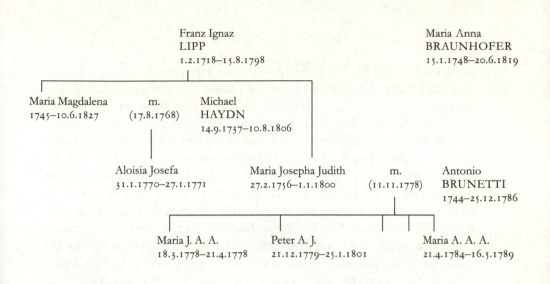

Franz Ignaz
LIPP
1.2.1718–15.8.1798

Maria Anna
BRAUNHOFER
15.1.1748–20.6.1819

Maria Magdalena
1745–10.6.1827

m.
(17.8.1768)

Michael
HAYDN
14.9.1737–10.8.1806

Aloisia Josefa
31.1.1770–27.1.1771

Maria Josepha Judith
27.2.1756–1.1.1800

m.
(11.11.1778)

Antonio
BRUNETTI
1744–25.12.1786

Maria J. A. A.
18.3.1778–21.4.1778

Peter A. J.
21.12.1779–25.1.1801

Maria A. A. A.
21.4.1784–16.5.1789

Supplementary Information

Eberlin's children branch horizontally off the thick vertical line at the left. The dotted lines link them with their marriage partners. Children are only named when they are referred to in the text.

Johann Ernst Eberlin was Kappellmeister.
Maria Franziska Veronika Eberlin was court singer.
Nikolaus Meissner (senior) was violinist and horn player.
Joseph Nikolaus Meissner was bass singer.
Maria Elisabeth Sabina Meissner was court singer.
Anton Cajetan Adlgasser was organist.
Maria Anna Fesemayr was court singer.
Franz Ignaz Lipp was organist.
Maria Magdalena Lipp was court singer.
Michael Haydn was Konzertmeister, later organist.
Antonio Brunetti was violinist.
Maria Anna Braunhofer was court singer. She boarded with the Lipps for part of her childhood and was sent to Venice with Maria Magdalena Lipp to continue her education.
Maria Viktoria Adlgasser was a particular friend of Nannerl Mozart.
Maria Barbara Gertrudis Eberlin was another of her friends.
Members of the Mozart family acted as marriage witnesses and godparents for the Eberlins, Adlgassers, and Meissners on several occasions.

Note on Sources: The information comes from the *MBA* commentary; from Cuvay, 'Johann Ernst Eberlin'; and from Rainer, 'Adlgasser'. Where dates are not given, they could not be established; furthermore, the sources cited sometimes contain minor discrepancies as to dates.

children, but also for his honest good sense. He naturally thought that all this made him a desirable employee for Salzburg, one who would enhance its prestige. But on the other hand, he had stayed away far longer than had originally been intended, had contributed nothing directly to music in Salzburg in the past three and a half years, and almost certainly had it in mind to ask for more travel leave before long—something that, on the scale on which he had taken it so far, was not necessarily compatible with loyal service to his court.[38] This consideration cannot have been lost on him, for all that he appears to have persuaded himself that he and his family were fine ambassadors for the archbishop. In his letter to Hagenauer of 19 September 1765, after explaining what had made them decide to add on a journey to Holland, he asked if Fesemayr was still in Venice, indicating that it was 'so much the better' if she was. He probably meant that it was better for him, because he would not (as it seemed at that point, before the children were taken ill) have been away much longer than she.[39]

When the Mozarts were in Donaueschingen on the return journey, giving daily concerts for more than a week to Prince Fürstenberg, they met Leopold's colleague Meissner. He was on tour too, intending to go to Switzerland. He must have given Leopold all the important news about Salzburg, and it was perhaps these conversations that fuelled Leopold's fear that Schrattenbach was angry with him. At the end of his letter of 10 November 1766, he had acknowledged the possibility that their reception might be such that they would want to 'put their packs on their backs and move away'. He had also said that if the children were wanted by their fatherland, they could not be had for nothing.[40] On 22 November 1766, in the last letter written from this tour, he reverted to the subject:

for the rest, I can't conceal from you that the nearer I get to Salzburg, the more childish rumours reach my ears. which I would prefer to be spared. for a few years (praise God) I was at peace and free from such idiocy, and I want to remain so. In particular, our reception at court is spoken of in very strange terms. I can assure you that this seems really peculiar to me, and it would have an effect which many would not expect, because after great honours, insolence is absolutely not to be stomached.[41]

---

[38] This is not an ironic statement. Leave under Schrattenbach was encouraged for the purposes of self-improvement, so that though the Mozarts took more than anyone else, it is possible that Leopold was able to persuade himself that it was not an outrageous amount considering his mission.

[39] *MBA* 102/144–7 (not in *Letters*).   [40] *MBA* 112/93–7 (*Letters* 44).

[41] *MBA* 114/42–9 (not in *Letters*).

There could be no clearer hint that Leopold believed that he could have a future elsewhere if he wished. Curiously for a man who prided himself on a thorough knowledge of himself and of human nature generally, he seems to have taken the plaudits which had been heaped on them as a sign that they should be able to enjoy similarly favourable attentions at the court of their choice. He appears not to have considered that on tour they had been novelties, and that a large part of the children's charm was probably due to their age and the fact that they were no threat to any-one. As soon as Wolfgang began seriously to compete for commissions with adult composers, which he was to do only eighteen months later in 1768, he ran into problems of intrigue on the part of men who did not want their territory encroached upon; and the worse the problems became, the more stubborn, disagreeable, and counter-productive became Leopold's pride.[42] Leopold's self-assurance at this date was to suffer cruel disillusionment. Twelve years later, years in which his own career had stood still while he gave up all his time and energy to educate and advance his son, his pride had taken some heavy blows. As Wolfgang returned laden with debts from Paris, where his mother lay buried, Leopold had to negotiate a post for him under the same employer from whom Wolfgang had resigned in disgust. During this period, it was Wolfgang who wrote home spirited letters announcing that he would not tolerate any insolence from his employer, by now Archbishop Colloredo; but Leopold had had to accept the bitter truth that his own promise had not been fulfilled, and that he had no choice but to stay unrespected in Salzburg unless Wolfgang could at some future date secure an appointment elsewhere which would support them all.[43]

⁂

It was on 29 November 1766, after three weeks in Munich during which Wolfgang was ill again, that the Mozarts arrived back in Salzburg. Once they had left Munich, there were naturally no more letters written, and no family record of their reception exists. But the diarist Beda Hübner wrote two reports in quick succession on the homecoming of the Mozarts. In the first, dated 29 November 1766, he related the excitement of the whole town, outlined the chief triumphs of the tour, and commented that Nannerl was 'tolerably tall and almost marriageable already', that the journey was said to have cost 20,000 fl., and that in England and in other

---

[42] See Ch. 8.   [43] See Pt. III.

countries the children had appeared on public stages, 'just as foreign play-actors appear'.[44] This remark reveals how little the concept of a public concert was understood in Salzburg at this date, which was still almost entirely dependent on the court for the patronage of music.

By the time Hübner made his second report, on 8 December 1766, he had been to see the Mozarts at home, had heard Wolfgang give a keyboard performance, and had seen all the treasures they had brought back —nine gold watches, twelve gold snuff-boxes, numerous gold rings, and necklaces, ear-rings, knives, writing equipment, and toothpick boxes galore. Hübner estimated the value of the objects at 12,000 fl., and stated that in addition to the gifts, Leopold had also bought items for resale, in order to make a profit.[45]

How might the lives of the different members of the family be expected to proceed from this point? Leopold, Nannerl, and Wolfgang had been exposed to a variety of musical experiences which they could never have enjoyed in Salzburg, and these had widened and deepened the musical understanding of all of them. Furthermore, the need to present their own concerts regularly and effectively for discerning audiences had imposed a rigorous discipline on them which must have lifted them far above the level of many of Leopold's colleagues in Salzburg. In addition, all four of them had enjoyed the benefit of cultural experiences unimagined even by many members of the Salzburg nobility, let alone their own circle of friends. But while all this was intended to be merely the first stage of many similar experiences for Wolfgang, leading progressively to the clear goal of an outstanding musical appointment as Kapellmeister, for Nannerl the matter stood quite differently. Although it is not clear exactly what Leopold had in mind for her future, he had made it plain in his letter to Hagenauer of 10 November 1766 that the two children were to have different working patterns on their return. Even if Wolfgang had not possessed the remarkable talents which demanded special attention, his needs would almost certainly still have been different from Nannerl's. For though Leopold manifestly wanted Nannerl to be capable of earning money from music when she grew up, it was also an assumption of their society that she would marry for financial support. Wolfgang, on the other hand, would be responsible not only for his own upkeep but also, if they lived, for that of his parents, and any family of his own he might have.

---

[44] Deutsch, *Documents*, 67–9.

[45] Ibid. 71–2. There is no way of knowing how realistic Hübner's assessment of the value of the goods was.

Leopold had also told Hagenauer, in the same letter, how precious time was for young people. Perhaps this reflection was prompted by seeing his daughter, who had left Salzburg three and a half years earlier as a child of 12, 'almost marriageable already'. At any rate, he was clearly anxious to press ahead with Wolfgang's education. This would involve continued improvement in all the branches of music he had practised so far—organ, violin, and keyboard playing, together with the further keyboard skills such as transposition, figured bass, and improvisation—and an increasing concentration on composition, which in turn would involve familiarity with Latin and Italian. Competence in all these areas was necessary to a Kapellmeister.

As far as Nannerl was concerned, it seems likely that Leopold envisaged a number of developments which would give her a certain amount of versatility and enable her to earn small supplementary amounts of money within or without marriage (but preferably within). That she would continue to refine her keyboard playing was obvious, and it is possible that she would have paid some attention to singing. In addition she was soon to be expected to develop teaching skills. Of these activities, the only one which could be expected to furnish a woman with a secure salary was singing. Since there is no record of her singing being praised by her father or anyone else, it seems highly unlikely that Leopold could have had great expectations of her in this area. The remaining possibilities, therefore, were keyboard playing and teaching. Both would enable her to earn money, but not obviously to command a regular salary. It is more likely that they were seen as possibilities for a supplementary, irregular income, and Leopold's letter to Wolfgang of 6 April 1778 was to envisage just this possibility. He had in mind that Wolfgang might take a salaried post in Paris, in which case he and Nannerl could join him there. Both father and daughter would take some pupils, and Nannerl would play in the occasional public concert. In this way, they could all live together by pooling their income, and Nannerl would have a public platform of some sort.[46] But there was now an essential difference between her and Wolfgang which was caused by her sex and not by the fact that his talent was superior. He was thrust forward and had a clear goal to guide him as he worked, while she was forced to adopt a passive attitude, waiting until a man—either Wolfgang or a future husband—could provide the salary and the place of abode which would enable her to practise in the limited way described. At the age of 15, her most dazzling days were already behind

---

[46] *MBA* 444/49–55 (*Letters* 301).

her, and though she had been described as 'almost marriageable', it was to be nearly another eighteen years before she did in fact marry.

As for any reservations which might have been felt about the success of the tour, it is impossible to believe that Leopold could have felt at ease about every aspect of it. Musically, there was no doubt that his confidence in his children and his teaching had been triumphantly vindicated; but for the rest, only his meticulous planning, boundless energy, and a good deal of luck had brought them all home alive and without debts. When it is considered at how many points things could have gone badly wrong (the arrival in Paris with no capital; Leopold's near-fatal illness in London; the difficulty of earning enough money to move on from London; and the near-disaster in The Hague), it is not surprising that Leopold was to prefer to leave Maria Anna and Nannerl behind when he took Wolfgang to Italy. The family was to make one more trip together, and then the different members led divided lives for much of the time.

8

The Last Journey as a United Family:
The Visit to Vienna in 1767

~✦~

THE Mozarts were at home for ten months after returning from their grand tour. Little is known about their activities during this period, but they were clearly re-establishing themselves in court life. Despite the tensions among the musicians caused by real or imagined favouritism, they formed a close-knit group. Inter-marriage was common, and so was the performance of friendly duties such as acting as witnesses at weddings, or godparents at christenings. Musically talented children were given the occasional chance to perform at court, so that on gala days, when important guests were present and pride was at stake, the band could give the impression that it was one big, happy family.

When the Mozarts had met Meissner at Donaueschingen on their return home in October 1766, he was on tour and bound for Switzerland.[1] Leopold had received news from Salzburg that Meissner's wife Maria Cäcilia Barbara was ill, and had been the first to tell Meissner so. However, Meissner himself received a letter from her while still in Donaueschingen, and the news presumably reassured him, because he did not turn back.[2] But she died on 14 December while he was still absent, and on 15 December the court musicians performed a requiem for her at St Peter's.[3] She had been the oldest daughter of the deceased Kapellmeister Eberlin, who had had close ties with St Peter's. Since one of her sisters, the singer Maria Franziska Strasser, had died in January of the same year,[4] and another, Maria Josepha Katharina Adlgasser, had died in 1755, only one of Eberlin's six children was now still alive. The memory of Eberlin's importance, and the ties to other court musicians, lent this requiem special significance.[5]

---

[1] See Ch. 7.
[2] Leopold to Hagenauer, 10 Nov. 1766—*MBA* 112/29–39 (*Letters* 44, but the passage is not complete).
[3] See H. Klein, 'Unbekannte Mozartiana von 1766–67', *MJb* (1957), 179.   [4] See Ch. 7.
[5] See Fig. 1.

Wolfgang composed for at least three occasions during these few months. On 21 December 1766 a recitative and aria of his were sung in the court theatre after an opera performance,[6] on 12 March 1767 a performance was given of his *Die Schuldigkeit des ersten Gebots*,[7] and on 13 May 1767 *Apollo und Hyacinth* was given.[8] He would have been paid for some of these occasions, and was thus continuing to swell the family income at home as he had on tour.[9] But Leopold was not content for him to remain long in Salzburg, and on 11 September 1767 he took his family to Vienna again. He hoped that they would be able to play some part in the wedding celebrations of Maria Theresia's daughter, Archduchess Maria Josepha, to the king of Naples and Sicily, Ferdinand IV. It is probable too that he hoped for the offer of a Viennese court appointment. The wedding was supposed to take place on 14 October 1767, and Leopold was again allowed paid leave. But, as had happened on previous occasions, they were smitten by ill luck and their plans were thrown into confusion— in the first place, by rolling into Vienna at the beginning of an outbreak of smallpox. Among the many fatalities was the 16-year-old bride Maria Josepha, who died the day after her wedding should have taken place. The court went into deep mourning, and there was no prospect of being summoned to play to it. Later, in trying to retrieve the situation, Leopold attempted to enable Wolfgang to write an *opera buffa* for Vienna. But he was carried away by his pride, and made enemies of so many musicians that the opera could not be performed. He paid dearly for his stubbornness, for his absence from Salzburg was stretched from a projected three months to more than fifteen, the archbishop withheld his salary from April 1768 until he returned in January 1769, and it is even possible that he was threatened with dismissal. When the whole affair was over, his standing was considerably reduced, and he reported that he had never met with such frustration on all their travels.

The calendar of significant events in Vienna is as follows:

1767

11 Sept.	Left Salzburg.
15 Sept.	Arrived in Vienna and took lodgings with a goldsmith, Johann Schmalecker, on the second floor of his house in the Weihburggasse.

---

[6] See Deutsch, *Documents*, 71. The piece was K. 36.

[7] See Deutsch, *Documents*, 72–3. This was K. 35. Michael Haydn and Adlgasser composed other parts to it.

[8] See Deutsch, *Documents*, 75. This was K. 38.

[9] A payment from the *Schatulle* to Wolfgang of a gold medallion worth 12 ducats (60 fl.) is recorded on 18 Mar. 1767 for his oratorio. See Deutsch, *Documents*, 73–4.

7 Oct.	Archduchess Maria Josepha ill with smallpox.
14 Oct.	The wedding should have taken place between Maria Josepha and King Ferdinand IV of Naples. The Mozarts met Prince Kaunitz, the Austrian Chancellor.
15 Oct.	Maria Josepha died.
17 Oct.	Leopold and Wolfgang moved from the family's lodgings for fear that Wolfgang might catch smallpox, but Maria Anna and Nannerl remained.
23 Oct.	Fled Vienna for Brünn (now Brno).
26 Oct.	Travelled on to Olmütz (now Olomouc), where Wolfgang fell ill with smallpox on arrival.
28 Oct.	At Count Podstatsky's invitation, they moved from their inn to his home, and his doctor attended Wolfgang.
By 10 Nov.	Wolfgang had recovered.
By 29 Nov.	Nannerl had also recovered from smallpox.
24 Dec.	Back to Brünn, where they stayed with Archbishop Schrattenbach's brother, Franz Anton.
30 Dec.	Concert in Brünn.

1768

9 Jan.	Left Brünn.
10 Jan.	Arrived in Vienna, staying in a house on the Hohe Brücke.
19 Jan.	They were received at court. The emperor, Joseph II, may have suggested that Wolfgang write an opera.
End Jan.	Wolfgang started work on the opera *La finta semplice*.
c.24 Mar.	Concert at Prince Golicyn's.
From Apr.	Leopold's salary from Salzburg was withheld.
Before 20 Apr.	Concert to celebrate the wedding of Count Otto Wolfgang von Schrattenbach and Countess Isabella von Starhemberg.
27 Apr.	Letter from the Parisian salon hostess Mme Geoffrin to Prince Kaunitz asking him to support the Mozarts in their attempt to stay permanently in Vienna.
June–Sept.	Intrigue against Wolfgang's opera.
12 Sept.	Visited Dr Ignaz Parhamer, through whom was arranged Wolfgang's musical contribution to the ceremony to consecrate the church of the orphanage Parhamer managed.
21 Sept.	Leopold presented his *Species Facti* to Emperor Joseph, to complain about their treatment in connection with the performance of Wolfgang's opera.
7 Dec.	Wolfgang conducted a Mass, Offertory, and Trumpet Concerto, all of his own composition, at the orphanage church.
Late Dec.	Left Vienna.

1769

5 Jan.	Arrived home in Salzburg.
Early Mar.	Leopold petitioned for reinstatement of the lost salary.
8 Mar.	His request was refused—he was paid for January and February 1769 (when he was back at home in any case), but not for April–December 1768.[10]

On arrival in Vienna, the first thing to be done was to be presented at court, because until they had performed for the Empress Maria Theresia or her son the Emperor Joseph, they were forbidden by protocol to play elsewhere. But this was not so easily managed as it had been in 1762. Maria Theresia's husband Francis had died on 18 August 1765, while the Mozarts were in Lille, and since then Maria Theresia had withdrawn from society to spend what time was not taken up by affairs of state in pious remembrance of him. The Emperor Joseph, as Leopold reported to Hagenauer on 22 September 1767, had just returned from Hungary, and they hoped to be able to gain his ear in due course. Meanwhile, Vienna was bustling with preparations for the forthcoming marriage of Maria Theresia's daughter, the Archduchess Maria Josepha. Each day there was *opera buffa*, *opera seria*, or a play at the theatre, and in addition there were balls, fireworks, and illuminations at the various palaces of the nobility.[11] The Mozarts attended some of these events while waiting to be summoned to court, but by the time Leopold wrote to Hagenauer on 7 October 1767, it was clear that a major setback was threatened—the bride-to-be, the same age as Nannerl, had contracted smallpox.[12]

The background to her illness and death is that there had been an earlier outbreak of smallpox that year in Vienna. Josepha, the unloved second wife of the Emperor Joseph, had succumbed to it in late spring, and Maria Theresia herself had caught it from her. The empress recovered, but Josepha died on 28 May, and the sarcophagus containing her body was placed in the Habsburg vault in the Kapuzinerkirche. On the eighteenth of each month, the day on which her husband had died, Maria Theresia was in the habit of visiting the vault to pray for his soul. She did this as usual on 18 September 1767, and again on 4 October 1767, her deceased husband's name-day. On the second visit, her daughter Maria Josepha accompanied her. Following this visit, Maria Josepha fell ill with smallpox and there was a general belief, held among others by Maria Theresia herself and by Leopold Mozart, that the pestilential air in the vault

---

[10] The calendar is derived from Deutsch, *Documents*, and Eibl, *Chronik*.
[11] *MBA* 116 (*Letters* 47, but the passage is not complete).   [12] *MBA* 118 (not in *Letters*).

was to blame—in particular, the air from the unsealed coffin of her sister-in-law Josepha.[13]

Maria Josepha died on 15 October 1767, the day after she should have married, and Vienna was thrown into indescribable confusion. On 17 October Leopold wrote to tell Hagenauer all about it. He chose to link the manner of her death with specific circumstances pertaining at the time, suggesting that there was a divine pattern in it all. Beginning by announcing that the princess had become the bride of the Heavenly Bridegroom, he explained that the second opera planned for the wedding festivities told the story of Cupid and Psyche. Psyche was persecuted by Venus because Cupid had fallen in love with her. Venus was eventually moved by Psyche's beauty and virtue, however, and gave her to Cupid as a bride. Maria Josepha too had become a bride of heavenly love. Her illness had begun on the name-day of her departed father Francis, the opera in question was performed for the first time on the following day, and she had died on the name-day of her mother Maria Theresia.[14] Leopold was implying that the subject of the opera and the significant dates of her fatal illness were God's signs that her death had been divinely ordered.

In Paris in 1764, when it had been suggested that Wolfgang should be inoculated against smallpox, Leopold had emphatically expressed his belief that Wolfgang's well-being depended on the will of God. He said the same thing in Vienna in 1767, but as the disease raged around them, it would have required a will of iron to remain steadfast in the infected city. It comes as no surprise, therefore, that his next letter to Hagenauer was written on 10 November 1767 from Olmütz. It began by praising God for Wolfgang's successful recovery from smallpox, and continued:

You'll already have noticed from my previous letters that everything in Vienna was upside down and in confusion. Now I must tell you about some particular things which relate to us alone, and from which you'll see how divine Providence binds everything together in such a way that if we give ourselves up to it with complete trust, we cannot miss our destiny. You already know how dismal it was at the Viennese court, just at the time when it could have turned out for the best for us. At the same time another mischance befell us, which placed us in no small anxiety. the elder son of the goldsmith with whom we were living went down with smallpox immediately on our arrival, and we didn't discover this until it was almost over and the 2 little children had caught it too. I hurriedly

---

[13] This information comes from Leopold's letter to Hagenauer of 14 Oct. 1767 (*MBA* 119/ 36–42; not in *Letters*); and from D. Beales, *Joseph II*, vol. i: *In the Shadow of Maria Theresa* (Cambridge, 1987), 88.

[14] *MBA* 120 (*Letters* 50, but the passage is almost all omitted).

enquired about another lodging for us all, in vain. I was forced to leave my wife and daughter there, and I fled with little Wolfgang to my good friend, where we stayed ... In the whole of Vienna, nothing was spoken of except smallpox. If 10 children were on the death register, 9 of them had died from smallpox. you can easily imagine how I felt; whole nights went by without sleep, and I had no peace by day. I decided to go into Moravia just after the death of the princess bride, until the initial sadness in Vienna was in some degree over; Only they wouldn't let us go, since His Majesty the emperor spoke about us so often that we were never sure when it might occur to him to summon us: but as soon as the archduchess Elisabeth became ill, I wouldn't let anything hold me up any longer, because I could hardly wait for the moment when I could take my little Wolfgang out of Vienna, which was completely infected with smallpox, into a change of air.

Leopold went on to explain that they had left Vienna on 23 October, and had gone first to Brünn and called upon Archbishop Schrattenbach's brother, Count Franz Anton Schrattenbach. Schrattenbach wanted the family to stay and put on a concert, but Leopold decided, because of an 'inner urge', to travel on to Olmütz, and to arrange the concert in Brünn on their way back to Vienna. In the inn at Olmütz, Wolfgang showed the first signs of illness on their first evening, 26 October 1767. Two days later, Leopold sought out an acquaintance, Count Leopold Anton Podstatsky, after church, and explained the situation. Podstatsky was well known in Salzburg, being the nephew of a previous archbishop and having worked in Salzburg himself before being appointed dean at the cathedral in Olmütz. When Podstatsky learned that Wolfgang's illness was probably smallpox, he promptly moved the family into his house and arranged for his doctor to treat the child. Wolfgang recovered well, and Leopold laid particular stress on the fact that the pox themselves had appeared on his name-day, and were accompanied by a drop in fever and an improvement in his condition. But Leopold and Maria Anna were worried that Nannerl might yet catch it. As a younger child she had apparently had some spots which they hoped might have been smallpox ones, but they could not be sure.[15]

Sure enough, Nannerl did catch the disease, and Leopold wrote again to the Hagenauers on 29 November 1767 to say that, 'as he had already supposed', the few spots she had once had could not have been smallpox. However, she too was now better, and Leopold wrote:

You see that we didn't travel in vain after all! although we too had to share to a certain extent in the great grief of the Viennese court; the Dear Lord granted

---

[15] *MBA* 121 (*Letters* 51, but it is not quite complete).

us his divine protection in a different way, and was really exceptionally kind to us, more so indeed than we deserved; and so compensated us for the harm in an incomparably better way.[16]

When Leopold wrote these lines, he had received a number of letters from Hagenauer, at least one of which had been written since his own of 10 November, in which he had chronicled the flight and Wolfgang's illness. It seems likely, therefore, that Hagenauer had suggested that it had proved vain to flee Vienna, for Wolfgang had caught the disease anyway. Since Leopold was disputing this, and since he had already mentioned his inner urge to press on from Brünn to Olmütz, the conclusion seems inescapable that he attributed Wolfgang's recovery at least in part to the excellent accommodation and medical care he had received from Count Podstatsky. And the incomparably better way in which God had compensated them for their troubles was by ordering everything so that the children did catch smallpox but recovered unscathed, since they now had life-long protection.

The two passages quoted above throw interesting light on the relationship between acting to preserve health and believing that the outcome of illness was divinely predetermined. The two decisions Leopold made while in Vienna (moving Wolfgang from the infected house, and fleeing to Moravia with the whole family) had been intended to prevent the children from catching the disease, but hindsight showed that it had been better for them to have caught it. Did his decisions therefore imply panic which temporarily took away his trust in God, or did he believe at that stage that he was trying to reach the decision intended by God? Whatever the answer, it is clear that his nature was not passive and straightforwardly fatalistic.

Some degree of panic is suggested by Leopold's first decision, to move Wolfgang from the infected house, leaving Nannerl there. The inescapable interpretation of his actions is that, faced with a critical dilemma, he chose to try to make things safer for Wolfgang, but not Nannerl. Did he really do this because he hoped that she already had immunity to smallpox, or was it rather because Wolfgang was the more special child? At the same time he remained in Vienna for no better reason than that they might be summoned to court—and this despite the fact that it brought him no peace of mind, since apart from having left Nannerl at risk, there was still every likelihood that Wolfgang would contract the disease despite his removal from the house known to be infected.

---

[16] *MBA* 122 (*Letters* 52, but most of the letter is omitted).

As a postscript to the story of the Viennese smallpox epidemic of 1767, Leopold reported to Hagenauer, during the following year, that the Habsburg court was now being inoculated against it. On 6 August 1768 he described how the 'English inoculator' (it was Jan IngenHousz) had been assigned a house for inoculating poor children, whose parents were given a ducat (4 fl. 16 kr.) for agreeing to the procedure. Maria Theresia and Joseph were visiting almost daily, and the Viennese medical profession was resisting it because of the threat to business. 'Praise God!' wrote Leopold, at the end of his account, *'our inoculator was the best one'*.[17] About five weeks later, members of the imperial family itself were inoculated. On 13 September 1768 Leopold mentioned that the procedure had been carried out on Joseph's daughter Theresia and on Maria Theresia's youngest children, Maximilian and Ferdinand.[18] When it proved successful, Leopold reported on 24 September 1768 that everyone wanted to be inoculated.[19]

By the time Maria Theresia decided in 1768 on inoculation, her family had already suffered grievously from smallpox, and she and her son Joseph were anxious to protect those members of the family who had never had it. An important reason for Maria Theresia's and Joseph's interest in promoting inoculation among poor children was that by doing so, they could obtain safer inoculation for their own, by the system of removes.[20] The almost daily visits paid by Maria Theresia and Joseph to the house of inoculation, therefore, were not purely errands of goodwill—the empress and her son doubtless wanted to see for themselves how the process of inoculation affected IngenHousz's patients before they submitted their own children to it.

As for Leopold Mozart, his comments on inoculation were perceptibly milder in 1768 than they had been in 1764. His change of attitude was probably caused by a combination of factors: the experience of having been in the midst of an epidemic and of having seen both his own children contract the disease; the example of Maria Theresia, whom he saw as a model of Catholic piety; and the fact that inoculation was no longer such a novelty to him. Even so, he was clearly relieved that he did not have to take the decision to inoculate on behalf of his own children.

❦

[17] *MBA* 136/27–38 (not in *Letters*).   [18] *MBA* 137/13–16 (not in *Letters*).
[19] *MBA* 141/20–1 (not in *Letters*).
[20] See Ch. 5 for an explanation of removes. For important clients, more removes were used than for common people.

The Mozarts had not been the only members of the Salzburg court music to go to Vienna for the imperial wedding celebrations. Michael Haydn, the cellist Ignaz Küffel, and the horn players Joseph Leutgeb and Franz Drasil had all decided to try their luck too,[21] and Meissner was also on tour. The question now was what they would all do now that their trips had proved completely abortive. All must have invested money and seen little or no return. Should they merely return home, should they try to salvage something by remaining in Vienna a little longer, or should they travel on elsewhere? The question was complicated by the fact that the anniversary of Schrattenbach's consecration was 21 December, and a strong band would be wanted for the special musical celebrations.

As far as the Mozarts were concerned, the children's illnesses prevented them from returning in time for the consecration anniversary, but Leopold was concerned when he learnt that Meissner had decided to go on to Frankfurt and would also not be back,[22] because he was one of the jewels of the court music. Nevertheless, Leopold disregarded the ominous forewarning of Schrattenbach's possible displeasure, and did not return as quickly as he could even once the children were fit to travel. In Brünn, on the way back to Vienna, they gave a concert whilst staying with Schrattenbach's brother, and doubtless performed for him privately more than once during their fortnight there. But this could hardly compensate them for the disappointment of not having appeared in Vienna, and when Leopold wrote to Hagenauer on 12 January 1768, he had clearly decided to try to recover some of their losses by staying in Vienna some while longer.[23]

The Mozarts were asked to present themselves at court only nine days after their second arrival in Vienna and, according to Leopold's report to Hagenauer of 23 January 1768, were very graciously received. Maria Theresia spoke with emotion to Maria Anna about smallpox and other childhood ailments, while Wolfgang played to Joseph and discussed musical matters with him. Leopold did not mention Nannerl except to say that Joseph had made her blush.[24] It was this appearance at court which gave Leopold the idea which seemed to him such a brilliant opportunity at first, but which in retrospect was seen to be over-ambitious. It was that Wolfgang, just 12 years old, should write and conduct a comic opera for the Viennese stage. The background to Leopold's thinking was explained

---

[21] See Leopold to Hagenauer, 29 Nov. 1767—*MBA* 122/29–31 (*Letters* 52).

[22] Leopold to Hagenauer, 10 Nov. 1767—*MBA* 121/105–12 (*Letters* 51, but the reference to Meissner is omitted).

[23] *MBA* 123/33–5 (not in *Letters*).   [24] *MBA* 124/12–27 (*Letters* 54).

in his letter to Hagenauer of 30 January 1768—a long and revealing letter intended for Hagenauer alone, and purportedly seeking his advice, though actually probably tacitly asking for financial backing. In it can clearly be seen Leopold's over-zealous pride and stubbornness, which led him to fix determinedly on the operatic idea without informing himself adequately about the state of Viennese theatre and music, and their politics.

Leopold began by remarking that they were not in the healthiest of financial circumstances, but that the children were in good form and had made progress despite the setback of having had smallpox. He went on to give two of the main causes of their failure to advance themselves in Vienna, one being that the Viennese public was too frivolous to enjoy the serious musical fare offered by the Mozarts, and the other that high society was following the court's example of financial restraint and was not spending much on musical entertainment. The combination of these two circumstances made Leopold debate whether it would be better to cut his losses and return home, or to continue to try to make something worthwhile of the stay in Vienna. He was already more inclined to stay than leave, when he became aware of something which, on a man of his temperament, could have only the effect of making him dig in his heels. It was that he began to suspect that all the keyboard players and composers in Vienna were avoiding them, in order not to have to acknowledge Wolfgang's greatness. According to Leopold, they all wanted not to hear him play, so that they could continue to say that his talents were charlatanism. Nothing could have been calculated to raise Leopold's hackles more than this, since he could never tire of showing Wolfgang off even when the audience was already entirely converted.

In the first instance, he contrived a situation where one of Wolfgang's perceived detractors was forced to listen to the boy in company, and was then asked his opinion—the man was obliged to admit that Wolfgang's skill was unbelievable. But this did not satisfy Leopold, who wanted the whole of Vienna to be convinced of the truth of Wolfgang's greatness. This was the point at which Leopold had the idea of Wolfgang's writing an opera. He said that Emperor Joseph had first given him the idea by asking Wolfgang whether he would like to write and conduct one, but it seems more likely that the idea had been planted in Leopold's mind by Grimm's prophecy of 15 July 1766,[25] and by Leopold's own ambition for Wolfgang. The remark of the emperor's is more likely to have been a piece of polite jocularity, which Leopold seized upon as a foundation of sorts

---

[25] See Ch. 7.

for his own plans.[26] Leopold's final comments on the idea were that he would write to ask for an extension of his leave, and that it would be the best way to enhance the credit of the name Mozart not only in Germany, but also in Italy.[27]

Even at this early stage of the proceedings, it was clear that the Mozarts had not been guaranteed unambiguous support for the project from all the factions in Vienna's musical world which had the ability to cause trouble. On the contrary, Leopold had told Hagenauer how all the keyboard players and composers were against them. He hoped to get the singers on their side, as well as some aristocratic and influential patrons, and so to make a success of it, but he seems to have been too inexperienced to see that an operatic performance could founder in far more favourable circumstances than the ones in which he and Wolfgang were trying to operate. The management of the imperial theatres was leased to the entrepreneur Giuseppe Affligio, who had appalling financial problems in 1768, and could not afford the merest hint that an opera might not be a box-office success. When opposition to Wolfgang's intended opera *La finta semplice* surfaced, therefore, Affligio had not the slightest reason to exert himself to produce it well. From his point of view, it made much better sense to abandon the piece and produce something else instead.

For a little while, the project looked as if it might prosper—at any rate, when Leopold wrote to Hagenauer on 30 March 1768, he was more pleased that they had 'broken the ice in Vienna', and that the opera would be performed after the emperor's return from Hungary, than perturbed that Schrattenbach had ordered his salary to be stopped unless he returned in April. Leopold did not mention it, and it is not certain that he knew about it, but a similar warning had also been sent to Meissner and Küffel.[28]

But if Leopold was not concerned about his salary, Hagenauer was —perhaps merely from friendliness, or perhaps because the Mozarts were living partly on his credit. On 20 April 1768, Leopold wrote to tell

---

[26] Leopold's letter of 30 Jan. 1768 announced that Joseph had asked Wolfgang if he would *like* to write an opera (*MBA* 125/116–20; *Letters* 55). His letter of 30 July 1768 (by which time the project had struck opposition) claimed that Joseph had said that *he* would like Wolfgang to write one (*MBA* 135/26–8; *Letters* 62). But Leopold's eventual complaint (which he called *Species facti*—*MBA* 139; Deutsch, *Documents*, 80–4) to Joseph about the way in which they had been forced by intrigue to abandon the idea did not allude to any involvement by Joseph himself—though if Joseph really had encouraged Wolfgang's hopes, it would have been in Leopold's interest to point this out to him.

[27] *MBA* 125 (*Letters* 55).

[28] *MBA* 128 (*Letters* 57, but the passage about the salary is omitted). The decree applying to Leopold, Meissner, and Küffel is given in Deutsch, *Documents*, 78.

Hagenauer that they had entertained the wedding guests of Count Otto Wolfgang von Schrattenbach and Countess Isabella von Starhemberg in Vienna. Otto was a nephew of the archbishop, and Leopold appears to have taken patriotic pride in the fact that musicians from Salzburg could entertain such distinguished company in the imperial city for a whole evening to such delight.[29] When Hagenauer read this letter, it must have occurred to him that Leopold, relying on the consequent goodwill of Otto and his family, might petition the archbishop for the return of his salary; because in his next letter, on 11 May 1768, Leopold dismissed the suggestion. Acknowledging that it might be possible to capitalize on the friendship of Schrattenbach's relations, he nevertheless felt too proud to beg for the salary he was sure people were saying he was not earning. He went on to say that Schrattenbach's decree made future travelling easier, since it stated that he could absent himself at will, as long as he did not expect to be paid. He also specifically mentioned a journey he wanted to make to Italy which, 'taking all the circumstances into account, could now no longer be postponed'. He claimed that he had strong imperial support for this journey, and the alternative was to sit in Salzburg sighing for better conditions, while Wolfgang grew to an age which would rob his accomplishments of their miraculous nature. He regarded the Viennese opera commission as a preliminary step to an Italian journey, and though he expressed disdain for the formulation of the decree, he also claimed that the independence he would gain through not being paid during absences suited him well.[30]

The dissatisfaction with Salzburg voiced in this letter prompts the question whether Leopold had in mind from the beginning of his leave of absence that he might not have to return there. At the very least, there are suggestions in the correspondence of this period that Leopold did not think that people of talent were sufficiently appreciated by the archbishop. At the end of his letter of 10 November 1767, he had referred to Rochus Alterdinger, who had just received an appointment at the Salzburg court. Leopold indicated that it was high time that he had something, but hoped that the archbishop would not keep such a useful man in such a humble position for too long.[31] Later, at the end of the letter of 11 May 1768, Leopold expressed pleasure that two of the Salzburg female singers were doing so well and discovering how quickly it was possible to earn the equivalent of their annual salary in Salzburg.[32] Remarks of this

[29] *MBA* 129/8–15 (*Letters* 58).   [30] *MBA* 132/11–39 (*Letters* 59).
[31] *MBA* 121/116–20 (not in *Letters*).   [32] *MBA* 132/99–101 (not in *Letters*).

kind, taken together with the more specific references to his own family, suggest that Leopold saw the remuneration in Salzburg as a chronic problem which might never be resolved. In this respect, therefore, his attitude to the building up of a fine musical establishment in Salzburg was markedly less optimistic than it had been in 1764.[33] Leopold himself continued to promote sales of his own violin treatise when he was in Vienna in 1768, and tried to instigate its translation into Italian in readiness for his proposed journey to Italy (though the translation project never came to fruition).[34] On 14 October 1767, he mentioned sending a parcel of symphonies to Prince Fürstenberg at Donaueschingen, with whom they had stayed on their return from their grand tour.[35] And on 27 April 1768, their Parisian acquaintance Mme Geoffrin, presumably acting for Grimm at Leopold's request, wrote to the influential Austrian chancellor in Vienna, Wenzel Kaunitz. She announced that the Mozarts had decided to settle in Vienna, and asked Kaunitz to take them under his wing.[36] All this, together with the relative nonchalance with which Leopold viewed the suspension of his salary, suggests that he was trying to keep every option open for a better deal, and that he did not think at this stage that it would be difficult for him to improve on his Salzburg earnings.

Leopold's tone in his letter of 11 May 1768 had been confident and optimistic, but by the end of June he and Wolfgang had serious problems with the opera. In his letter to Hagenauer of 29 June 1768, he alluded darkly to intrigues, persecutions, and jealousies which were dogging them, but which he felt too weary to describe.[37] The full account of them was contained in his next letter, that of 30 July 1768. Leopold began by declaring that if he had known at the beginning what he knew now, he would never have let Wolfgang write a note. In particular, he seems to have appreciated only when it was too late that the patronage of the emperor and the nobility was of limited use to him, since Affligio, having leased the theatres at his own risk, was not answerable to anyone else. Leopold went on to chronicle some initial delays, which had been caused by alterations to the libretto and by Emperor Joseph's absence from Vienna in Hungary. While they were waiting, according to Leopold, all the composers in Vienna, led by Gluck, had set up a movement of organized resistance to the opera. These composers had incited the singers and the members of the orchestra not to co-operate, and the result was

[33] See Ch. 5, pp. 72–3, for his more enthusiastic viewpoint.
[34] Leopold to Hagenauer, 11 May 1768—*MBA* 132/89–99 (*Letters* 59).
[35] *MBA* 119/16–25 (*Letters* 49).   [36] Deutsch, *Documents*, 79.
[37] *MBA* 134 (*Letters* 61).

that a whole series of doubts was expressed about the work: the singers could not sing their parts; the orchestra did not want to be conducted by a boy; the music was no good; it was not composed according to the metre because Wolfgang had an insufficient grasp of Italian; and, when Leopold arranged for the rumours to be contradicted by the respected composer Hasse and the court poet Metastasio, that the music had been composed by Leopold rather than Wolfgang.

Leopold made strenuous efforts to dispel all these doubts, by arranging for Wolfgang to be given, in the company of composers and patrons, a book of librettos. One was chosen at random, and he began to compose it on the spot, in front of the whole gathering. The upshot was that it was decided that Wolfgang's opera should go ahead after all. But Leopold claimed that only the retrieval of their honour was keeping him in Vienna:

A hundred times I've wanted to pack up and get away from it all; and if this opera were an opera seria, I would have left instantly, yes at the first instant and laid it at the feet of His Princely Grace: Only since it's an opera buffa, and one in fact which demands special characteristics of the buffo singers, I have to redeem our honour here, cost us what it may. The honour of our most gracious prince is at stake too. His Princely Grace has no liars, charlatans or swindlers in his service, who with his most gracious permission intentionally go to other places and pull the wool over people's eyes like conjurors; No: rather he has honest men who to the honour of Prince and Fatherland are proclaiming to the world a miracle, which God caused to be born in Salzburg. I am responsible to Almighty God for this act, otherwise I would be the most ungrateful creature: *and if I have ever been responsible for convincing the world of this miracle, now is precisely the time, since everything which is called a miracle is made ridiculous and all miracles are denied.* For this reason, people have to be convinced: and was it not a great joy and great victory for me when I heard a voltairean say to me in amazement: *Now I have seen a miracle once in my life; that is the first*! But because this miracle is now too conspicuous, and consequently not to be denied, people want to suppress it: *They will not allow God the honour*, they think: it will only be a few more years, and then it will decline into something natural and cease to be a miracle of God. So they want to hide it from the eyes of the world: and how could it be more conspicuous than through a public spectacle in a great and populous city? — — — But why should we be surprised at the persecutions of strangers, when almost the same thing has happened in the birthplace of this child? — — what a disgrace! what inhumanity!

Leopold's lament continued, saying that Affligio blamed the singers for the trouble, and the singers blamed Affligio. He still believed, however, that the opera would be performed. Towards the end of the letter, he claimed that the trouble they had encountered in Vienna on this occasion had caused him more annoyance than anything else on all their travels. He still did not know when they might be home, because two of the singers were ill, and this was going to delay things further. Meanwhile, the name-day of Maria Anna and Nannerl had been and gone, and now it was Nannerl's seventeenth birthday. These were occasions which would normally have been spent with the Hagenauers in the garden of their country house in Nonntal, just outside Salzburg, and Leopold indicated how disappointed they were not to be able to do the same this year. Instead, they celebrated the occasions with Viennese friends.[38]

The fiasco of *La finta semplice* dragged on through the whole of August and much of September, and all the while Leopold was withdrawing money from Peisser, Hagenauer's banker in Vienna. On 6 August 1768 he affirmed his faith that God had some plan which would prove to be for their good, but when he next wrote, on 13 September 1768, his mood was again one of frustrated fury as the anniversary of their departure from Salzburg passed.[39] And on 14 September 1768 came the acknowledgement that they had lost the battle, and that he was giving up the fight for the staging of Wolfgang's opera. He had finally realized that the performance by people determined not to co-operate could make them a laughing-stock. Nevertheless, he intended to stay and present an account of his grievances to the emperor, in the hope of gaining financial recompense.[40] Leopold prepared a long document outlining his complaints, which he called *Species Facti*. It was given to Emperor Joseph on 21 September 1768. In it he asked for compensation of 160 ducats (682 fl. 40 kr.) and a proper examination of Wolfgang's musical powers.[41]

On 24 September 1768 Leopold reported to Hagenauer that he had been received most graciously by the emperor, and had been promised justice. But now a new problem arose. Hagenauer had evidently informed Leopold that there was trouble afoot in Salzburg. Leopold's letter began:

I've written to His Princely Grace today. I hope that the bruit you told me about is without foundation. But if God should have something else in mind for us; it wouldn't be in our power to alter it. But I hope that you wouldn't leave me for a single moment in ignorance.[42]

Since Leopold had already accepted the suspension of his salary, this new threat must have been something worse—perhaps his dismissal. Despite

---

[38] *MBA* 135 (*Letters* 62, but the reference to the name-day and Nannerl's birthday is omitted).
[39] *MBA* 136/2–12 (*Letters* 63); and *MBA* 137/3–6 (*Letters* 64).
[40] *MBA* 138/39–52 (*Letters* 65). [41] *MBA* 139; Deutsch, *Documents*, 80–4.
[42] *MBA* 141/2–5 (*Letters* 66).

the worry that this must have caused him, he pressed ahead with his effort for saving Wolfgang's reputation. The court, in a gesture of goodwill, arranged for Wolfgang to compose a Mass, an offertory, and a trumpet concerto to celebrate the consecration of the orphanage church on the Feast of the Immaculate Conception, 8 December. Leopold accepted the suggestion, even though it meant staying on in Vienna for another eleven weeks after he had learnt about the latest problem in Salzburg. Hagenauer was also asked to send secretly Leopold's own Sleigh-Ride Music.[43] That Leopold should ask Hagenauer not to tell anyone that he was sending it can perhaps best be interpreted as his desire not to irritate the Salzburg court further by giving it grounds for believing that he was seeking, through the promotion of his music, a court appointment in Vienna. It seems highly likely, however, that this was exactly what he did want. The orphanage concert took place on 7 December 1768 in the presence of the Austrian court, who would have had the opportunity to make some assessment of Leopold's ability and usefulness as well as the outstanding promise of Wolfgang. On 14 December 1768 Leopold expressed himself satisfied with the outcome. The admiration shown to Wolfgang had vindicated him in the eyes of the public, and Maria Theresia had given them a 'beautiful present'. At last they were able to leave the imperial city—as Leopold professed to believe, with their honour restored.[44]

On 5 January 1769, nearly sixteen months after leaving home, they arrived back again, but Leopold's salary was not re-established until he petitioned for it in late February or early March.[45] The fact that he was prepared to beg it back for the whole period of his absence, in contradiction of his earlier assertion that he would not do so, suggests that he might have been heavily out of pocket on his return. His request was not granted—on 8 March 1769 the answer came back that his salary should be paid for January and February (1769)—months during which he had in any case been in Salzburg—but he received no pay from April to December 1768.[46] As far as is known, this was the first time that his salary had been withheld in all the years of travelling. His fruitless petition

[43] Leopold to Hagenauer, 12 Nov. 1768—*MBA* 142/7–23 (*Letters* 67, but the reference to the Sleigh-Ride Music is omitted).
[44] *MBA* 143/16–23 (*Letters* 68).   [45] *MBA* 146; Deutsch, *Documents*, 88.
[46] Cf. commentary to *MBA* 146, and Deutsch, *Documents*, 88–9. The *MBA* commentary states that Leopold's appeal was allowed, but this seems to be a misunderstanding. Though the wording of the answer suggests that his request was being granted, it specifically states only that arrears were to be paid for January and February. This would exclude the period April to December 1768. Yet Leopold's petition makes it clear that he was seeking them for the whole period over which the salary had been withdrawn.

must have bolstered the belief which would grow ever stronger—that although a salary may be paltry, it was at least steady, regular income. For although the setbacks encountered during earlier periods of leave had contributed to his awareness of the fragility of a freelance income, it is only to be expected that the appreciation of his salary would be stronger once the stipend had been withdrawn than it had been when he was receiving it.

Taken as a whole, this period in Vienna had had the most damaging effect on the reputation of the Mozarts, and especially on that of Leopold. Although he claimed that the motive underlying the opposition to *La finta semplice* had been envy, this belief would not appear to be supported either by common sense or by what little other evidence exists. In 1768, Gluck (whom Leopold had cited as the ringleader of the troublemakers) was a highly successful, esteemed, and prosperous composer. At 54 years of age, it is hard to believe that out of envy of a 12-year-old he would act as Leopold claimed. When it is considered that Leopold had accused Schobert of envying Nannerl's playing in Paris in 1764,[47] it seems more likely that Leopold had a tendency to see envy in others—and even, in a perverse way, to welcome it as a manifestation of distorted admiration.[48]

But if Leopold imagined the envy, he did not imagine the opposition to the opera, and the origin of this is most likely to lie in a combination of two factors—first, the competition by composers to get their operas staged in Vienna, and secondly, the antagonism which Leopold aroused in people by the insistent manner in which he tried to make Wolfgang the centre of attention.

With respect to the first factor, an operatic commission in Vienna carried with it a fee which was not to be despised. The 100 ducats (426 fl. 40 kr.) which Affligio had promised Wolfgang for *La finta semplice* were more than Leopold's annual Salzburg salary of 354 fl. A sum of this kind must have been an extremely welcome extra to any composer in Vienna anxious to supplement his basic court income, and it would not be surprising if the Viennese composers resented this encroachment on their territory by a boy from elsewhere.

The second factor involved in the opposition to Wolfgang's opera was almost certainly Leopold's manner, and the way in which he chose to

---

[47] See Ch. 5.
[48] In the Preliminary Notice to the 2nd edn. of his *Violinschule*, written on 24 Sept. 1769, Leopold mentioned the incredible development of Wolfgang and claimed that he could call on the testimony of many of the greatest masters, and even the testimony of envy itself, in support of his remarks. See Deutsch, *Documents*, 91–2.

present his son to the public. His assertions about his belief in Wolfgang as a special gift of God may have been genuine, but they also functioned as an irreproachable justification for the way in which Wolfgang was thrust on the attention of the musical world. Far from being impressed by this refrain, many people apparently found it simply tiresome, and Leopold with it. This becomes clear from the correspondence slightly later between the Viennese composer Johann Hasse and his friend in Venice, Giovanni Ortes.

While Leopold had been in Vienna, one of his tasks was to obtain introductory letters for the proposed journey to Italy. Hasse was one of those to whom he turned, and on 30 September 1769 Hasse was to write to ask Ortes to help the Mozarts. He praised Wolfgang's musical achievements highly, and said that Leopold was refined in music and other areas, that the children were very well brought up, and that Wolfgang was charming. His only reservation about Wolfgang's future development was that Leopold might spoil him with excessive eulogies. On 2 March 1771, after Ortes had met Leopold and Wolfgang, he wrote to Hasse to say that Leopold had seemed piqued in Venice that Wolfgang had not been lionized more. Hasse's reply, on 23 March 1771, claimed that Leopold was probably equally discontented everywhere—he had behaved the same way in Vienna, and idolized his son too much.[49]

If Leopold was gaining himself a reputation among musicians as a sour man making himself somewhat ridiculous by expecting honours to be heaped on his son and himself wherever they went, his standing in aristocratic circles was perhaps becoming even worse. The period spent in Vienna from 1767 to 1769 shows that, faced with the conflicting claims on him by his son and his court, he chose to heed those of his son. What the Salzburg court thought about this was indicated by the refusal to repay his salary, but, more seriously, his reputation for being a less than desirable employee was spreading further afield than Salzburg. For all that he appeared to believe that the Austrian court had been very gracious and supportive in the matter of redeeming Wolfgang's honour, it was probably the view of him provided by this episode in his life which was to make Maria Theresia, in 1771, advise her teenage son, Archduke Ferdinand, not to employ Wolfgang. On 12 December 1771 the empress wrote to Ferdinand:

you ask me to take the young Salzburger into your service. I do not know why, not believing that you have need of a composer or of useless people. if

---

[49] Deutsch, *Documents*, 92–3, 132, and 134.

however it would give you pleasure, I have no wish to hinder you. what I say is intended only to prevent your burdening yourself with useless people and giving titles to people of that sort. if they are in your service it degrades that service when these people go about the world like beggars. besides, he has a large family.[50]

Nothing could show more cuttingly how completely Leopold's efforts to place his family on a higher footing than that of other musicians had failed. On the one hand, he was scorned by members of his own profession for his supercilious airs, and on the other he was cast by the most influential employer in the Austrian empire as a beggar who would degrade the service of his patron. For all that his opinion of his own abilities and usefulness had not diminished, Leopold had by this date damaged his own career prospects irreparably by the course he had chosen as the champion of his miraculous son.

As for Nannerl, Leopold's single-minded dedication to Wolfgang could not be without implications for her. During this period and for the next eight years or so, she had no role of her own which could in any way be considered commensurate with the successes of her childhood years or with her capabilities as a keyboard player. If her father could place a greater value on Wolfgang in a matter of life and death, it is not to be expected that in the normal course of everyday life her needs would receive extraordinary attention. In the sixteen months spent in Vienna, she was hardly mentioned in the letters home. Leopold was now concentrating single-mindedly on Wolfgang's compositional development. In pursuit of this path, Wolfgang had written several substantial compositions, and had had his talent put to the test in the presence of senior Viennese musicians. The battle for *La finta semplice* and Wolfgang's honour was more than enough for Leopold, and as far as Nannerl's public persona was concerned, she might almost as well not have been there. Leopold must have thought the same. When he next obtained leave from Salzburg, in December 1769, he was to decide to leave Nannerl and Maria Anna at home. A new phase then opened in the story of the family— one in which they led divided lives, and in which Nannerl's development was neglected. Not until 1777, when Leopold himself had to stay at home while Wolfgang and Maria Anna travelled, did he, with some surprise and emotion, begin to rediscover how much his daughter meant to him.

[50] Ibid. 138. See Ch. 10 for more detail on Leopold's attempt to have Ferdinand employ Wolfgang.

PART II

Leopold and Wolfgang
(1769–1777)

❦ 9 ❧

The Divergence of the Children's Paths:
Wolfgang's First Visit to Italy

❧❦❧

STRANGE though it might seem, Leopold and Wolfgang were back in Schrattenbach's favour only months after returning from Vienna. One important element in their rehabilitation must have been the opera score they brought back with them, for *La finta semplice* was performed at court on 1 May 1769, Schrattenbach's name-day. Evidently, then, they managed to get round the problems of the *buffo* characters mentioned by Leopold to Hagenauer on 30 July 1768.[1] Fesemayr, Braunhofer, and Lipp, the three female singers who had been educated in Italy, all sang in it, as did the male singers Meissner, Spitzeder, Hornung, and Winter.[2] Maria Magdalena Lipp had changed her name to Haydn, however; her marriage to Michael Haydn had taken place on 17 August 1768, while the Mozarts had been struggling in Vienna with the composition of the opera. In May 1769 she was in the early stages of pregnancy with their only child, Aloisia Josefa, who was to die just four days before her first birthday in January 1771, leaving a void in the life of her parents which was never to be filled.[3]

At the time of the production of the opera it is also likely that another marriage amongst the musicians was planned. Adlgasser's second wife, Maria Barbara, had died on 31 December 1768, probably from complications following childbirth, just before the Mozarts had returned from Vienna. The baby girl who had been born on 22 December followed her mother to the grave on 3 January 1769. On 19 June 1769 Adlgasser married the singer Fesemayr. He brought with him to the marriage three children: the 15-year-old Maria Viktoria, from his first marriage to Maria Josepha Katharina Eberlin; and the 7-year-old Joseph and 3-year-old Anna, sole survivors of the eight children of his second marriage.[4] But the newly

---

[1] See Ch. 8, p. 132.
[2] Deutsch, *Documents*, 89–90. Deutsch questions, however, whether the opera was performed on precisely this date.
[3] See Hintermaier, 'Hofkapelle', 166.   [4] See ibid. 3.

formed family seems not to have knit very happily. There were no children of the third marriage, and relations between Maria Anna Fesemayr/Adlgasser and her stepchildren seem to have been poor.[5] When Adlgasser died following his dramatic stroke at the organ in 1777, it was the plight of his children that Leopold was to use in order to impress on Wolfgang his responsibility for Maria Anna's and Nannerl's future upkeep. For Adlgasser's children were left by their stepmother to fend for themselves on a pittance of a pension, and Viktoria, Nannerl's close friend, had to struggle to support her half-brother and half-sister.[6] Witnesses at Adlgasser's third wedding were Meissner, Spitzeder, Nikolaus Strasser, and Leopold and Wolfgang Mozart; Meissner and Strasser were Adlgasser's brothers-in-law through their marriages with daughters of Eberlin.[7]

Wolfgang continued to compose prolifically throughout 1769, and in August he had two pieces of *Finalmusik* performed.[8] The genre was peculiar to Salzburg; it was a work of up to eight movements, written for performance in the open air to celebrate the end of the academic year and honour the university professors. Since it was organized by the students, they were among those in the band. The work was always performed first for the benefit of the archbishop at Mirabell, after which everyone trooped across the river to repeat the performance at the university. The piece tended to open and close with a march, while some of the inner movements resembled concerto movements for one or more instruments.

On 15 October 1769 Kajetan Hagenauer, who had entered St Peter's as a novice while the Mozarts had been in London, celebrated his *Primiz* or first Mass as Father Dominicus. The occasion was a grand one, and more worldly than might be expected. Wolfgang wrote the 'Dominicus' Mass (K. 66) for it, and the church was packed. Afterwards Wolfgang improvised at the organ. On the following day there was a grand meal for fifty guests at the Hagenauers' summer house in Nonntal, after which Nannerl and Wolfgang entertained the company with music. The diary entries reporting these events of 1769 suggest that Wolfgang, though still

---

[5] Babies were often instrumental in binding step-families together. Viktoria Adlgasser was devoted to her half-brother and sister from her father's second marriage, and if there had been a baby from the third for her to help care for, she might have got on better with her stepmother. Nannerl Mozart's stepdaughter, young Nannerl, had the care of Nannerl's son Leopoldl from just before the child's second birthday in 1787, and for this reason the two were to remain very close as adults. See Brno, MZA, Berchtold Family Archive, Family Chronicle, unpaginated, but p. 95 on my count.

[6] The story of the family following Adlgasser's death is told in Ch. 17.   [7] See Fig. 1.

[8] See Deutsch, *Documents*, 91.

only 13, had already made a name for himself in Salzburg as a reliable composer of music for special occasions.[9]

Perhaps it was all these high-profile activities that convinced Schrattenbach that Wolfgang's talents must be encouraged further. At any rate, he named him third Konzertmeister (the others were Michael Haydn and the ageing Ferdinand Seidl) in November, and allowed Leopold more leave to take Wolfgang to Italy. Wolfgang's new position was merely a title, but Kajetan Hagenauer wrote in his diary that Schrattenbach had promised him a salary on his return.[10] Leopold's salary continued to be paid while they were away, and in addition Schrattenbach gave them 120 ducats (600 fl.) from his *Schatulle* on 27 November.[11] With these arrangements made, Leopold and Wolfgang departed on 13 December on the journey 'that could now no longer be postponed'.[12]

The purpose of the trip was primarily educational, but the education was Wolfgang's and not Nannerl's; hers was considered virtually finished. During all the absences of Leopold and Wolfgang in the following five years, with the single exception of Nannerl's brief visit to Munich at the beginning of 1775 to see Wolfgang's opera *La finta giardiniera*, she and Maria Anna remained unwillingly at home. It was just this first journey undertaken without them that the women would most have enjoyed. Leopold's plans for Wolfgang involved his immersion in the Italian language, exposure to Italian church music of the highest quality, and further experience of Italian opera; all with the purpose of developing compositional skills. As on previous trips, they would give concerts with the dual aim of financing the next stage of the journey and of bringing Wolfgang's talent to the attention of discriminating and influential people. Finally, they would see a good deal of Italy. All these aims were achieved more or less successfully, but Maria Anna and Nannerl could only read the accounts in letters. Leopold and Wolfgang crossed the Alps and, travelling via Verona and Mantua, enjoyed a highly fruitful two months in Milan which culminated in Wolfgang's being awarded a contract to compose the first opera for the following winter's season. Thus they were able to spend most of 1770 travelling in Italy with the assurance of a handsome fee forthcoming on their return to Milan. They arrived in Rome, via Bologna and Florence, in time to witness the special

---

[9] Even the abbot of St Peter's, Beda Seeauer, who disapproved of the Hagenauers' ostentatious wealth and the fact that they were giving so little of it to the abbey, had nothing but praise for Wolfgang's music. See Deutsch, *Documents*, 93–4; and the fuller account of Seeauer's reactions to the occasion in H. Klein, 'Autobiographisches und Musikalisches aus dem Jugendtagebuch des späteren Abtes P. Dominikus Hagenauer', *ÖMz* (Sonderheft) (1967), 27–8.

[10] See Deutsch, *Documents*, 94–5.   [11] See ibid. 94.   [12] See Ch. 8, p. 130.

events of Holy Week; then they went to Naples for six weeks and saw Pompeii, Herculaneum, and a good many other antiquities; returning north through Rome they spent three months in Bologna, two of them in luxury on a country estate; back in Milan the opera was extremely successful; and the trip was concluded by visits to Turin and Venice, where they saw the end of the Carnival. This proved to be the last trip made by the Mozarts which could in any way be described as light-hearted. Not that it was without its risks and difficulties: but though Leopold occasionally brooded about their prospects in Salzburg, he still had high hopes of Wolfgang; and it was too soon for the necessity of Wolfgang's obtaining a good appointment of his own to be a crushing burden to them all. There was good reason, therefore, for the women to feel disgruntled at being left behind. But Leopold's reasons for not taking them were founded on his experiences of their earlier travels, when they had several times faced situations of acute anxiety. From his point of view it was natural to make the journey easier and cheaper by taking only Wolfgang.

~•≈•~

In many ways the Italian tour was easier to organize than the grand European one of 1763–6, because the links between Austria and Italy were such that the travellers were frequently on the familiar ground of Habsburg-administered Catholicism. The later part of the eighteenth century was a period of relative stability and peace in Italy, involving Habsburg influence acquired through tactical marriage-making.[13] In Milan the Mozarts made the profitable acquaintance of Count Karl Joseph von Firmian, the governor-general of Lombardy for the Habsburgs; in Florence they renewed their acquaintance with the Habsburg Archduke Leopold of Tuscany. Linking the territories of Lombardy and Tuscany were the duchy of Modena and the princedoms of Massa and Carrara, all of which were to be inherited by Princess Maria Beatrice Ricciarda d'Este; and it was to gain control of this land that a marriage contract was drawn up in 1753, when Maria Beatrice was 3 years old, between her and Archduke Leopold. When Leopold succeeded to Tuscany on the death of his father in 1765, however, his younger brother Ferdinand was designated her bridegroom instead. The commission won by Wolfgang at the end of his first Italian tour to write a *serenata* to celebrate this marriage, which took place in 1771, was to be one direct benefit accruing to the Mozarts from Habsburg influence in Italy, and Leopold did not quickly abandon his hope that

---

[13] See A. Wandruszka, *Österreich und Italien im 18. Jahrhundert* (Vienna, 1963), 39.

one or other of this numerous family would prove a long-term patron to Wolfgang. Even as far south as Naples, though the king was a Bourbon, his wife was a Habsburg, and Leopold apparently built his hopes of a profitable stay there on this fact.

On this trip Leopold did not take their carriage, and neither did he have a servant with him for the whole journey.[14] This increased considerably the amount of work he had to do himself. Travelling was uncomfortable at the best of times, and they were setting out in mid-winter. As early as 7 January 1770, Leopold was asking Maria Anna for a recipe for hand cream, because the inn dining rooms were unheated,[15] and in his letter of 11 January, he complained, 'I can't write to anyone, I'm a harassed man. nothing but dressing and undressing; packing and unpacking, and on top of that never a warm room, freezing like a dog, everything I touch is ice. And if you could just see the doors and locks on the rooms! just prisons—!'[16]

Leopold's most useful letter of introduction proved to be the one from the court official who had overall supervision of the musicians: the Obersthofmeister, Count Franz Lactanz Firmian. The letter was to his brother Karl Joseph, an extremely influential man, described by Burney as 'a sort of King of Milan'.[17] He was exceptionally cultured, apparently took a great liking to the Mozarts, and wrote them further useful letters of introduction to his acquaintances elsewhere in Italy.

The journey to Milan took six weeks, because Leopold and Wolfgang stopped several times to give concerts. On 17 December 1769 Leopold reported to Maria Anna the sum of 12 ducats (60 fl.) earned in Innsbruck.[18] For the first time, he used a cypher to disguise the information. The use of the substitution cypher became progressively more important in the family letters as the position of the Mozarts in Salzburg increased in difficulty,[19] but why it should have been used here to conceal a relatively

---

[14] In his letter to Maria Anna of 17 Feb. 1770, Leopold described himself as 'master, servant, and everything'—*MBA* 161/41–3 (not in *Letters*).

[15] *MBA* 152/104–9 (not in *Letters*).   [16] *MBA* 155/46–50 (*Letters* 76).

[17] See C. Burney, *Music, Men and Manners in France and Italy 1770*, ed. H. Edmund Poole (London, 1969), 55.

[18] *MBA* 149/35 (*Letters* 73).

[19] It was Nissen's biography of Mozart which first explained how the two cyphers used in the correspondence worked. In one, that used by Leopold here, the vowels were changed to consonants: m was used for a, l for e, f for i, r (though other sources give s—cf. commentary to *MBA* 149/35) for o, and h for u; conversely, a was used for m and so forth. The other was less easily spotted as a cypher, since the message was hidden in phrases that had a sense of their own: the initial letters of each noun were extracted to form the cyphered word. Cf. von Nissen, *Biographie*, Author's Preface, pp. xx–xxi. An example of the second type is Wolfgang's letter to Leopold of 13 Nov. 1780 from Munich, where Wolfgang was preparing his opera *Idomeneo* for performance. To conceal the nature of the exact relationship of Countess Baumgarten to the elector of Bavaria,

modest financial present is puzzling. Leopold had frequently mentioned far larger sums of money earned when he had written to Hagenauer on previous journeys. Either he did not want acquaintances in Salzburg to learn this information (which they would if Maria Anna were to circulate the letters in the way Hagenauer used to do), or he was worried that his letters would be intercepted by court officials on behalf of the archbishop.[20] In either case, the deed suggests that an atmosphere of suspicion and possibly resentment was developing between him and his colleagues or employer, or both.

Despite giving further concerts in Verona and Mantua, Leopold was not entirely happy. On 23 January 1770 they reached Milan, and on 26 January he wrote to Maria Anna to report on his financial position. He claimed that they had not taken in much money in Verona or Mantua, and warned her only to expect them to cover their travelling expenses, which were not cheap despite the fact that they were only for two people. In six weeks they had already spent 70 ducats (350 fl.). He went on to tell his wife how relieved he was that he had left her and Nannerl behind—not only could the women never have endured the cold, but the costs would have been frightening, and the accommodation in Milan would not have been so satisfactory. This was because they had obtained lodgings there at the Augustinian monastery of St Mark; though they were not free, they were very comfortable and convenient. Leopold and Wolfgang had three good, heated rooms, heated beds, and a monk to wait on them.[21] Presumably this accommodation would not have been available if women had been with them.

The Mozarts were lodged close to Firmian's house in Milan, but there was a delay of about a fortnight before they could meet him, because he had a cold. They were powerless to earn anything before he had received them. Leopold could still cope with this type of vexation, but there are

he wrote, 'Sie ist die *welche einen fuchsschwanz im Arsch stecken hat, und eine spitzige Uhrkette an ohr hangen, und einen schönen Ring, ich habe ihn selbst gesehen, und soll der tod über mich kommen, ich unglücklicher Mann ohne Nase.* sapient: pauca.' (*Favoritin*: U = V; the 'M' of 'Mann' is not used. The underlinings are mine.) Anderson's translation is, 'It is she *who has a fox's tail sticking out of her arse and, oh vanity, an odd-looking watch-chain hanging under her ear and a fine ring; I have seen it myself, though death should take me, unfortunate fellow, without a nasal extremity, sapienti pauca.'* See *MBA* 537/10–14 (*Letters* 358). This translation, though it inevitably has to sacrifice some of the relevant nouns, nicely conveys the tone of Wolfgang's message; the only important nuance missing which might also have been intended by him is that 'Schwanz' can mean 'prick' as well as 'tail'.

[20] In 1765 Hagenauer had told Leopold that one of his letters from London had been opened and fastened up again before he received it, and since Leopold had posted it himself, he had been convinced that this could not have happened in England. See Leopold to Hagenauer, 19 Sept. 1765— *MBA* 102/116–19 (not in *Letters*).

[21] *MBA* 157/66–93 (*Letters* 77).

hints that it had the power to make him quite dejected, and that he no longer had quite the old zest for travelling. At the end of his letter home of 26 January, after telling Maria Anna that the journey was easier without her and Nannerl, he told her to sell their old horse and carriage, explaining emphatically with a double negative that they would be making no more long journeys.[22]

Leopold and Wolfgang found their stay in Milan made congenial, once they had met Firmian, by his generous patronage and the friendship shown them by his secretary Leopold Troger and his steward Fernando Germani. The letters from Milan show that they were with one or other of these people almost every day; dining with Troger's married daughter, writing home from Germani's quarters, or making music. It was Troger who had arranged their agreeable lodgings at St Mark's, and Leopold asked Maria Anna to tell Troger's sister, who lived in Salzburg, how pleased they were with them.[23]

They first dined with Firmian, and played to him, on 7 February 1770, and the occasion had important consequences, because Firmian presented Wolfgang with the Turin edition of Metastasio's works in nine volumes.[24] On 18 February Leopold and Wolfgang gave another private concert at Firmian's house, this one attended by the duke of Modena and his granddaughter, Princess Maria Beatrice Ricciarda d'Este, the designated bride of Archduke Ferdinand, and thus important as a possible future patron. On 23 February they gave a public concert, and Leopold wanted to leave Milan soon afterwards. Firmian, however, persuaded him to stay and give another concert in his house on 12 March.[25] For this occasion Wolfgang wrote a recitative and three arias, using texts from the Metastasio edition which had been Firmian's gift. This concert, which was attended by the princess and a hundred and fifty members of the nobility, and at which Wolfgang's arias were evidently much enjoyed, produced the result that Wolfgang was invited to write the first opera for the following winter in Milan. The way in which the contract was gained serves as an example of Leopold's astuteness and his ability to grasp opportunities.[26]

[22] *MBA* 157/110–20 (not in *Letters*).

[23] Leopold to Maria Anna, 10 Feb. 1770—*MBA* 160/55–8 (*Letters* 79b).

[24] Firmian was a bibliophile who left a library of 40,000 books. See Wandruszka, *Österreich und Italien*, 64.

[25] Leopold to Maria Anna, 10 Feb., 17 Feb., and 27 Feb. 1770—*MBA* 160/4–15 (*Letters* 79); *MBA* 161/23–8 (*Letters* 80); and *MBA* 162/3–11 (*Letters* 81).

[26] Leopold to Maria Anna, 13 Mar. 1770—*MBA* 165/4–45 (*Letters* 83). The *MBA* commentary to 157/96 plausibly suggests that it was the impressions made on the duke of Modena and Princess Maria Beatrice by Wolfgang's concerts at Firmian's house which later won Wolfgang the commission of *Ascanio in Alba* to celebrate the marriage of the princess.

When Leopold wrote, they still had no contract for the opera, but hoped to obtain it on the following day. Leopold, in mentioning that Firmian had been exceptionally kind to them, said that he would write to the Salzburg Obersthofmeister, Count Franz Lactanz Firmian, on the following day. His reasons, as his next letter to Maria Anna of 24 March 1770 shows, were twofold: first to express gratitude for the hospitality shown to the Mozarts by the Milanese Firmian; and secondly to ask for permission for Wolfgang to write the opera which had been commissioned. The work was to be performed over Christmas, and they were to receive 100 gigliati (between 400 and 500 fl.) and free lodgings while it was being composed and rehearsed.[27]

The Mozarts left Milan on 15 March, after the usual hectic packing up and leave-takings. Leaving a town after an extended stay was always difficult; perhaps the most daunting aspect was the need to summon up the energy and courage to leave a place where the arrangements had favoured them, and start all over again in an unknown location among strangers.

Of the letters of recommendation provided by Karl von Firmian, the most useful was to Count Pallavicini in Bologna. Arriving in Bologna on 24 March, Leopold's situation could have been awkward, because though he wanted to give a concert there, he also wanted to press on to Rome so as to arrive in time to hear the Holy Week performances. Thanks to Pallavicini, both aims were realized; when the situation was explained to him, he organized a private concert for the day immediately following his interview with Leopold, 26 March. A hundred and fifty members of the nobility attended, together with Padre Martini, the acknowledged master of musical theory, history, and sacred composition. During the remaining few days in Bologna, to Leopold's satisfaction, Wolfgang took some lessons in counterpoint with Martini, and on 29 March they were able to leave with their purse replenished. Pallavicini gave Leopold letters of recommendation for Rome which he hoped would enable Wolfgang to meet the Pope;[28] on the return journey to Milan, the Mozarts were to be even more indebted to him.

From Bologna they proceeded to Florence, where Firmian's letter of recommendation to Maria Theresia's son Leopold, grand duke of Tuscany, resulted in an early audience with him, and a concert on 2 April. The fam-

---

[27] *MBA* 170/11–22 (*Letters* 84). A gigliato was a gold coin with a value akin to that of the ducat. Wolfgang Hess gives a useful list of sample currency conversions at the end of the small catalogue (also containing an essay by R. Angermüller) to the exhibition promoted in 1983 by the Internationale Stiftung Mozarteum in Salzburg, the Staatliche Münzsammlung in Munich, and the Bayerische Vereinsbank in Munich: *'Auf Ehre und Credit': Die Finanzen des W. A. Mozart.*

[28] See Deutsch, *Documents*, 112–13; and Leopold to Maria Anna, 27 Mar. 1770—*MBA* 171/5–37 (*Letters* 85).

ous violinist Nardini performed on the same occasion,[29] and arranged a meeting between his pupil Thomas Linley and Wolfgang. The boys were about the same age, and struck up a friendship which Leopold was happy to encourage. They made music together more than once, and Leopold reported admiringly to Maria Anna on 21 April that they played like men rather than boys.[30] When the Mozarts left Florence on 6 April, they thought of spending longer there on their way back to Milan, so that Linley and Wolfgang could meet again. But the arrangement foundered because of the accident which was to befall Leopold.

After a trying five-day journey in terrible wind and rain, through untended land with filthy inns and scanty food, the Mozarts arrived in Rome on Ash Wednesday, 11 April. Here they were found a private lodging, where they became such good friends with their landlady and her daughter that they were not permitted to pay for their accommodation when they left for Naples.[31] The month spent in Rome must have been relatively free from worry for Leopold. The accommodation was comfortable, the food good, and they had the use of a harpsichord. Wolfgang had good conditions for composing, and his performances attracted the usual admiration. Leopold received a letter from Count Franz Lactanz Firmian, presumably giving permission for Wolfgang to compose the opera for Milan. And they met Meissner, who was again on tour, and gave a concert with him at the German College, where other Salzburg friends were living.[32]

Leopold's main worries as they left Rome on 8 May were that there might be bandits on the road to Naples, and that their health might be affected by the weather. He claimed that they would spend only five weeks in Naples, and then return north via Loreto to Bologna and Pisa, in order to spend the hottest months in the healthiest places.[33] Leopold was not alone in worrying about the air around Rome. The road to Naples passed through the Pontine Marshes, which were a notorious health risk and virtually uninhabited. The lonely appearance of the untended land, together with its reputation, lent it an atmosphere of horror in the eyes of travellers. Everyone had his preferred method of travelling through this country, but most people seem to have agreed that it was necessary to keep awake, in order not to be caught unawares by the poor air. In

[29] Leopold to Maria Anna, 3 Apr. 1770—*MBA* 173/6–24 (*Letters* 86).

[30] *MBA* 177/47–65 (*Letters* 88).

[31] Leopold to Maria Anna, 29 May 1770—*MBA* 188/17–24 (not in *Letters*).

[32] Leopold to Maria Anna, 14 Apr., 21 Apr., 28 Apr., and 2 May 1770—*MBA* 176, 177, 181, and 182 (*Letters* 87, 88, 90, and 91, but not complete).

[33] Leopold to Maria Anna, 28 Apr. and 2 May 1770—*MBA* 181/23–34 and 182/9–17 (*Letters* 90 and 91).

October 1770, when Burney travelled the route, he doubted whether the land could ever be reclaimed; in February 1787, Goethe thought it could. In fact, it was finally conquered under Mussolini in the 1930s.[34]

It was presumably with some relief, therefore, that the Mozarts arrived in Naples on 14 May, having travelled in convoy with three other coaches, and having stayed in Augustinian houses for the overnight stops. On 19 May, Leopold wrote to Maria Anna to tell her that they had no choice but to stay five weeks or five months, and that their decision would depend on the circumstances.[35] They were required by the Milanese opera contract to be back in Milan by 1 November,[36] so he clearly meant that they would consider staying in Naples until it was time to leave for Milan if their stay there could be financed satisfactorily. If not, they would leave in five weeks, presumably in accordance with his previously expressed wish to get clear of Rome and into healthier air before the hottest part of the summer.[37]

But the satisfactory financing of a lengthy stay in Naples depended to a large extent on the patronage of the king and queen, and it was not long before it became apparent that the king was not interested in hearing them. They did not appear at court, and their chief income in Naples came from a concert given on 28 May in the house of the imperial ambassador, Count Kaunitz-Rietberg. Leopold hoped to take in 150 ducats (750 fl.) at this concert, but though he told Maria Anna on 29 May 1770 that it had passed off very well, he deliberately did not reveal the sum earned.[38] Returning to the subject on 5 June 1770, he claimed that his reason for secrecy about their earnings was that people in Salzburg would note only the income, and very few would understand how expensive travelling was. He assured her, however, that they had enough money to travel away from Naples in an honourable way.[39]

Once it was clear that the king and queen did not want to summon them, and once they had received the income from their concert together with some other presents of money, Leopold was free to plan the return jour-

---

[34] For impressions of the Pontine Marshes by other travellers, cf. Burney, *Music, Men and Manners*, 155; and J. W. Goethe, *Italienische Reise*, ed. H. von Einem (Munich, 1985); English trans.: *Italian Journey*, trans. and ed. W. H. Auden and E. Mayer (Harmondsworth, 1970), 180–1.

[35] *MBA* 184/60–1 (*Letters* 92).

[36] Leopold to Maria Anna, 24 Mar. 1770—*MBA* 170/22–4 (*Letters* 84).

[37] Anderson's translation of this passage is inaccurate. Whereas Leopold wrote, 'I have no other choice' ('ich habe keine andere wahl'), her rendering is, 'The matter is entirely out of my hands.' The effect of this is to make the figures mentioned in Leopold's next clause, 'to stay five weeks or five months', appear arbitrary, when he meant them to be specific.

[38] *MBA* 188/8–9 (*Letters* 95). Anderson's translation has Leopold say that the concert brought them in a considerable sum, but no clause to this effect is given in *MBA*.

[39] *MBA* 189/11–20 (*Letters* 96).

ney to Milan. His idea was to leave on 16 June, spend a week in Rome, and then travel to Loreto, perhaps going on from there to Bologna or Florence, and then via Pisa, Lucca, Leghorn, and Genoa to Milan. Loreto was a major detour, but he was keen to see the pilgrimage church of Santa Casa, and he relished the idea that this plan offered of seeing so much of Italy.[40] In fact, they did not leave until 25 June, after a period of sight-seeing in and around Naples. Travelling non-stop with two horses, they accomplished the journey to Rome (which often took four and a half days) in twenty-seven hours—but not without paying a price. Whilst dashing along the last stage to Rome, the postilion, by over-zealous lashing of one of the horses, caused it to rear up and then fall. The front of the two-wheeled *sedia* pitched forward and down and, in trying to stop Wolfgang from being thrown out, Leopold raked his right shin. The lower half of the shin received a cut 'the width of a finger', and by the following day was badly swollen. When writing to Maria Anna on the day after their arrival, however, he made no mention of it. Instead he merely reported how exhausted and famished they had been on arrival at the house of their old landlady. Even in his next letter he made light of it. He started by answering questions she had asked, revealing that Wolfgang was not yet even thinking of starting work on his opera, and hinting at the stories he could tell about the court at Naples. Only then did he describe how the accident had happened, and he wrote in very reassuring terms about the present state of the wound.[41]

The injury to Leopold's shin was none the less serious. No bones were broken, but the cut was long and wide and the bruising very heavy. All through the summer, his letters home recorded the progress of his recovery; and though he usually managed to describe his condition in a cheerful and stoical manner, it is clear that the situation affected him badly and brought on fits of depression. The injury forced them to change almost all their travel plans, and had it not been for the generosity shown them by Pallavicini when they reached Bologna, they might have had to spend five weeks at the inn there, with all the expense that that would have entailed. It was to take more than two months for the injury to heal completely.

The first worry confronting Leopold on arrival in Rome was that the injury might prevent their leaving as early as they wanted to; of all the unhealthy places he had wanted to avoid during the summer, Rome was

---

[40] Leopold to Maria Anna, 29 May 1770—*MBA* 188/11–28 (*Letters* 95).
[41] Leopold to Maria Anna, 27 and 30 June 1770—*MBA* 193 and 194 (*Letters* 99 and 100).

the one he most feared. In fact, they could not leave within a week in any case, because they heard soon after their arrival of the possibility of Wolfgang's receiving the papal Order of the Golden Spur, and they had to await developments. On 8 July 1770 they had an audience with the Pope, and the Order was conferred. Then they were free to leave, and did so on 10 July.

Despite the fact that his shin and foot were still extremely uncomfortable, Leopold did not give up his cherished idea of going to the pilgrimage church at Loreto. The journey there, however, and then onward to Bologna, was so trying, and made his injury so much worse, that on arrival in Bologna he accepted the necessity of staying there until it was completely healed. From Rome they had travelled to Loreto, and then along the coast as far as Rimini, before cutting inland to Bologna. They had left Rome in the evening and travelled all the first night without sleeping. On subsequent nights they got some rest, but always started off at about three o'clock in the morning. They would rest during the hottest part of the day and travel a little further from four o'clock until eight or nine in the evening. Their sleeping pattern was wrecked, the quantities of biting insects plagued them, the chaise jolted them around, and the lower part of Leopold's leg swelled to the same size as his calf, while the wound itself reopened. On arrival at the inn in Bologna, all Leopold could do was to lie on the bed.[42]

It was from this predicament that Pallavicini rescued them. First he offered surgeons and the use of his carriage. The surgeons were deemed at first unnecessary, but the carriage was gratefully accepted. Leopold, however, was surprised at how slow his shin was to recover, and reported that the swelling and pain had spread to the ball of his foot and his toes. Meanwhile their costs were mounting; on 28 July 1770 he estimated that the 'joke' was going to cost them 12 ducats (60 fl.), but on 4 August he revised the figure upwards to 20 ducats (100 fl.). Pallavicini must have decided around this time to take control of the situation, because on 11 August Leopold's letter to Maria Anna explained that he and Wolfgang were now living as Pallavicini's guests on his estate just outside Bologna.[43]

Pallavicini was married and had a son Wolfgang's age. Once installed in their new quarters, Leopold and Wolfgang were living in luxury. They

---

[42] Leopold to Maria Anna, 21 July 1770—*MBA* 199/9–43 (*Letters* 103, but virtually the whole passage is omitted). The impression given by the truncated report in *Letters* is that of an uneventful sightseeing trip.

[43] Leopold to Maria Anna, 28 July, 4 Aug., and 11 Aug. 1770—*MBA* 200, 202, and 203 (*Letters* 105, 106, and 107, but with omissions).

had cool rooms, sheets finer than noblemen's shirts, chamber pots and nightlights of silver, an abundance of summer fruits, and two servants. Leopold was treated with great consideration, and even in the chapel he was provided with a second chair for his bad leg. He thought that they might remain there for the rest of August;[44] in fact, they were to stay until 1 October.

Partly because of the injury, and partly because they had received the libretto and cast list for the opera (*Mitridate, rè di Ponto*) during their early days in Bologna, Leopold subsequently decided that it made better sense to stay with Pallavicini until it was time to leave for Milan. The recitatives had to be sent ahead to arrive by mid-October, so they now had their minds more on the writing of the opera than on further sightseeing.[45] The long spell with Pallavicini enabled Leopold to recuperate from the stresses he had endured since leaving Naples, and to ease his worries about money; a blessing, because his injury had brought with it spells of melancholy.[46] On 1 October they took leave of Pallavicini and moved for the last part of their stay in Bologna into the town. Here they saw Martini frequently, and here Wolfgang successfully sat his examination for entry to the Accademia Filarmonica. This accomplished, they left for Milan, arriving on 18 October.[47]

Wolfgang now got down to serious work on his opera. He tended to compose all morning, and after lunch they would walk to Firmian's to see their friends Troger and Germani. The first performance was to take place on 26 December, and rehearsals would start around the beginning of December. Wolfgang therefore had about six weeks in which to write the opera, though he had started the recitatives in Bologna. Although he could work fast, he was hampered by the demands of the singers, who were quite capable of declining to sing any aria he had written if it did not please them. Leopold, in writing home on 10 November, asked Maria Anna to persuade their friends in Salzburg to send Wolfgang light-hearted letters to rouse him from time to time from his serious mood. Troger and their other friends in Milan also provided light relief, Troger inviting them for the weekend at least once to the estate he had just bought outside Milan.[48]

No doubt the experience of trying to stage *La finta semplice* in Vienna increased the nervousness of Leopold and Wolfgang. The first hurdle to

[44] Leopold to Maria Anna, 11 Aug. 1770—*MBA* 203 (*Letters* 107).
[45] Leopold to Maria Anna, 1 Sept. 1770—*MBA* 206/2–15 (*Letters* 110).
[46] Leopold to Maria Anna, 11 Aug. 1770—*MBA* 203/56–9 (*Letters* 107). Leopold tended to brood about affairs in Salzburg when he was depressed.
[47] Leopold to Maria Anna, 6 and 20 Oct. 1770—*MBA* 213 and 214 (*Letters* 116 and 117).
[48] Leopold to Maria Anna, 10 and 17 Nov. 1770—*MBA* 218 and 219 (*Letters* 120 and 121).

be overcome was that of pleasing the singers. On 3 November 1770 Leopold wrote:

otherwise I don't know what else to write to you about, except that (praise God) we're well, and wish that it were New Year's Day already, or at any rate *Christmas*: because until then there's always something or other to do, or something to think about, maybe from time to time a little irritation that makes one want to shit oranges, and consequently unsettled days. Patience! An awful lot of this undertaking, blessed be God, is safely over, and, God be praised, once more with honour! With God's help we too will nibble safely through the unavoidable irritations, which every Kapellmeister has to endure from the virtuosi scum, like Hanswurst through the Mountain of Mu– –.[49]

The types of irritation Leopold meant were dissatisfaction on the part of the singers with the music that had been written for them; the late arrival of one of the singers, which made it impossible for Wolfgang to write his music until the last minute; attempts by other composers to persuade the singers to sing arias written by them rather than those by Wolfgang; and rumours that the opera would be no good.[50] Though Leopold professed to be capable of trusting in God and tackling each problem patiently as it cropped up, there can be little doubt that he found this a very trying period. Harassed by all his problems, he had little mental and emotional capacity to spare for those parts of his letters relating to Maria Anna and Nannerl.[51]

According to custom, Wolfgang had to conduct the first three performances himself from the keyboard. Accordingly, on the evening of 26 December, he took his place at the keyboard, dressed in his new costume of scarlet lined with sky-blue satin and edged with gold, while Leopold watched and listened from a box above. According to Leopold's reports, the opera was highly successful; the theatre was full each evening, and encores were requested. With the hard work and the worry behind them, they were free to enjoy some recreation. They stayed up till two every morning to see the opera, slept late in the morning, played in a concert at Firmian's house, and saw a good deal of their friend Troger and his daughter, who gave Wolfgang his requested meal of liver dumplings and

---

[49] *MBA* 217/15–24 (*Letters* 119). Anderson, however, translates 'to shit oranges' ('Pomeranzen scheissen') as 'to foam at the mouth', and omits the reference to Hanswurst and the Mountain of Muck ('Dr– – –berg').

[50] Leopold to Maria Anna, 17 Nov. 1770 (*MBA* 219; *Letters* 121), and 24 Nov. 1770 (*MBA* 220; *Letters* 122); Leopold to Martini, 2 Jan. 1771 (*MBA* 226; *Letters* 128).

[51] See pp. 160–1 below for an example.

sauerkraut.[52] Wolfgang was also made an honorary member of Verona's Accademia Filarmonica.[53] After a trip to Turin, and a final dinner with Firmian, they left for Venice. Here they saw the end of the Carnival, were handsomely entertained by Hagenauer's friends the Wider family, and played to many members of the nobility. Leaving Venice on 14 March, they made their way home via Padua, Vicenza, Verona, Rovereto, Bressanone, and Innsbruck; and from Verona, on 18 March 1771, Leopold wrote to Maria Anna to tell her he was expecting two pieces of good news. One proved to be a commission from Maria Theresia for Wolfgang to write a *serenata teatrale* to celebrate the forthcoming marriage of the Archduke Ferdinand with Princess Maria Beatrice Ricciarda d'Este (whom the Mozarts had met at Firmian's); the other was a contract for him to write the first carnival opera for Milan in 1773.[54] So when they arrived home on Maundy Thursday, 28 March 1771, Leopold was in possession of the documents which would enable them to go twice more to Italy, assuming he could obtain more leave from Salzburg.

❧❦❧

Leopold had little time for anything, during this first Italian journey, except managing the tour. His letters home were much shorter than they had been previously, and he hardly ever answered letters other than those from Maria Anna. Instead, she had to pass on his news and give greetings to their friends. Though he continued to be relieved that he had left the women behind, he nevertheless regretted that they were not sharing the experiences with him and Wolfgang. All down the length of Italy they met people they had known on their previous travels, and sent back greetings from them to Maria Anna and Nannerl. They wrote home about the operas and balls they were attending; mentioned the churches, museums, architecture, and paintings they were seeing; made new friends, especially in Milan, and were invited to stay on country estates; visited several famous pilgrimage churches which the women would love to have seen; met the Pope; saw Vesuvius smoking, and visited some of the antiquities near Naples; sailed on the Mediterranean and saw the Adriatic; and experienced the Venetian Carnival, and rode in the noblemen's gondolas. Though he had no time to write at length about everything,

[52] Leopold to Martini, 2 Jan. 1771 (*MBA* 226; *Letters* 128); and to Maria Anna, 29 Dec. 1770 and 5 Jan. 1771 (*MBA* 225 and 227; *Letters* 127 and 129).

[53] Deutsch, *Documents*, 131–2.

[54] Leopold's letters to Maria Anna from 2 Feb. to 25 Mar. 1771—*MBA* 230, 231, 232, 233, 234, 236, and 238 (*Letters* 131, 132, 133, 134, 135, 136, and 137).

Leopold often referred Maria Anna and Nannerl to the guidebook they had at home.[55] He particularly wished that they could see Florence and Rome, and, of course, Wolfgang's opera.

Naturally the women occasionally lamented that they were missing all these things,[56] but they did not pine away in complete boredom for the whole fifteen months. Though their letters have not survived, it is possible to deduce some of their activities from the letters of Leopold and Wolfgang; and it seems clear that Nannerl, at any rate, used her initiative to enjoy a fairly active social life. She was 18 years old when the others left, and 19 when they returned. Though the evidence is lacking to show that she had serious admirers, her company was certainly enjoyed by at least two young bachelors in Salzburg. With one of these, Joseph Joachim Ferdinand von Schiedenhofen, she apparently entered into a lightly conspiratorial relationship involving the 'stealing' (as she apparently expressed it to Wolfgang) of minuet melodies by Michael Haydn, and their arrangement for the keyboard.

During the first phase of the absence of Leopold and Wolfgang, it was Carnival time in Salzburg as elsewhere. Leopold wrote expressing pleasure that the women were having such a lively time, and Wolfgang wanted to know what kind of costumes had been worn by Herr von Mölk and Herr von Schiedenhofen.[57] Both these men were in their early twenties, both came from respected Salzburg families, both had promising official court careers before them, and both clearly spent a good deal of time with Nannerl and Maria Anna during this period. Schiedenhofen belonged to the minor nobility, and his family possessed estates at Stumm (in the Ziller valley between Salzburg and Innsbruck) and at Triebenbach (outside Salzburg). By 'Herr von Mölk' Wolfgang probably meant Franz, the eldest of several sons of the court chancellor.[58]

Piecing together all the fragments of information from Leopold's and Wolfgang's letters from Italy, it seems that Nannerl and Schiedenhofen

[55] J. G. Keyssler, *Neueste Reisen durch Teutschland, Böhmen, Ungarn, die Schweiz, Italien und Lothringen*, 3 vols. (Hanover, 1751; 2nd edn. by G. Schütze, 1752).

[56] See e.g., Leopold to Maria Anna, 18 Sept. 1770—*MBA* 209/58–9 (*Letters* 113).

[57] Leopold to Maria Anna on 27 Feb. and Wolfgang to Nannerl on 3 Mar. 1770—*MBA* 162/19–20 (*Letters* 81) and *MBA* 164/16–19 (*Letters* 82a).

[58] The choice lies between Franz and Anton, since Albert was studying at the German College in Rome (where Leopold and Wolfgang visited him when they gave the concert with Meissner), and the other sons were too young to be called 'Herr'. As the eldest son, Franz is more likely to have been referred to as 'Herr von Mölk' than Anton (for whom the customary designation would have been 'Herr Anton'). In 1781 Franz was to be involved in a scandal so shocking that it was not recorded in court documents, and was banished from Salzburg on its account—see *MBA*, commentary to 611/26.

had met at some of the Salzburg balls, heard twelve minuets by Michael Haydn, and decided to make keyboard arrangements of them. Since 'no one' in Salzburg could do this, they sent them to Wolfgang—though Nannerl did one of them herself, and Wolfgang praised it highly.

The saga of the minuets was spun out over the whole period of Wolfgang's absence, and he, meanwhile, was sending to Schiedenhofen and Nannerl dances he had encountered or composed in Italy.[59] This suggests that Nannerl and Schiedenhofen might have been dancing together at this time, and since Schiedenhofen also often listened to Nannerl practising the keyboard,[60] the two presumably had a fairly close friendship.

Both Schiedenhofen and Mölk wrote regularly to Leopold from Salzburg. Leopold seldom had time to reply to their letters, so he used to send greetings to them via Maria Anna. He also asked his wife to pass on his thanks to Schiedenhofen and his mother after Maria Anna and Nannerl had been invited for a short stay, in the autumn of 1770, out to the Schiedenhofen country house at Triebenbach. Among the entertainments to be enjoyed there were country walks, playing charades, and shooting. Various friends staying at the same time as Maria Anna and Nannerl composed a medley of letters and verses for the name-days of Wolfgang and Leopold.[61]

If Mölk and Schiedenhofen were admirers of Nannerl during this period, then Schiedenhofen was almost certainly her favourite of the two. On 26 January 1770 Wolfgang wrote to Nannerl:

I'm really heartily delighted that you enjoyed yourself so much on that sleigh-ride, and I wish you a thousand opportunities for enjoyment, so that you pass your life really merrily. But one thing annoys me, that you let Herr von Mölk suffer and sigh so endlessly, and that you didn't go sleigh-riding with him, so that he could have bowled you over: how many hankies won't he have used that day, crying because of you; he will, of course, have taken two ounces of cream of tartar beforehand, which will have purged the dreadful dirtiness of his body.[62]

[59] See letters of 24 Mar., 14 Apr., 21 Apr., 25 Apr., 19 May, and 7 July 1770—*MBA* 168/6–7 (*Letters* 84a); *MBA* 176/81–8 (*Letters* 87); *MBA* 177/87–93 (*Letters* 88a, but with some draft material omitted), *MBA* 179/28–9 (*Letters* 89a), *MBA* 184/87–97 (*Letters* 92a), and *MBA* 197/25–7 (*Letters* 102a). Cliff Eisen, in a private communication, points out that the same minuet melodies were so often used by more than one composer that they were effectively common coin. Perhaps the reference to theft suggests, nevertheless, that a certain amount of stealth was used to prevent the initial taking over of someone else's melodies appearing too blatant.

[60] Leopold to Maria Anna, 21 Apr. 1770—*MBA* 177/35–7 (*Letters* 88).

[61] Leopold to Maria Anna, 10 Nov. 1770—*MBA* 218/2–8 (*Letters* 120, but not complete).

[62] *MBA* 158/2–10 (*Letters* 77a). There is an ambiguity of meaning in Wolfgang's comments about Mölk; while I translate his verb 'umschmeissen' as 'bowl over', Anderson gives 'upset'. It can mean both to tip or knock over and to stun in a figurative sense; Wolfgang might have been

After Wolfgang had made such encouraging remarks about her har-
monization of one of the Haydn minuets, Nannerl evidently tried her
hand at more composition, because on 7 July 1770 Wolfgang wrote praising a song she had sent him: 'I've been really surprised that you can
compose so beautifully, in a word, the song is lovely, and try something
more often.'[63] She also played the keyboard to visitors passing through
Salzburg, and she took part in three academies or concerts.[64] Putting all
these snippets of information about Nannerl together with the fact that
she was able to amuse Wolfgang throughout his first Italian tour by her
sense of fun and her wit (notably by the Italian greeting she sent him for
his name-day in October 1770),[65] the overall impression is that she knew
how to enjoy herself as well as to work, and that her love of fun had not
yet been quenched by cares.

Maria Anna's situation was quite different from Nannerl's, and she does
not emerge from the correspondence of the first Italian tour in such a
positive light. Her duties while Leopold and Wolfgang were away were
chiefly household ones, which she must have been teaching to Nannerl.
Countless references from the Mozart correspondence, and from court
documents such as pension appeals, show that a woman's claim to respect
rested on an unimpeachable moral reputation and the ability to manage
a household economically. Since salaries were often barely adequate for
the needs of a family, women had to exercise skill and ingenuity to make
ends meet. As well as shopping carefully and cooking proficiently, they
had to be capable of preserving foods in season, making up commonly
needed medicaments such as lotions,[66] and all kinds of needlework. Old
clothes were cut up and made into something new, outworn knitted

---

suggesting that Mölk's sledge driving was poor, or that he would have wanted to make an impression on Nannerl. Given Wolfgang's love of word play, he probably intended both meanings to
be registered.

[63] *MBA* 197/24–5 (*Letters* 102a).

[64] Leopold to Maria Anna, 6 Oct. 1770 and 5 Jan. 1771—*MBA* 213/20–2 (*Letters* 116) and
MBA 227/11–15 (*Letters* 129).

[65] Wolfgang to Nannerl, 3 Nov. 1770—*MBA* 217/35–44 (*Letters* 119a).

[66] The domestic preparation of medicaments involved labour now difficult to grasp. The book
of household medicine used by the Mozarts vividly shows how alien are the ideas of medical care
then being practised. It specifies hosts of ingredients—a few of them familiar to modern kitchens,
many half-familiar as herbs, and others (animal droppings, horns, contents of glands, feathers) bizarre.
These were boiled, simmered, left to stand, boiled again, stood in the sun, stood in a cool place,
strained, skimmed, distilled, and so forth. The application was just as complicated, and often formed
part of a dietary, exercise, and rest routine that made normal life impossible. See Eleonora Maria
Rosalia, Duchess of Troppau and Jägerndorf, *Freywillig aufgesprungener Granat-Apffel des Christlichen
Samariters* (Leipzig, 1709). *MBA* 1026/86–7 (not in *Letters*) reveals this book to have been used by
the Mozarts.

garments were unravelled and reknitted, and patching and mending went on constantly. Within the Mozart family, Maria Anna apparently rose early and worked diligently to achieve all this, and Nannerl was later to follow her example, to the admiration first of Leopold and later of her husband.[67]

Maria Anna also offered prayers for the well-being of the travellers, worried about their health, and broadcast news of Wolfgang's triumphs to influential people in Salzburg. All these things were well within her sphere of competence. But she also had to handle the marketing of Leopold's *Violinschule*, and since a number of her letters to Leopold during this period evidently complained about rising prices in Salzburg,[68] the *Violinschule* sales were more than usually important. Here, however, she was slightly out of her depth. She did not like writing letters, and because Leopold insisted on controlling all business matters himself, she was not good at dealing with those areas of life habitually undertaken by him. As early as 7 January 1770, Leopold was sending her instructions about the *Violinschule*:

Have no letters come from Herr Lotter about the safe receipt of the money? — — hasn't Herr Breitkopf in Leipzig written to say whether he's received the 100 books? — — Have the books been sent to Vienna, and has Herr Gräffer reported their arrival? — — you only have to tell me about these things in a few words . . . Meanwhile, put together *12 copies of the Violinschule*, and send them to *Joseph Wolf's* bookshop, in Insprugg. if I'm not mistaken, the man who runs this business in Insprugg is called Felicius or Felicianus Fischer. You can find out from Mayr's printing house. You only need to enclose a short letter. something like this: *You receive here 12 copies of the Violinschule, which my husband, from Verona, has told me to send you. You may keep them on commission, according to the arrangement, and sell each one at 2fl. 15kr. tyrolean coinage, and reimburse my husband at 1 fl. 45 kr. in the same coinage for the ones sold: you may put this in the paper and charge the costs to my husband in this case.*[69]

And so it went on, Leopold reminding Maria Anna what to do when, and writing pedantic little letters for her to copy out. On 8 September 1770 he expressed irritation that she had not used her initiative to promote the sales:

---

[67] See Leopold to Maria Anna and Wolfgang, 27 Oct. 1777—*MBA* 357/68–71 (*Letters* 230a); and the will of Nannerl's husband, which specifically mentioned her capable housekeeping—Brno, MZA, Berchtold Family Archive, clause 2 of the will of Johann Baptist von Berchtold zu Sonnenburg.

[68] See Leopold to Maria Anna, 5 June, 11 Aug., 1 Sept., and 27 Oct. 1770—*MBA* 189/50–5 (not in *Letters*), *MBA* 203/57–9 (*Letters* 107), *MBA* 206/27–9 (*Letters* 110), and *MBA* 216/44–61 (*Letters* 118, with a slight omission).

[69] *MBA* 152/98–119 (not in *Letters*).

Have some books been sent to Herr otto in Frankfurt? — — It's high time. if they haven't been sent, and it's already too late for Herr Wallner to take at least 15 copies with him, or to send them on ahead, the safest way is to write immediately to *Herr Johann Jacob Lotter, printer and music publisher* in augsburg, *resident not far from the Voglthor,* and tell him that he should send 24 copies straight away to *Herr David otto, organist to the Barefeet, resident not far from the Leonardsthor in Frankfort am Mayn,* so that they'll still arrive for the Frankfort fair. you'll get this letter on the 15th; so you must write straight away on the 17th, that way Herr Lotter will get the letter on the 19th; and can make arrangements straight away. But if, as I hope, some books have already been sent to Frankfort; inasmuch as I wrote to you that I was amazed you'd asked about it, since you could see, or should have been able to see, from Herr otto's letter and from the specification I left behind, that he'd paid for all the books he'd had, consequently I told you from Naples that he should be sent some: so if, as I say, some have already been sent; Herr Wallner can still be given another *6 copies* or as many as he can take with him now. I can't think about everything, and I expected you two to deal with that kind of thing at home, to think about it, remind me in good time, and look after the interests of us all diligently, since you know how many things I've got to think about; and *NB* Frankfort is one of the best places.[70]

❧

Because the correspondence of the first Italian journey is the first surviving body of letters written by the members of the family to each other, some impression can be formed of the relationships within the family at this period. However, there are two main hindrances: the letters from the women have not survived; and there is virtually nothing from Leopold to Nannerl, or from Wolfgang to Maria Anna.

The pattern of letter-writing suggests that they had agreed that Leopold would write to Maria Anna, while Wolfgang would write to Nannerl. Leopold did not often write even short messages to Nannerl; he tended merely to include her in his stock final sentence, which typically sent them both a thousand, ten thousand, or a million kisses. Occasionally he told her where to find music, asked whether she was practising, suggested she sing (but only as much as was good for her chest), and exhorted her to write frequently to Wolfgang. Once he praised her industry, and once he told her that her playing had been praised by an acquaintance they had met in Italy.[71] He did not comment on the compositional exercises

[70] *MBA* 207/23–44 (not in *Letters*).
[71] Leopold to Maria Anna, 24 Mar. 1770 and 5 Jan. 1771—*MBA* 170/66–8 (*Letters* 84) and *MBA* 227/11–15 (*Letters* 129).

she sent for them to see. Doubtless his neglect of her was caused partly by the vexations he underwent on the journey, partly by preoccupation with the injury to his shin, and partly by occasional spells of depression. When he believed (mistakenly) that he had forgotten to send greetings for her name-day, he did not try to make amends by offering them belatedly, or by apologizing, but simply followed up his comment by saying that he had suffered melancholy thoughts while his foot was troubling him.[72] On the other hand, he rebuked Nannerl caustically (and unjustly) for having failed to send greetings both for his and for Wolfgang's name-day. Though his very next sentence stated that he now recollected that she had sent Wolfgang an Italian greeting, he did not apologize for his mistake, saying merely that his head had been full of business matters.[73] This aspect of his character was presumably well known to the other members of the family (later he was to be cutting to Wolfgang, too), but it is difficult to believe that it was not hurtful.[74]

Leopold wrote all the main news to Maria Anna. As well as the accounts of their activities, he reported on the state of the Church in Italy, expressed concern about her health and Nannerl's, urged her not to worry if she did not receive letters when she was expecting them, since the postal service was very erratic, and was pleased when she and Nannerl had been enjoying themselves. Though his manner was often curt, therefore, there was apparently no lack of underlying affection and consideration.

Wolfgang's messages to his mother on this Italian tour, like Leopold's to Nannerl, were almost non-existent. The first letter of all, that of 14 December 1769, included a merry passage written specifically to her;[75] but thereafter he tended simply to add a line of greeting for Maria Anna to his letters to Nannerl. Occasionally he asked Maria Anna to pray for him and, towards the end of his long absence, he expressed a longing for them all to be living together again.[76] It is possible that he was already finding that he had little to say to his mother. Certainly by the time he made the journey to Paris with her in 1777, he was apparently to find her company tedious and her presence little more than a nuisance.[77]

---

[72] Leopold to Maria Anna, 11 Aug. 1770—*MBA* 203/56–9 (*Letters* 107).

[73] Leopold to Maria Anna, 17 Nov. 1770—*MBA* 219/2–17 (*Letters* 121).

[74] Leopold hinted as much on 1 Dec. 1770—*MBA* 221/3–11 (*Letters* 123). In this passage, he explained that shortly after dispatching his complaint that the women had forgotten his name-day, he had received their greeting; whereupon Wolfgang had expressed concern that the women would be hurt by his letter.

[75] *MBA* 147/24–31 (*Letters* 71*a*).

[76] Wolfgang to Maria Anna, 20 Oct. 1770—*MBA* 214/57–65 (*Letters* 117*a*).

[77] See Chs. 17 and 18.

It is therefore in Wolfgang's letters to Nannerl that the best glimpses of his character through his own pen are given. On 14 December 1769, just after they had left Salzburg, he wrote in Italian, '... if I must confess the truth, I have to say that travelling is very merry, and that it's not cold at all, and that in our carriage it's as warm as in a room ... if you see Herr von Schidenhofen, tell him that I'm always singing: Tralaliera, Tralaliera, and tell him that it's not necessary to add sugar to my soup now, since I'm not in Salzburg ...'.[78] On 7 January 1770 he wrote, 'Dearest sister, I've had an aching feeling because I've been waiting so long in vain for an answer ...'.[79] On 17 February 1770 it was, 'I'm here too, now you've got me: I say, Mariandel, I rejoice with all my arse that you've been so frightfully merry ... addio, children, farewell, I kiss Mama's hands a thousand times, and to you, I send a hundred kisses or smackers on your wonderful horseface ...'.[80] And on 24 March 1770, 'Oh you busy thing you! ... Every post day, when the German letters come, my food and drink taste much better ...'.[81] On 19 May 1770 he wrote, 'I really like the twelfth minuet by haiden that you sent me, and you've composed the bass to it incomparably well, and without the slightest mistake, and I beg you try this kind of thing more often ...'.[82] On 16 June 1770 he wrote about the sea: 'I'm still alive too, and am always as merry as ever, and like travelling: now I've been sailing on the Muckyterranean Sea too.'[83] And on 4 August 1770 he teased her about her singing: 'Does Herr *Deibl* come often? does he still honour you both with his entertaining conversation? And the honourable Karl von Vogt? does he still deign to listen to your unbearable voice? *Herr von Schidenhofen* should help you diligently to write minuets, otherwise he won't get any sugar lumps!'[84] From Pallavicini's estate outside Bologna he wrote on 21 August 1770: 'I'm still alive too, and in fact very merry. today I had the urge to ride a donkey, because it's the custom in italy, and so I thought I really should try it too.'[85] And from Venice, on 20 February 1771, he sent a message to Hagenauer's son Johann Nepomuk Anton about the Wider daughters:

I'm still alive too ... tell Herr Joanes that the wider pearls are always talking about him, especially Mad^{lle} catharina, and he should come back to Venice soon NB: to submit to the attáca, that is, to allow his backside to be smacked on the floor, in order to become a real Venetian: they wanted to do it to me too,

[78] *MBA* 147/33–9 (*Letters* 71*b*).
[79] *MBA* 153/3–4 (*Letters* 75*a*).
[80] *MBA* 161/51–9 (*Letters* 80*a*).
[81] *MBA* 168/1–4 (*Letters* 84*a*).
[82] *MBA* 184/94–7 (*Letters* 92*a*).
[83] *MBA* 191/40–1 (*Letters* 98*a*).
[84] *MBA* 202/58–61 (*Letters* 106*a*).
[85] *MBA* 204/36–8 (*Letters* 108*a*).

all seven women got together to help, and yet they couldn't get me onto the floor....[86]

These and other passages suggest that Wolfgang was not only at the centre of the family on account of his extraordinary talents, but that he was also its life and soul. His disposition was affectionate, generous, and merry, and he was always able to entertain the others. At the same time, he was dependent on their loving attention to him. Despite all the problems of his later life, he was to keep both traits—his gaiety, and his need to be loved.

[86] *MBA* 232/33–9 (*Letters* 133*a*).

10

The First Quest for an Honourable Appointment: Wolfgang's Second Visit to Italy

⁓⤜⤛⁓

WOLFGANG's commission to compose a *serenata teatrale* to celebrate the marriage of Archduke Ferdinand to Princess Maria Beatrice Ricciarda d'Este was the visible purpose of the second trip to Italy. Beneath the news of the progress of the composition, rehearsals, and performances of *Ascanio in Alba* (K. 111), however, can be detected Leopold's desire to act to improve the working and financial conditions of his family. Wolfgang was now $15\frac{1}{2}$ years old and, though there was still ample time for him to secure a good appointment of his own, Leopold was now starting to look for suitable opportunities. The importance of this quest has often been overlooked in writing about this period of Wolfgang's life. The success of *Ascanio*, Wolfgang's extreme youth, and the fact that Leopold had a job which could still support them all, have contributed to a tendency to see the venture simply as the next in a long line of youthful triumphs, and to underestimate the difficulties facing Leopold at this time.

On the one hand there was the dissatisfaction with Salzburg, since observance of the careers of musicians there did not inspire confidence in Leopold that the outlook for Wolfgang was bright. On the other hand there was the difficulty of moving elsewhere, since this would involve two members of the same family seeking employment together. These problems need to be borne in mind in order to understand why Leopold, after years of hard work educating his son, could not afford to relax his efforts on Wolfgang's behalf.

To take first the events surrounding the composition of *Ascanio*, Leopold and Wolfgang left Salzburg on 13 August 1771 and travelled to Milan, arriving in the evening of 21 August. There they took lodgings in the same house they had inhabited when Wolfgang had been composing his opera *Mitridate* in the late autumn of 1770. Other musicians connected with the archduke's marital celebrations were also lodged there. On 24 August 1771 Wolfgang wrote to Nannerl, 'above our room is a violinist, beneath it another, next to it a singing master who gives lessons, in the last room by ours is an oboist. that's fun when you're composing! gives you plenty of ideas.'[1]

Milan was in a ferment of activity because of preparations for the wedding. The most important musical events were to be Hasse's grand opera *Il Ruggiero ovvero L'eroica gratitudine* and Wolfgang's work *Ascanio in Alba*. The wedding itself was to take place on 15 October, and when the Mozarts arrived in Milan, the libretto of *Ascanio* had still not arrived from Vienna. Until it did so, the music could not be written or the scenery and costumes made, but preparations for the public spectacles were under way, and Leopold reported seeing twenty thousand pounds of wax candles in readiness for the illuminations.[2] In Firmian's household there was also great activity. Germani, Firmian's steward and the Mozarts' friend from 1770, was about to enter the service of Archduke Ferdinand as his Controller. On 31 August Leopold was able to report the arrival of Wolfgang's libretto and also of Hasse;[3] and on 21 September he described their dealings with the singers, and the turmoil occasioned by last-minute preparations such as the decoration of the theatre, the illuminations, and the liveries, carriages, and horses.[4] By the end of September rehearsals were beginning for both Hasse's and Wolfgang's works, and on 12 October Leopold reported that important wedding guests (among them Count Joseph Gottfried Saurau, a canon of Salzburg Cathedral) had begun to arrive in Milan, that the town was swarming with people, and that the military was enforcing strict security precautions.[5] The wedding took place as arranged on 15 October, Hasse's opera (deemed grander and more important than Wolfgang's *serenata*) was given its first performance on the following day, and *Ascanio* on 17 October. Thereafter, both works were given a number of times more. According to Leopold, *Ascanio* was such a success that it was repeated on 19 October, a day originally set aside (with 18 and 20 October) for mourning the death of Maria Theresia's father on 20 October 1740.[6] Leopold had already, on 21 September 1771, implied that Wolfgang's

---

[1] *MBA* 242/48–50 (*Letters* 140*a*).
[2] Leopold to Maria Anna, 24 Aug. 1771—*MBA* 242 (*Letters* 140).
[3] *MBA* 243 (*Letters* 141, but not complete).   [4] *MBA* 246/2–24 (*Letters* 144).
[5] *MBA* 249 (*Letters* 147).
[6] Leopold to Maria Anna, 12 and 19 Oct. 1771—*MBA* 249/41–4 (*Letters* 147); and *MBA* 250 (*Letters* 148).

work was in effect not inferior to Hasse's in scale;[7] now on 19 October 1771, with typical barely concealed superiority, he wrote, 'The archduke has recently ordered two copies. all the noblemen and other people constantly address us in the street to congratulate Wolfgang. In short! *I'm sorry*, Wolfgang's Serenata has so crushed Hasse's opera that I can't describe it.'[8]

On 8 November 1771 Leopold and Wolfgang dined at Firmian's with Hasse, and both Wolfgang and Hasse were rewarded with presents for their work.[9] The Mozarts should now have been free to leave, but the archduke, absent for a short while in Varese, had indicated that he wanted to see them when he returned. Whilst waiting for him, they gave a concert at the house of Ferdinand's privy paymaster, Albert Michael von Mayr.[10] The reason for the interview with Ferdinand was almost certainly the possibility of Wolfgang's being taken on in the service of the archduke, but the Mozarts had to leave Milan before they had received an answer from him.[11] On 5 December 1771 they departed, and on 15 December they arrived home. The day after their arrival, Archbishop Schrattenbach died, so the Chapter entered into the *Sedisvacanz* routine, and the procedure for electing the next prince-archbishop was set in motion.

❧

The Mozarts had presumably hoped that Wolfgang would be given a salary for his duties as Konzertmeister on his return in March 1771 from the first journey to Italy. But he had not been, and to make matters worse Schrattenbach had decreed that Leopold's salary was not to be paid during his absence on the second journey to Italy.[12] Furthermore, as the correspondence from the first Italian trip shows, there was price inflation in Salzburg during the early 1770s, making life more difficult for everyone on low, static, court salaries. Leopold thus had grounds for increasing dissatisfaction with working conditions there, and there was

---

[7] *MBA* 246/12–15 (*Letters* 144). Leopold said that the *serenata* was really a small opera, and that the music in the opera only appeared longer because there were two ballets lasting three quarters of an hour each. He surely meant that Wolfgang's work (if one excepted the ballets in Hasse's opera) was on the same scale as Hasse's. Anderson's translation of this passage, however, misleadingly suggests that it was *Ascanio* which was padded out by ballets.

[8] *MBA* 250/5–9 (*Letters* 148). The *Notizie del Mondo* gave a report to the same effect on 26 Oct. 1771—see Eisen, *Documents*, 35.

[9] Leopold to Maria Anna, 9 Nov. 1771—*MBA* 255/4–9 (*Letters* 151).

[10] Leopold to Maria Anna, 16 and 24 or 23 Nov. 1771—*MBA* 256 and 257 (*Letters* 152 and 153).

[11] Leopold's remark to Maria Anna on 8 Dec. 1771, written from Ala on the way home, that the matter she had asked him about was 'not hopeless' ('nicht leer') probably refers to the interview with Ferdinand. See *MBA* 259/10–12 (*Letters* 155).

[12] See Deutsch, *Documents*, 135–6.

a hidden purpose in the second journey to Italy. His hope was that Wolfgang's activities there might lead either to advancement in Salzburg, or to a good offer at a different court.

When *Ascanio* proved so successful, Maria Anna must have written to express the hope that Wolfgang might be offered the next vacant salary in Salzburg. On 16 November 1771 Leopold replied that he very much doubted it.[13] The background to his pessimistic remark was his twenty-five years' experience of the vagaries of the employment conditions in Salzburg. For although there were some general trends in career progression, there were also gross inconsistencies, anomalies, and downright unfairnesses. These made it impossible to assess from precedent the likelihood of preferment, and fostered an atmosphere of seething discontent. A few examples from Leopold's lifetime may help illustrate some of the peculiarities of the system.

Among the composers, until the accession of Archbishop Colloredo in 1772, the career progression to the position of Kapellmeister was relatively orderly. A man tended to be engaged at a low level, as Leopold had been, and by composing diligently would work his way up to the position of Vice-Kapellmeister and then Kapellmeister. Strange things had nevertheless been known to happen. When the Kapellmeister Biechteler von Greiffenthal had died in 1743, Karl Heinrich von Bibern advanced to his position from Vice-Kapellmeister, and the then organist Eberlin expected to be promoted to Vice-Kapellmeister. But the tenor singer Lolli apparently pushed aside Eberlin by offering to occupy the position of Vice-Kapellmeister without a salary increase. The outrage this caused among the musicians was such that they had to be commanded to show respect to Lolli, and when von Bibern died in 1749 Lolli was not further promoted to Kapellmeister. He remained Vice-Kapellmeister, and Eberlin leapfrogged over him to occupy the position of Kapellmeister.[14] Not until Eberlin died in 1762 did Lolli advance to Kapellmeister in 1763, on the same occasion that Leopold became Vice-Kapellmeister.[15]

Questions of salary, leave, and other benefits such as *Schatulle* payments were even more inconsistent. Promotions and titles did not necessarily bring with them an increased salary. Lolli served ten years as Vice-Kapellmeister (admittedly at his own suggestion) before his salary

---

[13] *MBA* 256/15–17 (*Letters* 152).

[14] See Hintermaier, 'Hofkapelle', 75–80; and M. Cuvay, 'Beiträge zur Lebensgeschichte des Salzburger Hofkapellmeisters Johann Ernst Eberlin', *MGSL* 95 (1955), 182–3. The claim about Lolli's sly behaviour comes from the diary of the St Peter's monk Otto Gutrather. Cuvay cites the court document commanding the musicians to respect Lolli.

[15] See Ch. 3 for details of Leopold's promotion.

was raised and he was given free lodgings and an extra food allowance in 1753; and no further increase was forthcoming on his appointment to Kapellmeister in 1763.[16] Leopold served several years without pay as a young man, and did not receive a salary increase when he became Vice-Kapellmeister in 1763.[17] In 1769, when Leopold had not only been granted paid leave for the first journey to Italy, but had also been given 120 ducats (600 fl.) from the *Schatulle*, Meissner had also applied for leave to go to Italy, and for a loan of 300 fl. to help with his expenses. The leave was granted, but not the loan. Meissner had already submitted to the court a long and bitter set of complaints in August 1769. Among his grievances were the fact that he was being paid less than one of the instrumentalists, though as a singer he had more duties; he ought to be entitled to a free lodging; he had never been given anything from the *Schatulle*; the allowance of Tyrolean wine for the benefit of his voice had been withdrawn without compensation; and, unlike other musicians, he was given no help with the expense of educating his son at Kremsmünster. He also complained that, when opera was performed at court, he not only sang in it but helped coach the female singers; and that his teaching in the Kapellhaus was of such a high standard that boys could now sing the parts formerly taken by four castrati, thus saving the court some 3,000 fl. annually.[18]

There is some evidence to suggest that on occasions (perhaps when it was especially necessary to make economies), families living under the same roof with more than one member in court service were expected to accept a disadvantageous financial position, at least in the short term. In 1758 Eberlin's unmarried daughter Maria Franziska was appointed as a singer at a salary of 100 fl. annually. At that time her father, as Kapellmeister, was earning 581 fl. 40 kr. annually, a figure which included a wine, bread, and wood allowance. He also had a free lodging, and the joint emoluments of him and his daughter could therefore be said to be handsome by Salzburg standards. In 1760 or 1761 Maria Franziska's salary was increased to 120 fl. per annum, but when Eberlin died in 1762 his salary was lost to the family (though his widow would have received a pension). In 1763 Eberlin's widow died, and his daughter Maria Franziska was granted what she claimed to consider a salary increase of 60 fl. annually, giving her altogether 180 fl. But when she married Nikolaus Strasser in 1764 it became clear that the court thought of this extra 60 fl. as a pension, because it was promptly withdrawn.[19] Taking now the case of the Meissner family, Joseph Nikolaus

---

[16] See Hintermaier, 'Hofkapelle', 232.   [17] See ibid. 290.   [18] See ibid. 263–73.
[19] See ibid. 75–80 and 81–3.

Meissner's father Nikolaus served the court as violinist and horn player from 1723 until his death in 1760. From 1758 old Nikolaus's salary was 282 fl. annually, including the allowance for bread and wine; while his son the bass singer, who had been appointed in 1747, was earning 378 fl. plus the *Hoftafel* (dining rights) and his Kapellhaus teaching increment. Nikolaus's daughter, the unmarried Maria Elisabeth Sabina, was appointed as a singer in 1759 at the very low salary, even by comparison with the other female singers, of 60 fl. annually. It has been suggested that the reason for her exceptionally low salary was the fact that two other members of her family were also drawing salaries from the Salzburg court; and in support of this argument it has been noted that immediately after her father's death in 1760 her salary was increased to 120 fl. annually.[20] Tending to work against this argument, however, is the fact that Maria Franziska Eberlin had been appointed only a year before Maria Elisabeth Sabina Meissner at a higher starting salary, even though her father was in receipt of a relatively high salary. Despite the lack of complete consistency in the cases of the Meissner and Eberlin female singers, however, they show that, on occasions at least, emoluments were determined according to the perceived need of a family rather than to the deserts of the employees.

When an employee died in Salzburg, and a salary was vacated, the results were various. Dependants were generally provided with a small pension, and the rest of the money saved might be used either to create a new post, or to give increases to some of the colleagues of the deceased, or—for nothing of any advantage to the department concerned. In 1765 the three female singers Braunhofer, Fesemayr, and Lipp had been appointed. Each started at a salary of 100 fl. annually, though their female colleagues Eberlin and Meissner were by this time both receiving 120 fl. But when Maria Franziska Eberlin (who had changed her name to Strasser on her marriage in 1764) died in 1766, Braunhofer, Fesemayr, and Lipp immediately had their salaries increased to 120 fl. annually, bringing them up to the same level as Meissner. They profited financially, therefore, by the death of their colleague.[21] On the other hand, when Eberlin died, the court saved his salary of 581 fl. 40 kr. without apparently using much of it elsewhere in the court music; neither Lolli, who succeeded Eberlin as Kapellmeister, nor Leopold Mozart, who succeeded Lolli as Vice-Kapellmeister, gained any increase in salary.[22]

---

[20] See ibid. 263, 274, and 277.   [21] See ibid. 45, 109, and 227.
[22] See ibid. 232 and 290.

The difficulty facing those awaiting a salaried appointment or an increase in salary was that there was no way of knowing from precedent how likely such preferment was. Leopold had learnt directly from his own experience that when money was saved by someone's death, other colleagues did not necessarily benefit. He therefore had no grounds for optimism in 1771 that Wolfgang might soon gain a salary of his own, and must have thought himself justified in seeking an appointment for Wolfgang elsewhere. It is this desire which almost certainly lies behind some of the laconic remarks in his letters from the second Italian journey. On 7 September 1771, for example, he wrote to his wife,

It was nothing extraordinary to me that the archduke Maximilian has been made a canon: after all, since my return from Italy I've been saying everywhere in Salzburg that it would happen. the rest will come to pass too: just have patience! I'm sorry I can't write everything. Salzburg is not the only object of this first step! — — — — —[23]

This passage, obscure though it seems at first, can cautiously be interpreted in accordance with Leopold's ambitions during this period. Maria Anna had obviously reported the news about Archduke Maximilian, who was the youngest son of the empress and the same age as Wolfgang; he was destined for the Church. Leopold was in the habit of making predictions, and rarely missed the opportunity of boasting when one of them proved accurate. In this passage, therefore, it seems highly probable that 'the rest' which would also come to pass was another prediction of his, already well known to Maria Anna; and since it was obviously of a private family nature and was appended to his reference to Maximilian, it is highly plausible that it concerned the likelihood of Wolfgang's gaining service with one or other of the Habsburgs. The last sentence, about Salzburg, almost certainly means that one result of the composition of *Ascanio* might be an improvement in their position there, but that Leopold had his eye on opportunities elsewhere too.

Leopold had always been indefatigable in wooing possible patrons, and from now on he pursued the same policy with more fervour than ever, in order to maximize Wolfgang's chances of a promising appointment. The Habsburg interests in Italy, and the fact that there were members of the empress's family still to be settled or only recently settled, meant that there were interesting possibilities of patronage to be exploited. Archduke Ferdinand, for whose wedding *Ascanio* was composed, was just setting up

[23] *MBA* 244/14–18 (not in *Letters*).

his own household and might be persuaded to take on Wolfgang.[24] Because of Ferdinand's extreme youth (he was 17 years old on marriage), it is reasonable to believe that he might take advice from Firmian or his new Controller Germani, both of whom Leopold had done his best to befriend. When Leopold and Wolfgang had arrived in Milan, Firmian and his secretary Troger were out of town, and were to pass through Salzburg on their way back. In his letters of 18 and 31 August 1771, Leopold told Maria Anna and Nannerl to be sure that Troger presented them to Firmian in Salzburg.[25] Behind his instructions almost certainly lay more than mere politeness and gratitude for past favours; Leopold also had his mind on the possible future usefulness of these people. A similar motive probably lay behind Leopold's letter of 19 July 1771 to Pallavicini, a letter whose ostensible purpose was to bring Pallavicini up to date with Wolfgang's achievements and commissions since they had spent the summer of 1770 with him on his estate outside Bologna.[26] They did not expect to see Pallavicini on this trip to Italy, but the fact that he was a prominent Italian nobleman in the service of the Habsburgs was sufficient reason for the letter; Leopold was astute and energetic enough to lay long-term plans.

But the situation facing Leopold was one of considerable difficulty because of Wolfgang's youth. It is hardly conceivable that he would have allowed his 15-year-old son to take up an appointment which involved his living away from his family. Although many young Salzburg people did so, Leopold was not the man to believe that anyone else could supervise his children as well as he could. On 18 March 1771, writing from Verona on the way home from the first Italian journey, Leopold had sent a message to the Salzburg merchant Kerschbaumer through Maria Anna. Kerschbaumer's son Franz Xaver was in Verona and was about to go to Venice; so Leopold recommended Kerschbaumer to place Franz Xaver under the protection there of Wider, the friend first of the Hagenauers and then of the Mozarts, in order to safeguard him from the perils of 'the most dangerous place in the whole of Italy'.[27] Franz Xaver Kerschbaumer was 27 years old at the time, but as a single man he was still in need of the guidance of safe company, according to Leopold.

---

[24] On 28 Sept. 1771 Leopold had told Maria Anna that singers had already been recruited for Ferdinand's new establishment—*MBA* 247/9–13 (*Letters* 145). Anderson's translation, however, is incorrect, giving the impression that the recruitment of singers was for the archbishop's musical establishment in Salzburg.

[25] *MBA* 241/41–3 (*Letters* 139) and *MBA* 243/30–2 (not in *Letters*).

[26] *MBA* 239 (not in *Letters*).   [27] *MBA* 236/38–46 (*Letters* 136).

How much more delicate, therefore, would Wolfgang's age and situation have appeared to Leopold; quite apart from the fact that he had invested so much time from his own best years in bringing up his children that he was more emotionally dependent on them than many parents.

Bearing in mind this difficulty, Leopold almost certainly had his eye on two possibilities. Either he and Wolfgang might gain a dual appointment; or Wolfgang might gain a title which would allow him to continue to live in Salzburg until he was older, meanwhile supplying his new patron with compositions in return for money. The fact that Leopold took two copies of his *Violinschule* to Italy with him on this second visit, bound in the Italian way (as he mentioned to Maria Anna on 21 September 1771), supports the supposition that he wanted to promote his own work as well as Wolfgang's.[28] But the difficulty in obtaining a dual appointment was more than twice that of a single one, because if both Mozarts were to be taken on they would inevitably bring two dependent women with them, with all that that implied in terms of possible future pensions. On 12 December 1771, while Leopold and Wolfgang were on their way home from Milan still hoping that their interview with Ferdinand might produce the desired result, Maria Theresia, whom Ferdinand had asked for advice on the matter, replied in extremely negative terms, stating that the Mozarts were useless beggars who would degrade the service of their patrons, and that Wolfgang had a large family. Behind the particular remark about the size of his family might have lain her concern about pensions.[29] Her reply as a whole, which Leopold would have found crushing had he known of it, suggests a number of possibilities about the kind of service the archduke had been considering for Wolfgang. Since Leopold was not mentioned, a dual appointment was apparently not envisaged; but Wolfgang might perhaps have commanded a salary greater than Leopold's 354 fl. in Salzburg, enabling Leopold to offer his own services as it were for nothing, with the possibility of his and Nannerl's gradually acquiring private teaching as supplementary forms of income. Alternatively, Wolfgang might have been offered a title in return for compositions, enabling him to continue living in Salzburg until he became old enough to leave his parents' household. Whatever the situation was, it does seem certain that his family was considered a negative factor in the decision; and, more ominously, the Mozarts were considered by Maria Theresia highly undesirable as employees, a fact that could well blight all future attempts to establish Wolfgang with any

---

[28] *MBA* 246/73–8 (not in *Letters*).   [29] The passage is quoted in Ch. 8, pp. 136–7.

member of the Habsburg dynasty, and render all Leopold's efforts in these directions futile.

❧

On 7 September 1771 Leopold asked Maria Anna whether she had received his salary for August.[30] What seems to have happened is that he had been informed verbally before leaving home in mid-August that his salary would be stopped during his absence; but that this verbal decision was not relayed to the Court Pay Office immediately, and the salary was mistakenly paid for the whole of August and September. On 16 October 1771 a decree was issued which cancelled it;[31] but Count Saurau, a canon of the cathedral in Salzburg, after witnessing the success of *Ascanio* (whose first performance took place on 17 October), wrote a favourable report of the events in Milan to the court chancellor, Franz Felix von Mölk. Mölk passed on the news to Archbishop Schrattenbach, and on the basis of this report, Leopold hoped to have his lost salary for October and November restored when he arrived home in mid-December. Schrattenbach, however, was dying as they returned and the petition, written after his death, had therefore to be addressed to the cathedral Chapter, which governed Salzburg during the *Sedisvacanz*. There is some scope for misunderstanding in the wording of Leopold's submission,[32]

---

[30] *MBA* 244/39 (*Letters* 142).   [31] Deutsch, *Documents*, 135–6.

[32] The relevant part of the petition in German (*MBA* 261/17–29) reads: 'HöchstGedacht S:ᵉ hochf: Gnaden ertheilten uns zwar die Erlaubniß zur Reise doch mit Zurückhaltung meiner ohnehin nur in 28f 30 xʳ bestehenden Besoldung, die jedoch aus übersehung noch anderthalb Monat ausgefolgt wurde. nachdem aber ein Schreiben von S:ʳ Hochgräfl. Excellenz H: Grafen von Sauerau an tit: H: HofCanzler erfolgte, durch welches erstgedacht S:ᵉ Excellenz S:ʳ Hochf: Gnaden die vergnügte Nachricht von dem allgemeinen Beyfall und der Ehre, der sich mein Sohn gemacht, zu geben glaubte; so gaben S:ᵉ Hochf: Gnaden also gleich Befehle die Besoldung einzuhalten. Es gelanget demnach an Euer Hochwürden Hochgräf: Excellenzien meine gnädige Herrn das unterthänigste Anlangen und Bitten mir diesen nur aus 2 Monaten bestehenden Abzug *pr: 59f*, nämlich *pro Octobre und Novembre* gnädigst ausfolgen zu lassen...' Anderson's translation of this passage (*Letters* 157) reads: 'His Grace gave us leave to travel but at the same time suspended my salary which, as it is, amounts only to 28 gulden 30 kreuzer a month, and which, through an oversight, I was permitted to draw for a further month and a half. His Excellency the Count von Sauerau wrote, however, to the Court Chancellor and sent him the pleasant news of the unanimous applause and the honour which my son had won for himself. Whereupon His Grace immediately gave me leave to retain the sum already paid. I am submitting, therefore, to Your Excellencies and most gracious Lords my most humble request that the small amount deducted, that is, 59 gulden for the months of October and November, be paid to me in full.' Deutsch (*Documents*, 138–9), however, gives: 'It is true that His Serene Highness most considerately granted us permission to travel, but withheld my salary which in any case amounts to only 28 florins 30 kreuzer, though by an oversight I was paid for another month and a half. When, however, in a letter from his Excellency Count Sauerau, addressed to the Court Chancellor, the former thought to acquaint His Serene Highness with the

but the eventual outcome was that his salary for October and November was restored to him, though without precedent for the future. The success of his appeal probably owed something to the care which Leopold took to stay on good terms with people of influence in Salzburg. Saurau had helped on this occasion, and after he was made dean of the cathedral in 1772, Leopold was to ensure that polite attentions were paid to him at appropriate times.[33]

※

There is not a great deal of information about the activities of Maria Anna and Nannerl during this four-month absence of Leopold and Wolfgang. Leopold had urged the women not to neglect being presented by Troger to Karl von Firmian when he passed through Salzburg; but when they did meet Troger, and Troger reported back to Leopold on the interview, Leopold was not pleased with what had happened.

On 21 September 1771, writing from Milan, Leopold had described the frenzy of activity directed towards the imperial marriage. In the same letter he announced the arrival of the Davies family, whom the Mozarts had first met in England. There were two sisters, Marianne and Cecily, and their parents. Marianne played the glass harmonica and Cecily was a singer. They lived in the same house in Vienna as Hasse, and Cecily received singing lessons from him. Both girls were friendly with Hasse's daughter, and the whole party asked after Nannerl and Maria Anna. Later in the same letter Leopold commented on the beautiful sights to be seen in Milan, and made a veiled reference to the possibility of people coming from Salzburg to enjoy them. He claimed that a carriage for four

good news of the general applause and honour accorded to my son, His Serene Highness at once gave orders for my salary to be stopped. Your most reverend and most noble Excellencies are accordingly most humbly requested and besought graciously to have paid to me this deduction of only 2 months at 59 florins, *i.e.* for October and November . . .' With regard to these two contradictory English translations, it should be noted (*a*) that 'einzuhalten' is more likely to mean that *Leopold* should be allowed to keep his salary than that it should be kept *from* him (the decree stopping his salary had been issued on 16 Oct. 1771 and Saurau cannot have reported on the success of *Ascanio* until after 17 Oct. 1771, so the only logical development arising from Saurau's letter would have been to reverse the earlier decision); (*b*) that there is no justification for Anderson's invention of the phrase 'sum already paid', which only serves to confuse the matter further; and (*c*) that the most satisfactory understanding of the passage is that it was tacitly assumed by all parties that Leopold would keep the sum paid in error—his appeal was based on the claim that Schrattenbach, moved to reverse his decision of 16 October by Saurau's favourable report, had ordered verbally that Leopold be permitted after all to draw his salary for October and November. It was this verbal decision of Schrattenbach's that Leopold wanted the Chapter to ratify.

[33] See Chs. 11 and 13 for details of some of these attentions.

people would not cost much money, but that accommodation would be a heavy item. Then he said that he could help with accommodation by taking in anyone who came. If meals were cooked at home, it would be more economical (he and Wolfgang tended to eat at an inn when they were not invited out).[34] Even before such an enticing letter had arrived, Maria Anna and particularly Nannerl were wishing that they could go to Milan to see the celebrations and meet old acquaintances; and when they met Troger, whose sister lived in Salzburg and was among the fortunate few intending to go, they mentioned their wish to him. He duly relayed it to Leopold who, if he had been hinting on 21 September that the women might come, had obviously reconsidered matters and was far from pleased that they had expressed their desire to Troger. On 5 October 1771 he wrote:

Herr Chaplain Troger told me, when he was giving me the pills, that you and Nannerl would have liked to come with us. If you were completely in earnest about this, you did very wrong not to tell me so straight out. although the difference, just as far as the return journey is concerned, would definitely have been *60 ducats*. Anyway, you don't really need to regret it very much. Because you would have had to endure incredible heat: and although a lot of big things are being organized here; when all's said and done, they're partly things that you've seen even better already, or they're things which, because of the crowd, you'll only see with great discomfort, maybe even at the risk of your life if you're determined to see every piddling little thing.[35]

This passage, taken together with his letter of 21 September 1771, shows a tendency of Leopold's to oscillate between generosity and financial caution. This was no doubt understandable considering how necessary caution still was to the Mozarts, but it was nevertheless rather hard on his family. Even though, from the dates involved, Maria Anna and Nannerl had almost certainly expressed their wish to Troger before receiving Leopold's tantalizing letter of 21 September, the contradictions in his two letters indicate a man who could not make up his mind to do something liberal. On 21 September, he had said the travel costs would not be great; on 5 October they would add at least 60 ducats (300 fl.). On 21 September he had mentioned the wonderful things that were being organized; by 5 October these had all lost their lustre. During the first Italian journey, the women would never have been able to stand the cold; now they would not be able to bear the heat. Exactly the same tendency in Leopold was to crop up in Vienna in 1773 and in Munich in

[34] *MBA* 246/16–48 (*Letters* 144).   [35] *MBA* 248/18–27 (*Letters* 146).

early 1775: in 1775 there was a danger that Nannerl might not be able to go to Munich to see Wolfgang's opera *La finta giardiniera* because of the difficulty of finding a respectable lodging for her; in 1773 Maria Anna and Nannerl could not accompany Leopold and Wolfgang to Vienna because two different families wanted to accommodate them and the situation would be embarrassing.[36]

Leopold continued to put objections to a trip to Milan by the women in some of his later letters. On 12 October 1771 he repeated his assertion that to see anything would involve gross discomfort and perhaps danger, and insisted that there would be better future opportunities to see Italy. He also described how unpleasant the security operations made Milan appear.[37] On 19 October 1771, two days after the first performance of *Ascanio*, he again alluded to Nannerl sighing for Italy, and repeated his assurance that the women would see Italy at some future date under better conditions;[38] in fact, neither was ever to do so. By 26 October 1771, Leopold could feel a little happier about them for knowing that they had been invited by the Schiedenhofen family to the Triebenbach estate, as they had been the previous autumn. This invitation provided a diversion from the routine in Salzburg itself, and at no cost to Leopold. Ever anxious to prove his predictions right, he was able in this letter to report loss of life and limb in Milan following the collapse of an overcrowded grandstand at some of the wedding festivities. He went on to urge them to have new clothes made for the festive occasions following the archduke's marriage, and not to stint on the expense;[39] these, and the entertainments at Triebenbach, were to be their consolation.

---

[36] See Chs. 12 and 13 for details of the visits to Vienna and Munich.
[37] *MBA* 249 (*Letters* 147).   [38] *MBA* 250 (*Letters* 148).
[39] *MBA* 251 (*Letters* 149, but the passage about the collapsing grandstand is omitted).

❦ 11 ❧

The Intensification of the Quest:
Wolfgang's Third Visit to Italy

❦❧

THE election of the new prince-archbishop in Salzburg did not proceed smoothly. Local feeling favoured Count Ferdinand Christoph Waldburg-Zeil, the dean of the cathedral. He was a native of Salzburg, and was well known and liked. Count Joseph Gottfried Saurau, who had interceded for Leopold to have his salary restored at the end of 1771, also offered himself as a candidate. But Zeil had close connections with the Bavarian court, and because of Salzburg's awkward position between Austria and Bavaria, his election would have been unacceptable to Austria. Imperial agents were therefore dispatched to Salzburg to put pressure on the canons to vote for Count Hieronymus Colloredo, Austria's choice. After a number of voting sessions had failed to produce the required majority for any of the candidates, Zeil and Saurau were persuaded that their positions were hopeless, and Zeil reluctantly offered his allegiance to Colloredo, who was finally elected on the following day, 14 March 1772. On 29 April Colloredo made his solemn entrance into Salzburg,[1] and on 21 August Wolfgang began to draw a salary for his services as Konzertmeister. He was paid 150 fl. annually.[2]

Colloredo's election was a bitter blow to Zeil, and worse was to follow. Because Zeil's position as dean made him the second most powerful man in the prince-archbishopric, one of Colloredo's early acts, on 30 September 1772,[3] was to appoint him bishop of Chiemsee instead. Although this brought Zeil the title of prince, it was common knowledge that the move was demotion; he was being robbed of his main sphere of influence, and the bishopric of Chiemsee carried with it a residence-in-Salzburg requirement, which was intended as a curb on the bishop's

---

[1] F. Martin, 'Die Salzburger Chronik des Felix Adauktus Haslberger', pt. 2, *MGSL* 68 (1928), 52.

[2] Deutsch, *Documents*, 142.   [3] Martin, 'Die Salzburger Chronik', pt. 2, 52.

independence.[4] The bad feeling between the two men was to persist until Zeil's death in 1786, and when Colloredo made himself unpopular by the reforms he implemented in Salzburg, Zeil was often seen as a focus of opposition to him. In time the Mozarts were to be among those who tried to capitalize on Zeil's loathing for Colloredo. They courted Zeil's goodwill in the hope that he would be able to help Wolfgang gain an appointment at the more prestigious Bavarian court, and thus snub the archbishop.[5]

The pleasure the Mozarts must have taken in Wolfgang's salary was considerably dampened by Colloredo's approach to replacing the ageing Kapellmeister Lolli. Lolli was by now over 70 years old, and more than ripe for retirement. Precedent suggested that Leopold ought to have been confident of succeeding him,[6] but instead Colloredo started to look for an outsider. This decision must have signalled to Leopold that unless Colloredo predeceased him, his chances of promotion to Kapellmeister were probably gone for ever.

In July 1772 Colloredo, through the head of his finance department Karl Maria Erenbert von Moll, opened negotiations with Domenico Fischietti, who was an Italian composer (chiefly of operas), and was a few years younger than Leopold. Fischietti had been in the service of the elector of Saxony, but his contract there had not been renewed, and from May 1772 he was in Vienna without a salaried appointment. Colloredo wanted Fischietti to undertake not only the organization of the music at court, in the theatre, and in the cathedral, but also to instruct any new female singers that might be appointed, and to take charge of the teaching in the Kapellhaus. Colloredo presumably felt that his aim of improving the organization of the court music through strong leadership would best be achieved by bringing in new blood. In return for these duties, Fischietti was offered a salary of 800 fl. annually, which included allowances formerly offered as extras. Not since Eberlin had the Kapellmeister received a comparable sum. Eberlin had been drawing 581 fl. 40 kr. from 1753, and had enjoyed the extras of the *Hoftafel* and a free lodging; 200 of Fischietti's 800 fl. were supposed to replace the *Hoftafel*. Lolli had been Kapellmeister since 1763 on a salary of 456

---

[4] For further information about the relative weight of the incumbents of clerical positions in Salzburg, see J. Graf von Moÿ, 'Die Hintergründe der Fürstungen im Salzburger Domkapitel: ein Beitrag zur Verfassungsgeschichte des Erzstiftes im 18. Jahrhundert', *MGSL* 119 (1979), 231–59, esp. 237–41; and M. Heim, *Bischof und Archidiakon: Geistliche Kompetenzen im Bistum Chiemsee (1215–1817)* (St Ottilien, 1992), 17–19.

[5] See Ch. 16 for more information about this.

[6] See Ch. 10 for details about the career progressions of Salzburg musicians.

fl. plus the *Hoftafel* and a free lodging;[7] and Leopold Mozart had been Vice-Kapellmeister since the same date on a salary of 354 fl. without either of these extras. The offer to Fischietti was therefore generous by Salzburg standards; yet Fischietti, despite his unemployment, hesitated about accepting it and made it clear that he wanted more money. This request was rejected, but Colloredo undertook to provide Fischietti with a free lodging once Lolli had 'gone to compose for the chosen in Heaven'. Fischietti was given a three-year contract on these terms, though not without reservations on Colloredo's part when he subsequently discovered that the new Kapellmeister was to bring with him the additional burden of a wife.[8]

The fact that the Mozarts were together at home during the period of Colloredo's election and its immediate aftermath means that there is no correspondence documenting Leopold's reaction to Fischietti's appointment. But there can be little doubt that it was a bitter blow to him, and one which must have made him look back on his own career as one of lost opportunities. In 1764 he had enthusiastically expressed his desire that Salzburg should become famous throughout Germany as a court excellently staffed by native talent.[9] His subsequent dissatisfaction with his salary, and the choice he had made to devote so much time to Wolfgang, had been interlinking factors in his waning commitment to service at Salzburg. Now he must have seen the effect of this on his own career with brutal clarity. Leopold was 52 years old when Colloredo was elected, and increasingly, from this time on, his hopes of adequate provision for a comfortable old age for himself and Maria Anna, together with support for Nannerl until she married, were centred on Wolfgang.

When Leopold and Wolfgang left home for Milan on 24 October 1772, therefore, they had again two ends in view; the successful composition and production of the opera that had been commissioned in the spring of 1771 on their way home from the first journey to Italy and, if possible, the procurement of a good appointment for Wolfgang. If there was any change in Leopold's attitude to this trip, it was almost certainly that the second aim had become a little more urgent than it had been on their previous visit to Milan.

Arriving in Milan on 4 November 1772, they took a different lodging from the one formerly used, and on 21 November Leopold described it as more comfortable, nearer the theatre, and very close to the d'Asti

---

[7] See Hintermaier, 'Hofkapelle', 232.   [8] See ibid., 117–19.
[9] See Ch. 5, pp. 72–3, for details about this.

family (Troger's daughter and her husband, who had become such friends during the previous two visits). The opera was to be *Lucio Silla*, and when Leopold wrote, the castrato Rauzzini had arrived, and Wolfgang was able to start composing his music.[10] However, the prima donna Anna Lucia de Amicis did not get there until 4 December, and Leopold wrote on 5 December 1772 that the tenor had been taken ill and that another one was being sought. The late appearance of de Amicis and the lack of a tenor for the title role meant that most of the music could not yet be composed, though the first performance was to be given on 26 December.[11] By 12 December the only pieces outstanding were those for the tenor, who was expected from Turin around 15 December; the recitative rehearsals had to begin without him.[12] When Leopold next wrote, on 18 December, the tenor had at last arrived, Wolfgang was writing his arias at breakneck speed, and rehearsals were in full swing. They had seen Karl von Firmian to offer their congratulations, because his brother Leopold Ernst had just become a cardinal; they were to dine on the following day with Albert Michael von Mayr, Archduke Ferdinand's privy paymaster; and they intended to spend Christmas Eve with Ferdinand's Controller, Germani, and his wife.[13] To this letter Wolfgang appended one of his zany postscripts to Nannerl, writing every other line upside down:

I hope you're well, my dear sister. When you get this letter, my dear sister, the same evening, my dear sister, my opera will be performed. think of me, my dear sister, and imagine it, my dear sister, very hard. you're seeing and hearing it, my dear sister, too. admittedly this is difficult, as it's already 11 o'clock. Otherwise I believe, and don't doubt at all, that during the day it's lighter than at Easter. My dear sister, tomorrow we're dining with Herr von Mayer, and why do you think? Guess, because he's invited us. the rehearsal tomorrow is in the theatre but the impresario, Sig. Castiglioni, has asked me not to say anything about it, because otherwise everyone will come running in, and we don't want that. So I beg you, my child, don't tell anyone anything about it, my child, because otherwise too many people will come running in, my child. A propos, do you know the story of what happened here? I'll tell you now. today we came away from Count firmian's to go home, and as we entered our street we opened the door of our house, and what do you think happened? we went inside. farewell, my little lung. I kiss you, my liver, and remain as ever my stomach your unworthy brother Wolfgang frater, please, please, my dear sister, I'm itching, scratch me.[14]

[10] *MBA* 267 (*Letters* 162, but not complete).   [11] *MBA* 269 (*Letters* 164).
[12] *MBA* 270 (*Letters* 165).   [13] *MBA* 271 (*Letters* 166, but not complete).
[14] *MBA* 271/21–49 (*Letters* 166a).

On 26 December 1772 the first performance of *Lucio Silla* was given. Prior to going to the theatre for it, Leopold and Wolfgang dined with Troger's daughter, Frau d'Asti, and wrote a letter home. Leopold reported that the dress rehearsal had gone very well, and that he had written to Archbishop Colloredo and the Obersthofmeister, Franz Lactanz von Firmian, to send them the libretto. He also described the celebrations taking place in Milan in honour of the new cardinal, Count Leopold Ernst von Firmian—three important musical gatherings had taken place on consecutive nights at the residence of Karl von Firmian, and Wolfgang had played at them. Archduke Ferdinand and Princess Maria Beatrice had spoken to them, the best houses had been illuminated for three days, the church bells had played pieces like the carillons in the Netherlands, and there had been music in the street. Leopold was in such a state of nerves about the opera as he wrote this letter that he forgot to enclose New Year greetings to the women.[15]

Leopold's letter of 26 December could not be kept back long enough to report the outcome of the first performance of the opera, because the weekly post from Milan to Salzburg left on that day. It was not until 2 January 1773, therefore, that he was able to report the success of the opera despite various initial setbacks. He claimed that on the first night the performance should have begun at six o'clock and that the theatre was therefore filling up from half past five. It had been very hot, the singers were nervous, and many in the audience were standing. Archduke Ferdinand, however, only rose from his dining table shortly before five o'clock, and then had to write five letters with New Year greetings ('and NB', added Leopold drily, 'he writes very slowly etcetc.'); consequently the opera could not start until eight o'clock and was not over until two the following morning. In addition a performance mishap had occurred which led to a quarrel between the prima donna, de Amicis, and both the tenor, Morgnoni, and the castrato, Rauzzini; de Amicis had to be pacified on the following day by an audience with Ferdinand and Maria Beatrice before the opera could proceed smoothly.[16]

Subsequent performances thrived. On 9 January 1773 Leopold reported that the theatre was still full, an unusual circumstance for the first opera of the season. Arias were being repeated, and all the Milanese friends sent their greetings to Maria Anna and Nannerl, and wished for their presence. Leopold and Wolfgang intended to stay on a little longer to see the second opera (Paisiello's *Sismano nel Mogol*), and Leopold must have applied

[15] *MBA* 272 (*Letters* 167).   [16] *MBA* 275 (*Letters* 168).

to Colloredo for extended leave of absence in order to do this, because on 16 January he told Maria Anna that Colloredo had answered his letter very graciously and given him some commissions to fulfil in Milan. The opera was still going splendidly, and was so popular that the first performance of the second opera was to be postponed.[17]

As had been the case during the previous visit to Milan, however, Leopold had an ulterior motive for the extension of the visit. He was busy trying to secure an appointment for Wolfgang, this time with Maria Theresia's son Leopold, grand duke of Tuscany. All through the period of Wolfgang's activity with the opera, Leopold had been brooding about the position of himself and his family in Salzburg. On 14 November 1772 he mentioned a few old ailments which had been troubling him and which tended to bring on feelings of depression about Salzburg, which he then had to exert himself to banish. He regretted the death of 'poor Winter', the bass singer in Salzburg; but predicted that Hornung, another bass singer, might 'now snap up something, unless perhaps a bass singer is ordered from the West Indies'.[18] This remark was almost certainly a sarcastic allusion to Colloredo's appointment of the outsider Fischietti in preference to Leopold. On 28 October 1772 Leopold had told Maria Anna (who had presumably written to say that she had been asked by someone in Salzburg for symphonies) that if absolutely necessary she could surrender some, as long as she made a careful note of which they were;[19] then on 28 November 1772 he told her she had done right about the music, and that the Kapellmeister would be writing symphonies.[20] Whether these two remarks are connected and hint at a policy of non-cooperation with Fischietti, whereby Leopold and Wolfgang would withhold their own compositions as far as possible in order to force him to write enough music for the court requirements, is unclear; but it is fairly obvious that father and son felt personal animosity towards Fischietti. On 5 December 1772 Wolfgang wrote to Nannerl, 'fischietti will probably soon start work on his opera buffa (in German) on his idiotic opera.'[21]

---

[17] *MBA* 277 and 279 (*Letters* 169 and 170).

[18] *MBA* 266/13–21 (*Letters* 161, but the reference to Winter and Hornung is omitted).

[19] *MBA* 264/33–5 (not in *Letters*).

[20] *MBA* 268/24–5 (not in *Letters*). The Kapellmeister mentioned in this passage is tentatively identified in *MBA* as Wolfgang Mozart, but Fischietti is surely a likelier candidate.

[21] *MBA* 269/50–1 (*Letters* 164a, but with an eccentric translation). Wolfgang's German is, 'der fischietti wird wohl bald anfangen an seiner opera buffa (auf Teutsch) an seiner närrischen opera zu arbeiten'; Anderson gives, 'I suppose Fischietti will soon be setting to work at an opera buffa, which, when translated, means "crazy opera".' The parenthesis 'auf Teutsch' is surely a way of intensifying the expression of scorn for Fischietti's work; presumably Wolfgang thought the idea of this particular Italian setting a German text ludicrous.

There was little Leopold could do about his frustrating position in Salzburg except continue to keep the favour of anyone there who had any influence, until Wolfgang could earn an appointment elsewhere. On 28 November 1772 Leopold expressed pleasure at Maria Anna's news that Count Saurau had been appointed Zeil's successor as dean of the cathedral;[22] Leopold continued to place great importance on his patronage. Similarly important were the Obersthofmeister Count Franz Lactanz von Firmian, and Countess Maria Josepha Viktoria von Arco, wife of the court Kämmerer and mother of Countess van Eyck, the woman who had given the Mozarts their accommodation in Paris in 1763. Countess Arco had long been well disposed towards the Mozarts, was a senior member of court society, and was valued by the musicians for her ability to intercede for them.[23] On 26 December 1772 Leopold told Maria Anna that he had written both to Firmian and the archbishop, but that she should not neglect to call on Countess Arco with New Year greetings.[24]

It was also on 26 December 1772, the date of the first performance of *Lucio Silla*, that Leopold first mentioned his application to Grand Duke Leopold of Tuscany, an application presumably for an appointment for Wolfgang. As with the previous year's appeal to Archduke Ferdinand, it is unknown what kind of position Leopold had in mind; Wolfgang was still only 16 years old, so the same arguments against his leading a life independent of his family would have applied. In his letter, Leopold used the cypher to tell Maria Anna of the dispatch of the application to Florence. He also revealed that it was strongly supported by their Milanese patron Count Karl von Firmian, that its arrival had been delayed, and that they now had to await the answer.[25] This had to be done without arousing the suspicion or wrath of Colloredo, which may partly have been Leopold's reason for writing to the archbishop to ask permission to stay and see Paisiello's opera. On 9 January 1773 Leopold reported, again in cypher, that the grand duke was considering the application, and that he, Leopold, was quite hopeful.[26] By 16 January 1773 he had received notice of the commissions from Colloredo which would detain them legitimately in Milan a little longer, but had also heard discouraging news through Troger about the prospects of an opening in Florence. He hoped that they would at least get a letter of recommendation from Grand Duke Leopold, but

---

[22] *MBA* 268/18–21 (not in *Letters*).
[23] Meissner's appeal in 1769 (discussed in Ch. 10) had alluded to Countess Arco's help in obtaining a temporary lodgings allowance—see Hintermaier, 'Hofkapelle', 267.
[24] *MBA* 272/17–20 (*Letters* 167, but without the reference to Countess Arco).
[25] *MBA* 272/20–6 (*Letters* 167).   [26] *MBA* 277/38–40 (*Letters* 169).

urged Maria Anna and Nannerl to practise the utmost economy in order to save money for future travelling; Leopold's attitude to continuing service in Salzburg is revealed by his words, 'I begrudge every kreuzer that we spend in Salzburg'.[27] From this date his spirits were sinking, and he had to start to consider what his next move might be; but without a definite answer from the grand duke he did not want to leave Milan. During this period of anxious waiting, they attended rehearsals for the second opera, enjoyed the company of their friends, and gave instructions to copyists in Milan for works requested by Colloredo. Wolfgang also composed a string quartet and the motet *Exsultate, jubilate*, K. 165. On 23 January 1773 Leopold told Maria Anna that he had sent Wolfgang's opera to the grand duke—this was presumably part of a final effort to secure the hoped-for appointment—and that he was writing from his bed because of severe rheumatism. He reiterated the hope he had expressed on 16 January that at the very least they would obtain a recommendation, and alluded to further plans and his trust in God if all failed.[28]

Once Colloredo's commissions were completed, there was no further pretext for remaining in Milan. But the attack of rheumatism gave Leopold the idea for a lie designed to give them an excuse for staying longer. From this date until the time of their actual departure on 4 March 1773 he resorted, with increasingly ludicrous effect, to this deception, which must surely have been known to Wolfgang. On 30 January he described his sufferings but added a passage in cypher to reassure Maria Anna that in fact he was fine, and had only been confined to bed for a few days. She should, however, spread the report of his illness around Salzburg and cut off the cyphered portion of the letter so that it could not fall into the wrong hands (Maria Anna did not do this).[29] On 6 February he described his continuing indisposition and announced that they could not contemplate the return journey through the icy Tyrolean mountains until he was better. He told Maria Anna to see Firmian and the new dean Saurau, or Countess Arco, to explain the situation. These three names crop up repeatedly as well-disposed patrons and mediators of the Mozarts in the correspondence of this period, and Leopold presumably hoped to forestall gossip about his tardy return by having Maria Anna give them his version of events immediately. In particular he urged his wife to keep on good terms with Saurau.[30] On 13 February he acknowledged for the first time that people in Salzburg would be getting suspicious about his

---

[27] *MBA* 279/25–31 (*Letters* 170).   [28] *MBA* 281/28–32 (*Letters* 171).
[29] *MBA* 282 (*Letters* 172).   [30] *MBA* 283 (*Letters* 173).

prolonged attack of rheumatism, and would be assuming that he was remaining in Milan for his own pleasure; again, therefore, he urged Maria Anna to report on his condition to Firmian, claiming that he himself could hardly write.[31] On 20 February the saga reached its preposterous climax when Leopold told Maria Anna that he had written to Firmian himself, but that unfortunately the letter had been barely legible because of his stiffness.[32] By 27 February, however, the long wait for an answer from Florence was over, and there was nothing more to detain them. They had been offered nothing by the grand duke. In an expression of emotion unusual for him, Leopold confessed to his wife that he was finding it hard to leave Italy. But leave they must, and as fast as possible, because Colloredo was sure to be angry if they were not back to contribute to the Election Day celebrations on 14 March. To signal to people in Salzburg that he really was now on the way back, Leopold did not address this letter to Maria Anna, but instead enclosed it in one to his colleague Franz Anton Spitzeder. He claimed that by doing this Maria Anna would be able to let it be known in Salzburg that she had received no letter since that of 20 February, and was therefore assuming that Leopold and Wolfgang had already left.[33] What pretext Leopold used to Spitzeder in asking him to pass on his letter to Maria Anna is unknown, but the episode demonstrates Leopold's belief that he could be damaged by gossip. Whether feelings of guilt about his deception made him exaggerate this danger, or whether serious harm really could be done in this way, Leopold evidently felt insecure about his position there; this feeling was to increase in the years to come.

If the journey home proceeded as Leopold planned, the travellers arrived in the nick of time on 13 March 1773, the eve of the first anniversary of Colloredo's election. Leopold must have known that, for the time being at least, there was no prospect of employment in Italy. The two most promising Habsburg patrons there, Archduke Ferdinand and Grand Duke Leopold, had been tried in vain. Through all the hard work of their three visits Wolfgang had covered himself in glory and they had many new friends, some of whom ought to have been influential, but they had failed to secure the object of their greatest desire. For the time being there was no point in trying to obtain other commissions there; their energy would have to be directed somewhere with the prospect of employment. It is not known whether Grand Duke Leopold was influenced by Maria Theresia's opinion of the Mozarts in declining to employ Wolfgang;

[31] *MBA* 284 (*Letters* 174).   [32] *MBA* 286 (*Letters* 175).   [33] *MBA* 287 (*Letters* 176).

but it was probably as well for Leopold, as he began to lay plans for an attempt at a position in Vienna, that this opinion was hidden from him.

～≫⅄≪～

One of the pieces of Salzburg news relayed by Maria Anna and Nannerl while Leopold and Wolfgang were in Milan was the forthcoming marriage of a family friend, Optatus Basil von Amann.[34] Though none of them yet knew it, a net of marital relationships was already being woven which in 1784 was to link the Mozarts with the Amanns, and to make the disasters which befell Basil's young family from 1784 to 1787 a matter of concern for Nannerl. Basil's father, Franz Anton von Amann, was a respected court official in Salzburg. As General-Einnehmer he had responsibility for handling large sums of money collected as taxes. He and his wife had nine children, of whom Basil was the seventh. The younger children were roughly contemporary with Nannerl and Wolfgang Mozart, and were their childhood friends. Basil was placed in his father's office as an underling, and in the autumn of 1772 was 25 years old when he applied for permission to marry Maria Franziska Polis, daughter of a well-to-do merchant. It was granted, and his salary was increased to 300 fl. annually. The young married couple set up house and, counting on future help from their families, began to live beyond their means, to the disquiet of Basil's father. By 1782, some two years before news of calamitous disgrace broke, Basil and Maria Franziska were to be the parents of five living children.

In 1769 Maria Franziska Polis's sister Maria Margarethe had married Johann Baptist Berchtold von Sonnenburg, Pfleger of St Gilgen. They too were producing a young family all through the 1770s, and bringing up their children in the house where Maria Anna Mozart had been born. But in 1779 Maria Margarethe died, on the same day that their ninth child was born. Berchtold remarried, but his second wife died even younger, also from childbirth complications. When he married Nannerl Mozart in 1784, the four surviving children from his first marriage were to provide continuing links both with the Amanns and the Polises, despite the death of their mother.[35]

---

[34] Wolfgang to Nannerl, 28 Nov. 1772—*MBA* 268/37–45 (*Letters* 163*a*).

[35] The information in these two paragraphs comes from F. Pirckmayer, 'Basil von Amann: Ein Kulturbild aus der letzten Zeit des geistlichen Kleinstaates', *MGSL* 48 (1908), 45–59; F. Martin, 'Beiträge zur Salzburger Familiengeschichte', *MGSL* 82 (1942), 70–2; and J. H. Eibl, 'Zur Familiengeschichte der Berchtold zu Sonnenburg und der Amann', *MM* 19 (1971), 12–17. Details of the deaths of Berchtold's first two wives are in Brno, MZA, Berchtold Family Archive, Family Chronicle,

On 21 November 1772 Leopold alluded to his twenty-fifth wedding anniversary. He rarely expressed sentiment in letters to his wife (and was rarely to do so to Nannerl, though he would to Wolfgang), but he did remark that their idea of getting married had been a good one. He also said that they had had to wait 'many years' to do so, and that all good things took time.[36] Just as Leopold and Maria Anna must then have had to contain their impatience to marry until Leopold had an adequate salary in Salzburg, so during this period they had to try to calm their frustration in Salzburg until Wolfgang should enable them to improve their circumstances. Nannerl was already grown up, and Wolfgang nearly so, and Leopold was beginning to fret about getting them settled and securing a peaceful old age for himself and Maria Anna. Meanwhile he wanted Nannerl to amass some teaching experience as well as to keep up her performance skills. On 12 December 1772 he wrote:

How's it going with M[lle] Zezi, is she learning? Is Nannerl conscientious with her? — — Greet Nannerl for me and tell her that she should practise diligently: and that she should teach little Zezi with care and patience. I know that it's for her own good, if she accustoms herself to demonstrate something to someone else thoroughly and with patience. I'm not writing this idly.[37]

In urging Nannerl to become a good teacher, Leopold probably had in mind a communal benefit as well as the advantage that would accrue to her personally; her contribution to a joint family income might be needed in the future.[38]

On 6 February 1773 Leopold mentioned two people known to them who had just inherited large sums of money.[39] The amounts involved in both cases were vastly outside the financial experience of the Mozarts, and his mention of the cases does not necessarily indicate that the subject was preying on his mind; but legacies, provision for dependants, and other related matters occur increasingly in the correspondence from this date. During his next trip away from Salzburg with Wolfgang, to Vienna in the summer of 1773, he was to be seriously shaken by the death of his contemporary Dr Niderl, who left a son almost three years younger than Wolfgang. From then until Nannerl's marriage in 1784 Leopold was to

unpaginated, but pp. 35 and 39 on my count. See Fig. 2 for a diagram of the relationships discussed, and Chs. 27 and 30 for further details about the plight of Basil's family in the 1780s.

[36] *MBA* 267/16–19 (*Letters* 162).   [37] *MBA* 270/34–8 (*Letters* 165).
[38] See Ch. 7, pp. 116–18, for an explanation of Leopold's idea about how the family might live if Wolfgang got a job outside Salzburg.
[39] *MBA* 283/42–4 (not in *Letters*).

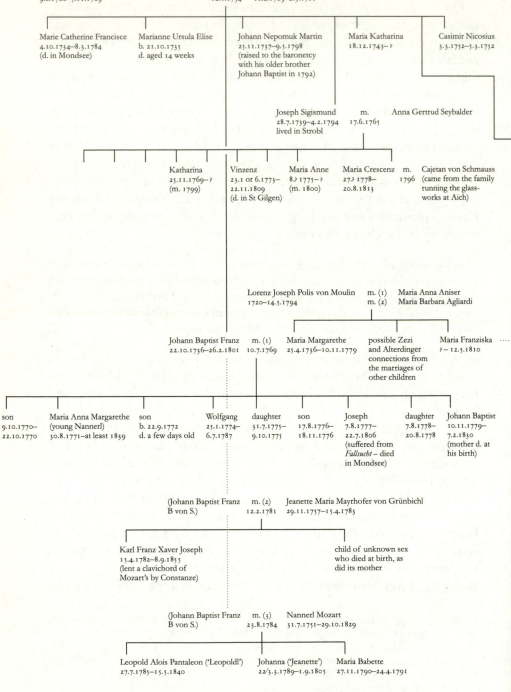

FIG. 2. Some interrelationships among the Berchtold von Sonnenburg, Polis von Moulin, and Amann families in Salzburg

AMANN

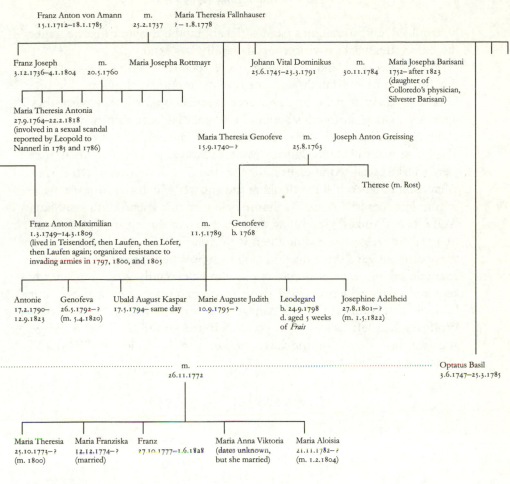

Franz Anton von Amann · m. · Maria Theresia Fallnhauser
15.1.1712–18.1.1785 · 25.2.1737 · ?– 1.8.1778

Franz Joseph · m. · Maria Josepha Rottmayr
3.12.1736–4.1.1804 · 20.5.1760

Johann Vital Dominikus · m. · Maria Josepha Barisani
25.6.1745–23.3.1791 · 30.11.1784 · 1752– after 1823
(daughter of
Colloredo's physician,
Silvester Barisani)

Maria Theresia Antonia
27.9.1764–22.2.1818
(involved in a sexual scandal
reported by Leopold to
Nannerl in 1785 and 1786)

Maria Theresia Genofeve · m. · Joseph Anton Greissing
15.9.1740–? · 25.8.1763

Therese (m. Rost)

Franz Anton Maximilian · m. · Genofeve
1.3.1749–14.3.1809 · 11.5.1789 · b. 1768
(lived in Teisendorf, then Laufen, then Lofer,
then Laufen again; organized resistance to
invading armies in 1797, 1800, and 1805

Antonie
17.2.1790–
12.9.1823

Genofeva
26.5.1792–?
(m. 5.4.1820)

Ubald August Kaspar
17.5.1794– same day

Marie Auguste Judith
10.9.1795–?

Leodegard
b. 24.9.1798
d. aged 5 weeks
of *Frais*

Josephine Adelheid
27.8.1801–?
(m. 1.5.1822)

m. · Optatus Basil
26.11.1772 · 3.6.1747–25.3.1785

Maria Theresia
25.10.1773–?
(m. 1800)

Maria Franziska
12.12.1774–?
(married)

Franz
27.10.1777–1.6.1828

Maria Anna Viktoria
(dates unknown,
but she married)

Maria Aloisia
21.11.1782–?
(m. 1.2.1804)

Note on Sources: The information comes from Eibl, 'Zur Familiengeschichte'; Martin, 'Beiträge zur Salzburger Familiengeschichte: Amann'; H. Schuler, 'Nannerl Mozarts Stiefkinder', *AM 23* (1976), 30–5; Hummel, *Nannerl*; Pirckmayer, 'Basil von Amann'; Brno, MZA, Berchtold Family Archive, Family Chronicle; and *MBA* commentaries.

The source information is sometimes confusing and inaccurate; even within the Berchtold Family Chronicle an event may appear twice with slightly different dates. However, it is hoped that the diagram is accurate enough to illuminate some of the connections among the families mentioned in the book.

be troubled, and sometimes panic-stricken, by the thought that he might die before financial provision for his family was secured.

Yet, as Leopold and Wolfgang made their way home from Milan, the situation of the family was not one of unmitigated gloom. Despite Leopold's claim that he resented every kreuzer spent in Salzburg, they were negotiating during this period the rental of a large apartment on the Hannibalplatz (now called the Makartplatz) on the east side of the Salzach. The house was called the Dancing-Master's House, and the apartment they were to take consisted of eight rooms on the first floor, one of which was a handsome dance hall overlooking the square, which the Mozarts were to turn into a music room. The house belonged to a friend of theirs, Maria Anna Raab ('Mitzerl'), and they were to move in during the late autumn of 1773. As well as providing them with more comfort, light, and space, the apartment gave them the potential to supplement their income by, for example, taking resident pupils. It was almost certainly Wolfgang's newly acquired salary which enabled them to contemplate such a move, but Leopold and Nannerl were to manage to continue living there even after Wolfgang had left Salzburg for good. Nannerl stayed until her marriage and returned there for the birth of her son Leopoldl, and Leopold remained until his death.

Wolfgang's Viennese Sojourn in 1773

WOLFGANG had become 17 in January 1773, and for some time it had been impossible to continue calling him a child prodigy. Thanks to his talent and his tailor-made education, he already had all the musical qualities needed by a Kapellmeister, but there was no way forward to cater adequately for his situation. To the world outside his family, he was just a youth who would have to climb the career ladder patiently from the bottom, like other boys his age. Since he had always been protected from drudgery, had never had to be one of many, had been accustomed to have the plans of the whole family revolve around his artistic development, and had been encouraged to believe that a magnificent future awaited him, this must have been deeply frustrating for him. It is possible that the conceit which was to be one of his adult characteristics developed partly as a response to these circumstances; reports of him as a child had frequently commented on his modesty.

There are hints in the correspondence that Wolfgang was restless in Salzburg during the period 1773–7, and repeatedly asked Leopold about the possibility of further travelling.[1] After returning from Milan in March 1773, the next trip Leopold was able to arrange was a summer one later the same year to Vienna, and he and Wolfgang left in mid-July.

The exact purpose of this visit is shrouded in mystery, because Leopold's letters home are couched, at least so far as the most important parts of them are concerned, in cryptic terms. But what does seem clear, since there was no compositional commission to fulfil, is that it was an outright attempt to obtain a post of some sort for Wolfgang. It is difficult to imagine what other benefit was to be hoped for from the visit; the members of the aristocracy, as Leopold would well have known, were all out of town on country estates, so there could be little possibility of earning money by giving concerts. Conceivably Leopold hoped that Wolfgang might

---

[1] See Leopold to Wolfgang, 18 Dec. 1777 (*MBA* 392/13–16; *Letters* 262); 11–12 Feb. 1778 (*MBA* 422/33–5; *Letters* 285); and 11 June 1778 (*MBA* 452/98; *Letters* 308).

obtain an operatic commission for Vienna (in which case they would secure the opportunity to return there at a more propitious season); but he was hardly the man to spend so much money on one trip solely for those purposes, and it seems overwhelmingly likely that his chief aim was to petition Maria Theresia for a court post.

Although Leopold had tried to conceal from people in Salzburg his attempts to obtain a post for Wolfgang in Italy, it seems that on this occasion Colloredo was told the true purpose of their journey. The reason why Leopold should at any time have wanted to hide his ambitions of a better post for Wolfgang or himself was that he did not want to make plain his lack of commitment to Salzburg, for fear of further damage to his prospects there. On previous occasions the compositional commission had given them an adequate pretext for the journey, and it might have been the lack of one this time which had forced Leopold to be more open with Colloredo.

In August 1777 Wolfgang was to petition Colloredo for his discharge in order to travel to obtain an appointment elsewhere. His appeal mentioned two points which have a bearing on his visit to Vienna in 1773: he was considered only 'half in service'; and he had been told three years earlier, when he had asked leave to go to Vienna, that he had nothing to hope for in Salzburg, and would do better to seek his fortune elsewhere.[2] Since nothing is known of any plans to go to Vienna in 1774 ('three years ago'), it seems likely that the visit of 1773 was meant. If this is so it implies that Leopold had asked explicitly in 1773 about Wolfgang's prospects in Salzburg of a full and properly paid post, and had been told that they were minimal. It is thus very plausible that he should have been granted leave to go to Vienna to seek work for him there.[3] The timing of the visit was decided not by Leopold's convenience but by the fact that an absence of the archbishop, who also planned to go to Vienna, meant that they would not be needed in Salzburg for a few weeks.

When Leopold and Wolfgang arrived in Vienna, they took up lodgings with the Fischer family, friends from a previous visit. Maria Anna Barbara Fischer, roughly contemporary with Leopold and Maria Anna Mozart, was the widow of a chef in imperial service; she had a daughter,

---

[2] *MBA* 328 (*Letters* 206).

[3] It has been suggested that the purpose of the visit to Vienna could not have been to seek a post for Wolfgang, because Colloredo would never have released him from Salzburg service, and Leopold would never have been able to prevent Colloredo from discovering any attempt to gain such a position in Vienna. See A. Orel, 'Zu Mozarts Sommerreise nach Wien im Jahre 1773', *MJb* (1951), 45. But this argument ignores the evidence of the petition of August 1777.

also called Maria Anna Barbara, who had recently married a prospering coppersmith. When Leopold wrote home to Maria Anna on 21 July 1773, he was able to give news of a number of old friends and acquaintances.[4] One was Dr Franz Anton Mesmer, who made the Mozarts very welcome, and whose house and garden in the Landstrasse suburb provided an attractive location for amateur music-making. He had a large circle, some members of which had potentially useful connections; Franz Reinhard von Heufeld, for example, was the director of the German theatre in Vienna.

Pleasurable though it might have been in more settled circumstances to spend the summer in Vienna with friends vying with each other to entertain them, and urging them to send for Maria Anna and Nannerl too, Leopold's purpose was serious business. On 24 July the empress returned from a visit to Eisenstadt; on 26 July the Mozarts spent St Anne's day, the name-day of Maria Anna and Nannerl, with the Mesmers in their garden; on 31 July Colloredo arrived in Vienna; on 5 August Maria Theresia received Leopold and Wolfgang in audience; and on 12 August Leopold reported the negative result of this event:

Her Majesty the Empress was very gracious to us, it's true, only that's all as well, and I'll have to wait for our return to tell you about it verbally, because I can't write it all down. As far as that enclosure is concerned, that contained nothing advantageous either, because this gentleman himself lives on his own far from any courts, otherwise the letter was uncommonly polite, and he suggested something to me that I'd already had in mind for a long time in any case, only everything has its obstacles.[5]

The identity of the 'gentleman' mentioned in this letter is unknown, as is the nature of the suggestion made by him to Leopold. Presumably, though, they had been given to understand that there was to be no opening at the Viennese court, at any rate for the time being. One possibility for the suggestion made by the unknown man, and already considered by Leopold, is that Wolfgang might obtain some post in Vienna unconnected with the court—as organist at one of the churches, for example. Leopold might have been prepared to consider this, since it would provide a basic income to be supplemented by freelance work done by the two of them and Nannerl. But the solution to the mystery remains in the realm of speculation; the only thing known is that Leopold thought it worth

---

[4] *MBA* 288 (*Letters* 177).

[5] *MBA* 289/4–10 (*Letters* 178, but not complete). The dates of the empress's movements are taken from Orel, 'Sommerreise', 34–5.

while to try to stay longer in Vienna despite their lack of success with the empress.

After their audience with Maria Theresia, Leopold and Wolfgang had to report to Colloredo for instructions. When they spoke to him, on 12 August, he allowed them to extend their leave of absence. This was probably because, although he was returning to Salzburg, he did not intend to stay there long before making another trip away. At any rate, from the date of the archbishop's departure from Vienna until that of the Mozarts', Leopold wanted Maria Anna to report each post day on what she could learn of Colloredo's plans, so that Leopold could make his own accordingly.[6]

The reasons for assuming that Colloredo knew the true reason for the Mozarts' presence in Vienna are first that (as already mentioned) Wolfgang's petition of August 1777 suggests that there had been mutual agreement that he might look elsewhere for employment; and secondly that Colloredo himself saw Maria Theresia after she had given audience to the Mozarts, making it unlikely that their plans could have been concealed from him.[7] It is also probable that he knew more about the reasons for their lack of success than they did, since other evidence, already mentioned, suggests that Maria Theresia's gracious manner masked contempt for the Mozarts.[8]

But though it is probable that Colloredo knew that Leopold was seeking a position in Vienna for Wolfgang, it also seems likely that Leopold was keen to give the impression that he was not seeking anything for himself. This is suggested by a significant passage in Leopold's letter home of 21 August 1773. On that date, the Mozarts now being in the period of extended leave, Leopold wrote to Maria Anna to explain why she and Nannerl could not join them in Vienna as they wanted to. His descriptions of the delightful hospitality they were receiving, together with the pressing invitations from both the Mesmers and the Fischers, had obviously whetted the appetites of the women. Leopold wrote:

I've just this moment received your letter. If I'd known Frau von Messmer's circumstances, which, as you know, *were very doubtful*, I could have brought you with us. only, I couldn't have known them. then there's the fact, firstly, that the

---

[6] Leopold to Maria Anna, 14 Aug. 1773—*MBA* 290/5–7 and 21–4 (*Letters* 179, but not complete).

[7] A third reason is that Leopold said so himself on 8 Sept. 1773—*MBA* 295/34–7 (not in *Letters*). However, the context of this remark is one of mutual mistrust between him and gossips in Salzburg, so that by itself it would have to be treated with caution.

[8] See Ch. 8, pp. 136–7 and Ch. 10, pp. 172–3.

Messmers wanted to have you in the Landstrasse and fr. fischer with her: and finally, how would we get back home? — — you could come down on the river and more quickly, but uncomfortably enough, with the mail coach. and going back up? — — and what an amazing sensation it would make in Salzburg! you can rest assured that it would be a great pleasure to us and all our good friends in Vienna: but it's not worth the trouble any longer, and we're not in a position to meet large costs; if we'd had any prospects or income, I would certainly have written to you that you should come. Only there are a lot of things I can't write about. and on top of that we've got to avoid everything that could cause a stir or raise suspicion as much here *NB*, as in Salzburg, and provide the opportunity for a spoke to be put in our wheel. We don't know ourselves when we'll leave. it might happen really soon, but it might drag out a little while yet. It depends on circumstances that I can't mention. We'll quite definitely be home, god willing, by the end of September. The situation will and must change. Be comforted, keep healthy! God will help! — — — — —[9]

Despite the appearance this passage gives that Leopold was seizing on any excuse he could think of to prevent himself being saddled with the additional inconvenience of his womenfolk (and indeed he was surely doing this), his comments about suspicion should not be dismissed as a fabrication devised solely for this purpose. Neither is it adequate to dismiss them or to underestimate their importance by reference to a developing paranoia of Leopold's with respect to his position in Salzburg. For even if he did delude himself about the interest shown in his affairs by his colleagues (and this is far from certain when the troubled atmosphere of the whole of the court music is considered), account would still have to be taken of any inner logic involved in his delusion in order to understand precisely what he was worried about. To attempt a better understanding of these worries, it is helpful to consider this passage in conjunction with the circumstances of the next absence from Salzburg, to Munich in the winter of 1774/5.

On that occasion Leopold and Wolfgang were to go without the women to Munich, because Wolfgang had been commissioned to write the opera *La finta giardiniera*. Nannerl was keen to go too, but had to endure a tantalizing delay while Leopold searched for a respectable lodging for her. Even when one was found, he worried that her absence from Salzburg would attract comment, and insisted that she keep Count Saurau, the dean, fully informed about her plans. Because she was dependent

[9] *MBA* 291/46–66 (*Letters* 180). The translation of the end of this passage in *Letters* gives an incorrect emphasis. It reads: 'Moreover we must avoid anything which might create a stir or provoke suspicion either here or, in particular at Salzburg . . .'; whereas Leopold's 'NB' refers to Vienna rather than Salzburg.

on Salzburg friends for transport to Munich, she could not choose her departure date, and it was by coincidence rather than design that she was able to leave Salzburg at precisely the right time to arrive in Munich to see the postponed first performance of Wolfgang's opera. When Leopold realized that this would be so, he was mightily relieved, because this fact gave Nannerl a genuinely 'innocent' reason for her journey—namely, to see her brother's work.[10] Nowhere is it recorded why Maria Anna did not go too, but it seems highly likely that she sacrificed her own pleasure in order not to attract further suspicion in Salzburg. In view of the way in which Leopold expressed his worries about this Munich trip, it seems unlikely that his comments to Maria Anna in August 1773 about attracting suspicion were entirely fabrications designed to dissuade her from further attempts to travel to Vienna.

But what were the suspicions that Leopold was so worried about? Passages from the letters both from Vienna in 1773 and from Munich in 1774–5 suggest that his thinking ran along the following lines. Wolfgang was of an age where it was necessary to establish him in some position, and since he did not have an adequate one in Salzburg it was natural that Leopold should travel with him in order to help him obtain one. If the women were to go too, however, it could easily give the impression that the whole family intended to move with him. If this suspicion were allowed to develop, it would damage Leopold's position in Salzburg by undermining his commitment to his post there, and, more importantly, it would damage Wolfgang's prospects of employment in Vienna or Munich by arousing the fear in potential employers that they would be saddled with pension arrangements for Wolfgang's dependants. Only by reasoning of this kind can sense be made of all the passages relating to the arousal of suspicion in the correspondence of these periods; in particular, of Leopold's emphasis at the end of his letter of 21 August 1773 on the need to avoid such suspicion in Vienna.

Thus it was that Maria Anna and Nannerl were used as a type of hostage during this period, their only hope of an amelioration of their lot being that Wolfgang would soon obtain an appointment in some livelier place so that they could all join him there. Until this could be so, they were to live their lives in suspension. For Nannerl in particular, it must have been tremendously frustrating to have her talent lying dormant and her urge to enjoy a more stimulating social life suppressed, while reading the reports sent back by father and brother from Vienna about walks on

---

[10] See Ch. 13 for more details about this.

the ramparts to meet acquaintances, outings to the spa town Baden, out-door concerts in the garden of the Mesmers' house in the Landstrasse, and so on.

At the end of the letter of 21 August 1773, after telling Maria Anna that he did not yet know when they would leave Vienna, because it de-pended on circumstances that he could not mention, Leopold said that he intended to remain as long as necessary, provided that Archbishop Colloredo continued to be absent from Salzburg.[11] What the unmen-tionable circumstances were is unknown, but clearly Leopold still had hopes of some kind in Vienna. And since it is not known exactly what the empress had said to Leopold during the audience of 5 August, it may be that they still concerned a post at court. On 4 September 1773 Leopold wrote towards the end of his letter, 'Herr Gasmann was ill; but is better. I don't know what sort of connection this is supposed to have with our stay in Vienna. Fools are everywhere simply fools! . . . We won't stay here very much longer now, with the next post I'll give you more details.'[12] And on 8 September 1773 he wrote, 'I'm greatly indebted to the people of Salzburg, that they're so very concerned about my return. it means that I'll arrive in Salzburg with more pleasure, and then immediately perambulate around the lit-up or illuminated town all night, so that the lights don't burn in vain.'[13]

These two passages reveal that there was in fact gossip about Leopold and Wolfgang circulating in Salzburg, and that Maria Anna was report-ing it to her husband. Florian Leopold Gassmann was a Kapellmeister at the Viennese court, so the rumour connecting his illness with the Moz-arts' prolonged stay in Vienna presumably centred on the suspicion that Leopold was waiting to try to snap up a post for Wolfgang if Gassmann should die. Despite Leopold's disdainful refusal to acknowledge this possibility, it seems more than likely that it did indeed form at least one of his motives for remaining in Vienna; the supposition is supported by the fact that he claimed to be on the point of departure after he had reported the improvement in Gassmann's condition.

During the period following their audience with the empress, Leopold and Wolfgang were as musically active as the quietness of the season allowed. It seems likely that Leopold wanted to use the time to demon-strate the widest possible range of Wolfgang's performing and composi-tional abilities. Wolfgang already had his Italian theatrical successes to

---

[11] *MBA* 291/67 (*Letters* 180).   [12] *MBA* 294/69–74 (*Letters* 183).
[13] *MBA* 295/14–17 (*Letters* 184).

recommend him as a competent composer for the stage, and now Leopold conducted a performance of Wolfgang's 'Dominicus' Mass, K. 66, in the Jesuitenkirche. On another occasion, Wolfgang borrowed a violin and a concerto from their musical friends the Teybers, and played in public in the Kajetanerkirche.[14] Among the works he wrote during this period were the six string quartets, K. 168–73, some at least of which were probably performed at private concerts at the Mesmers' house. They met the Kapellmeister Giuseppe Bonno, the ballet-master Jean Noverre, the actor and playwright Johann Gottlieb Stephanie (future librettist of Wolfgang's opera *Die Entführung*), and the dramatist Tobias von Gebler (with whom Wolfgang arranged to collaborate on a heroic drama, *Thamos, König in Ägypten*).[15]

It was not until 24 September, some three weeks after Leopold had reported himself ready to leave, that they departed from Vienna. Meanwhile two unrelated occurrences had taken place, either or both of which might have caused the delay in their departure. One was that the Emperor Joseph had returned unexpectedly early from his visit to Poland, and Leopold may have hoped that there might be some advantage to be obtained from him.[16] The other was more mundane. One of the medical doctors in Salzburg, Franz Joseph Niderl, had come to Vienna early in September because of long-standing agonizing indisposition with a stone, and Leopold and Wolfgang became caught up in his fate. Whatever the reason for this final postponement, Leopold must have been aware as they left that another Habsburg court had to be crossed off their list of possible opportunities, at least for the time being.

⁓⁂⁓

Apart from reporting their own activities, Leopold wrote home about various topics he thought would interest Maria Anna. Some were of general concern, such as the disbanding of the Jesuit order in Austria,[17] but most concerned their own acquaintances. Judging by Leopold's speculations about the sexual reputation of the Salzburg portrait painter Rosa Hagenauer-Barducci, who was in Vienna at the same time, the Mozarts

---

[14] Leopold to Maria Anna, 12 Aug. 1773—*MBA* 289/37–44 (*Letters* 178).

[15] Leopold to Maria Anna, 12, 14, and 28 Aug. 1773—*MBA* 289 (*Letters* 178); *MBA* 290 (*Letters* 179); and *MBA* 293 (*Letters* 182).

[16] Leopold to Maria Anna, 15 Sept. 1773—*MBA* 297/35–7 (*Letters* 186).

[17] The main account was given by Leopold to Maria Anna, 4 Sept. 1773—*MBA* 294/4–30 (*Letters* 183).

were at least as keen on gossip as any of their neighbours.[18] They were also interested in other people's financial affairs: Leopold commented that the sisters Maria Katharina and Franziska Auenbrugger, two fine keyboard players, did not receive a pension from Maria Theresia;[19] and that the younger Maria Anna Barbara Fischer had been exceptionally fortunate in marrying a man of means who had been generous enough to make her a handsome settlement immediately.[20] Maria Anna was also later to display the same curiosity about other people's incomes, writing home from Mannheim to tell Leopold about the salaries of the musicians there.[21] Their inquisitiveness probably stemmed partly from dissatisfaction with their own financial situation, and their worries about settling Nannerl and Wolfgang in the world.

But after their own activities, what affected Leopold most during this visit to Vienna was the illness and death of Niderl. In the summer of 1773 Niderl, like Leopold, was 53 years old. He came from a family of apothecaries in Salzburg, and had been a contemporary of Leopold's at the university in the late 1730s. He had made a good career as a physician in Salzburg, and had probably treated the Mozarts. His wife, who was profoundly deaf, had gone to Bad Gastein with Maria Anna Mozart in 1750. Niderl had suffered for years from stones, and by 1772 his illness was incapacitating him to the extent that he could not work. He therefore decided to go to Vienna for medical treatment, and after making his will travelled there with his wife and his sister's husband Joseph Günther, a surgeon practising in Salzburg.[22] Leopold was informed about these events from an early stage, and on 8 September 1773 he reported that Niderl and his wife had arrived and were surrounded by surgeons, physicians, and apothecaries, and that a decision had been taken to operate on the following day.[23] The operation went ahead as planned, but on 11 September 1773 Leopold's letter home was headed by a black cross:

I hope you'll have prepared yourselves before Dr. Niderl's departure for an occurrence which at best is sad, so that it won't fall so painfully on you to hear of his death as it did on me, since I went to visit him and found him already departed. On thursday the 9th, between 10 and 11 o'clock in the morning, he

---

[18] Leopold to Maria Anna, 4 Sept. 1773—*MBA* 294/31–68 (not in *Letters*).

[19] Leopold to Maria Anna, 12 Aug. 1773—*MBA* 289/28–32 (*Letters* 178).

[20] Leopold to Maria Anna, 21 July 1773—*MBA* 288/13–23 (not in *Letters*).

[21] Maria Anna to Leopold, 7 Dec. 1777—*MBA* 386/63–70 (*Letters* 256a).

[22] See H. Schuler, 'Dr. med. Franz Joseph Niderl, Hausarzt der Familie Mozart: ein Beitrag zu seiner Familiengeschichte', *MM* 26 (1978), 4–11.

[23] *MBA* 295/3–13 (not in *Letters*).

was operated on in the presence of all the specialists, and so successfully that in a minute and a half, in fact even faster, everything was over. Straight afterwards I had the stone, which was larger than a large Italian nut, in my hands. I left him the same afternoon, as well as a patient like that can be, because at that time there wasn't the slightest bad sign. on friday the 10th between 10 and 11 o'clock in the morning we went to enquire about his condition and in good hope too. Picture to yourself the shock when I saw him laid out on the bed, and found the people engaged in washing him, because he'd just departed, so that was 24 hours after the operation.

so far as I could gather in the haste and appalling consternation everything changed after midnight, so that they then predicted his death.[24]

Leopold went on to say that he had lost three nights' sleep because of Niderl's operation; the first in worrying about it in advance, the second wondering how he was after it, and the third reliving the shock of seeing him in the process of being laid out. He then became involved in all the necessary duties. He arranged for Rosa Hagenauer-Barducci to paint Niderl, since his family had no portrait of him, he attended the funeral, and he visited Niderl's widow, Maria Kunigunde, to try to console her. He also took an interest in what would become of Niderl's 14-year-old son, believing that it might be best for the boy if he were to remain in Vienna rather than return with his deaf mother to Salzburg.[25]

Leopold continued to be extremely cast down by Niderl's death. His dejection stemmed partly from the fact that the two had been friends, but also surely from Leopold's increased awareness of his own mortality. In particular, the question of what would happen to Niderl's son must have weighed on Leopold's mind, and made him wonder how his family would fare if he too were suddenly to die.

Leopold had originally thought of returning home from Vienna via Mariazell and St Gilgen, in order to take Wolfgang to Maria Anna's birthplace and to the pilgrimage church of his namesake St Wolfgang, across the lake from St Gilgen.[26] But the deeply unsatisfying nature of this visit to Vienna caused him to change his mind. He had put on weight (as he had during his longer and even more frustrating visit to Vienna in 1768), his money was gone, and he was in no mood for pleasure-seeking.[27] After visiting the Mesmers at their country estate Rotmühle, therefore, and buying various small presents for Maria Anna and Nannerl as partial compensation for having been left behind, he and Wolfgang left Vienna

[24] *MBA* 296/3–18 (not in *Letters*).   [25] *MBA* 296/19–51 (not in *Letters*).
[26] Leopold to Maria Anna, 8 Sept. 1773—*MBA* 295/21–6 (*Letters* 184).
[27] Leopold to Maria Anna, 25 Aug. 1773—*MBA* 292/25–8 (*Letters* 181).

around 24 September and travelled home by their usual route of St Pölten, Linz, and Lambach.[28] Wolfgang apparently never did see St Wolfgang or St Gilgen, despite the fact that Nannerl was to live in the latter village for seventeen years following her marriage.

[28] Leopold to Maria Anna, 15, 18, and 22 Sept. 1773—*MBA* 297, 298, and 299 (*Letters* 186, 187, and 188, but with omissions).

❦ 13 ❧

La finta giardiniera in Munich

❦

It was some time in the second half of 1773 that the Mozarts moved from their rooms in the Hagenauers' house to their new accommodation on the other side of the river in the Dancing-Master's House. The house was opposite the building that was to be turned into a public theatre in 1775. On the east side of the square was the Holy Trinity Church, which housed the Virgilianum in its south wing. The house had been owned by the dancing-master Franz Karl Gottlieb Speckner, and in the handsome first-floor dancing hall Speckner had taught the better class of young people in Salzburg to dance, and instructed them in court etiquette. Here he had given balls and masked redoubts (assemblies with dancing, cards, and refreshments, at which everyone wore masks and costumes to disguise identity). On Speckner's death in 1767, the house passed to his cousin Maria Anna Raab (called 'Mitzerl' by the Mozarts), who let out the dancing hall for wedding breakfasts and other parties.[1] When the Mozarts rented their apartment, they got eight rooms, including the dance hall. This they turned into a music and general entertainment room.[2] They used it for domestic concerts and for the rehearsal of works such as *Finalmusik* pieces that Wolfgang had written for outdoor summer performances. Here they also held their regular *Bölzlschiessen* contests, which involved a group of friends firing airguns at a target set up in the room. And Leopold, who did a little business buying keyboard instruments on behalf of third parties, kept the new instruments here while their pitch settled, before transferring them to their new owners. At the back of the house was a courtyard garden, where skittles was played. Because the former dancing hall was a good size and had once been a semi-public room,

---

[1] See R. Angermüller, 'Der Tanzmeistersaal in Mozarts Wohnhaus, Salzburg, Makartplatz 8', *MM* 29 (1981), 1–2. The Dancing-Master's House has just been completely renovated by the Internationale Stiftung Mozarteum. See the extensive illustrated article by R. Angermüller, ' "Können Sie denn noch ein paar Zimmer anbauen lassen?": Zur Geschichte des Mozart-Wohnhauses', *MM* 44 (1996), 1–83.

[2] See Ch. 16 for more detail on *Bölzlschiessen*.

the Mozarts occasionally allowed it to be used by others. In the spring of 1785, Leopold was to offer it to the officials who had the melancholy task of auctioning off property that had belonged to the Amann family.[3]

After their move, the Mozarts had as close neighbours a branch of one of the most important noble families in Salzburg, the Lodrons. In 1631 Archbishop Paris Lodron had founded a Primogenitur-Majorat for his younger brother. This later became tied to the hereditary court position of Oberst-Landmarschall. Both titles were to pass to the eldest son, as long as he kept the Catholic faith. Later, in 1653, a Secundogenitur-Majorat was founded for the second son. The Lodron Primogenitur palace was merely a stone's throw from the Dancing-Master's House, and the Lodron inhabitants during the Mozarts' occupancy were Ernst Maria von Lodron (called 'Count Potbelly' by the Mozarts),[4] his wife Maria Antonia (daughter of the Kämmerer Arco), and their children.[5] The relationship between Countess Maria Antonia Lodron and the Mozarts was to be crucially important, for not only was she very musical, but she enjoyed an extremely close relationship with Colloredo, and had substantial influence over him. Although Salzburg was an ecclesiastical court, women played an important role in its life. They dined regularly, attended nearly all its social functions, and gave their own assemblies which the archbishop attended. When the ladies dined, the *Edelknaben* waited at table as pages, bringing extra warmth to the occasion through the way they were petted by the women. Perhaps Countess Lodron had not been a great favourite with Schrattenbach, because she had hardly been mentioned by the Mozarts while he had been archbishop; then it had been her mother, old Countess Arco, who had interceded for the musicians, and who had had to be kept sweet with New Year greetings and so forth. When Colloredo became archbishop, however, Countess Lodron gradually became the first lady of the court. She and Colloredo must have been friendly long before he came to power, because he was godfather to her son Hieronymus, who had been born in 1766. Count and Countess Lodron had at least eight children, born between 1759 and 1771, and four of the daughters were to become keyboard pupils of Leopold and Nannerl Mozart. Furthermore, Wolfgang's compositions for the countess and her daughters were to earn the Mozarts a special place in her regard, so that despite finding her cold, proud, and false, they

---

[3] See Ch. 27.

[4] 'Graf Baucherl'—Leopold to Wolfgang, 1–3 Nov. 1777—*MBA* 362/85–8 (*Letters* 234). The well-judged translation 'Count Potbelly' is Anderson's.

[5] See Fig. 3 for the relevant relationships in the Arco, Firmian, and Lodron families.

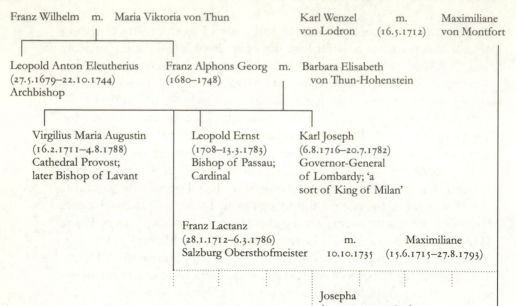

Supplementary Information

The dotted lines show the important marriage links between one family and another; the offspring of these marriage links are shown with the same dotted lines.

Note on Sources: The information comes from Schuler, 'Lodron'; id., 'Die Herren und Grafen von Arco und ihre Beziehungen zu den Mozarts: Anmerkungen zu Mozart-Briefen', *MM* 32 (1984), 19–34; and id., 'Mozart und Mailand: Archivalisch-genealogische Notizen zu den Mailänder Mozartbriefen, zugleich ein Beitrag zur Trogerforschung', *Genealogisches Jahrbuch*, 22 (Neustadt a. d. Aisch, 1982), 7–119.

FIG. 3. Some interrelationships among the Firmian, Lodron, and Arco families in Salzburg

Georg Anton Felix von Arco   m.   Maria Josepha Viktoria
(24.4.1705–2.9.1792)   17.4.1731   von Hardegg
Salzburg Oberstkämmerer   (2.3.1710–31.12.1775)

Leopold Julius Felix
(1.2.1732–1803)

m. 22.6.1762

Leopold Ferdinand
(19.8.1764–29.5.1832)
lived with his grandfather
Georg Anton Felix von Arco;
Leopold Mozart's pupil

— Joseph Adam (27.1.1733–1802)
Bishop of Königgrätz. Helped
Mozart obtain his organist
contract in 1778

— Franz Anton (16.3.1735–1795)
General: took a special interest
in 'Louise' Lodron, and fought
his own father's attempts to
force her into an unsuitable
marriage in 1780

Ernst Maria Joseph Nepomuk   Maria Antonia
(30.5.1716–18.2.1779)   (13.10.1738–14.12.1780)
'Count Potbelly'   m.   'the' Countess Lodron

Sigmund ('Sigerl') (16.6.1759–1.4.1779)	Hieronymus Maria ('Momolo') (21.5.1766–7.9.1823)	Maria Antonia ('Tonerl') b. 23.6.1767	Maria Anna Aloysia b. 28.6.1769	Maria Theresia b. 13.8.1771

Aloisia
('Louise')
b. 3.4.1761

Giuseppina
(Josepha, 'Peperl')
b. 11.10.1764

Joint dedicatees, with their
mother, of K. 242

— Maria Anna Felicia
(17.12.1741–1764)
Countess van Eyck,
the Mozart's hostess in
Paris in 1764; died
while they were staying
with her

— Karl Joseph Felix
(9.3.1743–1830)
was present at Mozart's
second resignation in
1781

managed to remain on good terms with her. The first important allusion to her in the correspondence was when Leopold told Maria Anna to send her New Year greetings at the beginning of 1775.[6]

On returning from the fruitless visit to Vienna in the summer of 1773, Leopold and Wolfgang had to bide their time in Salzburg again, awaiting the next opportunity of improving the family's position. During the interval between their return and the next departure, this time to Munich for Wolfgang to compose and conduct the commissioned opera *La finta giardiniera*, Wolfgang's compositional activities continued apace. Among his works were symphonies, concertos (including his first original keyboard concerto, K. 175), sacred music, a serenade, a keyboard sonata, and much of the *opera buffa* for Munich. His compositional diversity, which must have been encouraged by Leopold, was intended partly to provide him with maximum advantage when seeking new employment. When he and Leopold left for Munich on 6 December 1774, he had a stock of compositions of various types on which he could draw if an appropriate opportunity arose.

Nannerl had never been allowed to go to Milan, but the Munich Carnival was something quite different, because it was an event that many Salzburg people could hope to see at least once in a lifetime. Munich at that time was a mere two days' journey from Salzburg, with an overnight stop in Wasserburg am Inn. Many Salzburgers had business connections in Munich, and tended to use the carnival period to go there and attend to their interests, so that they could also enjoy some of the masked balls and other events. Consequently, it is not surprising that the 23-year-old Nannerl, balked of three opportunities of seeing Italy and one of spending a summer in Vienna, should have entered a strong plea for being allowed to go with Leopold and Wolfgang. But Leopold, despite the relative ease with which this could be arranged (Wolfgang was being paid for the composition, and Nannerl was able to travel respectably and free of charge with the family friend Frau von Robinig in the chaise of another friend Herr Gschwendtner) was still half-reluctant to have her with them. She could not share the accommodation which had

---

[6] Leopold to Maria Anna, 30 Dec. 1774—*MBA* 308/16–19 (*Letters* 194). The information in this paragraph is from H. Schuler, 'Mozart und das hochgräfliche Haus Lodron: eine genealogische Quellenstudie', *MM* 31 (1983), 1–17; details of court social life are to be found in H. Wagner, 'Das Salzburger Reisetagebuch des Grafen Karl von Zinzendorf vom 31. März bis zum 6. April 1764', *MGSL* 102 (1962), 167–90; observations about the Mozarts' view of Countess Lodron's character are from numerous passages in the correspondence. Mozart scholarship has hitherto accorded Colloredo's sister Countess Wallis the position of first lady at court in the 1770s, but my own view is that it was Countess Lodron. See Ch. 18 for my reasons for this.

been offered to her father and brother, presumably because it was too small, and Leopold therefore had to find a room for her elsewhere. Despite the slight nuisance that this caused him, however, it seems fairly clear from the sequence of events that this was not his main worry, and that his chief concern was that her presence in Munich could arouse suspicion that the whole family planned to move there if possible; as already mentioned, this might well have been the reason for Maria Anna's remaining at home.[7] When Leopold and Wolfgang left Salzburg, it was on the understanding that they would try to find a lodging for Nannerl and that, if they were successful, she might join them later.

Leopold's first letter home from Munich was dated 9 December 1774, and with regard to Nannerl's visit he wrote, 'About Nannerl, whom I greet, I can't write anything. I haven't got any prospect yet of anywhere I could place her. And the time's been too short for me so far as well . . .'.[8] If Nannerl thought this first letter discouraging, the next, written on 14 December 1774, must have been even more so. For in addition to the continuing problem of finding a respectable room, Leopold indicated for the first time that ideally her presence in Munich should be linked to seeing Wolfgang's opera, and he had begun to doubt whether she would be able to do so because of the way in which the succession of carnival operas ran in Munich. Some twenty operas were to be given in rotation, and Leopold still did not know when Wolfgang's might be performed.[9]

The difficulty caused Nannerl by the uncertain timing of Wolfgang's opera was exacerbated by the fact that she was not free to make her own travel arrangements, being dependent on Frau von Robinig and Herr Gschwendtner for her transport. However, when Leopold wrote on 16 December 1774 the accommodation problem at least had been solved. Franz Ignaz von Dufraisne, an acquaintance who had met Leopold in Munich and asked him why Nannerl was not with them, suggested Frau von Durst, a respectable young widow, whose main room overlooked the market place in Munich. She could provide a bedroom and a keyboard instrument for Nannerl, and the arrangement seemed eminently satisfactory, particularly since she had made a point of mentioning that her main reservation was that Nannerl might attract unsuitable male visitors to her house.[10] This comment was sure to impress Leopold.

Although one problem was now solved, Leopold's later letters reveal that he was still not happy about the suspicions that might be aroused in

---

[7] See Ch. 12, pp. 194–6.   [8] *MBA* 300/12–14 (*Letters* 189).
[9] *MBA* 301 (*Letters* 190).   [10] *MBA* 302 (*Letters* 191).

Salzburg by her presence in Munich. Perhaps it was these misgivings that caused him to be less than generous in announcing that she could join them:

Now comes the point where Nannerl will see how wretched it is not to be able to put on her own cap, and not to be able either to make herself up or do other little things of that kind. You can't always have other people's servants to wait on you. I imagine that the lady will be used to arranging her own hair most of the time. So Nannerl must get used to putting on a negligé cap neatly herself and to making herself up and practise the keyboard really hard. especially the Paradies and Bach sonatas etc: and the concerto by Luchesi etc.[11]

The postscript to the letter foreshadowed the Salzburg suspicions which were weighing on Leopold's mind. He wrote, 'Above all, Nannerl must seek an opportunity of telling Count Sauerau that she would like to travel to Munich in the company of Md^me von Robini and Herr gschwend-ner. We must above all show confidence in him by telling him that.'[12] Because so many of the musicians' duties were cathedral ones, the dean and Chapter had partial jurisdiction over the members of the court music. This was one reason for keeping the confidence of the dean; it was presumably to counter the potentially destructive force of gossip about a Mozartian plot to take flight from Salzburg that Leopold wanted Nannerl to see Saurau personally and explain herself.[13]

When Leopold next wrote, on 21 December 1774, he sent instructions intended to ensure that Nannerl would keep warm during the journey. Wolfgang had had to stay indoors for nearly a week on arrival in Munich, because of severe toothache which had probably been brought on by the bitter cold. The chaise Nannerl was to travel in was apparently only half-covered, so Leopold advised her to cover her head well, to wear a man's fur coat and warm boots, and to have Herr Gschwendtner lay down some hay in which she could bury her feet. He also gave her further instructions about which music to bring with her, mentioning sonatas and variations by Wolfgang but discouraging her from packing many concertos, since they already had one with them (K. 175) and it was

---

[11] *MBA* 302/30–8 (*Letters* 191).

[12] *MBA* 302/51–4 (*Letters* 191b). Anderson's translation, however, is misleading. It reads, 'Nannerl should find an opportunity of telling Count Sauerau that she would like to go to Munich with Madame von Robinig and Herr Gschwendner. It is important that he should know of our arrangements.' The urgency of Leopold's tone is watered down, thus virtually removing the curiosity aroused in the reader of the German text as to why Leopold deemed it so necessary to confide in Saurau.

[13] See Ch. 12, pp. 194–6, for a discussion of similar worries of Leopold's in Vienna in 1773. The Mozarts probably used music as one means of keeping the friendship of Saurau; the diary of their friend Schiedenhofen mentioned that Nannerl had gone to an academy of Saurau's on 24 Dec. 1774. See Deutsch, 'Schiedenhofens Tagebuch', *MJb* (1957), 18.

not certain that she would need one. Leopold expected her visit to last only twelve days and, at the end of the letter, he again urged her not to keep her plans secret from Count Saurau.[14]

But it was in his next letter, written on 28 December 1774, that Leopold was able to report news which relieved him of the greater part of his fears. Wolfgang's opera had received its first rehearsal on the same day that Nannerl and Maria Anna had seen Count Saurau to tell him of Nannerl's plans. Though it had been very well received by all involved, the first performance had been postponed until 5 January 1775, in order to do it justice by allowing more rehearsal time. Leopold followed this news directly by saying, 'So it turned out to be a really good opportunity to give His Excellency Count Sauerau news of the journey. I'm pleased about it. I can easily believe that everyone's polite, that's their policy, and they suspect all kinds of things.'[15] The sequence of Leopold's remarks makes it almost certain that his relief stemmed from the fact that the postponement of the opera meant that Nannerl would see it after all, and that Count Saurau would therefore have less reason to suspect some ulterior motive for her visit to Munich.

Nannerl did not leave Salzburg until 3 January 1775, and Leopold's letters in the interval gave her instructions for obtaining a letter of credit from Hagenauer, for finding Frau von Durst's house in Munich, for putting together some kind of costume for the masked balls, and for packing various articles such as copies of the Parisian portrait of Leopold, Wolfgang, and herself. Wolfgang also mentioned music she should bring, and repeated the injunction that she should keep warm on the journey. Meanwhile, another new year was approaching, and on 30 December 1774 Leopold, in accordance with his policy of cultivating patronage among the more influential of the nobility in Salzburg, reminded Maria Anna to send cards to Count Saurau and Countess Lodron. In the same letter, Leopold reported that Wolfgang's opera would be performed for the first time on the day after Nannerl's arrival, but then not until Easter. The Munich carnival began with Epiphany on 6 January 1775, but the most boisterous of the entertainments would not take place until the last week, culminating in a wild climax on Shrove Tuesday. Thus he expected Wolfgang's opera to be slipped in just before the carnival began. The composer of the *opera seria* for the same season was Antonio Tozzi, court Kapellmeister in Munich; and Leopold, just as he had in Milan in 1771 when comparing Wolfgang's work with Hasse's, feigned regret at a

---

[14] *MBA* 305 (*Letters* 192).   [15] *MBA* 306/6–16 (*Letters* 193).

circumstance which must have delighted him—that people were saying that Wolfgang's work was going to destroy Tozzi's.[16]

Nannerl duly arrived on 4 January 1775 and took up her quarters with Frau von Durst. Meanwhile, as Leopold wrote to Maria Anna on 5 January 1775, Wolfgang's opera had been postponed again—this time until 13 January 1775. Leopold was of course keen for as many Salzburg people as possible to see the work, but the way in which the Munich theatre rotated performances of so many different operas made this a hit-and-miss affair. Colloredo, for example, was one of the many people from home who were in Munich for part of the carnival, but not at the right time to see Wolfgang's work.[17]

On 11 January 1775 Wolfgang wrote to Maria Anna to tell her that the dress rehearsal would take place on the following day, and that everything augured well. She had written fearing that the theatre manager, Count Joseph Anton Seeau, might harm the opera in some way, and Wolfgang assured her of Seeau's friendliness and expressed pain that she should have entertained such suspicions.[18] It is hard to imagine why she thought Seeau might have had this intention. With a subsidy from the elector of Bavaria, Seeau ran the court theatre at his own risk. He engaged and paid composers and performers, took all the receipts, and made the income and expenditure balance.[19] It could therefore hardly have been in his interest to wreck an opera which had got as far as the dress rehearsal at the risk of his own money. It is possible that Maria Anna's suspicion stemmed from too much overwrought family talk about persecution, and from hearing too much gossip in Salzburg about her family. But though on this occasion it seems likely that her fears were groundless, this fact does not necessarily mean that all the remarks about persecution in the correspondence are similarly unfounded.

Even before the first performance had taken place on 13 January 1775, Leopold was telling Maria Anna that all the signs suggested that Wolfgang would be commissioned to write the *opera seria* for the following year's Carnival in Munich.[20] This was not in fact to be, but meanwhile Wolfgang professed himself pleased with the reception of *La finta giardiniera*. On 14 January 1775 he described the applause and compliments to his

[16] Leopold to Maria Anna, 28 and 30 Dec. 1774—*MBA* 306 and 308 (*Letters* 193, 194, and 194*a*).
[17] Leopold to Maria Anna, 5 and 18 Jan. 1775—*MBA* 309 and 312 (*Letters* 195 and 198).
[18] *MBA* 310 (*Letters* 196).
[19] See the commentary to *MBA* 342/32 about the way in which Seeau operated.
[20] Leopold to Maria Anna, 11 Jan. 1775—*MBA* 310/19–20 (*Letters* 196*a*).

mother, picking out for special mention the praise of the electress and the dowager electress, and of Count Waldburg-Zeil, the former dean of Salzburg. Wolfgang proceeded to express for the first time his frustration in Salzburg; he told his mother that they would not return immediately and that she should not wish them to, since she knew how good it was for him to breathe freely. Furthermore, his opera was to be given again shortly, and he had to stay to supervise it or it might be changed beyond recognition.[21] This remark is a clear reference to the risk of sabotage, though no enemies were mentioned by name. In fact, the second performance was postponed because of the serious illness of one of the female singers.

Particularly galling to Leopold and Wolfgang must have been the fact that Colloredo arrived in Munich only just too late to see *La finta giardiniera.* Leopold claimed that Colloredo was overwhelmed with embarrassment at the compliments heaped upon him because of Wolfgang's work,[22] but that could only be partial compensation to them for his not having heard it himself.

By the time Leopold wrote again, on 21 January 1775, he had heard from Maria Anna that there was gossip circulating about them in Salzburg, to the effect that Wolfgang had entered the elector's service.[23] Leopold reacted with disdain to the childishness of the rumours. His analysis was that they stemmed from their enemies and from people whose consciences told them that Wolfgang would have good grounds for leaving the archbishop's service. He gave no indication who the enemies might be, but he probably had in mind colleagues; perhaps, in particular, musicians who feared that their own prospects of promotion were blocked while the Mozarts lived in Salzburg, and who therefore spread rumours such as these to try to give the impression that the commitment of the Mozarts to the Salzburg court was weak.[24]

Although the delay in performing the opera for the second time meant that many people would not see it, it also meant that others would, and some were potential employers. In his letter of 21 January 1775 Leopold told Maria Anna that the two dukes of Zweibrücken and the elector of the Palatinate were expected in Munich, and that Wolfgang and he must

---

[21] *MBA* 311 (*Letters* 197).   [22] Leopold to Maria Anna, 18 Jan. 1775—*MBA* 312 (*Letters* 198).
[23] *MBA* 313/2–4 (*Letters* 199).
[24] It is worth considering Nannerl's letter to Wolfgang of 23 Oct. 1777 (*MBA* 354/96–101; *Letters* 227a) in conjunction with this passage. Wolfgang had again been in Munich hoping to be offered an appointment, and rumours again circulated in Salzburg that he and Leopold were to be engaged by the elector. Nannerl blamed Maria Magdalena, Michael Haydn's wife, for instigating them, claiming that the motive was to rid Salzburg of the Mozarts so that her husband, Haydn, might become Kapellmeister.

therefore stay to supervise the second performance.[25] Of the people he mentioned, the elector Palatine Karl Theodor was an exceptionally important possible patron. Leopold also commented on the fact that the Salzburg court sculptor, Johann Baptist Hagenauer (husband of the Italian portrait painter Rosa Hagenauer-Barducci, who had painted Niderl's portrait in death in 1773),[26] was to leave for another post, and that word was getting around that Salzburg did not offer the conditions which could attract and keep talented people.[27] It seems highly probable that Leopold himself fuelled this kind of gossip, in order to promote the idea that the responsibility for any lack of status experienced by the Mozarts in Salzburg lay with their mean employer rather than any failings of theirs.

Leopold had envisaged that Nannerl would only stay in Munich twelve days, though he and Wolfgang had always intended to remain longer. He had expected her to travel back as she had come, in Herr Gschwendtner's chaise. But for some reason this was not possible, and Leopold only discovered the fact when he tried to make arrangements for her return journey. Perhaps the women had feared that if there had been any doubt in Leopold's mind about how Nannerl would get home, he would have used it as a further argument against her going. Though he chided Maria Anna for not having told him this earlier,[28] there was nothing to be done, and Nannerl was able after all to stay on in Munich for the rest of the carnival and return home with Leopold and Wolfgang. She went out and about sightseeing with various Salzburg friends who were still there,[29] and participated in the carnival celebrations with Leopold and Wolfgang. At one of the masked redoubts Nannerl appeared as an Amazon,[30] a costume presumably more to her taste than the Salzburg national dress suggested by Leopold when he had written to her at home before her departure to tell her to get together an outfit.[31] Having stayed far longer than had originally been intended, she had to send messages through her mother to her pupils (now two in number—Barbara Zezi and the daughter of Johann Ernst von Antretter) that they should continue to practise.[32]

---

[25] Because of the illness of one of the singers, the second performance had to be abridged as well as postponed. See Leopold to Maria Anna on an uncertain date in Feb. 1775—*MBA* 314/12–14 (*Letters* 202*a*).

[26] See Ch. 12. [27] *MBA* 313 (*Letters* 199).

[28] Leopold to Maria Anna, 18 Jan. 1775—*MBA* 312/25–8 (not in *Letters*).

[29] Leopold to Maria Anna, 21 Jan. 1775—*MBA* 313/16–20 (*Letters* 199).

[30] Leopold to Maria Anna, 15 Feb. 1775—*MBA* 316 (*Letters* 201).

[31] Leopold to Maria Anna, 30 Dec. 1774—*MBA* 308/11–15 (*Letters* 194).

[32] Nannerl to Maria Anna on an uncertain date in Feb. 1775—*MBA* 314 (*Letters* 202*).

During this same period Leopold twice conducted Masses by Wolfgang in the court chapel of the elector,[33] and Wolfgang wrote the motet K. 222 in order to show the elector more of his contrapuntal church music.[34] The second performance of Wolfgang's opera took place towards the end of February, Shrove Tuesday fell on 28 February, Lent began on 1 March, and a third performance was given on 3 March. Leopold intended them to leave on 6 March, and mentioned the possibility that they would bring a girl back with them as a resident pupil. He was not keen on the idea, and claimed to have been trying to refuse the arrangement.[35] In the event it did not materialize. Now that they had ample accommodation, the idea was sure to be on a list of possible ways of supplementing their income, but perhaps Leopold was not keen at this date because of the hindrance a resident pupil would cause to any future travel plans. Since the visit to Munich had not produced an offer of employment, he was certain to want to obtain more leave as soon as possible to try again—unless the outlook for them in Salzburg showed signs of improving.

⸎

Meanwhile, in Salzburg, Fischietti's long-term position as Kapellmeister was in doubt. He had been appointed above Leopold in September 1772, initially for three years, so his contract did not expire until the end of August 1775. In his letter to Maria Anna of 16 December 1774, Leopold had alluded to Fischietti and the fact that the Kapellmeister was choosing a text to set to music. The occasion for which he was expected to write the piece in question was the projected visit to Salzburg in the spring of 1775 by Archduke Maximilian. Wolfgang was also required to write some music for the occasion, but Leopold claimed that they had not even started to think about it, because there was still plenty of time. On the other hand, he congratulated Fischietti for getting down to work so early;[36] a sly reference, perhaps, to the fact that Wolfgang could compose so much more quickly than his Kapellmeister.

But though Fischietti may still have been in Salzburg in April 1775 to direct the performances in honour of Archduke Maximilian,[37] Leopold

---

[33] Leopold to Maria Anna, 15 Feb. 1775—*MBA* 316 (*Letters* 201).

[34] See Wolfgang's letter to Martini of 4 Sept. 1776—*MBA* 323 (*Letters* 205).

[35] Leopold to Maria Anna, 1 Mar. 1775—*MBA* 318 (*Letters* 203).

[36] *MBA* 302/59–62 (not in *Letters*).

[37] Deutsch, *Documents*, 152, asserts this without adducing any documentary evidence; Hintermaier, 'Hofkapelle', 120, claims that it is not established.

had heard while the Mozarts were still in Munich that the Kapellmeister would soon be leaving. On 15 February 1775 Leopold wrote at the end of his letter to Maria Anna that he had heard that Fischietti was letting it be known that he had been summoned to Naples for the end of March; and Leopold scornfully claimed that this boast of Fischietti's was made merely so that he could depart from Salzburg in glory, giving the impression that he had a compositional contract in Naples.[38] It is not known exactly when Fischietti left Salzburg, but he must have been in Naples by November 1775, because his opera *Nitteti* was given there during that month; and he apparently never returned to Salzburg, though his name continued to appear in the court calendar as Titular Kapellmeister from 1775 until 1783.[39] Despite the few but derisive comments about his musical abilities made by Leopold and Wolfgang, therefore, this fact suggests that he went of his own volition rather than because he feared his contract would not be renewed in Salzburg.

Whatever the reasons for Fischietti's departure, the post of Kapellmeister in Salzburg would obviously be vacant again and, though documentary evidence showing that Leopold applied for the post is lacking, there are grounds for believing that he may have done so. At the very least, he probably tried to obtain a salary increase for himself, Wolfgang, or both of them.[40] This attempt, however, was not to take place until March 1777, some two years after Fischietti's probable departure. It is not known what was happening in the intervening period. The Mozarts were all at home for two and a half years after returning from Munich, so no letters of theirs exist to shed light on the question. Possibly the archbishop was doing what he was to do in 1778 after the departure of Fischietti's successor Rust—writing to all the musical centres of Italy to try to persuade someone to take on the post.[41] What is almost certain is that with Fischietti about to go, and no successor chosen, there could be no question of the Vice-Kapellmeister Leopold obtaining any more leave for the time being. He must have known as he and Wolfgang returned to Salzburg that he would have to undertake Fischietti's duties, and despite his disillusionment with his own career in Salzburg, he must have had at least some hope that by doing so efficiently he might win the vacant post himself.

[38] *MBA* 316/29–32 (not in *Letters*).
[39] See Hintermaier, 'Hofkapelle', 117–22, for details about Fischietti's career.
[40] See Ch. 14, pp. 221–3, for more details about this.
[41] See Leopold to Maria Anna and Wolfgang, 11 June 1778—*MBA* 452/155–63 (*Letters* 308).

❧ 14 ❧

Escalating Grievances in Salzburg

❧❧❧

OLLOREDO was by all accounts a difficult character. Even his admirers admitted that he had trouble being pleasant to the people around him.[1] So when he started to introduce his Enlightenment reforms in Salzburg, the resistance they provoked was intensified by the paradox that measures intended to improve the lot of man on earth were imposed by a man who appeared to have no love of humanity.[2] Adaptation of the populace from Schrattenbach's ('the pious archbishop's') reign to his was slow and painful, and many people had grounds for personal animosity towards him. Among them, now famously but then unexceptionally, were the Mozarts. And it was during the period from spring 1775 to autumn 1777 that the first big confrontation with him was brewing up. Since the Mozarts were then all at home together, however, there are no family letters to comment on the events, and knowledge of them is sketchy.

The recorded evidence that does survive from this period allows two aspects of the Mozarts' lives to be glimpsed. One is the round of social activities, partly chronicled by the diaries of Nannerl and of the family friend Schiedenhofen; the other is the increasing resentment felt by the family at their treatment by the archbishop, charted by a very small but significant body of miscellaneous documents.

The main part of Schiedenhofen's diary covers events from October 1774 until April 1778.[3] Nannerl's covers a longer period, but does not survive complete. Its exact size and scope is unknown because Mozart's wife Constanze, into whose hands it was later to pass, removed and gave away individual pages at different times. What has been recovered today is

---

[1] See Wagner, 'Aufklärung', 114. Wagner cites a diary entry by Franz Pichler, who always defended Colloredo, but commented that he was not liked because his manner lacked kindness, and he did not offer practical help when it was called for.

[2] See ibid. 105–6. Wagner cites the diary of Felix Adauctus Haslberger, who noted in Mar. 1783 the circulation of a subversive flysheet parodying titles of theatrical works. One such parody was 'Enlightenment and love of mankind on paper'.

[3] See Deutsch, 'Schiedenhofens Tagebuch', 15–24. Deutsch gives all the entries which have a bearing on music or the Mozarts. Not all of these are in Deutsch, *Documents*.

a set of incomplete entries from 1775, 1776, 1777, 1779, 1780, and 1783. They record events in Salzburg within and without the family, but without comment. The purpose of the diary has not been satisfactorily determined. Mozart's nineteenth-century biographer Otto Jahn thought that Leopold had encouraged both children to keep diaries for pedagogical reasons, so that they could look back and see what they had achieved;[4] but though this is a reasonable hypothesis for Nannerl's girlhood travel diary, none of the surviving entries from her adult one chronicles anything that could support the claim. Nannerl did not write down what she read, summarize the contents of sermons, say what music she played, or indicate in any other way her musical, intellectual, spiritual, social, or emotional development. The entries cover marriages, births, and deaths; arrivals in and departures from Salzburg; aspects of her daily routine such as church-going, hair-dressing, and teaching; processions and other celebrations; and the social activities of the Mozarts. The diary may originally have been conceived as an *aide-mémoire* for the purpose of letter-writing or when recounting verbally events that had taken place during the absence of another member of the family. Maria Anna and Nannerl had written one for this purpose during at least one of the absences of Leopold and Wolfgang in Italy;[5] Nannerl, Leopold, and Wolfgang had kept another when they were in Munich without Maria Anna during the carnival of 1774/5;[6] Nannerl was to incorporate her diary entries into her letters to Wolfgang and Maria Anna when they travelled alone in 1777;[7] and Leopold was to ask Wolfgang to write a diary in order to make his letter-writing more methodical.[8] Clearly, if this had been the initial purpose of keeping a diary, the habit had persisted even when the family was all together, as it was from 1775 to 1777.

The reason for the mutilation and dispersal of Nannerl's diary in the nineteenth century was that some entries had been written by Wolfgang, and leaves containing his writing were given away to people seeking a sample of his hand. The style of his entries is quite different from that of Nannerl's, and perhaps betrays among other things impatience with life in Salzburg. The diary has been mined for what it can tell about performances of Wolfgang's works, but has otherwise generally been found

---

[4] See W. Hummel, 'Tagebuchblätter von Nannerl und Wolfgang Mozart', *MJb* (1957), 207.
[5] See Leopold to Maria Anna, 14 Nov. 1772—*MBA* 266/10–11 (not in *Letters*).
[6] See Leopold to Maria Anna, 15 Feb. 1775—*MBA* 316/23–4 (*Letters* 201).
[7] See Nannerl to Maria Anna and Wolfgang, 4 Oct. 1777—*MBA* 343 (*Letters* 215a, but not complete). The diary entries were copied into the letter on this occasion. Apart from these few entries, the diary has not been translated into English.
[8] See Leopold to Maria Anna and Wolfgang, 17 Nov. 1777—*MBA* 374/20–6 (*Letters* 244).

disappointing.[9] Yet the laconic entries yield more of interest than first sight would suggest. Taken all together, they enable basic patterns of daily life in the Mozart household to be seen; they show the occasional events such as church festivals, carnival celebrations, summer serenades, name-days, and markets, all of which punctuated and enlivened the daily round; they give an indication of the considerable extent of the Mozarts' sociability and hospitality; they record the forms taken by the religious piety of women; they show the passion, of Leopold and Nannerl as well as Wolfgang, for getting up music and for the theatre; and they make a valuable contribution to knowledge of what it was like to be a resident pupil in the Mozart household.[10] Perhaps most important of all, the pictures they build up both of hectic times when friends were staying, and of quiet times when only the ordinary routines were being followed, offer insight into what it must have been like for Leopold after Wolfgang and Nannerl had moved away.[11]

The first big event for the Salzburg court musicians after the return of Leopold and Wolfgang from Munich in March 1775 was the visit from Archduke Maximilian in April. Fischietti and Wolfgang had both been commissioned to write music specially for the visit. Naturally the archbishop wanted to show off his musical personnel, and during Maximilian's visit concerts were given at court on 22, 23, and 24 April. On 22 April Fischietti's piece was performed, though it is not clear whether Fischietti was actually present to direct his work or whether he had already left Salzburg;[12] on 23 April Wolfgang's *Il rè pastore*, a *dramma per musica*, was given; and on 24 April, the evening before the archduke's departure, the music-making was more informal, involving amateur musicians of noble birth, including the archbishop and the archduke themselves. On this

---

[9] See e.g. the commentary to *MBA* 761, about the entries made while Wolfgang and his wife Constanze were visiting Salzburg in 1783. First, it is regretted that the exact date of Wolfgang's arrival is not known, because the relevant pages are missing; the non-survival of other pages while he was in Salzburg is also regretted, but with the postscript that they no doubt recorded only trivial events. Then the assertion is made that the diary records only two events of any note—the first performance of the C minor Mass, K. 427, and Wolfgang's meeting with the blind keyboard player Maria Theresia von Paradis (for whom he was to write a concerto). Next, the commentary lists the 'trivial' types of event noted by the diary—visits, outings, church-going, bathing, and shooting; and regrets that there is nothing about Wolfgang's collaboration with Varesco about the opera *L'oca del Cairo*, or about the two duos (K. 423 and 424) Wolfgang supposedly wrote to help Michael Haydn out of a difficulty. Finally, in a belated acknowledgement that it was Nannerl's, rather than Wolfgang's, diary, its main use is seen as showing that Nannerl and d'Ippold (the man she wanted to marry) were still serious about each other. In fact, the entries made in 1783 richly depict the Mozarts' daily domestic routines in Salzburg—see Ch. 23 for more details.

[10] Leopold was to take his first resident pupil in 1781.

[11] See Pts. 4 and 5, esp. Chs. 23, 26, and 27, for more details.   [12] See Ch. 13.

occasion, Wolfgang performed on the keyboard.[13] Leopold organized at least part of the music for these three days, engaging the castrato Consoli and the flautist Becke from Munich.[14]

Among the amateur musicians drawn from the nobility for the concert on 24 April were Count Johann Rudolph Czernin and his sister Countess Antonie Lützow. Their father was Count Prokop Adalbert Czernin, and their deceased mother had been Colloredo's sister. Both Count Johann Rudolph Czernin and Countess Antonie Lützow had recently arrived in Salzburg. Countess Lützow was 25, and her husband Johann Nepomuk Gottfried had just been made commander of the fortress. Count Johann Rudolph Czernin was 17 and was to attend the university, under Colloredo's supervision. Countess Lützow was a fine keyboard player, and her brother an aspiring violinist. The Czernin family was soon afterwards to enter into an arrangement with Wolfgang which hints at the type of career he was later to envisage as desirable. For during this relatively long period in Salzburg, he wrote a considerable number of compositions which had nothing to do with his duties at court; they were for family friends or for members of the nobility other than Colloredo. Though payments are not documented, he must have received gifts of money for most of them. And given that his court salary was only 150 fl. annually and even Leopold's was only 354 fl., it is quite possible that his private commissions were not only assuming an economic importance greater than his current court post, but that he believed that they could be more significant even than a fully-paid position. No compositions during this period can be shown to have been written specifically for Count Johann Rudolph Czernin, who was soon to be indefatigable in his efforts to enlarge the sphere of his amateur music-making in Salzburg,[15] but the Keyboard Concerto, K. 246, was written in 1776 for Countess Lützow. And by December 1776 Count Prokop Adalbert Czernin had made up his mind to pay Wolfgang 20 ducats (100 fl.) annually in return for a regular supply of compositions.[16]

---

[13] See Deutsch, *Documents*, 152–3.   [14] See ibid. 151 and 154.

[15] For one of Czernin's initiatives, see Leopold to Maria Anna and Wolfgang, 12 Apr. 1778—*MBA* 446/28–56 (*Letters* 302). The violin concertos K. 207, 211, 216, 218, and 219 were written between Apr. and Dec. 1775. The occasions are unknown, but it is possible that Czernin had something to do with them.

[16] See the letter from Count Johann Rudolph's supervisor Karl von Petermann to Count Prokop Czernin, 13 Dec. 1776—Deutsch, *Documents*, 157–8; and T. Volek and I. Bittner, *The Mozartiana of Czech and Moravian Archives* (Prague: Archives Department of the Czech Ministry of the Interior, 1991), 5 and 18–19. Volek and Bittner claim that it cannot be considered certain that the annual fee of 20 ducats was for compositions alone; it might have been intended partly for music lessons given by Wolfgang to Count Johann Rudolph. However, in a letter to Leopold of 19 Dec. 1780, Wolfgang alluded to the Czernin composition plan in such a way as to suggest that

When 'Old Czernin', as the Mozarts called Count Prokop Adalbert, visited Salzburg to see his children, efforts were made to provide musical entertainment. Nannerl recorded his arrival on 29 May 1775,[17] but since her diary is not extant for the period from this date until 8 August 1775, no details survive about the length of the visit, the family's activities, or whether, perhaps, Count Johann Rudolph Czernin played any of Wolfgang's new violin concertos. In May 1776 a number of Colloredo and Czernin clan members visited Salzburg, and probably heard Countess Lützow play the Concerto, K. 246, which Wolfgang had just written for her.[18] In 1777 Schiedenhofen's diary noted a rehearsal of country dances at the Lützows' on 1 February, at which Leopold and Wolfgang Mozart, Count Johann Rudolph Czernin, and friends from the Barisani, Robinig, and Mölk families were also present. They were apparently planning a ballet for performance on Carnival Monday, but the death of Count Prokop Czernin in Prague on 31 January 1777 plunged the family into mourning and put paid to the plan.[19]

With the death of 'Old Czernin', Wolfgang's prospects of an annual income from him in return for compositions were over almost before they had begun, but the idea for this kind of revenue did not leave him. The Czernin family was by no means the only one for whom he composed during this period (though it provided the first recorded example of a regular annual sum); but whereas at first he apparently considered his fees as a welcome addition to his salary (following Leopold's cautious example),[20] he was later to differ significantly from his father by arguing that, in conjunction with income derived from teaching and concert-giving, they were sufficient even without a basic salary. It was the divergence of opinion on this point that was to cause so much trouble in 1781.[21]

Following Archduke Maximilian's visit, the next important musical events chronicled by the diaries of Nannerl and Schiedenhofen were the

it covered compositions only. See *MBA* 565/28–34 (*Letters* 378). It is also unlikely that Wolfgang would have been Czernin's teacher in preference to Leopold, yet Petermann's letter referred specifically to a financial arrangement with 'petit Motzard'. The ducat/florin conversion of 5 fl. to the ducat, which had applied in Salzburg from 1766 at the latest, was still in force in 1777. See Wolfgang to Leopold, 29–30 Sept. 1777—*MBA* 339/37–40 (*Letters* 212a).

[17] *MBA* 319/20.

[18] See Volek and Bittner, *Czech and Moravian Mozartiana*, 5; and H. Schuler, 'Zur Dedikationsträgerin von Mozarts "Lützow-Konzert" KV 246', *MM* 33 (1985), 1–2. The arrivals of Countess Lützow's relations are recorded by Nannerl's diary in May 1776—*MBA* 321/57, 62, 64–5, and 69. But Nannerl does not mention any performance of the concerto.

[19] Deutsch, *Documents*, 159.

[20] See the passage from Wolfgang's letter to Leopold of 19 Dec. 1780 mentioned in n. 16 above.

[21] See Ch. 21 for more details.

performances of *Finalmusik* in August 1775. A rehearsal was held at the Mozarts' house on 8 August 1775 for Wolfgang's work (probably K. 204), written for the first-year logic students to offer in honour of their professors. At 8.30 p.m. on 9 August the serenaders left their assembly point at the Dancing-Master's House and made their way to Mirabell. Having performed the music there, they moved on to the university and performed it again for the professors. The evening's entertainment did not draw to a close till after 11.00 p.m. Schiedenhofen went to both venues with his sister Aloysia (Louise) and a friend, and met the Barisanis, the Loeses, and the Robinigs.[22] On 23 August Schiedenhofen's diary again mentioned *Finalmusik* by Mozart, and again he met up with the Robinigs and Barisanis.[23] Silvester Barisani was the personal physician of Colloredo. He lived with his large family in a house in the grounds of the Lodron Primogenitur palace. Schiedenhofen's diary frequently mentioned the names of Robinig and Barisani in connection with the Mozarts, suggesting that all four families were on friendly terms during this period. They all contained young people more or less contemporary with Nannerl and Wolfgang Mozart.

In February 1776 Schiedenhofen recorded details of some of the carnival balls he attended, which often went on until nearly six in the morning. On 18 February he attended one dressed as a lackey, while Leopold Mozart went as a porter and Wolfgang as a hairdresser's boy; on 19 February Schiedenhofen, dressed as a Tyrolean girl, attended another at which music by Leopold Mozart was apparently played.[24]

On Palm Sunday and Easter Sunday 1776, Schiedenhofen's diary recorded performances of church music by Wolfgang in the cathedral; these would have constituted a part of his official court duties. Then, with the return of summer, private music-making resumed. The date 13 June was St Antony's Day, and since at least two members of Salzburg's top nobility, Countess Lodron and Countess Lützow, were called Antonia, it was celebrated in style. Typically the music written for name-day serenades would be performed outside, under the window of the person being honoured. Schiedenhofen's diary recorded going on 18 June 1776 to hear Wolfgang's music (the Divertimento, K. 247) composed for the occasion; although this was not the name-day itself, it was still within a week, or octave, of it, and celebrations and greetings continued within this

---

[22] *MBA* 319/25–31; and Deutsch, *Documents*, 154.   [23] Deutsch, *Documents*, 154.
[24] Ibid. 155–6. This was the only occasion on which Schiedenhofen indicated that music by Leopold Mozart was performed at any of the events he noted in his diary. Michael Haydn, Hafeneder, and Adlgasser were the composers he tended to name other than Wolfgang Mozart.

period.[25] The Mozarts were evidently proud of the pleasure they could give by Wolfgang's music, and their complete control over the performances probably meant that these occasional pieces were better rehearsed than his compositions for the court. They were also probably more impressive than most similar ventures arranged by other musicians; at any rate, Leopold was to make much of the fact that Countess Lodron's name-day serenade in 1778, when Wolfgang was in Paris, was a fiasco. Count Czernin, who had insisted on organizing the music (written by Hafeneder) on this occasion, committed one blunder of etiquette after another, and seriously offended the countess and Colloredo.[26]

Schiedenhofen's diary for the rest of the summer of 1776 records music-making with the Mozarts at the Antretter house, and a performance of the music written by Wolfgang for the marriage of Elisabeth Haffner. She was the daughter of the wealthy (but by this date deceased) merchant and former mayor of Salzburg, Siegmund Haffner. The bridal music, the 'Haffner' Serenade, K. 250, had been commissioned by her brother Siegmund the younger, and was performed at their summer residence in Loreto, on the outskirts of the town.[27]

Other occasions on which Schiedenhofen paid social visits to the Mozarts and made music with them were recorded for August 1776, but he made no mention of St Anne's Day, 26 July, the name-day of Maria Anna, Nannerl, and many other women, including his own future wife, Anna Daubrawa. Since Nannerl's diary is not extant for July 1776, it is not known how the occasion was marked by the Mozarts, although it is customary to assume that Wolfgang wrote the septet divertimento, K. 251, for it.[28] Certainly he tended to mark the occasion of his sister's name-day with a composition when he had time.

Such was the round (or some of it) of the social and musical activities of the Mozart family in 1775 and 1776, but there survives very little information about what was being done during this period to appoint a new Kapellmeister. Fischietti must have departed at the latest in the autumn of 1775, leaving Leopold in charge of the court music. It seems highly likely that Colloredo was looking around for another Italian Kapellmeister, as he was to do after the departure of Fischietti's successor Rust in 1778, and failing to find one; but while his search remained fruitless, it is hard to believe that Leopold did not hold out hope of obtaining the appointment, even if he acknowledged to himself the likelihood that this would

---

[25] Ibid. 156–7.   [26] See Ch. 18 for the details.
[27] Deutsch, *Documents*, 157.   [28] Ibid. 157.

be, from the archbishop's point of view, *faute de mieux*. Whether he petitioned unsuccessfully for the post in 1776 is unknown, but on 4 September 1776 he wrote (as if from Wolfgang) to Martini in Bologna. With the
letter was enclosed the Motet, K. 222, written by Wolfgang in Munich early
in 1775 for performance before the elector of Bavaria, together with a
request for Martini's comments on its quality. The letter also mentioned
the Munich carnival opera *La finta giardiniera*, and expressed the desire to
see Martini again. It went on to enumerate the problems of music in Germany, and to say that Leopold had served the Salzburg court for thirty-
six years, but that the archbishop had no interest in his older employees.
For these reasons Leopold no longer had his heart in his work, but
was increasingly pursuing his interest in literature.[29] The letter's chief
purpose was clearly to elicit something useful from Martini, perhaps a tes-
timonial. Leopold might have written it in the aftermath of an unsuccessful petition for promotion for himself, or prior to appealing for a
better-paid post for Wolfgang, or as a precaution in case a forthcoming
petition were rejected, or simply with the general aim of increasing their
options.

If Leopold had petitioned unsuccessfully for promotion before writing to Martini, was it true that his failure was caused by his age? He would
hardly have mentioned to Martini the fact that Italians were valued far
more highly in Salzburg than Germans, so he might have used his age
as a convenient and face-saving reason for his low standing there. But
there is some evidence to suggest that his age may by now really have been
a factor in Colloredo's reluctance to promote him. In 1778, after the
ignominious departure of Giacomo Rust,[30] the archbishop's choice of a
successor to Fischietti, Leopold's letters to Wolfgang were to dwell for a
time on the possibility of Michael Haydn's being groomed for the post
of Kapellmeister.[31] Haydn, born in 1737, was eighteen years younger than
Leopold.

Whatever had or had not happened in the autumn of 1776, Leopold
did hand in a petition to the archbishop on 14 March 1777, and it was
rejected. What was he asking for? Neither the appeal nor any reply to
it has survived, so the answer remains speculative.[32] Knowledge of the

---

[29] *MBA* 323 (*Letters* 205). [30] See Ch. 17 for more details about this.

[31] See Chs. 16, 17, and 18 for details of Leopold's initial enthusiasm for Michael Haydn's promotion, and his later withdrawal of support.

[32] Deutsch asserts that the request 'clearly concerned leave for father and son to travel once again'—
Deutsch, *Documents*, 159. In fact, as I argue in the main text, this is what it is *unlikely* to have concerned. The *MBA* commentary to 326 argues that it was a request for an increase in salary for Leopold

appeal comes from Wolfgang's petition to Colloredo (which was actually penned by Leopold) of August 1777. In this request, Wolfgang alluded to the dismal circumstances of the Mozart family, and claimed that these were already known to the archbishop from Leopold's petition of 14 March 1777. He went on to say that since the response to Leopold's request in March had not been favourable, Leopold would then have asked for leave in June 1777, so that they could travel in order to improve their affairs,[33] had the archbishop not ordered everyone involved in the court music to stand by for a visit from the emperor. The wording of Wolfgang's request of August suggests that Leopold's petition of March had not asked for leave, but for promotion and/or an increase in salary for either or both Mozarts; the desire for leave followed the unsuccessful petition of March.[34] Further evidence for the likelihood that the Mozarts had asked for an improvement in Wolfgang's situation during this period comes from the correspondence of autumn 1777, when Wolfgang was in Mannheim, and from Leopold's letter to Martini of 22 December 1777. In the family correspondence are allusions to the unjust court treatment of Wolfgang, which included a suggestion that Colloredo had dismissed the idea that Wolfgang knew how to compose,[35] and in the letter to Martini Leopold claimed that Wolfgang had been paid a miserable pittance in Salzburg, and that Colloredo had rejected his plea for better terms on the grounds that he knew nothing and ought to enter a conservatory in Naples to continue his musical education.[36]

But if the Mozarts felt aggrieved on Wolfgang's account, they also had grounds for discontent on Leopold's. By March 1777 he had been doing Fischietti's job without extra pay for almost two years. While there was no Kapellmeister, he could not get away from Salzburg to help Wolfgang win a post elsewhere—the archbishop would neither reward him nor release him. However, by June 1777 a new Kapellmeister was in the offing. It is not known exactly when Colloredo opened negotiations with

and Wolfgang. This is almost certainly right, though the possibility that Leopold was also requesting promotion (either for himself or Wolfgang or both of them), and that he was pointing out the unfairness of their position, should be borne in mind.

[33] The wording of *MBA* 328/17–18 is 'um dadurch uns wieder in etwas aufzuhelfen'. *Letters* 206 translates this imprecisely as 'in order to enable us to make some money'. It is not certain that Leopold's main wish was for more money; he was anxious for Wolfgang to gain a good appointment. The translation in Deutsch, *Documents*, 162–4, is more accurate.

[34] *MBA* 328 (*Letters* 206); Deutsch, *Documents*, 162–4.

[35] See Wolfgang to Leopold, 4 Nov. 1777—*MBA* 363/20–6 (*Letters* 235); Wolfgang to Leopold, 8 Nov. 1777—*MBA* 366/84–9 (*Letters* 238*a*); and Leopold to Wolfgang, 17 Nov. 1777—*MBA* 374/85–93 (*Letters* 244).

[36] *MBA* 396 (*Letters* 266).

Giacomo Rust, but he was appointed on 12 June 1777 at a salary of 1,000 fl. annually—120 fl. more than Fischietti had received, and over 600 fl. more than Leopold.[37] It is thus highly unlikely to have been coincidence that Leopold wanted to request leave to travel in the same month that Rust was appointed—the salary differential and the fact that Rust was another Italian outsider must completely have disgusted the 'honest German', while at the same time he must have felt that there was no need for him and Rust to be in Salzburg simultaneously.

These events, hazy though the knowledge of them is, form the background to the summer music-making of 1777 which was again recorded by Schiedenhofen, and suggest that behind the apparent idyll of outdoor serenading and social gatherings in the country gardens of friends lurked a smouldering resentment in the Mozart family at the treatment they were receiving. On 13 June, the day after Rust's appointment, Schiedenhofen noted a rehearsal at the Mozarts of the music composed by Wolfgang for Countess Lodron's name-day; and on 16 June, still in the octave of her name-day, the performance of this music, which was probably K. 287 or 288. It took place at Barisani's, and Schiedenhofen walked home afterwards with his future wife Anna Daubrawa. July brought with it the return of St Anne's Day on the 26th, and Schiedenhofen mentioned a rehearsal on the 25th for the music Wolfgang wanted to have performed for Nannerl. A good deal was made of the occasion in 1777. The rehearsal took place at the house of a friend called Gussetti, presumably for the sake of secrecy, and the performance probably in the courtyard behind the Mozarts' house. All the music was by Wolfgang, and consisted of a symphony, a violin concerto (which he played himself), and a flute concerto. Since Anne was a common name, Schiedenhofen spent part of the day calling with friends to congratulate the Annes of his acquaintance—among them members of Barisani's family, and Anna Daubrawa. Other social events during this summer included walks, more music-making (including an academy in which Wolfgang and Nannerl played together on one keyboard and their friend Josepha Duschek from Prague sang), and an afternoon and evening in the country garden of the Robinigs just outside the town in Schallmoos, from which Schiedenhofen walked home with Wolfgang.[38]

---

[37] Hintermaier, 'Hofkapelle', 343. Though Fischietti had been appointed in 1772 at a salary of 800 fl., he had been granted an extra 80 fl. annually in March 1773 as a lodgings allowance—see ibid. 117.

[38] See Deutsch, *Documents*, 160–2.

Between 21 August and 6 September 1777 Schiedenhofen wrote nothing about the Mozarts, but his entry for 6 September is a stark reminder of all that must have been on Leopold's mind since at least March: 'In the afternoon I visited the Mozarts, where I found the father ill, because he and his son are dismissed the service because of the request which the latter made to His Grace for permission to travel.'[39] The request Schiedenhofen meant was Wolfgang's petition of August 1777, which was actually written by Leopold. This was the petition mentioned above which, after stating that Leopold's request of 14 March had been rejected, explained that Leopold had wanted to ask for leave in June, but had been prevented by the imminent visit of the emperor. After this was over, Leopold had submitted a request for leave to travel. He himself had been refused such leave, though Wolfgang, being 'only half in service', might go alone. The petition continued by stating that Leopold had pursued this idea with Colloredo, who had, however, then raised some objection even to Wolfgang's departure. The appeal now being submitted was the Mozarts' response to this objection. Wolfgang invoked the Gospel to support his plea that he be allowed to repay God for the talents he had been given. He said that his duty was to place himself in a position where he could support himself and his parents; Leopold had devoted enormous effort to his education for this purpose, and Wolfgang also wanted later to be able to support his sister, who would otherwise not be able to make use of her musical training. After reminding Colloredo that he himself had told Wolfgang three years ago that he had no expectation of advancement in Salzburg, Wolfgang asked to be discharged.[40] It was in response to this petition that the Mozarts received a double dismissal.

Or did they? Schiedenhofen suggested as much, but in fact the wording of the reply received by Leopold was: '. . . father and son shall have permission to seek their fortune elsewhere . . .'. An internal court memorandum added a sarcastic detail: 'To the Exchequor with the observation that father and son have permission to seek their fortune elsewhere, according to the Gospel.' And a note was sent to the pay office so that Wolfgang's salary could be stopped if he did leave; Leopold was not

---

[39] Ibid. 164.

[40] *MBA* 328 (*Letters* 206); Deutsch, *Documents*, 162–4. The petition is undated, but must have been written in mid or late Aug. 1777. It was after the emperor's visit on 31 July 1777 that Leopold submitted his first request for leave. Following this came the discussion about whether Wolfgang might be allowed to go by himself, and only when Colloredo had raised objections to this plan did Leopold write the petition from Wolfgang which caused all the trouble. The devastating answer was written on 1 Sept. 1777.

mentioned.[41] Leopold was reinstated as a formality after petitioning for his job back, and the paymaster told him that he had not received unequivocal instructions to stop his salary.[42] The initial reply, therefore, was probably intended merely as a reminder of authority by an employer heartily sick of being bothered by the woes of his employees. That Schiedenhofen referred to it as a dismissal is probably a reflection of the effect it had had on Leopold, who must have seen in it the horrifying possibility of the withdrawal of all the family's income while there was as yet no prospect whatever of employment elsewhere.

The famous petition of August 1777 had mentioned not only Wolfgang's duty to use his talents to support his parents, but also to help his sister; and the wording suggests that it was not only financial help that he wanted to provide for Nannerl, but also an opportunity for her to use her own musical skills. Given that the object of his appeal was leave to travel, the most plausible meaning of this passage is that Leopold envisaged the situation where Wolfgang would obtain a salaried appointment somewhere other than Salzburg, where there would be a platform for Nannerl. Not only did Leopold therefore show himself aware of the difficulty of Nannerl's position, and express his reliance on Wolfgang to ameliorate it, but the fact that he built this argument into the official petition suggests that he thought of it as incontrovertibly respectable in the context of the current Salzburg culture.[43]

Almost prostrated though he was by the response to the petition, Leopold must have exerted himself to make plans for Wolfgang to leave, and for Maria Anna to go with him. On 19 September 1777 Schiedenhofen recorded a farewell visit to the Mozarts, because Wolfgang and Maria Anna were to leave on the following Monday (in fact they went on Tuesday, 23 September). Leopold was ill with a heavy catarrh and, no doubt, a heavy heart.[44] During this short period of preparation they appear not to have received any interventionary help from members of the nobility, some of whom apparently did not even know about the affair until later—Countess Lodron, for example, was not in town.[45] Had some of their sympathetic aristocratic patrons been involved, the matter might have been resolved less drastically. Leopold must have been packing music and arranging

[41] Deutsch, *Documents*, 163–4.

[42] Leopold to Wolfgang, 27 and 28 Sept. 1777—*MBA* 335/34–9 and 337/40–57 (*Letters* 210 and 211).

[43] It is important to bear in mind cultural expectations of Wolfgang, and not to fall prey to the psychological anachronism of judging the family relationships according to present-day assumptions.

[44] Deutsch, *Documents*, 164.

[45] Leopold to Wolfgang, 11 June 1778—*MBA* 452/123–38 (*Letters* 308).

letters of credit and recommendation; but above all, with the memory of all the dangers and difficulties of travelling, he must have been trying to instil in Wolfgang some idea of the best way to proceed in every contingency. The shock he had received so recently was not a good omen for the journey, and he must have needed all his courage to prepare for a separation which involved trusting his inexperienced son to act in such a way as to be able to provide for the whole family.

PART III

The Fractured Family
(1777–1780)

❧ 15 ❧

Hopes of a Mozartian Exodus

❧❧❧

THE journey begun in September 1777 was to become one of the
most famous disasters in musical biography. Almost everything that
could go wrong did. Wolfgang could not earn anything like enough to cover
the expenses, Maria Anna (who went with him because Leopold could
not) fell ill and died in Paris, and Wolfgang had to give away some of
her property to pay the nurse. By the time he returned with the utmost
reluctance to Salzburg in January 1779, he had plunged his father into debts
of more than twice Leopold's annual salary. For Leopold, all this confirmed his growing belief that the only sensible way to make a living was
through a secure, salaried position. The unnegotiable aspect of this belief
was to become the main bone of contention between him and Wolfgang
in 1781.

Although the Mozarts were already so well travelled, this journey
involved greater difficulties than previous ones. One reason for this was
that the childhood tours had not had as their chief aim the obtaining of
an appointment. The family was used to arriving at a new destination and
assessing quickly the chances of making a court appearance or giving a
concert, but Wolfgang would now have in addition to calculate the likelihood of being offered a post if he stayed long enough. His plan of
action on arrival at a new destination therefore involved more speculation than previously. If it was a place without a court, he had simply to
try to put on a concert which would produce enough money to pay at
least the expenses of the next stage of the journey. But if it was a place
with a good court, such as Munich or Mannheim, he had to decide how
long it was feasible to stay. He needed to pay all necessary attentions to
the people who could secure him performance opportunities before the
ruler, and having obtained such opportunities, he had to perform music
which demonstrated as many of his skills as possible, to prove his versatility. He also had to plan ahead by having performance copies made
of works which he had brought with him in incomplete form. It was
too expensive to travel with complete sets of parts for orchestral works,

so he tended to carry only a single set; Leopold expected him to have the other parts copied as necessary, and when possible to sell them to recover the copyist's fee before moving on.[1] If there were any likelihood that by staying longer he stood a chance of obtaining an appointment, he was to do so; in this case, he must move from the inn to a cheaper private lodging, take some pupils to earn money, and compose music designed to appeal to the court in question. If the prospects did not seem favourable, he had to press for the earliest possible delivery of the present due for any performances he had given, and move on before the inn bill swallowed up the money he had earned. One difficulty in all this was gauging the prospects; the procrastination before rulers' decisions were made and communicated could be very frustrating, and precious funds could be consumed to no avail while waiting. Another was that the family circumstances meant that he could not spare the time to be as patient as was probably necessary. Leopold expected him to need to stay several months in one centre to show his abilities, but to do this Wolfgang needed to be able to earn enough by way of temporary income to meet his expenses. And if no offer seemed imminent at the end of this period, Leopold started to fret that Wolfgang should be moving on to somewhere more promising.

A second reason for the increased difficulty of this journey was that Leopold could not go with Wolfgang. Not only were his powers of planning superlative, but he was Wolfgang's social equal and they could act as a team. While Wolfgang was practising or composing, Leopold could be having music copied, paying visits to people of influence, studying the opportunities which might be exploited, planning the next stage of the journey, writing letters, and removing all practical duties from Wolfgang. Above all, his maturity meant that he could help his son to be taken seriously, and he had the discipline and experience to keep tight control of the finances. Because Leopold was not happy about Wolfgang travelling alone, he sent Maria Anna with him, but she could give virtually no help of this kind. Her role appears to have been to undertake domestic duties such as the care of clothes, to offer advice where possible, and to safeguard Wolfgang's morals. She could not accompany him into society or do anything to promote his fortunes.

In addition to the extra difficulties of this tour, Wolfgang was hampered by its risks. The aim was that he should obtain an appointment at a different court, so that the whole family could move from Salzburg.

---

[1] See Leopold to Wolfgang, 15 Oct. 1777—*MBA* 350/59–103 (*Letters* 222).

If he was not successful, he was expected at any rate to increase his fame by performance and composition in a number of European musical centres, and to earn enough money to pay at least for his travel expenses.[2] But his Salzburg salary of 150 fl. annually was now lost to the family, so that if he could not earn its equivalent over and above these expenses, the others would suffer financially. Furthermore, it appears that Leopold had no capital to hand with which he could fund the initial stages of the journey until Wolfgang could be expected to earn something. He therefore had to borrow 300 fl., and was thus in debt almost to the extent of one year's salary even before Wolfgang set out.[3] This situation was to cause great trouble between father and son; on the one hand, Leopold wanted Wolfgang to gain first-hand experience of organizing so complicated an undertaking, but on the other it was difficult for him not to interfere when Wolfgang's experience was being bought at the expense of the whole family.

The combination of factors outlined above made the burden on Wolfgang very great. He had to have a rational plan for the journey based fundamentally on the two big questions of where to spend the winter and how to survive the quiet summer period; to behave with influential people in such a way as to maximize the likelihood that they would help him; to have suitable music always ready, not only for his own performance but also for presentation to patrons along his route; to make sure that the travel expenses for the next stage could be earned; to arrange letters of introduction and credit for the next destination; to spend as little as possible; and to keep track of his money, the coinage of which would constantly be changing. He and Maria Anna had to plan the most economical route possible, but they might make a detour if by doing so they

---

[2] See Leopold to Wolfgang, 11–12 Feb. 1778—*MBA* 422/35–50 (*Letters* 285).

[3] See Leopold to Wolfgang, 20 Nov. 1777 and 19 Nov. 1778—*MBA* 375/70–1 and 505/67–8 (*Letters* 246 and 340). It is unlikely that Leopold was completely without means, despite taking out this loan. In his letter of 29 Apr.–11 May 1778, although complaining about the debt he owed, he suggested that overall he did have the means to pay everything. Perhaps he had lent sums of money out to individuals at interest, a common way of investing at the time, and could not easily realize the capital from them. But Leopold intended this money in any case to help Maria Anna and Nannerl if he died before other adequate provision had been made for them—see *MBA* 448/207–9 (*Letters* 304). A note of any loan agreements of this kind still running at the time of Leopold's death would have been recorded in the inventory and *Sperr-relation*, two of the official documents always produced after someone's death. But in Leopold's case, these two documents are lost. Mozart's biographer Maynard Solomon expresses great scepticism about Leopold's repeated claims in the correspondence of 1777–9 that the money he provided for Wolfgang plunged him into debt. Solomon sees Leopold's laments about lack of money as a deceitful ruse to instil guilt into Wolfgang and so gain a hold over him. See M. Solomon, *Mozart: A Life* (London, 1995), ch. 9. It will become clear that I disagree profoundly with this thesis.

could travel via a court, abbey, or town where money could be earned. Leopold knew about most of the promising ones, and suggested routes which provided the best potential, but Wolfgang still had to check before leaving anywhere that the ruler of any establishment under consideration was in residence.

The potential disasters against which Wolfgang had to guard were financial failure, loss of honour, and illness. When he set out, Leopold was already worried that Maria Anna and Nannerl were not adequately provided for in the event of his death. His unease had almost certainly been increased by the new fact that Wolfgang was no longer in Salzburg employment, for although his salary had not been large, precedent suggested that it would have been increased on Leopold's death. Until Wolfgang again had a salary, or Nannerl married, the only things standing between the women and penury were the salary hanging on Leopold's own ageing life, and any money he could save for them. For this reason, he viewed the sum he initially provided for Wolfgang as an investment, which he hoped would increase in value as Wolfgang made his court and public appearances, but which he expected at the very least to be returned to him intact.[4] Quite apart from the fact that Leopold wanted the money for future contingencies concerning the women, financial credit and honour were inextricably linked in his mind, and he was to suffer terrible anxiety about both when he could see no way of reducing his debts. Also at stake was Wolfgang's personal and professional honour, since he had resigned in circumstances which made it extremely desirable that he should be offered a post dignified enough for them to show to the world that Colloredo had spurned a jewel. And because Leopold was still living in the midst of the Salzburg courtiers, this aspect of Wolfgang's honour meant even more to him than it did to Wolfgang. He felt he would be a laughing stock if Wolfgang's behaviour did not produce a result which would vindicate all the efforts Leopold had made on his behalf.[5] Finally, Leopold had the constant background worry that illness would afflict the travellers. For this contingency, which the family had experienced so many times, extra funds were ideally always at hand, so that proper care could be afforded, and financial worries did not add themselves to the other fears.

[4] See Leopold to Wolfgang, 20 Nov. 1777—*MBA* 375/79–81 (*Letters* 246). Solomon suggests that Leopold's anxiety about money was pathologically unreasonable—he had plenty, but was fearful that others would take it from him. See Solomon, *Mozart*, 155–6. This view, however, completely ignores Leopold's fears for Maria Anna and Nannerl.

[5] See Leopold to Wolfgang, 29 Dec. 1777—*MBA* 399/5–13 (*Letters* 268).

It was Leopold who took most of the decisions in the Mozart family, and since he was very anxious to guide Wolfgang's life at this time, it is not surprising that the first period in which they had ever been separated from each other should have given rise to correspondence of exceptional interest. Since Wolfgang lacked familiarity with all the practical aspects of the venture, Leopold's letters were filled with advice on these topics, offering a wealth of information about how musicians lived and worked. More importantly still, nearly all Leopold's letters had a moral purpose; the time had come for Wolfgang to show himself capable of taking responsibility both for his outstanding talent and for the upkeep of his family. Since Wolfgang often did not act as Leopold thought he ought to, the correspondence is a rich source of information about the characters of both men, and about the relationships within the family during this period. These benefits to posterity are increased by the fact that both sides of the correspondence survive for the period during which Wolfgang was absent, from September 1777 to January 1779.

At 21 years of age, Wolfgang lagged behind his contemporaries in independence. Many of the Mozarts' acquaintances had been sent away from home to study or work when they were far younger, and were completely self-reliant by the time they were Wolfgang's age. Why was Leopold so protective, and why did he think Wolfgang should still be grateful for his advice? There were probably several factors at work. His own father had died when he had been 17, so he may not have experienced at first hand the frustrations of not being permitted to choose his own course; only two of Leopold's children had survived, so he was able to do more for each;[6] he believed that Wolfgang's outstanding talents obliged him to achieve something exceptional; his belief that Wolfgang was incompetent in practical affairs may have been well founded; the fate of the whole family hung on the success of the venture; and he had a strong emotional dependence on Wolfgang, which had been strengthened by their closeness during his upbringing.

From the letters written by Leopold to Hagenauer when Nannerl and Wolfgang had been small, it is clear how tenderly Leopold and Maria Anna

---

[6] One example of a family in which the children had to be more independent because there were more of them is that of the Teybers. Leopold and Wolfgang had seen a good deal of them in Vienna in 1773. Matthäus Teyber was a Viennese court violinist with at least six surviving children. The girls became singers, and two of the boys professional musicians. Matthäus's son Anton, born like Wolfgang Mozart in 1756, was studying in Italy with Martini while the Mozarts were in Vienna. Anton's younger brother Franz worked as an itinerant musician in theatrical troupes during his early career. In the essay she wrote for Schlichtegroll in 1792, Nannerl said that Leopold had taught his children himself because only two of them had survived—see Deutsch, *Documents*, 454.

loved their children; but the correspondence of 1777–9 shows unequivocally for the first time Leopold's dependence on his family, and his suffering at being parted from his wife and son. From these letters and the ones he wrote to Nannerl after her marriage, it is clear that he lived for his family. Even at times of gross financial anxiety while Wolfgang and Maria Anna were away, he would still urge Maria Anna to buy herself a fur to keep warm,[7] or to pay more to eat better.[8] His words professing loving care were based on genuine and realistic intentions to provide whatever was needed. In this respect, they form a strong contrast with those of Wolfgang, whose deeds frequently belied his words. No less striking is Leopold's fortitude, and his ability to keep outwardly calm whilst inwardly quailing at the terrifying possibilities of disaster which were present from an early stage of the enterprise. Thanks to these qualities he was to accomplish the noteworthy achievement of easing Wolfgang's return to Salzburg after sixteen months (which involved overcoming the pride both of Wolfgang and Colloredo), with salary increases for himself and Wolfgang which gave the family a combined income of 904 fl. annually, compared with their previous 504 fl.[9]

One feature of Wolfgang's character emerging from the correspondence of this period is that his upbringing and education had to some extent spoilt him for earning his living in the tough world of court musical establishments. The attention Leopold had lavished on him since early childhood, tailor-made to his requirements at every stage, had been ideal for his musical development, but less so for adapting his character to acceptance of the donkey-work required of most court musicians. It is striking that Wolfgang more than once during this absence haughtily asserted his desire to be nothing but a Kapellmeister,[10] and equally disdainfully spurned the idea of undertaking duties such as playing the violin, which made him merely one of many.[11] On this trip, for the first time in his life, his character was put severely to the test as he was forced to undertake drudgery in order to try to survive financially. The merriness, vivacity, and love of his family which had been such a feature of his childhood were shown up as products of an environment which had never yet

[7] See Leopold to Maria Anna, 11 Dec. 1777—*MBA* 389/117–20 (*Letters* 259).
[8] See Leopold to Maria Anna, 12–20 Apr. 1778—*MBA* 446/168–75 (*Letters* 302).
[9] See Hintermaier, 'Hofkapelle', 290 and 296.
[10] See Wolfgang to Leopold, 7 Feb. and 3 July 1778—*MBA* 419/53–4 and 458/107–8 (*Letters* 283a and 311).
[11] See Wolfgang to Leopold, 11 Sept. 1778—*MBA* 487/33–5 (*Letters* 331).

required anything difficult of him; once such a requirement was made, his deeds could not match his words. Leopold recognized his arrogance as a fault, but was nevertheless careful to give him the impression that the agreement he had negotiated with Colloredo for Wolfgang's return to Salzburg after this disastrous trip to Paris offloaded the more irksome duties on to other people.[12] In this display of readiness to protect his son can perhaps be glimpsed some of the roots of Wolfgang's superciliousness.

Maria Anna's position on this journey was one of considerable difficulty because of the lack of a well-defined role, and because Wolfgang apparently found her company dull. Perhaps he felt embarrassed in front of the people he mixed with that his parents believed him to be in need of a minder whose services were little more than those of a nursemaid. Maria Anna was separated from him socially, and often sat in lodgings alone while he was invited out. In Mannheim and Paris she endured at least for a time cold and dingy rooms, in which she had to sit all day with little to do. She appears not to have engaged very actively in the organization of the journey, or to have had much influence over Wolfgang, but rather to have followed plans suggested by others. Though she often had time to spare, her letters home did not contain as much detailed news as Leopold would have liked; and she, as well as Wolfgang, was capable of writing letters without considering what their effect on Leopold might be.

Nannerl's role during the travellers' absence was to keep house and cheer Leopold when he was depressed. Having been neglected by him to some extent since the end of 1769, she now enjoyed far more of his attention. Rising with aplomb to the new challenges facing her, she surprised and moved her father by her industry and steadfastness. As he gradually learnt Wolfgang's faults, Leopold increasingly recognized her virtues and became steadily more concerned for her future security. One result of this concern was his effort to train her in branches of musical knowledge hitherto neglected by her, apparently in the hope that it would increase her chances of supporting herself if he died before she was provided for. By the time Wolfgang returned to Salzburg in 1779, Leopold and Nannerl

---

[12] The terms Wolfgang eventually accepted when he returned to Salzburg were markedly less good than those Leopold had led him to expect. It is not clear whether Leopold did initially negotiate a package whose more attractive aspects were then whittled away; whether he lied to Wolfgang in order to make him accept the terms; or whether he could reshuffle the duties informally for Wolfgang despite the contractual obligations. Possibly there were elements of all three circumstances. See Ch. 18, pp. 312–16, for details.

were much closer than they had been, and the faults Wolfgang had displayed while away were not forgotten. A remembrance of them surfaced again when Wolfgang made his second break with Salzburg in 1781, and again when he married in 1782. After this, Leopold and Nannerl knew that they could count on no further financial help from him, and would have to make what arrangements they could for their futures. Big changes in the family relationships thus began during this period.

En route to Paris: The Journey to Mannheim

A T six in the morning on 23 September 1777 Wolfgang and Maria Anna set off in the family chaise for Munich. The departure was so hectic that there was hardly time to say goodbye, a fact that grieved Leopold deeply when he later learnt that he would never see his wife again. Leopold was ill with a catarrhal chest, but nevertheless bore the brunt of the packing, staying up till two in the morning to do so; not surprisingly in these circumstances, various articles were left behind. Leopold and Nannerl were so cast down when the travellers had gone that they returned to their beds and hid from the world until the following day;[1] their only visitor was apparently Joseph Bullinger who, since his arrival in Salzburg as tutor to the young Count Leopold Arco in the mid-1770s,[2] had become an intimate friend. He was a musical, viola-playing, ex-Jesuit, and appears to have won the confidence of the Mozart family to such an extent that he alone was permitted to share all Leopold's anxieties about money and the family honour while Wolfgang was absent with Maria Anna. It was Bullinger who had provided the loan of 300 fl. with which the travellers set out.[3]

Though Munich was the first destination, and the Mozarts had hopes that Wolfgang might be appointed at the court there, Leopold's plans went further. At the very least he expected Wolfgang to be given a present of money for performing in Munich, but if there were no chance of an appointment there, he wanted Wolfgang to leave promptly and move north-west towards Mannheim,[4] the other main opportunity for

---

[1] Leopold to Wolfgang, 25 Sept. and 15 Oct. 1777, and 11–12 Feb. 1778—*MBA* 331, 350, and 422 (*Letters* 208, 222, and 285).

[2] It has been suggested that Bullinger arrived in Salzburg between 1774 and 1776, after the dissolution of the Jesuit Order in 1773, and that he might have tutored Wolfgang in some branches of his education. See E. F. Schmid, 'Der Mozartfreund Joseph Bullinger', *MJb* (1952), 18–19.

[3] See Leopold to Wolfgang, 20 Nov. 1777 and 19 Nov. 1778—*MBA* 375/70–1 and 505/67–8 (*Letters* 246 and 340).

[4] Though there is evidence to suggest that had Prince Carl Anselm of Thurn and Taxis been resident in Regensburg, Leopold might have wanted Wolfgang to go first north-east to Regensburg—see Wolfgang to Leopold, 11 Oct. 1777 (*MBA* 347/191–2; *Letters* 219d), and Leopold

obtaining a position. And right from the beginning he almost certainly had in mind the possibility of a journey further than Mannheim.[5] The route from Munich to Mannheim had to be organized in such a way as to earn the travel expenses as they went, and Leopold's idea was that they would go via Augsburg, Dischingen (where Prince Carl Anselm of Thurn and Taxis was staying), the Cistercian abbey of Kaisheim, Wallerstein or Hohen-Altheim (both residences of Prince Kraft Ernst of Oettingen-Wallerstein), Ansbach, Mergentheim, and Würzburg. Augsburg offered the possibility of giving public performances, and all the other places private ones.[6] In 1763, travelling from Salzburg to Mannheim, they had taken in money only in Munich and Augsburg, but on that occasion they had gone on from Augsburg through Ulm and Ludwigsburg; Leopold probably suggested this different route in order to exploit what he hoped would be better opportunities. Naturally he did not expect them to be successful at each of the places mentioned, but he did expect them to earn something somewhere. In fact, the route taken by Wolfgang was quite different from the one suggested by Leopold:

1777

23 Sept.	Left Salzburg.
24 Sept.	Arrived in Munich. No record of any earnings.
11 Oct.	Left Munich and arrived in Augsburg. Small earnings.
26 Oct.	Left Augsburg and arrived in Hohen-Altheim. Could not play before Prince Kraft Ernst, who was mourning the death of his wife.
28 Oct.	Left Hohen-Altheim.
30 Oct.	Arrived in Mannheim, via Nördlingen, Cannstatt, Bruchsal, and Schwetzingen. Earned nothing on the journey.

Wolfgang's spirits on leaving Salzburg were high, and his early letters home breathed merriness, excellent humour at being released from service to the 'prick' Colloredo (Leopold was much alarmed by this epithet), and an incipient sense of his responsibility to act for the good of the whole

to Wolfgang, 12–13 Oct. 1777 (*MBA* 348/40–5; *Letters* 220). The purpose of such a journey is not clear, since Regensburg was a major detour in a journey from Munich to Mannheim; and the question of whether the aim was only that of earning travel expenses must therefore remain open; see n. 6 below.

[5] See Leopold to Wolfgang, 12–13 Oct. 1777—*MBA* 348/40–72 (*Letters* 220). Here Leopold gave suggestions for a promising route to Mannheim, and mentioned Darmstadt, Frankfurt, Mainz, and Koblenz beyond Mannheim.

[6] See immediately preceding note for ref. Cliff Eisen, in a private communication, points out that Leopold may have had a little-known connection with the Thurn and Taxis house, concerning the dissemination of his music, and that he may have had an idea for exploiting it now; also that he certainly had a prior connection with Oettingen-Wallerstein.

family.[7] On arriving in Munich, his early steps were directed to approaching the elector through Count Seeau (the theatrical manager), Prince Waldburg-Zeil (Salzburg's former dean, and fellow enemy of Colloredo), and Wotschitka (a cellist and personal valet of the elector's). Seeau had the budget of the theatre under his control, and was therefore to be courted on his own account as well as for his usefulness in easing Wolfgang's approach to the elector. Leopold's ideas on how Wolfgang should proceed were many and various. He should be exceptionally polite to all the nobles; offer to put on a concert in Seeau's garden; offer to write music free of charge for Seeau's theatre; persuade their acquaintance, the castrato Consoli, to sing one of Wolfgang's scenas for the elector; befriend Wotschitka and discover from him the elector's taste in gamba music before writing a suitable piece for him; try to ensure that the elector experienced all Wolfgang's skills, especially the contrapuntal ones; and offer to supply testimonials from Hasse and Martini. If there was any hope of a permanent appointment, Wolfgang should stay longer.[8]

Wolfgang had no success from any of these leads, but it took him two and a half weeks to accept the situation and leave. The difficulty lay in the fact that, although the elector told him firmly on 30 September that there was no vacancy, he hoped that by staying longer in Munich, an appointment at some future point would be forthcoming. Wolfgang therefore tried to arrange for a temporary freelance income from two main sources, and wrote home to ask Leopold's advice. One source was theatrical commissions from Count Seeau; the other was a (hypothetical) consortium of ten people of means, who would pay Wolfgang 600 fl. annually in return for compositions. This latter plan was propounded by Albert, the music-loving landlord of the inn where the Mozarts were staying. Wolfgang was very keen to stay in Munich, and suggested that his total income from these two freelance sources would be in the region of 800 fl. annually, a sum which would support them all.[9]

Leopold did not immediately dismiss the ideas put forward by Wolfgang, though he did express reservations about the certainty of the money and the quality of the work for Seeau.[10] However, Wolfgang himself began to realize that the plan was not progressing, and his next letter was less confident. When he wrote that the 800 fl. he expected to earn would be

---

[7] See Wolfgang to Leopold, 23 Sept. 1777—*MBA* 329 (*Letters* 207, where Wolfgang's epithet 'Schwanz' is translated as 'idiot').
[8] Leopold to Wolfgang, 28 Sept. 1777—*MBA* 337/77–101 (*Letters* 211).
[9] Wolfgang to Leopold, 29–30 Sept. 1777—*MBA* 339 (*Letters* 212a and c).
[10] Leopold to Wolfgang, 4 Oct. 1777—*MBA* 343/4–28 (*Letters* 215).

fine if it were a question of supporting himself alone, the implication must surely be that he was not after all certain that he could earn so much. Nevertheless, he was reluctant to abandon the idea of staying in Munich. He had complained about the prejudice there against any musician who was not Italian, but now he began to get enthusiastic about composing for Munich's German stage, and praised in glowing terms the principal singer in the *Singspiel*, Margarethe Kaiser. Although accepting that he must move on, Wolfgang still hoped that Albert would continue to work at his plan once he had left, so that he could return to Munich on these terms if he failed to do better elsewhere.[11]

Leopold's response now was that the plan probably would support Wolfgang alone, but that it was not honourable enough, and that Colloredo would mock; there was no need to throw himself away in this manner, and he should move on to Augsburg. Nannerl echoed his sentiments,[12] and that was the end of Wolfgang's first attempt to support a family on a freelance income.

Other activities undertaken in Munich were visits to the theatre (where Wolfgang and Maria Anna were separated socially, she attending in the parterre while he visited the boxes of the nobility); visits to the sick composer Mysliveček, who was supposed to be arranging an opera commission for Wolfgang in Naples, in return for Leopold's help in eliciting money owed to Mysliveček by Colloredo; the writing of keyboard music for Nannerl, and the dispatch of duets by Schuster for her to play with Leopold; the investigation of the possibility of Leopold's taking as a resident pupil the 13-year-old daughter of the nobleman von Hamm; unsuccessful attempts to chase up an old debt owed to Wolfgang by Baron von Dürnitz; and various small-scale musical events. In the two and a half weeks that they were there, however, Wolfgang apparently did not play at court or receive any present, so that by the time they left, all they had to show for the stay was a hefty inn bill. The amount is unknown, but Leopold's irritation at the less than satisfactory outcome in Munich was based partly on his experience of mounting expenses when staying in inns.[13] In 1763 they had taken 175 fl. in ten days in Munich, but Leopold was perhaps slightly unfair in thinking that Wolfgang could have done the same this time, given that his purpose was different and he needed time to try to arrange the funding that would allow him to stay longer. The

---

[11] Wolfgang to Leopold, 2–3 Oct. 1777—*MBA* 342/25–37 and 91–6 (*Letters* 214 and 214*b*).
[12] Leopold and Nannerl to Wolfgang, 5–6 Oct. 1777—*MBA* 344/3–7 and 94–8 (*Letters* 216 and 216*a*).
[13] Leopold to Wolfgang, 12–13 Oct. 1777—*MBA* 348/34–40 (*Letters* 220).

overall impression of Leopold's attitude is that he could to some extent stand back and let Wolfgang take his own decisions; but if they proved unsuccessful, he was apt to use the benefit of hindsight to reproach his son for them.

In any case, as Wolfgang attended one last theatrical performance, leaving Maria Anna to sweat alone over the packing for Augsburg,[14] none of them realized how soon any lingering hopes of a future appointment in Munich would be destroyed by the untimely death from smallpox of the elector.

As Maria Anna and Wolfgang prepared to leave Munich for Augsburg, Leopold was doing what he could to plan their programme there, and their onward journey. In addition, he was casting around for alternative openings for Wolfgang. One was the pursuance of the attempt through Mysliveček to obtain an opera commission from Naples. Wolfgang had written from Munich to beg Leopold to allow him to accept any such offer that might be made,[15] and Leopold agreed. He also tried to get an opera commission for Venice, believing that whether or not Wolfgang soon obtained an appointment, prestigious Italian opera contracts could only help his career.[16]

Leopold had seen from newspapers that Augsburg had recently had a glut of concerts, so he did not rate highly their chances of earning a handsome sum of money there. He therefore warned them that if Wolfgang could not give more than one concert, they should not stay long.[17] His instructions for the journey beyond Augsburg to Mannheim involved a host of money-making possibilities, the most important of which was to call on Prince Carl Anselm of Thurn and Taxis at Dischingen.[18] Leopold was already frustrated at not being with Wolfgang to make sure everything was done as he wished; he sympathized with Maria Anna's fatigue at packing, wished he were there to do it for her, and admitted his difficulty in remaining patient.[19]

The story of how Wolfgang fared in Augsburg is well known. They arrived in the evening of 11 October, and left on 26 October. During the fortnight there, Wolfgang gave a concert for the councillors, and also a public concert. He took in 100 fl. from the two occasions (a sum which

---

[14] Wolfgang and Maria Anna to Leopold, 11 Oct. 1777—*MBA* 347 (*Letters* 219a, c, and d).

[15] Wolfgang to Leopold, 11 Oct. 1777—*MBA* 347 (*Letters* 219).

[16] Leopold to Wolfgang, 12–13 Oct. (*MBA* 348/76–82; *Letters* 220); and 15 Oct. 1777 (*MBA* 350/123–41; *Letters* 222).

[17] Leopold to Wolfgang, 9 Oct. 1777—*MBA* 346/36–44 (*Letters* 218).

[18] Leopold to Wolfgang, 15 Oct. 1777—*MBA* 350/144–7 (*Letters* 222).

[19] Leopold to Wolfgang and Maria Anna, 12–13 Oct. 1777—*MBA* 348/120–3 (*Letters* 220).

did not cover the expenses of the journey so far), was disgusted with the behaviour of the councillors, and (despite his abhorrence of court service in Salzburg) expressed his longing to arrive in a place with a court again.

Wolfgang's first step on arriving in Augsburg was to call on his uncle, Leopold's brother Franz Alois, and his cousin Maria Anna Thekla, the *Bäsle*.[20] Next day, he visited the Stadtpfleger, Jakob Wilhelm Benedikt Langenmantel, whom Leopold had known in his youth. Despite the haughty reception from Langenmantel, the possibility of putting on a concert for the councillors was proposed, and Wolfgang was introduced to Langenmantel's son Jakob Alois Karl, who was in charge of organizing such events. It was the younger Langenmantel who entertained himself by mocking Wolfgang's papal Order of the Golden Spur, which Wolfgang was wearing on Leopold's instructions; and Wolfgang was so offended that his first thought was to leave Augsburg immediately without performing. He was persuaded to stay, however, by the family friend and maker of keyboard instruments Johann Andreas Stein, with whom Wolfgang enjoyed warm relations. The concert for the councillors, which took place on 16 October, was apparently an indifferent affair, with a poor orchestra and a present for Wolfgang of only 2 ducats (10 fl.). Meanwhile, Stein suggested that Wolfgang also give a public concert. This took place on 22 October, and brought in 90 fl. Stein and the cathedral organist Demmler joined Wolfgang in a performance of his Concerto for three keyboards, K. 242, which he had written for Countess Lodron and her two older daughters, Aloisia and Giuseppina. Stein provided the instruments, which Wolfgang praised highly to Leopold. At this concert, unknown to Maria Anna and Wolfgang, was their great Parisian friend Grimm, who was passing through Augsburg. Other activities in Augsburg included several visits to the monastery of Heilig-Kreuz, where Wolfgang played the Stein organ, and many occasions of music-making at Stein's in the company of the *Bäsle*.[21]

Before Leopold had even received Wolfgang's first letter from Augsburg, he was writing with more advice on how to proceed there and on how to prepare for the next stage of the journey, to Mannheim. He did not expect Wolfgang to be able to give a concert in Augsburg in under a week, but was keen that he should manage one or two as quickly as possible, to repair the damage done by the too-long stay in Munich. He also asked what the inn bill had been in Munich, so that he could

[20] *Bäsle* means 'little cousin'—see Glossary.
[21] Wolfgang and Maria Anna to Leopold, 14, 16–17, 17, and 23–5 Oct. 1777—*MBA* 349 (*Letters* 221), *MBA* 351 (*Letters* 224), *MBA* 352 (*Letters* 225), and *MBA* 355 (*Letters* 228 and 229).

evaluate the financial situation; but Wolfgang and Maria Anna apparently never sent him this.[22] Leopold was very keen that a newspaper article about Wolfgang should appear in the Augsburg press, so that it could be used to annoy Colloredo. He was also concerned that Wolfgang should be making sure that he had music ready copied for the next stage of the journey, so that it could be presented to patrons in return for a gift of money. Since Leopold hoped that between Augsburg and Mannheim Wolfgang might be able to present compositions to Prince Taxis, Prince Oettingen-Wallerstein, and the abbot of Kaisheim, he wanted Wolfgang to make these advance preparations in Augsburg.

Leopold was also concerned about the timing of the next stage of the journey. Above all else, he wanted Wolfgang to visit Prince Taxis, of whom he had high hopes. The difficulty was that 4 November was St Charles's Day; and, this being the name-day of the elector of the Palatinate, there would be a grand opera in Mannheim on that date in honour of the event. Leopold knew that Wolfgang would badly want to see the opera, but thought that it was not now possible for him to get to Mannheim in time unless he hurried his journey there (which would involve the risk of tearing himself away early from Prince Taxis and having to omit Würzburg from his plans). Since this would run directly counter to the good of the family finances, Leopold was strongly against the idea. He therefore urged Wolfgang not to hurry to Mannheim for the sake of the opera, but nevertheless to make sure that he called on Prince Taxis and Prince Oettingen-Wallerstein as soon as possible, in case they themselves intended to go to Mannheim for the event. Having seen them, Wolfgang should proceed to Mannheim via Würzburg, and should accept the fact that he would miss this performance of the opera; it would be repeated during Carnival, and he would be able to see it then.

As Wolfgang's letters about his unsatisfactory progress in Augsburg reached Salzburg, Leopold expressed doubt about whether the two weeks they would be there would justify the expense. When he learned the financial outcome of the two concerts, and saw the review, however, he was tolerably pleased.[23] The review praised all aspects of Wolfgang's composition and performance in the highest terms,[24] and was welcome material for the anti-Colloredo faction in Salzburg; and the income from the

---

[22] The information in this paragraph and the next is from Leopold's letter of 15 Oct. 1777—*MBA* 350 (*Letters* 222). Leopold's claim that they never told him the amount of the inn bill in Munich is in his letter of 18 Dec. 1777—*MBA* 392/130–1 (*Letters* 262).

[23] Leopold to Wolfgang, 23 and 29–30 Oct. 1777—*MBA* 354/31–8 (*Letters* 227) and *MBA* 359/76–91 (*Letters* 231).

[24] See Deutsch, *Documents*, 167–8.

two concerts of about 100 fl., while not covering all the costs of the trip so far, helped to make up for the long stays in Munich and Augsburg.

It was in reporting their financial position prior to leaving Augsburg that Wolfgang and Maria Anna probably practised their first deception on Leopold. It is not possible to reconstruct with certainty from the letters the progression of earning and spending on this journey, but some idea of it can be extracted with a tolerable degree of accuracy. Leopold had borrowed 300 fl. as starting capital, about 100 fl. of which was used to buy the chaise and other necessities, and two hundred of which was carried with them by Wolfgang and Maria Anna.[25] Nothing was earned in Munich, and the inn bill there is unknown, but on leaving Augsburg Wolfgang claimed that they had 'now lost *in all* 26 or 27 fl.'[26] By this, he seems to have meant that, after paying for everything on the journey so far, they had eaten into their capital of 200 fl. by 27 fl. He did not make it completely clear whether he had deducted the Augsburg concert costs of 16 fl. before making this calculation, but since the letter was written on the point of their departure from Augsburg and Wolfgang emphasized the words 'in all', Leopold would probably have assumed that he had done so, and that the Augsburg inn bill was also included in the assessment. Either this was not the case, however, or the journey from Augsburg to Mannheim cost more than Leopold had expected and the travellers were not prepared to admit as much; because in replying from Mannheim to Leopold's projection that if they had left Augsburg with 170 fl. they should have arrived in Mannheim with 100 fl. of their capital intact,[27] Maria Anna claimed that in fact they had arrived with only 60 fl. She accounted for this by saying that Wolfgang had omitted to mention the concert expenses of 16 fl. and the inn bill of 38 fl. on leaving Augsburg.[28] When she wrote these words, it was already clear to her and Wolfgang that Leopold was highly displeased about the route they had taken from Augsburg to Mannheim (which had disregarded all his advice, earned nothing, and was not even the shortest way); so it is possible that the journey had cost more than the 70 fl. Leopold had estimated, and they did not want to incur his further wrath by admitting as much. Whatever the truth of the matter, this was only the first of several examples of Leopold

[25] See Leopold to Wolfgang and Maria Anna, 5 Jan. 1778 (*MBA* 401/78–81; *Letters* 270); and to Wolfgang on 27 Aug. 1778 (*MBA* 478/195–200; not in *Letters*).
[26] Wolfgang to Leopold, 23–5 Oct. 1777—*MBA* 355/113–7 (*Letters* 229).
[27] Leopold to Wolfgang and Maria Anna, 24 Nov. 1777—*MBA* 378/30–4 (*Letters* 248).
[28] Maria Anna to Leopold, 10–11 Dec. 1777—*MBA* 388/105–11 (*Letters* 258a, which appears to misprint the figure for the Augsburg inn bill, giving 300 fl. instead of *MBA*'s 38 fl.).

calculating the financial situation as finely as possible from Salzburg, while Maria Anna and Wolfgang constantly failed to meet his projections, but tried to avoid admitting as much by trusting that Wolfgang would earn more in future and thereby make such an admission unnecessary.

At the time that Wolfgang and Maria Anna left Augsburg, Leopold was annoyed at what he considered excessively long stays both there and in Munich. Furthermore, it was clear to him, from their announcement (without explanation) that they intended to travel straight from Augsburg to Wallerstein,[29] that they were not going to see Prince Carl Anselm of Thurn and Taxis in Dischingen. Nevertheless, his comments on these disappointments were quite mild. He conceded that something had been set in motion in Munich, and that they had recovered some money in Augsburg, and merely warned them of how carefully they would have to tread in Mannheim in order to be successful. It was a very expensive place, and if they were not careful, Wolfgang would not be able to perform at court and collect his present before they had spent its equivalent on accommodation. Leopold therefore advised them to stay in a private lodging rather than an inn. With respect to the possibility of a permanent appointment there, he strongly advised Wolfgang not to tell any musician there that this was what he had in mind, because to do so would immediately arouse the enmity of people jealous of their own positions. Instead, Wolfgang should ensure that the elector heard what he could do, and only then should approach him direct about an appointment.[30]

Leopold's moderate comments were drawn forth by the relatively successful eventual outcome of the stay in Augsburg; but later on the journey, when things were going from bad to worse, he was to revert to his criticism of Wolfgang for what had happened in Munich, and to build it into a devastating attack on Wolfgang's handling of the whole enterprise.

As Wolfgang and Maria Anna were moving on from Augsburg, Leopold was still pursuing all possible leads. He was still in correspondence with Mysliveček about the Neapolitan opera commission, and Mysliveček was still simultaneously trying to enlist Leopold's help in eliciting the money owed him by Colloredo. Leopold succeeded in getting the money paid to him, but the opera contract was never forthcoming, and Leopold later sourly remarked that Mysliveček only wrote when he wanted Leopold's help.[31] Leopold still had hopes that something might

[29] Wolfgang and Maria Anna to Leopold, 23–5 Oct. 1777—*MBA* 355/18–23 (*Letters* 228a).
[30] Leopold to Wolfgang, 29–30 Oct. 1777—*MBA* 359/80–111 (*Letters* 231).
[31] Leopold to Wolfgang, 25–6 Jan. 1778—*MBA* 410/56–9 (*Letters* 276).

be forthcoming in Munich for Wolfgang, and was in contact with Prince Waldburg-Zeil who, in turn, was enlisting the support of Counts Seinsheim and Berchem (both influential courtiers in Munich).[32] Rumours were circulating in Salzburg that Leopold and Wolfgang had both been taken on in Munich at a joint salary of 1,600 fl. annually; Nannerl claimed that Michael Haydn's wife was behind them, and that her motive was a desire to drive the Mozarts from Salzburg; Leopold, on the other hand, thought that Zeil's servants were circulating similarly flattering rumours to needle Colloredo.[33]

Leopold had given Wolfgang plenty of advice since leaving home, from the need to practise his Latin, and the correct way to write an orderly letter, to more important matters such as the best way to proceed with the next stage of the journey. Every letter had expressed his love, and he frequently revealed how anxious he was about their well-being. When writing for Wolfgang's name-day, Leopold added advice on another plane by revealing how keenly he felt his responsibility to God for Wolfgang's upbringing. The name-day greeting was a separate, more formal, part of a longer letter filled with the usual news. In this greeting, Leopold urged Wolfgang to live as a true Catholic Christian, and not to neglect the care of his soul, so that Leopold, at the solemn moment of death, need not reproach himself for having disregarded the salvation of Wolfgang's soul. He also urged Wolfgang to treasure Maria Anna, whose old age had been made so difficult by this journey.[34] The references to preparation for death in the Mozart correspondence show that Leopold followed convention and believed it to be a formal, learnt affair, in which earthly matters were arranged in an orderly way and the soul was prepared to meet its maker. To die suddenly, without the opportunity to make these arrangements, was thought at best unfortunate.[35]

Leopold was concerned that travelling would become steadily more difficult with the approach of winter. His hope was that they would be

---

[32] Leopold to Wolfgang, 18–20 Oct. 1777—*MBA* 353/21–6 (*Letters* 226).

[33] Nannerl to Wolfgang, 23 Oct. 1777—*MBA* 354/96–101 (*Letters* 227*a*); and Leopold to Wolfgang, 12–13 Oct. 1777—*MBA* 348/26–32 (*Letters* 220).

[34] Leopold to Wolfgang, 23 Oct. 1777—*MBA* 354/68–82 (*Letters* 227).

[35] Cf. Leopold's regret on 21–2 Dec. 1777 that Count Berchem had died so suddenly that he would take 'a good deal of baggage with him into Eternity' (*MBA* 395/14–17; not in *Letters*); and his description to Nannerl on 12 Apr. 1786 of the more 'correct' death of Zeil, discussed in Ch. 29 (*MBA* 948/5–38; not in *Letters*). Leopold's own death may have taken place without the sacraments—see Brno, MZA, Berchtold Family Archive, Family Chronicle, unpaginated, but pp. 42–3 on my count. For detailed information about preparing for death in the 18th c., see J. McManners, *Death and the Enlightenment: Changing Attitudes to Death among Christians and Unbelievers in Eighteenth-Century France* (Oxford, 1981; paperback edn. 1985).

able to spend the coldest months in Mannheim,[36] having earned some more money on the way there. What he did not expect was that they would arrive there so soon, travelling with only overnight stops from Augsburg in complete disregard of all his route suggestions. He had already sent Wolfgang some general advice about how to proceed in Mannheim, but had intended to supplement it. The actions of the travellers balked him of this opportunity.[37]

Leaving Augsburg in the morning of 26 October, Wolfgang and Maria Anna arrived in Mannheim in the evening of 30 October. Next day, they wrote to report their arrival, but despite having taken a completely different route in almost every particular from the one suggested by Leopold, they did not make any attempt to explain why. This insensitivity of them both to what Leopold would think about the news they reported was a fairly constant feature of their behaviour, and caused Leopold a great deal of anxiety, irritation, and frustration. Only later, after he had complained that he had not received any explanation for the route they had chosen, did it become clear that most of the people he had hoped they would call on were not in residence.[38] Their first overnight stop was in Hohen-Altheim, where they had to stay two nights because Maria Anna had a cold; Wolfgang could not play to Prince Oettingen-Wallerstein because he was mourning his recently deceased wife. His Kapellmeister, Ignaz von Beecke, suggested a route from Hohen-Altheim to Mannheim which proved unsuitable for carriages, and this resulted in an unnecessarily circuitous (and therefore more expensive) journey.[39] When Wolfgang's affairs in Mannheim failed to prosper, Leopold was to cast this journey in his teeth, and even express the belief that Beecke, an old keyboard rival of Wolfgang's, had suggested it from malevolence.[40] Kaisheim, Ansbach, Würzburg, in short nearly all the places suggested by Leopold, were omitted; instead, the travellers went from Hohen-Altheim round by Ellwangen, Cannstatt, and Bruchsal, and earned not a kreuzer. Having arrived in good time for the grand opera on 4 November, they paid their first calls and prepared to implement their plans for Wolfgang to be engaged by the elector.

---

[36] Leopold to Wolfgang, 18–20 Oct. 1777—*MBA* 353/119–21 (*Letters* 226).
[37] Leopold to Wolfgang, 13 Nov. 1777—*MBA* 369/109–16 (*Letters* 240).
[38] Maria Anna and Wolfgang to Leopold, 26 Nov. 1777—*MBA* 379/3–9 (*Letters* 249).
[39] Wolfgang and Maria Anna to Leopold, 31 Oct. 1777—*MBA* 360/3–27 (*Letters* 232).
[40] Leopold to Wolfgang, 20 Nov. 1777—*MBA* 375/16–28 (*Letters* 246).

While Wolfgang was trying to take his first steps towards independence, Leopold and Nannerl were doing their best in Salzburg to pass the time without the liveliest member of the family. Each of them had duties which claimed a considerable part of the day. Leopold had his court, cathedral, and teaching obligations, while Nannerl had domestic tasks. Although they kept a maid who cooked for them (called Therese or 'Tresel'), Nannerl had to supervise her closely, and had duties of her own such as ironing and various forms of needlework. She attended Mass early each morning, had her hair dressed at home several times a week, gave private lessons, did music practice, and took the dog, Miss Pimpes, for a walk. But after all the work of the day was done, there seems to have been ample time for recreation. For the Mozarts this took the form chiefly of domestic music-making, card-playing, shooting, and going to the theatre. The family was very sociable, and hardly a day went by without a visit being paid or received.[41]

When Wolfgang left Salzburg, a large dent was inevitably made in the music-making capabilities both of the court and of Leopold's household. At court, although apparently mainly used as a violinist, he had been one of the two most respectable keyboard accompanists; so when he had gone, the other, the 48-year-old organist Cajetan Adlgasser, served this function on his own. To accompany at court involved possessing not only all the necessary skills but also a presentable appearance and demeanour, because of the conspicuousness of the position. At home, the loss of Wolfgang was even greater, because Nannerl's keyboard skills were not as wide-ranging as his. She had apparently hitherto concentrated on *galanterie* playing and had neglected accompaniment skills. This meant that she was strong at playing keyboard sonatas and concertos which she had had time to prepare, but was not so confident at sight-reading and playing from a figured bass. In particular, she was not equally at ease in every key.[42] Once Leopold was deprived of Wolfgang's company, he naturally devoted more time to Nannerl, and encouraged her to develop the accompanying skills which were needed for them to make music together. He was astonished at her burgeoning talent, and was to claim on 6 April 1778 that she could accompany as well as any Kapellmeister.[43]

The essential ingredient of the Mozarts' domestic music-making was a voracious appetite for playing anything they could get their hands on,

---

[41] The information permitting this outline of the family's activities to be made is mainly from Nannerl's diary entries.

[42] See Leopold to Wolfgang, 25–6 Feb. 1778—*MBA* 430/89–102 (*Letters* 291).

[43] *MBA* 444/131–2 (*Letters* 301).

and this promoted versatility and ingenuity. The staple minimum while Wolfgang was away was Nannerl at the keyboard and Leopold on the violin, so that they could play violin sonatas and the like; but they needed very little more in terms of resources before they would attempt much more ambitious orchestral works in scaled-down form. With one more violin, for example, they were playing keyboard concertos in April 1778; Leopold and the new castrato Francesco Ceccarelli took the parts of first and second violin, and Nannerl filled in all the other important orchestral parts, as well as playing her solo part. The same three people also performed arias and motets, Ceccarelli this time taking the vocal part and Nannerl filling in as necessary on the keyboard.[44] Among the grandest domestic concerts given by the Mozarts for which documentation survives were to be those arranged in the autumn of 1786, when Leopold's friends Theobald and Magdalena Marchand visited him from Munich. Leopold and Nannerl had taught the Marchands' children Heinrich and Margarethe ('Gretl'), and their niece Johanna ('Hanchen') Brochard, as resident pupils until Nannerl's marriage in 1784. The visit in 1786 was a grand reunion and provided rich musical resources; apart from Leopold and Nannerl, there was Heinrich to play the keyboard and violin, Gretl to play the keyboard and sing, their brother Daniel to play the cello, and sundry Salzburg court instrumentalists gathered up by Leopold.[45] These two cases give some idea of the extremes of the range of forces which might be assembled in the Dancing-Master's House, and there were obviously numerous intermediate combinations. In short, every opportunity was seized; if they got hold of new music, the Mozarts rounded up the essential instrumentalists, and if travelling singers or instrumentalists visited Salzburg, appropriate music was chosen to exploit their particular talents.

Although the Mozarts paid and received visits almost every day, Sunday was the day most given over to leisure activities. Presumably the day started with attendance at a church service, and Leopold must sometimes have had official duties in the cathedral. At eleven o'clock, at any rate during the period directly following the departure of Wolfgang and Maria

---

[44] See Leopold to Wolfgang, 12–20 Apr. 1778—*MBA* 446/8–16 (*Letters* 302). This tendency of the Mozarts to play orchestral works with minimal forces was perpetuated by Nannerl after her marriage and move to the village of St Gilgen. Her determination then to play Wolfgang's latest keyboard concertos was to involve Wolfgang, Nannerl, and Leopold in a curious three-way concerto traffic, one part of which entailed packing the parts along with lard, candles, and other goods into the backpack of the glass-carrier or other messenger travelling on foot between Salzburg and St Gilgen. It has received little attention from historians of music. See Pt. V for more details.

[45] See Ch. 29 for more details.

Anna in 1777, a domestic concert was given in the Dancing-Master's House.[46] After lunch the members of the shooting company arrived, and the *Bölzlschiessen* took place. Following this, the friends assembled might go for a walk, attend a rehearsal or performance at the theatre opposite, or play cards. Other friends might turn up at any time to join in one or more of the activities, and some might stay for supper.

Whereas Leopold's colleagues were inevitably involved in the domestic music-making arranged by the Mozarts, they were not generally included in the other leisure activities. Membership of the shooting company fluctuated, but during the absence of Wolfgang and Maria Anna the only member belonging to the court music was the new castrato Ceccarelli, whom Leopold took under his wing when he arrived in Salzburg in October 1777. The *Bölzlschiessen* proceeded approximately as follows. The company (of which there were many in Salzburg) consisted of some six to ten members, all of whom would turn up with their air guns. Each member in rotation was *Bestgeber*, which involved providing a sum of money for the prizes, a painted target, and possibly refreshments. The target was shot at and the prizes distributed. Absent members were represented by attending ones, so that Nannerl and Leopold shot for Wolfgang and Maria Anna while they were away. But perhaps the greatest fun was in the choice of a target, which depicted a scene involving someone known to all the members, together with appropriate doggerel. Some idea of the flavour of the targets can be obtained from the Mozarts' correspondence. After Wolfgang had been insulted by the younger Langenmantel in Augsburg, he asked Leopold to have a target made which was probably intended to represent him and his antagonist:

The *targets*, if it's not too late, like this, please. a little man with fair hair stands there bending over, and showing his bare arse. from his mouth come the words. *good appetite for the feast*. the other is done in boots and spurs, a red frock coat, a fine fashionable wig; he must be of medium build. he's depicted in just the right position to be licking the other's arse. from his mouth come the words. *oh, there's nothing to beat it*. like that, please. if it can't be this time, another time.[47]

Similarly derived from Wolfgang's experiences while travelling was a target provided by Leopold on Wolfgang's behalf just after he had left Augsburg for Mannheim. It showed the parting of Wolfgang from his Augsburg cousin Maria Anna Thekla Mozart,[48] with whom he had

---

[46] See Wolfgang to Leopold, 11 Oct. 1777—*MBA* 347/202–9 (*Letters* 219d).
[47] Wolfgang to Leopold, 4 Nov. 1777—*MBA* 363/108–16 (*Letters* 235b).
[48] Leopold to Wolfgang and Maria Anna, 17 Nov. 1777—*MBA* 374/52–65 (*Letters* 244).

apparently had sexual relations of some sort, and to whom he wrote the famous earthy 'Bäsle' letters. But most of the targets depicted people in Salzburg, and Nannerl's friend Katharina ('Katherl') Gilowsky was often the butt of the Mozarts' humour. She was a year older than Nannerl, and the eldest daughter of the barber and surgeon Wenzel Andreas Gilowsky. She had a reputation for being a husband-hunter, and was variously depicted being courted by two men simultaneously, biting her nails during a card game through anxiety about remaining an old maid, and (more politely, when Ceccarelli was *Bestgeber*) lying in a cradle while Ceccarelli played a lullaby on his violin, because it had just been her birthday.[49] She continued to be something of a laughing stock in the Mozart household, and was later to be depicted tripping over a step in Kerschbaumer's shop and showing her bare buttocks.[50]

The card games that the Mozarts played daily with or without their friends formed a necessary social accomplishment for all but the poorest classes of society, and the same games were played by nobility, clergy, and musicians alike.[51] The social circle of the Mozarts was made up of people from very different walks of life. Members of the highest nobility were generally not a part of it unless the occasion was music-making, although Leopold's teenage pupil Count Leopold Arco (a member of one of the most illustrious Salzburg families) shot with the Mozarts' company on occasions, probably partly because his tutor was the Mozarts' friend Bullinger. On the other hand, the Mozarts were involved socially with some members of the minor nobility or *wilde Adel*; these were families such as the Schiedenhofens.[52] Other friends were the court paymaster Franz Vinzenz Lankmayr and the doctor's son Franz Anton Prex, who was an administrative assistant of Nannerl's future husband in St Gilgen. Among the women were Schiedenhofen's sister Louise, her companion Nannerl Kranach, Katherl Gilowsky, and Rosalia ('Sallerl') Joly, an old friend of Maria Anna's. All these women except Louise von Schiedenhofen led lives of domestic service, something that was difficult to avoid except by wealth or marriage (hence Katherl's desperation to catch a man). Nannerl Mozart was educationally and musically accom-

---

[49] Leopold to Wolfgang and Maria Anna, 27 Nov. 1777 (*MBA* 380/114–24; not in *Letters*), 5 Jan. 1778 (*MBA* 401/100–9; not in *Letters*), and 12–20 Apr. 1778 (*MBA* 446/165–8; not in *Letters*). See Plate 11 for yet another target depicting Katherl.

[50] See Leopold to Wolfgang, 11 Nov. 1780—*MBA* 536/20–4 (not in *Letters*).

[51] See G. G. Bauer, 'Bölzschiessen, Brandeln und Tresette: Anmerkungen zum spielenden Menschen Mozart', *MM* 39 (1991), 21–40.

[52] Schiedenhofen's diary shows that the Mozarts and the Schiedenhofens made up card parties together. See Deutsch, 'Schiedenhofens Tagebuch'.

plished, morally unimpeachable, domestically competent, and beautiful. But though her matrimonial sights were set higher than Katherl's,[53] she too worried that she might have to seek domestic service if Leopold died before she married.[54]

Inevitably, considering the amount of time spent together with their friends, the Mozarts needed a good stock of small talk, so it is not surprising that the correspondence regularly reported gossip. And in 1777, for the first time, the Salzburg end of the correspondence is preserved, so that the local stories appear in full. Though the gossip has been dismissed as trivial, and irrelevant to a view of Mozart,[55] it makes an important contribution to understanding the mentality of his family, friends, colleagues, and neighbours.

Sometimes the stories simply gave details of births, marriages, and deaths; sometimes they concerned sexual peccadilloes, financial indiscretions, and other weaknesses of character. The stories of death are often particularly revealing. The underlying insecurity of everyone's life, from pauper to noble, caused by the stern authority of death, repays the trouble of attempted reconstruction. Families were regularly broken up, people might marry three times and produce more than half a dozen children each time, step families often cohered in the most fragile way, and women and children could be rendered homeless paupers overnight. On 9 October 1777, Leopold gave Wolfgang and Maria Anna the first instalment of the story of the marriage of Nikolaus Strasser to the apothecary's daughter Therese Ruprecht.[56] Strasser had previously been married to Eberlin's daughter Maria Franziska, who had been spitefully treated by some of her singer colleagues, and had died following a miscarriage in 1766.[57] Strasser invited only relatives and close friends to the wedding feast, and this meant that Adlgasser and his daughter Viktoria were included because Adlgasser's first wife, Viktoria's mother, had also been a daughter of Eberlin.[58] But Adlgasser's third wife, the singer Maria Anna Fesemayr/Adlgasser, was excluded, and was invited only to the dance following the feast. She made such a fuss about it that Adlgasser eventually decided to let her go to the meal instead of him. His effort to keep the peace was much derided by Leopold, who called him a 'silly

---

[53] In Aug. 1778 Katherl tried to snap up the valet Johann Joseph Adam just after he had been rebuffed by Nannerl. See Leopold to Wolfgang, 27 Aug. 1778—*MBA* 478/36–49 (not in *Letters*).
[54] See Ch. 17, p. 286, for more details.
[55] See the Introduction to *Letters*, p. xvii, n. 3. Here Anderson lists gossip with 'rather tiresome descriptions of illnesses, and long lists of greetings' as 'purely extraneous and irrelevant matter'. The Publisher's Preface to the Third Edition, p. v, repeats the view.
[56] *MBA* 346/25–9 (not in *Letters*).   [57] See Ch. 7 for the account.   [58] See Fig. 1.

sausage'.[59] Little did any of them know then how soon afterwards larger cracks were to appear in the Adlgasser family, or how the changed circumstances were to affect the state of mind of Leopold and Nannerl Mozart.[60]

On 23 October 1777 Leopold reported a death whose repercussions illustrate some of the constraints placed on marriage in Salzburg, and suggest reasons why it may not have been easy for Nannerl Mozart to find a suitable partner. The deceased was Eleonore, wife of the court Oberbereiter Gottlieb von Weyrother. Eleonore was pregnant, and died suddenly on her wedding anniversary, the day of Leopold's letter, after suffering violent abdominal pains during the visit of her midwife. Since she left behind children, her husband immediately thought of remarrying. During the emergency precipitated by Eleonore's collapse, her physician Dr Silvester Barisani was absent from Salzburg because he was on duty at Laufen, the autumnal residence of the archbishop. Weyrother's choice for his second bride fell on Barisani's daughter, Maria Anna Constantia ('Tonerl'), and it was probably a love match;[61] but Silvester Barisani, perhaps annoyed that he had not been present when his patient Eleonore had needed him, incurred Colloredo's displeasure by indicating that he did not want to stay any longer in Laufen. Colloredo thereupon informed Weyrother that if he were thinking of remarrying, he should choose (because of the children that would be born) either a woman with money or an older woman experienced in housekeeping and child care. Tonerl Barisani was neither of these, being only 23 years old and apparently no heiress.[62]

During the same period that these events were taking place, the Mozarts' acquaintance Franz von Mölk also wanted to marry. His intended bride was almost certainly another daughter of Barisani's, Maria Josepha,[63] but his request for permission to marry was turned down flat by Colloredo at just the same time that Colloredo was stipulating the type of woman who would make Weyrother a suitable wife. Leopold believed that

---

[59] Leopold to Maria Anna and Wolfgang, 17 Nov. 1777—*MBA* 374/35–51 (not in *Letters*).

[60] See Ch. 17 for more details.

[61] Wolfgang to Leopold, 23–5 Oct. 1777—*MBA* 355/118–21 (*Letters* 229).

[62] Leopold to Wolfgang and Maria Anna, 23 Oct and 13 Nov. 1777—*MBA* 354/4–23 (not in *Letters*); and *MBA* 369/27–42 (not in *Letters*).

[63] Mölk's sweetheart was always called 'Peberl', 'Pepherl', or 'Pepperl', all being pet forms of 'Josepha'. Nowhere is a surname for the woman indicated in the Mozart correspondence. In the commentary to *MBA* 400/33, it is suggested that she was the daughter of Countess Lodron, but this seems unlikely. In 1777 Giuseppina Lodron was only 13 years old; furthermore, Leopold alluded to Mölk's desire to marry in the middle of his description of Colloredo's displeasure with Barisani, making it more likely that Mölk's sweetheart was Barisani's 25-year-old daughter Maria Josepha.

Colloredo was acting from spite towards Barisani, but he conceded that the stated reasons for the stipulation were good ones. In fact, Weyrother was eventually to defy Colloredo, and marry Tonerl Barisani in April 1778, but the penalty was that he did not receive the usual present of money from the court.[64] In general it was not considered prudent to cross the archbishop in such cases. Hence it is possible that Nannerl Mozart, young and without wealth like Tonerl Barisani, did not have a large choice of suitable marriage partners.

Just as important to an understanding of the underlying attitudes of the members of the Mozart family, and hence of the relationships within it, is the news transmitted by Leopold to Wolfgang and Maria Anna about the court music. If Leopold's accounts are accurate, the musical establishment sank to increasingly bestial levels after Wolfgang left, and was only promising to improve when there was a prospect of his returning. This view must be treated with caution, since Leopold's state of mind was quite different directly after Wolfgang's departure from its condition during the second half of 1778. When Wolfgang left, family hopes were high that he need never return, and that the whole family would also be able to leave; in this state of mind there was a grim satisfaction in relating the faults of the place they all expected to escape. But as it became less clear that Wolfgang could obtain employment elsewhere, and that there was a real possibility of his returning to Salzburg with an increased salary, Leopold's thoughts were bent more towards making the best of things and building up the Salzburg music to an acceptable standard. Nevertheless, even when allowance has been made for Leopold's changing outlook, it seems clear that there was a real decline in standards and morale during Wolfgang's absence. The failure of the new Italian Kapellmeister, Rust, to settle in Salzburg, the unexpected death of the organist Adlgasser in December 1777, and the loss of Wolfgang, left important gaps in a band that could not afford them. Further, individually less serious, losses catalogued by Leopold can be confirmed from other evidence,[65] so that even after discounting his more vivid descriptions of, for example, Michael Haydn's tipsiness and the Italian violinist Brunetti's womanizing, more than a grain of truth remains in his portrayal.[66] It is

---

[64] Leopold to Wolfgang and Maria Anna, 16 Mar. 1778—*MBA* 438/62–3 (not in *Letters*).

[65] Most conveniently from Hintermaier, 'Hofkapelle'.

[66] Leopold's characterization of Haydn as a tippler is contradicted by other reports. After Haydn's death the St Peter's monk Gabriel Hutter wrote of him, 'His character was quiet, discreet modesty. Drink and gambling were far removed from him, moderation in thinking, speaking, even in judging other musical works, were what made him beloved and valued.' Cited in Croll and Vössing, *Johann Michael Haydn*, 79.

essential that the more important events affecting the court music in Salzburg are borne in mind if any assessment of Leopold's relations with Wolfgang during this period is to be attempted, because Leopold had his eye on possibilities both at home and abroad, and his idea of what the future held for them all was affected by events in Salzburg as well as by Wolfgang's actions elsewhere in Europe.

While Wolfgang was in Munich, various matters relating to the court music were afoot. Most importantly for Leopold, he had to petition for the continuance of his job, following Colloredo's invitation to him to leave along with Wolfgang. The petition does not survive, but the reply was copied out by Leopold in his letter of 28–9 September 1777 for the benefit of Wolfgang and Maria Anna. It alluded in general terms to the archbishop's desire for harmony among his musicians and a good attitude to the new Kapellmeister Rust. Leopold professed to be nonplussed by it, because it was completely irrelevant to the points he had raised in his petition; but the very irrelevance, coupled with the fact that the paymaster had received no formal instructions to cancel Leopold's salary, supports the argument proposed previously that Colloredo had not intended to dismiss Leopold so much as to show his power in order to stifle expressions of discontent in which he had not the slightest interest.[67] As for Wolfgang's departure, that continued to be a talking point in Salzburg for some while afterwards. Members of the nobility who might have prevented matters from reaching such a dramatic crisis had been absent from the city on their country estates. When they discovered what had happened, there was some consternation, and Leopold claimed that the Obersthofmeister Firmian had rebuked Colloredo for allowing Wolfgang to leave.[68]

Even at this early stage, Rust's sojourn in Salzburg did not augur well. He had arrived in June 1777, and was on poor terms with Michael Haydn as early as September. On one occasion related by Leopold, Haydn had expressed irritation when he was required to attend a rehearsal he considered unnecessary, and this involved waiting for Ferlendi and Brunetti, two Italian members of the band who were late in arriving. Haydn's epithet on the latecomers, 'Italian asses', spoken in Rust's hearing, was clearly intended to needle the new Kapellmeister, and succeeded.[69] Yet despite this, and despite Colloredo's desire for peace among his musicians, Haydn seems to have enjoyed the archbishop's favour during the

---

[67] *MBA* 337/40–57 (*Letters* 211). Leopold's 'dismissal' was discussed in Ch. 14.
[68] Leopold to Wolfgang and Maria Anna, 4 Oct. 1777—*MBA* 343/39–52 (*Letters* 215).
[69] Leopold to Wolfgang and Maria Anna, 25 Sept. 1777—*MBA* 331/96–100 (*Letters* 208).

early part of Wolfgang's absence. His incidental music to Voltaire's *Zaire*, which was performed in the theatre in Salzburg shortly after Wolfgang's departure, won high praise from both Colloredo and Leopold (though the remuneration, according to Leopold, was insulting).[70] With Wolfgang gone, this period could have been one when Michael Haydn's career progressed. As Vice-Kapellmeister, Leopold had had considerable control since 1763 over whose music was performed in the cathedral and at court, and it seems that when the Mozarts were in Salzburg Wolfgang's music had predominated. When they were away, on the other hand, Haydn had composed and performed more.[71] At the beginning of Wolfgang's absence, when Leopold expected him to obtain an appointment somewhere else, Haydn's career looked set to move upwards, perhaps partly because Leopold felt that he could now afford to be generous to him. Colloredo talked of sending him to study in Italy as part of the process of grooming him for the post of Kapellmeister,[72] and Leopold thought so highly of Haydn's 'Oboe Mass' that he was prepared to support Haydn should a cathedral Kapellmeister post be formed.[73] Whether Haydn's personal attributes were responsible for the fact that neither plan came to fruition, or whether Leopold withdrew his support once he decided that it would be best for Wolfgang to return to Salzburg, is not clear. Perhaps a combination of both factors was involved; at any rate, Leopold's praise for Haydn's music soon changed into censure of his personal life and connections, and consequent unfitness for any respectable post. Haydn's tipsiness was frequently mentioned in the correspondence, and when his wife's sister bore an illegitimate daughter fathered by the Italian violinist Brunetti, Haydn's career seemed sure to stagnate.[74] Reading a little between the lines of Leopold's accounts of the way in which he was to manipulate influential members of the nobility during 1778, in order to promote Wolfgang's chances of obtaining the post of organist vacated by Adlgasser's death, it seems that Leopold's tactics involved pointing up Michael Haydn's moral defects.[75] The whole business thus reveals interesting details of how favour was curried at court.

[70] Leopold to Wolfgang and Maria Anna, 30 Sept.–2 Oct. (*MBA* 340/3–10 and 70–4; *Letters* 213); 5–6 Oct. (*MBA* 344/24–32; *Letters* 216); and 9 Oct. 1777 (*MBA* 346/52–5; *Letters* 218).
[71] See C. Eisen, 'Salzburg under Church Rule', in N. Zaslaw (ed.), *The Classical Era: From the 1740s to the end of the 18th Century* (Basingstoke, 1989), 182–3.
[72] Leopold to Wolfgang and Maria Anna, 4 Dec. 1777—*MBA* 385/134–7 (*Letters* 255).
[73] Leopold to Wolfgang and Maria Anna, 1–3 Nov. 1777—*MBA* 362/4–41 (*Letters* 234).
[74] See Leopold to Wolfgang and Maria Anna, 11 June 1778—*MBA* 452/167–76 (*Letters* 308).
[75] See Ch. 18 for more details.

One major change afoot in the musical personnel during the early part of Wolfgang's absence was the reintroduction of castrati. Colloredo's predecessor Schrattenbach had tended to appoint female singers rather than castrati, so this reversal of policy shows that Colloredo did not altogether lack the will to fund the improvement of his musical establishment. Castrati commanded salaries vastly higher than those of the female singers, and indeed of anyone else except the Kapellmeister; Ceccarelli was given a six-month contract from November 1777 with 100 fl. monthly.[76] The advent of a castrato opened up theoretical possibilities of performing opera in Salzburg, a point which Leopold did not neglect to emphasize to Wolfgang when trying to tempt him back home in 1778.

Occupied though Leopold and Nannerl were, there can be little doubt that a large dent was made in their happiness by the absence of the travellers. Leopold missed Wolfgang terribly, and was prone to fall into the same mood of melancholy as he had occasionally experienced when travelling in Italy. His feelings of sadness were now particularly aroused when, on returning home, he remembered that he would not hear Wolfgang playing the keyboard or violin.[77] Since Leopold had long been disillusioned with his job, and since his happiness had for some time come almost entirely from the company of his family, it is not surprising that the lustre should have gone from his life. His warnings to the travellers to look after their health, warnings reiterated in almost every letter, were not idle conventions but deeply felt entreaties which reflected his fear that a joyful reunion could not be taken for granted: and behind that fear itself lay his conviction that his own life depended on such a reunion.[78]

[76] See Hintermaier, 'Hofkapelle', 59.
[77] Leopold to Wolfgang and Maria Anna, 5–6 Oct. 1777—*MBA* 344/48–52 (*Letters* 216).
[78] Leopold to Wolfgang and Maria Anna, 27 Sept. 1777—*MBA* 335/41–4 (*Letters* 210).

The First Major Conflict between Leopold and Wolfgang: In Mannheim

❧❧❧

P ERHAPS it was fortunate for Leopold that he did not at first know how depleted the travellers' purse was on arrival in Mannheim on 30 October. Whereas he expected them to arrive with 100 fl. of their capital intact, they actually had only 60 fl.; and, given that their fortnight in Augsburg had resulted in an inn bill of 38 fl., this was not a particularly healthy sum.

It seems fairly clear from the order of events that Wolfgang and Maria Anna hoped that Wolfgang would soon earn a handsome present of money from the elector of the Palatinate, and that this would render a confession of the state of their finances unnecessary. The approaching name-day of the elector made for an auspicious start, because it was celebrated with gala days filled by operatic, theatrical, and musical events. Sure enough, after introducing himself to Christian Cannabich and other members of the Mannheim musical establishment, it was arranged that Wolfgang should play to the elector and his wife at an academy on 6 November. While preparing for this event, Wolfgang was assessing the state of music in Mannheim, together with his own chances of being taken on there.

Wolfgang's chief strengths were keyboard and organ playing, and composition. Mannheim's chief pride was its orchestra. The organists there were apparently weak, and there was no keyboard player to match Wolfgang. The Kapellmeister, Ignaz Holzbauer, was ageing, and the other main composer, the Vice-Kapellmeister Georg Vogler, was held in contempt by Wolfgang. Vogler, however, was high in the elector's favour. Wolfgang, having suffered so much from the fact that he was not Italian and had not completed a formal, recognized, course of study in Italy, saw that in Mannheim he might be valued for his ability to write for the German stage there. The opera performed for the elector's name-day was a German one, Holzbauer's *Günther von Schwarzburg*, and

Wolfgang expressed great interest in it. The type of arrangement that would have suited him would have been one where he was invited to stay for a few months to compose a German opera. This would give him the chance to show the elector all his abilities, and perhaps be taken on permanently.

Wolfgang began to cultivate friendships with the musicians he was introduced to, and at first everything looked promising. Cannabich, the Konzertmeister, had a teenage daughter, Rosina ('Rosa'), and Wolfgang began to instruct her in keyboard playing free of charge. He also wrote a sonata for her, K. 309. In return, Cannabich and his wife invited Wolfgang and Maria Anna to spend large parts of each day with them, and introduced Wolfgang to other musicians. Perhaps the most useful of these to Wolfgang was the flautist Johann Baptist Wendling. Wolfgang reported early on to Leopold that Wendling's daughter Elisabeth Augusta had once been a mistress of the elector's, but this did not (yet) prevent him from developing his friendship with Wendling, and nor did it cause Leopold to forbid such a friendship.

There were four gala days to celebrate the elector's name-day. On the first, Wolfgang met the electress, who remembered him from fourteen years previously; on the second, Wolfgang and Maria Anna saw the German opera; on the third, there was a grand academy at which Wolfgang played extensively and was highly praised by the court; and on the fourth, Wolfgang and Maria Anna attended the theatre with the Cannabichs. Following his successful performance before the court, Wolfgang was introduced to the illegitimate children of the elector (two of whom were learning to play the keyboard), in the presence of the elector himself, and was repeatedly asked to play to them. Wolfgang was able to express his desire to write a German opera for Mannheim, and the elector suggested that this might be arranged.[1]

Now that the travellers were so far from home, letters in each direction took six days, making it awkward for Leopold to write with advice. He had no idea how Wolfgang would get on in Mannheim, and therefore how long he would stay. Because the journey from Augsburg to Mannheim had been so rushed, Leopold had been unable to prepare and send instructions for their further travels if they decided to leave Mannheim very soon. This, coupled with the fact that the prospects of progressing satisfactorily beyond Mannheim were not certain, made him

---

[1] The information in this paragraph and the preceding two is from the letters of Wolfgang and Maria Anna, 4 and 8 Nov. 1777—*MBA* 363 (*Letters* 235) and *MBA* 366 (*Letters* 238 and 238*a*).

anxious and irritable, and if he then did not receive on a regular post day
a letter from Wolfgang, his own letter expressed his frustrated annoyance. He was angry because he was sending what advice he could for their
onward travels without knowing whether, by the time his letter reached
Mannheim, they would still be there. The thought that they might already
have left was vexing, not only because he did not believe that there was
an obviously satisfactory way to proceed, but also because he believed that
if Wolfgang went about things in the right way, he should be able to stay
the winter in Mannheim. Leopold's ideas for their onward travel were pessimistic. He had two possible destinations in mind, Holland and Paris, but
the journey to either was not certain to pay the travel expenses. He had
discovered that the prospects of giving concerts in Frankfurt (which they
had done in 1763) no longer existed. Money might be earned in Mainz
and Koblenz, but after that Leopold's ideas dried up. He therefore made
a number of suggestions designed to help them stay in Mannheim if they
had not already left. As well as urging Wolfgang to cultivate friendships
with everyone influential, he told him to ask the elector for a temporary
appointment, and suggested that Maria Anna be used as a reason for not
wanting to travel further in winter. Wolfgang's age and small physical stature
were not conducive to his being taken seriously, but Leopold believed that
if he could stay long enough to show what he could do, he would be
retained by the elector.[2]

By the time Leopold next wrote, however, he had received Wolfgang's
report about the successful academy and the meeting with the elector and
his children, and was thus feeling much happier. He regarded the meeting with the children as especially fortuitous, and alluded to the prospect of their all enjoying a glass of Rhenish wine together before long.
Reiterating his conviction that if Wolfgang could stay a few months he
would be offered an appointment, he finished: 'for my part, I shall never
leave off caring for the welfare of my children as much as I can, telling
them what I can, teaching them, and using all my efforts for them, the
same way that I've done so far, up until I die, as the old faithful husband
and father Mozart.'[3]

Leopold was not to enjoy this mood of satisfaction for long. A few days
after giving his academy, Wolfgang was summoned to receive his present. Instead of the hoped-for gift of money, it was a gold watch whose
acknowledged value was almost useless to him. As Wolfgang wrote to

---

[2] The information in this paragraph is from Leopold's letter to Wolfgang, 13 Nov. 1777—
MBA 369 (*Letters* 240).
[3] Leopold to Wolfgang, 17 Nov. 1777—*MBA* 374 (*Letters* 244).

Leopold to report this, he had been building up an inn bill in Mannheim for nearly two weeks, despite the fact that Leopold had urged them almost as soon as they arrived to move to a private lodging.[4] To pay it from the money they had arrived with would leave them virtually nothing. Wolfgang therefore approached the Mannheim merchant Schmalz, hoping to obtain a cash advance, but here, too, he was unsuccessful. He had mismanaged the credit system, and Schmalz refused to pay him anything. On leaving Salzburg, Wolfgang had been given a letter of credit from Hagenauer to his business contact Herzog in Augsburg. Had Wolfgang presented this letter to Herzog in Augsburg, he could have obtained money in return, but at that point he did not need the cash. On leaving Augsburg, therefore, he should have arranged to have this credit extended to Mannheim by asking Herzog for a letter to a contact there. Herzog's contact in Mannheim was Schmalz, but since Wolfgang apparently did not ask Herzog specifically for the credit to be extended to Mannheim, all Herzog gave him was a letter of introduction to Schmalz. Without explicit instructions from Herzog about money, Schmalz was not authorized to pay out cash.[5]

Wolfgang therefore had to write to Herzog in Augsburg and ask him to authorize Schmalz to give him money. Though Wolfgang could hardly be blamed for having been given a watch, the fact was unfortunate enough to warrant the greatest tact when relaying the news to Leopold; yet Wolfgang apparently did not consider the effect the news would have on him. He made light of the gift of the watch, merely remarking that 'on a journey you need money'. And before reporting the unsuccessful attempt to draw cash from Schmalz, he wrote a parody of a confession, in which he described cracking all manner of scatological jokes in the company of the Cannabichs and others. In reporting the Schmalz affair, Wolfgang alluded to the fact that he now had to wait for an answer from Herzog, and that therefore Leopold could continue to write to Mannheim. Finally, in his next letter, he continued the account of the credit from Schmalz by relating that Herzog had set everything right by arranging for Schmalz to advance 150 fl.; Wolfgang's tone was flippant in the extreme, and he claimed to have referred to Schmalz (which means 'lard') in his letter to Herzog as 'Herr Butter', 'Herr Milk', and 'Herr Cheese'. He also wrote down a riddle concerning different possibilities about his future, and how both he and Leopold might react to each; here, too, his tone was

---

[4] Leopold to Wolfgang and Maria Anna, 10 Nov. 1777—*MBA* 367/27–9 (*Letters* 239).

[5] Wolfgang to Leopold, 13 and 14–16 Nov., and Leopold to Wolfgang, 24 Nov. 1777—*MBA* 370/39–47 (*Letters* 241); *MBA* 373/81–96 (*Letters* 243a); and *MBA* 378/4–16 (*Letters* 248).

frivolous, and the riddle seems insoluble.[6] Furthermore, his remark that Leopold could continue to write to Mannheim must have implied to Leopold that Wolfgang was only waiting for his money from Schmalz before leaving; and since Wolfgang made no mention of any plans beyond Mannheim, Leopold was sure to wonder what would become of him next. Lastly, if Wolfgang had been successful in drawing money from Schmalz at his first attempt, the debt would have bounced back to Salzburg to catch Leopold unawares; and since he already owed money to Hagenauer, this would have been embarrassing.

Sure enough, Leopold's reaction to these letters was one of outrage. He assumed that prospects in Mannheim were non-existent, and that Wolfgang was preparing to leave. From previous experience, he knew how much forward planning was necessary in order to cover travel expenses and accommodation costs in a new destination while preparing to earn money. He already owed 300 fl. to Bullinger, 100 fl. to the merchant Weiser, about 40 fl. to the merchant Kerschbaumer, and an unspecified amount to Hagenauer, and was expecting tailors' bills in the new year.[7] The family's total debt was well in excess of one year's salary, and he did not know how to reduce it, let alone provide more travel money for Wolfgang and Maria Anna. Nevertheless, this was obviously going to be necessary, and he gave suggestions for a route to Paris which would provide maximum earning opportunities and would also enable them to draw cash from the merchant Bolongari in Frankfurt. Every suggestion was accompanied by an urgent exhortation to earn as much as possible while spending as little as possible, and above all to stop treating the journey like a joke. He laid great emphasis on the difficulties of earning money, living on an irregular income, keeping well, and warding off crooks; Leopold had had ample experience of all these things.

In his exasperation, Leopold not only castigated Wolfgang for his frivolity with regard to Schmalz, Herzog, and Hagenauer (because it was essential to keep the respect of merchants, on whom the financial aspect of the whole venture depended), but also brought up grievances which

---

[6] Wolfgang to Leopold, 22 Nov. 1777—*MBA* 377 (*Letters* 247). Wolfgang said that one of the three possibilities would be very good for Leopold, but only good for himself; one would be very bad in Leopold's eyes, but tolerable in his; and the third would be tolerable to Leopold, but very good, dear, and valuable to him. The commentary to *MBA* 377/34 ff. suggests that one or more of the possibilities was perhaps connected with the Weber family, whom Wolfgang had not yet mentioned to Leopold.

[7] The Weiser, Kerschbaumer, and Hagenauer debts appear to have been on regular goods accounts which had not yet been settled. However, the amount owed to Hagenauer was increased by 150 fl. at one fell swoop by Wolfgang's activation of the credit letter to Schmalz.

would not have played so large a part if other things had gone well. Thus he reproached Wolfgang for the route chosen from Augsburg to Mannheim, for not yet having told him why they had not called on Prince Taxis, and for wasting time at every stage of the journey so far, so that the beautiful autumn days had now disappeared, and they were being forced to undertake a risky journey to Paris without even the benefit of good weather and long days to help them. Above all, he was incensed because he was not being kept informed of their plans or their financial situation, despite the fact that he was responsible for all the debts; and he went so far as to suggest that they did not want to involve him.[8]

Yet despite the impression Wolfgang had given Leopold of being about to leave Mannheim, he was in fact still trying to stay for the winter. His hopes were centred on being allowed to teach some of the elector's children. The elector's musical intendant, Count Savioli, was the proper channel for negotiation, and Wolfgang was maintaining pressure on him for an early answer. Meanwhile, he expressed himself weary of 'speculating' about what the future held for them; though they did not know what would happen, it was sure to be God's will. He intended to withdraw 150 fl. from Schmalz so that he could pay the innkeeper, and then to wait for the elector's reply. If they did have to leave Mannheim, they would go to Kirchheimbolanden to play to Princess Caroline von Nassau-Weilburg, whom they had last seen in The Hague. They could expect a present from her of 6 louis d'or (66 fl.),[9] and would stay as long as the officers' table pleased them. The rest of the space on the paper of this letter was used to give a greeting to all their acquaintances in Salzburg, in which Wolfgang thought of someone for every letter of the alphabet.[10]

Because it took twelve days to receive the answer to each letter written, Wolfgang was still receiving Leopold's indignant outbursts long after he had reported the events to which they were reactions. Perhaps

---

[8] Leopold to Wolfgang, 20, 24, and 27 Nov., and 29 Nov.–1 Dec. 1777—*MBA* 375 (*Letters* 246); *MBA* 378 (*Letters* 248); *MBA* 380 (*Letters* 250); and *MBA* 382 (*Letters* 252). I believe that my acceptance of Leopold's veracity with respect to the poor state of the family finances is not naïve. Solomon thinks that Leopold had a fortune hoarded away which, miser-like, he kept secret even from his own family; and he indirectly criticizes all biographers who take Leopold at his word in his statements about the debt. See Solomon, *Mozart*, 155. But Solomon consistently fails to take into account the enormous discrepancy between touring expenses and Leopold's salary in Salzburg (together with the loss of Wolfgang's salary); the incontrovertible fact that Wolfgang did not earn enough on this tour to cover his expenses; and the question, already mentioned in Ch. 15 of this book, of saving to make provision for dependants.

[9] Leopold converted a louis d'or at 11 fl. during this journey of Wolfgang's—see his letter of 19 Nov. 1778—*MBA* 505/54–61 (*Letters* 340).

[10] Wolfgang to Leopold, 26 Nov. 1777—*MBA* 379 (*Letters* 249a).

because Wolfgang was vexed at his frustrating wait for an answer from the elector, and perhaps because he felt that Leopold's ill humour at the situation was causing him to apportion blame unfairly, he retaliated by writing that it was evident that Leopold could not adapt himself to adversity with equanimity. He also defended himself against the charge that he was careless, saying that he was merely prepared for anything, and therefore capable of waiting patiently. Finally, he begged Leopold not to anticipate happiness or sorrow; as long as they remained healthy, all would be well, since happiness lay entirely in the imagination.[11]

Leopold was stung by Wolfgang's remarks on unnecessary speculation, and patience and trust in God, and retaliated with a sermon of his own. He made plain his view that the fact that all things happened in accordance with the will of God did not relieve man of the responsibility to plan ahead as far as he could. He scorned the idea of going to Kirchheimbolanden only, because it would make much better sense to combine this trip with visits to Mainz and Koblenz, where they had put on successful concerts in 1763. He castigated Wolfgang for having relied too much on a present of money from the elector, so that when the watch was forthcoming instead, Wolfgang had been placed in an embarrassing financial position; and he emphasized the fact that it had been his own 'speculation' in providing a letter of credit to Herzog in Augsburg that had enabled Wolfgang to extricate himself from this embarrassment by drawing money from Schmalz in Mannheim. His indignation with Wolfgang's attitude to planning ahead reached its climax when he recalled that he had already incurred debts of 450 fl. for Wolfgang's sake; and he also reproached Maria Anna for not having given a proper account of their expenditure. He seems to have feared that Wolfgang had been lulled into a false sense of security in Mannheim by the fact that he was on good terms with people like Cannabich and Wendling, because he also gave a serious warning about the rarity of true friendship, and the speed with which so-called friends tended to make themselves scarce when approached for financial help.[12]

Nevertheless, when Leopold learned that Wolfgang was trying to stay in Mannheim, he felt calmer, not only because the plan would solve their problem about where to spend the winter, but also because he was still convinced that it was a sure way to an appointment there. He therefore wrote a more conciliatory letter, in which he explained that nothing had

---

[11] Wolfgang to Leopold, 29 Nov. 1777—*MBA* 381 (Letters 251).
[12] Leopold to Wolfgang and Maria Anna, 4 Dec. 1777—*MBA* 385 (*Letters* 255).

the power to upset him more than uncertainty about the people dearer to him than life itself. He was still perturbed both by Wolfgang's remarks about idle speculation, and his idea that Leopold could not adapt himself to misfortune. Leopold stated that the only time when he could so adapt himself was when it befell him despite everything he had done to prevent it, so that there was nothing for which he could reproach himself. As examples, he gave his serious illness in London (when he had had a plan prepared for getting his family safely home in the event of his death); the dangerous illness of both children in The Hague (when, thanks to a credit note, he had been able to draw 600 fl. with which to pay an inn bill vastly higher than he had envisaged); and the attack of smallpox in Olmütz (where again a credit note which he had not anticipated needing had come to their rescue). Leopold's choice of examples is revealing, indicating as it does the chief fear always lurking at the back of his mind: that illness might strike one of them at any time, and bring disaster on the enterprise. Against the illness itself there was little they could do, but against the financial consequences of it there was much; this view of his is clearly shown by his statement that in The Hague and in Olmütz, though he and Maria Anna could only try to comfort one another, they had at least known how to get hold of money.[13]

An early answer from Savioli about teaching the elector's children was not forthcoming. Despite Wolfgang's cultivation of the goodwill of their governess (which resulted in a contrived meeting between Wolfgang and the elector, as Wolfgang was teaching the children to play music he had composed for them), Savioli repeatedly made excuses about why the elector could not yet give his decision. Meanwhile, Wolfgang was discussing other possibilities with Cannabich. He wanted to obtain more pupils to boost the income he hoped to get from the elector, and he also wanted to set things in motion for obtaining a permanent appointment. He had been in Mannheim since 30 October, and had been given the watch before the middle of November. By the time Savioli finally told him that the elector would not pay him to stay to teach his children, it was 8 December, and he and Maria Anna had been living in the inn for more than five weeks.

From Wolfgang's letters to Leopold about all this, it is clear that he thought he was doing all he could, that the things that had gone wrong were not his fault, and that patience and trust in God were necessary.[14]

---

[13] Leopold to Wolfgang, 8 Dec. 1777—*MBA* 387 (*Letters* 257, but not complete).

[14] Wolfgang to Leopold, 6–7 and 10–11 Dec. 1777—*MBA* 386 (*Letters* 256); and *MBA* 388 (*Letters* 258).

But though he and Leopold had appeared to agree that it was necessary to be prepared for any eventuality, and to trust in God, they did not mean the same thing as each other. To Leopold, being prepared meant foreseeing eventualities and having plans ready to cope with them; to Wolfgang, it meant waiting until they arose and then tackling them as necessary, a conception that seemed to Leopold to involve being prepared for no eventuality at all. In short, Leopold's trust in God was much less passive than Wolfgang's. From Leopold's point of view, Wolfgang was at fault not only because his contingency plans were virtually non-existent, but also because he did not communicate to Leopold any ideas he was pursuing, thus rendering Leopold helpless. To a man who had been used to being in control of every situation, this was bound to be exceedingly frustrating.

The difference in attitude between Leopold and Wolfgang can be explained largely by Leopold's experience and Wolfgang's lack of it. Wolfgang had encountered no problems so far which were not already familiar to Leopold from past travels, and Leopold had developed his approach to a journey of this kind by his hard-won experience of its problems. But the correspondence of this period also suggests that Wolfgang's moral and religious upbringing had not been helpful to his independence, since certain remarks of Leopold's show that his reasoning about the workings of the will of God, and the contribution of man's choices to his own destiny, could be extremely confusing.[15] Perhaps the combined facts that previous journeys had been largely successful, and that Leopold had been accustomed to attribute this success to the grace of God, had fostered passivity in those members of the family not required to make the decisions; Maria Anna at least seems to have relied chiefly on prayer for a happy outcome to their problems.[16] Thus they could mouth assurances that they were prepared for all contingencies, without being fully engaged in the practical implications of such assurances.

Fortunately for all concerned, Wolfgang's letter reporting that the elector would not pay him to stay to teach his children was also able to unfold a different plan, one which was to restore the travellers' rocking boat to an even keel for a short while. All the time that Wolfgang had been waiting for Savioli's answer from the elector, he had been becoming more friendly with the flautist Wendling; and Wendling had suggested that if Wolfgang could stay in Mannheim until Lent, he might

---

[15] Examples are given later in this chapter, at pp. 289–90, and in Ch. 18, pp. 307–9.
[16] Two examples occur later in this chapter, at pp. 271–2 and 289.

then make one of a foursome, and go to Paris with Wendling, the oboist Ramm, and the ballet-master Lauchérey. Expense would be cut considerably if they travelled together, and Wendling had experience of the concert season in Paris, and knew the Mozarts' friend Grimm. When the elector decided not to retain Wolfgang, Wendling's plan was at risk, since Wolfgang was a useful fourth member who could only go with them if he could support himself in Mannheim until they were ready to leave. Wendling therefore made an arrangement which was to solve all Wolfgang's problems for the next two months. He procured a commission for Wolfgang to write three flute concertos and two flute quartets for a Mannheim acquaintance, De Jean, in return for 200 fl.; he arranged free accommodation for Wolfgang with the court councillor Serarius; and he invited Wolfgang to take his midday and evening meals with him. For Maria Anna, he said they would find a room, and she would travel home as they left for Paris. In outlining this plan to Leopold, Wolfgang asked him to get letters of recommendation for Paris from their acquaintances in Vienna. In addition, since the idea of a permanent appointment in Mannheim seemed to have dwindled for the time being at least, Wolfgang wanted to write to Prince Waldburg-Zeil to see if the idea of a post in Munich could be revived.[17]

Leopold's reaction was one of cautious approval, but he was seriously worried by the lack of success of the journey so far. It was a bitter blow that Wolfgang had not managed to get even a temporary appointment at either of the courts of which they had had such hopes, Munich and Mannheim; and the fact that they had not covered their expenses either was deeply disturbing. The long period during which the elector had left Wolfgang without a decision had already caused Leopold to anticipate that the attempt to teach his children would be unsuccessful, and he had castigated Wolfgang for not having explored more possibilities in Mannheim;[18] now he showed his dejection by giving a long and detailed exposition of the situation of the family. His words state unequivocally that they were all dissatisfied with life in Salzburg under Colloredo, but suggest that the impetus for the journey had come primarily from Wolfgang, who had wanted them all to leave; that Leopold's cautiousness had refused to countenance this; and that he had even been doubtful about letting Wolfgang go, because of his inexperience. Moving on to the Parisian idea, he tried to temper Wolfgang's enthusiasm for Wendling's

---

[17] Wolfgang to Leopold, 3 and 10–11 Dec. 1777—*MBA* 383 (*Letters* 253); and *MBA* 388 (*Letters* 258).

[18] Leopold to Wolfgang, 11 Dec. 1777—*MBA* 389 (*Letters* 259).

kindness by pointing out that it was in Wendling's own interest to help Wolfgang stay in Mannheim until he was ready to go to Paris. However, he agreed to the plan on certain conditions. First and foremost, he wanted to be sure that the fee of 200 fl. from De Jean was a firmly agreed figure that could be relied upon. Leopold used this figure as the basis for a financial calculation which suggested to him that the arrangement would both support them in Mannheim for the next two months and provide capital with which to travel; Wolfgang to Paris, and Maria Anna home to Salzburg. Secondly, he refused to allow Wolfgang and Maria Anna to live separately in Mannheim, on the grounds that Wolfgang had a duty to look after his mother. He therefore suggested that they pay slightly more for a lodging for her, so that Wolfgang could sleep there too.[19]

In Leopold's second condition can be seen his tenderness and concern for Maria Anna. Not long before, she had complained of how cold their room at the inn was, and how expensive it was to have a fire lit. To economize, she was only having one fire made in the morning on rising, and one in the evening. The rest of the day she sat there freezing so badly that she could hardly hold a pen to write, and frequently alone, because Wolfgang was usually invited out to dine.[20] Leopold's response had been sympathetic, and he had made various suggestions which he hoped would help:

my dear wife I pity you, that you have to endure so much cold for 24 kr. a day in money for heating: and it must be even worse now, since we've had the most incredible cold for a little while. if I were in your place, I'd visit someone who has a warm parlour; and if I were at home, I'd sit myself in bed, rest my back on the pillows, and cover myself up to the waist, then read or knit in this position, or sew, or even sleep, or tell my future fortune or misfortune with the cards. if anyone happens to come, you say I've got a slight headache etc: or something else etc: I'd definitely do that, and not suffer any cold. —[21]

He had also urged her, despite the lack of money, to buy herself a man's fur if they had to travel on from Mannheim in the winter.[22] Despite a lifelong need for strict economy, Leopold wanted his family to have the necessary comforts, and was prepared to provide these even when deeply in debt.

[19] Leopold to Wolfgang and Maria Anna, 18 Dec. 1777—*MBA* 392 (*Letters* 262).
[20] Maria Anna to Leopold, 7 Dec. 1777—*MBA* 386/45–51 (*Letters* 256a).
[21] Leopold to Maria Anna, 15 Dec. 1777—*MBA* 391/32–41 (*Letters* 261).
[22] Leopold to Maria Anna, 11 Dec. 1777—*MBA* 389/117–20 (*Letters* 259).

The new lodging arrangements made by Wolfgang were even more satisfactory than his initial outline had suggested, though they entailed a good deal of work on his part. He was offered a pleasant room big enough for both of them, with wood and candles supplied, in Serarius's house. In return, he was to give keyboard lessons to the 15-year-old daughter of the house, Therese Pierron. Here at last Maria Anna had somewhere warm to sit, and was soon being invited for most of the day to join Serarius's wife and daughter, whose company she enjoyed. Wolfgang took his midday meals with Wendling, and Maria Anna took hers with Christian Danner, a 20-year-old Mannheim violinist whose family they knew from 1763. In return for her meals, Wolfgang instructed Danner in composition.[23] Since he was also still teaching Rosa Cannabich, and had to get down to serious work on his compositions for De Jean, Wolfgang was now very busy. The lessons, at least to the two girls, were given daily, and his routine was to rise at eight and compose from ten until around half past twelve. He would then go to Wendling's, and compose a little more there until lunch, which lasted from half past one until three. From there he would go to an inn to give keyboard lessons to a Dutch officer for cash, and then home to teach Therese Pierron from half past four until six. He spent the evenings with the Cannabichs, where he gave a lesson to Rosa and had his meal.[24] Wolfgang also had it in mind to write some sonatas for publication, and a Mass which could be presented to the elector to keep alive the hope of gaining an appointment in Mannheim.[25]

There was little slack time, and the routine had to be kept up from week to week simply in order to live. The money promised by De Jean for the flute music was not an enormous sum, considering that Maria Anna had to travel home and Wolfgang to Paris. By the time they moved into Serarius's house, they had been in the inn for six weeks, and the bill came to 114 fl. including tips. In writing to tell Leopold this, Maria Anna adopted a defensive tone. She pleaded that they could not have known how long they would have to wait for a decision from the elector about staying on, and also claimed that though the inn had been expensive, private lodgings were also very dear. She stated that she could not have lived more economically; she had bought herself virtually nothing and had sat day after day in a miserable freezing garret. Now, by contrast, she was delighted to have a comfortable, warm room; she attributed her good fortune to the protection of her two favourite images, the Virgin Mary

[23] Maria Anna and Wolfgang to Leopold, 14 Dec. 1777—*MBA* 390 (*Letters* 260 and 260*a*).
[24] Wolfgang to Leopold, 20 Dec. 1777—*MBA* 394/39–51 (*Letters* 264*a*).
[25] Wolfgang to Leopold, 10–11 Dec. 1777—*MBA* 388/88–90 (*Letters* 258).

at the pilgrimage church of Maria Plain, and the Loreto Christ child, to both of whom she had been praying, and in whom all her trust was vested. She also explained that they had drawn 150 fl. from Schmalz in order to pay the bill at the inn, and now had 72 fl. in total. Despite the excellent lodging and meal arrangements, they still had outgoings in Mannheim, for items such as washing, shoes, and hair powder; and therefore anything Wolfgang could earn in cash would be extremely necessary for these and the future travel expenses.[26]

Leopold was delighted with their new arrangements, and began to think out ways for Maria Anna to travel home. In sending greetings to the travellers for the new year, he expressed his confidence in God's mercy and in Wolfgang's industry, talent, and goodheartedness. Indicating how troubled the outgoing year had been, he declared his reliance on Wolfgang to bring the family fame, honour, and money, and to preserve him from the scorn and mockery of his enemies. Such mockery would be his death.[27]

Maria Anna, in her New Year greetings, also referred to the outgoing year in extremely negative terms, while Wolfgang assured Leopold that there was no doubt about the firmness of De Jean's financial offer for the flute music, and begged him to continue to bestow his love on Wolfgang, who would endeavour to deserve it in the year to come.[28] Right at the end of 1777, therefore, the family had been restored for a time to a position from which it believed it could yet emerge triumphant. Despite the debt and the differences between them which had been shown up by the pressures of the journey, the new arrangements in Mannheim offered them a chance to regain their equilibrium; while Wolfgang's projected journey to Paris held out hopes of large financial gains, and movements were still afoot to gain Wolfgang an appointment either in Mannheim or in Munich. Though they did not know it at the time, however, two deaths which took place in December 1777 were to contribute to the eventual reluctant return of Wolfgang to the detested service in Salzburg.

❦

During the early, shaky weeks in Mannheim, a good deal had been happening in Salzburg. Leopold and Nannerl had been continuing their music-making, and he was full of praise for her progress. He claimed that

[26] Maria Anna to Leopold, 18 Dec. 1777—*MBA* 393 (*Letters* 263).
[27] Leopold to Wolfgang and Maria Anna, 29 Dec. 1777—*MBA* 399/5–13 (*Letters* 268).
[28] Wolfgang to Leopold, 20 Dec., and Maria Anna and Wolfgang to Leopold, 27–8 Dec. 1777—*MBA* 394/28–36 (*Letters* 264a); and *MBA* 398 (*Letters* 267 and 267a).

if she kept up her practice, she would be able, by the end of the winter, to accompany anything; be it figured or unfigured, in any key, and no matter how difficult the modulations. For this practice, he said that they chose compositions by Wolfgang because of the challenges posed by his style; and he mentioned specifically pieces in C and F 'with the minor 3rd'.[29]

Leopold and Nannerl had also taken in a lodger, as an act of charity. There had been a shuffling round among the tenants in the Dancing-Master's House, with the final result that the landlady Mitzerl had vacated her room on the same floor as those occupied by the Mozarts, and moved downstairs. She could not easily let the empty room, because it was so closely related to those of the Mozarts; so Leopold rented it from her for 8 fl. annually, and promptly sublet it to Maria Clara Susanna Auer (called 'Sandl'). Sandl Auer, aged 35, was the youngest daughter of the deceased cathedral chapter Verwalter (administrator) at Traunstein. She eked out her living by mending women's caps. Caps formed a very important part of women's dress; a clean one was worn each day, a plain costume was smartened up by a fine cap, and judgements about social class and the standard of housekeeping were made on the basis of the cap worn. Sandl's previous lodgings had been costing her 12 fl. annually, and Leopold let her have his room for the 8 fl. he was paying. In addition she was to pay the maid Tresel 3 fl. annually for small tasks such as making her fires, so that she was better off by 1 fl. a year. Leopold arranged for her meat to be bought and cooked with theirs, and for a space to be cleared for her firewood; and on fast days she was given a portion of their soup and the other fast-day dish that they were to eat. The net saving to Sandl by these arrangements gives some indication of how poor it was possible to be in Salzburg. Her father's position had been similar to that of Maria Anna's father and Nannerl's future husband, and was by no means menial; yet she was virtually destitute, just as Maria Anna Mozart's mother had been when her husband had died. Sandl was also, as later events were to show, almost completely uneducated.[30]

At about the same time, Leopold was also considering taking a fee-paying resident pupil into his house, but nothing came of this idea. The impetus had come from Wolfgang in Munich. He had met there a

---

[29] Leopold to Wolfgang, 17 Nov. 1777—*MBA* 374/68–76 (*Letters* 244). The commentaries both of *MBA* and of *Letters* suggest that the pieces Leopold meant were the keyboard sonatas K. 279 and K. 280, both of which have slow movements in the minor. But Leopold was describing Nannerl's practice of accompaniment skills, which solo sonatas did not offer.

[30] Leopold to Wolfgang and Maria Anna, 1 Dec. 1777—*MBA* 382/52–69 (not in *Letters*). See Ch. 18 for the continuation of Sandl Auer's story.

nobleman called von Hamm, whose daughter was almost 13; the arrangement with Leopold was apparently intended as an alternative to a convent education. Leopold's reaction to Maria Anna and Wolfgang was concern that the girl would not fit in with their frugal life-style; von Hamm's offer was 150 fl. annually, and this was to cover everything from her board and lodging (not forgetting a cup of coffee and a white roll for breakfast each day) to her tuition in every subject. More importantly, however, Leopold wanted to know what her musical capabilities were, and in particular whether she had a good ear for rhythm, since he was only prepared to take pupils who would do him credit. When Leopold wrote back to von Hamm, he said that he could not contemplate the idea for under 200 fl. annually, and Maria Anna supported him, saying that in a convent she would pay 100 fl. for her board and lodging alone. Leopold was to be much more at ease with his later resident pupils the Marchand children, because they lived in every respect as members of the family.[31]

Leopold was still involved in correspondence with Mysliveček, and hoped that as well as obtaining the Neapolitan opera contract for Wolfgang, he would be able to help recommend Wolfgang to the elector in Mannheim. Mysliveček knew Anton Raaff, an ageing but influential tenor in Mannheim, and Martini, who was also in high favour with the elector of the Palatinate. For a reason that remains unexplained, Leopold's efforts to reciprocate Mysliveček's supposed efforts on behalf of the Mozarts, by helping him obtain money owed him by Colloredo for compositions, were bound up with Countess Lodron. Leopold presented Mysliveček's request for money to her rather than processing it in the normal way through the Obersthofmeister, and his description of what he had done suggests that there was something clandestine about the relationship between Colloredo, Countess Lodron, and Mysliveček's music; at any rate, he made it clear to her that if she could not help in the matter, he would give Mysliveček's letter to the Obersthofmeister. Whatever the reason for his tactics, they worked; Countess Lodron soon afterwards told him that Colloredo had sent Mysliveček a present of money.[32]

---

[31] Maria Anna to Leopold, 11 Oct. 1777 (*MBA* 347/128–36; *Letters* 219a); Leopold to Wolfgang and Maria Anna, 12–13 Oct. 1777 (*MBA* 348/92–106; *Letters* 220); Leopold to Wolfgang and Maria Anna, 1 Dec. 1777 (*MBA* 382/100–19; *Letters* 252); and Maria Anna to Leopold, 6–7 Dec. 1777 (*MBA* 386/52–7; *Letters* 256a). Nine years later, Leopold was to comment to Nannerl on his pupil Heinrich Marchand's unfastidiousness; Heinrich would happily eat up the remains of Nannerl's infant son's baby food. See Ch. 29 for more details about how Heinrich fitted in to the household.

[32] Leopold to Wolfgang and Maria Anna, 29–30 Oct. and 1–3 Nov. 1777—*MBA* 359/67–75 (*Letters* 231); and *MBA* 362/81–5 (*Letters* 234). But Anderson's translation of *MBA* 359/72 omits five important German words. Following his assertion that if Countess Lodron would not deal with

During his conversation with Countess Lodron about Mysliveček's present on 2 November 1777, Leopold also discussed Michael Haydn's new 'Oboe Mass', which had just received its first performance. In fact, its title was *Missa S. Hieronymi*, and had clearly been written to please Hieronymus Colloredo. It used six oboes, two of which were soloists, and Leopold had already described its somewhat complicated performance in detail and with warm admiration of the music to Wolfgang and Maria Anna. The musical forces in the cathedral were disposed in five places, or 'choirs'. One was on high at each angle of the crossing, and one at ground level near the altar. Each choir had its own organ, and specified instrumentalists and singers were allotted to each. There was also a sixth organ over the west entrance, but this was used mainly for preludes on grand occasions.[33] Keeping time when the musicians were spatially separated in this way could be problematic, and part of Leopold's description had been taken up by an account of how it had been managed. Colloredo and Countess Lodron had conversed together about Haydn's music, and it was in the aftermath of the performance that Leopold expressed to Wolfgang his hope that a post of Kapellmeister, 'which had been worked at for so many years', might be created at the cathedral. His implication was that if it were, it might go to Michael Haydn. The current difficulty, however, seemed to be Rust. Less than six months after his appointment as Kapellmeister, he wanted to leave and return to Italy, so Colloredo was yet again facing the problem of finding a Kapellmeister. Leopold presumably meant that while there was this uncertainty, Colloredo would not apply his mind to the creation of a new post at the cathedral.[34]

the matter, he would take it up with the Obersthofmeister, Leopold wrote 'and she knows it at least' ('und sie weis es wenigst'); Anderson does not translate this phrase, which gives quite a different character to the tactics Leopold employed, suggesting a veiled threat. Countess Lodron was probably the most influential of the members of the nobility in Salzburg who desired to see Wolfgang return; but her exact role in achieving this end is obscure because Leopold tended to refer to her simply as 'the countess', and the *MBA* commentary assigns different identities to the countess at different times. The question is important because the countess who was responsible for easing Wolfgang's return to Salzburg evidently commanded great authority and was extremely close to Colloredo. Perhaps for this reason the *MBA* commentary assumes that some of Leopold's references to 'the countess' mean Countess Wallis, Colloredo's sister; but this identification is unsatisfactory in a number of respects, and it must be considered possible that Leopold was referring always to Countess Lodron. I shall therefore address the question of which countess was meant wherever it is pertinent to the story of obtaining a new post for Wolfgang in Salzburg.

[33] For a compilation of descriptions of the disposition of the musical forces in the cathedral, see Hintermaier, 'Hofkapelle', pp. xii–xvi. See also Fig. 4.

[34] I have been able to discover nothing about whether the creation of a cathedral Kapellmeister post really had been under discussion for years in Salzburg. If it had, Leopold must at some point have thought of it as a desirable post for Wolfgang, offering the theoretical possibility that father and son might occupy the two most prestigious positions in Salzburg. The post was never created.

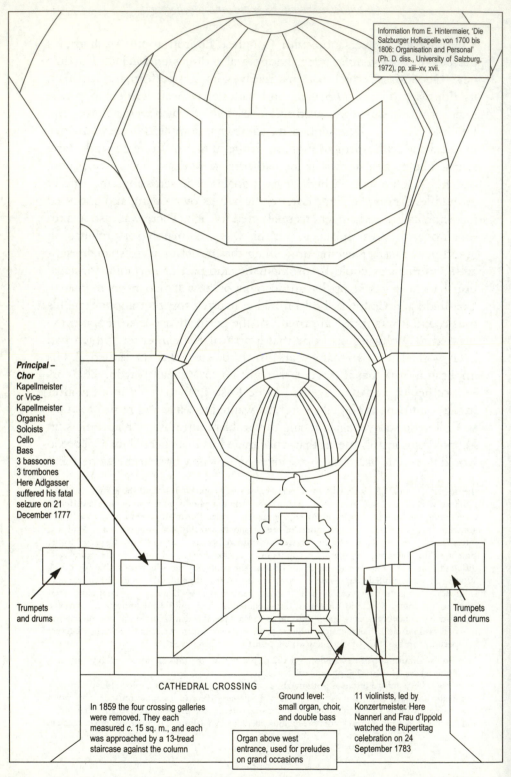

Information from E. Hintermaier, 'Die Salzburger Hofkapelle von 1700 bis 1806: Organisation and Personal' (Ph. D. diss., University of Salzburg, 1972), pp. xiii–xv, xvii.

Principal –
Chor
Kapellmeister
or Vice-
Kapellmeister
Organist
Soloists
Cello
Bass
3 bassoons
3 trombones
Here Adlgasser
suffered his fatal
seizure on 21
December 1777

Trumpets
and drums

Trumpets
and drums

CATHEDRAL CROSSING

In 1859 the four crossing galleries were removed. They each measured c. 15 sq. m., and each was approached by a 13-tread staircase against the column

Ground level: small organ, choir, and double bass

Organ above west entrance, used for preludes on grand occasions

11 violinists, led by Konzertmeister. Here Nannerl and Frau d'Ippold watched the Rupertitag celebration on 24 September 1783

FIG. 4. Disposition of the musical forces in Salzburg Cathedral during the time of the Mozarts

Rust's health was apparently poor, and his doctor Barisani had told him to return to Italy immediately unless he wanted to leave his bones in Salzburg. Rust therefore applied for his resignation, but Colloredo at first refused, and, in anger with Barisani, sent a second doctor to him instead. This man, Buchmann, gave Rust a prescription in which Rust had so little faith that he dragged himself to Barisani for his opinion. Not surprisingly, Barisani told Rust that if he took this medicine he would simply die a few weeks sooner. Leopold drily commented that it would be cheaper for Colloredo to pay 15 fl. for a night burial for Rust than to give him 20 ducats (100 fl.) for his travel back to Italy, especially since it would be such a waste of the money if Rust were anyway to die on arrival.

But the most interesting part of Leopold's conversation with Countess Lodron concerned Wolfgang. She correctly assumed that he would go to Mannheim from Augsburg, and alluded to the openings offered by the German opera there, and to the fact that the elector valued people of talent. The tutor to her children, Abbé Henri (who, like Bullinger, was an ex-Jesuit, and occupied in the Lodron household a position similar to Bullinger's in that of Arco), had also reported to Leopold her apprehension that Wolfgang would remain permanently in Mannheim.[35] The knowledge of her fear that Wolfgang would win a good appointment elsewhere was to prove useful to Leopold long after Wolfgang's chances in Mannheim had come to an end, and he was able to use his acquaintance through Bullinger with Henri to obtain inside information about the countess's wishes and powers with respect to a new Salzburg appointment for Wolfgang.[36]

The news from the court music which caused the greatest sensation, and involved the most complicated repercussions, while Wolfgang was in Mannheim, was the dramatic death of Adlgasser. On 21 December, while playing the organ for Vespers in the principal crossing choir of the cathedral, the 48-year-old organist, whom Leopold had known for at least twenty-seven years, suffered some kind of seizure.[37] It was not immediately apparent what was wrong with him, because he did not collapse; rather, he continued to play, at first randomly, 'as if a dog were running

---

[35] The information in this paragraph and the two preceding ones is from Leopold to Wolfgang and Maria Anna, 1–3 Nov. 1777—*MBA* 362 (*Letters* 234, but not complete). Anderson translates the phrase about the attempt to create a cathedral Kapellmeister post ('daran so viele Jahre gearbeitet wird') in such a way as to suggest that it was only Haydn who had been pressing for such a post.

[36] See Ch. 18 for more details.

[37] See Fig. 4, which shows the choir in which Adlgasser was taken ill.

over the organ', and then by holding down the clenched fist of his left hand while still playing psalm melodies with his right. Leopold eventually lifted up his left hand out of the way, while the tenor singer Spitzeder played a bass as best he could to the melody which Adlgasser continued to play with his right hand, and in this way they put an end to the temporary cacophony. They thought at first that he might be drunk, because he could speak, was rolling his eyes, and vomited. It was difficult to get medical help to him, because the space was so confined and the service was still going on, but when he could decently be removed, he was carried home and seen by Barisani. It then became clear that he was seriously ill. Leopold met his weeping 24-year-old daughter Viktoria, Nannerl's friend and hairdresser, running to the chemist's to fetch spirit of hartshorn for him, but despite this and all the other remedies tried, he died on 22 December 1777.[38]

For his family, this was of course disastrous, though financially it should not have been quite as bad as Leopold Mozart's death would have been for his family at the same time. Adlgasser's annual salary of 448 fl. was lost at one cruel blow, but his wife, Maria Anna Fesemayr/Adlgasser, was still drawing her annual court singer's salary of 120 fl.,[39] whereas Leopold was the sole breadwinner in the Mozart household. On the other hand, the Adlgasser family was not so united as the Mozarts were, and Maria Anna Mozart expected Viktoria Adlgasser to leave her stepmother's home now that her father could no longer hold everything together.[40] In fact, the outcome was to be worse than this for Viktoria. Her half-brother Joseph was 17 and her half-sister Anna 11, but Joseph went off the rails after his father's death and for two years was incarcerated in the fortress, because of his complete lack of self-discipline. On St Michael's Day (29 September) 1779, one of the dates on which house rents were due, Maria Anna Fesemayr/Adlgasser left all her stepchildren and returned to her father's house. Perhaps she felt that with Viktoria and Joseph grown up, she had done enough for them, and was no longer prepared to use her pension-sized salary to subsidize their accommodation. Viktoria then tried to support alone her younger half-brother and half-sister whom, according to their guardian Rochus Alterdinger, she loved as much as if she were their complete blood sister. Both Viktoria and Anna were sickly, but Viktoria would have been placed in a situation if she had

---

[38] Leopold to Wolfgang and Maria Anna, 21–2 Dec. 1777—*MBA* 395/20–54 and 84–95 (*Letters* 265, but only the bare fact of Adlgasser's death is given).

[39] The salary figures are from Hintermaier, 'Hofkapelle', 3 and 109.

[40] Maria Anna to Leopold, 3–4 Jan. 1778—*MBA* 400/18–21 (*Letters* 269).

not been needed to care for Anna and mend Joseph's clothes for him. Joseph died young in 1787, but Viktoria continued to look after Anna, and Alterdinger had nothing but admiration for her love and steadfastness. Immediately on Adlgasser's death, the three children had jointly been allowed a court pension of 8 fl. per month for one year, but because Viktoria and Anna were too frail even to earn a living by taking in sewing, Alterdinger had repeatedly to appeal for its extension, and was successful. The half-sisters Viktoria and Anna thus grew old together in poverty and ill health.[41]

The effect of this death on the court music was also substantial. Adlgasser and Wolfgang Mozart had been the foremost organists, Adlgasser having the official title, and the same two men had been the principal keyboard players. In addition, Adlgasser had been organist at Holy Trinity, the church in the square where the Mozarts lived, and he had taught the boys in the Kapellhaus, and the daughters of Countess Lodron. A good deal of reorganization was therefore necessary, and it was not to be completed until Wolfgang returned more than a year later.

No less significant to the Mozarts than the death of Adlgasser was that, on 30 December 1777, of the elector of Bavaria, Maximilian III Joseph. Only an hour or so after the event, the elector Palatine, Karl Theodor, was declared his successor. The political repercussions were considerable, and brought the threat of large-scale war in Europe for some time to come; at the level of the musicians and other court employees, the outcome was extremely disadvantageous for most. Karl Theodor decided to move his court from Mannheim to Munich, and so where there had been employment opportunities at two prestigious courts, these opportunities shrank abruptly. For a while, the Mozarts continued to hope that Wolfgang might be offered an appointment in the reorganization of the personnel of both places; but Leopold eventually decided that this was neither likely nor even desirable, since the absence of a legitimate heir to Karl Theodor made the employment situation risky. As 1778 began, therefore, though the Mozarts did not immediately suspect it, the deaths of the elector of Bavaria and of Adlgasser had lessened the likelihood of Wolfgang's obtaining an appointment away from Salzburg, and increased that of his returning there.

<hr />

[41] See Rainer, 'Adlgasser', 205–37. See also Fig. 1 for the relationships within the Adlgasser family.

In the middle of January 1778, Wolfgang wrote to Leopold that he was making a short excursion to Kirchheimbolanden from Mannheim to visit Princess Caroline of Nassau-Weilburg. He had arranged to go with Fridolin Weber and his second daughter Aloysia, and he expected to earn 8 louis d'or (88 fl.). Weber was the court copyist in Mannheim, and Wolfgang said that he was struggling to support a wife, five daughters, and a son on a salary of 400 fl. annually. The Webers' chief hopes of improving their lot were vested in the promising voice of the 17-year-old Aloysia. Wolfgang praised Aloysia's musical talents and her respectable demeanour.[42]

Since Leopold's financial worries were meanwhile increasing, his reaction was to hope that the princess's present would be a good one. He had received the two tailors' bills he had been expecting, and did not know how to pay the 21 fl. 24 kr. they amounted to. Their servant Tresel also had to be paid, the house rent was due, and he was wondering if he would have to find more money for the approaching journeys of Wolfgang and Maria Anna. In the same letter, Leopold told Maria Anna to bring home any old clothes of Wolfgang's, which they would be able to use for the sake of economy.[43]

Both Leopold and Maria Anna were very worried at the thought of Wolfgang in Paris without parental guidance. Leopold's worry was based on his conviction that Wolfgang had not been capable of managing a journey alone when he left Salzburg; however, he hoped that the experience he had gained so far, together with all the paternal letters of advice, had made the necessary difference.[44] Maria Anna's worries were probably similar, but she was also unhappy about the company of Wendling and Ramm, although she did not mention this fear to Leopold until later. She simply expressed her wish that Grimm could look after Wolfgang in Paris, and her regret that they had not heard from him and did not know where he was.[45]

Leopold's letter expressing hope that the Kirchheimbolanden present would be handsome crossed with Wolfgang's report of the trip. Wolfgang's interest in the Weber family had ripened into overwhelming love for Aloysia while they had been away together, and his mind was in turmoil. He completely put aside all thought of his own family, overturned all Leopold's plans, and begged him to set in motion his new idea

[42] Wolfgang to Leopold, 17 Jan. 1778—*MBA* 405/19–45 (*Letters* 273a).
[43] Leopold to Maria Anna, 2 Feb. 1778—*MBA* 414/5–13 and 26–30 (*Letters* 280).
[44] Leopold to Maria Anna, 18 Dec. 1777—*MBA* 392/147–9 (*Letters* 262).
[45] Maria Anna to Leopold, 1 Feb. 1778—*MBA* 413/8–12 (*Letters* 279).

of establishing Aloysia on the Italian stage. Going to Paris with Wendling and Ramm was out of the question, because both were libertines, and
men of no religion (this was also the argument he had used to try to win
Maria Anna over to his point of view). Instead, he thought of staying
on in Mannheim to finish his music for De Jean, and meanwhile Weber
would organize a concert tour to be undertaken by himself, Wolfgang,
Aloysia, and her older sister Josepha, who was also a singer. Leopold's
role was to arrange some engagements for Aloysia in Italy, including that
of prima donna at the Ascension opera in Venice. Wolfgang would write
operas for half the usual fee, simply in order to give her the opportunity
to make her fortune. They would call in to see Leopold for a fortnight
on their way through Salzburg, and would make plenty of money on the
other journeys they planned to make together. The letter chattered on about
the jolly time they had had in Kirchheimbolanden; the present, however, had been only 7 louis d'or (77 fl.), and Wolfgang had paid some of
the Webers' expenses as well as his own. For the sake of cosiness, they
had eaten at the inn on some of the occasions when they might have
received free meals at the officers' table, and his net profit was 42 fl.[46]

It was already ironic enough that this letter should have crossed
with Leopold's anxious one, but the crossing of the next few letters too
reveals vividly the different perspectives of father and son, and shows how
apt Wolfgang was to forget the viewpoint of his family when not being
reminded of it by letters.[47] Before Leopold had received Wolfgang's
bombshell, he wrote again; and since it was the last letter he expected to
write before Wolfgang left for Paris, it expressed his heaviness of heart
at the thought of Wolfgang moving even further away from him, without even his mother. Leopold recounted the course of events which
had brought them all to this dangerous position. He started by asserting
that his worries about Wolfgang in Paris were not the result of a timid
nature, but of his experience of all that could go wrong, and he supported
his argument by reminding Wolfgang of the risks he had undergone
when travelling while the children were young. Everything done then, he
said, had been to advance Wolfgang and, through him, the whole family.
He had sacrificed all his time to educate both children, with the aim of
rendering them able to provide for themselves, and of furnishing himself

---

[46] Wolfgang to Leopold, 4 Feb. 1778—*MBA* 416 (*Letters* 281).

[47] In circumstances like these, when letters were taking so long to reach their destination, the
normal editorial practice of ordering the letters chronologically according to the date on which they
were written means that the reply does not immediately follow the letter to which it was reacting,
and the reader has to be alert to the significance of the fact that the recipient's knowledge of events
on a given date lagged behind the recounting of them.

with a comfortable old age. This he had wanted to be free from petty worries, so that he could prepare spiritually for his death, and account to God for the upbringing of his children; yet now he was forced to undertake once again the wearisome labour of giving private lessons (Leopold had just begun to teach Countess Lodron's daughters, following Adlgasser's death). He recalled the financial difficulties of his married life; the income of 20 fl. per month,[48] the support of Maria Anna's mother, the keeping of two servants, the seven children, the childbeds, illnesses, and deaths. During all this time, not only had he never been able to spend a kreuzer on his own pleasure, but he had had to work himself to the bone to pay for everything; yet despite this, he had never been in debt before. Now the debt was 700 fl., and he did not know how he could support Maria Anna and Nannerl; therefore everything depended on Wolfgang. After more in the same vein, and a warning against becoming entrapped by women, Leopold repeated that he did not want to have to reproach himself on his death-bed for failing to bring up his son as a true Catholic Christian.[49]

In a postscript, Leopold told Maria Anna that he had wept while writing this letter, and had not allowed Nannerl to read it. He also warned them about Wolfgang's diet and health, and the fact that everything 'heating' in his diet and life-style was inimical to him.[50] Leopold clearly had a terrible fear that Wolfgang might die before the family finances could be saved; or that he might be led astray and abandon his family; or that he, Leopold, might die. The debt was now the equivalent of two years' salary, and he had recently had a horrifying reminder of the possibility of sudden death in the form of Adlgasser, who had been ten years younger than Leopold.

Just as Leopold had written this letter before receiving Wolfgang's about the Webers, so Wolfgang wrote again before receiving this letter or Leopold's previous one (which had mentioned the hope that he would earn a handsome present from Princess Caroline). He therefore had little to temper his enthusiasm for helping the Webers; but even allowing for this, his tone was sure to strike Leopold as breathtakingly thoughtless and arrogant. He gave three reasons to justify his refusal to go to Paris with Wendling: one was the company; one was the fact that they had heard nothing from Grimm; and the third was that he had realized that he would have to give lessons to make progress there:

---

[48] From his marriage in 1747 until 1756—see Hintermaier, 'Hofkapelle', 290.
[49] Leopold to Wolfgang, 5 Feb. 1778—*MBA* 417 (*Letters* 282).
[50] *MBA* 417/179–211 (*Letters* 282a).

I couldn't really get along in anything except through pupils, and I wasn't born for that work. I have a living example of it here. I could have had two pupils; I went to each three times, then I found one of them out, so I didn't go back. I'll gladly give lessons as a favour, especially when I see that someone has talent, pleasure, and zest for learning. but to have to go to a house at a given time, or to have to wait for someone at a house, I can't do that, however much it might bring me. that's impossible for me. I leave that to people who can't do anything else except play the keyboard. I am a composer, and was born to be a kapellmeister.[51]

How could Maria Anna have allowed Wolfgang to write such letters to Leopold? She was disturbed enough by his ideas for travelling with Aloysia to add a confidential anxious postscript to Wolfgang's first letter outlining these, but she seems to have been so relieved that he would not after all travel to Paris with Wendling that she overlooked the effect that the letter would have on Leopold. She admitted that she did not like Wolfgang's friendship with Wendling and Ramm, but said that she had never tried to prevent it; she had no influence over Wolfgang, and he did not enjoy her company. Since there was nothing to be lost by staying in Mannheim, however, she declared herself content to do so, and to accompany Wolfgang to Paris later if necessary, when they might have heard from Grimm.[52]

Leopold was horrified by Wolfgang's new ideas, which caused him sleepless nights and palpitations. He reminded Wolfgang of the twofold purpose of the journey; to win a good appointment or at least to earn a handsome sum of money, in order to help his parents, sister, and himself. He depicted two alternative outcomes which depended on Wolfgang's choices: to live a Christian life, bringing pleasure and honour to a well-provided family and earning a place in history; or to be a common musician with a room of starving children sleeping on straw. He criticized Wolfgang's handling of almost every detail of the journey so far. He poured scorn on the idea that an unknown German teenager could get anywhere on the Italian stage. And he could hardly bear to think of Wolfgang travelling round Europe giving concerts with Aloysia. This would involve putting aside his aged parents and loving sister, and exposing them to the mockery of Colloredo and the whole town, the more so since Leopold had told everyone that he was about to go to Paris.

Having enumerated all these reproaches, Leopold tackled the subject of Paris, which was the only sensible destination. New plans had to be

---

[51] Wolfgang to Leopold, 7 Feb. 1778—*MBA* 419 (*Letters* 283a).
[52] Maria Anna to Leopold, 5 Feb. 1778—*MBA* 416/140–56 (*Letters* 281a).

made, since the old ones had all been handled by Wendling; and Leopold applied himself to this task by writing to an Augsburg merchant currently in Paris, Arbauer, to ask what he could suggest by way of accommodation for Wolfgang and Maria Anna. Leopold was also concerned about the fee of 200 fl. from De Jean for the flute music; the arrangement had been made by Wendling, and Leopold's fear was that his annoyance at having his plans spoilt by Wolfgang's last-minute refusal to join him might affect the money owed. He therefore asked for an assurance that the 200 fl. was secure.

Finally, he made some suggestions as to how Aloysia might be helped. He told Wolfgang to introduce her to Raaff in Mannheim, because he had great influence with Italian impresarios. And she should acquire some experience in acting there, even if it was unpaid. Leopold also declared himself willing to write to impresarios in Italy. He made it clear that if Wolfgang earned fame and money in Paris, a trip to Italy could be countenanced afterwards. The letter ended by reporting how upset Nannerl, too, had been made by Wolfgang.[53]

Leopold's fears about the fee from De Jean proved justified, though not because of any involvement of Wendling's. Wolfgang reported that Wendling, Ramm, and De Jean were about to leave for Paris, and that De Jean had given him only 96 fl. The reason Wolfgang gave was that only two concertos and three quartets had been finished. He was unwilling to accept the blame for this, saying merely that De Jean was obliged to pay him the whole amount, since he could send the outstanding pieces on after him; and that the reason he had not finished them was that he had had insufficient free time, hated the instrument, had not always been in the mood, and was not prepared to scribble any old music.[54] At this point, Wolfgang had not received Leopold's reaction to his new plans, but had received the letter which had been intended to prepare him for his responsibilities in Paris. Presumably because this letter had reminded Wolfgang of the needs of his family, he made it clear that he was still thinking of going to Paris, but on his own. Hence De Jean's reduced fee was a blow to him. He could not even afford to pay for Maria Anna's journey home, and he declared his intention of trying to earn more money

---

[53] The information in this paragraph and the preceding two is from Leopold to Wolfgang, 11–12 Feb. 1778—*MBA* 422 (*Letters* 285).

[54] Though some of the reasons put forward by Wolfgang might appear inadequate, given the needs of his family, his claim that he was not prepared to scribble any old music was probably sincere. For despite all his later appalling financial problems, he was not to compromise his artistic integrity.

in Mannheim for this purpose. He asked Leopold to arrange the journey to Paris, and to send some arias for Aloysia.[55]

By the time Wolfgang next wrote, he had received Leopold's reaction to his ideas for helping the Webers, and he responded to some of the criticisms. He did so in a rather off-hand way, though admitting that he had been partly at fault. He reminded Leopold about the arias for Aloysia, and sent a curt message to Nannerl to the effect that if she cried over every 'piddling little thing' he would never come home again. (This remark was to draw a sharp rebuke from Leopold.) Maria Anna's part of the letter reported that the sum total of their cash was 140 fl., and that they intended to sell the chaise and travel together to Paris with the mail-coach. She begged Leopold not to take things so much to heart, assuring him that nothing had been lost but bad company.[56]

As Wolfgang's letters filtered through, Leopold was filled with indignation at the contents. He accused Wolfgang of lying about the extent of his commitment to De Jean; he thought this because De Jean had paid approximately half of the agreed fee, yet the work Wolfgang claimed to have completed (two concertos and three quartets) was far more than half that which he claimed had been agreed (three concertos and two quartets). He also lamented that Wolfgang's experience was being bought at the expense of the rest of them. He was incensed at Wolfgang's arrogant claim that teaching was beneath him, and sharply reminded him of the teaching he was undertaking in his old age in order to finance Wolfgang's journey. He accused Wolfgang of treating him more cruelly than Colloredo, and said that Bullinger and Nannerl were the only two people in whom he could confide; before everyone else he had to pretend that everything was fine. This was difficult because of the money he owed and could not begin to repay. Hagenauer, for example, who had loaned the 150 fl. drawn from Schmalz, had been told by Leopold that Wolfgang was to earn 200 fl. from De Jean, and had expressed the greatest confidence that Wolfgang would do his duty as a son. Leopold was now in the embarrassing position of having to prevaricate before him. Above all, he despaired of Wolfgang's fecklessness, and reminded him of the responsibility attached to a gift such as his.[57]

Leopold had no choice but to support Wolfgang in every way possible until he arrived in Paris, for this plan offered the best chance that

---

[55] Wolfgang to Leopold, 13–14 Feb. 1778—*MBA* 423 (*Letters* 286a).

[56] Wolfgang and Maria Anna to Leopold, 19 Feb. 1778—*MBA* 426 (*Letters* 288). Anderson translates 'every piddling little thing' ('jedem Dr[eck]') as 'every silly trifle'.

[57] Leopold to Wolfgang, 23 Feb. 1778—*MBA* 429 (*Letters* 290).

the situation could be rescued; but he did more than was necessary. As well as thinking out all the practical arrangements that occurred to him, he complied with Wolfgang's request that he should have arias copied for Aloysia. This was done at his expense, because Wolfgang had begged him to make a present of them to the impoverished family. Leopold, however, did not neglect to point out his generosity in doing this at a time when his clothes were all in rags. He also claimed that he and Nannerl could not contemplate going to the theatre, or to any of the carnival balls in Salzburg, and mourned the fact that on top of all his worries he had no idea when he might see his wife and son again. He wrote fondly of Nannerl as his support, and detailed her progress in keyboard accompaniment. She could by now accompany everything at sight, even fugal pieces; her knowledge of harmony and modulation had increased vastly; she could move at will from one key to another; and could even extemporize. Leopold claimed that it was the fear of her father's death which had spurred her on to learn these skills. He mentioned the Adlgasser children's pension of 8 fl. per month for a year, but claimed that Maria Anna and Nannerl would get nothing if he died, because Wolfgang had voluntarily given up his appointment and Colloredo had simultaneously dismissed Leopold; Nannerl would have to go into service, and Wolfgang would have to support his mother. Leopold used this grim prospect facing Nannerl to demonstrate to Wolfgang that she had not been crying over a 'piddling little thing', and went on to tell him that she had offered her savings of 50 fl. as the security for a further loan from Hagenauer (since it was clear that the travellers were going to need more money to get to Paris). Her savings consisted of money she had earned from giving private lessons. He also said that Nannerl had started to pray so earnestly in church that people had commented on it to him, and drew the moral that Wolfgang had never before had to think of other people, and had therefore forgotten what it must be like for his family in Salzburg.[58]

Wolfgang's response to this letter was crestfallen and penitent. He was grateful for the arias for Aloysia, and for the loan from Nannerl, and shocked by Leopold's description of his clothes. He begged them tenderly to rely on him to lift them all out of the morass they were in, and produced particularly kind words for Nannerl, urging her not to forget

[58] Leopold to Wolfgang, 25–6 Feb. 1778—*MBA* 430 (*Letters* 291). I have not been able to determine whether Leopold was right when he said that the women would get no pension from Colloredo, but he spoke the truth about the pension of the Adlgasser children. It is not clear how Nannerl could have earned her living by her accompaniment skills. She might have entered a noble house as governess, in which case they would have been useful for domestic music-making; whether she would have been asked to accompany at court is difficult to evaluate.

her skill in *galanterie* playing now that she was practising so much score-reading. He claimed that he told everyone that she played with more precision than he. Nevertheless, he did not accept the blame for the present predicament—rather, he blamed the stinginess of German princes, and said that he and Maria Anna had been living as economically as possible, with board, lodging, wood, and candles free, and that Leopold knew how important it was for his appearance to command respect.[59] The letters, however, many containing information supplied by Wolfgang himself, suggest that he was deceiving himself when he claimed he could not have done more. In mid-December 1777, after paying the inn bill in Mannheim and moving into Serarius's house, he and Maria Anna had claimed to have 72 fl. Since then, Wolfgang had claimed to earn 42 fl. profit from Princess Caroline and 96 fl. from De Jean; but by mid-February 1778 they said they had only 140 fl. They had therefore spent 70 fl. in two months, even though the most important items of expenditure had not required the outlay of cash. Annually, this would work out at 420 fl., a sum greater than Leopold's annual salary in Salzburg of 354 fl.[60] Since Wolfgang had mentioned the importance of his appearance, it is possible that some of the money had been spent on clothes. It certainly seems to have been the case that Wolfgang tended to receive the lion's share of fine costumes; while the others scrimped and saved, and altered his old clothes for their own use, he was provided with everything needed to cut a fine figure in society, because the hopes of the family's fortunes were vested in him. Furthermore, in addition to having spent more than was desirable, Wolfgang had paid some of the Webers' expenses in Kirchheimbolanden, had passed over the chance to teach more, and had failed to earn the agreed sum from De Jean.

The preparations for Paris continued. Leopold had agreed with Maria Anna that they must both go together, and gave them all manner of instructions. He had heard that Grimm was there, which relieved his mind considerably, but he was nevertheless worried about money, and also about their health. He told them to renew their stock of black powders in Mannheim, where they would be easier to find than in Paris, and to seek out a German doctor. He also hoped they would be able to sell the chaise for 5 louis d'or (55 fl.), but was doubtful even so whether they would have enough, and arranged for them to draw 5 louis d'or (55 fl.)

---

[59] Wolfgang to Leopold, 7 Mar. 1778—*MBA* 435 (*Letters* 296 and 296a).

[60] Leopold's letter of 18 Dec. 1777, in which he had given a projection of how much they might spend in two months in Mannheim, revealed that he thought 50 fl. a month a generous sum, even if it were to include a lodging for Maria Anna and her food. See *MBA* 392/63–72 (*Letters* 262).

in Mannheim before leaving. This was presumably the loan secured by Nannerl's savings.[61] Having done all this, however, he was still worried that they might arrive in Paris with little cash, and hastily arranged through the Salzburg merchant Gschwendtner, whose brother was in Paris, for them to be able to draw money from him if absolutely essential.[62] Leopold's financial desperation can be judged from the fact that he wrote to Breitkopf to beg him to send as soon as possible money owed to Leopold for the sale of his *Violinschule*; this amounted to 37 fl. 30 kr.[63]

While Leopold was fretting about the poor start they would be making in Paris with so little capital behind them, and warning Wolfgang that if he did not apply himself with the greatest industry to his mission he might have to pawn possessions and they might all be made destitute, Wolfgang and Maria Anna were making heavy weather of selling the chaise. Eventually they struck a bargain with a coachman whereby they were driven to Paris by him in the vehicle, which he then kept. By this means, their transport to Paris cost 81 fl. instead of 121 fl., though food and accommodation on the way added another 4 louis d'or (44 fl.). Wolfgang's last letter to Leopold from Mannheim detailed the travel arrangements, and asked him to be sure to copy more arias for Aloysia on to small-format paper, so that Fridolin would not have to pay so much to receive them.[64]

❧

The main Salzburg news in the new year was the continuing confusion following Adlgasser's death. Spitzeder had temporarily taken over his teaching duties in the Kapellhaus, and Michael Haydn (to the Mozarts' disgust) had been given his post of organist at Holy Trinity.[65] Leopold Mozart had taken over the teaching of the daughters of Countess Lodron. He seemed to claim that he was doing so reluctantly—at any rate, he gave her the impression that he was doing her a great favour—but the

---

[61] Leopold to Wolfgang and Maria Anna, 28 Feb.–2 Mar. 1778—*MBA* 433 (*Letters* 294).
[62] Leopold to Wolfgang and Maria Anna, 16 Mar. 1778—*MBA* 438/7–15 (*Letters* 298).
[63] Leopold to Breitkopf, 13 Mar. and 4 Oct. 1778—*MBA* 437 and 495 (not in *Letters*).
[64] Wolfgang to Leopold, 11 and 24 Mar. 1778—*MBA* 436 and 439 (*Letters* 297 and 299).
[65] Leopold to Wolfgang and Maria Anna, 29 Dec. 1777—*MBA* 399/131–4 (*Letters* 268). It is not clear why the Mozarts should have objected to Haydn's appointment at Holy Trinity, unless Leopold had had designs on it himself and thought that Haydn, who lived much further away, was poaching it from him. Leopold contented himself with commenting on Haydn's tipsiness during services, but Maria Anna was indignant at his 'baseness' in taking the post, and asked what had become of the idea of sending him to Italy to be turned into a Kapellmeister (*MBA* 400/27–30; *Letters* 269).

reluctance might have been calculated to make himself more desirable.[66] With this move began the manipulation of the well-disposed nobility which was to lead to Wolfgang's return. Leopold had a reputation as a teacher which made him extremely valuable in the eyes of the nobility, and his fees were modest. By indicating that Wolfgang was being very successful, he planted the fear in Countess Lodron and her father Count Arco (whose grandson Leopold was also Leopold Mozart's pupil) that Wolfgang was highly likely to be engaged elsewhere. The assumption was that if this were to happen, the rest of the Mozarts would follow Wolfgang away from Salzburg, and a fine teacher would be lost to the town.

When Adlgasser died, it was clear that had Wolfgang still been in Salzburg he would have been the obvious successor. Leopold was asked by the Obersthofmeister if he had any suggestions for an organist who was also a good keyboard player, and had a respectable enough manner to teach ladies. Because the criteria so exactly fitted Wolfgang, Leopold and the Obersthofmeister enjoyed a joke about it, and Leopold gave the impression that Wolfgang was making his fortune in Mannheim.[67] Despite all his worries in the course of the next year, Leopold was to succeed in keeping up this brave front in Salzburg, and thus made Wolfgang far more sought-after.

As the travellers were on the way to Paris, both Leopold and Maria Anna were congratulating themselves on having escaped sending Wolfgang there with Wendling. Their attitudes to this deliverance are illuminating. Maria Anna claimed that she had prayed daily to God to prevent the journey, and that her prayers had been answered;[68] but she could have taken direct action herself to prevent it, by writing about Wendling's morality to Leopold. Leopold also expressed relief that the danger had been averted, thanks to God. He said (though he had not done so when Wolfgang had first mentioned that Wendling's daughter had been the elector's mistress) that a man who could sacrifice his own daughter from self-interest was loathsome. He also chided Maria Anna for not having done what was in her power to prevent the journey with Wendling, so that God had instead had to work his will by causing Wolfgang to become intoxicated with love.[69] But Leopold was later to change this

---

[66] Leopold to Wolfgang and Maria Anna, 5 Jan. 1778—*MBA* 401/116–27 (*Letters* 270). In this passage, Leopold mentioned the countess's 'false friendliness', so perhaps he really was reluctant to have anything to do with her.

[67] Leopold to Wolfgang and Maria Anna, 12 Jan. 1778—*MBA* 403/43–50 (*Letters* 272).

[68] Maria Anna to Leopold, 22 Feb. 1778—*MBA* 428/62–3 (*Letters* 289a).

[69] Leopold to Wolfgang and Maria Anna, 25–6 Feb. 1778—*MBA* 430/11–22 (*Letters* 291, but the most revealing part of the passage is omitted).

view and tell Wolfgang that he (Leopold) *would* have trusted Wolfgang to make the journey safely with Wendling, had he been informed of all the circumstances in time to give his judgement. The reason for this change of view was that the outcome of the Parisian trip was disastrous, involving as it did the death of his wife, which Leopold believed would not have occurred if she had not gone there. His attempts after her death to reconcile the will of God with decisions taken by man were to involve him in tortuous reasoning.[70]

[70] See Ch. 18.

❦ 18 ❧

Explaining the Unacceptable:
Maria Anna's Death

❦❧

A FTER a tedious nine-day journey, Maria Anna and Wolfgang arrived in Paris on 23 March 1778, and took up lodgings with Mayer, the Parisian agent of the Augsburg merchant Arbauer. Wolfgang carried with him Fridolin Weber's parting gift, an edition of Molière, and the memory of the sad leave-taking of Mannheim friends such as the Webers and Cannabichs. Maria Anna, who had disliked Paris on her first visit in 1764, and had not wanted to make the journey again, brought with her a dress, a fan, and an amethyst ring given to her on the previous occasion by Grimm's long-standing companion, Mme d'Épinay.[1] They may have arrived with as little as 100 fl., and Wolfgang had to set about immediately to earn money.[2]

Paris offered vastly more opportunities for this purpose than Mannheim. There were two independent series of public concerts, both of which needed a continuing supply of music. One was the Concert spirituel, organized by Joseph Legros, and the other was the newer Concert des amateurs, which had been founded by François-Joseph Gossec (though the musical director while Wolfgang was there was Joseph Boulogne). Both series commissioned symphonies, but the Concert des amateurs tended to promote new music more vigorously than the Concert spirituel. The public platform

---

[1] See Leopold to Maria Anna and Wolfgang, 6 Apr. 1778—*MBA* 444/127–9 (*Letters* 301); and Wolfgang to Leopold, 18 Dec. 1778—*MBA* 510/98–116 (*Letters* 345).

[2] According to Wolfgang, transport and accommodation on the way had cost 125 fl. Cash in hand on leaving Mannheim may have been no more than 228 fl. This was made up of 140 fl. the travellers claimed still to have on 19 Feb., the credit of 55 fl. secured by Nannerl's savings, and 3 louis d'or (33 fl.) given by Baron von Gemmingen to Wolfgang for music just before Wolfgang left Mannheim; see Ch. 17, pp. 285–8, and Wolfgang to Leopold, 24 Mar. 1778—*MBA* 439/16–25 (*Letters* 299). However, it is possible that they had sold more music or other belongings before leaving, to raise a further sum. Though financial projections of this sort are generally not very reliable, they can be useful when there is other evidence about the overall picture of the financial situation at a given point. In this case, for example, there is other evidence to show that Wolfgang never found his feet financially in Paris.

offered by these institutions meant that for the composer or performer who could please the audience, other opportunities in the form of teaching and private commissions were sure to follow. Printed music for domestic purposes was also in demand, and Wolfgang had been writing violin and keyboard sonatas for this market while he had been in Mannheim. Opera and ballet commissions were theoretical possibilities, and the French court offered patronage and employment opportunities.

For these reasons, Paris attracted musicians from far and wide, and competition was intense. Daunting though the process of infiltration was to a new arrival, however, Wolfgang was not entirely without support. Grimm was at hand, and Wendling was already there with his Mannheim friends. He apparently bore Wolfgang no grudge for having pulled out at such short notice from his own travel plans, and was prepared to help him establish himself. Having experienced the Parisian Lenten concert season before, he already had useful contacts. Wolfgang therefore buckled down to making what acquaintance he could, on the advice of Wendling and Grimm, and at first expressed optimistic determination to make good in Paris. He asked Leopold to show cheerfulness in his letters, and urged him to come and join them there if war should break out in Germany.[3]

Meanwhile, Maria Anna had to make the best of the lodgings arranged by Leopold through Arbauer. The room looked on to an inner courtyard, and was so dark that she could get no inkling of what the weather was like. Even knitting was difficult. The stairs were too narrow to admit a keyboard instrument, so Wolfgang went to Legros to compose, leaving Maria Anna on her own all day. The arrangement did not last long, because the room was too far from the houses of the nobility and from the theatre, and in early April they moved to more convenient lodgings in the rue du Gros Chenêt; but Maria Anna suffered again, as she had in Mannheim, from having virtually no role, and from being socially separated from Wolfgang. He soon had a number of houses where he could dine, but she was dependent on the food sent to their room by the cookshop, and found it all but inedible.

By early April, Wolfgang had a number of projects under way. At the instigation of Legros, he was rewriting choruses for a Miserere by Holzbauer, for performance in Holy Week. He had met the ballet-master Noverre and the composer Gossec, and the idea of his writing

---

[3] Wolfgang to Leopold, 24 Mar. 1778—*MBA* 439 (*Letters* 299). This letter also contains details about the departure from Mannheim, and the journey.

an opera was mooted. He was starting work on a Sinfonia Concertante for flute, oboe, horn, and bassoon, to be played by Wendling and some of his friends in one of Legros's concerts. He was continuing work on a set of violin and keyboard sonatas, which he intended to have printed. Finally, he was writing a concerto for flute and harp, commissioned by the duc de Guines for himself and his daughter, and was giving the daughter lessons in composition. Despite their admission that they had little money, therefore, Wolfgang and Maria Anna hoped not to need to draw any from Gschwendtner. Maria Anna claimed that Wolfgang was already well known and liked, and he expressed confidence in his ability to work hard and earn money, though he already detested the French language and singing.[4]

Leopold's attitude to the beginning of the stay in Paris was simple encouragement. He urged Wolfgang to view Grimm as a father-figure, and was sure that if Wolfgang took his advice, he would prosper. He too hoped they would not have to draw money from Gschwendtner, not only because the debt was already frightening, but also because it would harm their honour in Salzburg if it became known that Leopold was still having to support Wolfgang. He sketched a situation whereby they might all be able to live in Paris; his idea was that if Wolfgang could obtain a salaried appointment with a prince, the foundation would be laid for a move from Salzburg for the whole family. Using the salary as basic security, Wolfgang would be able to earn additional sums from the theatre, the Concert spirituel, the Concert des amateurs, and from printed compositions; while Leopold and Nannerl would be able to give lessons, and Nannerl would have a public platform. For Leopold, the salary was crucial to the scheme, because it would be paid even in times of sickness. He had held this belief for a long time, but the experiences of this journey were to make him even more cautious. By the time Wolfgang was returning to Salzburg later in 1778, Leopold thought that one salaried appointment was hardly enough for his peace of mind, and was urging the return home because both father and son would have the security of a salary, thus easing Leopold's fears about what would happen to Nannerl if one of them died before she married.[5] In reply to Wolfgang's request that he should write cheerfully, and should come to Paris if war broke out, Leopold reminded him that it would be impossible to leave

[4] The information in this paragraph and the preceding one is from Maria Anna and Wolfgang to Leopold, 5 Apr. 1778—*MBA* 440 (*Letters* 300 and 300*a*). The violin and keyboard sonatas were K. 301–6.

[5] See Ch. 19, pp. 325–7, for more details about this point.

Salzburg while he owed so much money there; and that his peace of mind depended on the success of Wolfgang's actions.[6]

Wolfgang's optimism about his prospects in Paris was short-lived. At the beginning of May, he was writing in despondent terms about the futility of paying visits to the nobility; the distances were too great, the streets too dirty, the people were out, or if they were in they thought they had paid him by exclaiming at his talent. He gave a vivid description of the rudeness he had endured when playing to the duchesse de Chabot, to whom he had been introduced by Grimm; he had been made to wait in a freezing room until he could no longer feel his fingers, and when he eventually started to play it was to the chatter of conversation and card-playing. The choruses he had written for Holzbauer's Miserere had been wasted to the extent that only two of them had been performed and it had not been indicated that they were by him. Moreover, Legros had failed to produce the Sinfonia Concertante Wolfgang had written, and had given no explanation. Finally, his initial dislike of French taste had ripened into disgusted antipathy and, though he asserted his intention of staying in Paris for the sake of earning money to help Leopold, he begged his father to arrange for him to go to Italy as soon as possible. In the same letter, Maria Anna reported having been unwell with a head cold, and asked if Leopold could send more black powders and digestive powders, since their supply was running low.[7] The black powders were *pulvis epilecticus niger*; they had the effect of reducing fever, and were a staple of the Mozarts' medicine chest.

Leopold responded in the only way he could. Though he was sympathetic to the difficulties Wolfgang had enumerated, their finances and the political situation made it impossible to leave Paris, and Wolfgang therefore had to fight his way through all the obstacles and make the best of it. He advised Wolfgang to study French taste before writing anything, to set the words carefully, and to be prepared to revise his work. Any music written for engraving should be light and popular, and he should ensure that he was paid for everything he did. Once he had earned money and fame, a journey to Italy would be possible. He also reminded Wolfgang of the antagonism they had had to contend with when Wolfgang had been writing his first and third operas. He could see no way of sending the black powders at present, and suggested that they try to buy them in Paris; and

[6] The information in this paragraph is from Leopold to Wolfgang and Maria Anna, 6 Apr. 1778—*MBA* 444 (*Letters* 301).

[7] Wolfgang and Maria Anna to Leopold, 1 May 1778—*MBA* 447 (*Letters* 303 and 303*a*).

he urged Maria Anna not to forget to be bled, especially since she was not in her accustomed environment.[8]

Leopold's points were unanswerable, and Wolfgang consequently continued to persevere. By mid-May he had three pupils, one of whom was the daughter of the duc de Guines, through whom there was a possibility of introduction to the French court. The queen was pregnant, so that grand celebrations, offering work to musicians, could be expected in due course. The plan to write an opera was still in existence, and Wolfgang intended to write some ballet music for Noverre. Most interestingly of all, he claimed to have been offered the post of organist at Versailles. It involved being in residence there for only six months of the year, and the salary was 2,000 livres (915 fl. 45 kr.) annually; but Wolfgang said that the cost of living was such that it was not as well paid as it seemed, and he did not think he would accept it.[9]

Not surprisingly, Leopold was more interested in this post than Wolfgang. He pointed out the security of the salary in sickness and in health; the fact that six months of the year were free for other projects; the proximity of the French court and other noble families; the opportunities for composition; the fact that he would be on the spot if a Kapellmeister post became available; and the fact that he would always be able to leave if something better cropped up. He did not urge Wolfgang to take it, however, but only to take Grimm's advice on its desirability.[10]

By the end of May, Wolfgang was no happier. He told Leopold that although he was not ill, he had no zest for life. He spoke warmly about the discriminating musical taste of Count Sickingen, the Palatine ambassador to Paris, to whom he had been introduced by Mannheim acquaintances, but hinted that he still disliked the French. Other news reported in this letter was that he had seen a French edition of Leopold's *Violinschule* for sale, and that Maria Anna was looking for a barber she could trust, in order to be bled.[11]

This time Leopold was less patient with Wolfgang's complaints. He assumed that the dissatisfaction came from the grind of having to earn one's own living instead of relying on someone else, and pointed out that Wolfgang was now experiencing what had been a fact of life for

---

[8] Leopold to Wolfgang and Maria Anna, 6–11 May 1778—*MBA* 448/185–247 (*Letters* 304).

[9] Maria Anna and Wolfgang to Leopold, 14 May 1778—*MBA* 449 (*Letters* 305 and 305a). The livre/fl. conversion is Wolfgang's own.

[10] Leopold to Wolfgang, 28 May 1778—*MBA* 450/231–48 (*Letters* 306).

[11] Maria Anna and Wolfgang to Leopold, 29 May 1778—*MBA* 451/45–78 (*Letters* 307 and 307a).

Leopold for thirty years. He drew attention to the five pupils he himself had to take against his wishes, and to the fact that it had been Wolfgang who had been so keen to leave Salzburg. He acknowledged the difficulty of making headway in Paris, but insisted that it was possible to earn money there. He also complained, not for the first time, about the haphazard way in which Wolfgang wrote his letters home, and urged him to answer letters and give news methodically. His own method was to jot down points as reminders on a piece of paper kept for the purpose, and write about them bit by bit as he had time. By the time the post day arrived, all he had to do to finish the letter was to add a greeting. Wolfgang and Maria Anna never acquired this habit, however, so that Leopold was frequently frustrated by letters which failed to continue topics begun in previous ones.[12] Finally, he mentioned the supposed offer of the post of organist at Versailles. He assumed it had not been a real offer so much as a 'pious wish' on the part of Rudolph, the man who had first mentioned the subject to Wolfgang; but he had nevertheless used it in his campaign to win a new appointment for Wolfgang back in Salzburg. By the time Maria Anna was bled, on 11 June, Leopold had his greatest diplomatic triumph—the winning of a good post for Wolfgang in Salzburg at a considerably enhanced salary, in the face of the pride of Wolfgang and of Colloredo—well in hand.[13]

❧

While Wolfgang was struggling to make progress in Paris, life for Leopold and Nannerl in Salzburg was not without incident. Because Maria Anna missed her home, she was always keen to read news of Salzburg events, and Leopold reported it all faithfully. At the beginning of May, the cap-mender Sandl Auer, to whom he had recently offered a room, was the subject of one of his stories. Though she was descended from a noble family, she was poor and had had little education. The only hope of improving her lot lay in marriage. Johann Andreas Lasser, the Oberschreiber (chief clerk) of Gnigl just outside Salzburg, had taken advantage of her simplicity by teasing her with expressions of love. The

---

[12] Though Leopold's exhortations with regard to letter-writing may seem fussy, patronizing, and pedantic, it has to be remembered that a letter from Paris to Salzburg could take ten days, and that there was no significantly faster way of sending news. If something of importance were omitted from a letter, therefore, it could take almost three weeks from the date of receipt before the recipient, having reminded the other person to send the information in question, received it.

[13] Leopold to Wolfgang, 11 June 1778—*MBA* 452/86–123 (*Letters* 308).

daughter of the customs officer in Gnigl had joined in the game by carrying letters between the two, and had inflamed Sandl's fear and jealousy by telling her of other women in Lasser's life. The result was that Sandl became completely hysterical one evening, so that the combined efforts of Leopold, three women from the Dancing-Master's House, and the rosary were powerless to calm her, and they were up all night while she raved away. Next day, Barisani suggested she be bled and prescribed some medicine, and a priest came to hear her confession, but she did not improve, and had to be removed to hospital for several days. She recovered and came home, but Leopold's analysis of the case reveals the vulnerability of poor women when they lacked the support and advice of a family. He ascribed her temporary insanity to her delusion of nobility (presumably because it made her unwilling to accept her humble situation), her poverty, a ray of hope that she might become a wife, the destruction of this hope through the mischief of a third person, and her inability to think rationally (which had prevented her from exercising enough scepticism about Lasser's declarations of love).[14]

The domestic music-making of Leopold and Nannerl had been enhanced for some while by Ceccarelli, the castrato who was in Salzburg on a short contract. The advent of Ceccarelli seems to have been partly responsible for spurring Nannerl on to even greater efforts at the keyboard, and early in May Leopold reported how hard she was working at her *galanterie* playing, accompaniment, taste, and expression. She had also written a bass to a violin solo of Ceccarelli's, and Leopold was so surprised and pleased by it that he was encouraging her to do so more often.[15] The other stimulus to Nannerl's playing for a few months during this period was Count Czernin's newly formed amateur orchestra. Czernin, as nephew of Colloredo, played the violin at some of the evening concerts at court on Tuesdays, Thursdays, and Sundays. This was a common practice, and Colloredo himself also sometimes played along with his court orchestra. Now, according to Leopold, Czernin wanted to be involved in something more ambitious, and to direct an orchestra himself. His band comprised people from virtually every social class in Salzburg. There were nobles, canons, court councillors, tradesmen, students, *Turnergesellen* (musicians employed for civic musical functions), three court musicians (Leopold Mozart being one), ex-Jesuit tutors, lackeys—and one woman,

---

[14] Leopold to Maria Anna and Wolfgang, 29 Apr.–11 May 1778—*MBA* 448/7–92 (not in *Letters*).

[15] Leopold to Maria Anna and Wolfgang, 29 Apr.–11 May 1778—*MBA* 448/232–6 (*Letters* 304).

Nannerl Mozart, who accompanied everything at the keyboard. Other women were involved as amateur soloists, either singing or at the keyboard, but Nannerl was the only one with any pretensions to professional standards. The concerts took place each Sunday afternoon in the hall of the Lodron palace, so it was natural that the Lodron daughters (of whom Leopold was now teaching the elder two and Nannerl the younger two) should often be involved as soloists. Leopold was full of scorn for much of the playing, and suggested that hitherto unknown time-signatures were being discovered. The problem was that some of the nobles involved were determined to promote themselves as soloists despite woeful inadequacies in their playing. However, one aspect of the venture that was probably useful to the Mozarts was the fact that they, as linchpin members, gained even closer contact with the Lodron household.[16]

Czernin's band is interesting among other reasons for the musical roles it made possible for Nannerl in Salzburg; not that the standard of music-making was anything special, but she was able to demonstrate her newly acquired accompaniment skills in a semi-public environment. Since Adlgasser's death, the keyboard player at court had been Franz Ignaz Lipp, Michael Haydn's father-in-law. That this was from the beginning of the arrangement seen as an interim measure is suggested by the fact that Colloredo had started immediately after the loss of Adlgasser to hunt for a new organist and keyboard player whose demeanour was respectable enough to accompany at court and to teach ladies. Since Lipp was not offered the post, he was presumably not such a man; so Leopold's comments on his frequent inebriation may not have been exaggerated. In December 1777, when telling Maria Anna and Wolfgang that Michael Haydn had been appointed organist at Holy Trinity, Leopold had mentioned that he drank on duty, and that he sent the equally bibulous Lipp to play at the services he could not manage.[17] Now Leopold described the 'bestiality' of the court music with Lipp as accompanist, and reported how Ceccarelli openly criticized Lipp when he had to sing with him.[18] On the other hand, Ceccarelli enjoyed being accompanied by Nannerl; he made music privately with her and Leopold daily during this period, and the inaugural concert given by Czernin's band opened with an aria sung by him and accompanied by Nannerl. Though a number of female amateurs played keyboard concertos in Czernin's series, Nannerl did not,

---

[16] Leopold to Wolfgang and Maria Anna, 12–20 Apr. 1778—*MBA* 446/28–56 (*Letters* 302).

[17] Leopold to Maria Anna, 29 Dec. 1777—*MBA* 399/131–4 (*Letters* 268).

[18] Leopold to Wolfgang and Maria Anna, 11 June 1778—*MBA* 452/150–2 (*Letters* 308, but Anderson tones down Leopold's comment on the bestiality).

because Countess Lodron would not grant them the use of her best harpsichord (which Leopold pointedly said was reserved for her music-making when Colloredo was present). Instead, she provided one made by the court organ-builder Egedacher, which Nannerl considered too poor to do her playing justice.[19] Nannerl did, however, coach some of the women and girls who were to perform, so that they could do themselves credit.[20] All this suggests that from Adlgasser's death until Wolfgang's return she may have been the Salzburg keyboard player who best combined high standards with appropriate social graces. Leopold had been encouraging her to develop the skills required of a professional keyboard player leading an ensemble, had stated specifically that the purpose of this was to enable her to earn a living if necessary, and had claimed that she could accompany as well as any Kapellmeister.[21] If his reports of the Czernin concerts are accurate, they suggest that the occasions gave her the opportunity to show her newly acquired skills in a household where it might have been possible for her to find employment which used them, were she to need it.

By mid-June 1778 Colloredo had still not found a Kapellmeister to replace Rust, or an organist and keyboard player to replace Adlgasser. Leopold claimed that there was no longer any question of promoting Michael Haydn, because his sister-in-law Judith Lipp had given birth to an illegitimate daughter fathered by the violinist Brunetti, and the two miscreants had frequented Haydn's house.[22] He also claimed that, but for Czernin's patronage, Brunetti would be dismissed by Colloredo, because it was his second such offence.[23] Leopold saw Czernin, together with Count Starhemberg, as particular protectors of Brunetti and other Italian musicians in Salzburg; and Michael Haydn belonged to the Italian 'camp' too, through his friendship with Brunetti. The Mozarts' particular benefactors, on the other hand, were members of the Arco and Lodron families.[24] When Colloredo's cousin Anton Theodor Colloredo celebrated his consecration as archbishop of Olmütz in Salzburg Cathedral on 17 May 1778, Brunetti tried through Czernin and Starhemberg to obtain a commission from Colloredo to produce one of Haydn's Masses for the service. They were

---

[19] Leopold to Maria Anna and Wolfgang, 12–20 Apr. 1778—*MBA* 446/43–5 and 50–3 (*Letters* 302).
[20] Leopold to Maria Anna and Wolfgang, 11 June 1778—*MBA* 452/21–40 (*Letters* 308).
[21] See Ch. 17, p. 286, and Leopold to Wolfgang and Maria Anna, 6 Apr. 1778—*MBA* 444/131–2 (*Letters* 301).
[22] See Fig. 1 for a diagram of Brunetti/Haydn/Lipp relationships.
[23] Leopold to Maria Anna and Wolfgang, 11 June 1778—*MBA* 452/155–76 (*Letters* 308).
[24] See Fig. 3 for a diagram of Arco/Firmian/Lodron relationships.

not successful, however, and Leopold had music by Wolfgang performed instead.[25] In this act may be seen the withdrawal of any generous gestures Leopold might for a time have been inclined to make towards Haydn, now that he was thinking along the lines of Wolfgang's return to Salzburg.

Czernin seems not to have been as close to Colloredo as the chief protectors of the Mozarts, Count Arco and his daughter Countess Lodron. Czernin's age may have had something to do with this; he was a year younger than Wolfgang Mozart, and still a student, while Colloredo and Countess Lodron were more or less contemporaries. At any rate, the Mozarts' letters suggest that Colloredo and Countess Lodron were very close during this period. Leopold exploited this relationship for his own ends, calculating that the countess would first recognize the necessity of keeping the Mozarts in Salzburg, and then mediate between him and Colloredo to make this possible. He claimed to Wolfgang and Maria Anna that the playing of her daughters had improved vastly since Adlgasser's death because he had been teaching them, and the results of this teaching were made public when the girls performed as soloists at Czernin's amateur concerts.[26] This question of a teacher for her daughters, coupled with the fact that there was no organist or decent accompanist at court, made the solution to Salzburg's difficulties obvious; if Wolfgang could be tempted back, the Mozarts would all stay. When the countess's name-day came round again in June, Leopold told a story which indicates further his belief that Salzburg's nobles had nothing but grief to expect from special occasions unless the Mozarts were in charge of the music. Since Wolfgang (who had written and produced the music for the countess's name-day in both the preceding years) was away this year, Czernin led his amateur band in a ham-fisted attempt at serenading her. First he committed the *faux pas* of having the music played for his sister Countess Lützow before it was played for Countess Lodron, although Countess Lodron's rank was superior. Then his playing was decidedly indifferent. Finally, Brunetti encouraged him to believe (falsely) that Countess Lodron was snubbing him by refusing to appear at her window, and in high dudgeon he marched the band off in mid-serenade, as if the intention were to insult her. The fiasco was witnessed by many courtiers and councillors who had accompanied the musicians to pay their respects, and the countess was furious. Next time she saw Brunetti, she dressed him down in public, and Colloredo ceased speaking to him.[27] Leopold, who because of the

[25] Leopold to Maria Anna and Wolfgang, 28 May 1778—*MBA* 450/140–9 (*Letters* 306).
[26] Leopold to Maria Anna and Wolfgang, 11 June 1778—*MBA* 452/21–40 (*Letters* 308).
[27] Leopold to Wolfgang and Maria Anna, 29 June 1778—*MBA* 457/121–45 (not in *Letters*).

low standard had made an excuse to Czernin so that he would not have to be in the serenading party,[28] told the story in such a way as to suggest that Countess Lodron could not but have compared Czernin's bungled attempt with the serenades offered by the Mozarts in previous years.

Even before the name-day débâcle, Countess Lodron had moved into action to initiate the negotiations which were to bring Wolfgang back to Salzburg. The immediate spur was a passing conversation on her staircase with Leopold, who in answer to her question about the travellers, had told her that Wolfgang had been offered a post of organist at Versailles. Soon afterwards, she sent the tutor Henri to tell Leopold through Bullinger that if Wolfgang would return to Salzburg, he would be appointed Konzertmeister and organist at a salary of 50 fl. per month, and would certainly become Kapellmeister in due course. Leopold's response was cool. He deliberately took his time in passing a message back to Henri for the countess, and when he did it was simply to the effect that he had not mentioned the Versailles opening with the intention of making Wolfgang seem more desirable to Salzburg.[29]

Nevertheless, Leopold must have been excited at the possibility of Wolfgang's returning at an annual salary of 600 fl., and he continued to help members of Salzburg's nobility understand that this would be the best solution to all their problems. On Trinity Sunday, Leopold, Colloredo, Count Starhemberg, and others were present at the service in Holy Trinity, where Michael Haydn was now organist. According to Leopold, Haydn's organ playing was an uncoordinated shambles because he was not sober. Following the service, Starhemberg asked Leopold to visit him next day to discuss the question of a new court organist. At this interview, Leopold claimed that they discussed the deficiencies of Haydn and other court musicians, and he told Starhemberg bluntly how Wolfgang had been driven from Salzburg by the shoddy treatment he had received. When Starhemberg indicated that Wolfgang would be the most

---

[28] Leopold to Maria Anna and Wolfgang, 11 June 1778—*MBA* 452/199–210 (*Letters* 308, but not complete).

[29] Leopold to Wolfgang and Maria Anna, 11 June 1778—*MBA* 452/120–50 (*Letters* 308). Leopold referred to the woman with whom he had this conversation simply as 'the countess'. The *MBA* commentary identifies her as Countess Wallis, Colloredo's sister, but without any explanation. Here and at *MBA* 457/67 it simply remarks that Countess Wallis represented the feminine aspect of the court. Perhaps this assumption is made because the countess who negotiated Wolfgang's new contract evidently wielded great authority. Since other passages show that Countess Lodron was very close to Colloredo during this period, however, and that they had musical interests in common, there is every reason to believe that she may have been the countess meant by Leopold. Furthermore, Henri was tutor in her household. Anderson also identifies the countess in these passages as Wallis.

suitable candidate for the post of organist, Leopold said that he could not possibly write to tell him this unless he could tell Wolfgang the salary; Wolfgang would not return for the money that Adlgasser had received (448 fl. annually), and even 50 fl. per month might not tempt him. Leopold knew the strength of his position. Salzburg's perennial problem in attracting good outsiders was that salaries tended to be poor, and Leopold was mindful of the fact that no new organist/keyboard player could be offered a low salary with the promise of extra income from private teaching, because the few wealthy pupils were already being taught by himself. Having done this much, Leopold waited to see whether a firm offer for Wolfgang would be forthcoming. Meanwhile, he asked Wolfgang if he could send any music from Paris; he was longing to have some of his new compositions.[30]

❧

This was approximately the stage Leopold's campaign had reached when Maria Anna was bled on 11 June. A week or so later she was ill with a headache, fever, and diarrhoea. She and Wolfgang had not managed to replenish their stock of black powders, so the early treatment of her illness did not proceed according to their accustomed routines. A little later still she lost her hearing, and on 29 June, when Leopold reported the result of his conversation with Starhemberg, she was dying. Only very gradually after her death was Leopold able to piece together from Wolfgang's reports some of the circumstances of their life during her final illness, and these were distressing enough. What he probably never discovered in detail was that Wolfgang had had a secret agenda in Paris involving the Webers, and that this must to some extent have distracted him from concerns for his own family. What follows here is a reconstruction of what is known about the events, though some of the information only came to light several months later.

On 10 June, the day before Maria Anna was bled, Wolfgang was dining with Grimm and Raaff, who was visiting Paris from Mannheim. Maria Anna dined with Haina, husband of the music publisher Gertrude Haina. After the meal, Haina walked with her in the Luxembourg Gardens, and then escorted her home. The day was very hot, and she was tired. Next day she was bled, and on the following day she was writing to Leopold

---

[30] Leopold to Wolfgang and Maria Anna, 29 June 1778—*MBA* 457/5–73 and 170–9 (*Letters* 310, but not quite complete).

with an aching arm, while Wolfgang was out trying over the symphony he had written for Legros, K. 297, to Count Sickingen and Raaff. It was to be performed at the Concert spirituel on Corpus Christi, 18 June.[31] By the date of this concert, Maria Anna was already unwell with diarrhoea, and it was the last day on which she was up. Wolfgang said that on 20 June she was still unwell, but refused a doctor. Part of the problem was that the doctor had to be German. By the time she would have accepted that she needed a doctor, Maria Anna was too ill to be left while Wolfgang went out searching. Hence no doctor visited her until 24 June. On 26 June Wolfgang was told she should make her confession, which she did a few days later; and she died soon after ten in the evening on 3 July.[32]

At first sight, Wolfgang's account seems straightforward, and the description of his distress during her illness convincing. Yet his other activities during the period of her illness suggest that his mind was partly engaged elsewhere, and the subsequent disclosures of his financial position suggest that he may also have lacked the money to give her the care she needed.

Taking first the suggestion that his attention was not wholly fixed on his own family, Wolfgang told Leopold in his letter of 31 July that during Maria Anna's illness he had had plenty of time for composition but could not have written a note. He clearly intended to convey to Leopold his distraught state caused by anxiety for his mother. It is difficult to believe that he was not being entirely sincere, yet he was able to write to Weber in Mannheim on 27 June, 29 June, and the day of Maria Anna's death, 3 July. These letters do not survive, but they were apparently not concerned only with his distress about his mother, because a later letter to Weber which does survive (dated 29 July 1778) indicates that Weber and Wolfgang had been corresponding about the ways in which Wolfgang might help his friends in Mannheim.[33] From Wolfgang's letter to Leopold of 31 July 1778, it is clear that Weber had told Wolfgang that the Mannheim musicians had been told to choose either to move to Munich to serve the elector there, or to remain in Mannheim. Since the elector was going to reside in Munich, it was evident that Mannheim would die and that the best prospects were going to be in Munich. Weber's problem was that though there was some chance that Aloysia would be engaged for the Munich stage if he moved there, his debts in Mannheim were such that he did not think his creditors would let him go out of their

---

[31] Maria Anna and Wolfgang to Leopold, 12 June 1778—*MBA* 453 (*Letters* 309 and 309*a*).
[32] Wolfgang to Leopold and Nannerl, 31 July 1778—*MBA* 471/34–109 (*Letters* 319).
[33] *MBA* 469 (*Letters* 317). It is in this letter that the three other letters to Weber are mentioned.

reach.[34] Weber therefore, as Wolfgang's letter to him of 29 July shows, had hinted in his desperation that he might allow Aloysia to join Seyler's troupe of travelling players in Mainz. This idea horrified Wolfgang because of its lack of respectability, and he begged Weber to put it out of his mind. He suggested that Weber stay in Mannheim and continue to press for a better salary for himself and for an engagement for Aloysia; but at the same time that he try to obtain an appointment at the court in Mainz. In case of urgent need, Wolfgang wrote that they might come to Paris, where he would try to obtain engagements for Aloysia; but this was to be a last resort. He even hinted that if absolutely necessary, and if his circumstances permitted it, he would provide their board and lodging in Paris.[35] When he wrote these lines, he was virtually destitute himself, and was living as the guest of Mme d'Épinay.

It was precisely at this time that Wolfgang was himself still thinking of being taken on in Mannheim (he was hoping that Raaff would successfully recommend him to the elector), or alternatively that he would gain an appointment in Mainz (through Count Sickingen, whose brother had influence there). Thus Wolfgang's society with Raaff and Sickingen in Paris almost certainly had more to do with his plans to help the Webers, and to obtain a position that would enable him to be with them, than with loyalty to his own family. For although a post at either of these courts would have been beneficial to his family too, Wolfgang's letters do not suggest that it was of them that he was thinking first. At the end of his letter to Weber of 29 July, he said that if he were not obliged to support his father and sister, he would like nothing better than to devote himself entirely to the Webers.[36] Furthermore, Wolfgang indicated in his letter to Leopold of 31 July his awareness that Grimm believed he would not succeed in Paris because he did not take enough trouble to cultivate the right people; it therefore seems likely that by spending so much time with Raaff and Sickingen he had passed up chances to earn more money.

As for the travellers' financial situation when Maria Anna fell ill, it must have been grim. Only gradually, as Wolfgang made his homeward journey, did Leopold learn something of their plight. Though it is not possible to piece together a detailed picture of this, it gradually emerged that they had after all had to borrow money from Gschwendtner, and Leopold only discovered this loan of 10 louis d'or (110 fl.) when

---

[34] *MBA* 471/219–53 (*Letters* 319).   [35] *MBA* 469 (*Letters* 317).
[36] *MBA* 469/200–7 (*Letters* 317).

approached for the money by Gschwendtner's brother in Salzburg.[37] Furthermore, Wolfgang had borrowed 15 louis d'or (165 fl.) in bits and pieces from Grimm,[38] had moved into Mme d'Épinay's house after Maria Anna's death,[39] had pawned Maria Anna's watch and perhaps sold two of his own, and had given the amethyst ring (gift to Maria Anna from Mme d'Épinay) to the nurse who attended his mother in her final illness, because otherwise she would have taken Maria Anna's wedding ring.[40] This surely implies that Wolfgang had no cash with which to pay her. Since there were important matters which Wolfgang concealed from Leopold during this disastrous visit to Paris (the dissipation of his energies, and the true state of his finances), the thought cannot be ignored that the delay in calling in the doctor may have been caused partly by lack of funds. Leopold believed from the first that the doctor should have been called as soon as the diarrhoea appeared,[41] but it was only later that he learnt something of the extent of their poverty. Though he never in his letters challenged Wolfgang on the point of lacking the money to pay a doctor, it is difficult to believe that the suspicion did not occur to him, given how exhaustively he tried to reconstruct the events, and how good he was at reading between lines and winkling out inconsistencies, half-truths, and lies.

Wolfgang's behaviour on Maria Anna's death has been described as indicating a new maturity and sensitivity.[42] Immediately after the event, he wrote to tell Leopold that she was very ill, while writing to Bullinger to report her death, and to ask him to tell Leopold and Nannerl the whole truth.[43] His motive was to prepare them more gradually for the appalling news. Yet apart from this one piece of consideration, his letters reveal not only the thoughtlessness natural in someone so young

---

[37] Leopold to Wolfgang, 10 Sept. 1778—*MBA* 485/99–105 (not in *Letters*). Though the passage appears to show that Leopold thought of these 10 louis d'or as 100 fl., he may have been rounding the figure down; I convert the sum at 11 fl. per louis d'or to accord with his more commonly used conversion during this period. In his letter of 19 Nov. 1778, he converted the sum for the same debt to give 110 fl.—cf. *MBA* 505/70 (*Letters* 340).

[38] Wolfgang to Leopold, 11 Sept. 1778—*MBA* 487/77–9 (*Letters* 331).

[39] Wolfgang to Leopold, 9 July 1778—*MBA* 462/39–42 (*Letters* 313).

[40] Wolfgang to Leopold, 18 Dec. 1778—*MBA* 510/98–116 (*Letters* 345). Wolfgang actually claimed that he had swopped two of his watches for a better Parisian one, but in view of his problems in Paris, this claim should perhaps be regarded with scepticism. More likely is that he was given the Parisian one that he took home, and that he sold the other two for much-needed cash. It needs to be borne in mind that he constantly earned less and spent more than Leopold expected, so that this act would provide money which he did not have to declare to his father.

[41] Leopold to Wolfgang, 12–13 July 1778—*MBA* 464/77–86 (not in *Letters*).

[42] See S. Sadie, *The New Grove Mozart* (London, 1980), 58.

[43] Wolfgang to Leopold and to Bullinger, 3 July 1778—*MBA* 458 and 459 (*Letters* 311 and 312).

and inexperienced at comforting the bereaved, but also a more disturbing preoccupation with himself. The first trait is shown by his failure to appreciate that Leopold and Nannerl would want to piece together all the details of Maria Anna's illness in order to come to terms with it. He gave a full description only right at the end of July after Leopold had specifically asked for it;[44] before that, he had concentrated on urging them to believe simply that she had had to die because it had been the will of God.[45] The second trait is shown by his deliberately enigmatic references, one of which was even given in the very letter written directly after his mother's death and reporting how gravely ill she was, to his hopes for the future. He asked Leopold not to speculate about what he meant (it was almost certainly his idea of obtaining a situation which would allow him to be with the Webers), since he would tell him about it in detail when the time was ripe.[46] Yet he well knew that there was nothing Leopold hated so much as to be kept guessing about his plans. And if Leopold was not to speculate, why did Wolfgang mention the subject to him at all? The only answer would seem to be his engrossment in his own prospects of future happiness, even during this time.

❧

On 12 July, nine days after Maria Anna's death, Leopold began a letter to her, writing affectionate greetings for her approaching name-day on 26 July. Next morning, just before ten o' clock, he was going to continue with the letter when he received Wolfgang's telling him of Maria Anna's dangerous illness. He and Nannerl were, of course, deeply distressed, and Nannerl was prostrated by attacks of weeping, which gave her a headache and made her vomit, just as they had when Wolfgang and Maria Anna had left home in September of the previous year. She retired to her room just after lunch, but Leopold was strong enough to host the shooting party in the afternoon. The event was subdued, however, by the bad news. Bullinger was present, and he had received Wolfgang's letter reporting Maria Anna's death. After all the other guests had gone, Bullinger showed Leopold the letter which removed any hope.[47]

---

[44] Wolfgang to Leopold, 31 July 1778—*MBA* 471/34–106 (*Letters* 319).

[45] Wolfgang to Leopold and Nannerl, 3 and 9 July 1778—*MBA* 458/17–29 (*Letters* 311); and *MBA* 462/13–26 (*Letters* 313).

[46] Wolfgang to Leopold, 3 and 31 July 1778—*MBA* 458/80–8 and 471/115–32 (*Letters* 311 and 319).

[47] Leopold to Wolfgang, 12–13 July 1778—*MBA* 464 (*Letters* 314).

It was clear from the moment Leopold learnt the news that he was going to want all the details of the illness, in order to try to reconcile himself to his loss. Wolfgang's appeals to him to accept that nothing could have helped her, because the hour of her death had been fixed by God, were of little avail, despite the fact that he was repeating standard doctrine which he must have learnt from his parents. Indeed, these appeals may have exacerbated Leopold's grief by suggesting to him that Wolfgang's attitude to her illness had been too fatalistic and that he might not have done enough to save her life. Even before he had been told the full progression of the illness, Leopold was asserting that she had been bled too late and probably too little, that the combination of fever and diarrhoea was extremely serious, and that the doctor had been called in too late.[48] As the further news filtered through (for example, Wolfgang's specific admission on 31 July 1778 that the doctor had not attended until she had been in bed five days, because Wolfgang had been unable to leave her to summon one), Leopold became more and more convinced that she would not have died if she had been at home. No doubt he thought back to the dangerous illnesses when the children had been young, and how they had been rescued from the jaws of death by intelligent and devoted nursing. In Maria Anna's case, he believed the combination of fever and diarrhoea to have indicated the urgent necessity of a doctor, whose expertise alone could decide whether to reduce the fever, or whether to let it run its course so as not to aggravate the diarrhoea. Hence to Leopold the delay in calling the doctor was extremely significant and, furthermore, could be laid at no one's door but Wolfgang's; while Wolfgang gave the impression that he was trying to divert attention from his role by attributing everything to the will of God.

Leopold's further remarks about the causes of his wife's death show how convoluted reasoning could become when the attempt was made to reconcile the significance of the actions of men with God's purpose. He accepted that the hour of her death had been appointed by God, but nevertheless believed that she would not have died if she had been in Salzburg. Thus God's will had worked in such a way as to force her from her home. Leopold's explanation to Wolfgang was that she should have been able to return home in February, when Wolfgang should have gone to Paris with Wendling. It had not been doubts about Wendling's company which had caused Wolfgang to refuse to travel with him, but

---

[48] Leopold to Wolfgang, 12–13 July 1778—*MBA* 464/54–60, 77–86, and 154–8 (*Letters* 314, but not quite complete).

his love for Aloysia Weber; and he had told Leopold of his revised plans so late that Leopold had been unable to write in time for Wolfgang to travel with Wendling after all. If Leopold *had* been asked in time, he would have told Wolfgang to go to Paris with the others, and would have trusted to his good sense and morals to keep him safe there. Maria Anna would then have returned home as arranged, and would not have died. Because, however, she had to die when she did, Wolfgang had acted as he did, and prevented her return home.[49]

This reasoning cannot but have struck Wolfgang as confusing. In the first place, Leopold contradicted his earlier conviction that Wolfgang had had a lucky escape from travelling to Paris with such a dangerous companion as Wendling;[50] and secondly, since Leopold was now accusing Wolfgang's faulty decisions (especially his impetuous behaviour after he had fallen in love with Aloysia) of causing Maria Anna's death, it is far from clear what he thought would have happened if Wolfgang had acted so that she could have returned to Salzburg. Would she still have died on 3 July if she had then been in Salzburg?—he specifically said not. Would she then have survived that fateful day?—again, he specifically said not. Yet if Leopold really believed that Wolfgang had acted as he had *in order* that God's purpose could be fulfilled and she could die on the predestined date, how could Wolfgang be held responsible for his decision not to go to Paris with Wendling? The only clear result of Leopold's reasoning was that he could lay the blame on Wolfgang, and that seems to have been his motive. That he was not being entirely sincere, however, is suggested by his letter to Count Ignaz Joseph Spaur (prince-bishop of Brixen, and a long-standing acquaintance of Leopold's in his capacity of canon of Salzburg Cathedral), reporting the death of his wife. Here he again alluded to the fact that Maria Anna's days had been numbered, but this time the tyrannical Colloredo was the instrument through whom a happy family had been torn apart and the mother forced into her grave in a distant land.[51] Clearly Leopold could have presented this interpretation to Wolfgang if he had chosen to, or he could simply have accepted Wolfgang's suggestion that it was straightforwardly a question of divine will. The fact that he did not shows how deep was his general displeasure with Wolfgang, and how much he wanted to impress on his son the possible dire consequences of the neglect of his family. Wolfgang did

---

[49] Leopold to Wolfgang, 27 Aug. 1778—*MBA* 478 (*Letters* 326, but the letter is substantially cut, and an important part of Leopold's reasoning (*MBA* 478/84–94) about his wife's death is omitted).

[50] See Ch. 17.   [51] Leopold to Spaur, 31 July 1778—*MBA* 472 (not in *Letters*).

not respond to the individual points raised by Leopold about his behaviour and decision-making, but it is difficult to believe that he can have looked forward to a reunion with his father with anything but dread. This is the more likely because in his letter to Wolfgang of 27 August 1778, in the middle of the explanation about the cause of Maria Anna's death, Leopold revealed to Wolfgang (verbatim in every important respect) the confidential postscript written by Maria Anna in Mannheim, in which she had expressed her worries about Wolfgang's impulsiveness and her perception that he disliked her company and would not listen to her advice.[52]

Leopold was desolate at the death of his wife. He thought back to the moment of parting from her in September of the previous year, when he had been too ill and too busy packing to say goodbye to her properly. He reminded Wolfgang how she had nearly died bringing her youngest child into the world, how much she had loved and lived in her son, and how she had been destined to sacrifice herself for him in a different way. He prophesied that Wolfgang would only appreciate all that she had been to him now that she was dead, just as he would one day love Leopold better when he too was dead. He spoke of the sadness of the whole town and especially of their close friends, and praised the ways in which Nannerl was trying to comfort him. He begged Wolfgang to pack up Maria Anna's belongings carefully and send them home in a trunk, and suggested that Wolfgang might put some of the music he had been promising in the same trunk.[53]

Maria Anna's death also brought straight to the surface all Leopold's fears about the fragility of life. Distraught though he was at losing his wife, the prospect of Wolfgang succumbing to illness was even worse, for on him rested Leopold's hopes of paying his debts, and of security for Nannerl. Leopold therefore redoubled his exhortations to Wolfgang to look after his health, and sent some black powders to Paris.[54]

For his part, Wolfgang wrote letters intended to be consolatory. He spoke gently to them of his love, and urged them to rely completely on him to support them. He promised to answer Leopold's letters more methodically. He wrote a long description of the successful first performance of his symphony (K. 297) on Corpus Christi Day at the Concert spirituel,

---

[52] Maria Anna to Leopold, 5 Feb. 1778—*MBA* 416/140–56 (*Letters* 281*a*). See also Ch. 17 for details of the decisions taken in Mannheim.

[53] Leopold to Wolfgang, 12–13 July (*MBA* 464; *Letters* 314); 20 July (*MBA* 467; *Letters* 316); and 3 Aug. 1778 (*MBA* 473; *Letters* 320). However, the passages are not all complete in *Letters*.

[54] Leopold to Wolfgang, 20 July 1778—*MBA* 467 (*Letters* 316).

knowing how much this would please Leopold. He reported that his violin and keyboard sonatas were being printed and that he would earn 15 louis d'or (165 fl.) from them. Several times he promised to send all manner of music, knowing how comforted Leopold always was to play his new compositions. And he sent Nannerl a 'praeambolum' or capriccio as a present for her name-day, and regretted that he could not be with her to celebrate the event with music.[55]

These protestations of dutiful affection, together with the extravagant promises to send so much music, suggest a genuine desire to do what would please Leopold and Nannerl. Wolfgang had said he would send the engraved sonatas, the French edition of Leopold's *Violinschule*, a treatise on composition by Vogler in which Leopold had expressed interest, sonatas by Hüllmandel and concertos by Schröter, some of his own keyboard sonatas, the symphony that had been composed for the Concert spirituel, the Sinfonia Concertante which should have been performed at one of Legros's concerts, two flute quartets, and the concerto for flute and harp.[56] Yet it was little more than a week later that Wolfgang was regretting to Weber the fact that he had to support his father and sister, and pledging his assistance should Weber and Aloysia come to Paris. And all this in the dismal financial situation described above. Furthermore, there is something very suspicious about the discrepancy between the music promised and that actually sent. Wolfgang claimed that he was waiting for a suitable (he meant primarily economical) opportunity to send it, but when one arose he apparently sent virtually nothing of his own composition. Leopold had mentioned that he might enclose music in the trunk bringing Maria Anna's belongings home, but when this trunk eventually arrived in Salzburg in December 1778, the only composition of Wolfgang's acknowledged by Leopold was an aria written for Aloysia.[57] And, writing from Nancy on the way home, Wolfgang was to say that he was not bringing home many compositions because he had not been able to compose very much. He claimed that De Jean had left the flute music in Mannheim when he had gone to Paris, so that it would have to be forwarded from there; and he further claimed that he had sold to Legros two symphonies and the Sinfonia Concertante, though he would

---

[55] Wolfgang to Leopold and Nannerl, 3, 9, and 18–20 July 1778—*MBA* 458 (*Letters* 311); *MBA* 462 (*Letters* 313); and *MBA* 466 (*Letters* 315, 315*a*, and 315*b*).

[56] *MBA* 466/163–72 (*Letters* 315*a*). The keyboard sonatas mentioned by Wolfgang have often been taken to be K. 330, 331, and 332, but these were written later than this. See W. Plath, 'Beiträge zur Mozart-Autographie II: Schriftchronologie 1770–1780', *MJb* (1976–7), 131–73, esp. 171.

[57] Leopold to Wolfgang, 10 Dec. 1778—*MBA* 509/54–6 (not in *Letters*).

be able to write them out from memory when he returned home. Thus he was only bringing his sonatas with him as new music.[58] The second of the two symphonies Wolfgang claimed to have left with Legros has not been identified, though it has been plausibly suggested that the work was an old one already known to Leopold.[59] More importantly, it has been shown that his statement that he left K. 297, the symphony first performed at the concert on Corpus Christi, with Legros, was a partial lie. Though he did leave a version of it with Legros, he also took it with him (albeit in several different parts) when he left Paris.[60] What motive could he have had for this particular lie? One would expect that, since he was not bringing back anything like what had been promised, he would have been only too pleased to have at least a new symphony to show Leopold. Perhaps he hoped to be able to sell the work to a patron on the way home, and earn money which would not have to be declared to Leopold; in this way, his shattered finances might be made to seem a little less disastrous.[61] Whatever the reason for the lie, the fact that he told it casts doubt on all his other statements to Leopold about the music supposedly composed in Paris.

Thus Wolfgang's behaviour to his family during his stay in Paris was not straightforward, the reason apparently being that he was being pulled one way by considerations of filial duty and another by his desire to help the Webers and unite his life with Aloysia's. This conflict confused his intentions when Leopold started to suggest that he consider returning to Salzburg. He still proclaimed his intense dislike of Paris, and said that he had rejected the idea of the post at Versailles because he wanted to be a Kapellmeister (and well paid, to boot) rather than an organist. He also complained that he was losing pupils because they tended to leave Paris for the summer, and that he had not been paid for the work he had done for the duc de Guines. Nevertheless, he was starting to plan for the approaching concert season in Paris, and was talking about opera and oratorio possibilities in fairly optimistic terms.[62] He professed that

---

[58] Wolfgang to Leopold, 3 Oct. 1778—*MBA* 494/59–69 (*Letters* 335).

[59] See N. Zaslaw, *Mozart's Symphonies: Context, Performance Practice, Reception* (Oxford, 1989), 329–34.

[60] See A. Tyson, 'The Two Slow Movements of Mozart's "Paris" Symphony, K. 297', in A. Tyson, *Mozart: Studies of the Autograph Scores* (Cambridge, Mass., 1987), 106–13. Tyson's case rests on a study of the paper of all the known authentic sources of the different movements of the symphony, together with an examination of the later fate of these documents where known.

[61] Tyson suggests a different possible motive for this lie—see A. Tyson, 'Mozart's Truthfulness', *MT*, 119 (1978), 938–9.

[62] Wolfgang to Leopold, 3, 9, and 31 July 1778—*MBA* 458/76–108 (*Letters* 311); *MBA* 462/83–104 and 147–55 (*Letters* 313); and *MBA* 471/145–215 (*Letters* 319).

he would be prepared to consider a return to Salzburg under the conditions outlined by Leopold, though he would much prefer to work elsewhere (Mannheim, for example, of which he had not given up hope). He was also exploring his secret plans (outlined above) for joining Aloysia, and these ranged from winning a salaried post at Mannheim or Mainz to bringing her to Paris (and possibly even London) to make her fortune.[63] Since his overwhelming desire was to find some way of being near her, it seems curious at first sight that he should indicate any kind of willingness to return to Salzburg. The reason seems to have been that he simply did not believe that Leopold could negotiate the salary and conditions he had discussed with Countess Lodron;[64] at any rate, once the Salzburg prospect began to look more real, Wolfgang was to be dismayed by it, and started to talk about how he might prefer to stay in Paris.

❧

Leopold had guessed that the hints Wolfgang had been dropping about an idea of his that he would disclose to Leopold when the time was ripe concerned marriage to Aloysia Weber. He knew how little Wolfgang liked Paris, and he was worried about Wolfgang's continuing residence there without either of his parents. When Grimm wrote to Leopold expressing his fear that Wolfgang would never make headway there, and effectively withdrawing his support for him,[65] Leopold's thoughts became even more concentrated on the possibility of a return to Salzburg. The next stage of the negotiation process was made possible by the death of Fischietti's predecessor, the pensioned Kapellmeister Lolli, because by that event his salary of 456 fl. annually was saved.[66] Leopold continued to tell Countess Lodron and everyone else who asked him that Wolfgang was getting on famously in Paris, and meanwhile started to apply gentle pressure on Wolfgang to make him think more favourably of returning home. His tactics were persuasive. He indicated that he knew Wolfgang's secret hope, and that it could materialize only if Wolfgang obtained a good

---

[63] Wolfgang to Weber, 29 July 1778—*MBA* 469/150–2 (*Letters* 317).

[64] *MBA* 462/89–104 (*Letters* 313). The commentaries on this passage in both *MBA* and *Letters* state that the countess referred to is Countess Wallis, Colloredo's sister. Neither gives any reason why this should be assumed. Wolfgang's reference was simply to 'the crested goose', and he urged Leopold to be on his guard against her falseness. Since the Mozarts apparently shared the view that Countess Lodron was false (see Ch. 17, n. 66), I take this as a small piece of contributory evidence that Countess Lodron was the countess responsible for the negotiations with Leopold about Wolfgang's return.

[65] Leopold to Wolfgang, 13 Aug. 1778—*MBA* 476/5–62 (*Letters* 323).

[66] See Hintermaier, 'Hofkapelle', 232.

2. (*below*) Maria Anna Mozart, née Pertl. Oil-painting by Rosa Hagenauer - Barducci, *c.*1775. Maria Anna is holding a length of lace.

1. (*above*) Leopold Mozart, engraving by Jakob Andreas Friedrich, after Matthias Gottfried Eichler, 1756. Frontispiece to Leopold's *Violinschule*. The musical compositions depicted are all by Leopold: a symphony, an offertory, a Mass, a trio, a fugue, a pastoral, a divertimento, a march, and what appear to be some litanies. The Latin caption is from the *Rhetorica ad Herennium*, 3. XV. 26, a work then still thought to be by Cicero. The passage from which Leopold's quotation is taken is a discussion of gesture in oratory, and translates: 'In our gestures, therefore, there should be neither ostentatious charm nor coarseness, in order that we may avoid giving the impression of being either actors or menials'.

3. Leopold Mozart and his children, water-colour by Louis Carrogis de Carmontelle, Paris, November 1763.

4. Salzburg, print by Anton Amon, after Franz von Naumann, 1791.

5. The interior of Salzburg Cathedral during a Solemn High Mass, engraving by Melchior Küssel, *c*.1680. This view shows the four musicians' galleries at the crossing.

6. The exterior of the Dancing-Master's House, lithograph after G. Pezold, *c.*1840. The Mozarts lived here from 1773; the music room overlooked the Hannibalplatz (now Makartplatz) on the first floor.

7. The former dance hall of the Dancing-Master's House, after restoration in 1996. The room was used by the Mozarts as a music room.

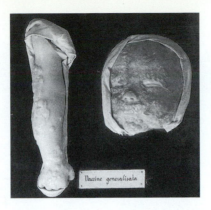

8. A virulent reaction to smallpox vaccination, wax and linen cast, late nineteenth century.

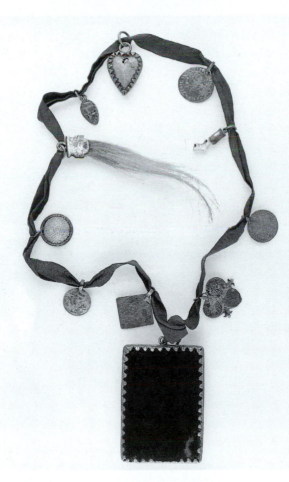

9. *Fraiskette*: silken band with eleven pendants thought to help ward off *Frais*. Salzburg, sixteenth to eighteenth century. The pendants include a breviary, commemorative coins (the earliest from 1566, the latest from 1765), and objects from the natural world such as stones with special attributes.

10. *Loretokindl*: wax model of the renowned Christ-child figure, arrayed in costly garments, residing in Salzburg's Capuchin Convent of St Maria Loreto, Salzburg, eighteenth century. The *Loretokindl* was thought to have miraculous powers, and was venerated by the Mozarts.

11. Reconstruction of a *Bölzscheibe*, a target for a *Bölzlschiessen* occasion in 1778. Katherl Gilowsky stands holding the wax model of a man. To her right is the pilgrimage church of Altötting, to her left that of Maria Plain. A rough verse translation reads:

> At every pious pilgrim church to which I wend my way,
> I carry something from my hopes for which alone I pray:
> Will heaven not at last relent to hear a poor soul's plea?—
> And for my sacrifice and prayer bestow a man on me?

The description on which the reconstruction is based is in Leopold's letter to Maria Anna and Wolfgang of 29 June 1778—*MBA* 457/234-42; not in *Letters*.

12. Maria Anna ('Nannerl') Berchtold von Sonnenburg, née Mozart, anonymous oil-painting, c.1785.

13. Johann Baptist Franz Berchtold von Sonnenburg, Nannerl's husband, anonymous oil-painting, c.1785.

14. St Gilgen and the Abersee (now Wolfgangsee), looking south-east, c. 1800. On the left are the Falkenstein and the Schafberg; on the right the Zwölferhorn.

15. (*left*) The *Pflegerichtsgebäude* in St Gilgen from the lake, with the church of St Ägidius in the background, drawing by E. Heermann, 1906. Birthplace of Maria Anna Mozart, and Nannerl Mozart's home after her marriage in 1784 until her husband's death in 1801.

16. (*above*) The *Pflegerichtsgebäude* in St Gilgen from the road, as it appears today, photograph, 1983. The building now houses the *Mozart Gedenkstätte*.

17. The Berchtold Family Chronicle entry showing details of Leopold Mozart's death. An English translation is provided in Ch. 30, pp. 542–3. and a transcription of the German in Ch. 30, n. 63.

18. The first and last pages of Nannerl Berchtold von Sonnenburg's essay about Mozart for Schlichtegroll's *Nekrolog* of 1792. The first page shows predominantly her hand, though with corrections and additions by a different one. The last page shows the postscript in this second hand (now presumed to be that of Albert von Mölk), together with the later obliteration (most probably by Nissen) of the passage about Mozart's marriage to Constanze.

appointment. While appearing still to sanction the idea that Wolfgang might win a post in Mainz or Mannheim, he pointed out that Mannheim/ Munich jobs were insecure because the elector had no obvious heir, and that Mainz suffered by comparison with Salzburg because the church music was not as good, and it was not so conveniently situated for journeys to Italy. He reminded Wolfgang about the debt he owed, about Nannerl's lack of security, and about the vulnerability of freelancing when a person might be perfectly well one day and ill the next; and again criticized him for his desire to help the Webers before he had provided for his own family. He also told Wolfgang that Countess Lodron, from fear that Leopold might leave Salzburg and deprive her family of such a good teacher, had indicated that Leopold could be offered Lolli's salary and Wolfgang Adlgasser's (making 1,000 fl. annually in total);[67] and that Wolfgang could be guaranteed leave to go to Italy every two years. Leopold thought that Colloredo would find it hard to agree to this, but told Countess Lodron that if he did, Wolfgang would accept for the sake of returning home to cheer his father.[68]

Only four days after reporting this conversation with Countess Lodron, Leopold had received a firm offer for Wolfgang from Colloredo. The details, according to Leopold, were that Wolfgang would receive a salary of 500 fl. annually. Leopold also gave Wolfgang the impression, without stating so explicitly, that Colloredo would make him Kapellmeister in due course. The junior organist, Paris, was to be given a small increase in return for carrying out most of the cathedral duties, releasing Wolfgang to be Konzertmeister. And Wolfgang was to be allowed travel leave if he obtained operatic commissions. Now that Leopold had this offer, any other possibilities open to Wolfgang looked unsatisfactory, and he took it for granted that Wolfgang would agree. He pointed out the proximity of Munich, Vienna, and Italy, and even held out the hope that Aloysia

---

[67] Lolli's and Adlgasser's combined incomes amounted to 1,000 fl. only if Lolli's perk of the *Hoftafel* (dining rights)—which was worth 100 fl. annually (see Hintermaier, 'Hofkapelle', 3)—was included. Leopold was eventually given Lolli's salary but without this perk, so that his and Wolfgang's combined income was 904 fl. annually. See n. 72 below.

[68] Leopold to Wolfgang, 27 Aug. 1778—*MBA* 478/113–239 (*Letters* 326, but with important omissions). This is the passage which seems to me most convincingly to suggest that the countess who eased Wolfgang's return was Countess Lodron, and that Countess Wallis was not involved in any significant way. In it, a woman is referred to as 'the countess' four times. Two references concern her evident authority and closeness to Colloredo, and the other two mention the loss to her if Leopold and Nannerl (who were now teaching her four daughters) should leave Salzburg. Countess Lodron had four daughters, and Countess Wallis did not; and Leopold appears to mean the same countess throughout the passage. The *MBA* commentary, however, unconvincingly oscillates between identifying 'the countess' as Lodron and as Wallis, according to whether it is her authority or her need of a teacher that is under discussion.

might also be engaged in Salzburg, since Colloredo was looking for a new female singer for operas. He also mentioned Salzburg's advantage over Munich that it was a cathedral court, so that the employees were better protected in the event of the death of the ruler.[69]

While Leopold was in the thick of these negotiations, Wolfgang was in Saint-Germain on a short visit from Paris, and since Leopold's letters were being sent to Paris, could not reply promptly. The delay in securing his son's consent made Leopold highly agitated, and each post day he sent off another letter reiterating all the advantages he had already mentioned, and adding more for good measure. On 3 September he compared the ordered life Wolfgang would be able to lead in Salzburg with the ceaseless uncertainty of freelancing in Paris. He pointed out that Wolfgang could not afford to leave the place he hated, and that it had been Leopold who had arranged everything so that Wolfgang's future with Aloysia looked more optimistic. He did not rule out the possibility that Wolfgang could call in at Munich on his way home to see if the elector would improve on the Salzburg offer. After promising again that the junior organist Paris would undertake the most irksome of the duties, he also promised that Wolfgang's Konzertmeister duties would not be linked with the violin any longer—he could perform them from the keyboard. He listed the entertainments that would be open to them on such an augmented income, and promised to permit the friendship with Aloysia. And he portrayed himself and Nannerl as beggars if Wolfgang did not comply, and reminded Wolfgang of how he had claimed to long to see his family again.[70]

In his next letter, still before receiving any reaction from Wolfgang, Leopold went over much of this ground again. This time, however, he sent Wolfgang a list of the musicians who had decided to leave Mannheim for Munich, and pointed out that there were no keyboard players or organists, and no Kapellmeister, on it; Wolfgang might therefore stand some chance of being taken on there. Leopold also claimed that Colloredo intended Wolfgang to direct the court music from the keyboard, and Leopold to do everything else (he seems to have meant all the other duties normally undertaken by the Kapellmeister), and that this arrangement would obviate the need for a new Italian Kapellmeister. Finally, he mentioned that he had just received a request from Gschwendtner for payment of the money drawn by the travellers in Paris; but instead of

---

[69] Leopold to Wolfgang, 31 Aug. 1778—*MBA* 480 (*Letters* 328, but not complete).
[70] *MBA* 482 (*Letters* 329, but most of it is omitted).

rebuking Wolfgang roundly for having kept silent about this, his reaction was fairly mild. He simply used the fact as further ammunition to support his case that Wolfgang's life in Paris could not go on in this way.[71]

Either Leopold was not being entirely honest when he put all these points to Wolfgang, or the situation changed in some respects during the period between the oral agreement and the new written employment decrees for himself and Wolfgang. Leopold had initially elicited from Wolfgang a cautious indication that he would be prepared to consider a return to Salzburg on the basis of a salary of 600 fl. annually and the promise that he would in time become Kapellmeister. By the time Leopold was writing the three letters mentioned above, the 600 fl. had shrunk to 500 (though Leopold was now to receive an increase of 100 fl. annually, making the net result to the family the same). The final decree, however, made it clear that Wolfgang was technically expected to replace Adlgasser in almost every detail—that is, his salary was to be 450 fl. annually, he was to perform all the organist's duties in the cathedral, and he was to teach in the Kapellhaus. Nothing was written in about leave to travel, the likelihood of becoming Kapellmeister in due course, or the undertaking of the Konzertmeister duties from the keyboard instead of the violin. Leopold, on the other hand, was granted a position something akin to the deceased Kapellmeister Lolli's—his salary rose from 354 fl. to 454 fl. annually, in return for which he was expected to superintend all the Kapellhaus teaching until a new Kapellmeister was appointed. These conditions belie Leopold's positive claims to Wolfgang that he would not have to cover all the cathedral services as organist, and that Colloredo was not seeking a new Kapellmeister because he intended Wolfgang to take on the post in due course. It may be that Leopold knew that the formal agreement was flexible, and that some of the duties not relished by Wolfgang could be delegated to others; but the agreement that Wolfgang was eventually forced to accept was very different from what Leopold had led him to expect. The suggestion can hardly be ignored that Leopold, in his desperation to get Wolfgang home in order to have a sufficient income to pay the debts, lied to him about the conditions of service.[72]

Wolfgang's reaction to Leopold's supposedly seductive letters indicates why Leopold might have found it prudent to lie to his son. For on 11 September 1778, after writing of his longing to be home with his family,

---

[71] Leopold to Wolfgang, 10 Sept. 1778—*MBA* 485 (*Letters* 330, but incomplete).

[72] For Adlgasser's conditions of service, see Hintermaier, 'Hofkapelle', 3–7; for Lolli's, ibid. 232–7; for Leopold's, ibid. 290–5; and for Wolfgang's, ibid. 296–8.

Wolfgang faithfully enumerated all the advantages of the Salzburg post —the security, the permission to travel, and the relatively light duties. Suddenly, however, he gave expression to an outburst of rage and disgust at the thought of the indignities he knew would be involved—the coarseness of the other musicians, and the disdain with which they were treated by Colloredo. He claimed that he would certainly not accept the post without the permission to travel, that he would no longer play the violin, and that it would be best if Leopold could obtain a written promise that he would become Kapellmeister. He indicated that he would not take the post even to get away from Paris, if it were not for the sake of seeing Leopold and Nannerl again; and then he talked of how much better he was now getting on in Paris. The same letter also contained bitter complaints about the condescension with which Grimm was treating him. He owed Grimm 15 louis d'or (165 fl.), and clearly found the obligation irksome. He was trying to arrange his affairs in preparation for leaving, and this involved collecting money owed to him, and selling what music he could in order to earn travel funds. He hoped to repay Grimm with the 165 fl. he expected to earn from his printed violin and keyboard sonatas. He asked Leopold to allow him to make his own arrangements for travelling, rather than entrust them to Grimm, and he specifically asked for permission to call at Mannheim on the way home if the Webers should still be there, even though it was a diversion from the most direct route.[73]

While Wolfgang was reluctantly arranging to leave Paris, the Webers' position had abruptly improved out of all recognition. Aloysia had won an appointment in Munich, and the family now enjoyed a total income of 1,000 fl. annually. Leopold had learnt this from one of his correspondents in Munich, who had been keeping him informed about the way in which the Mannheim and Munich bands were being merged. Because the elector's court was about to go to Munich, Leopold considered Wolfgang's request to be allowed to visit Mannheim irrelevant. However, he did still sanction the idea of trying to obtain a position in Munich better than the one on offer in Salzburg.[74] Was this sanction genuine, or was he simply pulling out all the stops to achieve the first and most essential part of his plan—to induce Wolfgang to leave Paris? On the one hand, the Salzburg offer promised a joint secure income of 904 fl. annually, which was exceptionally high at that court for German musicians living under the

---

[73] *MBA* 487 (*Letters* 331).
[74] Leopold to Wolfgang, 17 and 24 Sept. 1778—*MBA* 490 (*Letters* 332); and *MBA* 491 (*Letters* 333).

same roof; so it is no wonder that Leopold was delighted with it. On the other hand, he himself was very dissatisfied with the same aspects of life in Salzburg as Wolfgang was, and he wanted Nannerl to have the opportunity to exhibit her skills; so he may still have been genuinely interested at this point in the possibility that Wolfgang might be appointed to a post in Munich. Whatever his motives for encouraging Wolfgang's hopes of being taken on there (and he claimed he was still pressing Martini and Raaff for recommendations), the fact was that Wolfgang, though he acquiesced in leaving Paris, was still far from reconciled to a return to what has been called serfdom in Salzburg.[75] What with Leopold planning his homeward journey in as much detail as possible, refusing in no uncertain terms to allow him to travel via Mannheim, reproaching him for his arrogance in specifying conditions in Salzburg, and enumerating the ways in which their lives would be improved by his return; and Grimm racing around to bundle him out of Paris even before his sonatas were printed and paid for, Wolfgang's feelings as he sat in the slow coach to Nancy on 26 September were probably confused and rebellious.

[75] See N. Zaslaw, *Mozart's Symphonies*, ch. 10, entitled 'Salzburg III: Serfdom (1779–1780)'.

❧ 19 ❧

Returning to Serfdom

❧❧❦

THE travel arrangements made by Grimm on behalf of Wolfgang suggest that the relationship between the two men had been deteriorating rapidly during the period following Maria Anna's death. Grimm paid for the journey as far as Strasburg, and apparently chose the cheapest mode of travel. But because the coach was so slow, more overnight stops were needed, and Wolfgang had to pay for these; furthermore, the starting times were highly inconvenient, and the journey therefore very tiring. Wolfgang had hoped to wait in Paris until his sonatas were printed, and to repay Grimm the 165 fl. he owed him with the income from these. He wanted them with him so that he could present them to the elector's wife as he passed through Munich. But Grimm arranged the journey so hurriedly that this was impossible, and Wolfgang could only fume that he would not be able to make any corrections before they appeared. Leopold, too, was extremely annoyed about the haste, because he had sent Wolfgang a credit letter for use in Strasburg, and Wolfgang had left before it arrived in Paris.[1]

Once Leopold understood the situation, he bustled around and rearranged the credit letter so that it was awaiting Wolfgang's arrival in Strasburg, and sent suggestions and instructions for the onward journey from there. Though the new conditions to which Wolfgang was returning meant that their financial problems would be solved, Leopold was nevertheless keen for Wolfgang to earn as much as possible and spend as little as possible on the way home, to prevent the debt growing any larger. He therefore told Wolfgang in no uncertain terms not to waste money by travelling to Mannheim; urged him not to stay long in Strasburg if the prospect for earning money was not favourable; and suggested a route from Strasburg through Stuttgart, Dischingen, Kaisheim, Eichstätt (all

---

[1] Leopold to Wolfgang, 1 Oct. 1778 (*MBA* 493; *Letters* 334, but heavily cut); and Wolfgang to Leopold, 3 Oct. (*MBA* 494; *Letters* 335); and 15 Oct. 1778 (*MBA* 496; *Letters* 336).

of which offered possibilities of earning income), and Augsburg (where he would be offered free accommodation).[2]

Leopold's nerve had been greatly shaken by the events of the previous year, and he was both longing to have Wolfgang at home again to enable him to start paying off the debts, and living in dread of new disasters. Travelling was in any case more dangerous at this time of year, because of the short daylight hours and the risk of being robbed after dark, and Leopold feared that the risk was greater than usual because the political situation meant that there were army deserters at large.[3] But the correspondence suggests that, rational fears notwithstanding, Leopold was excessively overwrought, and strained almost to breaking point. The minuteness with which he was to complain about almost every detail of Wolfgang's journey home seems obsessive, even though the complaints themselves (which addressed among other points Wolfgang's failure to give basic information about where he was) do not seem unreasonable. Wolfgang, on the other hand, appears not to have appreciated how desperate Leopold's state of mind was becoming; his letters suggest that his main concern about their reunion was with its effect on himself.

At first Leopold had hoped that Wolfgang would be home for his name-day, 31 October; when this began to look impossible, he hoped to see him in Salzburg for Leopold's name-day on 15 November; then for Christmas; then for the New Year.[4] In fact, it was to be the middle of January 1779 before Wolfgang set foot in his native city again.

By the time Wolfgang reached Nancy, he had had enough of the slow coach. He therefore abandoned it and rearranged his journey. On 3 October he wrote from Nancy to tell Leopold this, but indicated that he would be leaving for Strasburg 'tomorrow', in the company of an older man whom he had met on the coach from Paris to Nancy.[5] Leopold repeated this information in a letter to the merchant brothers Frank of Strasburg, and asked them to keep any mail for Wolfgang (including the rearranged letter of credit addressed to another merchant, Scherz) until he arrived. But Wolfgang then delayed his departure from Nancy without telling Leopold, and the Frank brothers wrote to Salzburg to report Wolfgang's non-arrival on the expected date. Leopold therefore imagined

---

[2] *MBA* 493 (*Letters* 334, but most of the information is omitted).

[3] *MBA* 493/67–82 (not in *Letters*).

[4] Nannerl to Wolfgang, 10 Sept. 1778 (*MBA* 485/90–1; not in *Letters*); and Leopold to Wolfgang, 31 Dec. 1778—*MBA* 515/21–33 (*Letters* 349).

[5] *MBA* 494/38–48 (*Letters* 335).

Wolfgang lying ill in Nancy, or stranded there, having been robbed by his new travelling companion. The panic into which he was plunged lasted several days, until he received Wolfgang's first letter from Strasburg.[6]

Meanwhile, Leopold had heard news from his correspondent Becke in Munich which was casting doubt on both the likelihood and the desirability of Wolfgang's gaining an appointment there as he passed through on his way home. Becke wrote that Cannabich of Mannheim had been appointed the director of the merged Mannheim and Munich bands, and that the Munich contingent was to be subordinate to that from Mannheim. There were to be three divisions—the actual musicians, on full salaries; a group of reserves, most of whom were old and were expected to die before being called on; and a group of emeritus musicians with no duties. In the second and third groups, salaries were being cut by at least 100 fl. annually, and all the *Accessisten* (musicians serving without pay in the hope of being appointed at a later date) had been released without prospects because of the number of young Mannheimers. Of the thirty-two members of the orchestra at the German theatre, only three were survivors of the original Munich band. One of the few Munich instrumentalists lucky enough to be kept on was the oboist and cor anglais player Joseph Fiala; but he was so worried about the instability of his prospects there that he was trying to negotiate a position in Salzburg. Leopold was not slow to realize that there was a battalion of superfluous musicians in Munich, all dependent on the health of one man, the elector.[7]

Wolfgang eventually arrived in Strasburg, but behaved just as thoughtlessly with regard to his onward travel plans as he had when reporting his departure from Nancy. His first letter home, written on 15 October, implied that he would leave after giving a concert two days later; but he then decided to stay for a further concert, without informing Leopold immediately. Heavy flooding then intervened to keep him even longer in Strasburg, and he gave a third concert; and Leopold, who knew about the floods but had no idea where Wolfgang was, was plunged into a second fit of panic which lasted another few days until he received Wolfgang's next letter of 26 October–2 November, giving his revised plans for leaving Strasburg.[8]

Unluckily for Wolfgang, the concerts were apparently not very profitable; he claimed that he cleared 7 louis d'or (77 fl.) altogether, and he

---

[6] Leopold to Wolfgang, 19 Oct. (*MBA* 500/69–109; *Letters* 337); and 19 Nov. 1778 (*MBA* 505/9–14; *Letters* 340).

[7] *MBA* 500/34–69 (not in *Letters*).

[8] *MBA* 496/80–2 (*Letters* 336); and *MBA* 503/3–4 and 60–5 (*Letters* 338).

drew another 8 louis d'or (88 fl.) from the merchant Scherz on Leopold's credit letter as a precaution for the journey to come. Despite the fact that the Webers were now in Munich, and that he had received Leopold's letter forbidding him to travel via Mannheim, he had decided to do so —he claimed on the advice of local people who said that the roads and coaches were better on this route. He sent Leopold greetings for his approaching name-day, and bemoaned once again the fact that he had still not received his printed sonatas from Paris. The reason he felt so strongly about them was that he hoped not only to be given a present for them from the elector's wife in Munich, but also that they might induce the elector to offer him an appointment.[9] This consideration may partly explain why he displayed such rank disobedience to Leopold in travelling to Mannheim; he might have wanted to slow down his journey in the hope that the sonatas would catch up with him before he reached Munich. He might additionally have counted on earning money in Mannheim which would help pacify Leopold.

Despite the fact that Wolfgang had told Leopold that he was, after all, travelling via Mannheim, Leopold was expecting his next letter to come from Augsburg. This may have been because he could not believe that Wolfgang would actually stay in Mannheim, even if he was passing through; he had expected that Wolfgang would be planning to arrive in Munich in time for the elector's name-day on 4 November. At any rate, he alerted people in Augsburg to Wolfgang's imminent arrival there, and waited to hear that this had occurred. Each post day, however, brought him a letter from Augsburg saying that Wolfgang was not yet there, and eventually one of these letters (dated 13 November, and perhaps from his brother's family) reported that Wolfgang was not intending to go to Augsburg at all. Leopold therefore had to endure a third fit of panic, in complete ignorance as to where Wolfgang might be.[10]

In fact, Wolfgang had arrived in Mannheim on 6 November and had been offered hospitality by Cannabich's wife, who had not travelled to Munich with her husband. Wolfgang had received Leopold's letter explaining the far from promising prospects under the elector, but he was still obstinately set on trying to get an appointment almost anywhere other than in Salzburg. In Mannheim, this stubborn hope led him

---

[9] *MBA* 503 (*Letters* 338). It seems that Wolfgang also incurred another debt to Scherz of 12 louis d'or (132 fl.) on this visit to Strasburg. Somehow Scherz neglected to reclaim the money from Leopold until much later, so that Leopold did not know of it on Wolfgang's homeward journey. See Wolfgang to Leopold, 6 Dec. 1783—*MBA* 770/7–42 (*Letters* 500).

[10] Leopold to Wolfgang, 19 Nov. 1778—*MBA* 505/30–40 (*Letters* 340).

to listen to people who flattered themselves, despite all evidence to the contrary, that the elector would return and make his court in Mannheim again. He therefore entertained the idea that he might be retained there; he took some pupils, and started to think about composing the music for a duodrama, *Semiramis,* which would be performed by Seyler's troupe. On 12 November (which was not even the first post day after his arrival),[11] he wrote to Leopold to tell him that he hoped to earn 40 louis d'or (440 fl.) from this, and would have to stay six or eight weeks to compose it. He repeated his expressions of disgust at the idea of service in Salzburg, indulged in bluster at the thought that Colloredo might try to act as a great lord before him, and asked Leopold to use the duodrama commission to try to make Colloredo fear that he would not come home after all, and to induce him to increase the salary offered. His farewell greeting, 'take care of your health, which is so precious to me',[12] vividly illustrates how little he was engaged with Leopold's point of view; for Leopold's letters were amply indicating his enormous anxiety to have Wolfgang home as soon as possible, and this exhortation must surely have struck Leopold as hollow.

It was only when Leopold received this letter on 19 November that he was released from the third terrible anxiety that had been oppressing him, and it is thus hardly surprising that his reaction to Wolfgang's news was of impotent fury. He was in no mood to take an indulgent view of the latest dreamy idea, and wrote a witheringly critical letter. He began by pointing out that the departure date from Paris should have allowed Wolfgang to be home by his name-day on 31 October (when he was in fact still in Strasburg). He continued by recounting the three deadly shocks he had suffered as a result of Wolfgang's inconsiderate letter-writing. He mentioned the 8 louis d'or (88 fl.) drawn in Strasburg, and asked if Wolfgang intended to use the money to take his ease in Mannheim. And at the thought of Wolfgang attempting to obtain an appointment in Mannheim, despite everything that Leopold had written, he was beside himself with fury. He then listed the debts that Wolfgang had run up since leaving home (300 fl. provided initially, 200 fl. drawn from Schmalz in Mannheim, 110 fl. from Gschwendtner in Paris, 165 fl. from Grimm, and 88 fl. from Scherz in Strasburg), which amounted to 863 fl. in fourteen months. He had worked out that these could be paid

---

[11] The post days from Mannheim for Salzburg letters were Thursday and Saturday (see Maria Anna to Leopold, 20 Dec. 1777—*MBA* 394/20–3; *Letters* 264), and Wolfgang had arrived in Mannheim on Friday, 6 Nov. 1778.

[12] *MBA* 504 (*Letters* 339).

off in two years, but only from a double salary; and he gave a veiled threat to reveal this state of affairs to Mme Cannabich if Wolfgang did not leave immediately. He also hinted again that the responsibility for Maria Anna's death lay at Wolfgang's door, and said that Wolfgang might soon have his father's death on his conscience. He reminded Wolfgang of Nannerl's wretched position, and of the fact that no one could know when he might die. Finally, he accused Wolfgang outright of a lack of love towards him, in that Wolfgang could have been back in time for Leopold's name-day on 15 November, but had chosen not to be. The devastatingly bitter attack made it clear that unless Wolfgang changed his ways forthwith, he would be met with reproaches rather than joy on his arrival home.[13]

Four days later, before Wolfgang could have received this letter, Leopold was writing again to reinforce what he had already said. It is indicative of his frustration and desperation that this letter was written despite the fact that there were no new circumstances—its purpose, like that of the previous one, was to try to instil in Wolfgang the sense of duty Leopold felt he patently lacked. The tone, however, was slightly less harsh, and he tried to make Wolfgang understand that the two considerations which hindered him from thinking coherently (his love for Aloysia and his detestation of Salzburg) need not do so. The service in Salzburg was essential if Wolfgang was to avoid the wickedness of abandoning his father to shame and mockery; but it was also to Wolfgang's advantage, in that he would be close to Aloysia in Munich, and also close to Italy. Furthermore, Wolfgang could invite other Munich friends (Cannabich, Wendling, Ramm, and Ritter, all of whom had moved from Mannheim to Munich) to stay with them in Salzburg. Leopold then described how miserably he had passed his wedding anniversary on 21 November, thinking about Wolfgang in Mannheim, and how Nannerl had tried to cheer him by inviting Ceccarelli, Fiala (the new oboist, just arrived from Munich), and his wife to dine. He repeated his threat to expose Wolfgang's behaviour to the Cannabichs, and said that he wanted to live a few more years to pay his debts—then Wolfgang might bang his head against the wall if he wished.[14]

Meanwhile, in Mannheim, Wolfgang's hopes of being paid to stay and write a duodrama were not materializing. The work was apparently available, but not the money, and while Leopold was writing himself blind

[13] Leopold to Wolfgang, 19 Nov. 1778—*MBA* 505 (*Letters* 340, but much of Leopold's attack is omitted).

[14] Leopold to Wolfgang, 23 Nov. 1778—*MBA* 506 (*Letters* 341, but with substantial omissions).

in the effort to get Wolfgang to leave, Wolfgang was vainly pestering Baron Heribert von Dalberg to try to extract from him a promise of 25 louis d'or (275 fl.) for his work.[15] On receiving Leopold's bitter letter he did not answer immediately, later implying that he had been too wounded by it to do so. When he did reply, he did not answer any of Leopold's points, but instead merely suggested that Leopold was in the wrong to have written so severely. However, in view of the fact that the money he had hoped to earn was not forthcoming, and that Leopold was commanding him to leave, there was little alternative open to him. He therefore reported his plan of travelling via the abbey of Kaisheim with the abbot, and said that he would continue his work on the duodrama in Salzburg for no pay. He also expressed his dissatisfaction with the state of the court music in Salzburg—the lack of clarinets,[16] and the large number of performances, which militated against quality.[17]

The news that Wolfgang had plans for leaving, and that he was being invited to Kaisheim, calmed Leopold. He advised Wolfgang to note the style of church music there, as well as the names of all the influential people, so that the future possibility of writing church music for the abbey would be created. He also tried to keep up Wolfgang's spirits by suggesting that his duodrama might be performed in Salzburg by the troupe of players engaged for the winter, and encouraged the hope that they might obtain clarinets in Salzburg.[18]

When Wolfgang left Mannheim, his sonatas had still not arrived from Paris, and he was wondering if they had been sent to the *Bäsle*, his cousin Maria Anna Thekla in Augsburg. His route home would have taken him through Augsburg if the abbot of Kaisheim had not offered Wolfgang a ride to Munich in one of his carriages. The offer was too good to refuse, so Wolfgang wrote to his cousin to ask her to forward the sonatas to him if she had them. Evidently she did, because he then reported to Leopold that he had received them on the day before leaving Kaisheim.[19] On this day, 23 December, he wrote to the *Bäsle* suggesting that, since

---

[15] Wolfgang to Dalberg on 24 Nov. 1778—*MBA* 507 (*Letters* 342).

[16] Though clarinets did exist in Salzburg at this date, they were not used in the court music departments for which Wolfgang was required to write; they were older instruments with restricted range, used primarily in military and folk music. Wolfgang was almost certainly lamenting the lack of the more modern clarinet with a larger range and a timbre more suited to cantabile lines. See K. Birsak, 'Salzburg, Mozart und die Klarinette', *MM* 33 (1985), 40–7.

[17] Wolfgang to Leopold, 3 Dec. 1778—*MBA* 508 (*Letters* 343).

[18] Leopold to Wolfgang, 10 Dec. 1778—*MBA* 509 (*Letters* 344, but not complete).

[19] Wolfgang to Leopold, 18 and 29 Dec. 1778—*MBA* 510, esp. lines 77–82 (*Letters* 345); and *MBA* 513/8–11 (*Letters* 348).

he could not after all travel via Augsburg, she might come to Munich to see him. She must have had some acquaintance of her own there, because he made it clear that he would not be able to provide accommodation for her. He was not sure where he would be lodging himself (though he presumably hoped that it would be with the Webers), and he said that it was precisely on this account that her presence would be so necessary to him—she might have a great role to play.[20]

Was the suggestion that the *Bäsle* visit him in Munich a real desire of Wolfgang's, or merely a semi-sincere proposal to appease her disappointment that he would not see her in Augsburg? Since his letters to her were always filled with zany absurdities (in marked contrast to his formal and serious style when writing to Aloysia), it is difficult to say whether the remark about her possible role in Munich was genuine. If it was, there are two plausible possibilities for his wish that she should be there. One was that he might already have begun to fear that Aloysia was no longer interested in him as a lover. Leopold had warned him gently in his letter of 23 November that he feared that Weber was one of the many ungrateful people who abandoned friends who had helped him when he had been down on his luck, once his fortunes improved.[21] This remark might have been made in response to news (which could have reached Leopold on the grapevine) that Aloysia considered her attachment to Wolfgang over. If Wolfgang had begun to doubt his reception by her, it might mean both that the uncertainty he expressed to the *Bäsle* about his Munich lodgings was genuine, and that he would be cheered by the *Bäsle*'s company if Aloysia were to reject him. The other reason he might have wanted her to be there is that it could already have occurred to him that she might be persuaded to return to Salzburg with him, and help him over his fear of the first meeting with Leopold. It was just at this time that he was having to confess to Leopold that he had pawned, sold, and given away possessions in Paris, and he was well aware that Leopold was far from satisfied with his handling of almost every aspect of his journey. The letters he was to write from Munich suggest that the closer he got to Salzburg, the greater his dread of meeting Leopold became.

By the time Wolfgang was making his way from Kaisheim to Munich, Leopold had decided that an appointment at the elector's court there

---

[20] Wolfgang to Maria Anna Thekla Mozart, 23 Dec. 1778—*MBA* 511 (*Letters* 346).

[21] *MBA* 506/84–90 (*Letters* 341, but the phrase '. . . und dann in Glücksumständen nicht mehr kennen' is translated: '. . . and, when they become prosperous, lose their heads completely'). Though Leopold's German phrase does not convey an unambiguous meaning, it seems to me more likely that he meant that it was Wolfgang whom Weber might no longer 'know' (i.e. acknowledge) than himself.

was no longer desirable, given the political situation and the family's circumstances. One of his reasons was that Europe was still teetering on the brink of wholesale war in the aftermath of the death of the elector of Bavaria, Maximilian III Joseph. If war were to break out, Bavaria would be in the thick of it, but Salzburg would be a relatively quiet corner in which to sit it out. Furthermore, Leopold's dread of untimely death, already well developed, could only have been increased by the events of the last fifteen months, when the deaths of Maria Anna, Adlgasser, and the elector had all impinged on the fortunes of the Mozart family. This dread now made him realize with new appreciation the advantage of what was being offered in Salzburg, for both he and Wolfgang were to receive approximately equal salaries. This meant not only that while they both lived the debts could be paid in two years, and then they would be very well off; but also that if either died, Nannerl would not immediately be destitute. By contrast, if Wolfgang were to be offered an appointment in Munich, and the others were to follow him there, Leopold's and Nannerl's security would be dependent solely on Wolfgang's appointment, which itself would be dependent solely on the health of one man, the elector. Since the oboist Fiala had just moved from Munich to Salzburg for precisely this reason, and Leopold had been seeing a good deal of him through helping him to settle in, this consideration must surely have impressed itself powerfully on his mind. Leopold knew, however, that Wolfgang was extremely keen to win an appointment in Munich, so he wrote to him there, on 28 December 1778, to explain why there could no longer be any question of attempting to do so.

The tone of Leopold's letter was cold, perhaps because of his annoyance that Wolfgang would not be home for the New Year. He acknowledged that the latest setback (staying longer in Kaisheim in order to take advantage of the offer of a ride to Munich at the end of December) was justified, but was fretting at the slowness of the journey as a whole. This was because he had repeatedly given dates for Wolfgang's return to people in Salzburg, only for Wolfgang to 'make him a liar' by failing to meet them; he was worried that Colloredo might lose patience and withdraw the offer to Wolfgang; and he could already have paid off 100 fl. of the debt if Wolfgang had returned more quickly. He knew that Wolfgang had many reasons for prolonging his stay in Munich (Aloysia, other friends, the question of an appointment, and the superior entertainments), and therefore explicitly forbade such a stay, and forestalled any ruses of Wolfgang's designed to make him change his mind. He warned him, for example, not to ask Cannabich to intercede for him, and threatened to reveal to Cannabich Wolfgang's less than dutiful behaviour if Wolfgang did so. He also warned him not to make an excuse of staying to present his sonatas to the elector's wife. He gave instructions that Wolfgang was to come home on the first coach of the New Year, forbade him to indulge in any more 'merry dreams', and explained why there was no question of accepting an appointment in Munich even if it were offered. To account for his change of opinion on this point, he said that when the family had been living in Salzburg on one meagre salary, nothing would have been lost to them in following Wolfgang to a salaried appointment elsewhere. Now that they were each to have a good salary in Salzburg, however, there was far less reason to move. To hammer home this point further, he stated that the only Munich offer which could match the Salzburg one would be 1,000 fl. annually, of which 400 fl. was settled on Leopold, and 600 fl. on Wolfgang. Finally, he threatened Wolfgang with the extreme step that he would come to Munich himself to fetch him if Wolfgang disobeyed his instructions.[22]

Wolfgang, who had arrived in Munich on 25 December, must already have been very worried about his reception in Salzburg even before he received this letter. For on 29 December, before Leopold's letter had arrived, he and the family friend Becke both wrote to Leopold. Wolfgang's mood was lower than it had ever been in a letter to his father, but he did not specifically explain why; he merely asked Leopold for comfort. The depression has usually been attributed to the combination of misery at his rejection by Aloysia (which apparently occurred during this visit to Munich),[23] and dread at the thought of facing Leopold and Salzburg. Becke's letter certainly suggests that the dread of Leopold was very real. Its only purpose was to plead with Leopold for understanding of Wolfgang's fine, loving qualities, and he stated that Wolfgang feared his reception from Leopold. If work did not prevent it, he would have been prepared to travel home with Wolfgang.[24]

What had Wolfgang told Becke, that an outsider should write such a letter to Leopold? It was presumably his worry that he was being blamed for Maria Anna's death, and perhaps too for the debt that had accumulated; in any case, Wolfgang must have presented his case in the most favourable possible light to Becke. The suggestion that Becke should travel

[22] The information in this paragraph and the previous one is from *MBA* 512 (*Letters* 347, but most of it is omitted, and what is included gives a completely inadequate idea of Leopold's reasoning).

[23] See von Nissen, *Biographie*, 414–15.

[24] *MBA* 513 (*Letters* 348); and *MBA* 514 (Becke's letter; not in *Letters*).

home with him had probably come from Wolfgang, who was soon to ask Leopold if he might bring the *Bäsle* to Salzburg.

Nevertheless, Wolfgang did not plan to leave Munich early, despite the fact that to fail to do so could only make things worse with regard to Leopold. In the same letter he said that he was going to present his sonatas to the elector's wife, to see something of the opera (Schweitzer's *Alceste*), and to write a Mass before travelling home. Even at this stage, he probably could not relinquish what remained of his hope that he might be taken on there, and would not need to return to Salzburg.

If this had been Wolfgang's state of mind before he received Leopold's cold and angry letter of 28 December telling him not even to think of remaining long in Munich, his mood can only have worsened subsequently. When he next wrote, he claimed that Becke had spent a good deal of time persuading him of Leopold's paternal love, only to have his good work undone by Leopold's letter. As was Wolfgang's wont, he did not reply to specific criticisms of his behaviour (except to take offence at Leopold's scorn of his 'merry dreams'), but instead implied that the letter showed Leopold's lack of tenderness towards him. While he was writing the letter, he received another one from Leopold telling him of an opportunity for leaving almost immediately,[25] but he refused to do so. He claimed that he would give up the pleasure of seeing the opera if Leopold insisted, but that he was determined to stay until he had presented his sonatas and received a present for them.[26]

Meanwhile, Leopold had received the letters written on 29 December by Wolfgang and Becke, and was disconcerted by them. He assured Wolfgang that his reception at home would be loving, and tried more gently to get Wolfgang to see things from his point of view. He explained his fear that Colloredo might revoke the offer if Wolfgang did not return soon, because it was beginning to look as if Wolfgang wanted to make a fool both of Colloredo and of Leopold. He turned round Wolfgang's desire for comfort from Leopold by stressing his own need of comfort from Wolfgang. He acknowledged that Wolfgang was giving up a more interesting life to return to Salzburg, but claimed he was doing all he could to organize entertainments at home for the benefit of them all, and was trying to arrange a trip to Italy. And, perhaps stung by the suspicion that

---

[25] This letter is lost. *MBA* numbers it 514*a* (in accordance with the editorial policy of assigning numbers even to lost letters if it is certain that they were written), but when Wolfgang replies to it in *MBA* 516/31–7, the *MBA* commentary calls it 515, which is Leopold's surviving letter of 31 Dec. 1778.

[26] Wolfgang to Leopold, 31 Dec. 1778–2 Jan. 1779—*MBA* 516 (*Letters* 350).

Wolfgang's narration of his woes to Becke had been very one-sided, he challenged Wolfgang to show Becke his letter of 28 December (in which he had commanded Wolfgang not to stay long in Munich), so that Becke could see how reasonable his arguments were. Though his tone was far softer than it had been, he nevertheless likened Wolfgang to a horse, who would allow himself to be ridden, and would docilely pull the carriage, as long as he was fed and stabled.[27]

By 8 January 1779 Wolfgang had presented his sonatas to the elector's wife, and had therefore run out of reasons for remaining in Munich. He wrote to Leopold that he now felt easier about his return home (although he was already disgusted by the provincial behaviour of Salzburg acquaintances whom he had met in Munich), but asked if he could bring the *Bäsle* with him. He admitted that his fear of returning had been a fear of his reception, and stated that he was not aware of having done anything deserving of reproach.[28]

Leopold agreed that the *Bäsle* might come, but refused to allow Wolfgang to wait in Munich until her father had been approached for permission. He wanted Wolfgang to travel home with their acquaintance Gschwendtner (with whom Nannerl had been given a lift to Munich in January 1775), who would probably leave on 14 or 15 January; the *Bäsle* could follow, if her father agreed, with the mailcoach on 20 January. Leopold emphasized that he would be extremely angry if Wolfgang did not follow his travel instructions.[29]

Leopold's letter marked the end of the correspondence from this testing period. Whether the *Bäsle* did indeed follow on behind Wolfgang and Gschwendtner, or whether she accompanied Wolfgang, what passed between father and son on their reunion, and how soon Wolfgang was disabused of any idea he had been encouraged by Leopold to cherish that Colloredo was now going to treat him with new respect, is undocumented. One of his first jobs on returning must have been to sign the petition which Leopold had already written, to ask formally for his job of organist.[30] Once this had been granted, Leopold no doubt breathed more easily. Yet the omens were not good. Wolfgang had been brought home against his will only with the greatest difficulty. His actions had at several critical points belied his assurances of unbounded love for his family. When Leopold had compared him with a horse, who would allow

[27] Leopold to Wolfgang, 31 Dec. 1778—*MBA* 515 (*Letters* 349, but with substantial omissions, including the comparison with a horse).

[28] Wolfgang to Leopold, 8 Jan. 1779—*MBA* 520 (*Letters* 351).

[29] Leopold to Wolfgang, 11 Jan. 1779—*MBA* 521 (*Letters* 352).   [30] *MBA* 522 (*Letters* 353).

others to use him as long as he was stabled comfortably, he had followed up his unflattering remark with the offer to provide the stable and hay himself; and had invited Wolfgang to confirm that he would prefer his father's stable to any other. Yet Wolfgang's brief taste of freedom, and his evident unfettered enjoyment of the company of other friends, suggests that this was far from being the case. Leopold's letters had catalogued the entertainments that they would be able to enjoy as a family in Salzburg on the greatly increased income that he had won (Carnival balls, outings, card parties, the theatre, and the shooting competitions); but they have a sad ring about them when compared with the more vibrant society which Wolfgang had enjoyed in Munich and Mannheim, mainly because the company in Salzburg was so limited and dull. Leopold was later to acknowledge this himself, when he was left alone in the Dancing-Master's House after Nannerl's marriage;[31] but while his family lived with him, the lustre of the events came from the fact that he could enjoy them in the company of his children. It is thus hardly surprising that they should have meant more to the father than to the son.

The events of the period of Wolfgang's absence had also clarified the different perspectives of Leopold and Wolfgang on their employment. Both wanted to live and work in a livelier place than Salzburg: but with Wolfgang the desire to leave was so strong that he preferred almost anything else to what he perceived as slavery, and could do so even while enumerating the advantages to his compositional career of a quiet life in Salzburg;[32] while Leopold wanted first and foremost financial security, and was not prepared to give it up unless a similar arrangement (which now, for safety's sake, meant two respectable salaries) could be negotiated elsewhere.

Perhaps only because the enormous debt could be used as a hold over Wolfgang was Leopold able to force him back home at all; and even then, the deed could ultimately only be achieved by threats. The correspondence suggests that the Mozarts' acquaintances in Salzburg had a clear view of Wolfgang's duties as a son, and that these included behaving honourably and supporting his family financially.[33] But Wolfgang's

---

[31] See Chs. 26 and 27 for more details about Leopold's loneliness after Nannerl's marriage.

[32] See Ch. 18, pp. 315–16. Whether it would have been advantageous to his compositional development to stay in Salzburg must be doubted. He would presumably have composed under less stress, but without the stimuli that were surely partly responsible for the outpouring of masterpieces in Vienna.

[33] When Wolfgang had drawn the 150 fl. from Schmalz in Mannheim (see Ch. 17, pp. 263–4), Leopold had been embarrassed because the sum was entered as a debit on his account with Hagenauer in Salzburg, and he had to explain to Hagenauer why Wolfgang still needed financial

actions had frequently been at odds with his words, and nowhere can this be more clearly seen than in Leopold's threat to expose his unfilial behaviour to the Cannabichs. Not an actual sense of duty to his father and sister brought him back to Salzburg, but the fear that people he respected would discover its lack.

It is chiefly on the correspondence documenting the journey to Paris and back that analyses of the relationship between Leopold and Wolfgang are founded. The resulting portrayals are usually heavily to Leopold's disadvantage, since there is no shortage of his own words suggesting to those seeing the matter from a Wolfgang Mozart-centred perspective that Leopold was tyrannically possessive. Thus Solomon's biography perpetuates many familiar unsympathetic views of Leopold. Solomon claims, for example, that when Leopold commanded Wolfgang to return from Paris, he was breaking his promise to allow Wolfgang to lead a freelance life if the search for a good appointment failed; that he negotiated the Salzburg employment agreement for Wolfgang without his consent; that no third person was to be allowed any portion of Wolfgang's earnings or affections; that Leopold would not allow Wolfgang intimacy with any woman; that the list of women Leopold mentioned in his letter of 11–12 February 1778 (all four of whom Wolfgang had met and admired on his journey from Salzburg to Mannheim) shows that he distrusted without exception every woman named by Wolfgang; and that Leopold insisted that Wolfgang give up Aloysia Weber and his cousin Maria Anna Thekla Mozart, both of whom he loved. None of these particular interpretations can be obtained from a careful reading of the evidence.

When Leopold stated that if Wolfgang could not gain an appointment he could go to a big city and earn money from freelance work, he was writing before Wolfgang's departure from Mannheim for Paris. By the time he was commanding Wolfgang to return, Wolfgang had been in Paris several months, could barely support himself, and hated it so much that he was begging Leopold to try to arrange for him to go to Italy. From Leopold's point of view, he had had his chance of freelance work and failed to earn the sort of money which was the sole justification for it. And though the Salzburg employment agreement was negotiated without Wolfgang's consent (indeed with great dissatisfaction on his part), the larger context was that he was also extremely dissatisfied in Paris, and a journey to Italy

support. Hagenauer's response had been: 'For goodness' sake! I have complete faith in Herr Wolfgang, he'll do his duty as a son all right, just let him get to Paris; and keep calm.' Leopold to Wolfgang, 23 Feb. 1778—*MBA* 429/71–9 (*Letters* 290).

was at least more feasible from Salzburg.[34] Concerning Solomon's remarks about women, there is no surviving evidence to suggest that Leopold was implacably hostile to all intimate connections. He did not forbid the friendship with Aloysia; on the contrary, he had arias copied for her at his own expense, told Wolfgang that he would try to arrange for her to sing at the Salzburg court with a view to gaining her an appointment there, and said that Wolfgang could correspond freely with her and invite her to stay in Salzburg. The claim that Leopold required Wolfgang to give up his cousin is an invention. And the list of women detailed by Leopold in his letter of February 1778 as having been admired by Wolfgang was given not to show disapproval of any of them, but to demonstrate Wolfgang's fickleness to him; he had been enthusiastic about each in turn until he had met the next, which convinced Leopold that his plan of undertaking musical tours with Aloysia was impetuous.[35]

What Leopold was undeniably opposed to was the excessive dissipation of Wolfgang's energies while the financial future of himself and his parents and sister remained insecure. For this reason, all Leopold's remarks about the women Wolfgang loved, including those he was to make about Aloysia's sister Constanze from 1781, bear a different interpretation from that of possessiveness—namely, a belief that marriage was irresponsible without an adequate financial basis. Leopold and Maria Anna themselves had had to submit to this hard discipline, and Leopold did not live to see Wolfgang obtain such a basis.

The correspondence of this period shows that it was when things were going badly that Leopold would make his most wounding remarks, and the possibility should be borne in mind that some of his most hysterical and obsessive ones at this time were made when he was in a very poor nervous state. Insistently though they obtrude on the consciousness of the reader, therefore, it is important to balance them against the encouraging, admiring, generous, and loving comments that Leopold also made to Wolfgang in abundance. In short, though his own words make him an easy target for attack, and though they certainly cannot all be explained away to depict a father with a completely healthy attitude towards his son's desire for independence, it is possible to view him in a more even-handed way if the letters are read with careful attention to all their contexts.

---

[34] See Solomon, *Mozart*, 150–2. The letter containing Leopold's sanction of freelancing if he could not win an appointment is that of 11–12 Feb. 1778—*MBA* 422/35–50 (*Letters* 285).

[35] See Solomon, *Mozart*, 159, 172, and 175 for the above-mentioned remarks about women. Leopold's letter containing the list of women in whom Wolfgang had shown an interest since leaving Salzburg is *MBA* 422 (*Letters* 285).

Leopold had exerted himself to the utmost to make Wolfgang return. He had negotiated a package almost unprecedented at the Salzburg court for German musicians living under one roof; he had claimed to have secured protection for Wolfgang from the most tedious duties; he might well have lied about the working conditions; he had promised all manner of luxuries and entertainments, as well as another visit to Italy; and he had cajoled and threatened. When he had said that Wolfgang must return for two years in order that the debts might be cleared, and that after that he might bang his head against the wall if he wished, he probably never envisaged that Wolfgang might want to do just that.

PART IV

Wolfgang's Independence
(1780–1784)

❧ 20 ❧

The Next Hope of Freedom:
Idomeneo in Munich

❧

To the question whether Leopold's promises to Wolfgang of a more rewarding life in Salzburg were fulfilled, the answer must be a resounding 'no'. Although this was partly because the working conditions were not as favourable as Leopold had led Wolfgang to expect them to be, the most important sources of Wolfgang's dissatisfaction with Salzburg were in any case outside Leopold's control. His passion for composing was frustrated by the nature of the court music—his works were apparently little appreciated by Colloredo and many other courtiers, the orchestra was far from special, and there was virtually no scope for him to work at his chief love, opera.[1] When it is considered with what rapidity he was to pour forth all manner of new works once he had established his first toe-hold in Viennese society (responding in particular to the opportunities offered him by the theatre, the excellent wind players, and the Viennese love of keyboard music), these Salzburg years can be seen as confining his talents in a stoppered vessel which was ready to explode by the time he finally made the break with his native city.

Socially he was also restricted, wanting little to do with most of the other musicians, and later complaining that the people whose company he might have enjoyed did not think him good enough for them.[2] Thus when

---

[1] Reports on the quality of the Salzburg orchestra by outsiders give a mixture of complimentary and critical opinions. One states that the orchestral playing was of low quality, but that there were a few excellent solo instrumental performers, who could make the overall impression seem good. Zaslaw points out that Mozart's finest symphonic music of this period in Salzburg is contained in the orchestral serenades commissioned privately, rather than in the symphonies written for the court. He suggests that this may have been because the Mozarts had complete control over the choice of players and the rehearsals for these private events. See Zaslaw, *Mozart's Symphonies*, ch. 10, esp. 338–9. A comprehensive survey of the various orchestras known to the Mozarts in Salzburg is given in C. Eisen, 'Mozart's Salzburg Orchestras', *Early Music* (Feb. 1992), 89–103. See also following note.

[2] Wolfgang to Leopold, 26 May 1781—*MBA* 599/29–37 (*Letters* 406). This passage also summarizes some of Wolfgang's other complaints about Salzburg.

Wolfgang complained that his best years were being wasted in Salzburg,[3] it is impossible not to feel the truth of the remark.

From January 1779 until November 1780 there are no family letters to inform us about activities in Salzburg, because the three remaining members were at home together. Nannerl's diary survives for parts of the period, however, enabling some typical routines to be reconstructed.[4]

The family rose early and did most of the day's work in the morning. Nannerl, who went to church almost every day, was frequently at the seven o'clock Mass, though she rarely mentioned being accompanied by her father or brother. They no doubt had court duties in the morning—teaching at the Kapellhaus, playing for services in the cathedral, and rehearsing for concerts and services. Leopold must have had additional organizational duties, since he was acting Kapellmeister, and Wolfgang must have used some of the day for composition. While they were thus occupied, Nannerl spent part of the morning (and often the early part of the afternoon) giving private lessons. She had only two or three families to whom she went, but visited one of them daily except Sunday, and the others (broadly speaking) on alternate days. She also supervised the housekeeping. Usually the family lunched together at home, and devoted the bulk of the afternoon to recreation. Sometimes they visited friends, but more often they received visits; during all the periods for which Nannerl's diary survives, hardly a day went by on which they did not see at least one friend socially. On Sundays, and sometimes on weekdays too, the Mozarts hosted the shooting party; at other times they played cards, and probably often made music (the diary does not always indicate music-making, but there was frequently at least one musician among the visitors). If the weather was fine, they would then go for a walk, taking Pimpes the dog. On Tuesdays, Thursdays, and Sundays, there was music at court in the evening, at which Wolfgang and Leopold generally had to be present. For parts of the year, a visiting troupe of actors would be in town, staging plays, operettas, and ballets in the theatre opposite the Mozarts' house—the family always tried to befriend them, and seems often to have been offered free entrance to all the performances. During Carnival (between Epiphany and Lent), there were balls to dress up for, although no excerpts from

---

[3] Wolfgang to Leopold, 8 Apr. 1781—*MBA* 587/31–4 (*Letters* 397).

[4] Although Nannerl's diary has never been published in English, considerations of space have prevented its being given in full in this book. However, a table of entries for 1783, sorted into categories of activity, is given in Table 1. Though these are not the entries on which the material in this chapter is based, the underlying routines were much the same during all the periods for which the diary survives.

the diary survive to inform us about these in the winters of 1779 or 1780; during summer there were outings to nearby beauty spots, and serenading. The year was punctuated by church festivals and other occasional events such as the fairs, at which Leopold settled accounts with the visiting booksellers who marketed his *Violinschule*. In Lent, academies were given. Holy Week was particularly important to Nannerl—on Good Friday 1779 she and her friend Katherl Gilowsky embarked on a pious round of visits to sixteen different churches to mark the occasion. Beginning at eight in the morning at the cathedral, they kept it up all day with a mid-morning and a lunch break. At one church (the Kajetanerkirche) they climbed a stairway on their knees; the day was concluded by a visit to Holy Trinity to hear the special music for Good Friday. Occasionally the Mozarts would receive visits from friends or musicians passing through the town, in which case they would organize a concert or take them to see the sights in and around Salzburg, as appropriate.[5]

The leisure activity from which the Mozarts derived most pleasure was theatre-going, and the opportunity offered to Wolfgang in Salzburg to observe theatrical effectiveness should not be underestimated. The public theatre had been opened in Salzburg in 1775, at Colloredo's instigation, and was visited by a succession of travelling troupes. These had to negotiate with Colloredo's theatre commission for permission to stage their performances in Salzburg. Between 1775 and 1792 the theatre, which seated between six and seven hundred people, was host to about sixteen different troupes. Performances from a varied repertoire (including adaptations of works by Shakespeare) were given between three and five times per week, nearly always in German. There was usually a play or an operetta, followed by a ballet; sometimes melodrama was performed. The number of different pieces in production at any one time was large; Waizhofer's troupe had twenty-five operas and a melodrama up and running on the musical side alone in 1785/6, and most were performed only once. In one season it was therefore possible to see an enormous amount of drama, spoken and sung, and the Mozarts did not neglect the opportunity. Wolfgang also occasionally did small quantities of compositional work for some of the troupes. The theatre was an important draw, and administrative officials from outlying villages would make an effort to get into town for at least some of the performances (as Nannerl and

---

[5] The information in this paragraph is from Nannerl's diary entries from Mar. 1779–Dec. 1780—*MBA* 523, 526, 527, 528, 529, 529a, 530, 532, 533, 534, 544, 546, 547, 548, 550, 552, 554, and 564 (*MBA* 547 and 564 are actually letters from Nannerl to Wolfgang, but they are based on her diary entries).

her husband were to do from St Gilgen when Wolfgang's *Die Entführung* was being performed by Schmidt's troupe in 1784); but the results were not always financially satisfactory for the performers. The size of the troupes varied—Böhm's, which was in Salzburg in 1779/80, had about twenty-one members, while Schikaneder's, in 1780/1, had thirty-four. Of these, some would be actors, some singers, some dancers, and some instrumentalists. Compositional capability was required, as was also the ability to translate and adapt plays and operas for the particular require-ments of the troupe; members had therefore to be prepared to turn their hands to a number of different activities. Extensive wardrobes were car-ried from place to place, and were the chief asset of the troupe; when Böhm, dissatisfied with his Salzburg takings in 1779, asked Colloredo if he could be released early from his contract, Colloredo refused and threatened to confiscate his wardrobe and place him under arrest. There must have been a substantial number of hangers-on in addition to the performing mem-bers—children and other relations, and the tutors and servants to wait on them. It was small wonder, therefore, that life in Salzburg seemed rather flat whenever the players left town for their next venue. The Mozarts, who tended to cultivate the friendship of these people by inviting them to the Dancing-Master's House, and who attended virtually every performance (spoken and sung), must have experienced quite a void in their lives each time this happened.[6]

At some point in 1780 Wolfgang was commissioned to write a carni-val opera for Munich—*Idomeneo*. The librettist, Giambattista Varesco, also working in Salzburg, was recorded by Nannerl visiting the Mozarts on 22 August,[7] and since he was not among their regular callers, the occa-sion was probably connected with the collaboration. Colloredo grudgingly granted Wolfgang six weeks' leave to go to Munich to compose the work and supervise rehearsals,[8] and Wolfgang left on 5 November.

With Wolfgang's departure, the correspondence resumed, and it strongly suggests that the Mozarts were still extremely dissatisfied with their situation in Salzburg, and were hoping that Wolfgang, by showing his

---

[6] The information in this paragraph is from E. Hintermaier, 'Das fürsterzbischöfliche Hoftheater zu Salzburg (1775–1803)', *ÖMz* 30 (1975), 351–63; S. Dahms, 'Das musikalische Repertoire des Salzburger fürsterzbischöflichen Hoftheaters (1775–1803)', *ÖMz* 31 (1976), 340–55; and Nannerl's diary entries reporting the departure of Böhm's troupe by carriage and sledge for Augsburg in Feb. 1780—*MBA* 529, 530, and 529a. For an explanation of my reasons for placing most of these entries in February, rather than March as the *MBA* commentary states, see Appendix 1.

[7] *MBA* 533/54.

[8] Wolfgang to Leopold, 16 Dec. 1780—*MBA* 563/56–7 (*Letters* 376). Six weeks was an unreal-istic amount of leave for the work involved, and the earliest projected date for the first performance of *Idomeneo* was 20 Jan. 1781—see Wolfgang to Leopold, 13 Nov. 1780—*MBA* 537/90 (*Letters* 358).

abilities in Munich, might obtain a better position and enable them to leave. Wolfgang's hopes seem to have been centred on Munich itself as a possible source of employment, while Leopold appears to have had his eye rather on a Viennese appointment through the influence of various imperial ministers working in Munich.[9]

Leopold's attitude seems inconsistent with that in 1778, when he had been doing his utmost to persuade Wolfgang that a Salzburg post had great advantages over positions at other courts. Nannerl was still unmarried and dependent on Leopold and Wolfgang, so the considerations which he had then thought so important ought still to have applied; if Wolfgang took a post elsewhere and the others moved with him, Leopold and Nannerl would only have the security of one salary. Perhaps Leopold felt that since conditions for Wolfgang in Salzburg were just as unsatisfactory as they always had been, it was unfair to expect him to stay merely for the sake of their having two salaries. Perhaps, too, Leopold felt that the decreased security for Nannerl would be less important now that there were no longer debts to leave her. Almost two years on from Wolfgang's return from Paris, the debt must have been virtually cleared. And perhaps he reasoned that Nannerl's own employment possibilities, to say nothing of her marriage prospects, would increase if Wolfgang could secure an appointment which enabled the whole family to move to an animated centre such as Vienna.

Whatever the precise hopes of Leopold might have been, the Mozarts fairly clearly were very keen for Wolfgang to compose the opera. He seems to have undertaken the work for less than the usual fee,[10] and Leopold probably had to take on at least some of Wolfgang's court, cathedral, and teaching duties in order to secure from Colloredo the necessary leave for Wolfgang. Leopold also had the unenviable task of communicating to the librettist Varesco the changes to the libretto demanded by Wolfgang, and this required a good deal of tact, patience, and firmness.

On arrival in Munich, Wolfgang called on Count Seeau, the theatre intendant. Seeau was able to present him to the elector as early as 12 November, and on the following day Wolfgang consulted with Seeau, Cannabich

---

[9] It is not clear whether Leopold did not favour a post in Munich for Wolfgang, or whether he simply did not think it likely that Wolfgang could obtain one—in his letter of 24 Nov. 1780 (*MBA* 542/93–7; *Letters* 363), Wolfgang said that he knew that Leopold did not rate his chances of such an appointment highly, but there is no way of knowing what Leopold's reaction might have been had he considered one likely. In his letter of 2 Dec. 1780 (*MBA* 551/27–39; not in *Letters*), Leopold urged Wolfgang to remember the influence with the Viennese court of the imperial ministers working in Munich.

[10] Leopold to Wolfgang, 11 Dec. 1780—*MBA* 558/58–61 (*Letters* 373).

(the leader of the orchestra), Quaglio (who was in charge of the stage sets), and Legrand (the ballet-master), about the production of the opera.[11] After this, he set to work at the composition, as usual consulting the singers as to the kind of arias they wanted. Two major problems were the fact that Wolfgang's friend Raaff, who was taking the part of Idomeneo, was ageing and could not act, while the young castrato dal Prato, taking the part of Idamante, could neither sing nor act well, and was incapable of learning his role methodically. Wolfgang complained that he had to spend an enormous amount of time taking dal Prato through his part line by line,[12] and the deficiencies of these two singers caused Wolfgang to require even more changes to the libretto from Varesco than he other-wise would have done. In addition he had to be on his guard against the usual problem of cabals—at one point, for example, a rumour went round that his setting of the Italian words was deficient.[13] To ensure a fine performance, he had to keep the goodwill of all the singers while insist-ing that the dramatic requirements of the opera were not compromised too far. He also had to cultivate the goodwill of the orchestra because, as Leopold reminded him, his music needed careful rehearsal to produce its full effect.[14]

Rehearsals for *Idomeneo* began at the beginning of December, before the opera was completely composed, and the first performance was fixed for 20 January 1781, though it was later postponed to 29 January. All this time Wolfgang, although very busy, was enjoying the superior company offered by Munich society; he claimed that he was frequently invited out to dine, and was welcome in several noble houses.[15] This in itself must have formed quite a contrast with life in Salzburg, where Nannerl's diary and the family letters seldom if ever mentioned dining with members of the nobility.

Because Varesco was in Salzburg, Wolfgang did not communicate with him direct, but transmitted all his thoughts about the changes he wanted made to the libretto to Leopold, and asked Leopold to ensure that Varesco carried them out. This meant that Leopold was fully aware of the way in which the libretto had to develop in order to satisfy Wolfgang's dramatic requirements (which themselves were shaped by the shortcom-ings and demands of the singers), and he could not resist making suggestions

---

[11] Wolfgang to Leopold, 13 Nov. 1780—*MBA* 537 (*Letters* 358).
[12] Wolfgang to Leopold, 22 Nov. 1780—*MBA* 541/34–6 (*Letters* 362).
[13] Wolfgang to Leopold, 27 Dec. 1780—*MBA* 570/26–36 (*Letters* 381).
[14] Leopold to Wolfgang, 25 Dec. 1780—*MBA* 569/9–29 (*Letters* 380).
[15] Wolfgang to Leopold, 24 Nov. 1780—*MBA* 542/9–13 (*Letters* 363).

of his own as to how certain scenes might be staged, and what orchestration might be used. These suggestions have a quite different quality from his usual practical exhortations to Wolfgang to write music which could be understood even by musically uneducated people. Leopold made this kind of suggestion too, but his comments about the means of dramatic effectiveness reveal a desire to share in Wolfgang's compositional efforts. On his part, Wolfgang seems to have been quite willing for Leopold to be involved in this way, and the correspondence suggests that the two could discuss artistic matters amicably as equals, notwithstanding that Leopold was happy to acknowledge Wolfgang's inspired creativity. Feeling himself partly involved with the composition of *Idomeneo* was perhaps Leopold's chief consolation while Wolfgang was away in Munich, because apart from this his life was trying.

Leopold was longing to be able to follow on to Munich to observe the progress of the opera more closely, hear the fine orchestra, and share the society Wolfgang was enjoying.[16] But he had little idea when he might be able to do so. Colloredo was so awkward about granting leave that Leopold thought it likely he would not be able to arrive until the date of the dress rehearsal. On the other hand, it was known that Colloredo was planning a visit to Vienna to his sick father, and this raised hopes in Salzburg that if the visit materialized, a general exodus of musicians to Munich and elsewhere would be possible while the archbishop was away. These hopes were tempered, however, by the consideration that if Colloredo's father were to die, the proposed visit might be cancelled. To complicate matters further, the Empress Maria Theresia died on 29 November 1780, and for a short while Leopold and Nannerl feared that the mourning would interfere with the staging of the opera.[17] Meanwhile, Leopold was plagued by the negotiations about the libretto with Varesco, who complained that because of the repeated changes demanded he had had to copy it out four times, and who seemed to suspect the Mozarts of purloining part of his fee.[18] Leopold also negotiated the translation of the libretto into German by his Salzburg friend and colleague Andreas Schachtner, so that all in all he was quite harassed.

During this period all three of them had catarrhal complaints of one kind or another. Leopold was particularly worried about Wolfgang, partly

---

[16] Leopold to Wolfgang, 11 Nov. 1780—*MBA* 536/32–4 (*Letters* 357).

[17] Leopold's uncertainty about when he might be able to get away lasted well into January 1781—see Leopold to Wolfgang, 2 Dec. 1780 (*MBA* 551/4–14; *Letters* 368); Nannerl to Wolfgang, 18 Dec. 1780 (*MBA* 564/33–5; *Letters* 377); Leopold to Wolfgang, 29–30 Dec. 1780 (*MBA* 572/72–3; *Letters* 382); and Leopold to Wolfgang, 11 Jan. 1781 (*MBA* 578/18–22; *Letters* 388).

[18] Leopold to Wolfgang, 4 Jan. 1781—*MBA* 575/5–25 (*Letters* 385).

because he was not able to observe his condition personally, and partly because he believed that the mental strain of such a big composition was in any case a reason for being exceptionally vigilant about the onset of potentially dangerous symptoms. He begged Wolfgang to let him know if his indisposition became worse, saying that if it did he would come to Munich to nurse him. He also alluded to Maria Anna's death, repeating his conviction that she might not have died if he had been with her.[19] Nannerl's cold developed into a feverish cough, and Leopold nursed her himself and supervised the regimen of diet and medication prescribed for her. Her treatment involved being bled, and then following a course of medicines and foods designed to moisten and strengthen the chest. These were a mixture and a tea for the chest, barley water and barley porridge, and light moist meals. Regular careful observation of her symptoms was necessary, and appropriate adjustments to the regimen, and she also had to sleep in a heated room. Leopold too was unwell, and the combination of illness, extra work, uncertainty, and worry caused a tendency in him to sink into depression. His mood appears to have reached a low point on 20 November, the day before his wedding anniversary. Since Maria Anna must have been in his mind on this date, it was perhaps partly the thoughts of her death, from an illness he thought should have been curable, which increased his fears for the health of his children. He must also have remembered Nannerl's childhood illness in The Hague, which had begun as a chesty cough and had nearly killed her. In writing to Wolfgang about Nannerl, he complained that his own cold (which he later confessed was very severe) was having to be driven away by all the running around he was forced to do. He lamented the fact that at the age of 61 he still had to be the strong one of the family, and feared that he would never enjoy his old age in peace and quiet. In addition, the thought of his approaching wedding anniversary made him melancholy.[20]

Wolfgang's response to this letter shows that there was still an expectation within the family that he would be the means by which the positions of Leopold and Nannerl would be ameliorated. After expressing

---

[19] Leopold to Wolfgang, 25 Nov. 1780—*MBA* 543 (*Letters* 364, but not complete); and 30 Nov. 1780—*MBA* 547/106–14 (*Letters* 366a).

[20] Leopold to Wolfgang, 20 Nov. 1780—*MBA* 540/28–50 and 64–5 (*Letters* 361, but almost all Leopold's complaint is omitted, and Nannerl's illness appears much less serious than it evidently was). Though the Mozarts commonly talked about having 'catarrhs', it is clear from the descriptions of the symptoms that these were often more serious than the ailments now called colds; it seems likely that they were frequently more akin to bronchitis or pneumonia. See Leopold's letter to Wolfgang of 4 Dec. 1780 (*MBA* 553/25–73; mostly omitted from *Letters* 369) for a detailed analysis of the ways in which diet, medicine, and rest were thought essential for the safe dispersal of the harmful matter through expectoration, urination, and excretion.

concern about Nannerl's health, he begged Leopold not to write any more melancholy letters, since he needed a cheerful heart in order to compose. He went on to sympathize with Leopold's trials in Salzburg, and to regret that he was the unwilling cause of them, and tried to encourage his father to believe that the sacrifices Leopold was making for Wolfgang at present would ultimately be worth while, because the success of the opera might lead to an appointment for Wolfgang in Munich which would enable Leopold to leave Salzburg.[21]

Gradually, Leopold's problems and worries eased. Nannerl slowly recovered, and he chipped away at the difficulties over the libretto, and was rewarded by the promising reports of the early rehearsals in Munich. The main Salzburg news he and Nannerl reported to Wolfgang was about progress on the family portrait which was being painted,[22] about Schikaneder and his troupe (Nannerl sending a list of the plays performed since Wolfgang's departure, and Leopold nagging him to write the aria he had promised Schikaneder), and about the illness and death of Countess Lodron. She died a terrible death at the age of 42 in December 1780, and Leopold described her lingering illness with an abscess on her back, black pustules in her mouth and throat, and her blood completely corrupted.[23] With her death, the household of children was broken up. Her husband had already died in February 1779, shortly after Wolfgang's return from Paris, and her eldest son Sigmund (three years younger than Wolfgang) had also died a gruesome death on 1 April 1779, some four months after attempts by a number of specially summoned doctors and surgeons to clear his infected abdomen of stinking black matter by means of lancing his side in several different places.[24] On the death of the second parent, there were six surviving children ranging in age from 19 down to 9. The eldest, Aloysia or Louise, was marriageable, and Leopold reported marriage negotiations concerning her during this period. There was a general feeling of outrage at the fact that the groom was 61 years old, and the Mozarts, who knew all the children well through having taught them, expressed sympathy for Aloysia. Her uncle, Count Franz Anton Arco, son of the ageing Oberstkämmerer Georg Anton Felix Arco, championed her in the matter, even though his father threatened

---

[21] Wolfgang to Leopold, 24 Nov. 1780—*MBA* 542/88–97 (*Letters* 363).

[22] This is the oil-painting by Johann Nepomuk della Croce, showing Wolfgang and Nannerl seated playing at one keyboard, Leopold standing with his violin, and Maria Anna represented by her portrait hanging on the wall.

[23] Leopold to Wolfgang, 15 Dec. 1780—*MBA* 562/70–8 (not in *Letters*).

[24] Leopold to Wolfgang, 19 Nov. 1778 (*MBA* 505/109–15; not in *Letters*); and 23 Nov. 1778 (*MBA* 506/108–12; not in *Letters*).

to disinherit him if he did not cease his objections. The plans eventually foundered when the groom himself accepted that the marriage would be a gross mismatch.[25]

Most of the younger children, all girls except one, were to be dispersed to relations outside Salzburg, or to convents. Only the boy, Hieronymus ('Momolo'), aged 14, looked set to remain in Salzburg; Leopold suggested that he might attend the Virgilianum, the school for aristocratic children, where he would still be under the supervision of his godfather the archbishop and of his grandfather Count Arco, and close to his tutor Henri.[26] The dispersal of this young family shows how much at the mercy of death even the richest and grandest people were.

After the death of the countess, her effects and those of her son Sigmund (which she had evidently been keeping for sentimental reasons) were shared out according to her will. Bullinger's younger brother Franz Xaver, who had been Sigmund's tutor, was given a magnificent wolf fur that had belonged to Sigmund, and Leopold was hoping that he might borrow it for the journey to Munich, since his own was in tatters. He said explicitly that he had not enough money to replace it,[27] and this was not the only hint in the correspondence of this period that the Mozarts had little spare money. Despite the fact that Barisani had advised Nannerl to sleep in a heated room, and that Wolfgang had told Leopold that a stove could be installed for 4 or 5 fl. in the room she was to have in Munich, they eventually decided that it was too expensive, and that they would manage without it.[28] Furthermore, Wolfgang apparently had very little money with him in Munich while he was writing *Idomeneo*. As well as a small amount of cash, Leopold provided him with a credit note for 15 fl. at the beginning of his stay there, and this money lasted until the end of December. He needed the cash for breakfasts, laundry, hairdressing, and the barber.[29] When the mourning for Maria Theresia began, Leopold sent Wolfgang's

[25] Leopold to Wolfgang, 2 Dec. 1780 (*MBA* 551/23–7; *Letters* 368), but Anderson's note on the Lodrons is inaccurate; Wolfgang to Leopold, 5 Dec. 1780 (*MBA* 555/51–8; *Letters* 370); Leopold to Wolfgang, 8 Jan. 1781 (*MBA* 576/79–83; not in *Letters*); Leopold to Wolfgang, 11 Jan. 1781 (*MBA* 578/4–13; not in *Letters*; and Leopold to Wolfgang, 13 Jan. 1781 (*MBA* 579/7–9; not in *Letters*). See Fig. 3 for a diagram of Arco/Firmian/Lodron relationships.

[26] Leopold to Wolfgang, 11 Dec. 1780—*MBA* 558/25–36 (not in *Letters*).

[27] Leopold to Wolfgang, 11 Jan. 1781—*MBA* 578/26–31 (not in *Letters*). Though the *MBA* commentary identifies 'the preceptor Bullinger' as the Mozarts' main friend Joseph Bullinger, Schuler has shown him to be Joseph's brother Franz Xaver. See H. Schuler, 'Mozart und das hochgräfliche Haus Lodron: eine genealogische Quellenstudie', *MM* 31 (1983), 6–7.

[28] Wolfgang to Leopold, 24 Nov. 1780 (*MBA* 542/104–8; *Letters* 363); and 18 Jan. 1781 (*MBA* 580/28–30; *Letters* 390).

[29] Leopold to Wolfgang, 11 Nov. 1780 (*MBA* 536/14–18; not in *Letters*); and Wolfgang to Leopold, 15 Nov. 1780 (*MBA* 538/5–8; *Letters* 359).

black suit, which Wolfgang had to pay to have repaired, and in reporting that he was coming to the end of his money, Wolfgang used this expense to justify having spent it all, and assured Leopold that he had not been squandering it.[30] The remarks about money during this period suggest that the Mozarts were spending very thriftily, and that Leopold had no intention of allowing Wolfgang a free rein with his finances while he was in Munich. This in turn suggests that the debt was still being paid off.

Despite this, Nannerl made one very extravagant purchase, one whose expense suggests the significance to her of the carnival trip to Munich. She had no mourning dress fit for wearing at all the events she expected to attend there, so she had a new one made, at a cost of 70 fl. This was a fantastic sum by comparison with earnings, being approximately equivalent to two months' worth of Leopold's salary. Nannerl seems to have bought it from the money she earned from giving lessons, and Leopold reported to Wolfgang her hope that the elector would have to pay for it,[31] almost certainly an allusion to her desire for Wolfgang to be employed in Munich. She was expecting to play in public there, and to attend Carnival balls and dine out in fine society; she probably also had in mind her attraction to eligible men, since she was by now 29 and still unmarried.

As *Idomeneo* neared completion Wolfgang, who must have arrived in Munich with such a sense of freedom from Salzburg, and such hopes that he might not have to return, began to feel again the oppression of the prospect of life there. Towards the end of his period of six weeks' leave, on 16 December 1780, he wrote to ask Leopold what was going to happen about this, since the first performance of the opera was not scheduled to take place until after the middle of January. He said that the archbishop and the pride of the nobility made life in Salzburg unbearable, and that he could not even look forward to regular leave. He remarked on the difficulty they had encountered in obtaining leave on this occasion, and indicated that in future it would not be forthcoming without a very special commission. In Munich, on the other hand, he felt sure that he had enough acquaintance and patronage to make a living. Freelance work was not reprehensible for a talented single man, who would be sufficiently capable of withstanding possible blows to his career caused by the deaths of his patrons. His feeling, therefore, was one of complete indifference to the possibility of being dismissed from Salzburg service

---

[30] Wolfgang to Leopold, 30 Dec. 1780—*MBA* 573/53–9 (*Letters* 383).
[31] Leopold to Wolfgang, 8 Jan. 1781—*MBA* 576/73–7 (*Letters* 386, but not complete).

for overstaying his leave, and he expressed himself with his customary animation: 'by god, if it were up to me—I would have wiped my backside with the last *decree* before I came away this time . . .'. He urged Leopold to come soon to Munich to hear the opera and tell him whether or not he was wrong to be so dissatisfied at the idea of returning to Salzburg.[32]

Leopold's response was to ignore Wolfgang's complaints and restlessness, and merely to answer the point about the expiry of the leave. He said that he had decided to keep quiet about this unless challenged, and then to furnish an excuse if necessary.[33] Perhaps he did not respond to the more important point because Wolfgang's complaints were so familiar to him that he assumed Wolfgang would know his answer; perhaps there was simply very little he could say to reconcile Wolfgang to Salzburg service, now that it was clear that the working conditions would never be as satisfactory as Leopold had promised in 1778; perhaps he did not think it worth writing down his thoughts on the subject because he knew he would soon be able to gauge the situation in Munich for himself, exert himself on Wolfgang's behalf, and discuss the question with him there; or perhaps his silence was a manifestation of his authority, in that he did not expect Wolfgang to take a major decision without the advice and consent of his father. At any rate, Leopold did not betray any anxiety that Wolfgang might actually do what he was hinting at—provoke Colloredo to the point where a rupture was inevitable.

Whatever Leopold's reasons for ignoring the question uppermost in Wolfgang's mind, it is surely not conceivable that he would have agreed to Wolfgang's request to stay in Munich without an appointment. Leopold's hopes were centred on the offer of a salary, and he was working to promote this by ensuring that every influential person in Munich was aware of all Wolfgang's capabilities. If nothing ensued, however, he expected Wolfgang to return to Salzburg for the time being, and to continue to win renown by future opera commissions, the dissemination of printed compositions, and so forth.[34] The joint efforts of father and son to increase

---

[32] *MBA* 563/56–80 (*Letters* 376). Although Wolfgang expressed himself strongly, he nevertheless wrote the key words in cypher, suggesting that he still had some feelings of caution. His emphasis of the fact that he was a single man may indicate the staking of a claim to take control of his own life, without having to consider first and foremost his father and sister.

[33] Leopold to Wolfgang, 25 Dec. 1780—*MBA* 569/30–6 (*Letters* 380). This is a further example of Leopold's willingness to practise deceit on his employer to achieve his ends, and of Wolfgang's knowledge of it.

[34] The answer Leopold would almost certainly have made to Wolfgang's request can be inferred from his negative response to the same question once Wolfgang was in Vienna in the spring of 1781. See Ch. 21, p. 353.

Wolfgang's fame during this period included making known in Munich *Zaide*, the German *Singspiel* he had been working on.[35] Since the elector was known for his interest in the German stage, and since there were imperial officials in Munich, this move was clearly part of the campaign to bring Wolfgang to the attention of the two most prestigious courts in Catholic Germany which encouraged German drama. Casting the net wider, the Mozarts were also probably pursuing the hope of winning an opera contract for Wolfgang in Prague, through their friendship with the singer Josepha Duschek.[36] And Leopold was continuing to try to persuade the publisher Breitkopf to print music by Wolfgang.[37]

On 11 January 1781 Leopold reported to Wolfgang the preparations for Colloredo's departure for Vienna, which was after all to take place. He described the personnel who were to accompany Colloredo, mentioning in particular the fact that the castrato Ceccarelli and the violinist Brunetti might be sent for once Colloredo was established there. He did not refer to Wolfgang, although clearly neither Ceccarelli nor Brunetti could perform without a keyboard player. At this point, Leopold still believed that the dress rehearsal of *Idomeneo* would be taking place on 20 January, and was therefore keen to leave Salzburg on the 18th. He was putting off until the last minute asking for leave to travel, presumably because he did not want to remind Colloredo of the fact that Wolfgang was in Munich on an unofficial extension of his leave.[38] When Wolfgang wrote to report the postponement by a week of the dress rehearsal, this suited Leopold very well, because Colloredo was sure to be gone by 22 January, and the Mozarts would be able to depart for Munich without approaching him.[39]

This seems to have been what happened. Leopold and Nannerl arrived in Munich on 26 January, and the dress rehearsal took place on the following day. The first performance was on 29 January, and there were subsequent ones on 3 February and 3 March.[40] Other activities in Munich are undocumented, but Nannerl and Wolfgang perhaps gave one or more concerts together. Around 10 March the family was in Augsburg for a few days, where Nannerl and Wolfgang performed (probably on instruments provided by their friend Stein) music for two keyboards. One listener described the effect as 'indescribably enchanting'.[41] It may be, therefore,

---

[35] Wolfgang to Leopold, 18 Jan. 1781—*MBA* 580/33–5 (*Letters* 390).
[36] Leopold to Wolfgang, 15 Dec. 1780 (*MBA* 562/63–9; *Letters* 375); and Wolfgang to Leopold, 16 May 1781 (*MBA* 596/23–4; *Letters* 404).
[37] Leopold to Breitkopf, 12 Feb. 1781—*MBA* 582 (*Letters* 392).
[38] *MBA* 578/32–43 (not in *Letters*).
[39] Leopold to Wolfgang, 13 Jan. 1781—*MBA* 579/5–7 (*Letters* 389).
[40] Deutsch, *Documents*, 190–1.   [41] Ibid. 193.

that they had played the same music, which probably included either or both of the Concertos K. 242 and K. 365, at concerts in Munich. In Munich too, Leopold must have seen a good deal of Theobald Marchand, the director of the court theatre, and his family. For when he and Nannerl returned to Salzburg, they took with them Marchand's 11-year-old son Heinrich, who was to become a resident pupil. Meanwhile, Colloredo had summoned Wolfgang to Vienna, where he wanted him to complete the tiny band of musicians entertaining him there. On 12 March, therefore, Wolfgang started out for Vienna, and around the same date Leopold, Nannerl, and Heinrich left for Salzburg.

21

The Final Break with Salzburg

❧❧❧

ALL Leopold's and Nannerl's letters to Wolfgang after Wolfgang's departure from Munich for Vienna in March 1781 are lost. This causes problems in reconstructing the sequences of events and the thought processes of the various members of the family from this date. Greatly to be regretted is the loss of information (which was surely given) about the education of Heinrich Marchand. This would have supplied further evidence about Leopold's pedagogical methods, which had once been applied to Wolfgang. Equally frustrating is not to know the reasons for Nannerl's inability to marry the man of her choice, the story behind her acceptance of the man who was to become her husband, or exactly what Leopold thought about Wolfgang's dramatic resignation from Salzburg service and his marriage to Constanze Weber. These important events have to be reconstructed as far as possible from Wolfgang's letters home, which involves trying to determine which letters by Wolfgang answer particular (lost) letters by Leopold and Nannerl, and what the lost letters might have said. One obvious difficulty is that it is often far from certain whether Wolfgang was doing the epistolary equivalent of thinking aloud, or whether he was responding to something written by Leopold. Thus when he wrote a sentence such as 'I certainly can't let the emperor know that if he wants to hear me he'd better be quick about it',[1] the possibility has to be borne in mind that he was responding to a point made by Leopold; in which case, something of Leopold's line of argument would be indicated. Sometimes (though not in this case), a sentence such as this is the only signal in the whole letter of the possibility of a letter from Leopold. When Wolfgang's letters are not read closely enough to note these possibilities, the results can be biographically damaging. An example occurs in the biography of Mozart by Volkmar Braunbehrens, who asserts that from the time of his arrival in Vienna until his break with Colloredo, Wolfgang wrote eight letters to Leopold, but received answers

---

[1] Wolfgang to Leopold, 11 Apr. 1781—*MBA* 588/40–1 (*Letters* 398).

only to one or two. He then asserts that Leopold's silence was so extraordinary that it must have been a disciplinary measure; Wolfgang's letters were asking for Leopold's permission to resign from Salzburg service, and Leopold assumed that Wolfgang would not take this step without his consent.[2] In fact, my own check suggests that Leopold did answer all Wolfgang's letters, and Braunbehrens' error appears to have arisen partly through uncritical reliance on information supplied by the authoritative German edition of the letters.[3] In this work, the decision was taken to assign a letter number to each missing letter if its original existence (and date) could be shown by an explicit reference to it in a surviving letter, or if its existence could be deduced from the text of a surviving letter.[4] In practice, however, lost letters to which an explicit reference was *not* made by an existing letter were frequently not numbered, even when their existence can be deduced with near certainty. And unfortunately, the problem is large; dozens of missing letters have escaped being numbered, and it is impossible to rely on the information.[5] Furthermore, the Braunbehrens example given here shows how easily an error of fact can lead to a misjudgement of the character of relationships.

When Wolfgang left Munich for Vienna, he and Leopold agreed on one point—that this visit to the imperial city was his chance to win the

---

[2] V. Braunbehrens, *Mozart in Vienna 1781–1791*, trans. T. Bell (New York, 1990), 48–9.

[3] *MBA*. For the period in question, however, *MBA* indicates that Leopold wrote four replies to Wolfgang's letters, rather than Braunbehrens' 'one or two'.

[4] *MBA*, Foreword to vol. v, pp. xii–xiii. An example of an explicit reference would be something like: 'I've just received your letter of 11 June.' Examples of unexplicit references are given in the text of this chapter.

[5] See Appendix 2 for my list of letters, surviving and lost, in the period mentioned by Braunbehrens. In the list of letters given by G. Geffray as having been written from and to the Dancing-Master's House in Salzburg during the Mozarts' occupancy, Geffray notes only those which can be proven to have been written, apparently deriving her information from the *MBA* commentary. See Angermüller, '"Können sie denn noch ein paar Zimmer anbauen lassen?"', 16 and 20 for some examples. For the period mentioned by Braunbehrens (17 Mar. to 9 May 1781), Geffray (who compiled the list for this part of Angermüller's article) gives as missing letters written from the Dancing-Master's House only those indicated by the *MBA* commentary. Later in the article, in the list of missing letters written to the Dancing-Master's House, she gives only three written by Nannerl to Leopold during the period from Nannerl's marriage to Leopold's death. These three, too, are the only ones noted by the *MBA* commentary. Geffray's listing does not purport to include missing letters whose original existence can only be deduced from unexplicit references in surviving ones, and hence the confusion of *MBA*'s position is not perpetuated. Nevertheless, her compilation should be used with caution, and should not be assumed to be the most complete list possible of missing letters. For although deductions about some of the missing letters are based only on indirect references in surviving ones, most of the deductions can be made with near certainty. Each time Leopold alluded in one of his letters to Nannerl (and he did so in nearly every letter) to doing some shopping for her, it can confidently be assumed that she had written to ask him to buy the articles in question. See Appendix 3 for more detail about the ways in which Nannerl and Leopold communicated after her marriage.

appointment that had eluded him for so long, enabling the whole family to escape from Salzburg. The point on which they differed concerned what Wolfgang would do if the appointment were not forthcoming before it was time to return to Salzburg. For Leopold, the post was essential, and to stay in Vienna without it was out of the question. If Wolfgang did not manage to get one, he was to return to Salzburg, wait patiently (for he was still young), and continue to make a reputation for himself by publishing his compositions and seeking further opera contracts. In this way, his continued service in Salzburg would be sweetened, and in time he would be offered a better job.[6] The cost of living in Vienna was higher than it was in Salzburg, and it is possible that Leopold and Wolfgang had discussed the subject of a minimum safe income in Vienna, and the uncertainty of providing this from a freelance career, before they parted in Munich.[7]

Wolfgang's point of view was rather different. The near-disasters which had beset the family when they had all travelled together under Leopold's guidance could not possibly have made the impression on him that they had on Leopold, for he had then been a child, and not responsible for the success of the trips. Neither was the experience of his journey with Maria Anna from 1777 to 1779 necessarily imprinted on his mind as disastrously as it was on Leopold's. He may, for example, have had quite a different perception from his father's of what might have become of that trip, because he knew better than Leopold the amount of effort he had invested in it. It is possible that his dominant memories of Munich and Paris were the opportunities for earning money, rather than his failure to grasp them. It may be, too, that his idea of the tactics necessary to win a good court appointment elsewhere was more realistic than Leopold's. Leopold's plan depended on using every period of absence to the full, but then retreating to Salzburg if nothing came of it. Once back there, Wolfgang would obviously not be in such a strong position to take advantage of opportunities at other courts. For this reason Wolfgang was more inclined to stay by whatever means in the centre where he

---

[6] That Leopold used Wolfgang's youth to support his argument that he should be patient is suggested by Wolfgang's letter to him of 8 Apr. 1781—*MBA* 587/31–2 (*Letters* 397).

[7] This is suggested by Wolfgang's letter to Leopold of 8 Apr. 1781—*MBA* 587/19–30 (*Letters* 397). Wolfgang was asking Leopold for permission to resign, and claimed that he was sure of being able to earn 'his' thousand thaler in Vienna. The wording suggests that 'my thousand thaler' was a sum they had previously discussed (although it is also possible that it was a stock phrase simply denoting an adequate salary), but the nuance of this phrase is not rendered by the translation in *Letters*. However, if it did denote an actual sum discussed, it is impossible to say what the figure was, because Wolfgang did not indicate what kind of thaler was meant.

thought the opportunities for an appointment lay, because he was confident that this strategem would ensure that he was in the right place when the right time arrived, and that he could earn enough from freelance work while waiting. At any rate, on leaving Munich for Vienna Wolfgang was determined to do his utmost to ensure that he did not have to return to Salzburg.[8]

Colloredo was to spend almost five months in Vienna on this trip, and he took with him a court in miniature. Some of the people, including Count Karl Joseph Felix Arco,[9] Johann Michael Bönike, Johann Franz Thaddäus von Kleinmayr, and a member of the Moll family, were key members of his establishment. Others were lesser servants such as Herr Zetti, who administered the post for the entire household, and the cooks, valets, and musicians. The musicians numbered only three (the castrato Ceccarelli, the violinist Brunetti, and Wolfgang as keyboard player), and they did not accompany Colloredo from the start. He had left Salzburg around 20 January 1781, but Ceccarelli and Brunetti were summoned later, as was Wolfgang from Munich.[10] Not until Wolfgang's arrival on 16 March did Colloredo have the complement of musicians he wanted, by which time he had already been in Vienna about two months. Furthermore, he stayed about six weeks after sending the musicians home, so that he only had their services for about six weeks of his five months' stay. This suggests that they were not intended for his private amusement so much as for the sake of demonstrating the lustre of his court. He kept them on a fairly tight rein, partly for the sake of the reputation of his household, and partly perhaps to hinder their being poached by Viennese employers. They gave a number of private concerts at the house of the Teutonic Order, where Colloredo was living, and (in their capacity of servants of Colloredo) at the houses of some of the Viennese nobility, but were not allowed to appear in concerts other than these. They were expected to show their presence regularly for instructions, and to eat a midday meal with the valets and cooks at the lower of the two tables provided in the house by Colloredo. Their regular salaries were being paid, and each was given 3 ducats (12 fl. 48 kr.) to cover the cost of an

---

[8] Wolfgang to Leopold, 26 May 1781—*MBA* 599/9–11 (*Letters* 406).

[9] One of the sons of the Oberstkämmerer Count Georg Anton Felix Arco—see Fig. 3.

[10] Leopold to Wolfgang, 11 Jan. 1781 (*MBA* 578/35–7; not in *Letters*); and 13 Jan. 1781 (*MBA* 579/5–6; *Letters* 389). It is not known exactly when Ceccarelli and Brunetti arrived in Vienna, but Wolfgang's letter to Leopold of 17 Mar. 1781 (*MBA* 583/43–5; *Letters* 393) suggests that it was not long before Wolfgang's arrival on 16 Mar.

evening meal which had to be bought elsewhere.[11] Their letters home travelled with the rest of the court post.[12]

From the beginning, Wolfgang detested the arrangement, and fretted and fumed against it. His only desire was to get out and about among the Viennese nobility (many of whom he knew), to come to the notice of the emperor, and to set in motion his plan of action for staying in Vienna. His early letters home were filled with bitter complaints: he claimed that Colloredo was neither paying him nor allowing him to earn money by performing in concerts arranged by others; he hated the dining arrangements; he could not bear the company of Brunetti (whom he considered a coarse boor) and the valets; he chafed at the thought that he was supposed to appear in society only as a part of Colloredo's band; and so forth. The last straw came when Colloredo refused to allow him to play in a charity concert for the Tonkünstlersozietät—as far as Wolfgang was concerned, Colloredo's only motive could be spite, and Wolfgang became convinced that he would never, in the short time available to him, come sufficiently to the notice of the people he wanted to impress.[13]

Yet his complaints about money, at any rate, were not quite justified in the context of his position as a salaried employee. Colloredo was paying his salary in Salzburg, though Leopold was apparently drawing it rather than passing it on to Wolfgang.[14] Colloredo was also providing accommodation and board, and was paying modest presents of money for some at least of the concerts the musicians played in. At the first one, for example, he gave each musician 4 ducats (17 fl. 4 kr.), and his father gave them each 5 ducats (21 fl. 20 kr.).[15] Furthermore, the restrictions placed on the musicians were not so great that they were entirely confined to his service; Wolfgang was able to give lessons to Countess Rumbeke.[16] For

---

[11] This assumes that the ducats were imperial ones, being converted for use in Vienna, each one giving 4 fl. 16 kr. (See Ch. 3, n. 1 for the ducat/florin conversions provided by Dexter Edge.) It is not clear how many meals the sum was supposed to provide. Given Colloredo's known desire for economy, Wolfgang's indication (*MBA* 583/39–40; *Letters* 393) that it was a pittance, the fact that it was a supplement to the musicians' salaries, and that they did earn small sums from the concerts arranged by Colloredo, I incline to think that it was a single payment intended to last until they returned home.

[12] These arrangements are described in Wolfgang's letters to Leopold of 17 Mar. 1781 (*MBA* 583; *Letters* 393); and of 24–8 Mar. 1781 (*MBA* 585; *Letters* 395).

[13] These complaints are voiced in Wolfgang's letters to Leopold of 17 Mar. 1781 (*MBA* 583; *Letters* 393); 24–8 Mar. 1781 (*MBA* 585; *Letters* 395); and 4 Apr. 1781 (*MBA* 586; *Letters* 396). The Tonkünstlersozietät was a charity which provided for the distressed widows and children of musicians.

[14] Wolfgang to Leopold, 4 Apr. 1781—*MBA* 586/38 (*Letters* 396).

[15] Wolfgang to Leopold, 24–8 Mar. 1781 (*MBA* 585/133–4; *Letters* 395); and 11 Apr. 1781 (*MBA* 588/30–1; *Letters* 398).

[16] Wolfgang to Leopold, 24–8 Mar. 1781—*MBA* 585/134–5 (*Letters* 395).

any musician largely satisfied with his working conditions, the six weeks in Vienna could have been quite enjoyable. That they were not so for Wolfgang was due to the incompatibility of ostensibly serving Colloredo whilst doing his best to leave him.

The reason Wolfgang was so keen to appear in the charity concert was that it was a very large event which would be attended by all the nobility. His services would be given free, but if he could then arrange to give a concert of his own, he would already have had the chance to advertise his abilities to the public, and would stand a good chance of drawing an excellent audience. He had set about cultivating the patronage of noble ladies, who had kept him at the keyboard following the performances arranged by Colloredo, and he believed that these ladies would have distributed tickets for the concert he wanted to give. Thus he would earn a handsome sum (his projection at this point was 100 ducats, being 426 fl. 40 kr.), and win admirers from potential patrons. After initially refusing to let Wolfgang take part in the charity concert, Colloredo relented, and Wolfgang was delighted with his reception. There was, however, no question of his being allowed to give a Lenten concert of his own.[17]

The Tonkünstlersozietät concert took place on 3 April, two and a half weeks after Wolfgang's arrival in Vienna, but immediately it was over, there was already talk of the return to Salzburg. This must have been agony for Wolfgang, who had only just begun to make himself known, and he was determined not to accept it. Writing to Leopold on Wednesday 4 April to report his successful appearance in public, he said that Colloredo had ordered the musicians to return to Salzburg before Sunday. Anyone wanting to stay a little longer in Vienna might do so, but would no longer receive the archbishop's board and lodging. The musicians' reactions to this news were mixed. Brunetti, who had apparently been out of his element in Vienna, was keen to return; Ceccarelli wanted to stay if he could afford to; and Wolfgang was determined to. He told Leopold that there was nothing to be lost by it, since Leopold would continue to draw two salaries in Salzburg, while Wolfgang would be able to send home his Viennese earnings.[18]

Wolfgang must have hoped that in the extra time allowed him in Vienna, and being freer of Colloredo's demands, he would make the breakthrough he needed; either he would be offered a post, or he would earn so much money that he would be able to persuade Leopold that

---

[17] Wolfgang to Leopold, 4 Apr. 1781—*MBA* 586/7–17 (*Letters* 396).
[18] *MBA* 586/19–56 (*Letters* 396).

temporary freelancing was a viable option. The more he thought about the contrast between the two places, the more he fretted at the idea of returning, and only four days later, on Sunday 8 April, before he could have received an answer from Leopold to his letter of 4 April, he wrote again. This time he asked bluntly if he might resign. His plan was to give a grand concert and take four pupils—in this way he would be able to earn his thousand thaler. He must have known that one of Leopold's arguments against this drastic action would be that he was still young, and that life still held plenty of opportunities for him, because he made the point that it was nevertheless dismal to waste his youth in such a beggarly place as Salzburg.[19]

Leopold's reaction to both Wolfgang's letters was negative. Even the idea of staying on in Vienna a little longer did not meet with his approval.[20] His argument seems to have been that the extra two or three weeks for which Wolfgang wanted to stay would not be sufficient to make his fortune, and that there was therefore no point; while to give a concert during Colloredo's presence in the city would be a pointed insult which would harm Wolfgang in the eyes of the Viennese nobility. He probably suggested that Wolfgang try to play to the emperor before leaving, and he asked if Wolfgang had seen Bonno, the Viennese court Kapellmeister.[21] In short, he would only countenance the idea of staying on if Wolfgang were offered an appointment.

Wolfgang's reaction to Leopold's letter was one of great frustration. He was already building his hopes on Leopold's consent to his resignation, and instead he received a letter forbidding him to stay even temporarily. On 11 April he wrote in strong terms of his feelings. He claimed that when he had performed in one of Colloredo's concerts, for which he had written new music, he had not been rewarded for it. The event had prevented him from accepting an invitation to Countess Thun's, where the emperor had put in an appearance and paid two of the musicians 50 ducats (213 fl. 20 kr.) each. He indicated his extreme disinclination to continue to serve such a miserly, malevolent master for a salary of 400

---

[19] *MBA* 587/21–37 (*Letters* 397).

[20] The evidence for Leopold's disapproval even of a temporarily extended stay in Vienna is as follows. When Wolfgang was writing his letter of 11 Apr. (*MBA* 588; *Letters* 398), he had not received a reply to his 'last' letter, and was still hoping for one (see *MBA* 588/22–4). Since this 'last' letter was that of 8 Apr. (*MBA* 587; *Letters* 397), in which he had first asked if he might resign, his arguments in *MBA* 588 (*Letters* 398) must counter Leopold's reaction to the letter before that, the one of 4 Apr. (*MBA* 586; *Letters* 396), in which he had asked to be allowed to stay temporarily.

[21] I surmise that these were Leopold's arguments from Wolfgang's remarks on 11 Apr. (*MBA* 588/25–64; *Letters* 398) and 9 May (*MBA* 592/59–62; *Letters* 401).

fl. annually when the alternative was to stay in Vienna and earn 1,000 fl. from one concert.[22] He said that it was quite impossible for him to arrange for the emperor to hear him before he left, and that he would not be interested in staying on unless he could give a concert. Although it was true that he could better his Salzburg salary even if his only income came from two pupils, he wanted to give a concert in order to build up a sum of capital which would give him the freedom to select his pupils more carefully. He acknowledged that he would not make his fortune in Vienna in two or three weeks, but insisted that he would never make it in Salzburg, and that it was better to wait for the appointment he wanted on 1,000 fl. annually in Vienna than on 400 in Salzburg. He outlined the prospects of a post in Vienna if he could wait there patiently—these were centred on the death of old Bonno, whom Salieri would succeed, leaving Starzer to advance to Salieri's position, and a vacancy where Starzer's place had been. He indicated that he was in touch with Bonno by telling Leopold that his symphony for the Tonkünstlersozietät concert had been rehearsed in Bonno's presence.[23]

Meanwhile, Leopold had received Wolfgang's letter of 8 April, in which he had asked if he could resign. The answer, predictably, was negative. It is not clear what arguments Leopold used, but his letter seems to have been sympathetic, and to have contained words of comfort and encouragement for Wolfgang's future opportunities. He suggested that Wolfgang give a concert in Linz on the way home, and mentioned the possibility that *Zaide* might be completed for performance in Vienna, and that Wolfgang might make arrangements for this before leaving. This was probably suggested to kindle hope in Wolfgang that he would be able to return to Vienna.[24]

On receipt of this reply, Wolfgang must have known that he had exhausted all legitimate means of securing his resignation with Leopold's consent. On 18 April he wrote in apparent submission to say that he accepted Leopold's case by and large, and would therefore return. He could not yet specify his departure date, but it would not be as early as Sunday.

---

[22] Wolfgang's salary was actually 450 fl., and Braunbehrens (*Mozart in Vienna*, 32) uses the discrepancy as fuel for his argument that Wolfgang was unreliable about money. An alternative explanation of this particular disparity, however, is that Wolfgang was paying another member of the court music 50 fl. annually to carry out his teaching duties in the Kapellhaus. This was the standard fee for these duties when they did not form a contractual part of a salaried appointment —see Hintermaier, 'Hofkapelle', 413.

[23] *MBA* 588 (*Letters* 398).

[24] My conjecture about the contents of Leopold's letter is based on Wolfgang's reply of 18 Apr. 1781—*MBA* 590 (*Letters* 399).

He was lukewarm about the idea of giving a concert in Linz, and said that *Zaide* was not suitable for the Viennese stage, but that the librettist Stephanie was going to give him a different libretto, sending it on to Salzburg if necessary.[25]

As the remaining time in Vienna dwindled, however, Wolfgang increasingly could not reconcile himself to the return. As when he had been expected to return from Paris in 1778, there was a strong incompatibility between his desire to please Leopold and keep the peace, and his disgust at the thought of continued service in Salzburg. But this time he had more control over the situation. There was no longer the question of crippling debt, and he was convinced that he could earn his living in Vienna, and that he would enjoy being there. By the time he wrote his letter home of 28 April, although he was still writing of a joyful reunion with his family, he had embarked on the provocation of Colloredo which was to lead to the rupture. He claimed that in the most recent of Colloredo's private concerts, Colloredo had tried to prevent him from augmenting the orchestra to suit the music he wanted to play, and threatened that if Colloredo did anything else similar, he would resign. He criticized Colloredo heavily, and did not use the usual cypher, stating that he would be delighted if Colloredo could read his letter. If this letter travelled, as usual, with all the court post, this was probably indeed quite a bold step. He also asked for Leopold's permission to return to Vienna the following Lent, with or without the consent of the archbishop, and mentioned again the libretto to be provided by Stephanie. Finally, he said he still had no idea when he and Ceccarelli would be leaving, because they had to await orders.[26] This sentence suggests that Wolfgang was dissembling, however, because earlier in the same letter he had referred Leopold to Ceccarelli for further details about the concert. Thus he must have been expecting Ceccarelli to arrive home before him.

The concert mentioned by Wolfgang had taken place on 27 April, and was envisaged as the last by Colloredo. From this point, he had no further use for Ceccarelli and Wolfgang, and was almost certainly expecting them to leave. If Wolfgang's account is accurate, he was required to vacate the archiepiscopal lodging on 2 May, and on that date he took a room in the Webers' house.[27] He was also given court money to cover

[25] *MBA* 590 (*Letters* 399). (The departure date originally mentioned by Colloredo had already been overstepped by Ceccarelli and Wolfgang.)

[26] *MBA* 591 (*Letters* 400).

[27] The Webers had meanwhile moved from Munich to Vienna, where Aloysia was engaged as a singer. Fridolin had died, and Aloysia was married to the actor Joseph Lange.

his journey home. Though he claimed to Leopold that he had been prolonging his stay only in order to collect money owed to him, the intention is more likely to have been to provoke Colloredo's anger. A week
later, on 9 May, Colloredo sent to ask him to carry a parcel back to
Salzburg, and asked when he was leaving. When Wolfgang replied that
he had intended to go on that same day, but had been prevented by the
fullness of the coach, Colloredo's wrath was unleashed, and Wolfgang
resigned verbally.[28]

But this was by no means the end of the affair. Not until Colloredo
returned to Salzburg in mid-June had it been accepted on both sides that
Wolfgang was no longer in his service, and meanwhile the argument
between Leopold and Wolfgang raged back and forth. From the beginning, Leopold believed that Wolfgang's decision could be retracted, and
was determined that it should be. For more than four weeks, therefore,
Wolfgang was receiving letters intended by every possible means to
break his resolve, and Leopold also enlisted the help of Count Karl Arco
to bring pressure to bear upon his son.

Knowing that Leopold had countered all his previous arguments for
resigning, Wolfgang needed a different reason to present to his father in
justification of his deed. He therefore invoked his wounded honour,
claiming that Colloredo had humiliated him in all three audiences in
Vienna, and that the last occasion, after years of similar abuse, had been
the final straw. After such an insult, he would beg rather than serve such
a master. He also tried to persuade Leopold that he would be more use
to him in Vienna than in Salzburg, and that he would not have taken this
step if he had not been sure he could support himself; and he played down
the effect on Leopold of Colloredo's displeasure by assuring his father that
Colloredo would not be able to deprive Leopold of his salary.[29]

Leopold appears not to have been impressed by the wounded honour
argument, which he probably thought a transparent excuse. The remark
about preferring to beg must surely have struck him as hyperbole, given
its close conjunction to the statement that Wolfgang would not have
taken such a drastic step without being sure that he could earn a living.
Furthermore, Colloredo was notorious for his sarcasm and inability to be
pleasant to those serving him,[30] so that the extent of the offence Wolfgang
claimed to feel on this occasion lacked plausibility. Finally, Leopold knew
from Wolfgang's previous letters that his son had wanted to provoke the

[28] Wolfgang to Leopold, 9 May 1781—*MBA* 592 (*Letters* 401).
[29] Wolfgang to Leopold in two letters of 12 May 1781—*MBA* 593 and 594 (*Letters* 402 and 403).
[30] See Ch. 14, p. 215.

archbishop. Not surprisingly, therefore, his reaction was extremely negative. It is possible that he criticized the fact that Wolfgang had tendered
his resignation in Vienna rather than in Salzburg; reproached Wolfgang
for leaving his father; accused him of bedazzlement with Vienna; disapproved of the fact that Wolfgang was living with the Webers; and hinted
at consolations in Salzburg such as an increase in salary and the prospect
of producing an opera in Prague, if Wolfgang would return.[31]

None of Leopold's arguments had any effect on Wolfgang. He pointed
out that it would have been harder to resign in Salzburg (he seems to
have meant psychologically harder, because of Colloredo's unchallenged
power on his own territory), that the road to Prague was at least as accessible from Vienna as from Salzburg, that an increase in salary would not
have changed the basic working conditions, that he had not left out of
an unreasonable love of Vienna, and that Leopold's remarks about the
Webers (which might have indicated that Leopold believed them to
want to entrap him for one of Aloysia's three sisters) were not true. He
repeated his assertion that he could be more use to Leopold in Vienna
than in Salzburg.[32]

To this letter, Leopold reacted even more strongly. He asserted again
that it had been wrong to resign while in Vienna, and claimed that the
only way for Wolfgang to save his honour was for him to retract; but he
also accused Wolfgang of never having loved him, and of being unwilling to sacrifice any of his pleasures for his father's sake. He also mentioned
a debt which he expected Wolfgang to pay. All this suggests that he
believed Wolfgang had resigned purely for reasons of selfish pleasure. In
response, Wolfgang continued to insist that it had been the insult which
had been the decisive factor—that he would sacrifice his happiness,
health, and life for Leopold, but not his honour. To retract now would
ruin rather than save his honour, and it was much more sensible to
resign in a place where he could earn a living. He claimed he would send
home money to pay the debt mentioned by Leopold, and that the only
pleasure he was indulging in was that of working without being harassed by Colloredo. He outlined his plans for earning money, these being
centred on selling sonatas by subscription, writing an opera, and giving
a concert in Advent. Finally, he remarked that Leopold and Nannerl
would also be better off in Vienna, in that Leopold could earn 400 fl. anywhere, and there were many Viennese houses where Nannerl would be

---

[31] This is surmise based on Wolfgang's letter to Leopold of 16 May 1781—*MBA* 596 (*Letters* 404).

[32] Wolfgang to Leopold, 16 May 1781—*MBA* 596 (*Letters* 404).

a welcome teacher. He therefore urged them to join him if Colloredo should vent his displeasure on Leopold.[33]

Leopold's next sally concentrated on his reasons for thinking Wolfgang unfit for earning a freelance living in Vienna. He pointed out Wolfgang's faults, especially his idleness, procrastination, frivolity, and inability to handle money. He probably expressed scepticism about the subscription, the opera, and the number of pupils Wolfgang could get. Wolfgang acknowledged some of the faults, but claimed that he was a reformed character, and that the traits mentioned by Leopold had been caused by the fact that he had never been happy in Salzburg service, and had therefore been hindered from working steadily. With respect to Leopold's accusation that he could not handle money, he claimed (apparently not taking into account his journey to Paris with Maria Anna) that he had not had enough control over his own money. He enumerated the points on which he found Salzburg unsatisfactory (the poor entertainment, the lack of stimulus for his talent, and the lack of a good theatre), and once again said that he would be able to help Leopold better from Vienna.[34]

By this time it was the end of May, and Leopold, who had probably discussed the affair with old Count Arco in Salzburg, wrote to Arco's son Karl in Vienna to enlist his help in persuading Wolfgang to return. Karl von Arco was an important figure in the dispute, because Wolfgang could not submit his written resignation without Arco's approval, and Arco was apparently unwilling to become involved in this way. This was one reason why the affair dragged on for so long. Following the receipt of Leopold's letter, which had probably mentioned among other things Leopold's fear that the fickle Viennese public would not lionize Wolfgang for long, Arco had two interviews with Wolfgang. Both were unproductive, and it was the second which Wolfgang claimed ended with Arco kicking him out of the antechamber. To the first interview Wolfgang claimed he brought his letter of resignation and the money he wanted to return, his intended travel expenses back to Salzburg. Yet he also claimed that during this interview he had told Arco that he would even now return to Salzburg if a sufficient increase in salary were offered.[35] What could have been his motive for this claim? It is hard to believe that his nerve had been shaken by Leopold's reproaches to such an extent that he was prepared to consider returning after all. More likely is the idea that it was a clumsy attempt to pretend to Leopold that he was prepared to back down for

[33] Wolfgang to Leopold, 19 May 1781—*MBA* 598 (*Letters* 405).
[34] Wolfgang to Leopold, 26 May 1781—*MBA* 599 (*Letters* 406).
[35] Wolfgang to Leopold, 26 May–2 June 1781—*MBA* 601 (*Letters* 407).

his father's sake; there was little danger that he would actually have been offered a salary increase.

In his next letter, giving further details of the first interview with Arco, Wolfgang assured Leopold that Arco had not so much as hinted that Colloredo would persecute Leopold for Wolfgang's offence. Arco had warned Wolfgang of the fickleness of the Viennese audience (though Wolfgang countered this by commenting that this was only true of the theatre, and that as a keyboard player he would always be able to please); and he had told Wolfgang that Colloredo's manner could be harsh to others as well as to Wolfgang. Nothing he said caused Wolfgang to change his mind, and he urged Leopold to look on his resolve to stay in Vienna with a more optimistic eye. He was sure he could make good there, but if not he would consider moving elsewhere. Finally, he promised to send Leopold 30 ducats (128 fl.) with Zetti, and apologized that it was not more.[36]

Meanwhile, Leopold was still trying from Salzburg to change Wolfgang's mind; as long as the letter to Colloredo remained undelivered, there was still hope. He compared Wolfgang with Aloysia Weber—in what respect is not certain, but Wolfgang was deeply offended, and indignantly asserted that she had lived on her parents until she was capable of commanding a good salary, and had then left her widowed mother in the lurch without a kreuzer, and married an actor;[37] he, on the other hand, had no desire but to help his family. Yet again, he insisted that he would be more use to them in Vienna, and again he urged them to come and join him if the situation in Salzburg became intolerable. He described his second interview with Arco, which he regarded as bringing his Salzburg service conclusively to an end. He begged Leopold to stop writing such reproachful letters, because they disturbed his peace of mind and prevented him from composing. Finally, he said that Zetti had left unexpectedly, and that he would therefore send the sum of money he had promised with the mailcoach in a week's time.[38]

This offer was almost certainly insincere, and the true reason for not sending the money was that Wolfgang had found that he could not spare it. The Mozarts never sent valuables in this way, and Wolfgang must have known that Leopold would not want him to do so. Sure enough,

---

[36] Wolfgang to Leopold, 2 June 1781—*MBA* 602 (*Letters* 408).

[37] It is not true that Aloysia did this (see commentary to *MBA* 604/64), but it is not known whether Wolfgang knew the truth about the financial arrangement made for Frau Weber's benefit on Aloysia's marriage.

[38] Wolfgang to Leopold, 9 June 1781—*MBA* 604 (*Letters* 409).

Leopold seems to have written back to suggest some other way of remitting it.[39] By the time Leopold wrote this letter, in mid-June, he had had to accept that Wolfgang's breach with Colloredo was final. Wolfgang regarded Arco's kick as the end of the business, Colloredo was returning to Salzburg, and it seemed that nothing more could be done. Leopold's reproaches petered out for the time being with one last letter mentioning his belief that Wolfgang did not care for him, his fear that Wolfgang would not fulfil his duties as a Christian, and his belief that he still felt responsible for the care of Wolfgang's soul. Once Wolfgang had responded to this by denying the first charge, and defending his sexual morals and his observance of fast days and other Catholic requirements, his letters were used to tell Leopold of his plans and progress.[40]

Unfortunately for him, it was now summer, and there were very few opportunities for earning money. Not having managed to give the Lenten concert he had wanted to, he did not have much capital to see him through until the nobility returned from the country in the autumn. The subscription for his sonatas could make no progress without these people, there were very few potential pupils in town, and his opera plans were also longer-term. He had arrived in Vienna with his mourning clothes, but the mourning was now over, and he needed summer wear, which Leopold was apparently slow to send. He was presumably paying rent to Frau Weber, and otherwise living as economically as possible while preparing for the winter concert season. According to his letters to Leopold, he had only one pupil during this period, Countess Rumbeke, though he charged her a high rate. He claimed that he could subsist on her fees alone, but would prefer to have three pupils. He explained this financial position on 16 June by way of apologizing for the fact that he could not spare more than 30 ducats (128 fl.) at present; even these, however, were not sent.[41]

By the end of June Wolfgang had made the acquaintance of the Auernhammer family, and was teaching the talented daughter Josepha, apparently at least in part in return for some meals. He was asking Leopold regularly for music from Salzburg, some of which was for two keyboards, for performance with Josepha.[42] It must also have been at least as early as this that his flirtation with Constanze Weber was becoming remarked, but he had never yet mentioned her to Leopold. It is also

[39] Wolfgang to Leopold, 16 June 1781—*MBA* 606/12 (*Letters* 411).
[40] Wolfgang to Leopold, 13 June 1781—*MBA* 605 (*Letters* 410).
[41] *MBA* 606 (*Letters* 411).
[42] Wolfgang to Leopold, 27 June 1781—*MBA* 608 (*Letters* 413).

possible that he was flirting with Josepha Auernhammer—rumours on this topic began to circulate too.[43]

Directly after resigning, Wolfgang had sent Nannerl a present of ribbons. After she had written to thank him, and to ask whether he could send her any keyboard music, he wrote her an affectionate letter on 4 July, assuring her that he would be delighted to fulfil any commissions she had. He wished she could experience the Viennese theatre, which was of course far superior to anything they had had in Salzburg, asked for Salzburg news (in particular about the progress of her friendship with Franz Armand d'Ippold), and promised her some music—two violin and keyboard sonatas which would be new to her, and three sets of variations.[44]

Wolfgang's allusion to d'Ippold was the first explicit reference to him as a suitor of Nannerl's, though he had been known to the family since at least 1777. Since Nannerl's diary had begun to name him as an afternoon visitor in the late autumn of 1780, just after Wolfgang had left to write *Idomeneo* in Munich, this period might have marked the beginning of the particular friendship between him and Nannerl. He was some twenty years older than she, and was a captain in the imperial and royal army. In Salzburg he occupied the position of director of the Virgilianum from 1775 and, since this was housed in a wing of Holy Trinity Church, was a close neighbour of the Mozarts. At the end of 1777 he was named Hofkriegsrat ('court war councillor'), which meant that he was on the defence committee. By the time he died in 1790, he was high in Colloredo's favour.[45] Knowledge of his friendship with Nannerl is extremely limited. They apparently wanted to marry, but for some reason could not. During the summer of 1783, when Wolfgang and his bride Constanze were to visit Salzburg, Nannerl was still seeing d'Ippold frequently, but a year later she married Johann Baptist Berchtold von Sonnenburg. How this situation developed is unknown. Many biographers have suggested that Leopold put an end to the romance with d'Ippold, variously because d'Ippold's position as director of a boarding school was incompatible with marriage,[46] he did not earn enough money,[47] or he

---

[43] See pp. 366–7 below.

[44] Wolfgang to Nannerl, 4 July 1781—*MBA* 610 (*Letters* 415). The two sonatas which would be new to Nannerl were K. 376 and K. 379, and the variations were K. 352, K. 359, and K. 360.

[45] See H. Klein, 'Zur Herkunft Franz Armand d'Ippolds', *MM* 7 (1958), 2–3, and F. Breitinger, 'Mozart Nannerls unglücklicher Verehrer', *Salzburger Volksblatt* (9–10 Aug. 1958), 5.

[46] Cf. Klein, 'Franz Armand d'Ippold', 3.

[47] Cf. Breitinger, 'Mozart Nannerls unglücklicher Verehrer'. Breitinger called Leopold the 'practically despotic family dictator'.

was not good enough for Nannerl;[48] one author suggests that Leopold wanted to reassert his authority within the family, having recently been defied by Wolfgang.[49] None of these suggestions adduces any hard evidence, and while important questions (for example about d'Ippold's salary, whether or not he was obliged to live in at the Virgilianum, and whether or not he asked permission to marry) remain unanswered, no further progress will be made.[50]

On an unknown date in the summer of 1781, but probably soon after Wolfgang's enquiry on 4 July about her friendship with d'Ippold, Nannerl apparently mentioned practical hindrances to the affair. Her letter remained unanswered until mid-September; the only communication with her that Wolfgang found time for in the intervening period was a cursory greeting for her name-day.[51]

The summer of 1781 was a bad time for Leopold and Nannerl. When they returned from Munich in March with Heinrich Marchand, they must have been expecting Wolfgang either to release them from Salzburg by gaining an appointment in Vienna, or to return to cheer their company and help with the extra teaching involved because of Heinrich's arrival. Instead, they had to endure the protracted resignation affair, which finished with them both tied as firmly as ever to Salzburg, but without Wolfgang. Very soon after the return of Colloredo in mid-June, rumours began to circulate in Salzburg about Wolfgang and women, perhaps in particular Constanze Weber; they were apparently spread by Moll, who had been in Vienna at the same time as Wolfgang.[52] Before the middle of July, Leopold was demanding that Wolfgang leave the Webers' house, and Wolfgang agreed to do so, acknowledging that there was gossip about his love life, but denying that he had any intention of marrying.[53] For the rest of July and the whole of August, Leopold was uncertain where Wolfgang was living because Wolfgang was evasive about it, but in the course of the correspondence it emerged that there was also

[48] Cf. commentary to *MBA* 387/115.   [49] Cf. Rieger, *Nannerl Mozart*, 182–3.

[50] Particularly frustrating is the brevity with which Klein discusses this question; Klein was for many years the director of the Salzburger Landesarchiv, and had unsurpassed knowledge of the documents of Salzburg's history. As far as I know, it has not been suggested that d'Ippold was refused permission to marry by Colloredo, but this hypothesis would be at least as reasonable as the Leopold-as-despot one.

[51] Wolfgang to Nannerl, 25 July 1781—*MBA* 612/57–66 (*Letters* 417). On 19 Sept. 1781 (*MBA* 625/12–8; *Letters* 425), Wolfgang apologized to Nannerl for not having answered her letter about d'Ippold.

[52] Wolfgang to Leopold, 13 July 1781—*MBA* 611/18–23 (*Letters* 416).

[53] Wolfgang to Leopold, 13 July 1781 (*MBA* 611/8–23; *Letters* 416); and 25 July 1781 (*MBA* 612/4–18; *Letters* 417).

gossip about him and Josepha Auernhammer.[54] Added to this were the fact that Wolfgang never did send the 30 ducats (128 fl.) he had been promising Leopold, and the difficulty Nannerl was experiencing in her relationship with d'Ippold. The last straw came some time in late July or early August, when Nannerl fell seriously ill. Although almost nothing is known about her ailment, Leopold must have had to nurse her, as he had in the winter while Wolfgang had been in Munich. The combined worries affected his own health, and he suffered dizzy spells.[55] Early in September he unleashed a bitter attack on Wolfgang, in response to Wolfgang's admission of rumours about him and Josepha. He accused Wolfgang of leading a life of pleasure in Vienna, and berated him for not having sent the money he had promised, and for neglecting his family. He did not, however, mention Nannerl's illness at this stage.

Wolfgang attempted a dignified reply, in which he reproached Leopold for heeding too much other people's comments on his activities, and begged him to regard the differences between them as private, rather than discussing them with others. He had in a previous letter tried to explain away the fact that he had still not sent the money he had promised Leopold,[56] but now at last he frankly admitted that he had not got it. He denied that he was devoting himself to amusement, and expressed the hope that his affairs would improve in the winter. If so, he would certainly not forget Leopold; if not, he was thinking of going to Paris.[57]

Though the remark about Paris seemed fairly casual, it must have indicated to Leopold that Wolfgang was not only earning nothing to speak of at present, but also that he was not entirely confident about doing well in winter. By the time Wolfgang wrote this letter, he had at last moved into a new lodging. He was working on the opera (*Die Entführung*), whose libretto had been provided by Stephanie, and was hoping that it would be performed during the projected visit to Vienna of Grand Duke Paul of Russia. Around the middle of September, he received letters from both Leopold and Nannerl. Leopold reported Nannerl's serious illness and his own dizziness, and Nannerl reproached Wolfgang for not having answered her letters. Whatever the precise contents of their letters were, they seem to have suggested to Wolfgang a link between Nannerl's ailment and her unhappiness about d'Ippold. It is thus against this

[54] Wolfgang to Leopold, 22 Aug. 1781—*MBA* 619/48–82 (*Letters* 421).
[55] Wolfgang to Nannerl, 19 Sept. 1781 (*MBA* 625/4–7; *Letters* 425); and Wolfgang to Leopold after 19 Sept. 1781 (*MBA* 626/5–7; *Letters* 425*).
[56] Wolfgang to Leopold, 25 July 1781—*MBA* 612/45–56 (*Letters* 417).
[57] Wolfgang to Leopold, 5 Sept. 1781—*MBA* 621 (*Letters* 423).

background of unhappiness, illness, and anxiety on the part of Leopold and Nannerl that Wolfgang's reply to these letters must be read.

On 19 September Wolfgang wrote the letter which was meant to encourage Nannerl, d'Ippold, and Leopold to move to Vienna to join him. First he expressed his shock that Nannerl had been ill for some time without his having been told about it. Then he expressed his belief that her 'constantly recurring indispositions' would come to an end if she could marry soon. He then apologized for not having answered her earlier letters, adding that he had begun a reply to one, but had abandoned it because he had had no firm suggestion to make (this seems to have been a reference to the way in which his progress in Vienna might help Nannerl). Next he outlined his prospects, which were still very uncertain —all he could tell her was that he was sure his opera would be well received, and that once the winter was over he would know better how he stood. He then expressed his belief that d'Ippold and Nannerl would never have any future in Salzburg, and that d'Ippold should exert himself to get employment in Vienna. If he was willing to do this, Wolfgang would help through his Viennese connections. Nannerl and d'Ippold would then be able to marry, and Nannerl would also be able to earn money in Vienna by playing in concerts and giving lessons. The combined incomes of Wolfgang, Nannerl, and d'Ippold would be sufficient to support Leopold in his retirement, so that they could all live 'really happily together' in Vienna.[58]

No documentary evidence reveals what the reaction of Nannerl and Leopold was to this letter, which was meant to be so beguiling, and to offer Nannerl all the ingredients for her future happiness—marriage to the man she wanted, the company of her father and brother, and professional activity in the vibrant city of Vienna. But the overwhelming likelihood is that it can only have increased her unhappiness by offering a fairy-tale scenario which was certain to be rejected by Leopold. Wolfgang's experiences in Vienna to date had certainly not shown that he could make a living there—he had failed to send home a sum of money he had promised, was evidently struggling to make ends meet, and was talking about going to Paris if his affairs did not improve. Furthermore, Leopold doubted whether his character was suited to a freelance way of life. Any prospects d'Ippold might have had in Vienna were at this stage entirely imaginary, while Nannerl's putative earnings were sure to be uncertain if she married, because the presumption would be that she

---

[58] *MBA* 625 (*Letters* 425).

would enter the vulnerable state of repeated pregnancy and childbirth. Thus, though Leopold had a strong desire to retire, to leave Salzburg, to be with Wolfgang, to arrange a marriage for Nannerl, and to provide her with a public platform, these considerations must have been overridden by the thought that if he did as Wolfgang suggested, the family would lose the only secure income it had.

Though nothing came of Wolfgang's suggestion, Nannerl and d'Ippold continued to see each other at least as late as 1783, presumably in the hope that something would turn up. The main hope of Leopold and Nannerl must still have been that Wolfgang would win an appointment in Vienna. With the nobility returning from the country, the writing of the opera well under way (as Leopold thought), and the projected visit of the grand duke, there were certainly more opportunities than there had been during the summer.

Thus for a few weeks things simmered down again while Wolfgang put his mind to taking advantage of the changing situation. He sent home the first act of the opera, and in another letter gave a long description of it; he mentioned how much faster he could now compose than formerly; he gave a concert involving music for two keyboards with Josepha Auernhammer; he saw the appearance of his violin and keyboard sonatas; and he was courting imperial attention by a number of means related to the grand duke's visit.[59]

Grand Duke Paul was married to Princess Sophia Dorothea of Württemberg, who had a 14-year-old sister, Princess Elisabeth. Elisabeth was betrothed to the emperor's nephew Franz, and was about to enter a convent in Vienna until her marriage. The visit of the grand duke thus coincided with the arrival in Vienna of members of the Württemberg house accompanying Elisabeth, and both parties were to be entertained in grand fashion by the Viennese court. Leopold must have calculated the opportunities that might exist for Wolfgang once the visiting dignitaries reached Vienna, for he told Wolfgang something about them which he hoped Wolfgang might be able to make use of.[60] Wolfgang had originally hoped that *Die Entführung* would be ready for performance before the visitors, but works by Gluck were performed instead. However, Archduke Maximilian summoned Wolfgang to play before the Württemberg family,

---

[59] Wolfgang to Leopold in two letters after 19 Sept. 1781 (*MBA* 626 and 627; *Letters* 425* and 425**); 26 Sept. 1781 (*MBA* 629; *Letters* 426); 6 Oct. 1781 (*MBA* 631; *Letters* 427); 17 Nov. 1781 (*MBA* 641; *Letters* 433); 24 Nov. 1781 (*MBA* 644; *Letters* 434); and 5 Dec. 1781 (*MBA* 646; *Letters* 435).

[60] Wolfgang to Leopold, 15 Dec. 1781—*MBA* 648/11–12 (*Letters* 436).

and Wolfgang subsequently prepared some Russian folk-songs on which he could improvise variations, for performance before the grand duke. These events presumably brought him in some money, though he did not mention it to Leopold; but his main hope was that the emperor would appoint him to the salaried post of keyboard teacher to Princess Elisabeth. He would then have some secure income.

All the time Wolfgang was involved in these preparations, however, he was becoming more and more involved with Constanze Weber. He said nothing of her to Leopold, but all Vienna knew what was going on, and rumours had even reached his cousin in Augsburg.[61] It could only be a matter of time before Leopold heard the latest, and Wolfgang must have known it. Writing on 10 November for Leopold's name-day, he seems to have tried to hint at the subject which was so difficult for him to mention outright, by saying that he was sure that Leopold would be happy at anything that made Wolfgang happy.[62] And on 5 December, when he expressed his hope that he would be appointed keyboard teacher to Princess Elisabeth, he made an enigmatic reference to his immortal soul, saying that it was because he recognized its importance that he had not been able to carry out Leopold's wishes precisely as Leopold intended.[63] He had probably already been forced by Constanze's guardian to sign an agreement in which he promised to marry her within three years, and he must have been quailing at the thought that Leopold was going to discover this, for Wolfgang's last statement on the subject of women had been to the effect that nothing could be more disadvantageous to him than a wife. Writing this mysterious little sentence was his method of paving the way for the inevitable full confession.

---

[61] Wolfgang to Maria Anna Thekla Mozart, 23 Oct. 1781—*MBA* 635 (*Letters* 429).
[62] *MBA* 640 (*Letters* 432).   [63] *MBA* 646/58–62 (*Letters* 435).

22

Wolfgang's Marriage

FROM Leopold's point of view, the most interesting piece of news in Wolfgang's letter of 5 December 1781 must have been the prospect of his becoming keyboard teacher to Princess Elisabeth of Württemberg, because this would be a salaried position which could form the secure financial foundation allowing him and Nannerl to join Wolfgang in Vienna. On 12 December he replied, mentioning the Württemberg prospects, and also asking for an explanation of the mysterious passage about the way in which Wolfgang had (or had not) carried out Leopold's wishes.[1]

Unfortunately, by the time his letter reached Wolfgang, the emperor had chosen Salieri as teacher to the princess. According to Wolfgang, writing on 15 December, this was because Salieri could teach singing as well as keyboard playing. Wolfgang was thus forced into the admission of his love for Constanze Weber without the advantage of being able to report simultaneously that he now had a salaried imperial position. He began by saying that he was sending a watch, *Idomeneo*, the six newly printed Sonatas for keyboard and violin, the Sonata for two keyboards (probably K. 448, which he had written specially for the concert he had recently given with Josepha Auernhammer), and the cadenzas (probably to the Concerto for two keyboards, K. 365, which he and Josepha had played at the same concert). He then passed fairly quickly over the disappointing news about Princess Elisabeth, saying merely that Archduke Maximilian had recommended him to her, but that the emperor was besotted with Salieri. Next he poured out the reasons why he wanted to marry, claiming both that he did not feel fulfilled as a single man and could not live the life of a libertine, and that marriage was an economical choice for someone like himself, who liked domestic peace and was not used to attending to practical affairs. He characterized Constanze as the martyr of her family, doing most of the work but receiving the least

[1] The contents of Leopold's letter can be partly surmised from Wolfgang's to Leopold of 15 Dec. 1781—*MBA* 648/3–14 (*Letters* 436).

371

reward. Praising her housekeeping and good sense, and playing down her physical attractions, he specifically stated that he believed he would be better off on the same income with her than without her. Though he claimed to have taken into account extra expenses necessarily connected with marriage (he probably meant above all pregnancy and childbirth), he said that these could be anticipated and saved for. He insisted that they had not been in love at the time of his resignation, and expressed his desire to marry her once he had a certain income, in order to save her from her situation. He promised half of this fixed income to Leopold, and hoped that Leopold would give his consent once the income was secured.[2]

One of the banes of Wolfgang's adult life was that he and Leopold had many mutual friends and acquaintances, and for all that they lived three or four post days away from each other, Leopold could often receive as much news as he wanted of Wolfgang from third parties. Just at the time that Wolfgang was defensively confessing part of the situation he was in, Leopold received news from Peter Winter (a Munich musician currently studying with Salieri in Vienna) that Wolfgang had gone much further with Constanze than he had admitted to Leopold.[3] According to Winter, Wolfgang had made a formal promise to marry Constanze, but this was apparently not the worst that Leopold had to hear. Wolfgang's life-style was probably described as dissolute, and debts incurred by him might also have been mentioned. Winter apparently further claimed that Wolfgang was despised by the court and all the Viennese aristocracy, and that Constanze was a 'trollop'.[4]

Leopold's reaction to Wolfgang's letter and Winter's report must have been one of shock, dismay, and bitter disappointment. Just when he had been led to hope that Wolfgang might be about to make a break-through by being appointed to teach the princess, he had that hope, and with it the further one that he and Nannerl might soon be able to join Wolfgang in Vienna, shattered. Even more ominous to the prospects for him and Nannerl, however, must have been the mention of marriage. Having struggled himself for years with the expenses of a young family, a sickly wife, and seven pregnancies and confinements, not to mention the ailments of the children, he cannot have been impressed by

---

[2] *MBA* 648 (*Letters* 436).

[3] It is not clear how Winter's news reached Leopold, but the suggestion in the commentary to *MBA* 651/3–4 that Winter had been passing through Salzburg on his way from Vienna to Munich seems very plausible.

[4] Winter's remarks are surmised from Wolfgang's response on 22 Dec. 1781—*MBA* 651 (*Letters* 438).

Wolfgang's statement that the expenses brought by marriage could be anticipated and saved for. He knew that Constanze was far younger than Maria Anna had been at the time he had married her, and that she could have some twenty years of childbearing before her. Furthermore, he was familiar enough with Wolfgang's unrealistic financial projections to realize that he was being offered half of nothing. To cap it all, Winter's report must have unnerved him by planting the fear that if the court and the aristocracy really did detest Wolfgang, he would certainly never prosper in Vienna.

Leopold apparently put on a brave face before Winter, and did not condemn Wolfgang to him. But he also wrote directly to Wolfgang to tell him what Winter had said, and to ask for the whole truth about the promise to marry Constanze. When Leopold's letter arrived, Wolfgang was in the middle of writing an exceptionally friendly letter to Nannerl. He had already added a postscript for her benefit to his last letter to Leopold, making it clear that the music he was sending was mainly intended for her.[5] Now he mentioned the music again, and promised more when he had had some variations copied. He also told her that he could easily find her a lodging if she wanted to come and visit him in Vienna. He discussed the plays which she had been seeing in Salzburg, and whose titles she had sent him, and he relayed news about their acquaintances in Böhm's troupe of players. He asked about the shooting company, and sent greetings to d'Ippold.[6] This letter was apparently the first (apart from the above-mentioned postscript) he had written to her since 19 September, when he had outlined his plan for her and d'Ippold to come to live in Vienna with Leopold, and it has the air of design about it. It was not the first time, nor was it to be the last, that he was to write with particular tenderness when there was some way in which Nannerl could help him, or when he wanted to boost his credit at home. After Maria Anna's death in Paris, he had promised to send all manner of music, at a time when he badly needed to divert attention from the probable neglect of his family; the fact that the promise was not kept calls into question the sincerity of the offer. Throughout his courtship of Constanze, he was to send Nannerl all sorts of fashion trifles in which Constanze had a hand, in order to try to win his sister over to his bride, and probably also to induce her to intercede for him with Leopold. After Leopold's death, Wolfgang was to write to Nannerl with great affection at a time when he badly needed

---

[5] *MBA* 648/96–107 (*Letters* 436a).
[6] Wolfgang to Nannerl, 15–22 Dec. 1781—*MBA* 649 (*Letters* 437).

her co-operation so that he could inherit cash from his father's estate.[7] And he was to write her one of his increasingly rare letters just at the time when he wanted her to flatter Michael Haydn and get some music out of him.[8] In short, his apparently most thoughtful letters were written when there was an ulterior motive.

However this may be, the interruption to his letter to Nannerl occasioned by the receipt of the letter from Leopold caused him to fulminate against Winter and terminate his own letter abruptly. He immediately began a reply to Leopold in which he expressed his fury at Winter's 'lies', and put his side of the story. The formal promise to marry Constanze within three years (or failing that, to pay her 300 fl. annually) had been made at the insistence of her guardian Thorwart, who believed that she was already compromised. Wolfgang denied to Leopold that anything improper had taken place, and apologized for not having told him about the matter earlier—he said that he had not done so because he had wanted to obtain his certain income first. He then briefly indicated that Winter himself was immoral, and then launched into a description of his daily routine, which involved rising at six in the morning and composing until ten, and then giving lessons for the rest of the morning. He told Leopold his charges, which were high, and claimed that he owed nothing to anyone. He challenged Leopold to write to a number of members of the nobility to discover whether he was detested by the aristocracy in general, and gave him the address of Baroness von Waldstätten, who could also vouch for Constanze's character. He said that he had recently been praised by the emperor, who had sent him 50 ducats (213 fl. 20 kr.) for a joint appearance with Clementi, and he begged Leopold to believe that things would get steadily better.[9]

Early in January 1782 Leopold responded to this letter, and apparently expressed some sympathy for Wolfgang's predicament in the matter of the promise to marry. This did not mean that he was reconciled to the event, however. He asked for more details about Thorwart, and expressed disapproval of him for not having kept the matter confidential. He accused Frau Weber of keeping a disorderly house, and went so far as to suggest that mother and guardian should be publicly shamed as

---

[7] See Ch. 31 for more details about the settlement of Leopold's estate. Hildesheimer neatly and amusingly links the thousand kisses and greetings which Wolfgang sent Nannerl in the last of three affectionate letters considered in this chapter with the thousand florins he was hoping to get from her after the auction of Leopold's effects. See W. Hildesheimer, *Mozart*, trans. M. Faber (London, 1985), 210–11.

[8] Wolfgang to Nannerl, 2 Aug. 1788—*MBA* 1082 (*Letters* 557).

[9] Wolfgang to Leopold, 22–6 Dec. 1781—*MBA* 651 (*Letters* 438).

seducers of youth. It is possible that he also asked about the prospects of a stable income.[10]

In his next two letters, Wolfgang admitted that Thorwart had acted with unnecessary strictness, but denied that the Weber house had been opened freely to him in order to entice him into the situation he was now in. He professed to be hurt that Leopold could believe that he could frequent such a house, and dismissed the public shaming idea as exaggeration. He claimed that the emperor had spoken to him about his marriage, and he seemed to think that he might be on the brink of obtaining an appointment from him (despite the fact that from the emperor's point of view, his marriage was probably a negative factor). He mentioned the Lenten academy he hoped to give in the theatre, and told Leopold that he would produce scenes from *Idomeneo*, and play a keyboard concerto and then improvise. Next he outlined three possible sources of steady income which he had in mind. The first was that Prince Liechtenstein wanted to form a wind band, and Wolfgang was in hope that he might be appointed its composer—it would not pay much, but he would insist that it was a lifelong commitment. The second was an imperial appointment, of which Wolfgang had some hope—he was seeing the emperor's musical valet, Strack, in order to boost his chances. The third was a possible future appointment with Archduke Maximilian, who seemed very taken with him and would one day be elector of Cologne—the problem here was that he would not be able to offer any appointments until he had actually become so. Wolfgang then indicated that if he could have it in writing from God that he would not become ill, he would marry Constanze immediately, because his freelance income was sufficient for the purpose. He explained the new payment arrangement he had instigated for the lessons he gave—whereas previously he had allowed his pupils to pay him in twelve-lesson blocks (so that he received nothing if they cancelled a lesson), he now tried to get them to pay him a fixed sum each month. He claimed that he could earn 6 ducats (25 fl. 36 kr.) per pupil per month in this way, that he already had three pupils, and that he only needed four on these terms to yield enough for a married couple to live on in a quiet way. Additional earnings would come from writing an opera each year, from academies, from having music printed, and from subscription dissemination of compositions. The only snag was that illness would cause all these income possibilities to be interrupted. However,

---

[10] Leopold's comments can be surmised from Wolfgang's letter of 16 Jan. 1782—*MBA* 659 (*Letters* 441).

Wolfgang indicated that he would not wait for ever for a definite income, because it was imperative that he should 'save' Constanze.[11]

Leopold's next remarks seem to have been critical in some way of Constanze, and it seems likely that he had suggested that she was herself responsible for the situation she found herself in. To this, Wolfgang responded by begging Leopold not to think so badly of her—he could never love her if she were as Leopold described. He hinted, however, that Constanze's mother was a trouble-maker. He also reassured Leopold that *Die Entführung* would be given after Easter, and asked him for the libretto to *Idomeneo*, so that he could plan his Lenten academy.[12]

By now, it was the end of January 1782, and Leopold had gone to Munich for the Carnival. He presumably took Heinrich Marchand with him, for a reunion with his family; Nannerl, however, stayed at home. It is not known why she did not go too, but d'Ippold may have been the main reason. It was thus Nannerl, rather than Leopold, who sent the libretto Wolfgang had asked for, and she also complained that Wolfgang did not answer her letters, and suggested that he found hers tiresome. She may also have mentioned Wolfgang's neglect of her and Leopold. In response, Wolfgang claimed that he did care about her, and would never forget her and Leopold, but that he simply did not have time to write much. He compared his routine in Vienna with theirs in Salzburg, rather provocatively suggesting that they had so little to do that they had time to write whole litanies; he, however, with not a kreuzer of fixed income, had to work every hour of the day in order to support himself. He ran through his routine for her benefit—rising at six, composing from seven till nine in the morning, giving lessons from nine till one, dining (often out), writing again from five or six till nine (unless he was out at an academy), visiting Constanze from nine till ten-thirty or eleven (depending on her mother's unpleasantness), and composing again until one in the morning.[13]

One of the things Wolfgang never learnt to do, despite all Leopold's exhortations, was to write his letters in a more measured way. Especially once he had moved to Vienna, they give the impression of having been written hurriedly, just in time to catch the post, whereas Leopold tended to write a little news daily, and only had to finish off his letters on post day. Wolfgang's letter-writing habits belie his words about how much he thought of his family, suggesting rather that it was only the stimulus of Leopold's expectation and the departing mailcoach that induced him

---

[11] Wolfgang to Leopold, 16 and 23 Jan. 1782—*MBA* 659 and 660 (*Letters* 441 and 442).
[12] Wolfgang to Leopold, 30 Jan. 1782—*MBA* 661 (*Letters* 443).
[13] Wolfgang to Nannerl, 13 Feb. 1782—*MBA* 663 (*Letters* 444).

to write at all. On the other hand, he frankly admitted how much he depended on receiving letters from them, and always fretted if they did not come, or were too short.[14] How he could behave in such a professedly unreciprocal way is puzzling—was it simply disorganization, did he lack the sympathetic imagination to understand how much pleasure his letters gave them, or was he so self-absorbed that it came naturally to him to take but not to give? Perhaps there were elements of all three factors in his character; at any rate, as later chapters will indicate, Leopold and Nannerl seem to have become increasingly disenchanted with him as time went on and he did not change.

There is a striking gap in the surviving correspondence after this letter to Nannerl of 13 February and before Wolfgang's next letter to Leopold of 23 March, but evidently Leopold had meanwhile returned from Munich, bringing not only Heinrich but also his elder sister Margarethe ('Gretl'), and had written to Wolfgang to tell him this. When Wolfgang replied, he enclosed a newly composed Rondo (K. 382) for the Keyboard Concerto in D (K. 175), but insisted that it was for Nannerl only, and that not even Heinrich and Gretl should play it. He also sent two more copies of his sonatas, two caps made by Constanze for Nannerl, and sundry other trinkets, and asked for the cap-box to be filled with more of his Salzburg music when it was returned.[15]

❧

When Leopold had accepted the charge of young Heinrich Marchand during the Carnival of 1781, it must have been in the expectation that Wolfgang would share the extra work of supervising his studies, since Leopold had always envisaged that the family would stay together. After Wolfgang broke with Colloredo, his salary was lost to the family, as it had been in 1777, and so, although Leopold (and probably Nannerl too) had to bear more of the work of teaching Heinrich, the income he brought with him must have been even more welcome than it otherwise would have been. Presumably his first year had been reasonably successful, since Leopold was willing to add Gretl to the arrangement in 1782. The apprentice-type training of the Marchands is not well documented, because though Leopold must have written about Heinrich and Gretl

---

[14] There are a number of passages supporting this assertion, but perhaps the most clear-cut is his letter to Nannerl of 2 Aug. 1788 (*MBA* 1082; *Letters* 557), in which Wolfgang specifically stated that he disliked writing letters, but loved receiving them.

[15] *MBA* 665 (*Letters* 445).

to Wolfgang, his letters to Wolfgang from 1781 are lost. The children ceased to live as Leopold's pupils when Nannerl married in 1784, presumably because the arrangement could not function without her. However, Heinrich was later to return to Salzburg as a court violinist, and he lived with Leopold again from March 1786 until May 1787. During this period Leopold was corresponding with Nannerl, and since he still evidently thought of Heinrich as a pupil, his letters to her give some information about the type of arrangement that probably existed earlier. This, together with knowledge of the family routines, enables an attempt to be made at reconstructing the experience of being a resident pupil with the Mozarts.

It is not known what Leopold was paid by Heinrich's parents. In 1777 Maria Anna had told him that 200 fl. annually was not too much to charge for a similar arrangement involving the teenage daughter of Herr von Hamm, but she was from a noble family and was expecting higher-quality food than the Mozarts enjoyed themselves.[16] The Marchand arrangement was much more congenial to Leopold, because Heinrich and Gretl (and later their young cousin Johanna ('Hanchen') Brochard) lived in every respect as members of the family. They had their own rooms in the Dancing-Master's House,[17] but neither expected nor received any special dietary treatment. When the price of beef rose by 1 kreuzer, Leopold bought lower-grade meat at the older price, because Heinrich was not fussy,[18] and Heinrich was also to be quite willing to eat up any gruel left by Nannerl's baby, 'Leopoldl'.[19]

The Marchand parents were both actors, and had once been involved with travelling troupes of players. The children had thus been steeped in itinerant theatrical life during early childhood. By the time Heinrich came to Salzburg, however, his father Theobald was theatrical director to the elector Palatine, and was earning a good salary. He and Leopold struck up a warm friendship, and although Wolfgang was to express his fear to Leopold that Heinrich's moral failings (especially his precocious interest in sex) were caused by a faulty upbringing,[20] Leopold found the parents to be good, caring, and deserving of the respect of their children. Leopold's attitude to people who worked on the stage was ambivalent; on the one hand, he enjoyed being able to share his literary interests

---

[16] Maria Anna to Leopold, 7 Dec. 1777—*MBA* 386/52–7 (*Letters* 256a).
[17] Leopold to Nannerl, 22 May 1786—*MBA* 959/32–9 (not in *Letters*).
[18] Leopold to Nannerl, 26 Jan. 1787—*MBA* 1026/55–61 (not in *Letters*).
[19] Leopold to Nannerl, 17 Mar. 1786—*MBA* 940/35–6 (not in *Letters*).
[20] Wolfgang to Leopold, 4 July 1781—*MBA* 609/35–57 (*Letters* 414). Wolfgang was probably responding to some comment of Leopold's about Heinrich—see the undated fragment *MBA* 1203 (6) (not in *Letters*).

with them, but on the other was wary of what he considered the loose morals to which he thought they were prone.

Leopold seems to have treated Heinrich, Gretl, and Hanchen as if they were his own children, and their moral education was of paramount importance. He did not want to be seen as a killjoy, but when Heinrich was invited to dine at the Kapellhaus, in return for having taught there, Leopold accompanied him to make sure that he did not drink too much. He was also pleased when Heinrich witnessed the death of the violinist Brunetti, because such an event was worth ten sermons.[21] Leopold's care of the Marchands was later acknowledged by Gretl when she called him 'dearest Papa'.[22]

Since the children lived as part of the family, they must have fitted into the routines of Leopold and Nannerl. This meant that they rose early, and perhaps went to church with Nannerl. They must then have worked all morning. Leopold was teaching Heinrich to play the violin and keyboard (he became good enough to perform as a soloist on both instruments), to compose, and to become competent in French, Italian, and Latin. Gretl learnt to sing and to play the keyboard. She probably shared at least some of the language lessons, and Leopold encouraged her, too, to compose, overseeing for her the publication with Torricella in Vienna of her first sonatas.[23]

Heinrich was apparently a completely different character from Gretl —he was incurably lazy, and had to be forced to work and practise.[24] Some idea of the grounding he must have been given in violin playing (many procedural points of which were also applicable to keyboard playing) can be gleaned from Leopold's *Violinschule*, which stressed among other things complete mastery of one step before the next was attempted.[25] As far as the non-musical aspects of the children's education were concerned, Leopold believed that young people's minds should be trained by the reading of good books, and presumably encouraged his charges to read books in French and Italian once they had reached an adequate level. The Marchand parents sent books from Munich on loan, and these were read by everyone in the house in turn, and were later even sent out to Nannerl and her acquaintances in St Gilgen.

[21] Leopold to Nannerl, 29 Dec. 1786—*MBA* 1015/6–27 (not in *Letters*).
[22] Leopold to Nannerl, 12 Nov. 1784—*MBA* 824/39–43 (not in *Letters*).
[23] Leopold to Nannerl, 14 Jan. and 27 Oct. 1785—*MBA* 835/23–31 and 892/110–12 (not in *Letters*).
[24] Leopold to Nannerl, 9 Mar. 1787—*MBA* 1038/6–26 (not in *Letters*). See also Ch. 2 for complaints by Leopold that Heinrich was too little interested in learning to play sensitively.
[25] See Ch. 2 for details of Leopold's pedagogical methods as shown by the *Violinschule*.

In addition to the formal tuition, Heinrich and Gretl must have helped out where necessary, copying music, and later undertaking the teaching of younger pupils for Leopold if he was ill or busy. Gretl may also have helped Nannerl with household duties. The afternoons must usually have been devoted to the family entertainments of shooting, card parties, the theatre, walking, and music-making, and the Marchands were included in any pleasure outings. When their parents came to visit, the house was full of music, and special efforts were made to show off what they had learnt, and to gather together the necessary forces to do justice to the music performed—much of which, of course, was by Wolfgang. These occasions were enormous social and musical jamborees involving a whirl of activity, as Nannerl's diary for the summer of 1783 suggests.[26]

The 'turbulent creatures', the Marchand children, came to mean a great deal to Leopold. They filled the Dancing-Master's House with youthful activity again, and gave him the satisfaction of being able to direct every aspect of their education, as he had with his own children, and see the rewards of his work. With Gretl he was particularly pleased, because she was steady, sensible, and gave no cause for anxiety. Leopold followed her career with interest, and was delighted when she was engaged as a singer at the court in Munich. On Nannerl's marriage, when the Marchands were to return to Munich, and Leopold was left entirely on his own, the void in his life was enormous.

~❧~

When Leopold returned from Munich with Heinrich and Gretl, he was still far from reconciled to the idea of Wolfgang's marriage. He had presumably discussed the Weber family with his friends in Munich while he had been there—as members of the Mannheim band who had moved to Munich in 1778, Constanze's family was well known among the musicians and actors there. It might have been from friends in Munich, therefore, that Leopold heard that Frau Weber drank more than was wise, and he relayed the comment to Wolfgang, who partly admitted it. Yet despite the unfortunate first impressions of the family Leopold had received—the ideas that they were out to entrap men, that their morals were loose, and that they might be too fond of alcohol—it is by no means certain that his objections to the marriage were based primarily on these considerations. Everything known about Leopold's experience of

---

[26] See Ch. 23 and Table 1 for details.

managing money suggests that Wolfgang's lack of a salaried position was itself quite enough of a stumbling block. Leopold himself had waited to marry his own bride until he had secured his financial position at the Salzburg court; and when Wolfgang's friend and Katherl's brother Franz Xaver Wenzel Gilowsky was to make sorry attempts from 1785 to scrape together sufficient income to marry, Leopold scornfully referred to the folly of his plans, and told Nannerl that Gilowsky's marriage idea was even more harebrained than Wolfgang's had been, in that he did not enjoy one hundredth of the standing in his profession (surgery) that Wolfgang did in his.[27]

In the same letter mentioning Frau Weber's tendency to drink, Leopold expressed his and Nannerl's pleasure with the articles Wolfgang had sent on 23 March, and mentioned a rumour he had heard that Wolfgang was about to be taken into the emperor's service. In response, Wolfgang said that he had heard the same rumour, but that nothing definite had happened. He was still trying, as delicately as possible, to ingratiate himself with the emperor's valet, Strack. By now it was April, and the usually quiet summer season was approaching again. This year, however, augured better than the previous one, when Wolfgang had earned virtually nothing while the nobility had been out of town. He had now started to go regularly to Baron van Swieten's on Sundays to perform older (especially contrapuntal) music, and he asked Leopold to send various examples of such music from Salzburg. Partly as a result of these Sunday occasions, he started to write more contrapuntal music of his own, and sent Nannerl a prelude and fugue for the keyboard. He claimed that he was going to write a set of six such pieces and present them to van Swieten, presumably in the expectation of a present of money. He also claimed that Constanze had urged him to write more fugues, being very keen on them herself.[28]

Other summer events were the first performance of *Die Entführung*, and a series of amateur concerts in the Augarten (one of Vienna's parks)

---

[27] Leopold to Nannerl, 8 Apr. 1785—*MBA* 860/34–49 (not in *Letters*). Gilowsky had written to Leopold during Wolfgang's courtship of Constanze to plead for their love, and Leopold was remembering this piece of absurdity (as he thought it) when he wrote the above lines.

[28] Wolfgang to Leopold, 10 Apr., and to Nannerl, 20 Apr. 1782—*MBA* 667 and 668 (*Letters* 446 and 447). The piece he sent to Nannerl was the Fantasy and Fugue in C, K. 394. Though Constanze was clearly trying during this period to ingratiate herself with Nannerl and Leopold, this fact alone does not warrant the assumption that Wolfgang's comment about her interest in fugues was a pious lie designed to impress them (cf. e.g. the *MBA* commentary to 668/18 and 21 ff.). Too little is known about her musical interests and abilities to make any such assertion; the most that it is judicious to do is to note the possibility that Wolfgang was exaggerating her interest in counterpoint.

and of serenades in some of the finest squares. The tickets were sold by subscription, and Wolfgang hoped to earn at least 300 fl. from his involvement. Countess Thun (who was apparently also very supportive of his opera) and van Swieten were expressing interest in the project. A symphony by van Swieten was given in the first concert, and Wolfgang and Josepha Auernhammer played the Concerto for two keyboards, K. 365. On 29 May Wolfgang described the first concert as a tolerable success (though the letter is suspiciously short of details about the quality of the playing and the receipts), and mentioned the presence of Archduke Maximilian and Count Wallerstein as well as van Swieten and Countess Thun.[29]

Meanwhile, the courtship of Wolfgang and Constanze proceeded, despite a serious disagreement at the end of April occasioned by Wolfgang's disapproval of her behaviour during a parlour game, during which she allowed her calves to be measured by a man.[30] Nannerl and Constanze were now corresponding, and Wolfgang was introducing Constanze to his Viennese acquaintances such as Countess Thun. On 16 July 1782 the first performance of *Die Entführung* took place, and Wolfgang was paid 100 ducats (426 fl. 40 kr.) for it. It is very probable that Wolfgang (and Leopold too) had high hopes of this German opera as another step (perhaps the final one) on the route to an imperial appointment—the goal which, from Wolfgang's point of view, would enable his marriage to take place, and, from Leopold's, might enable him and Nannerl to leave Salzburg. The emperor's encouragement of the German-language theatre and opera company during this period meant that there was one respect at least in which German composers had an advantage over Italians.

On 20 July Wolfgang reported on the opera to Leopold. He mentioned cabals which, however, had failed to wreck the performances. He was pleased with the reception so far, despite the fact that a trio had fallen apart during the second performance. He sent Leopold the score and two librettos, mentioned how full the theatre had been, and explained that he was about to arrange it for wind-instruments. This work had to be done in little more than a week, otherwise someone else would beat him to it and steal his profit. He expressed some dismay that Leopold had just asked him to write a new symphony to celebrate the ennoblement of Siegmund Haffner in Salzburg, because this work too had to be written quickly; Wolfgang said that he would give up his nights to fulfil Leopold's request.

---

[29] Wolfgang to Leopold, 8, 25, and 29 May 1782—*MBA* 673, 674, and 675 (*Letters* 450, 451, and 452).

[30] Wolfgang to Constanze, 29 Apr. 1782—*MBA* 670 (*Letters* 448).

As he finished the letter, he was dashing off with Count Zichy to see Prince Kaunitz at Laxenburg, the summer residence of the Viennese court.[31]

Three days later, on 23 July, Wolfgang moved house from the Graben to the Hohe Brücke. Next day, he hastily wrote to congratulate Nannerl on her approaching name-day, saying that *Die Entführung* would be given again in her honour on that day. On 27 July he wrote to Leopold, enclosing the first movement of what was to be the 'Haffner' Symphony, K. 385. Apologizing for not sending more of it, he explained that he had had to write a wind serenade quickly; clearly he had far more work this summer than he had had during the previous one. After telling Leopold how popular the opera was, he begged to be allowed to marry Constanze. He claimed that the marriage was necessary for his peace of mind, that most people thought that they were already married, and that Frau Weber was very angry. He pleaded that life in Vienna was no harder than anywhere else, and that it depended only on good organization, which would come more easily if he had a wife. He said that Leopold should not worry about the possibility that he might be taken ill, because in that event members of the top nobility would support him—as a married man, he would have an even greater claim on them. Wolfgang also claimed that Prince Kaunitz had spoken warmly of him to the emperor and to Archduke Maximilian.[32]

It is not clear what the situation was between him and Constanze during the weeks leading up to his wedding on 4 August, or where Constanze was living. It has usually been assumed that she was staying with Baroness von Waldstätten, but Wolfgang's letter to the baroness shortly before 4 August suggests the possibility that Constanze was living in Wolfgang's new accommodation. If this was so, the situation was highly irregular, and might account for Frau Weber's threat (mentioned by Wolfgang in his letter to the baroness) to call in the police to force her to return home. At any rate, by the end of July or the beginning of August, the wedding seems to have become an urgent necessity.[33] If it is true, as seems likely, that Wolfgang had built his hopes on an imperial appointment following the success of *Die Entführung*, he must also have had high hopes that his marriage would soon become possible; and the fact that the appointment was not forthcoming was not likely to cool his ardour. His letters to Leopold in late July show that he was not prepared to wait any longer.

---

[31] *MBA* 677 (*Letters* 453). [32] *MBA* 678 and 680 (*Letters* 454 and 455).
[33] *MBA* 683 (*Letters* 457).

As for Leopold, it is unclear how much he knew about what was happening. He certainly heard some unfavourable rumour about Wolfgang, and this was apparently one reason for his writing in extremely cold terms on 26 July. He had received the score of *Die Entführung*, but instead of playing through it with delight, as he always did with any new music sent by Wolfgang, he said simply that he had not had time to look at it. He also revealed that he had heard that Wolfgang was disliked in Vienna by other musicians on account of his boastfulness, and it is possible that he was still raising objections to the marriage.[34]

Leopold tended to write peevishly or reproachfully after big disappointments, and it is possible that the tone of this letter was set by his feeling let down that the opera had not immediately brought an imperial appointment. His belief that Wolfgang was hated by other musicians in Vienna was sure to exacerbate his irritation that this coveted goal had not yet been reached, because he believed that friendship with people like the Kapellmeister Bonno was a helpful stepping-stone. Moreover, he had recently suffered another blow to his pride in Salzburg, because on 1 July Colloredo's new Kapellmeister Luigi Gatti had arrived to take up his duties, pushing Leopold once more into a subservient position. Colloredo had actually offered Gatti the post in February 1781, though it is not certain that Leopold knew about it at that time. As had happened when Fischietti and Rust had been appointed above him from outside, Leopold once again had to suffer the indignity of knowing that Gatti was drawing almost twice his salary (Gatti received 800 fl. annually), despite the fact that Leopold had been doing the job since Rust's departure in February 1778.[35]

Wolfgang was hurt by Leopold's lack of interest in the opera, because he had always relied on pleasing his father (whatever the differences between them) by sending new music. On 31 July he told Leopold that it was making a sensation in Vienna, and then went on to reject Leopold's accusation that he was making enemies among the musicians. Finally, he asked again for permission to marry, but this time more firmly. He said that there could be no legitimate objection to the marriage, because Constanze was an honourable girl of good family, and he was able to support her. He also said that he had gone too far with her to back out now, and that the only honest thing to do was to marry her as quickly as possible.[36]

[34] Leopold's comments can be surmised from Wolfgang's letter of 31 July 1782—*MBA* 681 (*Letters* 456).

[35] See Hintermaier, 'Hofkapelle', 131–43.   [36] *MBA* 681 (*Letters* 456).

It was presumably this letter which broke down the last shred of Leopold's vain resistance; he bowed to the inevitable and sent his blessing, though indicating his suspicion that Wolfgang had deceived Constanze about the financial expectations he had of his father. According to Wolfgang two letters from Leopold, one of which agreed to his request, arrived together on the day after the wedding had taken place, and Wolfgang was able to claim that he had gone ahead with the ceremony because he had known that such a loving father would sanction it. He expressed some indignation at Leopold's suspicion, claiming that Constanze had long known what he had to expect financially from Leopold, but was nevertheless willing to unite her life with his. He apologized for having anticipated Leopold's blessing, and gave some details about the ceremony and supper, which had been given by Baroness von Waldstätten. He said that Constanze was longing to come to Salzburg, and that he was sure Leopold and Nannerl would like her. He sent a march to supplement the 'Haffner' Symphony, and hoped that all the music had arrived in time. Finally, he announced that Gluck had requested another performance of *Die Entführung*, and had invited Wolfgang to dine with him on the following day.[37] Some of Leopold's missing letters had thus presumably discussed Wolfgang's eventual inheritance, which was not expected to be large, but unfortunately the documentation revealing the details is missing.[38]

The marriage contract was a simpler document than that which was to be drawn up when Nannerl married in 1784. Constanze brought 500 fl. to the union, which Wolfgang promised to augment by 1,000 fl., and on the death of either party the total sum was to pass to the survivor. Any further additions to their wealth, in any form, were to be shared equally.[39]

On receipt of Wolfgang's letter of 7 August, Leopold obviously picked up the comment about Gluck, and mentioned some way in which Gluck

---

[37] Wolfgang to Leopold, 7 Aug. 1782—*MBA* 684 (*Letters* 458).

[38] The obvious possibilities are that Leopold did not have much to leave in any case; that he was not willing to promise much (anything?) to Wolfgang while Nannerl was uprovided for; and that he wanted to punish Wolfgang for disregarding his wishes. It cannot be stressed too strongly that there is no way of knowing which is the most likely—Leopold's will and *Sperr-relation*, as well as several crucial letters about his intentions, are lost. Furthermore, whichever case was correct at the time of Wolfgang's marriage, the situation could have changed before Leopold's death; this observation is perhaps especially true of the first two possibilities. Thus the hint in 1782 that Wolfgang had little financial help to expect from Leopold cannot with integrity be built into an argument that Leopold disinherited him. See Ch. 31 for a full discussion of the settlement of Leopold's estate.

[39] See Deutsch, *Documents*, 203–4. See Ch. 32 for an outline of the settlement of Wolfgang's estate, to which the marriage contract is relevant.

might be useful to Wolfgang (he may have meant simply by dying, however). Responding to this point, Wolfgang wrote on 17 August agreeing with Leopold, but also suggesting that if he could not make the progress he wanted to in Vienna, he would go elsewhere. Although he would rather serve the emperor than anyone else, he would not wait for ever— he had written to Legros to explore the possibility of commissions in Paris for the following Lent, and was brushing up his French and learning English. His letter supports the hypothesis that he had held very strong hopes indeed of an imperial appointment following *Die Entführung*, and was feeling correspondingly let down; for he mentioned that Countess Thun, Count Zichy, Prince Kaunitz, and Baron van Swieten were all very displeased with the emperor for his lack of practical support for people of talent. He also claimed that some of his supporters had been making strenuous efforts to keep him in Vienna.[40]

It may be that Wolfgang's contact with Gluck had increased his pessimism about Viennese prospects, since he knew that Gluck had had to earn his fame in Paris before he had enjoyed success and wealth in Vienna. At any rate, this letter filled Leopold with new alarm, and he immediately dashed off letters of his own both to Wolfgang and to Baroness von Waldstätten in an effort to dissuade his son from doing anything so rash as leaving Vienna at this juncture. He seems to have reverted to his more confident mode of thinking, in which he believed that because of the age of certain key musicians at the Viennese court, it could only be a matter of time before Wolfgang was taken on. Flitting away to Paris or London could thus only be counter-productive. Leopold's letter to the baroness is famous, but is invariably used merely to state Leopold's assessment of Wolfgang's faults. Taken as a whole, however, it also offers important information about Leopold's perception of the effect Wolfgang's decisions had had on his father's life. It is a problematic letter, because although it was written directly after the marriage, Leopold did not specifically state in it that this was the event to which he was reacting. The possibility therefore has to be borne in mind that he was referring either to Wolfgang's previous decision to give up his Salzburg salary, or to both events simultaneously.

Leopold told the baroness that he had been forced to accept philosophically Wolfgang's action, since he had made countless lucid representations to his son on the subject, but they had been ignored. He also said that Wolfgang was quite well aware of the way in which Leopold

---

[40] *MBA* 686 (*Letters* 459).

was being sacrificed through his behaviour, and yet was determined to persist in it.[41] He made it clear that the sacrifice took the form of his continued enforced service in Salzburg, which was not only burdensome for a man of his age, but also morally degrading. Since Wolfgang chose to ignore all this, however, all Leopold could do was to give him his fatherly blessing and pray to God not to withdraw His divine grace from him. It was following this that he made the famous remarks about Wolfgang's character. After saying that he, Leopold, would continue to hope for the best, he claimed that he would be quite happy were it not for Wolfgang's main fault. This was that he had no golden mean between his indolence when things were going well, and his frenetic activity when he was required to exert himself. It was the latter state that Leopold recognized at present—because Wolfgang had still not gained an appointment in Vienna, he was too impatient to see reason and wait. Leopold went on to state that nothing could hinder his progress there if he would only be patient—Bonno and Gluck were both very old, and there were sure to be vacancies in due course. Leopold therefore begged the baroness to urge patience on Wolfgang.[42]

If Leopold meant merely that he was being sacrificed because Wolfgang had resigned his salary, the situation was simply what it had been ever since the spring of 1781. But the reference to bestowing his paternal blessing on a son who evidently wanted to be left to his own devices suggests that the marriage was a factor in his complaint.[43] He presumably thought that there had been no necessity for it to have taken place so soon, and that it would better have waited upon an appointment. He might have feared

---

[41] There is a problem with meaning here. Leopold's German runs: 'denn da ich als ein wahrer Vatter meine Schuldigkeit gethan,—ihm in so vielen Briefen über alles die klaren und begreiflichsten Vorstellungen gemacht,—ich auch überzeugt bin, daß er meine mühsame Umstände, meine bei einem solchen Alter höchstbeschwerliche Umstände kennt, und meine Herabsetzungen in Salzburg einsieht,—da er weiß, daß ich sowohl in moralischen als Physikalischen Verstande durch sein Betragen aufgeopfert bin,—so bleibt mir nichts anderes übrig, als ihn (da er es so wollte) sich selbst zu überlassen und Gott zu bitten, daß er ihm meinen väterlichen Seegen angedeyen lassen und ihm seine göttliche Gnade nicht entziehe' (*MBA* 687/9–18; *Letters* 460). Anderson translates 'ich . . . durch sein Betragen aufgeopfert bin' as 'I am being punished for his conduct', giving the impression that Leopold's complaint was that Colloredo was deliberately plaguing Leopold because of his displeasure with Wolfgang. A more accurate translation, however, would read 'I am being sacrificed through his behaviour'. Though this translation could still be made to fit the idea that Leopold was being persecuted in Salzburg for Wolfgang's resignation, it could equally mean that Leopold was being sacrificed through Wolfgang's decision to resign and/or to marry, both of which events lessened the likelihood that he would ever be able to support Leopold sufficiently for him to retire.

[42] Leopold to Baroness von Waldstätten, 23 Aug. 1782—*MBA* 687 (*Letters* 460).

[43] This does not, of course, necessarily mean that Leopold was opposed to any marriage for Wolfgang, at any time. A more detailed discussion of this point was given in Ch. 19, pp. 331–2.

that the marriage would actually lessen Wolfgang's chances of a court post, because of the question of a pension for his widow if he died. He might have felt that he and Nannerl, by being still in Salzburg, had missed their chance to stake their claim on Wolfgang's support, and that Wolfgang, with the inevitable growing expenses of a young family, would discover that he could not after all provide for them even if he did subsequently obtain an appointment. Or he might have taken Wolfgang's refusal, twice in fifteen months, to heed his advice on matters he considered supremely important as a sign that Wolfgang did not care enough about his family to prove a reliable support; in other words, the marriage might have been the last nail in the coffin of Leopold's and Nannerl's expectations of him. If this was the case, the repeated postponement during the year to come of the visit to Salzburg, which the bridal couple professed to be burning with desire to make, can only have increased Leopold's feeling that Wolfgang's deeds again indicated something quite different from his words.

23

The Bridal Visit to Salzburg in 1783

THE wedding an accomplished fact, and Nannerl and Leopold never having met Constanze, the next event they hoped for was a visit to Salzburg by the bridal couple. Because it was August, in the customary quiet season in Vienna's concert life, Leopold probably expected them to be able to travel straightaway, and stay until the aristocracy began to return to the city in late autumn. For Wolfgang, however, it was not so simple, however much he might profess his desire to see his family. Grand Duke Paul of Russia was said to be about to pay another visit to Vienna, and the possibility of being chosen as keyboard teacher to Princess Elisabeth of Württemberg was apparently again afoot; Wolfgang therefore did not want to be absent from Vienna while such opportunities of court preferment existed. Writing to Leopold on 24 August, he acknowledged the truth of Leopold's remarks about France and England (which had evidently been to the effect that those journeys would always be possible in future if his prospects in Vienna did not improve), and told him about the uncertainty of the dates of the Russians' visit. He also mentioned that he was still seeing the emperor's valet Strack, through whom he perhaps hoped to obtain the earliest possible certain information about the visit.[1]

For the whole of the year to come, this type of situation cropped up repeatedly—there was always some reason why the visit could not be paid yet. The main problem, naturally enough, was the lack of a certain income, and the consequent necessity of being on the spot to grasp every opportunity that occurred for earning money or an appointment. The year 1782 was apparently quite a good one for Wolfgang financially, but he had no way of knowing that he would always be able to earn so much. Moreover, the fact that fifteen months after leaving Colloredo's service he had still not been offered a post by the emperor, despite the success of *Die Entführung* and a number of other apparently satisfactory

---

[1] MBA 689 (*Letters* 461).

court and public appearances, must have signalled to him that he might have to continue with freelance work for a considerable time. He therefore had to assess and exploit every possible opportunity, and plan ahead constantly. There were a number of fronts on which he had to advance, in order not only to earn money for the present, but also to prove himself to the emperor a suitable candidate for an appointment.[2]

His bread-and-butter income came at first from pupils. While Leopold charged very low fees for private teaching in Salzburg,[3] Wolfgang (who claimed on more than one occasion that he hated having to teach) intended to set a high price, in order both to make himself desirable and to minimize the amount of teaching he had to do. Despite sporadic remarks in the correspondence about pupils, and income from teaching, it is not possible to suggest with much hope of accuracy what he actually earned from this source during any of the ten years he was in Vienna. What is more feasible, though still problematic, is to suggest an approximate annual figure from teaching which he might have aspired to earn. The main difficulty is the context of Wolfgang's most explicit statement on the subject; on 23 January 1782 he told Leopold that he had three pupils, each paying a fixed rate of 6 ducats (25 fl. 36 kr.) per month

---

[2] The possibilities for earning a living as a freelance musician in late 18th-c. Vienna, and Wolfgang's earnings for each of his ten Viennese years, have been much discussed. Cf. U. Kraemer, 'Wer hat Mozart verhungern lassen?', *Musica*, 30 (1976), 203–11; C. Bär, 'Er war...kein guter Wirth. Eine Studie über Mozarts Verhältnis zum Geld', *AM* 25/2 (1978), 30–53; J. Moore, 'Mozart in the Market-Place', *JRMA* 114 (1989), 18–42; A. Steptoe, 'Mozart and Poverty: A Re-examination of the Evidence', *MT* 125 (1984), 196–201; M. S. Morrow, *Concert Life in Haydn's Vienna: Aspects of a Developing Musical and Social Institution* (New York, 1988); D. Edge, Review Article of *Concert Life in Haydn's Vienna* by Morrow, *The Haydn Yearbook*, 17 (1992), 108–66; id., 'Mozart's Fee for *Così fan tutte*', *JRMA* 116/2 (1991), 211–35; W. J. and H. Baumol, 'On the Economics of Musical Composition in Mozart's Vienna', in J. M. Morris (ed.), *On Mozart* (Cambridge, 1994), 72–101; Braunbehrens, *Mozart in Vienna*; H. C. Robbins Landon, *1791: Mozart's Last Year* (London, 1988); id., *Mozart: The Golden Years* (London, 1989); and id., *Mozart and Vienna* (London, 1991). A useful concise summary of the views of many of these authors is given in Stafford, *Mozart's Death*, 228–60. Although some consensus has been reached, there is still lively debate about if and how the income can be estimated. Since my own view is that some of the most readily available evidence has not been used cautiously enough, I draw attention to particular examples of such cases in the course of reviewing the main income-earning possibilities open to Wolfgang. Further, since some of the authors named above have already suggested modifications to the views of others, I concentrate here on points of an arguable nature which I am not aware of having been contested to date.

[3] In 1785 Leopold was charging one of his violin pupils (young Joseph Wölfl) 12 kr. hourly (though he claimed that he always extended the lesson to an hour and a half and often two hours without charging extra). At this rate, he would have earned 2 fl. 24 kr. from a block of twelve lessons; and if they took place three times a week, the 2 fl. 24 kr. would also have been his monthly charge per pupil. If he charged all his pupils a similar rate, his lessons must surely have been one of the best bargains in 18th-c. music. See Leopold to Nannerl, 27–9 Oct. 1785—*MBA* 892/113–27 (not in *Letters*).

(instead of the traditional method where the pupil paid for a block of twelve lessons), and that though he intended to take several more on those terms, one more would provide enough for a quiet life-style for a married couple.[4] The statement was made to win round Leopold to his desire to marry, which strongly suggests that the figures he produced had been calculated to satisfy his father, whose cautious views he knew so well. Unfortunately, he was not specific about whether the sum (102 fl. 24 kr. per month) could be earned every month of the year, for though he made much of the fact that whimsically cancelled lessons would no longer affect his fee, he may have been obliged to suspend lessons and payment during the summer months, when the aristocracy tended to be out of town for long periods. If he intended to present the arrangement as a twelve-month one, four pupils would have yielded 1,228 fl. 48 kr. annually, a sum that would almost certainly have satisfied Leopold if it had been guaranteed. And even if Wolfgang thought rather of a nine-month arrangement, the yield would have been 921 fl. 36 kr., which would likewise probably have satisfied Leopold if he had been assured of it. These two figures therefore indicate a likely range for Wolfgang's annual teaching income aspirations (or perhaps, to be more accurate, for his perception of Leopold's aspirations on his behalf; it is possible that Wolfgang hoped to be able to earn the sum he wanted from more congenial work). The clearly felt need in this letter to persuade Leopold that he could support a wife on these terms (bar illness) means, however, that scepticism must be applied to his remarks, which were not necessarily realistic. Even if he was being truthful in asserting that he actually had three pupils prepared to accept his terms, there is no way of knowing how long he kept these three, how easy it was to add to them or replace them, or whether his experimental method of payment continued to be acceptable to them and other potential pupils. This is why I believe it to be pointless to suggest a figure for what he actually earned from teaching in any one year; the data are not adequate for the task even of estimating with a margin of error.[5] Moore argues that Wolfgang's finances during his

---

[4] *MBA* 660/46–54 (*Letters* 442). There were 4 fl. 16 kr. to the imperial ducat until 1783—see Ch. 3 n. 1 for the ducat/florin conversions provided by Edge.

[5] Moore counts as 'fairly certain' income 972 fl. from teaching in 1782, the year to which my remarks above apply. The figure is reached by taking Wolfgang at his word that he had three pupils paying the rate he asked each month for the twelve months of the year. The ducat/florin conversion rate is not quite accurate; she converts at 4 fl. 30 kr. per ducat when it should be 4 fl. 16 kr. See Moore, 'Mozart in the Market-Place', 20–1. See also p. 397 below for further doubts about the reliability of Moore's figure of 972 fl.

ten years in Vienna take the shape of an arch, with the most prosperous period occurring mid-way; Wolfgang's standard of living rose appreciably during the early years there, and he failed to adjust it to the lower income he was earning in the later years. This seems entirely reasonable, although she suggests that Wolfgang's popularity as a teacher declined during his later years in Vienna, and that he asked his benefactor Michael Puchberg in 1790 to find him more pupils,[6] a claim which may not quite represent the true picture. An earlier letter from Wolfgang to Puchberg reveals that it had been Puchberg's suggestion that Wolfgang take some pupils.[7] Since Wolfgang was repeatedly applying to Puchberg during this period for cash, he could hardly refuse the suggestion; and it may be that during his middle, more prosperous, period in Vienna, he had largely given up teaching, only to find later that he could not live without it.

A second way in which money could be earned was by accepting invitations to play at private concerts or salons. Wolfgang certainly did this, but it is impossible to form any assessment of what he earned from it, and (as Moore points out) he may well often have been paid with trinkets rather than cash.

Opera commissions represented a third income-earning possibility, and Wolfgang seems to have pursued any opening of this kind with vigour. The standard fee for the composer was 100 ducats (426 fl. 40 kr. in 1782), but this seems to have been a once-for-all payment (though it is possible that the composer sometimes also kept the receipts of one of the performances).[8] The theatre copyist would copy the score for sale, but the composer received nothing from these sales; nor did he receive anything from further performances of the work, regardless of its popularity. The most he could hope for was that by being quick off the mark and making keyboard and *Harmonie* (wind-band) arrangements of the work before anyone else could do so, he could add something to his original fee. Wolfgang's problem, one which he was finding frustrating as early as 1782, was that although the structure of musical life was moving towards one where freelancing was more common, and the number of salaried

---

[6] Moore, 'Mozart in the Market-Place', 20. The letter in question is Wolfgang's to Puchberg before or on 17 May 1790—*MBA* 1125/26–7 (*Letters* 580).

[7] Wolfgang to Puchberg in early May 1790—*MBA* 1123/5–9 (*Letters* 578).

[8] Moore suggests that this might have happened with *Die Entführung*, and that it would explain why Frau Weber was so keen to rush him into his marriage after the third performance. See Moore, 'Mozart in the Market-Place', 23–4. Whether or not Wolfgang profited from such an arrangement, however, the assertion that Frau Weber had financial motives for hastening the marriage is not justified; in the absence of further information about the situation (in particular about whether there was the risk of a sexual scandal), the reason for the urgency of the wedding can only be guessed.

posts was shrinking, the financial conditions for freelance musicians had not yet altered to give them a reasonable return for their compositions.[9] For anyone with a salary, a fee of 100 ducats (426 fl. 40 kr.) for an opera was a welcome windfall; to someone in Wolfgang's position, it was extremely necessary cash. When, as happened with *Die Entführung*, the opera was a great box-office success, it was naturally galling to see the theatre taking handsome profits night after night, while the composer had only received the same flat fee that was always paid. In September and October 1782, Wolfgang expressed his feelings about this situation to Leopold. He said that he had been approached for a copy of the score of the opera, which was wanted in Berlin. Wolfgang, seeing the chance of adding to the income he had already earned from it, asked Leopold to have the score copied in Salzburg from the music he had sent home—this arrangement would be cheaper and more secret than having it copied in Vienna. Leopold must have mentioned some scruple about doing this, presumably because it was an irregular arrangement which would damage Wolfgang's reputation if it were discovered (the Viennese score was in the hands of the theatre copyist, and hence completely at the disposal of the emperor, whose theatre it was); and in reply, Wolfgang revealed his resentment that the theatre had taken 400 ducats (1,706 fl. 40 kr.) in two weeks from his opera, while he had only been paid 100 ducats (426 fl. 40 kr.). He went on to outline a plan for his future opera-writing, saying that he would produce the works at his own expense, take at least 1,200 fl. in three performances, and then let the theatre buy them from him for 50 ducats (213 fl. 20 kr.).[10] Despite his intention, he continued to be subject to the traditional arrangement of a single fee for the later operas he was to write, with one or two possible exceptions—*The Magic Flute*, for example, which was written for a different theatre from the emperor's Burgtheater, in partnership with his librettist Schikaneder. What sort of financial arrangement was in force for *The Magic Flute* is unknown, but Wolfgang and Schikaneder may have had a profit-sharing agreement.[11] Wolfgang had told

---

[9] Ibid. 40–2.

[10] Wolfgang to Leopold, 25 Sept. and 5 Oct. 1782—*MBA* 695/19–36 and 700/5–33 (*Letters* 465 and 469).

[11] For a critical account of the evidence for the history of composition of *The Magic Flute*, see P. Branscombe, *W. A. Mozart: Die Zauberflöte*, Cambridge Opera Handbooks (Cambridge, 1991), 67–86. With operas that had not been commissioned by a court, the composer had more subsequent autonomy over the score and sales. Just after Wolfgang's death in 1791, Constanze was offering *La clemenza di Tito* as well as *The Magic Flute* for sale to Archduke Maximilian (by that time elector of Cologne) through Luigi Simonetti, a tenor singer in his employment—see Deutsch, *Documents*, 428–9.

Leopold that he would be able to write an opera at least once each year in Vienna, but this was an unrealistic hope, given the competition for the commissions. Nevertheless, he was continually sniffing out operatic possibilities; when the Italian opera recommenced in Vienna in 1783, he busied himself with trying to find a suitable Italian libretto, and pursued actively the quest to find a librettist with whom he could work. When he eventually paid the visit to Salzburg with Constanze in the summer of 1783, he had made advance preparations with Varesco (the librettist of *Idomeneo*) to work with him on an Italian libretto, *L'oca del Cairo*, while he was there.

A fourth possibility for earning money was to give official concerts or 'academies'. In Lent, when the Burgtheater offered no operas or plays, it could be booked for these events instead. Wolfgang tried to book the theatre once each Lent, but knowledge of how the concerts were organized is very slight, and it is not possible to calculate what his net profit might have been on any occasion.[12] Moore gives the sum of 1,600 fl. for Wolfgang's concert in the theatre on 23 March 1783, taking the figure from a report in Cramer's *Magazin der Musik*,[13] but this report did not indicate whether it was a gross or a net figure. It is thus almost meaningless; if it was gross, further knowledge about expenses and profit-sharing arrangements would be needed. Edge suggests that the theatre might have taken as much as 50 per cent of the net profit of such concerts.[14] The other concert of Wolfgang's in the theatre for which some knowledge of receipts survives is that of 10 March 1785. Leopold was to attend it, and reported to Nannerl that Wolfgang had taken 559 fl.[15] But even here it is not clear whether this was gross income or Wolfgang's profit; and, although Wolfgang had claimed that the theatre had been packed for the concert on 23 March 1783, Leopold did not give Nannerl any indication of numbers for that of 10 March 1785. If the theatre was as full in 1785 as it had apparently been in 1783, this might indicate (though even in this case there would be room for doubts, because of the lack of detailed knowledge of ticket prices and extra gifts of money from well-wishers) that Cramer was reporting gross receipts while Leopold was reporting profit; without even this information, it must be accepted that little can be concluded about

[12] For details of the loss of evidence about concert organization, see Morrow, *Concert Life in Haydn's Vienna*, 123; and Edge, Review Article on Morrow's book, 125.

[13] See Moore, 'Mozart in the Market-Place', 21; and Deutsch, *Documents*, 215.

[14] Edge, Review Article on Morrow's book, 125.

[15] Leopold to Nannerl, 12 Mar. 1785—*MBA* 850/17–21 (*Letters* 525).

the takings.[16] In addition to his own concerts in the theatre, Wolfgang took part in those of his friends, but there is no documented evidence for how (even if) the proceeds were divided when this happened; Leopold alluded to Wolfgang's appearance in the concerts of others as a favour, so perhaps friends reciprocated without money changing hands.[17]

Publication of printed compositions offered a fifth way of earning money, but again it is very difficult to estimate Wolfgang's earnings from this source. Moore states that they were not large, partly because the era of fast growth in the music printing industry had not yet arrived. The only sum for which documentation exists is 100 ducats (433 fl. 20 kr.) from Artaria in 1785 for the 'Haydn' Quartets.[18] The dissemination of music through manuscript copies, however, was very big business, though Wolfgang's income from this source cannot accurately be determined or estimated either. From the few pieces of documentation about his attempts to get subscription schemes for manuscript copies of his music off the ground, however, can again be seen his desire to cut out the profit earned by people other than the composer. On 28 December 1782, for example, Wolfgang told Leopold that he was writing three keyboard concertos (K. 413, 414, and 415) for sale by subscription, and that he was distributing the tickets at 6 ducats (25 fl. 36 kr.).[19] By the time he wrote next on 4 January 1783, however, he mentioned a price of 4 ducats (17 fl. 4 kr.) for the three concertos.[20] Leopold must have written to express the fear that this was still too much (and also to ask how the scheme was going to work, in particular how Wolfgang was going to protect himself against pirated copies which would rob him of his profit), because on 22 January Wolfgang wrote again saying that he deserved a ducat (4 fl. 16 kr.) for each concerto, and that no one could get them copied for less than a ducat. He also said that he was not going to release any copies

---

[16] Similarly, Leopold's reports about the subscription price and the number of subscribers to Wolfgang's Mehlgrube concerts in Lent 1785 do not allow an accurate assessment of his profits to be made; Leopold gave the cost of the hire of the room, but not the other expenses. See Leopold to Nannerl, 15–16 Feb. and 12 Mar. 1785—*MBA* 847/34–6 (*Letters* 523) and *MBA* 850/17–21 (*Letters* 525). Thus Moore's Table 3 ('Mozart in the Market-Place', 21), giving details about Wolfgang's income from 1781 to 1791, cannot be relied upon as an unfailingly accurate summary of the money Wolfgang 'fairly certainly' earned during this period, despite her claim to this effect in n. 5, p. 20.

[17] See n. 15 above for the ref. to Leopold's letter.

[18] See Moore, 'Mozart in the Market-Place', 24. The source for the fee from Artaria is Leopold's letter to Nannerl of 22 Jan. 1785 – *MBA* 840/15–22 (*Letters* 522), in which he was relaying information supplied by Wolfgang. Moore's Table 3 (p. 21) converts the sum at 4 fl. 30 kr. per ducat, but in 1785 there were 4 fl. 20 kr. per imperial ducat, yielding 433 fl. 20 kr. For the conversions of different types of ducat during different periods, see Edge, 'Mozart's Fee for Così fan tutte', 218.

[19] *MBA* 715/8–14 (*Letters* 476).   [20] *MBA* 719/49–50 (*Letters* 477).

ordered and paid for until he had a certain number of subscriptions.[21] His words suggest that the expenses to him, if the scheme succeeded, would be limited to the copyist's fee of about a ducat per set, and the advertisements he placed in the *Wiener Zeitung* offering the subscription tickets for sale. The first notice appeared on 15 January, and it shows that he was aiming at the amateur market, for he stated that the works could be performed either with a large orchestra including wind instruments or *a quattro* (i.e. with two violins, viola, and cello);[22] his words to Leopold on 28 December 1782 to the effect that he had aimed at a happy medium between the easy and the difficult reinforce this claim. The subscription was apparently not a roaring success, however, and on 26 April 1783 (a month after the expiry of the subscription deadline) he offered all three concertos to the publisher Sieber in Paris for a flat fee of 30 louis d'or (about 330 fl.).[23] If his net profit under the proposed subscription scheme had been about 3 ducats (12 fl. 48 kr.) per set of concertos, he would have had to sell about twenty-five sets under subscription to raise the sum he hoped to earn from Sieber. In fact, Sieber did not take them, and they were next advertised by Traeg (still in manuscript form) in Vienna in September 1783, at 10 fl. for all three.[24] How well they sold at this price, and what Wolfgang made from them,[25] is unknown; but they were eventually issued in March 1785 by Artaria in Vienna, who offered each (by now engraved) concerto separately at 2 fl. 30 kr. apiece.[26] Thus, two years after he had first attempted the subscription manuscript sale, the Viennese public could buy the same works (in engraved form) for a total of 7 fl. 30 kr., compared with 17 fl. 4 kr. under Wolfgang's scheme—despite the fact that the publisher as well as the composer now had to make his profit.[27] What Wolfgang received from Artaria is unknown, but his original pricing would appear to have been (as Leopold had feared) vastly over-optimistic.[28]

These were the main money-earning possibilities open to Wolfgang, but there were also sundry other opportunities such as serenades in summer, special occasional events such as the visits of foreign dignitaries,

---

[21] *MBA* 722/3–11 (*Letters* 479).   [22] Deutsch, *Documents*, 212.

[23] *MBA* 741 (*Letters* 487). The louis d'or is converted here at 11 fl., but this is an approximation.

[24] Deutsch, *Documents*, 218–19.

[25] If anything—Traeg's source might have been a pirated copy.

[26] Deutsch, *Documents*, 242. See also Eisen, *Documents*, 54, for an advertisement by Lausch of (probably) the same concertos.

[27] This is assuming that Artaria paid Wolfgang for them, rather than engraving them from a pirated copy.

[28] Unless the differential can be explained by the age of the works by 1785.

and arrangements such as that which Wolfgang had with van Swieten. It is therefore not surprising that with so much to press ahead with, the right time for leaving Vienna never seemed to arrive. In the late summer and early autumn of 1782, Wolfgang was preoccupied with the possibility of the Russian visit and of obtaining Princess Elisabeth as a pupil. By 5 October he knew that he had been passed over again, and that Summer had been appointed her teacher at a salary of 400 fl. annually. Wolfgang made light of the matter to Leopold, and claimed to disdain such a miserly sum, but Leopold predictably answered that as certain income it was not to be despised. Wolfgang's counter-reply was that he could earn as much from two pupils, at a fraction of the inconvenience. His reasoning was that almost 100 fl. of the salary for teaching the princess would be lost to expenses, because of the carriage ride out to the convent where she lived, and the cost of dining out of town. The inconvenience consisted in the fact that he would be completely at the beck and call of the princess, who might well keep him hanging around waiting in idle frustration until she felt inclined to take her lesson. Thus he was claiming that two pupils were earning him either 300 or 400 fl. annually (depending on whether he was thinking of the gross income from the princess of 400 fl., or the income of about 300 fl., net of expenses). Yet if he was charging 6 ducats (25 fl. 36 kr.) per pupil per month, as he had told Leopold on 23 January 1782,[29] his monthly earnings from two pupils should have been 51 fl. 12 kr.; and if they paid him every month of the year, his annual earnings from two pupils should have been 614 fl. 24 kr. Evidently this was not the case; but whether he had lowered his fees, or whether he was not counting the summer months, or both, is not known.[30]

It was also during this period that Wolfgang was arranging for *Die Entführung* to be copied for Berlin, so that all in all it was not a good time to leave town. The next possibility discussed for the visit to Salzburg was Leopold's name-day on 15 November. This was not convenient either, however, because the aristocracy was just returning from the country, and the busy season was about to begin. Wolfgang half-heartedly offered to go for a brief visit in November, but made it clear that he would prefer to wait until the New Year. When Leopold pressed the point about November, Wolfgang made a show of agreeing to it, but found excuses (the weather, and a headache of Constanze's) for pulling out at the last

---

[29] See pp. 390–1 above.

[30] At any rate, Moore's figure of 972 fl. from teaching in 1782 ('Mozart in the Market-Place', 21) looks increasingly improbable. The passages in question are Wolfgang's letters to Leopold of 5 and 12 Oct. 1782—*MBA* 700 and 702 (*Letters* 469 and 470).

minute. By the time the weather had improved, Leopold's name-day had already passed, and Wolfgang claimed that his pupils would not let him go. Instead he offered to go in March or April. Constanze was now pregnant, but Wolfgang claimed that they could visit in the spring, since she would not be confined until June.[31]

Leopold could presumably understand the reasons for Wolfgang's inability to leave Vienna, but it seems likely that he became impatient with the repeated and exaggerated claims about how much they were longing to see him (Wolfgang said on one occasion that Constanze was carrying Leopold's portrait round with her constantly, and kissing it twenty times a day,[32] and on another that Constanze had had to be forcibly restrained from following the carriage of a friend returning from Vienna to Salzburg).[33]

In December, Wolfgang was engaged to play in concerts of Prince Golicyn's, and was anticipating the return of the Italian *opera buffa* company the following Easter by hunting for a suitable libretto. By the end of the year, and at the beginning of the New Year, he was extremely busy, with a full morning of teaching, and evenings devoted to composition unless he had to go out to play. He was writing the three keyboard concertos K. 413, 414, and 415, for sale by subscription, was seeking older music for performance at van Swieten's, and was also starting to think about the programme for his Lenten academy.[34]

The busy period continued through Carnival and Lent until April 1783, when the academies were over. Wolfgang's and Constanze's circle included a number of people involved with Vienna's theatrical and operatic life—his sister-in-law Aloysia Lange and her actor husband Joseph, the singers Johann Adamberger and Therese Teyber, and Wolfgang's *Die Entführung* librettist Stephanie. These people co-operated with each other, and appeared in each other's academies. On 11 March Wolfgang performed a keyboard concerto in Aloysia's academy, where his 'Paris' Symphony (K. 297) was also performed;[35] on 23 March Aloysia, Therese Teyber, and Adamberger performed in his; and on 30 March he appeared in Therese Teyber's. The programme of Wolfgang's academy, which he communicated to Leopold on 29 March, gives an idea of the amount of preparatory work that must have been put in. It started with the first three

[31] Wolfgang to Leopold, 19 Oct., 26 Oct., 13 Nov., and 20 Nov. 1782—*MBA* 705, 707, 708, and 710 (*Letters* 471, 472, 473, and 474).
[32] Wolfgang to Leopold, 21 Dec. 1782—*MBA* 713/26–9 (*Letters* 475).
[33] Wolfgang to Leopold, 12 Apr. 1783—*MBA* 739/20–32 (*Letters* 486).
[34] Wolfgang to Leopold, 28 Dec. 1782 and 4 Jan. 1783—*MBA* 715 and 719 (*Letters* 476 and 477).
[35] Wolfgang to Leopold, 12 Mar. 1783—*MBA* 731 (*Letters* 483).

movements of the 'Haffner' Symphony, K. 385, which Leopold had sent back from Salzburg so that Wolfgang could have it copied. Aloysia then sang 'Se il padre perdei' from *Idomeneo*, and Wolfgang played the third of his subscription concertos, K. 415, which he had recently finished writing (he presumably hoped that this would be good publicity for the subscription sale scheme which was running simultaneously). Adamberger then sang a *scena* by Wolfgang, K. 369, and a 'concertant-Simphonie' from the *Finalmusik*, K. 320, was performed. Next, Wolfgang played the Keyboard Concerto (already well known in Vienna), K. 175, with the Rondo finale, K. 382, and Therese Teyber sang a *scena* from *Lucio Silla*. Following this, Wolfgang played alone for a while, performing a fugue and then two sets of variations (K. 398 and K. 455) on airs from operas popular in Vienna. After Aloysia had sung a Rondo, K. 416, the concert finished with the last movement of the 'Haffner' Symphony.[36] The programme had to be put together in the midst of Wolfgang's other commitments, such as his morning teaching and his evening appearances at salons. Some of the music had to be written, parts had to be copied, the orchestra engaged, and rehearsals held. The concert was a brilliant success, the theatre was packed, and the emperor sent a special gift of 25 ducats (106 fl. 40 kr.). This must have been very necessary money, because by February Wolfgang had contracted his first recorded debt (the amount is unknown), and had appealed to Baroness von Waldstätten for help in meeting it. He claimed to her that he had relied on the money for his subscription concertos coming in faster. Thus, although 1782 had appeared to be a better year for him financially than 1781, with the fee for *Die Entführung*, some pupils, and the series of summer serenades and Augarten concerts organized by Philipp Martin,[37] all this money was evidently gone by (at latest) mid-February 1783. The letter to the baroness suggests that Wolfgang regarded it as quite acceptable to borrow money to tide him over until expected cash arrived, for he said that if he had known how slowly the subscription money would come in, he would have raised his loan on a longer time-limit.[38]

Presumably the outstanding amount was cleared once Wolfgang had the income from his concert, and he also sent Leopold money to reimburse him for the expense of having had *Die Entführung* copied in Salzburg, and an extra sum as a gift, in the hope that it would be useful. The amount is unknown, but it was the first (and was to be the only)

---

[36] *MBA* 734 (*Letters* 484).   [37] These concerts were mentioned in Ch. 22.
[38] Wolfgang to Baroness von Waldstätten, 15 Feb. 1783—*MBA* 729 (*Letters* 482).

recorded payment of this kind since Wolfgang had moved to Vienna in 1781; he regretted that he could not send more, saying that he needed to save money for Constanze's confinement, which was due at the end of May or the beginning of June. The money went with their Salzburg acquaintance Daubrawa, who also took some music for Leopold and Nannerl.[39]

Once Lent was over, the journey to Salzburg could be considered again, but despite his earlier claim that they would be able to travel in April, Wolfgang now said that this was unsatisfactory because of the approaching birth. He therefore promised that they would set off as soon as Constanze had recovered from the confinement.[40] This time he seems to have taken the resolve more seriously, because in early May he asked Leopold to approach Varesco about the idea of collaborating on another Italian opera. Presumably he saw the opportunity to work steadily at it while he was in Salzburg, and have it well under way by the time he returned. The Italian *opera buffa* company in Vienna had started up again and was very popular. Wolfgang was discussing libretto possibilities with the Viennese librettist Da Ponte too, but was uncertain about whether anything would come of them.[41]

Meanwhile Wolfgang was approaching Sieber in Paris about his three keyboard concertos and also a set of six string quartets (the 'Haydn' Quartets). He offered the quartets for 50 louis d'or (550 fl.) and the concertos for 30 louis d'or (330 fl.). The quartets were not yet finished, but the concertos were ready and waiting. It was now the quiet season again; this year Wolfgang had no opera to produce, and he had the expenses of childbirth and the journey to Salzburg to anticipate. Nor, presumably, could anything much be earned during his absence. Details about his finances at this point are unknown, but when he returned from Salzburg to Vienna in October, he apparently had virtually no money; the winter earnings from 1782 and the Lenten ones from 1783 must therefore have been insufficient to see him and Constanze through the summer and autumn of 1783.[42]

The more arrangements that were made for the journey to Salzburg, the less Wolfgang liked the idea of it, and later in May he wrote to

---

[39] Wolfgang to Leopold, 29 Mar. and 3 Apr. 1783—*MBA* 734 and 736 (*Letters* 484 and 485).

[40] Wolfgang to Leopold, 12 Apr. 1783—*MBA* 739 (Letters 486).

[41] Wolfgang to Leopold, 7 May 1783—*MBA* 745 (*Letters* 489).

[42] See Wolfgang's letter to Leopold, 6 Dec. 1783—*MBA* 770/7–42 (*Letters* 500), in which Wolfgang had to ask Leopold to lend him the money to settle an old debt which had been lying dormant since 1778. Nissen, too, claims that the reason for postponing the journey to Salzburg was Wolfgang's distressed financial situation—see von Nissen, *Biographie*, 475.

Leopold to suggest that they meet in Munich instead. He claimed that he was worried about being arrested in Salzburg, since he had never formally been discharged from service there.[43] His fear was for a while obscured by other events—he became ill in late May,[44] and then a son was born to him and Constanze on 17 June.[45] Following the birth of the baby, Raimund Leopold, Wolfgang was involved with writing new arias to be inserted into an opera by Anfossi, because two of the singers, Aloysia Lange and Adamberger, were not satisfied with their parts.[46] Wolfgang seems to have envisaged having work to keep him in Vienna during August (or perhaps they were not happy to leave the baby while he was so young), because on 5 July he wrote to Leopold to say that they should be able to travel in September. However, this sentence was followed by a renewal of his fears about revisiting Salzburg, and he suggested that they think of a different way of meeting. Claiming to prefer one plan to all others, he said that something would have to be sacrificed in order to enjoy the greatest happiness.[47]

Perhaps he meant by this allusion to hint that Leopold might give up his job and come to live in Vienna; if so the suggestion fell on stony ground. In reply, Leopold poured scorn on his fears of Colloredo, and suggested that Wolfgang's real objection to travelling to Salzburg was disinclination to see his father and sister. He might also have assumed that because it was summer, Wolfgang could easily get away. Nannerl too seems to have written in the same vein, and the combined reproaches and challenges served to push Wolfgang and Constanze into a final decision to travel.[48] By 29 July, in the octave of Nannerl's name-day, they were in Salzburg, having left the six-week-old Raimund in Vienna, it is not known with whom.

⊰⊱

[43] Wolfgang to Leopold, 21 May 1783—*MBA* 747 (*Letters* 490).

[44] It is assumed that a copy from the 1830s of a letter from Constanze to Leopold is the letter that describes this illness. The letter appears, however, to be dated 30 Nov. 1783. Since it refers also to an imminent confinement, and since Wolfgang's letter to Leopold of 7 June 1783 (*MBA* 750; *Letters* 491) refers to a recent illness, it has tentatively been assigned the date 30 May 1783 instead. As a new find, it is not printed in either *MBA* or *Letters*, but a transcription is given by R. Angermüller, 'Ein ungedruckter Brief Constanze Mozarts an ihren Schwiegervater Leopold', *MM* 39 (1991), 45–6.

[45] Wolfgang to Leopold, 18 June 1783—*MBA* 752 (*Letters* 492).

[46] Wolfgang to Leopold, 21 June 1783—*MBA* 753 (*Letters* 493).

[47] Wolfgang to Leopold, 5 July 1783—*MBA* 756 (*Letters* 495).

[48] Wolfgang to Leopold, 12 July, and Constanze and Wolfgang to Nannerl and Gretl, 19 July 1783—*MBA* 758 and 760 (*Letters* 496, 497, 497*a*, and 497*b*).

Little detail survives about the activities of Leopold and Nannerl during the period between Wolfgang's marriage and his visit to Salzburg. Nannerl was, as ever, avid for keyboard music, and in January 1783 Wolfgang was promising to send her cadenzas and *Eingänge* (introductory flourishes or lead-ins for the keyboard on its entrance in a concerto movement). He did so in February; they were for the concertos in D, K. 175 (with the new Rondo, K. 382, that he had already sent her) and in E flat, K. 271.[49]

Leopold, as was becoming his wont, again went to Munich for the Carnival in 1783, and took back with him to Salzburg a third resident pupil, the Marchands' cousin Maria Johanna ('Hanchen') Brochard, who was only 8 years old. Life in the Dancing-Master's House presumably continued in the usual routines, but with a further increase in work (perhaps, in view of Hanchen's age and sex, especially for Nannerl). Nannerl's diary for part of this period survives, but does not record her activities—only miscellaneous events such as marriages and deaths, the introduction of lectures on experimental physics, the arrival and departure of visitors to the town, and the performances at the theatre. D'Ippold was never mentioned by name, but she did record news about his establishment, the Virgilianum, and must still have been seeing him, because the diary entries made later the same year during Wolfgang's and Constanze's visit mention him frequently. Among the recorded items which must most have affected the Mozarts were the death of their old friend Frau Robinig and the madness of Basil von Amann (who was already involved in the financial scandal which was to cloud the deaths both of his father and himself in 1785).[50] Nannerl also recorded, on 16 April 1783, the death of Jeanette Maria Berchtold von Sonnenburg (though Nannerl used her maiden name of Grünbichl), without realizing the significance that this event was to have for her—sixteen months later she was to marry Jeanette's husband Johann Baptist.[51]

But after the arrival of Wolfgang and Constanze, Nannerl reverted to her older method of keeping the diary, noting her activities for each day. The result is to illuminate different phases of activity for the period

[49] Wolfgang to Leopold, 22 Jan. and 15 Feb. 1783—*MBA* 722 and 728 (*Letters* 479 and 481). A partial explanation of how Nannerl's concerto parts were prepared for her use is given in Ch. 24, pp. 430–4.

[50] See Ch. 11 for an earlier instalment of the story of Basil's family, and Chs. 27 and 30 for later ones.

[51] The diary entries are *MBA* 717, 721, 723, 726, 730, 732, 735, 738, 740, 742, 744, 746, and 748. Some are in Leopold's hand. The period covered is Jan.–June 1783.

from late July to late October 1783.[52] Underlying everything were the 'constants'—Nannerl's church-going, Leopold's court duties, teaching (that of Heinrich, Gretl, and Hanchen has to be assumed, but lessons given by Nannerl to others are recorded), housekeeping, the afternoon habit of paying or receiving visits, and the punctuations afforded by occasional events such as fairs and religious festivals. Over these everyday events were placed further layers of activities from the moment Wolfgang and Constanze arrived. From 29 July (at latest) until 27 October, Leopold and Nannerl could include the two visitors in all their activities, not only adding a lustre to everything they did, and inducing the family to make more outings than it otherwise would have made, but significantly increasing the interest of the domestic music-making. From 12 September Leopold and Nannerl had not only the company of Wolfgang and Constanze, but also the added attraction of the theatre, because Kühne's theatrical troupe arrived to play in Salzburg until Advent. Then, during much of September until about 2 October, in addition to the above-mentioned enhancements to the daily routine, Gretl was involved in a court opera,[53] and her parents came from Munich (with Hanchen's father and another Munich friend) on 25 September to see her in it;[54] at about the same time, d'Ippold's sister and sister-in-law were visiting him, and Nannerl's time was considerably taken up with them.[55]

What can be learnt from the entries Nannerl made in her diary during the summer and autumn of 1783? Perhaps the most striking feature is the readiness of the family to be sociable, and to give itself up entirely to making the most of the visits of friends and family; looking at the list of visitors suggests that the door was always open. As soon as Wolfgang and Constanze arrived, special outings were arranged to show her some of the sights of the area, and special efforts were made to increase the scope of the domestic music-making in the large room of the Dancing-Master's House. The presence of Wolfgang and Constanze meant that, even without inviting anyone else, the musical forces in the house were

[52] See Ch. 14, pp. 215–17, for an account of the undervaluation of Nannerl's diary, with particular reference to the entries during the visit in 1783 of Wolfgang and Constanze.

[53] According to the commentary to *MBA* 765/37, it was probably Gatti's *Olimpiade*.

[54] It is characteristic of the *MBA* commentary in general that it invariably places Wolfgang at the centre of all the family activities; thus, in commenting on the arrival of the Marchand parents and other relations (*MBA* 765/91), it claims that they had come to Salzburg specially to see Wolfgang; no consideration is given to the fact that their daughter Gretl (whom they had probably not seen since Lent) was appearing in an opera.

[55] See Table 1 for these diary entries. The arrangement in categories is mine; Nannerl of course simply recorded a list of activities for each day.

considerable. Constanze and Gretl were singers; Wolfgang, Heinrich, Gretl, and Nannerl were keyboard players; Wolfgang, Leopold, and Heinrich were violinists; and Wolfgang also played the viola (apparently in preference to the violin).[56] But the range of people invited specially to make music swelled the numbers so that a small orchestra was often formed. Nannerl listed the people involved in music-making, but it is difficult to reconstruct precisely the kinds of band produced, partly because most people played more than one instrument, and partly because some were friends with amateur musical interests, about which detailed knowledge is not available. However, her reference to Haydn (Michael, of course) and Fiala playing quartets on 12 September suggests that on this occasion Fiala, who was a fine oboist, was playing the cello, his other main instrument. Haydn presumably played the violin, and it is likely that Wolfgang played the viola and Leopold the other violin part; also likely is that they played some of the quartets which were to form the 'Haydn' set, and which Wolfgang had recently been composing.[57] A further noteworthy point about the musicians mentioned by Nannerl is the fact that they were not only string players (though Wolfgang later suggested that it was unusual for Leopold to have wind players at his house),[58] but included a bassoonist (Sandmayer) and oboists (Fiala and Feiner).

The diary shows a pattern of fairly regular daily music-making involving invited friends, only interrupted when the rehearsals began for the opera Gretl was in, and when Kühne's theatrical performances started. Then the castrato Bologna was recorded coming to practise his operatic part with Gretl. In fact, Bologna was such a constant feature of these summer entries that it is tempting to look for a particular reason, such as the pos-

---

[56] Nannerl's entries for 23 and 26 Oct. 1783 referred to the rehearsal and performance of Wolfgang's C minor Mass, K. 427, and stated that Constanze sang 'the solo' (it is not known who took the other soprano part). It is probable therefore that Constanze was also regularly involved in the domestic music-making with the others. On 4 Jan. 1783, Wolfgang had written to Leopold about a vow he had made before his marriage, which seems to have been connected with marrying Constanze and making a journey to Salzburg with her; and he invoked the existence of 'the score of half a Mass' as proof of his sincerity. See *MBA* 719/10–17 (*Letters* 477); but cf. also von Nissen, *Biographie*, 476, where Nissen claims that the Mass was promised as a thank-offering in the event of Constanze's recuperation from childbirth. Though the work remained unfinished, it was performed at the service in St Peter's Church on 26 Oct. Nannerl unfortunately did not record many details of the rehearsal or performance, but she did say that 'the whole of the court music was present' (*MBA* 765/181–2 and 194–5). Since the Salzburg visit was of great significance to Wolfgang, who must surely have wanted to prove to his family, former colleagues, and acquaintances that his move to Vienna and his marriage were glittering successes, it seems likely that the performance of the Mass (including Constanze's singing) reached a high standard.

[57] They could, of course, also have played oboe quartets, but Nannerl did not list anyone other than Fiala on this occasion who was obviously a cellist.

[58] Wolfgang to Leopold, 15 May 1784—*MBA* 790/13–17 (*Letters* 513).

sibility that he had an arrangement to take his meals at the Mozarts',[59] or that his voice was particularly in demand for domestic operatic music-making.[60] Once the court opera preparations were under way, Gretl had to attend rehearsals at court, and here Nannerl escorted her, as she also did whenever Gretl went to Countess Wallis (Colloredo's sister) to try on her costume.

As soon as Kühne's troupe arrived, its members were drawn into the Mozarts' social life. In return, the Mozarts were probably offered free tickets for the performances; at any rate, they were frequently at the theatre. And once the Marchand relations arrived, things became even more hectic. There were four of them, and the Dancing-Master's House was already full of people with Leopold, Nannerl, Wolfgang, Constanze, Heinrich, Gretl, and Hanchen; Leopold therefore found the visitors accommodation close by in the Alberti-Haus in the Theatergasse.[61] They too went with the family to Kühne's performances at the theatre; probably they had acquaintances in the troupe. One of Marchand's party was Martin Lang, a horn player, and Kühne also had musicians in his troupe, so the possibilities for domestic music-making were further increased. On 1 October, just before the departure of the Marchand relations, Nannerl noted a concert which was perhaps the grandest of those performed that summer and autumn, and gave a partial programme for it. In addition to the half-dozen or so musicians living in the house, more than seven extra people were invited to play, and they performed a symphony, a

---

[59] It was quite common for single men in court service to live in one house but take meals with a family elsewhere.

[60] It is often noted, the information originating in a statement of Constanze's to the Novellos, that the quartet 'Andrò ramingo' from the third act of *Idomeneo* (in which Idamante expresses his grief that his father has commanded him to go into exile) was performed during this summer visit. According to the Novellos, Constanze described Wolfgang's emotional agitation and his precipitate exit from the room—see V. and M. Novello, *A Mozart Pilgrimage: Being the Travel Diaries of Vincent and Mary Novello in the Year 1829*, ed. N. Medici di Marignano and R. Hughes (London, 1955 and 1975; here cited from the 1975 edn.), 114–15. Heartz, in imagining the casting of the piece on this occasion, suggests that Wolfgang took the part of Idamante (a castrato part, but he could sing soprano lines when necessary), Constanze that of Ilia, Leopold that of Idomeneo, and Nannerl that of Electra. His proposals are made to support the psychological suggestion that there are emotional parallels between the story of *Idomeneo* and Wolfgang's own life, especially with respect to the father–son relationship; see D. Heartz, 'Mozart, his Father and *Idomeneo*', *MT* 119 (1978), 228–31. The basis of the suggestion may be valid, but the castings are not convincing in the light of Nannerl's diary evidence. For although she does not record details of this performance, it does not seem likely that Wolfgang would have sung Idamante when two castrati, Bologna and Ceccarelli, were frequently available. Furthermore, Gretl would have been a more likely second female singer than Nannerl, and there was probably also a more suitable Idomeneo (vocally speaking) than Leopold.

[61] Leopold to Nannerl, 25–6 Mar. 1785—*MBA* 854/26–8 (not in *Letters*).

quartet from 'the opera',[62] a keyboard concerto in C (perhaps Wolfgang's new one, K. 415), a violin concerto (with Heinrich as soloist), and an aria (sung by Bologna). For the Marchand parents, seeing their children actively involved in such lively music-making was probably the climax of their visit.

Nannerl had kept up her church-going and teaching during the early days of Wolfgang's visit, but in late September things became increasingly hectic. D'Ippold's relations occupied her from about 16 September until 5 October, and the Marchands were in town during part of the same period, when she also had to help Gretl with her preparation for the opera. The St Rupert's Fair or market was also taking place on 30 September, and she went to it with most of Marchand's party; it was an important event, because many goods were obtainable nowhere else. During this, the busiest part of the period of Wolfgang's visit, she dropped most of her teaching (unless she simply failed to record it) and missed church three days in a row from 30 September (something otherwise unheard of unless she was ill).

Thus, though her diary indeed records very little about Wolfgang's musical activities, it offers copious information about the domestic and social life of the family. Information about Wolfgang's compositional endeavours during this period is better sought from paper studies,[63] but the diary is a fortunate contribution to knowledge of how the Mozarts passed their time. In particular it offers information about virtually the only performance platform of Nannerl's in Salzburg, and shows the insatiable appetite of the family for making music. This was emphatically not a feature of family life only when Wolfgang was at home—when Nannerl had married and moved to St Gilgen, and the Marchands paid another visit, she and Leopold again grasped the opportunity offered by

[62] This could have been the one Gretl and Bologna had been involved in for the court, or it could have been *Idomeneo*; in this case, it might have been the occasion described by Constanze to the Novellos—cf. n. 60 above.

[63] Although it has long seemed logical to assume that Wolfgang used his three months in Salzburg to compose in readiness for the next busy season in Vienna, the evidence for what he actually wrote was very thin until Tyson's methods of dating based on the examination of manuscript paper had been developed. Using these techniques, Tyson suggests that the Keyboard Sonatas, K. 330, K. 331, and K. 332, the orchestral Minuets, K. 363, a further Minuet and Contredanse, K. 463, part of the C minor Mass, K. 427, part of the opera *L'oca del Cairo*, K. 422, the Contredanse, K. 610, some fragments of fugues for keyboard, K. 153 and K. 375h, and a Solfeggio for voice, K. 393, were (in some cases, might have been) written in Salzburg during this visit. See Tyson, *Autograph Scores*, especially chs. 8 and 14. A useful summary of Tyson's redatings of some works written between 1781 and 1791 is given in A. Tyson, 'Proposed New Dates for Many Works and Fragments Written by Mozart from March 1781 to December 1791', in C. Eisen (ed.), *Mozart Studies* (Oxford, 1991), 213–26.

the presence of fine musicians, and arranged for her to visit Salzburg at the same time, to make 'nothing but music'.[64] Small wonder that after Nannerl had married and the Marchands had left, Leopold often did not know what to do with his time, especially when the travelling players had departed for their next location.

[64] Leopold to Nannerl, 6 Sept. 1786—*MBA* 984/49–73 (not in *Letters*).

TABLE 1. Nannerl Mozart's diary entries, summer–autumn 1783

This table is derived from the entries as printed by *MBA* 761, 763, 764, and 765. Nannerl tended to give a laconic list of her activities for each day; the categories given here are mine. Sometimes it is not clear in which category a particular remark belongs—for example, Nannerl typically wrote entries such as 'at the Hermes'' ('beym Hermes'), leaving it unclear whether she had been paying a social call, or whether she had been giving a lesson. In the case of the Hermes entries, I have classed them as teaching visits on account of their relative frequency and regularity; but there is no certain evidence that teaching was their purpose. Where Nannerl gave a list of visitors who had come to make music, I have indicated the instruments played by each where known; this information is derived chiefly from the *MBA* commentary. In the case of friends who were or may have been amateur musicians, however, the information about what they played is often not available. Nannerl frequently noted the activities of 'Henry'—the *MBA* commentary identifies him as the

Date	Church-going	Lessons given	Domestic music-making	Other socializing
Tues. 29 July	7.00a.m. Mass.		p.m. Unspecified—involved Sandmayr (oboist and bassoonist), his son Hans, Bologna and Ceccarelli (both castrati), Schachtner (violinist and trumpeter), Biber, and Reitter.	a.m. Visits to Hagenauer, Schiedenhofen, and Barisani by Nannerl, Wolfgang, and Constanze. p.m. Visit to Katherl Gilowsky; Katherl and Herr and Frau von Schiedenhofen visited the Mozarts; Bologna joined the Mozarts for a walk.
Wed. 30 July	11.30a.m. Mass in Mirabell, with Constanze.	p.m. 'Seperl' (Joseph Wölfl) taught for Nannerl by Heinrich for the third day running.	p.m. Involved Bologna, Biber, 'tonerl' (probably Anton Paris, organist), Reitter, Bullinger (viola player), 'zahlmeister' (Franz V. Lankmayr), and Gatti (Kapellmeister).	p.m. Bologna walking with them.
Thurs. 31 July (Nannerl's birthday)	11.30a.m. Mass in Mirabell, with Constanze.	p.m. Seperl.	p.m. Fiala (oboist and cellist), Reitter, Bologna, and Tomaselli (tenor singer) were involved, and perhaps also Ceccarelli and Brunetti (violinist).	a.m. Visits from Bologna and Ceccarelli. p.m. Visits from Ceccarelli and Brunetti. Walk.
Fri. 1 Aug.	10.00a.m. Mass.	a.m. Nannerl visiting the Hermes family, perhaps to give a lesson. p.m. Seperl.	p.m. Involved Ceccarelli, Bologna, Reitter, and Bullinger.	a.m. Visit from Perwein (oboist) and Cassel (violinist and double bass player). p.m. Outing with Bologna and Ceccarelli to drink beer on the Mönchsberg.
Sat. 2 Aug.		p.m. Seperl.		6.00a.m. Outing to pilgrimage church of Maria Plain in two carriages with Bologna. p.m. Visit to Captain Hermes on the Kapuzinerberg.

ex-Jesuit tutor Abbé Henri, but I believe this to be mistaken, and that he was in fact Heinrich Marchand. This belief rests on the facts that 'Henry' in these entries was often recorded in activities which otherwise involved only the members of the Mozarts' household (Leopold, Nannerl, Wolfgang, Constanze, Gretl, and Hanchen); or he was noted as the substitute teacher of Nannerl's and/or Leopold's pupil Joseph Wölfl (Leopold was later to offload some of his violin tuition onto Heinrich after Heinrich had returned to Salzburg as a salaried employee and was lodging with Leopold again—cf. e.g. Leopold to Nannerl, 1–2 Sept. 1786—*MBA* 982/63–6 (not in *Letters*)); and that there are other references to 'Henry' in the correspondence which could only have denoted Heinrich Marchand (showing that he is a likely candidate for the identification)—cf., e.g., Leopold to Nannerl on 21–2 Feb. 1785—*MBA* 848/29; Letters 524 (although Anderson here gives a tacit interpretation of Leopold's 'Henry' by calling him simply 'Heinrich').

Time spent with d'Ippold	Court-organized opera	Public theatre visits	Miscellaneous
			Wolfgang served Nannerl with ices in the afternoon and punch in the evening.

TABLE I. *(cont'd)*

Date	Church-going	Lessons given	Domestic music-making	Other socializing
Sat. 23 Aug. (Wolfgang and Constanze's baby son Raimund had died on 19 Aug.)	7.00a.m. Mass.	a.m. Nannerl visiting the Hermes family, with Wolfgang and Constanze, perhaps to give a lesson. p.m. Seperl.	p.m. Involved Bologna, Bullinger, Tonerl, and Seperl.	p.m. Visit to the Gilowskys, with Wolfgang and Constanze. Bologna walking with them.
Sun. 24 Aug.	Cathedral.		p.m. Unclear who was involved—perhaps most of the shooters.	a.m. Whole family visiting Obersthofmeister. p.m. *Bölzlschiessen*, with Wegscheider as *Bestgeber*; winners were Wolfgang and 'Zahlmeister'. Visit from Obersthofmeister, and 'young Daubrawa'. *Tresette* played by Nannerl, Katherl, Bullinger, and Bologna; some sort of row involving Bullinger. To Mirabell without Wolfgang and Constanze. Visit to Hagenauer.
Mon. 25 Aug.	7.00a.m. Mass.	a.m. Hermes.		p.m. Sightseeing outing to the palace of Leopoldskron, property of the Obersthofmeister Firmian.
Tues. 26 Aug.	7.00a.m. Mass.	a.m. Hermes. p.m. Seperl.	p.m. Involved Bologna and Paris.	
Wed. 27 Aug.	7.00a.m. Mass.	a.m. Hermes (after Paradis visit).	p.m. Involved Bologna, Fink (organist), Daubrawa, Biber, and Bullinger.	
Thurs. 28 Aug.				
Thurs. 4 Sept.	7.00a.m. Mass.	a.m. Hermes; possibly several of the Mozarts and Ceccarelli were present.		a.m. Visit from Ceccarelli. Visit (by 'all of us') from 8 to 9.00 (unclear whether a.m. or p.m.) to Schiedenhofen.
Fri. 5 Sept.	7.00a.m. Mass.	a.m. Hermes.	p.m. Involved Tonerl, Schachtner, and Seperl.	
Sat. 6 Sept.	7.00a.m. Mass.	a.m. Hermes.	p.m. Involved Bologna and Tonerl.	

Time spent with d'Ippold	Court-organized opera	Public theatre visits	Miscellaneous
p.m. Visit from d'Ippold.			
p.m. Visit from d'Ippold.			a.m. Visit from Herr Grubner (flautist) and Maria Theresia Paradis (blind virtuoso keyboard player) with her mother.
			Visit to the Ursuline convent to see three novices admitted. Visit to Paradis at her inn. p.m. Return to convent for sightseeing and the litany.
			Wolfgang and Constanze bathing.
p.m. Visit from d'Ippold.			Wolfgang and Constanze bathing.

TABLE 1. (*cont'd*)

Date	Church-going	Lessons given	Domestic music-making	Other socializing
Sun. 7 Sept.	9.00a.m. at St Sebastian's.			p.m. *Bölzlschiessen*, but without other guests. Visit from Bologna. After returning from theatre, game of *Lotterie*.
Mon. 8 Sept.	Cathedral service.		Unclear who was involved—perhaps Ceccarelli, Schachtner, Bullinger, and Bologna.	a.m. Visit from Bologna and Ceccarelli. p.m. *Bölzlschiessen*; 'Josepha' (probably Barisani) was *Bestgeber*, Wolfgang and Wegscheider won. Nannerl, Leopold, Bullinger, and Bologna played *Tarock*. Visit from Barbara von Mölk.
Tues. 9 Sept.	7.00a.m. Mass.	a.m. Hermes. p.m. Seperl.		p.m. Visit from Bologna and Berhandsky. Leopold, Nannerl, Gretl, and Heinrich out walking.
Wed. 10 Sept.	7.00a.m. Mass.	a.m. Hermes. p.m. Seperl.	p.m. Involved Bologna, Biber, and Tonerl.	Evening card party, till 11.30p.m., with Schiedenhofens, Josepha Barisani, and Bologna.
Thurs. 11 Sept.	7.00a.m. Mass.	a.m. Hermes.		a.m. Visit from Tomaselli. p.m. Outing to visit Seperl's father, the administrator of the Johannis-Spital; dined out, returning at 10.00p.m.
Fri. 12 Sept.	7.00a.m. Mass.	a.m. Hermes.	p.m. Quartets with Michael Haydn and Fiala.	p.m. Visit from Bologna and from Herr and Frau Weiss, members of Kühne's theatrical troupe.
Sat. 13 Sept.	7.00a.m. Mass.		p.m. Involved Bologna, Fiala, and Robinig (a friend and amateur musician).	
Sun. 14 Sept.	Cathedral service			a.m. Visit from d'Ippold, Bologna, and Tomaselli. p.m. Visit from Haydn. *Bölzlschiessen*; Tomaselli on *Bestgeber*, Wolfgang and Zahlmeister won.
Mon. 15 Sept.	7.00a.m. Mass.	a.m. Hermes. p.m. Seperl.		p.m. Nannerl, Gretl, and Hanchen walking in the Mirabell garden with

Time spent with d'Ippold	Court-organized opera	Public theatre visits	Miscellaneous
		Visit to theatre.	
	Bologna practising his part with Gretl, probably in the Dancing-Master's House. The opera may have been Gatti's *Olimpiade*.		Leave-taking of Count Fugger and Baron Rechberg. Wolfgang, Constanze, and Paris shooting birds on the Mönchsberg.
p.m. Visit from d'Ippold.	Bologna practising his part at the Mozarts'.		
	Bologna practising his part at the Mozarts'.		
p.m. Visit from d'Ippold.	Visit from Bologna, perhaps to practise his part.	Nannerl, Leopold, Gretl, and Heinrich went to the theatre.	Visit from a young male keyboard player who used to be in Kühne's theatrical troupe.
	Nannerl and Gretl at court for recitative rehearsal, and to see Countess Wallis, Colloredo's sister. Home with Bologna in court carriage at midday.		
See 'Other socializing'.		p.m. Bologna and 'all of us' to the theatre.	
	a.m. Nannerl and Gretl at court for a recitative rehearsal; Leopold looked in.	p.m. Theatre visit.	

TABLE I. (*cont'd*)

Date	Church-going	Lessons given	Domestic music-making	Other socializing
				Pimpes the dog. Leopold, Wolfgang, Constanze, and Heinrich visited the Mölks at their house in Riedenburg.
Tues. 16 Sept.	7.00a.m. Mass.	a.m. Hermes. p.m. Seperl.		Bologna, Leopold, Wolfgang, Constanze, Heinrich, and Gretl went to a shooting range near the Mirabell gate.
Wed. 17 Sept.	7.00a.m. Mass.	a.m. Hermes.	Evening—music for two violas performed for Wolfgang by Pinzger (court violinist) and Widmann.	Visit from Bologna, and walk with him.
Thurs. 18 Sept.	7.00a.m. Mass.	p.m. Seperl.	Involved Bologna and Fiala.	After the music-making, cards till 11.30p.m.
Fri. 19 Sept.	7.00a.m. Mass.	a.m. Hermes. p.m. Seperl.		
Sat. 20 Sept.	7.00a.m. Mass.			a.m. Visit from Robinig. p.m. Bologna walking with the Mozarts. Visit from *Hofrat* Gilowsky (Katherl's cousin, Joseph A. E.), Robinig, Frau Starzer, and her brother Herr Hepp.
Sun. 21 Sept.	Cathedral service; Nannerl accompanied by d'Ippold.			*Bölzlschiessen*—Heinrich as *Bestgeber*, Wolfgang and Wegscheider won. Bologna, Katherl, Bullinger, and Nannerl played *Tarock*.
Mon. 22 Sept.	7.00a.m. Mass.	a.m. Hermes. p.m. Heinrich taught Seperl.		Visit from Bologna.
Tues. 23 Sept.	7.00a.m. Mass. p.m. Vespers in cathedral.			a.m. Visit from Bologna. p.m. Another visit from Bologna. Visit from Robinig and 'Herr Döbler'.

Time spent with d'Ippold	Court-organized opera	Public theatre visits	Miscellaneous
Visit from d'Ippold and his sister-in-law, to Nannerl alone.			
	Nannerl and Gretl at court for a rehearsal; Leopold looked in.		
a.m. Nannerl visited d'Ippold's sister-in-law at the house of the Kletzl family.	a.m. Bologna practising at the Mozarts', probably for the opera.		
	Nannerl and Gretl at court for a recitative rehearsal; Leopold looked in.	With Bologna to the theatre.	
	Leopold and Nannerl at the theatre for a recitative rehearsal. p.m. Nannerl and Gretl with Countess Wallis, for Gretl's dress to be tried.		
See 'church-going' and 'public theatre visits'.		Theatre visit with Bologna, d'Ippold's sister, and 'Trezi' (Anton Trezzi, former foster-son of d'Ippold).	
Nannerl walking in the Mirabell garden with d'Ippold and his sister-in-law. Then *Tarock* and supper with Frau d'Ippold (probably the sister-in-law), after which d'Ippold and 'trezy' (Anton Trezzi) walked Nannerl home.	9.00a.m.–1.00p.m. Aria rehearsal at court for the opera, with all the instruments.	Theatre visit by Leopold, Gretl, Heinrich, and Bologna.	p.m. Nannerl and Tresel (the Mozarts' servant) at the fair/market; held to celebrate *Rupertitag* on 24 Sept. (St Rupert was Salzburg's patron).
	a.m. Recitative rehearsal in the theatre.		

TABLE 1. (*cont'd*)

Date	Church-going	Lessons given	Domestic music-making	Other socializing
Wed. 24 Sept.	Colloredo celebrated *Rupertitag* in the cathedral; Nannerl and Frau d'Ippold watched from the violinists' gallery or choir (see Fig. 4).			*Bölzlschiessen*—Gretl as *Bestgeberin*, Heinrich won. Visit from Frau Kühne (wife of leader of acting troupe). Visit from Barbara von Mölk, after return from theatre.
Thurs. 25 Sept.		p.m. Seperl.		Visit from Bologna. Visit from Robinig. Arrival of Marchands—see 'miscellaneous'.
Fri. 26 Sept.	7.30a.m. Mass.			p.m. Visit from Bologna.
Sat. 27 Sept.	7.00a.m. Mass.			
Sun. 28 Sept.	11.30a.m. Mass in Mirabell.			*Bölzlschiessen*—Bologna as *Bestgeber*, Ceccarelli won. Wolfgang, Constanze, Frau Marchand, Herr Brochard, Herr Lang, and Heinrich on an outing to Hellbrun palace.
Mon. 29 Sept.	9.00a.m. Mass.		On returning from Aigen, unspecified music-making, perhaps involving Bologna.	p.m. 'All of us' on an outing to Aigen, in 3 carriages. Visit from Bologna.
Tues. 30 Sept.				
Wed. 1 Oct.			p.m. Involved Robinig, Ceccarelli, Bullinger, Bologna, Tomaselli, Fiala, Feiner, and others. Performed were a symphony, 'the quartet from the opera', a keyboard concerto in C, a violin concerto played by Heinrich, and an aria sung by Bologna.	a.m. Visit from Bologna and Bullinger.

Time spent with d'Ippold	Court-organized opera	Public theatre visits	Miscellaneous
See 'church-going'. Nannerl visited Frau d'Ippold after church. After visiting the theatre, Nannerl supped with Frau d'Ippold; d'Ippold and Trezzi walked her home.		Theatre visit with Bologna.	*Rupertitag*
	10.00a.m. Recitative rehearsal in the theatre.		6.00p.m. Arrival of Herr and Frau Marchand (Gretl's and Heinrich's parents), Herr Brochard (Hanchen's father), and Martin Lang; Leopold found them lodgings close by in the Alberti-Haus in the Theatergasse.
	10.00a.m.–3.00p.m. (Finish time not quite certain, because of a correction by Nannerl)—'all of us' at the theatre to see the instrumental rehearsal of the opera.	p.m. 'All of us' to the theatre.	
	10.00a.m.–1.00p.m. Aria rehearsal in theatre. p.m. Gretl getting costumed. 5.00p.m. 'All of us' at the opera in the theatre.		
		Leopold, Nannerl, Herr Marchand, Gretl, and Bologna to the theatre.	
	Theatre rehearsal.		
	p.m. Gretl to Countess Wallis to be costumed. 6.00p.m. Opera in theatre, till 10.00p.m.		a.m. To the fair/market with Frau Marchand, Herr Brochard, and Herr Lang. Colloredo's name-day (Hieronymus)
		Theatre visit after the music-making.	

TABLE 1. (*cont'd*)

Date	Church-going	Lessons given	Domestic music-making	Other socializing
Thurs. 2 Oct.				a.m. Visit from Bologna.
Fri. 3 Oct.	10.30a.m. Mass.			a.m. Visit from Bologna.
Sat. 4 Oct.	10.30a.m. Mass.			p.m. Bologna walking with them.
Sun. 5 Oct.	10.00a.m. Mass in cathedral.			*Bölzlschiessen*—Katherl as *Bestgeberin* and winner.
Mon. 6 Oct.	7.00a.m. Mass.	a.m. Hermes. p.m. Seperl.		p.m. Out walking. Visit from Bologna.
Tues. 7 Oct.	7.00a.m. Mass.	a.m. Hermes. p.m. Seperl.	p.m. After Bologna had gone to court, unspecified music-making.	p.m. Bologna walking with them in Gnigl, incorporating a visit to an inn to see some shooting. Return home at 7.00p.m.; Bologna to court.
Wed. 8 Oct.	7.00a.m. Mass.	a.m. Hermes. p.m. Seperl.		p.m. Visit from Fiala.
Thurs. 9 Oct.	7.00a.m. Mass.	p.m. Seperl.	p.m. Involved Schachtner, Bologna, Tomaselli, and Abbate Piccini (a visitor to Salzburg).	a.m. Visit to Frau von Schiedenhofen, because she was sick. p.m. Visit from Albert von Mölk.
Fri. 10 Oct.	7.30a.m. Mass.	p.m. Seperl.	p.m. (probably while Nannerl was at the theatre). Music-making involving Wolfgang, Fiala, Heinrich, and a servant of the Wallis family.	p.m. Visit from Schachtner.
Sat. 11 Oct.	7.00a.m. Mass.	a.m. Hermes.		p.m. Frau von Hermes (from the Kapuzinerberg) visited the Mozarts. Game of *Tresette* with Bologna and Bullinger.
Sun. 12 Oct.	Service at St Sebastian's.			*Bölzlschiessen*—Leopold as *Bestgeber*, Wegscheider won. Visit from Frau von Hermes (from the Kapuzinerberg).

Time spent with d'Ippold	Court-organized opera	Public theatre visits	Miscellaneous
	p.m. Gretl to Countess Wallis to be costumed. 'All of us' to the opera.		a.m. Visit to Barisani with Hanchen; may have been a social call, or may have had a medical purpose. Frau Marchand and Herr Brochard took leave of Frau Weiss and Frau Kühne (from the troupe of players).
		p.m. Theatre visit with Bologna.	
a.m. Visit to Frau d'Ippold. p.m. Visit from d'Ippold's brother and sister-in-law, with 'the girls'. Nannerl returned to sup with them, and d'Ippold walked her home.			p.m. Nannerl and Gretl at the fair/market.
Nannerl and Gretl taking leave of Frau d'Ippold.		Theatre visit with Bologna.	
		Theatre visit.	
p.m. Visit from d'Ippold.		Theatre visit with Bologna.	
		Theatre visit with Bologna.	
		Theatre visit with Bologna and Frau von Hermes.	

TABLE I. (*cont'd*)

Date	Church-going	Lessons given	Domestic music-making	Other socializing
Mon. 13 Oct.	7.00a.m. Mass.	a.m. Hermes.		a.m. Visit to Schiedenhofen. p.m. Visit to Barbara Eberlin. Visit from Bologna.
Tues. 14 Oct.	7.00a.m. Mass.	a.m. Possibly a lesson given to Hermes, but the visit might have been a social one. p.m. Seperl.	p.m. Involved Bologna.	a.m. Visits to Hermes and Hagenauer, to offer congratulations (15 Oct. was St Theresia's Day). p.m. Bologna walking with them.
Wed. 15 Oct.	7.00a.m. Mass.			a.m. Congratulations visits to Barisani and Wegscheider (St Theresia's Day). Visit from Bologna.
Thurs. 16 Oct.	7.00a.m. Mass.			p.m. *Bölzlschiessen*— Wolfgang won.
Fri. 17 Oct.	7.30a.m. Mass.	a.m. Hermes p.m. Seperl.		
Sat. 18 Oct.		a.m. Hermes.		a.m. Visit to Katherl. p.m. Dancing the contredanse—involved Bologna, Ceccarelli, Tomaselli, Frau von Hermes, '2 girls', Fichtl, 'nanerl', Frau von Daubrawa, Herr von Fichtl 'Zahlmeister,' Herr and Frau Kühne, Herr and Frau Schätzl, Frau Höpfler, and Fräulein Clementine (last 6 people were members of Kühne's troupe). 'tonerl' played the violin for them.
Sun. 19 Oct.	Cathedral service.			*Bölzlschiessen*—'Zahlmeister' as *Bestgeber*, Wolfgang and Zahlmeister won. 8.00p.m. Outing to the Eizenberger inn for supper; dancing there till 4.00a.m. Return home at 6.00a.m.
Mon. 20 Oct.				
Tues. 21 Oct.	10.00a.m. Mass.	a.m. Hermes.	p.m. Probably involved Herr and Frau Kühne.	a.m. Visit to Hagenauer, to offer congratulations to Ursula for St Ursula's Day. p.m. Bologna walking with them.
Wed. 22 Oct.	7.00a.m. Mass.	a.m. Hermes.		8.00a.m. 'All of us' at breakfast with Johannes (Johann Nepomuk Anton) Hagenauer. Visit to 'old Hagenauer' (Johann Lorenz).

Time spent with d'Ippold	Court-organized opera	Public theatre visits	Miscellaneous
		Theatre visit 'together' (i.e. perhaps with Bologna, Barbara Eberlin, or both).	
p.m. d'Ippold visited the Mozarts.	a.m. Opera rehearsal in the theatre.		
	p.m. Gretl to Countess Wallis to be costumed. Leopold, Nannerl, Heinrich, and Hanchen to see the opera.		
		Theatre visit.	
		p.m. Theatre visit with Bologna.	
		Theatre visit.	
		Theatre visit with Bologna.	Rose at 1.00p.m., dined at 2.00p.m.
p.m. Visit from d'Ippold.		Theatre visit with Bologna.	

TABLE I. (*cont'd*)

Date	Church-going	Lessons given	Domestic music-making	Other socializing
Thurs. 23 Oct.	8.00a.m. Mass.			2–7.00p.m. 'Grand' *Bölzlschiessen*; 3 targets, Wolfgang as *Bestgeber*, Johannes Hagenauer as main winner, Ceccarelli as winner of smaller prizes. Visit from Frau Kühne, Frau Hornung, Herr and Frau Höpfler, Herr Streibel, and Herr Holzmann (all members of Kühne's troupe), after the shooting. Stadler (colleague of Leopold's) had supper with them.
Fri. 24 Oct.	10.00a.m. Mass.	a.m. Hermes.		p.m. Walking, probably with Bullinger.
Sat. 25 Oct.	7.00a.m. Mass.	a.m. Hermes.	p.m. Probably involved the following afternoon visitors: Bologna, 'young' Daubrawa, Kajetan von Antretter, Schiedenhofen, Fiala, 'the controller and his wife from the king of Poland,' Streibel, Fräulein Clementine, and 'tonerl'. Some were court musicians, some amateurs, and some from the theatrical troupe.	p.m. Walking. p.m. Visit from Johannes Hagenauer.
Sun. 26 Oct.	St Peter's service; Wolfgang's C minor Mass performed, and 'the whole court music was there.'			p.m. *Bölzlschiessen*— Hagenauer as *Bestgeber*, Katherl won. Visit from Tomaselli, Ceccarelli, and Frau von Hermes from the Kapuzinerberg to take leave (of Wolfgang and Constanze).
Mon. 27 Oct.				a.m. Visit from Ceccarelli, Wegscheider, Hagenauer, and Varesco. p.m. Leopold, Nannerl, Heinrich, and Gretl eating fowl in Gnigl. Bologna with them.
Tues. 28 Oct.	7.00a.m. Mass.		p.m., after d'Ippold's visit. Probably involved Bologna and Streibel.	Leopold and Heinrich dined at St Peter's.
Wed. 29 Oct.	7.00a.m. Mass.	a.m. Hermes. p.m. Seperl.		p.m. Visit from Bologna.
Thurs. 30 Oct.	7.00a.m. Mass.	a.m. Hermes. p.m. Seperl.		p.m. Out walking. Visit from Bologna and Kühne.
Fri. 31 Oct.	7.00a.m. Mass.	a.m. Hermes.		p.m. Out walking. Visit from Bologna and Hermes.

Time spent with d'Ippold	Court-organized opera	Public theatre visits	Miscellaneous
			a.m. Rehearsal in the Kapellhaus for the Mass composed by Wolfgang (i.e. the C minor Mass, K. 427); Constanze took 'the solo'.
		Theatre visit with Bologna.	
		Theatre visit with Bologna.	
		Theatre visit, perhaps with Bologna.	9.30a.m. Departure of Wolfgang and Constanze.
p.m. Visit from d'Ippold.			
		Theatre visit with Bologna.	
		Visit to theatre for rehearsal of the *opera buffa*.	
		Theatre visit with Bologna and Hermes.	

❦ 24 ❧

Nannerl's Marriage

❦❧

HAD the visit to Salzburg been a success? From a single remark in Nissen's biography of Mozart has grown, often with embellishments unsupported by any evidence, the predominating view that it did nothing to reconcile Leopold and Nannerl to Wolfgang's choice of a bride. The remark was that Constanze had hoped to be offered some of Wolfgang's childhood trinkets and trophies still held by Leopold, but was not.[1] Yet clearly, if the observation was true, there are possible reasons other than dislike of Constanze for Leopold's disinclination to part with anything. He may have intended to leave the objects to Wolfgang in his will, and have considered that it was therefore unnecessary to part with anything at this point; or he may have suspected in the married couple the common youthful reluctance to attach sentimental value to childhood relics, and have feared that anything given away by him might simply be sold by them. It seems quite likely, given Leopold's inquisitiveness about money, that he was able to form a shrewd idea of Wolfgang's financial situation;[2] and if he had any reason to be dissatisfied with it, he is hardly likely to have wanted to dip into his collection of treasures only to fear that the objects would soon be converted to cash.[3]

Wolfgang and Constanze left Salzburg on 27 October 1783, and returned to Vienna via Linz, where Wolfgang wrote a new symphony (K. 425, the 'Linz') and had it performed in a concert in the theatre there on 4 November. It is not certain when they arrived in Vienna, and neither is it known when they discovered that their baby, Raimund, had died. He had suffered

[1] Von Nissen, *Biographie*, Author's Preface, p. xviii.
[2] When Leopold visited Wolfgang and Constanze in Vienna in 1785, he was to reveal a comprehensive interest in their financial affairs. See Ch. 27 for more details.
[3] Yet it might be argued that if Nissen's work, which was in general so reticent about family disagreements, mentioned disharmony at all, there must have been a strong foundation for the remarks. In answer to this case, I would still point out that though Leopold certainly seems to have been regularly critical of Wolfgang's financial dealings, and though it is quite easy to imagine Wolfgang and Constanze bearing a grudge about the trinkets issue, there is nevertheless no particular reason to infer that dislike of Constanze formed part of Leopold's motive.

from *Gedärmfrais* ('intestinal cramp') and died in Vienna on 19 August, aged two months. *Frais* was one of the commonest-named infant ailments, and though it seems to have been a factor in many illnesses, was treated as a specific evil requiring specific remedies, some of which were magical.[4]

Wolfgang's letter to Leopold of 6 December 1783, by which time they were back in Vienna, reveals that his financial position was not particularly healthy. He owed Leopold 4 ducats (20 fl.) for something,[5] and was dismayed to discover that a forgotten debt from Strasburg in 1778 had also resurfaced, and that the creditor (the merchant, Scherz) was demanding repayment with interest. The sum involved (excluding the interest, which Wolfgang insisted he was not bound to pay) was 12 louis d'or (about 132 fl.),[6] and Wolfgang frankly admitted to Leopold that he could not spare the money, and asked him to guarantee it with the Haffner firm (Scherz's contact in Salzburg) for a month. Thus Leopold could not have been unaware that Wolfgang had not managed to save enough during one concert season to tide him over comfortably until the next.

The plans Wolfgang outlined to Leopold, however, show that he was optimistically determined to apply himself with vigour to the new season in Vienna. He said that he would give six subscription academies in the coming Lent, as well as his theatre academy. He therefore asked Leopold for *Idomeneo*, which he would use for some of these concerts. Other music requested by him were some Bach fugues, and two violin duos. He was also still working on the opera *L'oca del Cairo*.[7]

In return, Leopold was asking for music from Vienna—concertos, and material by other composers for performance by Kühne and his troupe. He had also asked Wolfgang to speak highly of Heinrich Marchand, who was now 14 years old and could be thinking about applying for jobs and appearing in public. On 22 December Wolfgang played a keyboard concerto in a concert organized by the Tonkünstlersozietät, and in January 1784 he and Constanze moved to a new lodging in the Trattnerhof.[8] By

---

[4] See Bartelt, 'Anhänger und Amulette'; and E. Hutter, 'Abwehrzauber und Gottvertrauen. Kleinodien Salzburger Volksfrömmigkeit', *Jahresschriften Salzburger Museum Carolino Augusteum*, 31 (Salzburg, 1985), 198–359. (This exhibition catalogue contains many illustrations of magical and religious charms, such as *Fraisketten*, against sickness). See also Ch. 28 for an account of the part played by *Frais* in baby Leopoldl's near-fatal illness at about the same age. See Plate 9 for an illustration of a *Fraiskette*.

[5] This conversion assumes that the ducats were to be converted to florins for Leopold's use in Salzburg.

[6] This is an approximate conversion, being the one used by Leopold for louis d'or/florins while Wolfgang was away from 1777 to 1779.

[7] *MBA* 770 (*Letters* 500).

[8] See Eisen, *Documents*, 55, for details of Wolfgang's rent here, which was 150 fl. annually.

this time he was up to his ears in work for the Lenten academies, the music for which he could only compose in the evenings, because he gave lessons all morning. When at some point during 1784 he began to keep a catalogue of all his compositions, the first entry was for the Keyboard Concerto, K. 449, to which he assigned the date 9 February 1784.[9] Because of his heavy workload, he told Leopold that work on the opera *L'oca del Cairo* would have to be suspended—there was no prospect of an early performance, and he had other music to write which would bring in money immediately.[10]

The music he meant must have been his new Keyboard Concertos, K. 449, K. 450, and K. 451, and the Quintet for keyboard and wind, K. 452, all of which were used during the Lenten season in 1784. On 20 February he was promising to send the score of K. 449 to Salzburg, together with a symphony and a sonata. The concerto had been written for Wolfgang's pupil Barbara Ployer (daughter of the Salzburg agent in Vienna), and Wolfgang was concerned that it should not fall into anyone else's hands, since she had paid him well for it. Wolfgang was also thinking of having some of his music engraved at his own expense (this had been Leopold's marketing method with his *Violinschule*), and asked Leopold how he could ensure that the engraver did not run off extra copies and sell them for his own profit.[11]

In his next letter, written on 3 March, Wolfgang was able proudly to list all his Lenten engagements for Leopold—evidently this season promised to be more successful again than the last. He planned to give two academies in the theatre, three private subscription ones in the hall of the Trattnerhof, where his new lodgings were, he was playing in three Trattnerhof concerts of another keyboardist, Richter, and he was booked for fourteen private concerts given by members of the nobility; between Thursday 26 February and Saturday 3 April he was to be out twenty-two times at concerts. Wolfgang also gave Leopold the price of the Trattnerhof subscription concerts—6 fl. for the series of three, and he expected to get

---

[9] However, the first ten entries in this catalogue were almost certainly made retrospectively, as late as November 1784, which raises questions about the accuracy of the dates Wolfgang assigned to the works. See D. N. Leeson and D. Whitwell, 'Mozart's Thematic Catalogue', *MT* 114 (Aug. 1973), 781–3. The entries in the thematic catalogue are given in *MBA*—the first is *MBA* 774. There is also a published facsimile of the catalogue—*Mozart: Eigenhändiges Werkverzeichnis Faksimile* (British Library Stefan Zweig MS 63). Einführung und Übertragung von A. Rosenthal und A. Tyson; Lizenzausgabe mit Genehmigung der British Library, London. Serie X Supplement to *NMA* (Kassel, 1991).

[10] Wolfgang to Leopold, 6, 10, and 24 Dec. 1783 and 10 Feb. 1784—*MBA* 770, 771, 773, and 775 (*Letters* 500, 501, 502, and 503).

[11] *MBA* 776 (*Letters* 504).

130 subscribers. These were the concerts, then, for which he was writing new music as fast as he could; but now that the season was under
way, and he was out for so many evenings, he had less time to compose
even than formerly.[12] The hectic life-style during the busy Lenten season
was to be described by Leopold to Nannerl when he went to stay with
Wolfgang the following year.

Writing again on 20 March, Wolfgang enclosed a list of all his subscribers,
of whom there were over 170. By this time, his first Trattnerhof subscription concert, at which he had played a new keyboard concerto (probably
K. 450),[13] had been a triumphant success. He begged Leopold to have
patience with him until the end of Lent, when he would have more time
to answer letters properly.[14]

The triumphs apparently went on and on. Wolfgang played the two
Concertos, K. 450 and K. 451, and the Quintet for keyboard and wind,
K. 452, frequently that season, and was particularly pleased with the
Quintet, which he thought Leopold would have loved. Meanwhile, he had
finished writing another concerto for Barbara Ployer (K. 453), and even
after the concerts he had previously listed for Leopold were at an end,
he was still being asked to play at private events.[15] Towards the end
of April, when things should have been quietening down, the violinist
Regina Strinasacchi visited Vienna, and Wolfgang composed a sonata for
violin and keyboard (K. 454) to play in public with her.[16] This sonata
was to become a favourite of Nannerl's future husband.[17] By the time
Strinasacchi had been and gone, it was more than two months since
Wolfgang had first promised to send Nannerl the Keyboard Concerto,
K. 449, and a sonata and symphony.

Little is known about Leopold's and Nannerl's activities during this
period; Wolfgang, never a good letter-writer, was too busy to answer
their letters properly, and was in any case completely absorbed in his
own affairs. But one event that affected Leopold in an unwelcome way
was the death in January 1784 of the court violinist Joseph Hafeneder.
Leopold was evidently given Hafeneder's teaching duties in the Kapellhaus,

---

[12] *MBA* 778 (*Letters* 505).

[13] The commentary to *MBA* 780/74 suggests that the concerto Wolfgang played was K. 449,
but this seems unlikely—both because that was a small-scale concerto, and because he had written it specially for Barbara Ployer.

[14] *MBA* 780 (*Letters* 506).

[15] Wolfgang to Leopold, 10 Apr. 1784—*MBA* 783 (*Letters* 508).

[16] Wolfgang to Leopold, 24 Apr. 1784—*MBA* 786 (*Letters* 510). For Leopold's views on Regina
Strinasacchi's playing, see Ch. 2.

[17] Leopold to Nannerl, 7 Dec. 1785—*MBA* 907/29–51 (not in *Letters*).

at least until another violinist should be chosen. Since Wolfgang's letter of sympathy at this new development noted that Colloredo should
have given an increase in salary and either ordered the choirboys to go
to Leopold for their lessons, or given Leopold a free lodging in the
Kapellhaus, it can be inferred that Leopold was expected to carry out this
extra burdensome duty for no increase in remuneration.[18] At the same time,
of course, a replacement for Hafeneder was being sought, and Wolfgang
suggested the name of Zeno Franz Menzel to Ployer, who was supposed
to be looking for a new violinist to send to Colloredo.[19] It was agreed that
Menzel should go to Salzburg on trial, and Wolfgang promised Leopold
that he would send some music with him.[20] But when Menzel left for
Salzburg, Wolfgang did not send the promised music at all. Leopold probably wrote to complain about this, and seems to have hinted at some ulterior motive of Wolfgang's for not doing so. In response, Wolfgang sent
the music (the 'Linz' Symphony and the four new keyboard concertos)
by the mailcoach, and excused himself by saying that he had not trusted
Menzel to take it, and had also thought that apart from K. 449 the concertos would not be much use to Leopold and Nannerl, since they included
obligato wind instruments, which Leopold rarely had at his domestic
music-making sessions. Wolfgang also begged Leopold not to let the
four concertos fall into the hands of anyone else, and urged him to have
them copied at home, so that the copyist could not cheat him.[21]

   This letter, with its suggestion of reluctance to send them the concertos at all, may reveal suspicion on Wolfgang's part that they would
not take sufficient steps to prevent his music being pirated, or it may
suggest a musical distancing of Wolfgang from Leopold and Nannerl.[22]

---

   [18] Wolfgang to Leopold, 20 Feb. 1784—*MBA* 776/13–19 (*Letters* 504). The *MBA* commentary
claims that Leopold was already teaching the violin and keyboard playing at the Kapellhaus, and
had to take over Hafeneder's duties in addition to his own, but it is not clear if this is right. When
the Kapellmeister Lolli had died in 1778, Leopold had been awarded a salary increase to compensate him for his extra duties (which included overseeing the teaching at the Kapellhaus) until a new
Kapellmeister should be chosen. He had not, however, actually taught at the Kapellhaus since 1768,
and it is not clear that the new decree specifically required him to teach. It seems likely that
Leopold should have been relieved of all Kapellhaus duties following the arrival of the
Kapellmeister Gatti in 1783. If this is so, the imposition of tuition following Hafeneder's death must
have been a sore trial to the man who was constantly hoping for a quieter life. See Hintermaier,
'Hofkapelle', 131–43 and 290–5.
   [19] Wolfgang to Leopold, 10 Apr. 1784—*MBA* 783/23–35 (*Letters* 508).
   [20] Wolfgang to Leopold, 28 Apr. 1784—*MBA* 787/19–21 (*Letters* 511).
   [21] Wolfgang to Leopold, 15 May 1784—*MBA* 790 (*Letters* 513).
   [22] The translation in *Letters* does not quite convey the likelihood that Leopold had harboured a
degree of ill feeling about Wolfgang's failure to send the music when he had promised. The
German is: 'Übrigens weis ich nicht was sie sich dachten und nicht schreiben wollten; und um alles
unangenehme zu vermeiden, schicke ich ihnen hiemit alles Neue was ich gemacht habe' (*MBA*

Conceivably it was a combination of both factors—if he felt impatient at the thought of them playing through grand concertos containing obligato wind instruments, without the necessary resources and hence failing to do them justice, he may have resented all the more the risk that the works would fall into the wrong hands and become so widely known that he would not be able to sell them.[23]

Despite his lukewarm dispatch of the concertos, however, it was not long before he was keen to know their opinion of them. He reiterated the need for a good performance and the use of all the parts, and explained the difference between the small-scale one (K. 449) and the other three.[24] Nannerl started to play them through, but did not get far before writing to Wolfgang to ask him about bits and pieces missing from them, especially from the passage in C major from the slow movement of the D major concerto (K. 451). In reply, Wolfgang agreed that something should be inserted, and promised to send it with the cadenzas.[25] This he apparently did, shortly before Nannerl's name-day in July. Writing to greet her for this event on 21 July, he expressed his hope that 'everything' had arrived safely with the mailcoach, apologized that he had been too busy to send all the cadenzas she wanted, and asked again for her opinion of the three grand concertos. It is not clear exactly what was sent, but his use of the plural ('I would gladly have sent you the cadenzas to the other concertos too') shows that there were at least two concertos for which he did not send cadenzas.[26] It seems likely that what was sent was

---

790/17–19). Anderson's translation is: 'Well, I don't know what it was that you were thinking about and did not want to mention in your letter; and therefore to avoid all misunderstanding, I am sending you herewith all my new compositions' (*Letters* 513). 'Unangenehme' should probably be translated more strictly as 'unpleasantness' (rather than 'misunderstanding'), in order that the possibility of a grievance on Leopold's part is conveyed.

[23] Although Nannerl and Leopold were apparently adept at arranging large-scale pieces of music for small-scale domestic performance, and could accommodate some missing instrumental parts by playing them on the keyboard, it is difficult to see how their traditional practices could have been applied to these concertos. Although Nannerl would have been able to supply on the keyboard much of the material from the orchestral tutti passages, the orchestral parts in the solo passages were from this time on increasingly rich in thematic material, instrumentation, and interweaving with the solo part. It does not follow, however, that because Leopold and Nannerl may not often have been able to perform the works adequately they could not appreciate the music— Leopold was to report to Nannerl being moved to tears when he heard a concerto performance in Vienna in 1785. See Ch. 27, p. 472, for further details.

[24] Wolfgang to Leopold, 26 May 1784—*MBA* 793/4–24 (*Letters* 514).

[25] Wolfgang to Leopold, 9–12 June 1784—*MBA* 797/19–22 (*Letters* 515). The passage is bars 56–63.

[26] But not necessarily three, as Heussner claims. See H. Heussner (ed.), *NMA Kritischer Bericht* V/15/6 (Kassel, 1986), f/8. Wolfgang's letter mentioning the dispatch of the cadenzas is *MBA* 799/10–16 (*Letters* 516).

everything necessary for a performance of K. 451 and perhaps also of K. 450. The reason for this claim is, in the case of K. 451, that Wolfgang knew what Nannerl needed for it and had already promised it. In the case of K. 450, Leopold was to tell Nannerl only eight weeks later on 14 September 1784 (after she had moved to St Gilgen) to be prepared to play the Concerto in B flat (K. 450) with all the parts when she came to visit him in Salzburg.[27] She would have needed a complete keyboard part, including cadenzas, to give any kind of performance of the work.

What were all the missing passages from Wolfgang's keyboard concertos, without which Nannerl could not play the works? And why was a complete part not sent in the first place? Since these pieces were to be so keenly coveted by Nannerl, and were so frequently mentioned in the correspondence between Leopold and Nannerl after her marriage, the following digression attempts to explain something of the way in which the music travelled back and forth, and was prepared for her performance.

✺

When a parcel of music arrived for Leopold and Nannerl from Vienna on the mailcoach, it was almost always in the form of Wolfgang's autograph scores. And a keyboard concerto score did not include the keyboard part complete in every detail, despite the fact that Wolfgang would already have performed the work before sending the score to Salzburg. Missing from the solo passages of the keyboard part in the score would typically be the cadenzas, but also often elements such as *Eingänge*, re-entry fermatas, and the occasional fleshing out of skeletal indications of melody (such as the passage in K. 451 asked for by Nannerl and mentioned above).[28] Missing too would usually be the figurings for the bass of the solo part in tutti passages; these were needed to give the soloist a range of options for the performance of the work, and are discussed further below. In the Mozart family, it seems to have been accepted that Wolfgang would supply the cadenzas, *Eingänge*, and other embellishments (he usually did so after having sent the score), but that Leopold would add the figurings for the tutti passages.

Were it not for the fact that Nannerl and Leopold regularly demanded Wolfgang's new music for their own use, knowledge of how the concertos were performed would be very much poorer than it is, for the performance parts prepared for Nannerl from the concerto scores eventually

---

[27] *MBA* 808/2–5 (not in *Letters*).   [28] See p. 429.

found their way into the library of St Peter's Abbey in Salzburg, where most are still kept today.[29] Their importance is that they constitute the richest surviving single body of copies proven to have a connection with Leopold, Wolfgang, and Nannerl Mozart. They often supply material (such as cadenzas) missing from the scores. And they reveal, in a way that the autograph scores alone could not, that the question of how the works were performed is more complex than might be expected; one particularly important problem, which has implications for modern performance practice, is the soloist's role in the tutti passages. This is not to say that the parts are a better source than the scores, but rather that several types of evidence need to be considered together in order to approach an understanding of the way the concertos were performed around the time of their composition. Scores, performance parts, loose material such as cadenzas and *Eingänge* which lagged behind the dispatch of the scores,[30] early printed editions of the works in question, and references in the correspondence all have their part to play.[31]

Peculiar circumstances have hampered the study of performance practice with regard to the concertos, even though detailed understanding of this practice is an essential prerequisite for editions of the works. The now so-called *Alte Mozart-Ausgabe* was based on the scores, before the significance of the St Peter's parts had been recognized. Many of the autograph scores were sent for safe keeping from Berlin to Poland during the Second World War, however, and remained inaccessible for a long time afterwards. The *Neue Mozart-Ausgabe*, the latest complete

---

[29] See M. H. Schmid, *Die Musiksammlung der Erzabtei St. Peter in Salzburg. Katalog. Erster Teil. Leopold und Wolfgang Amadeus Mozart. Joseph und Michael Haydn. Mit einer Einführung in die Geschichte der Sammlung* (Schriftenreihe der Internationalen Stiftung Mozarteum 3/4; Salzburg, 1970); id., 'Nannerl Mozart und ihr musikalischer Nachlass: Zu den Klavierkonzerten im Archiv St. Peter in Salzburg', *MJb* (1980–3), 140–7; and id., 'Musikalien des Mozartschen Familienarchivs im Stift St. Peter', in P. Eder and G. Walterskirchen (eds.), *Das Benediktinerstift St. Peter in Salzburg zur Zeit Mozarts* (Salzburg, 1991), 173–85.

[30] Some of this loose material is also in the St Peter's collection.

[31] There is one particularly neat example of how the St Peter's material relates to remarks in the correspondence. On 15 Feb. 1783, in response to a request from Nannerl, Wolfgang sent her the three cadenzas to the 'Concerto in D' (K. 175), and the two *Eingänge* to the 'Concerto in E flat' (K. 271). See *MBA* 728/8–9 (*Letters* 481). In the St Peter's collection is a small-format, thin, creased piece of paper containing precisely these items. The paper shows every sign of having been enclosed in a letter. See M. H. Schmid, 'Musikalien des Mozartschen Familienarchivs', 173–4. Cliff Eisen, in a private communication, comments further about K. 271 that though the keyboard part in St Peter's is copied on to paper of *c.*1777, the orchestral parts are on paper of *c.*1783–4. These facts tie in with Nannerl's request in 1783 for *Eingänge* for K. 271, supporting the hypothesis that she had in mind a performance of the work during that year; they suggest that though she still had a keyboard part from 1777, Wolfgang had taken the orchestral parts to Vienna and she had to have them recopied.

edition of Mozart's works, therefore turned to the St Peter's parts for the texts of some of the keyboard concertos. Thus neither edition had the benefit of both parts and scores, although the critical reports which accompany the volumes of music in the *Neue Mozart-Ausgabe* note some findings from the scores.[32] Only recently, above all with the work of Eisen and M. H. Schmid, has there been determined engagement with the whole corpus of relevant evidence, such that received ideas about performance practice are having to be heavily revised.[33]

Perhaps the most interesting findings for the purposes of this book relate to the question of the soloist's role in the tutti passages of the keyboard concertos. When the works were performed at one of Wolfgang's grand academies in Vienna, he must normally have been able to obtain all the instrumentalists he needed, but when Nannerl performed them in the Dancing-Master's House in Salzburg the conditions were usually less ideal, probably especially with respect to the wind players. She therefore had not only to play her own solo part, but also supply the parts of any missing instruments during the tutti sections. After her marriage, when she was living in St Gilgen, the musical forces available to her must usually have been even smaller than those in Salzburg, yet she continued to pester Leopold for Wolfgang's latest concertos, and even at times had complete sets of parts for them out there.[34] Since Leopold had long ago mentioned that she played concertos with a two-violin orchestra consisting of him and Ceccarelli,[35] it seems clear that the range of forces available to her was very wide, and her part had to try to accommodate all the options. On some occasions she might even have played the whole work unaccompanied, supplying a complete keyboard arrangement of the tutti passages; on others she might have strengthened the bass during tutti passages and supplied the parts of missing wind instruments; she might sometimes have realized a figured bass during tutti passages

---

[32] Some of the critical reports were published after the scores had again become available.

[33] See C. Eisen, 'The Mozarts' Salzburg Copyists: Aspects of Attribution, Chronology, Text, Style, and Performance Practice', in C. Eisen (ed.), *Mozart Studies* (Oxford, 1991), 253–307; id., 'The Orchestral Bass Part in Mozart's Salzburg Keyboard Concertos: The Evidence of the Authentic Copies', in N. Zaslaw (ed.), *Mozart's Piano Concertos: Text, Context, Interpretation* (Ann Arbor, 1995), 411–25; and M. H. Schmid, 'Zur Mitwirkung des Solisten am Orchester-Tutti bei Mozarts Konzerten', *Basler Jahrbuch für Historische Musikpraxis*, 17 (1993), 89–112. The rudimentary outline of the situation in this paragraph does not attempt to address the complexity of the history of the editorial principles, or the details of which sources were used for specific works, in the *NMA*. For details of sources, see the relevant *NMA* volumes themselves; for details of problems in the *NMA*, see the works cited in this note by Eisen and Schmid, esp. M. H. Schmid, 'Zur Mitwirkung des Solisten', 90–3.

[34] Further details are given where appropriate in Pt. V.   [35] See Ch. 16, pp. 250–1.

to add body when each instrumental part was represented but numbers were small; and she might sometimes have kept silent during tutti passages, if she had an adequate orchestra.[36] Her 'performance platforms' after her marriage, if such humble situations as must sometimes have existed may be dignified by the term, ranged from her husband's house in St Gilgen, with her as sole performer and him as audience, to the Dancing-Master's House in Salzburg during a visit of the Marchands, when Leopold gathered together the best forces he could, to do the music justice. In between was a host of other situations, depending on which friends and relations could be rounded up, and whether Nannerl wanted to offer special entertainment to people staying in or passing through St Gilgen.

Because the keyboard part in the score was not complete, the copyist Leopold would order in to prepare Nannerl's music for her could obviously not supply her with a copy of a complete keyboard part. The reason why *Eingänge*, cadenzas, and other embellishments were not in the score was probably that Wolfgang would usually give the first performance himself and would improvise them on the spot.[37] As far as the keyboard role in the tutti passages was concerned, the keyboard part in the score was usually merely marked (for example, *col basso*) to indicate what its bass-line should be. Figurings above this bass-line were usually not given, and Leopold tended to write them into Nannerl's part after the copyist had finished work. Only when this had been done, and Wolfgang had sent the extra bits and pieces, could Nannerl play the whole work.[38]

---

[36] See M. H. Schmid, 'Zur Mitwirkung des Solisten', 112.

[37] Whether the fact that Leopold and Nannerl expected him to supply them indicates that they were considered integral elements of the composition which had to be conceived by the composer is another question. And linked with this is the further question of the extent of Nannerl's own keyboard skills such as extemporization at this point. As noted in Ch. 16, pp. 250–1, and Ch. 17, pp. 272–3 and 286, she had received training from Leopold in improvisation and accompaniment, but the evidence for her actual accomplishment has not yet been satisfactorily assessed.

[38] The remarks in this digression are greatly simplified and are intended only to sketch the general outline. They do not do justice to the variety of interesting situations demonstrated by the source material and discussed in the literature by Eisen and Schmid cited above. Topics tackled by these authors include the identity of the Salzburg copyists used by the Mozarts, which in turn illuminates important questions about the works concerned; the different function of a score from a set of performance parts, which has implications for the way composer and copyist worked together and for the question of how far the score indicated the composer's *requirements* (as opposed to performance options); and the dual function of some performance parts, one surprising result of which is that music written into a solo part was not always necessarily intended to be played. Particularly impressive is the detective work done by both authors on a wide range of evidence in order to try to understand the sometimes contradictory messages in the source material about how Mozart's music was performed.

Eisen points out that the textual and performance evidence and ambiguities of the St Peter's performance copies have not yet all been identified and discussed; the web of evidence is more complex than once was believed.[39] One task which could profitably be done would be to dedicate a detailed examination of the parts (in conjunction with all the other evidence) specifically to the quest for more knowledge of how the works were played by Nannerl, what her own input into the preparation of the parts was, and what can be learnt from them about her musical abilities.[40]

It is impossible, despite the clues offered by the correspondence and all the other source material, to build up a complete picture of all the comings and goings of the keyboard music sent by Wolfgang to Nannerl. Identification of concertos mentioned in the correspondence cannot always be made with certainty.[41] After Nannerl's marriage, the correspondence was triangular, with concerto scores travelling from Vienna to Salzburg, and the copied parts travelling from Salzburg to St Gilgen. Even when they arrived there, they might be sent back for corrections, or Nannerl might take them with her when she visited Salzburg. Furthermore, Gretl Marchand sometimes wanted to play the works in Munich, Wolfgang sometimes urgently needed a concerto or some cadenzas back for his own purposes, and when Heinrich Marchand returned to work in Salzburg, he wanted to play them too. A prominent and fascinating feature of the correspondence between Leopold and Nannerl after her marriage was to be this great, many-faceted concerto traffic.[42]

❧

When Wolfgang wrote on 21 July 1784 for Nannerl's name-day, there was no hint that any big change in her circumstances was imminent. Yet four weeks later, on 18 August, he was writing again to congratulate her on her approaching marriage.[43] Nothing is known of how, why, or when her

---

[39] See Eisen, 'The Orchestral Bass Part', 413.

[40] I greatly regret that more details about Nannerl's concerto parts and performances cannot be given in this book, but reading the work of Eisen and Schmid convinced me that this was not something that should be attempted without a prior careful study of the source material, specifically addressing questions concerning Nannerl.

[41] One problem recurring frequently in the correspondence is that concertos are often referred to as 'new'. The *MBA* commentary in these circumstances almost always takes a Wolfgang Mozart-centred view of what Leopold meant when he described a concerto as new, and identifies the concerto in question as the latest that Wolfgang had written. It should always be borne in mind, however, that Wolfgang's perception of what was new was often different from Leopold's and Nannerl's. To them, 'new' typically meant 'most recently received'.

[42] It is mentioned at several points in Pt. V.   [43] *MBA* 801 (*Letters* 517).

attachment to d'Ippold was broken and the engagement to her husband formed, but on 12 August a marriage contract was drawn up and signed in Salzburg.

Nannerl's suitor was Johann Baptist Berchtold von Sonnenburg, whom the Mozarts had known since 1776 at the latest.[44] He came from a family of administrators in Salzburg service. His father, Franz Anton Virgil, had been Pfleger of St Gilgen from 1745 until his death in 1769, on which event Johann Baptist succeeded him. The post of Pfleger (literally, 'carer') involved a host of fiscal, magisterial, and pastoral duties, and required, among other things, a thorough knowledge of law and taxation. Johann Baptist had been born in Salzburg in 1736, the eldest son in a family of eight children. He had been educated from 1748 (by which time the family was living in St Gilgen) at the Benedictine monastery of Mondsee, some fourteen kilometres north of St Gilgen, and then at Salzburg University (also Benedictine), where he studied philosophy and law. Following two years' practice in the Hofrat (court councillors' department) in Salzburg, he had gone back to St Gilgen in 1761 as his father's assistant. Two of his brothers, Joseph Sigismund and Franz Anton Maximilian, followed broadly similar careers in local administrative service. Johann Baptist had been married twice before his marriage with Nannerl. In 1769, the year in which he took over the full Pfleger duties in St Gilgen, he married Maria Margarethe Polis von Moulin, and they had nine children before she died in 1779 after the birth of the ninth. Fifteen months later, with four of these children still living, he married Jeanette Maria Mayrhofer von Grünbichl, and a son was born to them before she died in 1783 following a miscarriage or stillbirth.[45] This son also survived, so that when Nannerl married Johann Baptist, there were five children whose care she had to take over. They ranged in age from 13 down to 2, the eldest being a girl and the others boys.[46]

---

[44] Schiedenhofen's diary recorded meeting Berchtold at the Mozarts' on 28 Sept. 1776—see Deutsch, 'Schiedenhofens Tagebuch', 21.

[45] See Brno, MZA, Berchtold Family Archive, Family Chronicle, unpaginated, but p. 39 on my count. The entry suggests that Berchtold had been very attached to Jeanette—it described her as 'a real jewel among all women, and his most beloved wife' ('ein wahres Kleinod von allen Frauen, und seine allertheuerste Gattin').

[46] The information about Berchtold and his family is from Brno, MZA, Berchtold Family Archive, Family Chronicle; J. H. Eibl, 'Der "Herr Sohn"' *MM* 14 (1966), 1–9; H. Schuler, 'Nannerl Mozarts Stiefkinder', *AM* 23 (1976), 30–5; and the Berchtold family tree in Ziller, *Geschichte St. Gilgens*, i. 296. The *MBA* commentary on the members of Berchtold's family is riddled with inaccuracies and inconsistencies, and cannot be relied upon. Also confusing is the fact that Berchtold's brother called Joseph Sigismund by *MBA* and Eibl, and Johann Joseph Sigmund by Ziller, is called Joseph Erasmus Ignatzius by the Family Chronicle in the Berchtold Family Archive. Though the

No inkling is given of what Nannerl or Leopold thought about her marriage. The correspondence between Leopold and Nannerl after the event suggests that the relationship between husband and wife during the early years was not easy, but the exceptional strain placed on families during the years of childhood, and the particular difficulties of bringing up stepchildren, and children in outlying villages such as St Gilgen, should not be underestimated. Furthermore, it is only the first two and a half years of the marriage about which a reasonable amount of information survives, since Leopold died in 1787, breaking the last regular correspondence pattern within the Mozart family. How Nannerl and Berchtold adapted themselves to each other after that has gone largely unrecorded; when Berchtold made his will in 1798, however, he was to write with great tenderness of Nannerl's qualities as a wife, while she was prostrated after his death, and described him as her 'most dearly beloved husband'.[47]

One aspect of the marriage that seems inescapably negative from the point of view of Nannerl and Leopold is the fact that it involved their living in different places. St Gilgen lay some thirty kilometres east of Salzburg, and took about six hours to reach, regardless of whether one travelled in a vehicle or on foot. Leopold, who had relied on Nannerl for company and comfort since 1777, and had always cherished hopes that they would be able to live together with Wolfgang, would be left quite alone for much of the time; and Nannerl, for whom even Salzburg had offered little in the way of a performing platform, would now have still less scope for her playing. What she gained was status, the challenging

Chronicle is more likely to have given the name accurately, I refer to him as Joseph Sigismund in order not to differ from the *MBA* index. In general, Christian names can be very confusing—many were given, and others could be added at the time of first communion. Official documents did not always list them all, and spellings varied too. See Fig. 2 for a diagram of Amann/Berchtold/Polis relationships, including the Berchtold children.

[47] Berchtold's will was drawn up on 25 Sept. 1798; clause 2 relates to Nannerl and reads in part, 'I settle on my dear wife and marriage partner Anna Maria, née Mozart, those emoluments designated for her in the marriage contract drawn up between us, and leave her, as partial recognition of the marital loyalty, love, tenderness, and good housekeeping shown to me by her, which unfortunately I am not in a position to repay adequately, an annual stipend from my fortune as long as she lives of 300 fl. . . .' ('Bestättige ich meiner lieben Frau Ehegattin Anna Maria, gebohrene Mozart jene Emolumente, welche derselben in unserm errichteten Heuraths Pacten bestimet sind, und vermache ihr zu einiger Betrauung der mir erwiesenen ehelichen Traue, Liebe, Zärtlichkeit und guten Hauswirtschaft, die ich gehörig zu vergüten leider außer stand bin, aus meinem Vermögen einen jährl. Fruchtgenuß so lang sie lebet mit 300 f. . . .'). See Brno, MZA, Berchtold Family Archive, Závěť Jana Baptisty a neúplný inventář pozůstalosti (Will and Inventory of Johann Baptist). Another copy of the will is in the SLA, Verlassakt Stadtgericht Salzburg Nr. 1.713/1822. Nannerl's comment about Berchtold is in her letter to Breitkopf & Härtel of 27 May 1801—*MBA* 1335/4–7 (not in *Letters*).

task of setting five children on the right path, the possibility of having children of her own, and the financial support of a court employee (not forgetting his pension rights) younger than her father. Berchtold, whose family belonged to the minor nobility, and whose first two wives had also done so, gained a wife whose culture and education compensated for her modest social background as the daughter of a musician.

The contract was more complex than Wolfgang's and Constanze's, since it had to take account of the inheritance rights of Berchtold's existing children. Nannerl brought 500 fl. to the marriage, and Berchtold promised 1,000 fl., with an extra 500 fl. as *Morgengabe*, a reward for virginity. The money he promised her was not immediately paid in full; rather she received annual interest on the amount, as pin money, and the capital remained intact until Berchtold died. One clause specified that anything passing from a third party to the bride or groom, either during the engagement or the marriage, should be classed as a separate, rather than as a joint, benefit. Thus, for example, Nannerl ought not legally to have been obliged to share any part of her future inheritance from Leopold with her husband. There were various clauses specifying how things were to be divided in the event of the death of either party. Witnesses to the contract were Leopold, the old family friend J. B. J. Joachim F. von Schiedenhofen, Franz Anton Reisiegl, Johann Kajetan Mayr von Mayregg, and Joseph Stephan Haslberger (guardian of Berchtold's children).[48]

On the same date that the contract was signed, an application was made to speed up the official pre-marital procedures, and on 23 August the wedding took place in St Gilgen. Details of how everything was arranged are not known, but it seems likely that Leopold gave Nannerl a new fortepiano as a wedding present.[49] Leopold travelled out there with various Salzburg friends, and the service took place at ten in the morning. It was attended by Johann Kajetan Mayr von Mayregg and his wife, Franz Anton Reisiegl, Gretl Marchand and Hanchen Brochard (who were specifically mentioned as being Nannerl's keyboard pupils), Katherl Gilowsky, Berchtold's brother Franz Anton Maximilian, and Berchtold's

---

[48] A copy of the contract is in the SLA, Verlassakt Nr. 1.713/1801/17, Johann Baptist v. Sonnenburg, 'Marriage Contract'. See Ch. 31, n. 32, for a translation of the clause concerning the rights of each partner over gifts and inheritances. Documents produced after Berchtold's death give further details about the financial arrangements set up in the marriage contract—see Ch. 35, pp. 614–16.

[49] A letter from Leopold to Nannerl of 9 June 1785 (*MBA* 871/64–76; not in *Letters*) refers to a fortepiano bought for Nannerl for use in St Gilgen from the organ and keyboard instruments maker Johann Evangelist Schmid.

eldest child Maria Anna ('Nannerl', like her stepmother). Heinrich was not mentioned as having attended,[50] and Wolfgang did not do so. On Leopold's return to Salzburg, he had immediately to make arrangements to return the Marchand children to their homes in Munich, and Nannerl had to take charge of her new responsibilities, in the house where her mother had been born and had spent her first four years. When Wolfgang had written to congratulate Nannerl on her approaching marriage, he had expressed unease at the thought that Leopold would now be entirely on his own. He suggested that Leopold ask Colloredo for permission to retire, so that he could draw his pension and go to live with Nannerl in St Gilgen; failing that, he should resign, and join Wolfgang in Vienna.[51] Leopold took neither piece of advice, and the three surviving members of the Mozart family now all lived in separate places, in circumstances as different as possible from those originally envisaged by Leopold.

[50] See Brno, MZA, Berchtold Family Archive, Family Chronicle, unpaginated, but pp. 39–40 on my count.

[51] Wolfgang to Nannerl, 18 Aug. 1784—*MBA* 801 (*Letters* 517).

PART V

Leopold and Nannerl

(1784–1787)

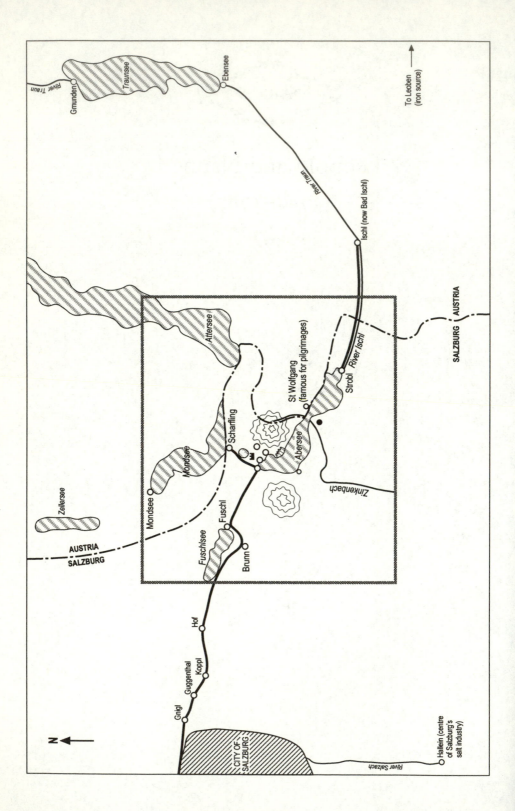

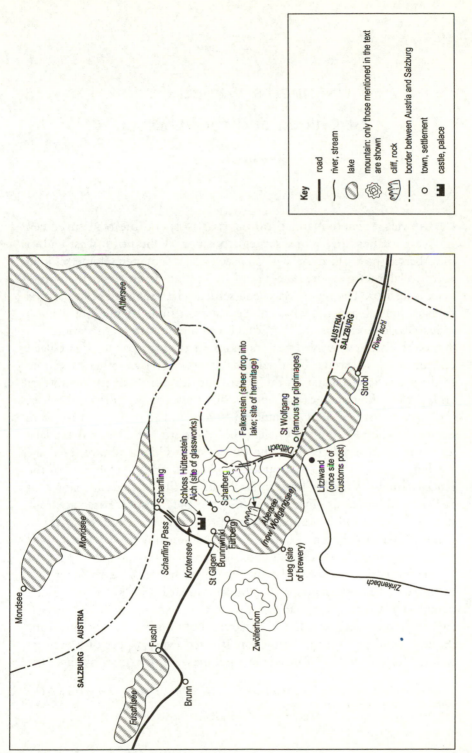

Key

—— road

／ river, stream

◯ lake

✿ mountain: only those mentioned in the text are shown

⟋⟍ cliff, rock

–··– border between Austria and Salzburg

○ town, settlement

▮ castle, palace

Mondsee

SALZBURG   AUSTRIA

Attersee

Mondsee

Fuschl

Fuschlsee

Brunn

Scharfling Pass

Scharfling

Krotensee

St Gilgen

Brunnwinkl

Fürberg

Schloss Hüttenstein

Aich (site of glassworks)

Schafberg

Falkenstein (sheer drop into lake; site of hermitage)

Dittbach

St Wolfgang

(famous for pilgrimages)

Abersee (now Wolfgangsee)

Zwölferhorn

Lueg (site of brewery)

Litzlwand (once site of customs post)

Strobl

AUSTRIA

SALZBURG

River Ischl

Zinkenbach

MAP 3. St Gilgen, the Abersee, and the Salzkammergut, with enlargement of central section.

Nannerl's Wilderness:
St Gilgen and the Abersee

❧

THE village where Nannerl Mozart was to spend the next seventeen years of her life lay in a strategic position at the north-west end of the Abersee (now called the Wolfgangsee), a lake some ten kilometres long and two kilometres wide, except at its mid-point, where a narrow bottleneck is formed. The region had been settled relatively late because of the forested hills all around, which made access difficult. A number of local industries depended on the lake, which was able to offer a precarious living to the people who lived near its shore. In 1780 the parish of St Gilgen contained some twelve hundred inhabitants, but two other lakeshore settlements, St Wolfgang on the north side and Strobl at the south-east end, swelled the number of people trying to wrest a living from the area. Only seventy-six of the two hundred houses in the parish in 1780 were actually in the village of St Gilgen; the rest were dotted round the lake and in the surrounding hills.[1] The Pfleger at St Gilgen administered the Salzburg court-owned land around the lake, but at the Strobl end of the Abersee much of the land was in the hands of the Cathedral Chapter, of St Peter's Abbey, or of private families such as the Lodrons. Based at Strobl, therefore, was another administrator representing these interests.[2] When Nannerl married Berchtold, the Strobl administrator was Berchtold's younger brother, Joseph Sigismund.[3]

The industries supported by the area were linked to each other in a complex and interdependent way, but the most important factor in the complexity was the fact that part of the north shore, including the village of St Wolfgang, was not in Salzburg, but Austria. The potential for disputes resulting from this situation affected every aspect of life incessantly, often in details of impressive pettiness. In the first instance, the

---

[1] Most of the material in this chapter is from Ziller, *Geschichte St. Gilgens*. The population figures in this paragraph are from ibid. ii. 189.

[2] Ibid. i. 23–7.   [3] See Map 3 for St Gilgen and the Abersee area.

Pfleger of St Gilgen had to try to reach an agreement with his counterpart in St Wolfgang; if this was unsuccessful, the archbishop of Salzburg had to negotiate with the abbot of Mondsee (who had jurisdiction over St Wolfgang); and in particularly intractable cases, even higher authorities (ultimately, the emperor) had to be invoked.

The Abersee lay in the Salzkammergut, and the salt industry was crucial to the prosperity of Salzburg. Salzburg's most important salt mines were actually at Hallein, due south of Salzburg, but the Abersee was nevertheless involved in a number of ways. There were complex agreements involving Salzburg, Austria, and Bavaria about the import and export of salt, and about the quotas (destined for more distant locations) which were permitted to travel through the several territories. Interwoven with the question of quotas was that of the use of the Abersee forests for the purposes of the salt industry, be it that of Austria or Salzburg. Austrian salt pans at Ischl (twelve kilometres east of Strobl) and Ebensee (sixteen kilometres north-east of Ischl) were granted wood from these forests for use in the salt extraction process, in return for an agreement with Austria about the quota of Salzburg salt which could be sold to Bohemia. The wood was fired in the evaporation process, and was also used to make barrels to contain the salt. When an area had been designated for felling, woodcutters set up camp and used streams to float the cut wood down to the lake, where it was transported on by water to Ischl or Ebensee. As the wood was carried down the streams, it sometimes broke bridges lower down, and this led to disputes between the local farmers and the salt officials. The Pfleger had to intervene in these disputes. He also had to use his judgement when, in the second half of the eighteenth century, the Abersee could no longer supply enough wood for the Austrian salt industry. Austria wanted to supplement it with wood from the Mondsee (which was Austrian), but the best transport route from the Mondsee to Ischl was by road over the Scharfling Pass, then into the Krotensee, and on down streams, entering the Abersee at Brunnwinkl and Fürberg. From these places, it would travel across the lake on barges equipped with sails, or (in winter) on sledges. In return for permission to use this route, the Austrian salt officials (who had a big base at Gmunden) offered to bear the expense of maintaining the road through the pass, even in winter, which would be to the advantage of the Abersee iron transporters. Under Berchtold's father, the request was refused, because he did not believe that the Austrians would keep their promise to maintain the road; but under Berchtold himself, the plan was put into action—perhaps partly because his second wife Jeanette was the daughter of an Austrian salt official.

Apart from supplying wood for the salt industry, the Abersee forests played a role in boat-building, in the production of pitch and charcoal, in the cottage industry of wood-turning, and in court hunts. The boats were needed for fishing, for carrying pilgrims across the lake to St Wolfgang, and for freight traffic and the transport industry along the River Traun; the charcoal was used locally by smiths and in the glass industry. Wood-turning was carried out by many farmers as a supplementary source of income; the wooden artefacts were loaded into backpacks (*Krächsen*) and carried long distances for sale at markets in Austria, Hungary, and Croatia. Because of the archbishop's hunting interests in the forests, the court hunting department under the Obristjägermeister also had its eye on the Abersee woods, and the Pfleger therefore had dealings with this office, as well as with salt officials.[4]

The Abersee region was also important to the iron trade. From the fifteenth century the iron route had passed through the Salzkammergut via Ischl and the Abersee, on its way from the mines in Leoben (east of the Abersee) to Salzburg. The route was already a well-worn one for salt. Most of the Abersee farmers supplemented their income by undertaking transport work, and since the distance from Leoben to Salzburg was about 160 kilometres, local farmers would take responsibility only for the stretch of the route near their own homes. Because the load was transferred so frequently from one group of farmers to the next, iron depots were built at strategic places, so that the iron could be checked and stored before it made the next stage of its journey. One such depot was at Strobl, where Berchtold's brother took charge of the iron in addition to his other administrative duties. He had to check the quantity, rebind any load that had come undone, and (at his own risk) transport it across the lake on flat barges to St Gilgen. Abersee and Fuschl farmers then took it over, and got it by road to Hof (rather more than half-way to Salzburg), and Hof farmers carried it into Salzburg. Because part of the route east of Strobl passed through Austria, and because St Wolfgang people also wanted an opportunity to earn money from the trade, there were countless possibilities of friction. At one point, the Austrian carriers refused to accept Salzburg coinage for their services, and tried to insist that they should be paid with Austrian money; at another, St Wolfgang launched a vigorous attempt to have the Abersee depot located on the Austrian shore of the lake instead of at Strobl. Ultimately the attempt was

---

[4] The information in this paragraph and the preceding one is from Ziller, *Geschichte St. Gilgens*, i. 70–94.

unsuccessful, but the details suggest that the opportunities for earning a living round the lake were so insecure that if one failed, the people who depended on it were likely to try to seize other people's livelihoods from them. Since St Wolfgang was heavily dependent on income from pilgrims, it suffered badly in years of war or sickness, when borders were closed; and at these times, it competed even more aggressively than usual with people from St Gilgen. Had the iron depot been moved from Strobl to the Austrian shore, the Salzburg farmers might have had to reduce the number of horses they kept, and this in turn would have affected the transport of salt.[5]

The Abersee supplied fish for the court kitchens in Salzburg, and in addition one of the many taxes was paid in fish. The lake was staked out, and fishing rights allocated in the form of *Seege* or nets. These were of specified dimensions, and the right to a *Seege* carried the duty to provide fish for the court and the fish tax in accordance with the rules laid down by the court Fischmeister. Twice a week, the choicest fish were chosen for court consumption and transported to Salzburg. Any fish rejected for this purpose were permitted to be sold at market. Here too there was enormous scope for ill feeling. In the first place, there was the problem that St Wolfgang fishermen were subject to slightly different rules from St Gilgen ones—for example, they were permitted to fish on St Rupert's Day, while the St Gilgen fishermen were not, because this was an official Salzburg holy day. Secondly, the St Wolfgang men did not always recognize Salzburg regulations. Once a year, on St George's Day, there was a meeting in St Gilgen in the presence of the Fischmeister and the Pfleger. All the fishermen using the lake were required to attend it—the rules were read out, and complaints could be made. But the St Wolfgang men rarely appeared at the meeting, and it was therefore more difficult to apply sanctions to transgressors of the rules on the Salzburg side. Thirdly, the man who chose the fish for the court kitchens had fishing rights of his own in the lake, so the system was often abused. Each catch, for example, would consist of larger and smaller fish, and he would tend to assign his own smaller fish to the kitchens quota, and choose the requisite number of larger ones from the catches of the other fishermen. This meant not only that they had no big ones left over to sell at market, but also that they fell into arrears with their fish tax, which also required fine, big fish. Berchtold's father had tried to reform the fishing regulations to make things fairer for his fishermen, but the difficulties caused by the peculiar nature

[5] Ibid. i. 110–27.

of the sharing of the lake, and by the rights of the fish buyer, proved intractable.[6]

Countless Abersee inhabitants lived from the lace industry. Lace-makers had to be married property-owners, but this requirement in no way implied that they were people of a certain means. Properties were divided and subdivided in order to meet the requirements, and widows worked at the craft to eke out a pitiful living when the family's main bread-winner had died. Whether Maria Anna Mozart's mother, or Maria Anna herself, had made lace is not known, but Maria Anna is depicted holding a length of lace in the portrait by Rosa Hagenauer-Barducci. Like the wooden artefacts, lace was carried in backpacks (usually by two men travel-ling together on six-week round trips) to markets in Austria, Carinthia, Steiermark, and Croatia. In 1776 its import into Austria was banned, and a serious decline set in. Miserable though the living had been, it had probably made the difference between survival and starvation for thou-sands of women—in the first few decades of the nineteenth century, the number of completely impoverished women rose sharply.[7]

The Pfleger's headquarters for the Abersee had originally been at Schloss Hüttenstein near the Scharfling Pass but, after a good deal of shilly-shallying about the best place for the Pfleger to live (caused in part by the delapidated condition of Schloss Hüttenstein), were finally moved down to the lakeside in St Gilgen in 1703. This move coincided approximately with the building at Aich of the first glassworks in the archbishopric in 1701. Aich was very close to Schloss Hüttenstein, so the abandoned building could be used as accommodation for the glass workers. In 1703 imported glass was banned in Salzburg, and the glass-works at Aich supplied the court and other Salzburg needs, and also sent glass as far afield as Bavaria, Austria, Bohemia, and Steiermark. Glass carriers took the fragile wares in backpacks, and it was one such person whom Leopold and Nannerl used as a channel of communication. After a poor start and a period of closure from 1724 to 1733, the glassworks was relaunched under private enterprise by Johann Wolfgang Schmauss. This time it prospered, so that in 1776 Berchtold reported that the Schmauss family had brought employment to over sixty adults and children. Although Aich had originally been chosen as a site because there was plentiful wood on the Schafberg, the demand eventually out-stripped the supply, and a second glassworks was built at Zinkenbach, where there was more wood. The wares produced were somewhat crude, and

---

[6] *Geschichte St. Gilgens*, i. 52–69.   [7] Ibid. i. 204–11.

included rosary beads and blue bottles into which was poured miraculous eye salve. Both products were sold to pilgrims by St Gilgen's sexton and schoolmaster.[8]

Pilgrims were also partly responsible for the ability of the Abersee to support a brewery, which was situated at Lueg. Here there was good cellarage in the cliffs, and plentiful wood, and the iron road passed by, making transport relatively convenient. Beer was cheaper than wine, so the pilgrims crossing the lake to St Wolfgang bought large quantities of it. By-products of the business were used in other Abersee industries —the ash, for example, was passed on to the glassworks. However, the important ingredients for the brewery (barley and hops) had to be imported, so that this was one more enterprise under threat when borders were closed in times of sickness or war.[9]

There was a long tradition of pilgrimages to St Wolfgang, and they were extremely important to the economy of the area. The inhabitants of St Wolfgang obviously benefited more than those of St Gilgen or Strobl, because of the board and lodging requirements of the visitors. However, there was also the question of their transport across the lake, and here there was open competition among all the boat-owners in the area. Not all pilgrims were poor—some were members of the nobility with money to spend. Artefacts and refreshments were therefore offered for sale at strategic places, and there were four embarkation points round the lake—at St Gilgen, Fürberg, Strobl, and Aigen. Though none of these places was in Austria, an agreement allowed St Wolfgang boat-owners a certain quota of pilgrims to carry, in return for co-operation with the Salzburg carriers in matters such as landing on the St Wolfgang side. There was constant friction, however, especially in lean years. The income from pilgrims was so important that the St Gilgen school was closed in May and October, the busiest pilgrimage months. This was partly because the schoolmaster was also the sexton, who had a stall selling rosary beads and other artefacts to the visitors, and partly perhaps because the children also often had pilgrim-related work to do. Under Colloredo's Enlightenment reforms in the 1780s, the number of permitted pilgrimages was cut drastically, as was their length, and local incomes suffered as a result.[10]

Because of the proximity of the borders with Austria, the question of customs was very important. The customs house serving Salzburg was originally located at Litzlwand, overlooking the narrowest part of the lake, so that all the shipping could be controlled. In the sixteenth century,

<hr />

[8] Ibid. i. 28–52 and 211–18.   [9] Ibid. i. 218–40.   [10] Ibid. i. 94–102.

however, it was moved to St Gilgen, and later still the post of customs officer was combined with that of Pfleger, who then hired a Schreiber or clerk to help with the work. A subsidiary customs house was situated on the Scharfling Pass, to prevent the circumvention of the St Gilgen control by traffic landing at Fürberg and going on to Mondsee and beyond via Aich. The list of goods subject to duty was very long, from lard and soap to iron and cattle. The customs officer kept part of each duty, but the remainder was used chiefly to pay for road maintainance in the area—the main road for which this particular customs post was responsible stretched from Koppl through Brunn, Fuschl, and St Gilgen to Strobl. The road through the Scharfling Pass, as far as the Austrian border, was also the responsibility of the St Gilgen customs officer. Because both roads formed part of the iron route, they were not only very important, but also subject to very heavy use. The duty on iron was payable both at Strobl and St Gilgen, so the respective administrators were constantly having to reckon up with each other.[11]

The multitude of ways in which the lake was used meant that there was endless scope for friction between the people of St Wolfgang and those of St Gilgen and Strobl. The questions of competition for livelihoods, smuggling, wear and tear on jointly used roads and bridges, and so forth meant that almost any incident could provoke a disagreement which the Pfleger had to try to resolve. Suspicion between the two sides, even at a high level, sometimes amounted almost to paranoia—as, for example, when the abbot of Mondsee offered to maintain a shrine on the Scharfling Pass. His offer was refused because Salzburg feared that he might later make a claim to the land on which it stood. Among the humbler local inhabitants, perhaps the most extreme examples of pettiness concerned disputes between St Wolfgang and St Gilgen over the right to recover the bodies of people who had drowned in the lake, and bury them. On one occasion, the body of a St Wolfgang girl had to lie in a chest in the middle of the Ditlbach bridge (which marked the border) while arguments raged about who should be allowed to bury her. Though both sides mounted a guard, the body was eventually 'stolen' by St Wolfgang people and buried on their land. Nor was this the end of the matter—so much had already been invested in the dispute that the two sides then argued about the question of expenses.[12]

As Pfleger, Nannerl's husband had to try to resolve all disputes before they became too acrimonious. He had to maintain good relations with

[11] *Geschichte St. Gilgens*, i. 102–10.   [12] Ibid. i. 153–65.

all the other officials with jurisdiction in the area, and know what was going on in every part of the land for which he was responsible. He also had to uphold the law. Minor transgressions were tried and punished by him, but more serious cases were referred to the court at Salzburg. Thus he did not deal with cases of murder, manslaughter, robbery, rape, incest, arson, witchcraft, poisoning, rebellion, or desertion (all of which were capital offences). He did, however, handle cases such as fornication, adultery, smuggling, poaching, and fraud, unless the offence had been committed repeatedly, in which case it was serious enough to be referred to Salzburg. He employed an underling called a Gerichtsdiener or Amtmann to help him. This man lived in the Amtshaus next to the Pfleger's house by the lake. The building, which commanded a view of the vessels embarking and disembarking, also contained three cells and a torture room. The Gerichtsdiener supervised the inmates of the cells, and administered the punishments, including torture, meted out by the Pfleger. His salary was meagre, but he was allowed to keep a proportion of each fine levied. The bulk of his income seems to have come from fines for fornication and adultery, and, no doubt because of the 'piecework' element of his pay, the cells were rarely empty. As late as the early eighteenth century, fornication was punished even in cases where the couple subsequently married; and the Gerichtsdiener would check a marriage date against the baptism date of the first child, and report the couple to the Pfleger for retrospective punishment if there were any suspicion of pre-marital sexual relations. Other offences punishable by the Pfleger were transgressions against the fast-day laws, brawls, illegal dances, working on Sundays, swearing, and the careless use of fire.[13]

Another major element of the Pfleger's job was tax collection, an exceedingly complicated procedure. Although by the later eighteenth century, some of the taxes in kind had been replaced by financial ones, the administration involved in assessing and collecting tax was still considerable. One problem was that where a specific tax had once been paid in kind but had been converted to cash, the assessment was based on the cash value of the original goods. Thus if the tax was the cash value of ten hens, and the hens were valued at a price the farmer thought too high, he naturally resented it, and wanted to give the hens instead. This type of situation arose many times over, because there were so many different taxes—a basic tax, a tax on people living on land not owned by the court, a cheese tax on dairy farms, a tax to support the dogs of the hunting

13 Ibid. i. 166–91.

449

master, a church tax, a fish tax, a tax when land changed hands, a hefty once-only levy each time there was a new archbishop, and so forth.[14]

Yet, in addition to his authoritative roles of administering justice, collecting taxes and customs duties, and sending reports to Salzburg, the Pfleger had to be the friend and defender of his people. When a tax or other demand was too onerous, he had to argue for an amelioration; in years when the harvest was bad, he had to take steps to see that the villagers did not starve; and he had to organize and lead attempts at defence in times of danger.

Among the qualities necessary for the job of Pfleger were a sense of fairness, patience and tact, firmness, good record-keeping, and a high degree of organization. In return, he received a salary, the house, and a number of emoluments whose value it is now impossible to calculate. These included a proportion of the fines he levied, and of the customs duties he took, and also benefits in kind such as fish, game, beer, and other similar goods. The office of Pfleger had originally been leased—the Pfleger paid the court an annual sum, and was then allowed to raise money as he wished by private taxation, enforced labour, fines, and other means. Because of the scale of abuse which this system encouraged, the conditions changed so that the post attracted a court salary in the seventeenth century. At first, in St Gilgen, this was 400 fl. annually, but the takings (in taxes and fines) could not support such a high sum. Various other systems were tried—first, the post was simply abandoned, and the clerk (a man called Lürzer) took over the work for a salary of only 200 fl. annually, making up his income by working as clerk to the brewery and the iron depot too. However, there must have been too much work for one clerk, because by 1687 Lürzer had advanced to the position of Pflegsverwalter (effectively Pfleger again), and had been given his own clerk. By 1708 the then Pflegsverwalter Schnedizeni was given a salary of 350 fl., after complaining that he could not possibly live on 200 fl. The rate for a clerk, however, remained 200 fl. By Berchtold's time, therefore, the post was paid for by a combination of salary and other benefits, and it seems likely that Berchtold was better off than Leopold Mozart, though he had five children to support on his income.[15]

St Gilgen could not supply all the necessaries of life, and the correspondence between Leopold and Nannerl after her marriage always mentioned goods which he was sending her from Salzburg. By contrast, those that she sent him from St Gilgen were not essentials, but local specialities

---

[14] *Geschichte St. Gilgens*, i. 28–52.   [15] Ibid.

such as fish, duck, or sausages. The village had a church, a school, three inns, a public bath-house (where routine surgery such as blood-letting and tooth extraction was practised), and a Saturday market with twelve bakers' stalls, two butchers', a grocer's, and the sexton's stall selling candles and rosary beads.[16] Dairy produce and fruit and vegetables were obviously available locally, and Nannerl's new family kept its own poultry.

It is likely but not certain that Nannerl's stepchildren initially went to the village school. Many remarks in the correspondence suggest that their early education was problematic, and certainly the school was very far from satisfactory. At the root of the problem was the question of the schoolmaster's pay. Judging from the earliest known reports, it was far too meagre to allow him to devote his time to teaching alone. In the middle of the seventeenth century, for example, the church paid him 5 fl. annually, with a supplement of 10 kr. per week. He had to collect more money from the pupils' parents to reap a more respectable sum. In 1687 the then schoolmaster also became sexton, and the two posts were combined for the next two hundred years. Since the emoluments of the sexton were far greater than those of the schoolmaster, teaching was accorded a lower priority than the sexton's duties. In 1626 the tiny church on the Falkenstein was built, and from 1659 the Falkenstein was inhabited by hermits. Since pilgrims going to St Wolfgang now also wanted to visit the Falkenstein, a new opportunity was created for the sexton to earn money. In 1704 he was given permission to man a stall near the church selling devotional artefacts, and also to sell them on the Falkenstein. But even during the periods which were not busy with pilgrims, the sexton was frequently otherwise engaged. One of his duties was the care of the devotional vessels in the church, and since the number of services was so great (there were many baptisms and funerals), this alone was quite time-consuming. In addition, he was responsible for collecting the church tax in kind for himself and the priest, and this involved visiting farms around the parish.

A further problem was that in 1761 a church was built in Strobl, and a school was started there too. As a result, the post of priest in St Gilgen became far less attractive, since the priest's income dropped with the number of his parishioners. There was a fast turnover of priests in St Gilgen (six came and went between 1788 and 1806), and this had a negative effect on the school, which was closely linked with the church.

The number of pupils in the late eighteenth century oscillated between twenty and thirty, a figure representing about a quarter of all school-age

---

[16] Ibid. i. 127–53.

children in the parish. Not until 1804, after Berchtold had died and Nannerl had returned to Salzburg, was there a dedicated school building. Until then, two venues were used simultaneously—one in the house of a cobbler in the centre of the village, and the other the upper floor of the house next door. This might have been to allow segregation of the sexes. The curriculum was extremely basic—above all it consisted of religious education (especially the catechism), with elementary reading, writing, and reckoning. From the mid-1770s, Colloredo attempted to get to grips with the question of education in the archbishopric, but it seems that virtually no progress was made under him in St Gilgen. In 1774 he set up a school commission, later placing it in the capable hands of Franz Michael Vierthaler. The aim was to contribute to the implementation of his Enlightenment reforms through the education of children. Vierthaler set up a plan whereby every teacher would be trained centrally in a specified curriculum, but the improvements were painfully slow to percolate through to many village schools. Above all, their implementation depended on attracting and keeping young men who were not already set in their ways and did not have vested interests in preserving the status quo. In a village like St Gilgen this was hard to achieve. The school was controlled by the priest and the sexton, who were not only both too old to retrain, but who for ages past had been encouraging their parishioners to believe that they stood under the special protection of St Wolfgang and his miraculous powers. Rather than learn to think and act for their own improvement, the people seemed happy to rely on their traditional superstitions, and there was little interest in the expansion of the curriculum proposed by Colloredo and Vierthaler. Furthermore, even when a younger man who had passed through Vierthaler's seminary was appointed teacher around 1800 (too late in any case for Berchtold's family), it proved impossible to keep him long because the conditions were so poor. Vierthaler had campaigned for better wages for teachers, and had insisted that existing teacher-sextons appoint an assistant so that the teaching would be less interrupted; but it was simply too expensive to effect quickly the types of change that would make the job really attractive. Above all, the lack of a suitable building was demoralizing.[17]

[17] The information in this paragraph and the preceding two is from L. Ziller, *300 Jahre Schule St. Gilgen: Geschichte einer Salzburger Dorfschule* (St Gilgen, 1965). The details of attempted reforms by Colloredo and Vierthaler are from L. Hammermayer, 'Die Aufklärung in Salzburg (ca. 1715–1803)', in H. Dopsch and H. Spatzenegger (eds.), *Geschichte Salzburgs: Stadt und Land*, vol. ii, pt. I (Salzburg, 1988), 375–452.

There were very few children in St Gilgen whose parents believed they needed more than the rudiments of literacy, and these few (the children of the Pfleger, and perhaps those of the handful of clerks, and the managers of the glassworks and the brewery) tended either to have a private tutor or to go to school in Salzburg. In fact, however, though it was a regional trend for the children of Pfleger to board in Salzburg, Berchtold was slow to arrange satisfactory schooling for his children, and the correspondence between Leopold and Nannerl reveals that it was impossible to attract good private tutors to such a quiet place, that Berchtold was reluctant to pay much for education (even for his sons), and that his daughter was barely literate at the age of 13. This was to be one of the difficult situations with which the education-conscious Mozarts, Leopold and Nannerl, had to grapple.

It was important for Leopold and Nannerl that they should be able to communicate with each other regularly, and there were a number of channels open to them. None of them was fast. The roads were very poor, and could be virtually impassable even in August.[18] The ascent from Gnigl to Guggenthal, on leaving Salzburg, and the south side of the Fuschlsee, were steep and treacherous. Vehicular traffic travelled no faster than that on foot—both took about six hours. There was nothing like a mailcoach service between the two places at this date. In order, however, that the Pfleger's reports could reach Salzburg regularly, there was a Gerichtsbote (a carrier in court service)—a local St Gilgen man who took official court documents and packets to Salzburg once a week.[19] He also carried private letters and goods, and was the main messenger used by Leopold and Nannerl. They also communicated through the glass-carrier, a woman who carried glassware from Aich into Salzburg, and through anyone else who happened to be travelling between the two places.[20]

The lakeshore house into which Nannerl moved, the one built in the time of her grandfather Wolfgang Pertl, was a large two-storey building, which had been extended under Berchtold's father.[21] Berchtold's business as Pfleger was conducted downstairs, where there was a room for public hearings, an archive for all the documents, and a number of

[18] See Ch. 26, p. 457, for a description of Leopold's homeward journey from Nannerl's wedding.

[19] In all discussion of communications between Salzburg and St Gilgen, the Gerichtsbote will henceforth be designated simply 'carrier'. Other messengers will be distinguished from him by specific reference to the type of goods they carried.

[20] See Appendix 3 for more details about the communications arrangements.

[21] See Ziller, *Geschichte St. Gilgens*, i. 37–41.

offices. The house had a tendency to dampness, and the family rooms were upstairs. The entrance was on the south-east, the lake, side, and the garden ended at the water's edge. When the inventory of Berchtold's belongings was compiled after his death in 1801, the family rooms named were a writing room, a 'clavier room', a bedroom, a print room, the 'prince's room', a 'summer room', a children's room, a kitchen, and a *Vorhaus* (an entrance hall). From the list of furnishings in each room, it seems that the prince's room was the grandest; it was a sitting room with five sets of curtains (more than were listed in any other room), and contained the grand portrait of Archbishop Schrattenbach, which had allegedly been given by that prince to the Berchtold family. The next finest room (in terms of the value of the furniture) was the summer room, which was also a sitting room. Neither of these rooms, nor the writing room, contained beds; the clavier room and the print room (so called because of its collection of engravings), on the other hand, had beds in them, as did the children's room, the kitchen, and of course the bedroom. A further bed was downstairs in the *Kanzlei*, one of the offices; this might have been for Berchtold's clerk, while the two beds in the kitchen were probably for domestic servants, and one of the beds in the children's room was also for a servant. Information about the contents of the clavier room is unfortunately thin; it was probably a small room, since it contained only one pair of curtains, but otherwise little can be learnt about it. This is most likely because the inventory was strictly of Berchtold's effects, so that any musical instruments in the house would only be listed if they were his. Since none was listed, either in the inventory or as bequests in his will, it can tentatively be inferred that he did not play anything himself. Because of the restricted nature of the information transmitted by the inventory, it is unknown which rooms in the house were used for making music. Presumably the clavier room was, but given its apparently modest status it seems likely that one of the public rooms was also used, if only on occasions.[22]

When Nannerl moved to St Gilgen, the five surviving Berchtold children were Maria Anna Margarethe (young Nannerl), aged almost 13; Wolfgang, aged 10; Joseph, aged just 7; Johann Baptist the younger, aged 4; and Karl Franz Xaver Joseph, aged 2. Young Nannerl was to become very close to Leopoldl, Nannerl's baby, whom she helped to bring up after

---

[22] See Brno, MZA, Berchtold Family Archive, Will and Inventory of Johann Baptist. The museum called the 'Mozart-Gedenkstätte', occupying a small part of the house in St Gilgen and dedicated to those members of the Mozart family who lived in it, is disappointing; it does not attempt to give details of the arrangement of the house, or of daily life within it.

Leopold's death. As an adult, she was also later to care for her brother Joseph, who was frail; he suffered from the *Fallsucht* (literally 'falling sickness', and usually interpreted as epilepsy), had to give up his education because of it, and died young in 1806. Young Wolfgang, who with his sister young Nannerl was mentioned frequently in Leopold's letters to Nannerl, was to die even sooner; he was already ailing before Leopold's final illness in the spring of 1787, and died aged 13 only a few weeks later than Leopold, of *Gliedersucht* (literally 'limb sickness' or 'joint sickness', a condition which among other symptoms made his joints swell painfully).[23]

From the date of Nannerl's marriage, Leopold's incoming correspondence is largely unpreserved; only one of Wolfgang's letters to him survives, and none of Nannerl's, though she wrote every week. Because of this, details of her life there have to be deduced from Leopold's letters to her, and there are many frustrating gaps in the reconstruction. One of these concerns her social life in the village, and especially her music-making. Although almost nothing is known about the musical forces she might have been able to muster there, and although she herself once called her situation 'a wilderness',[24] it is quite possible that she could gather together a few instrumentalists with whom to make music. Given the Mozart family practice of scaling down larger works to fit the instruments they had to hand, she would not have been doing anything very exceptional. Among the better-educated people close to the Berchtolds in the Abersee area were Berchtold's brother's family in Strobl at the other end of the lake, with four surviving children roughly contemporary with those of Berchtold; the priest and the sexton/schoolteacher; the clerk and the Amtmann who worked with Berchtold on a daily basis and must often have been in the house; Franz Karl von Schnedizeni, the owner of the brewery at Lueg; members of the Schmauss family, who ran the glassworks; and Joseph Bartholomäus von Riethaller, the salt official in Gmunden, who had a musical daughter. In addition, the facts that the lake was part of an important transport network, and that St Wolfgang attracted so many visitors, meant that there must occasionally have been acquaintances passing through the village, quite apart from those specifically invited by the Berchtolds to stay with them. Those passing through presumably stopped at the house and some of them probably played music with Nannerl. Furthermore, Salzburg musicians sometimes went

---

[23] See Brno, MZA, Berchtold Family Archive, Family Chronicle, unpaginated, but p. 43 on my count. See also Chs. 30 and 31 for more details about young Wolfgang's illness and death, and Fig. 2 for a diagram of Amann/Berchtold/Polis relationships.

[24] Nannerl to Breitkopf & Härtel, 24 Nov. 1799—*MBA* 1268/52–60 (not in *Letters*).

out into country areas to play at wedding dances and other celebrations; Nannerl would have known some of these, and some probably called on her.[25] And, of course, Leopold visited her periodically for the first few years, on one occasion accompanied by the new court organ and keyboard instruments builder and tuner, Johann Evangelist Schmid, and perhaps also by Heinrich Marchand.[26] Thus, although the indigenous music-making was probably of a very humble kind,[27] it may be that someone like Nannerl, with a passion for playing everything she could get her hands on, could make more of the situation than might be expected.[28] Certainly her appetite for new music did not diminish in St Gilgen, despite all the new demands on her time. And the fact that she sometimes had out there all the parts of her brother's latest keyboard concertos suggests that she might have tried (ludicrously? heroically?) to give some sort of performance even of these advanced works.

[25] Leopold mentioned a *Turner* of the Mozarts' acquaintance who, passing through St Gilgen, had wanted to call on Nannerl but had been too shy. Leopold's comments show that he thought the lad should certainly have paid the visit. See Leopold to Nannerl, 14 Jan. 1785—*MBA* 836/21–9 (not in *Letters*). The *Turner* in Salzburg were musicians under the jurisdiction of the city *Turnermeister*. They fulfilled a number of civic musical functions, such as blowing fanfares from the tower of the town hall, and were also leased out to play for weddings. See Hintermaier, 'Hofkapelle', p. xviii.

[26] See Leopold to Nannerl, 31 Mar. and 12 Apr. 1786—*MBA* 947/4–26 and 948/6–7 (neither passage in *Letters*).

[27] In a private communication of 27 June 1994, Professor Leopold Ziller informed me that the village musicians were string players and trumpeters who confined themselves to playing from memory folk music at wedding dances and similar events, and would not have been able to read music. Professor Ziller also said that although he had worked extensively on the history of the Abersee area, he had never discovered any material linking Nannerl with local musicians.

[28] Though it does not seem likely that a significant amount of information about music in St Gilgen remains to be found, it is possible that a search of the estate inventories and wills of the Berchtolds' relations, neighbours, and acquaintances would suggest something of their amateur musical interests. It would not be known, for example, that Berchtold's son Karl had had musical interests were it not for the information in Constanze Mozart's will showing that she lent him a clavichord of Mozart's. See E. Valentin, 'Das Testament der Constanze Mozart-Nissen. Mit biographischen Notizen über Constanze und Georg Nikolaus Nissen', *Neues MJb* 2 (1942), 134.

❧ 26 ❧

Nannerl's First Months in St Gilgen

❧

THE journey back to Salzburg from St Gilgen after Nannerl's wedding was not easy; clearly August had been a wet month. On his return with the Marchand children, Leopold began his first letter to Nannerl:

I can't describe our journey home properly in a hurry. Enough that the carriage collapsed on one side *four times*, because the through strap gave way, and chains had to be pulled through underneath, with help from farmers. then we stumbled along on foot through mud and over rocks; in short, we were in the house at *ten o' clock* . . .[1]

Gretl also wrote to Nannerl, thanking her warmly for all the kindness Nannerl had shown her from the beginning of their acquaintance. She had been only about 14 when she began her education with the Mozarts. She too touched on the frightful journey, suggesting that their lives had been in danger.[2]

Leopold's letter opened the next phase in the family correspondence, whereby he and Nannerl wrote to each other once every week. Since Leopold relayed Wolfgang's news to Nannerl, a small amount of information about his activities has been preserved despite the loss of his letters to Leopold from this time.[3] The bulk of the correspondence, however, concerns topics other than Wolfgang. It offers a picture of rural and domestic life, covering situations such as servant problems, sickness, child care, difficulties caused by poor communications, and relations between husband and wife; a glimpse of the changed relationships within the Mozart family, now that Leopold and Nannerl had abandoned the hope that Wolfgang would provide for them; amplification of Leopold's views

---

[1] Leopold to Nannerl, 30 Aug. 1784—*MBA* 803/5–9 (not in *Letters*).
[2] Gretl to Nannerl, 31 Aug. 1784—*MBA* 804 (not in *Letters*).
[3] It is this second-hand information about Wolfgang which has been given in *Letters*, while almost everything else Leopold wrote about to Nannerl has been omitted. This gives the impression that Wolfgang's activities were still of central importance to his father and sister, whereas this was not the case; many of Leopold's letters did not mention him at all.

on the upbringing of children, caused by the fact that he was advising Nannerl and Berchtold about their family; moving confirmation of his often-repeated assertion that he would strive for his family until his dying day; and the curious situation of the virtuoso Nannerl, who insisted on performing even the later keyboard concertos of her brother, despite the disadvantageous conditions.

Immediately on his return from St Gilgen, Leopold became involved in hectic activity, trying to find new servants for Nannerl, and arranging to return the Marchand children to their parents; presumably the resident pupil arrangement could not function without Nannerl. The servant question was pressing, because Michaelmas (29 September) was approaching, a time when servants routinely left their employment to take up new posts. It was also of crucial importance to Nannerl to hire good servants, because they were the key to her ability to run the household satisfactorily. Berchtold's five surviving children had apparently been running more or less wild since the death of his second wife Jeanette sixteen months previously, in April 1783. Furthermore, the spacing of the children conceals the situation of domestic turbulence that must have been a feature of the household since Berchtold's first marriage in 1769. For in almost every year someone had been born or had died, and two of the deaths had been of mothers, the mistresses of the house, who were not immediately replaced.[4] Leopold's letters to Nannerl suggest that Berchtold regarded the upbringing of his children as the province primarily of his wife and servants. Good servants, however, were difficult to obtain and keep, and the ones that could be hired easily were generally coarse and uneducated. Since the children's schooling was also unsatisfactory, it was almost impossible to provide an appropriate environment for them without a mistress in the house. One index of the uphill nature of the challenge facing Nannerl when she entered the household is her attempt to teach her stepdaughter Nannerl to play the keyboard, when the girl was completely unused to any task requiring concentration, and could hardly read or write. Nor was that all—the children were apparently physically neglected in terms of personal hygiene, so that Leopold felt it necessary to exhort even the 13-year-old Nannerl (who was supposed to be learning to care for her younger siblings) to clean her teeth and stop running

---

[4] See Fig. 2 for the full picture of births and deaths during Berchtold's previous two marriages. Berchtold's own mother, Maria Anna Elisabeth, had however lived with the St Gilgen family until her death in Mar. 1781; this fact must have lent some stability to the family between the death of Berchtold's first wife in Nov. 1779 and the marriage to his second in Feb. 1781. See Brno, MZA, Berchtold Family Archive, Family Chronicle, unpaginated, but pp. 35–6 on my count.

around with chicken feed smeared all over her hands. And this was not to mention the behavioural shortcomings of the children.[5] The problematic nature of the situation was almost certainly a factor in the decision to have Nannerl's first baby, Leopoldl, brought up by Leopold in Salzburg; the correspondence suggests that although Leopold and Nannerl were willing to do their best for Berchtold's children, 'their' child Leopoldl must not be allowed to go the same way.[6]

Three women were employed in the house—a cook, a *Stubenmädl* (chambermaid), and an *Untermensch* (under-maid). The chambermaid was superior to the under-maid, and had to be able to dress hair and do all kinds of needlework; the under-maid seems to have had mainly cleaning and childcare duties. Leopold was looking for industrious, good-humoured, sensible women with good morals, because their influence over young Nannerl would be considerable. Once he had chosen suitable women, each was given a florin to secure her services, and Nannerl and Berchtold were to travel into Salzburg at Michaelmas to meet the new servants and arrange their transport to St Gilgen.

The question of servants never ceased to loom large in the correspondence between Nannerl and Leopold, because it was one of the greatest banes of Nannerl's new life. Servant problems in times past have become such a cliché that an active imagination has to be employed in order to grasp the difficulties of being dependent on three other people for the smooth running of the household. Nannerl's tasks were to supervise the domestic economy and to direct the upbringing of the children. Though she probably did not have a heavy physical workload, her mental problems were considerable, as she struggled to run this large and unruly household economically, respectably, smoothly, and harmoniously. Not only had she to make sure that all the physical work was done well and economically, but she had to take responsibility for what the servants were teaching the children, to deal with feuds among the servants, and to set them a good example and instruct them morally. If she could not do all this, there was trouble between her and Berchtold.

It might be expected that all Nannerl's time was taken up with domestic duties, but this was not the case. She practised the keyboard as

---

[5] See Chs. 28, 29, and 30 for more details about Nannerl's stepchildren.

[6] Though it is clear that Leopold played the role of Leopoldl's father to the extent that he had the daily care of him for almost two years, I wish to distance myself from Solomon's suggestion of a 'barely veiled incest scenario' between Leopold and Nannerl. See Solomon, *Mozart*, 394–8. It was not then uncommon for children to be brought up by people other than their parents; all kinds of practical considerations led to such situations.

keenly as ever, and was constantly asking Leopold for more music. In early September, she wrote detailing her daily routine,[7] and Leopold replied:

Now I really must marvel that the days are almost too short to write a letter once a week, and the last one *without a date* to boot,—and that there's hardly time to read the news. I don't object to anything in the daily routine except playing the keyboard for three hours, from two o'clock till five, and then only going out walking for one hour.[8]

Leopold continued by mentioning the fine weather, boasting about how long he had been out in it, and accusing them of sitting around indoors. To take three or four hours' break from work (as they had after lunch in Salzburg, and as even Wolfgang claimed he did in Vienna) was evidently legitimate, perhaps because it was linked with good digestion,[9] but Leopold considered that more of it should be devoted to exercise in fresh air. Nannerl's priority, however, seems to have been her playing.

❧

While Nannerl was settling into her new routines, Leopold too had to adapt to enormous changes in his life. On Wednesday, 1 September, just over a week after the wedding, he left Salzburg with the Marchands to return the children to their families, and on Friday of the same week he was back home and describing it all to Nannerl:

On *Monday* and *Tuesday* I had enough to do sorting out all the junk, and as we were still being hindered by visits and the most important of the return visits, it couldn't really be otherwise than that on the 31st the night before our departure, I chased everyone off to bed at nine o' clock, and packed two cases, two seat chests, Heinrich's violin case, and a couple more big boxes full all on my own till half past midnight . . . We got up at half past four on the 1st of September, Heinrich was at the five o'clock Mass: and even so I had trouble managing to get out of Salzburg at seven o'clock with these turbulent creatures: because every moment something else that they'd forgotten turned up to be packed . . .

---

[7] Nannerl's letters to Leopold after her marriage have not survived, and their contents have to be surmised from his replies. One type of clue indicating that Leopold had received a letter from Nannerl concerns shopping; when he wrote a sentence such as '*Now the carrier has come*. I'm supposed to buy felt shoes, *using the pattern shoes*. But *where are the pattern shoes, then?*' (Leopold to Nannerl, 3 Dec. 1784—*MBA* 827/49–51; not in *Letters*), it is virtually certain that he was responding to a letter from Nannerl asking him to buy the shoes. Hardly any of the missing letters are numbered or noted in any other way by *MBA*. The problems of taking account of missing letters were discussed in Ch. 21, pp. 351–2.

[8] Leopold to Nannerl, 9–10 Sept. 1784—*MBA* 806/65–9 (not in *Letters*).

[9] Wolfgang to Leopold, 28 Dec. 1782—*MBA* 715/2–9 (*Letters* 476). In other descriptions of Wolfgang's daily routine in Vienna, too, the afternoon appears to have been relaxation time.

The plan was to hand over the children to the Marchand parents at Obing, which was between Munich and Salzburg just east of Wasserburg; everyone would stay at the inn there overnight, and they would separate on the following morning. When they arrived at Obing, they found that their numbers in the inn were to be swelled by the Munich musicians Ramm, Danzi, young Cannabich, and Lang, who happened to be on the road at the same time, travelling to Salzburg. Twelve people therefore sat down to supper at the inn (because Leopold had taken with him from Salzburg Nannerl's old friend Katherl Gilowsky, and there was a stranger too). Mme Marchand had brought a bottle of Rhenish wine as a present for Leopold, and that was drunk in company. After a convivial evening, people bedded down where they could—the Munich musicians had made up impromptu beds with palliasses on the floor of the room used for wedding dances. At four next morning they all rose again, and Ramm's party set off first for Salzburg:

now there were tears, as we took leave of the others. Mme Marchand, Gretl, Hanchen cried and cried. The thanks and the *asking of pardon*, which they repeatedly asked me to convey to my daughter too, had no end. It really did come from the heart, — Gretl asking a thousand pardons of my daughter, Hanchen too, and thanks for everything etcetcetc: then they were gone too! . . .

Katherl and Leopold then made their way back to Salzburg, where Leopold invited the Munich musicians to dine and make music with him, and busied himself undertaking various commissions for Nannerl and Berchtold (these were still mostly concerned with choosing servants). At the end of the letter, he wrote:

It's true, I'm now quite alone in eight rooms, in a really deathly silence. By day, to be sure, it doesn't bother me at all; but at night, as I write this, it's rather melancholy. if only I could at least still hear the dog snoring and barking. but all that doesn't matter, as long as I know that you're living happily together, — then I'm happy too.[10]

Leopold put a brave face on it, but the fact was that the new situation did matter terribly to him. In 1781 he had lost Wolfgang; now, at one fell swoop, he had lost Nannerl and the Marchands, and with them a tremendous amount of musical life. One of the big deprivations Leopold suffered was that he could not now hear Wolfgang's music whenever he

---

[10] Leopold to Nannerl, 3 Sept. 1784—*MBA* 805 (not in *Letters*). In the passage describing the leave-taking of the Marchands and Leopold, I translate 'die Fr: Tochter' as 'my daughter' to try to convey the formality of the Marchands' reference to Nannerl.

wanted to. Four years previously, when Wolfgang had been in Munich for *Idomeneo*, and Leopold had been nursing Nannerl at home, he had been bemoaning the fact that he could not enjoy his old age in peace because he still had to be the strong one of the family.[11] At that time he had still been hoping that Wolfgang would enable them all to leave Salzburg—he would retire, and they would all live together. Wolfgang's decision to leave his salaried employment, and his subsequent decision to marry, had meant that Leopold had had to be far more cautious about the idea of giving up his own post, or encouraging Nannerl to depend on her brother. Her marriage relieved him of the anxiety of financial provision for her, and gave him the comfort that she would not be alone when he died, but the cost for both of them was high. Nannerl's departure coincided with a decline in liveliness of the shooting parties—Katherl Gilowsky took up a post as governess in a local noble family and could no longer always attend, and without all the young people the events were not the same.[12] Leopold's house was no longer such an attraction, and he himself derived little enjoyment from the traditional family entertainments once he could not share them with his family. From this time on, the only entertainment in Salzburg that he really enjoyed was to be the theatre.[13]

❧

When the carrier left St Gilgen each Friday morning with his official court mail, he also had with him Nannerl's letter to Leopold and any gift of fish, game, or poultry she might want to send her father. He would deliver this to Leopold at or just after midday on Friday, leaving Leopold the rest of the day in which to carry out Nannerl's requests. Leopold usually had some shopping to do for her, and she often asked for more music, or mentioned some problem with her keyboard. If a new servant was needed, she would ask Leopold to look out for one, and he also got involved in trying to sell for Berchtold some jewellery that had belonged

---

[11] See Ch. 20, p. 344.

[12] Leopold to Nannerl, early Nov. 1784—*MBA* 820/38–44 (not in *Letters*). In Appendix 3 I argue that the exact date of this letter was almost certainly 5/6 Nov.

[13] Rieger rejects the idea that Leopold was excessively lonely after Nannerl's departure, and hints that he was indulging in self-pity. She points to the facts that Heinrich Marchand returned to Salzburg, that Leopold was still active teaching noble ladies, and that he received frequent visitors (such as Wolfgang's friend, the singer Nancy Storace). See Rieger, *Nannerl Mozart*, 203. This is an idiosyncratic view when one considers that his family had been the whole purpose of Leopold's life. Heinrich's return did help, but this did not take place until March 1786.

to one of his former wives. Leopold would usually have begun his letter to Nannerl earlier in the week, so that when her letter arrived, he merely had to answer any points raised by her. The carrier then returned to St Gilgen on Saturday morning, taking Leopold's letter to Nannerl and any goods he had for her. The cost of the shopping was reckoned up to the last kreuzer, and Nannerl would send the money the following week.[14]

Berchtold wanted Nannerl to keep an extremely tight grip on the family finances, and even the thrifty Leopold sometimes thought it excessive. The situation was difficult for Nannerl, because typically she would ask Leopold to buy something for them, Berchtold would complain at what it had cost, and Nannerl would have to query the price with Leopold, who would then write to justify the expense. His tone was always blunt, and he sometimes added a short sermon on parsimony. A typical situation arose during Nannerl's first winter in St Gilgen, when young Nannerl needed a new pair of felt shoes. Berchtold had expected them to cost 36 kr., but in fact they were 55 kr., and Leopold wrote:

my son-in-law is dissatisfied with the felt shoes; yes, I've often been dissatisfied during my life, and yet I've had to pay when I've wanted to have something. I can certainly remember a time when you paid 36 kr., then they went up to 45 kr., last year I had to pay 50 kr. and *NB* you can't even get ones of your own choosing, they're proud with it as well . . .[15]

Though Leopold had always managed his own affairs economically, he was not stingy, and there were some expenses which he regarded as an investment. One such was a better class of servant, for which he believed it was worth paying a little more. The first cook to work for Nannerl after Michaelmas 1784 did not stay long, and in November Leopold was looking for a new one for the Berchtolds. He liked the look of a particular woman because of her quiet piety, but she had a stunted foot which rendered her unfit for heavy work. Foreseeing that Berchtold would not want her unless she could do all the cook's work, including the carrying of water and firewood, Leopold wrote to try to persuade him that it would be worth hiring an extra local woman to undertake these heavy

---

[14] The carrier's routines, and other details of the ways in which Leopold and Nannerl communicated after her marriage, are given in detail in Appendix 3.

[15] Leopold to Nannerl, 10 Dec. 1784—*MBA* 829/51–5 (not in *Letters*). I have given 'my son-in-law' as a translation of the German 'Der Herr Sohn' to try to convey Leopold's formality with respect to Berchtold. There is no completely satisfactory way of rendering the phrase in English, and 'my son' had to be avoided in order not to confuse Berchtold with Wolfgang.

duties. Though he began by declaring that he did not want to interfere in their lives, he admitted that he could not resist giving his opinion. This was that servants were one of the worst tribulations of married life, and that it was increasingly difficult to get good ones. They were now better paid than they had been a generation previously, and yet they deceived their employers more; times had changed, and it was no use trying to live the way one's parents had. He continued:

then my son-in-law must reflect, and think: *I have young children*. If Nannerl learns something about *sewing, trimming a cap*, and suchlike *whitework*, and sees *good presentable cooking*, and at the same time is around servants who just have slightly better behaviour, and where she doesn't see bad examples, and isn't always hearing stupid love stuff; it will be more beneficial to her than if she has *such coarse peasant oafs* or *silly love-sick fillies* around her, where they're talking pretty peasant talk and she's picking up manners which will always stick with her, if not completely, still always very noticeably. *Oh, everything will turn out all right!*: I know the proverb well. No, dearest son-in-law! it doesn't turn out all right with every child. *Not all children have the same understanding* . . . you can't be too careful with the upbringing of children. These days you won't get a good clever cook who can also turn her hand to fine work if she's still supposed to do all the heavy work as well:—and even if you could, the finer work would lie there undone, when really any peasant woman, of whom you've got a whole village full, can help carry wood. you'll recoup the little bit you pay her because your daughter will be cleverer: In general I always had my whole attention on the education and development of my children, good manners and knowledge, good enlightened human understanding and skill is *No. 1*. Money and means is only *No. 2* in the eyes of any sensible person.—*the first* remains and no one can take it away from you. *The second* you can waste, lose, be defrauded of etc . . . my son-in-law might perhaps be surprised that I'm so thorough in all these things and make such a meal of them. but (my daughter knows me) that's just my way; with me everything has to be clear . . . and with this—Amen![16]

Leopold naturally wanted to see as much of Nannerl as possible, and there are signs that he was trying to disentangle himself from his court duties in order to have more leisure to visit her in St Gilgen. As early as 10 September he was telling her that the fine weather would have tempted him

---

[16] Leopold to Nannerl (but intended for Berchtold too) in late Nov. 1784—*MBA* 826/35–116 (not in *Letters*).

out to them if the archbishop had not ordered him to prepare a list of musicians and their salaries.[17] The first opportunity that presented itself for a reunion, therefore, was Michaelmas, when Nannerl and Berchtold planned to come in to Salzburg. Leopold must have envisaged a resumption of their intensive music-making, because on 14 September he wrote to her:

I'm sending three concertos, but only the keyboard parts, which my daughter can bring back with her when she comes in, in particular so that she can try the Concerto in B flat here with all the parts: also the new one that's already out there.[18]

The concertos he intended Nannerl to play were K. 450 and probably K. 451 ('the new one that's already out there'), both of which had been sent by Wolfgang from Vienna, with K. 449 and K. 453, on 15 May 1784.[19] Since Leopold was only at this juncture sending her the keyboard parts to three of these four, there had presumably been time for him to have only K. 451 copied before Nannerl had moved to St Gilgen. The visit duly took place; new servants must have been introduced to the Berchtolds, shopping and other business must have been conducted at the market, and the Dancing-Master's House must have been full of visitors and music again. Leopold then returned with them for a week's visit to St Gilgen. Very soon after he had left for St Gilgen, a letter arrived for him in Salzburg from Wolfgang, asking for some of his keyboard music back urgently for a concert. Leopold's servant Therese Pänckl ('Tresel') did not bother to forward the letter to St Gilgen, so that when Leopold returned there was barely time to do what Wolfgang asked, because the music he wanted (K. 453 and the cadenzas at least of K. 451) was with Nannerl in St Gilgen. On returning to Salzburg and finding Wolfgang's request, therefore, Leopold told Nannerl to send in K. 453 at the first possible

---

[17] *MBA* 806/70–3 (not in *Letters*).   [18] *MBA* 808/2–5 (not in *Letters*).

[19] See *MBA* 790/2–19 (*Letters* 513). Both Deutsch and Paumgartner and the *MBA* commentary identify 'the new one that's already out there' as K. 453, perhaps because it was the last of these four concertos to be composed. Cf. O. E. Deutsch and B. Paumgartner (eds.), *Leopold Mozarts Briefe an seine Tochter* (Salzburg/Leipzig, 1936), 495; and the commentary to *MBA* 808/2. I believe K. 451 to be a likelier candidate, however, for the following reasons. First, I argued in Ch. 24 (pp. 429–30) that Wolfgang probably sent all the extra material for K. 451 just before Nannerl's name-day, so she did have everything she needed for a performance of this concerto. Secondly, Nannerl was querying tempo indications for K. 453 later than this, in November 1784; if she had played through it during her Michaelmas visit to Salzburg, these should already have been clarified. See Leopold to Nannerl, 19 Nov. 1784—*MBA* 825/77–8 (not in *Letters*). K. 449, 450, 451, and 453 had all arrived together in Salzburg, and were thus all equally new to Leopold and Nannerl; Leopold's designation 'new', therefore, does not by itself enable a distinction to be made among these four works.

opportunity so that he could get it copied in time, and to copy out herself the cadenzas to K. 451 and send them in with the carrier.[20]

Following the Michaelmas visit, Leopold did not see the Berchtolds again until Christmas. His name-day was for the first time spent without any member of his family. However, he did have the pleasure of seeing Wolfgang's opera *Die Entführung* just after his name-day. In September a new theatrical troupe had arrived in Salzburg. The leader was Ludwig Schmidt, who brought ten different operas for the autumn and winter season in 1784/5. *Die Entführung* was far and away the most popular, with eight performances, compared with two or three of each of the other works.[21] At the time that Nannerl and Berchtold had paid their Michaelmas visit, *Die Entführung* had not yet been produced, so Nannerl was naturally keen to return to Salzburg to see it. On 19 November Leopold reported the tolerable success of the first performance.[22] He elaborated on the pleasure it was giving when he wrote after the second one, expressing particular gratification that Michael Haydn had praised it publicly.[23] Yet despite Leopold's general enthusiasm for the performances (which went so far as to report to Nannerl that people who had seen the work in Vienna, Berlin, Mainz, and Mannheim agreed that the Salzburg production was livelier and better acted), it seems clear that musically much was lacking. It was not performed with all the instrumentation for which it had been written, Haydn qualified his enthusiasm by saying that the work required a fuller orchestra, and Leopold later revealed to Nannerl that the grand aria 'Martern aller Arten' had not been sung complete, because the singer had not been sufficiently capable.[24]

Leopold told Nannerl after the second performance that the opera would now rest until Christmas, and it was then that she planned to return to Salzburg to see it. Thus, though Leopold would like to have been in St Gilgen shooting duck on his name-day,[25] he could console himself

---

[20] The two letters which describe the bustling about on the part of Leopold and Nannerl (*MBA* 813 and 820; neither in *Letters*) are undated, but I argue in Appendix 3 that *MBA* 813 should almost certainly be dated Fri. 22/Sat. 23 Oct. 1784, and that *MBA* 820 should be dated Fri. 5/Sat. 6 Nov. 1784.

[21] See S. Dahms, 'Das musikalische Repertoire', 345–6.

[22] *MBA* 825/21–37 (*Letters* 520).

[23] Leopold to Nannerl, late Nov. 1784—*MBA* 826/4–20 (*Letters* 521).

[24] Leopold to Nannerl, 7–10 Dec. 1785—*MBA* 907/60–82 (not in *Letters*). On the other hand, this aria, which includes virtuoso instrumental parts as well as the voice, was apparently a challenge even for Viennese musicians. In Nov. 1784 the *Wiener Kronik* reported that since the virtuosi for whom Mozart had written it were out of town, the aria had had to be replaced with one by Teyber for a performance of *Die Entführung* at the Kärntnertor Theatre on 5 Nov. See Eisen, *Documents*, 57.

[25] Leopold to Nannerl, late Nov. 1784—*MBA* 826/120–3 (not in *Letters*).

by looking forward to this visit. Furthermore, Theobald Marchand was pressing him to go to Munich and Vienna during the Carnival of 1785:

I've got a *long letter*, or rather *two letters* of Marchand's to answer, for which I'm going to need a week to set everything out in the right order, as I can't write much at once. I've to go *to Munich* — — I've to go *to Vienna* and God knows where. Oh, if only I were my own master! I'd soon have my bags packed.[26]

Nannerl and Berchtold travelled in to Salzburg again around Christmas, in time to see the performance on 26 December.[27] Meanwhile, Nannerl had been complaining that her keyboard needed tuning, and Leopold had promised to try to arrange for the court tuner Johann Joseph Egedacher to go out to St Gilgen and see to it. At first it seemed a routine affair, but it developed into an extremely frustrating problem for Nannerl. In the first place, Egedacher and his son Rochus were the only tuners in Salzburg, and Leopold soon discovered that the older man was now too infirm to work. This meant that Rochus had to undertake all his father's work—the court instruments had to be tuned three times weekly, on Tuesdays, Thursdays, and Sundays (the days of the court concerts), and there were other instruments in the town which were also his responsibility. Furthermore, he had clerical duties, being a priest. Since a visit to St Gilgen necessitated an overnight stay because of the travelling time, this was awkward. Moreover, the journey out there in winter was no bagatelle. When Nannerl returned to St Gilgen after Christmas, no arrangement had been made for Egedacher to visit her, and Leopold predicted both that none was imminent, and that there was no prospect either of a journeyman tuner being engaged. He also expressed despair at the sluggishness in court procedures which was responsible for the situation.[28]

Leopold was simultaneously busy arranging to go to Munich and Vienna. He intended to go to Munich first to see the Marchands, and then take Heinrich with him to Vienna, where Wolfgang was trying to arrange for Heinrich to give a Lenten concert. For some reason, Nannerl opposed the plan—perhaps because she depended heavily on Leopold for practical and moral support, or perhaps because she did not want to miss seeing him when she and Berchtold next visited Salzburg. On 14 January 1785, Leopold wrote:

[26] Leopold to Nannerl, 19 Nov. 1784—*MBA* 825/52–6 (not in *Letters*).
[27] See Leopold to Nannerl, 16 Dec. 1784—*MBA* 832 (not in *Letters*).
[28] Leopold to Nannerl, 14 Jan. 1785—*MBA* 836/6–14 (not in *Letters*).

I fully appreciate that you don't like it, on your account it's not pleasing to me either: but I really can't turn down a journey like this for the sake of a few days' visit from you, a journey which, though it comes at an inconvenient time of year for me, gives me the opportunity in Munich to hear the opera of a new maestro, whom I don't know; and to travel to Vienna at no expense to myself, to admire the fine affairs of your brother, and to arrange the engraving of the Marchand children's keyboard sonatas, and one or two other matters. if the journey's going ahead I'll leave here on the 28th.[29]

Five days later, Leopold reported that he now had leave from Colloredo,[30] but his letter reveals that Nannerl was continuing to object to his absence, for he wrote:

I can easily believe that you think this journey is very disagreeable, I myself, as you know, didn't have any great zest for it: but I think it should be more useful than harmful to my health. Once the theatre people have gone, I don't know what I'm supposed to do in the evening, I could rot away for *brooding* and *boredom*. I've been at Hagenauer's three times, and stayed in the little parlour at the back with the daughters, because in the front room there were already two professors, — the regent of the priests' seminary, the buildings intendant, and the priest from Gnigl playing a double round of *Brandeln*, — because this is now the usual evening's entertainment they arrange for the old man, — but I'm no lover of *Brandeln*, and nor do I have the slightest desire to gamble away four stakes twice over, making 45 kr. — 1 fl. — 1 fl. 15 kr., often coarsely disputed (with the exception of the clerics) into the bargain—I also take little pleasure in looking on at the game for a couple of hours in an *overheated oven of a room*, and listening to old *players' proverbs* which I've heard a hundred times before, and which are supposed to be amusing.[31]

More than twenty years previously, in 1762, Leopold had greeted Frau Hagenauer for her name-day by wishing her whole family a long life, followed by an eternal *Brandlspiel* to be enjoyed by the Mozarts and the Hagenauers.[32] Even after making allowance for the jocular politeness of his greeting, there are many passages in the correspondence which suggest that Leopold was reasonably happy with Salzburg entertainments when he could share them with his family, and when they were a restful diversion from work and the more purposeful leisure activity of making

---

[29] *MBA* 835/23–32 (not in *Letters*). Leopold used the plural form of 'you', suggesting that Nannerl had complained that his absence would make it awkward for her whole family (or at any rate for Berchtold as well as herself), rather than herself alone.

[30] Leopold was granted six weeks' leave, but was absent for about fourteen without seeking an extension. See Deutsch, *Documents*, 245–6.

[31] Leopold to Nannerl, 19–21 Jan. 1785—*MBA* 838/29–43 (not in *Letters*).

[32] Leopold to Maria Theresia Hagenauer, 16 Oct. 1762—*MBA* 34/71–7 (*Letters* 2).

music. Now that he was on his own, however, the entertainments which had formerly seemed adequate were shown up in all their futility.

Leopold had a number of things to attend to before he could leave. First and foremost, he had to arrange for his court duties to be done by others. He asked Michael Haydn to conduct in the cathedral, hinting to him that he would like Colloredo to allow Haydn to take Leopold's place permanently. His Kapellhaus teaching was to be undertaken by his pupil Breymann, and Leopold specifically said that he hoped these arrangements would facilitate his disentanglement from his duties, and give him more freedom. Leopold told Nannerl that Breymann would also be willing to make music with her on many days from five till eight, while she was in town, because this had been his usual lesson time with Leopold.[33]

Leopold also had things to do for Nannerl. He was figuring concertos as fast as possible with the intention of sending them out to her at the first opportunity, whether by the carrier or the glass-carrier; presumably she wanted to practise her accompaniment in tutti passages before she arrived in Salzburg and played them with anyone else. And he was still trying to get Rochus Egedacher out to St Gilgen to tune her keyboard. His first idea was to arrange for Egedacher to travel with the Graz carrier on Saturday 22 January, Egedacher having rearranged his court tuning schedule and his clerical duties. The carrier could not oblige, however, so Egedacher had to start investigating the possibility of making the journey in two stages—he talked of accepting a ride to Hof, and deciding on arrival there whether to pay the innkeeper another 48 kr. to be taken on to St Gilgen, or whether to walk the remaining fourteen kilometres.[34] Leopold also had to leave ready in his house everything that the Berchtolds would need, do the usual weekly shopping for them, and arrange his own journey. On 22 January he received a short letter from Wolfgang giving the dates of his Lenten concerts, urging Leopold to come soon, mentioning that he had just begun writing another keyboard concerto, and telling him about his six 'Haydn' Quartets, which he had performed before Haydn and sold to Artaria for 100 ducats (433 fl. 20 kr.).[35]

Because of the loss of Wolfgang's letters home, not a great deal is known of his activities during the first few months following Nannerl's marriage. Leopold reported some of his news to Nannerl, but sometimes he simply enclosed Wolfgang's letter with his own instead; and if

---

[33] Leopold to Nannerl, 19–21 Jan. 1785—*MBA* 838/43–55 (not in *Letters*).

[34] Leopold to Nannerl, 19–21 and 22 Jan. 1785—*MBA* 838/97–104 and 120–6, and 840/2–12 (not in *Letters*).

[35] *MBA* 840/15–22 (*Letters* 522).

a letter from Wolfgang arrived while Nannerl was visiting Salzburg, there was obviously no need for Leopold to write to her about it. Thus he told her on 14 September 1784 that Wolfgang had been very ill,[36] and on 19 November that Wolfgang had given a concert on his name-day;[37] but not that Wolfgang's second child, Carl Thomas, had been born on 21 September,[38] nor that Wolfgang and Constanze had moved to magnificent new lodgings in the Schulerstrasse on 29 September (Michaelmas).[39] Assuming Wolfgang wrote to Leopold about these important events, the letter probably arrived just when Nannerl was paying her Michaelmas visit to Leopold. Wolfgang entered a number of masterpieces in the catalogue of his works during these six months—the Keyboard Concertos, K. 456 and K. 459, the Keyboard Sonata, K. 457, and the 'Haydn' Quartets, K. 458, K. 464, and K. 465.[40] As Nannerl retreated even further from public life, and was getting to grips with all the problems of her new domestic economy, therefore, Wolfgang was entering his most productive, high-profile, and prosperous period in Vienna. But there was one feature of Nannerl's circumstances that was to assume great importance not only for her but also for Leopold, though it had not yet been articulated in the correspondence between them—when he left Salzburg for Munich and Vienna on 28 January 1785, she was expecting her first baby.

---

[36] *MBA* 808/7–18 (*Letters* 518).   [37] *MBA* 825/2–8 (*Letters* 520).
[38] See Deutsch, *Documents*, 228.   [39] See Eisen, *Documents*, 55.
[40] See *MBA* 811, 830, 814, 819, 834, and 837.

27

Leopold's Visit to Vienna in 1785

❦

LEOPOLD went first to Munich to collect Heinrich Marchand. There he enjoyed a lively reunion with the Marchands, the Brochards, and other Munich friends, and went to some of the carnival events. He also learnt of the disgrace of Nannerl's and Wolfgang's Augsburg cousin Maria Anna Thekla, the *Bäsle*, which accounted for the fact that they had heard no news from Augsburg for a long time—she had borne an illegitimate child. Nannerl meanwhile was in Salzburg, and Leopold left her in charge of selling copies of his *Violinschule* at the fair, and asked her to report on any performances of *Die Entführung* that took place while she was there.[1] It was five months since the Marchands had ceased to be Leopold's resident pupils, and Leopold found that Heinrich's playing left much to be desired. As they left Munich for Vienna on 7 February, therefore, he must have been prepared to coach Heinrich intensively before Heinrich's first public appearance there.[2]

The winter of 1784/5 was exceptionally bitter and long, and the journey from Munich to Vienna was four and a half days of trials. The snow was so deep that in places the road was virtually indistinguishable from the surrounding land, and the carriage sank into the ditch at the side. At one point Leopold and Heinrich had to climb out into waist-deep snow and fight their way across fields to Haag. The horses were worked practically to death, and on the stretch of road between Haag and Lambach local farmers formed road gangs to clear some of the snow away. Two labourers waded beside the carriage to hold it up until the next gang was reached, from which another two men were taken for the same purpose, until Lambach was reached.[3]

---

[1] Leopold to Nannerl, 2 Feb. 1785—*MBA* 844 (not in *Letters*). Eibl suggests that Nannerl and Berchtold stayed in Salzburg for the whole of Leopold's absence and a short while after his return, from late January until 23 May. See Eibl, *Chronik*, 84. This is not so, however; Leopold's letters to Nannerl show that she went to Salzburg and returned home twice while he was away, and then went a third time to await his return from Vienna and stay with him until 23 May.

[2] Leopold to Nannerl, 21 Feb. 1785—*MBA* 848/59–62 (not in *Letters*).

[3] Leopold to Nannerl, 15–16 Feb. 1785—*MBA* 847/4–30 (not in *Letters*).

Not surprisingly, Leopold went down with a cold shortly after arriving in Vienna, and had to miss some of the early social engagements. However, he was soon caught up in Wolfgang's frenetic Lenten activities, and could certainly not complain of boredom. He and Heinrich had arrived on Friday 11 February, and Lent had begun two days previously. Judging from Leopold's letters to Nannerl, however, there was nothing austere about a Viennese Lent. Dramatic performances in the theatres were suspended, but that was the only concession. The theatres and other concert rooms were busy with Lenten concerts; Wolfgang, who was by now on friendly terms with a good many instrumentalists and singers, took part in concerts other than his own, and many of his friends took part in his. His circle included a significant number of actors, playwrights, and opera singers, and there was frequent dining out. His days were so hectic that Leopold could hardly cope with the confusion: there was teaching, planning of and practising for concerts, composing and copying for them, giving them, and socializing around them. Wolfgang had a fortepiano with a specially built pedal providing extra bass notes, and both fortepiano and pedal were carried frequently from his house to concert venues. In the midst of all this, Leopold was trying to bring Heinrich's playing up to scratch for the concerts he was to give, get to know all Wolfgang's new music, arrange for keyboard music to be copied for Nannerl, and play with his grandson Carl, who was almost five months old.

The first concert Leopold went to took place on the evening of the day of their arrival, and by the time he wrote his first letter to Nannerl from Vienna on 15–16 February he had plenty to tell her. Wolfgang was giving one concert in the Burgtheater, and a set of six subscription concerts in the Mehlgrube, one of Vienna's other concert rooms. As Leopold arrived, the Keyboard Concerto, K. 466, was being copied for its first performance in the Mehlgrube that evening, and Leopold told Nannerl that Wolfgang had had no time to play through the Rondo. Next day, Joseph Haydn was present as three of the new 'Haydn' Quartets were played in Wolfgang's house, and Haydn made the famous comment to Leopold about Wolfgang's greatness as a composer. On Sunday, 13 February, Wolfgang played a keyboard concerto in a concert given by the singer Luisa Laschi-Mombelli, and Leopold was overcome with emotion at its beauty.[4] Two

---

[4] It is not certain which concerto this was. Leopold simply described it to Nannerl as a 'glorious concerto' and said that it had been written for Maria Theresia von Paradis 'for Paris'. His description suggests that neither he nor Nannerl knew it already; if this is so, it must have been a later one than K. 453, which seems to have been the newest they had in Salzburg at this date. K. 456 is usually suggested as an identification.

days later, K. 466 was played again, this time in the concert given by the singer Elisabeth Distler, and on 16 February there was a domestic concert at the house of Wolfgang's pupil Barbara Ployer.[5] Leopold did not fail to note the magnificence of Wolfgang's lodgings, nor to point out that his annual rent was 480 fl.;[6] he was also observing how Wolfgang stood with respect to the aristocracy, and mentioned the emperor's particular attention to him during Luisa Laschi-Mombelli's concert.[7]

Leopold next wrote to Nannerl five days later, on 21–2 February. By this time, he had been to more concerts, met a good many noble patrons of Wolfgang's, and dined out several times. The meals he described were lavish, and there was no question of fasting. Meat courses, oysters, glacé fruits, champagne, and coffee constituted the fare he was offered. True to his character, he was busy assessing the domestic economy of the people he met, and trying to gauge what all the musicians were likely to earn from their concerts, and what they would be left with after the expenses had been deducted. He noted that Wolfgang's friend, the actor Johann H. F. Müller, had eight children and a large apartment for which he paid 700 fl. annually; and that the playwright Stephanie (Wolfgang's librettist for *Die Entführung*) had a small apartment which yet cost 500 fl., because it was so near the theatre. Leopold was particularly struck by the popularity of the married couple Lebrun, who were both in Munich court service, he as an oboist and she as a singer; they were in Vienna to give three Lenten concerts, and Leopold prophesied that they were going to make a good deal of money.[8]

---

[5] Morrow notes in her Public Concert Calendar another concert of Wolfgang's, possibly in the Burgtheater, on 16 Feb. 1785. See Morrow, *Concert Life in Haydn's Vienna*, 259. This seems, however, to be a misunderstanding of the chronology in Leopold's letter to Nannerl of 15–16 Feb. 1785—*MBA* 847 (*Letters* 523). The letter was begun on 15 Feb. and finished on 16 Feb., and Leopold (unusually) did not make it clear which parts were written when. Consequently, his 'yesterdays' and 'todays' are confusing, but if it is assumed that everything up to and including the phrase 'dein Bruder spielt abermahl ein Concert' in *MBA* 847/67 was written on 15 Feb., and everything from the phrase 'Ich befinde mich nun viel besser' was written on 16 Feb., the chronology makes sense and shows that the concert Morrow gives for 16 Feb. was actually merely another reference to Elisabeth Distler's concert on 15 Feb. The fact that *Letters* omits several passages from the letter means that the chronology is harder to deduce from this edition, since the description of Leopold's cold in *MBA* 847/60–7 (which is one of the omitted passages) is helpful to it. A list of Addenda and Corrigenda to Morrow's concert calendars is given in Edge, 'Review Article on Morrow's book', 139–66; Edge notes this particular correction on pp. 147–8.

[6] Leopold paid 90 fl. annually for the Dancing-Master's House in Salzburg, with its eight rooms, including the magnificent music room. See Leopold to Nannerl, 27–9 Oct. 1785—*MBA* 892/114–27 (not in *Letters*).

[7] *MBA* 847/31–86 (*Letters* 523).

[8] *MBA* 848/4–39 (*Letters* 524). Leopold only mentioned two of the Lebrun concerts in this letter, but referred to three in his letter of 12 Mar. 1785—*MBA* 850/16–17 (not in *Letters*). Morrow's Public Concert Calendar also shows three appearances there, documented from a different source. See Morrow, *Concert Life in Haydn's Vienna*, 259–60.

As Leopold was writing this letter, he received one from Nannerl, who had returned from Salzburg to St Gilgen. Her letter evidently complained about her fortepiano, which had been temporarily ruined by the cold and damp while the St Gilgen house had been unheated during her absence, and was completely unplayable because of stuck keys. Leopold was shocked, but could suggest no remedy until Egedacher should get a journeyman to help him with the workload. He therefore told her to have his large clavichord tuned by Egedacher in Salzburg, and to have it taken out to St Gilgen. But this was more easily said than done, because the snow did not immediately permit such a journey.[9] While Wolfgang's magnificent instrument was being carried to and fro during the Viennese Lenten concert season, therefore, Nannerl was completely without the use of hers, and was trying unsuccessfully to arrange for Leopold's clavichord to be packed in straw and transported out on a wagon over roads choked with snow.

Leopold continued his letter by expressing his fears about the concert Heinrich was to give. He was worried first that Heinrich would not be good enough, and second that he would not attract enough of an audience to cover his expenses of almost 200 fl. Part of Heinrich's difficulty was that he was young and relatively unknown, and Lent was already packed with concerts given by Viennese favourites. One such was Lebrun, who was to give one of his concerts only two days before Heinrich's. Leopold was therefore toying with the idea of asking Lebrun to play in Heinrich's concert, to make the event more of a draw (whether he did so is unknown).

Finally, Leopold reported rumours that Berchtold's brother Johann Nepomuk Martin (who lived in Vienna) was a wife-beater, and he responded to some remarks in Nannerl's letter. She had mentioned that her friend Katherl Gilowsky was trying to ingratiate herself with the court chemist; Leopold's response was that it was entirely in character for her to lay claim to widowers. Nannerl must also have asked for the whole story about the *Bäsle*, at which Leopold had only hinted in his letter from Munich on 2 February. He replied:

you can easily imagine for yourself the story of the Augsburg cousin, a canon has made her fortune. — As soon as I have time I shall write a hellish letter from here to Augsburg, as if I'd discovered it in Vienna. The richest thing about it is,—that all the presents she got, which were obvious to the whole world, all

---

[9] *MBA* 848/39–50 (not in *Letters*).

of them, all of them were sent to her by her uncle in Salzburg. — what an honour for me![10]

Heinrich's first concert in the theatre took place on Wednesday 2 March, half-way through Lent. About a week later, on 10 March, Wolfgang gave his own Burgtheater concert, in which he played the just-completed Keyboard Concerto, K. 467; and on Sunday 13 March the theatre was booked for one of the two concerts given by the Tonkünstlersozietät, the charity that provided for widows and children of deceased musicians. Wolfgang was involved in this both as composer and performer; despite his hectic Lenten schedule, he had reworked part of the C minor Mass, K. 427, and had written two new arias, to form a cantata, *Davidde penitente*, K. 469. The day after this concert, Heinrich gave a second concert in the theatre, and on the following day another Tonkünstlersozietät concert was given, in which Heinrich played a violin concerto and Wolfgang's cantata was repeated. Leopold reported on Heinrich's first concert and Wolfgang's Burgtheater concert to Nannerl on 12 March; he probably wrote about the other concerts too, but only a fragment of his letter of 19 March survives.[11]

Leopold was fairly pleased with Heinrich's first concert. His fears had been that Heinrich might not play well enough to do his teacher credit, and that he might not earn enough to cover his expenses. Leopold was extremely sensitive on the first point, and felt a strong sense of responsibility on the second, since his own travel expenses to Vienna had been paid in full by the Marchands. He claimed that Heinrich had played magnificently, but that the audience had been disappointing, and the profit had only been 18 ducats (78 fl.) after 115 fl. expenses had been deducted.[12] However, Leopold must have been relieved to have covered the costs at all, and Heinrich's fine playing led him to hope that his second concert would be more successful financially. Wolfgang's concert in the theatre had been more profitable—Leopold claimed that he had taken 559 fl., though he did not explicitly state whether this was before or after expenses. He did suggest, however, that they had been agreeably surprised by the sum, given that Wolfgang was also involved in the

---

[10] The information in this paragraph and the previous one is still from *MBA* 848 (all is omitted from *Letters*).

[11] The list of concerts appears most conveniently in Morrow, *Concert Life in Haydn's Vienna*, 260–1. Leopold's letter to Nannerl of 12 Mar. 1785 also mentions them (*MBA* 850; *Letters* 525, but not complete). *MBA* 849 gives the entries in Wolfgang's thematic catalogue of the Concerto, K. 467, and the two arias for *Davidde penitente*.

[12] This conversion assumes imperial ducats, which converted at 4 fl. 20 kr. in 1785—see Edge, 'Mozart's Fee for *Così fan tutte*', 218.

six Mehlgrube subscription concerts. Perhaps the most successful concert-givers during this season were the Lebruns—Leopold claimed that they had taken 2,500 fl. in three concerts (though again it is not certain whether he meant gross or net).[13]

By the time Leopold wrote again to Nannerl on 19 March, Wolfgang had given his last Mehlgrube concert, and his profit from the complete Lenten season could be reckoned up. Leopold wrote:

> I think that my son can now deposit 2000 fl. in the bank *if he has no debts to pay*: the money is certainly there, and the housekeeping, as far as eating and drinking is concerned, is economical in the extreme.[14]

His figure was presumably based on the concert net receipts, together with his assessment of household expenses. The letter is problematic, however, because the original is lost. It is known only from the short extract quoted above, which was given in Nissen's biography of Mozart, and it is not clear that what was rendered by Nissen is even the whole of a sentence, since Nissen frequently edited the letters in order that his highly selective extracts should still make sense.[15] Particularly suggestive is Leopold's explicit reference to economy where food and drink were concerned, because he may have had quite different views about the household expenditure on clothes and other fashion items.[16] He had already hinted in his first letter from Vienna at the lavish furnishings in the apartment. Furthermore, it seems that Leopold and Nannerl recognized a need to be guarded in their correspondence between St Gilgen and Vienna when commenting on Wolfgang's and Constanze's affairs (presumably in case a letter fell into the wrong hands),[17] so it would be unwise to infer from this second-hand and out-of-context fragment that Leopold approved of their domestic economy in its entirety.

Whether Leopold had a strong suspicion that Wolfgang did actually have debts to pay is not clear, but it seems quite likely. His awareness in the

---

[13] *MBA* 850/5–21 (*Letters* 525, but only the news about Wolfgang's concert is given).

[14] *MBA* 852 (*Letters*, p. (not item no.) 889 n. 1) gives the figure mentioned by Leopold. *MBA* 852 appears in von Nissen, *Biographie*, 487; Leopold's phrase 'wenn er keine Schulden zu bezahlen hat' ('if he has no debts to pay') is rendered in italics in Nissen, but not in *MBA*. *Letters* reproduces the italics, however.

[15] It is not certain that Nissen himself actually wrote much of the biography which bears his name, but I use his name as the author in order to avoid awkwardness in referring to the work. For further information on the way the biography was written, see Ch. 35.

[16] It is quite easy to imagine, for example, that Leopold's sentence was incompletely rendered by Nissen, and continued with the word 'allein' ('only' or 'but'), introducing some qualification of his previous comments. Other letters incompletely rendered by Nissen which can be checked against the originals display comparably outrageous falsifications—see Ch. 35 for some examples.

[17] See pp. 482 and 484 below.

autumn of 1783 that Wolfgang did not have much money laid by to see him through until the main earnings season began again must surely have made him suspect that there might have been a pattern of borrowing against future expected receipts (as indeed there certainly was at times). If he did suspect this, he must have been deeply disturbed by it, because it would mean that teaching, the steadiest work Wolfgang had, was not enough to pay the daily expenses; the riskier 'windfall' income from concerts was being used for these instead of being saved for hard times. Furthermore, he could hardly fail to be aware that Wolfgang's situation was vulnerable compared with that of the theatrical people in his circle. These households frequently had more than one member capable of earning a good income, since women too could function lucratively in the theatre. Leopold had mentioned the actor Müller's eight children and high rent, but one of his daughters was already a paid actress in 1785; Joseph and Aloysia Lange had a double income, and so had the Lebrun couple. This meant not only more money in good times, but greater security when illness struck.

Wolfgang was trying to gain membership of the Tonkünstlersozietät during this period, but was ultimately unsuccessful. The society gave four concerts annually, two in Lent and two in Advent, and used the proceeds for its charitable works. Membership vouchsafed to musicians the comfort of knowing that in the event of their death, their widows and children would not be entirely destitute. For Wolfgang, without an imperial appointment and pension expectations, membership ought to have been all the more desirable. Exactly why he did not become a member is not certain. After he had applied for membership on 11 February 1785, he followed up his request with a reminder that he had often given his services to the society's concerts, and would continue to do so in future. His application was met by a demand for his birth certificate, which apparently he never produced.[18] It seems improbable that he was unable to do this, and more likely that he simply failed to get round to it. After his death, Constanze claimed in her application for a court pension that his perception of his youth and talent had made the risk of his own death before he had settled an adequate sum on his family seem slight; this was the consideration that had prevented his joining the Tonkünstlersozietät.[19] If this was true, Wolfgang had adopted his attitude despite numerous examples from his own acquaintance of young men being cut off in their

---

[18] See Deutsch, *Documents*, 236; and Eisen, *Documents*, 58.
[19] Constanze in her petition to the emperor for a pension on 11 Dec. 1791—*MBA* 1205/23–30 (not in *Letters*).

prime; but perhaps the attitude was nevertheless not uncommon among younger men.

When Leopold wrote his letter of 12 March, he was becoming weary of the demanding Lenten schedule, and longed for the concerts to be over. Nannerl was asking about music she hoped he would be able to bring back for her, including a keyboard arrangement of *Die Entführung*, and Leopold assured her that he would buy everything that was available. The publisher Torricella was supposed to be printing Wolfgang's own keyboard arrangement, but Leopold thought that Wolfgang had not yet finished it. He hoped, however, to obtain three sonatas from Torricella—K. 284, K. 333, and K. 454 (the last for violin and keyboard). But Wolfgang's newer music could only be obtained in the time available by having manuscript copies made. Leopold did not mention any copying in this letter, perhaps because there could be no question of having it done until the concerts were over, the house quieter, and the music fully available:

We never get to bed before 1 in the morning, never get up before 9, dine at 2 or half past 2. dreadful weather! daily concerts, always teaching, music, writing etc. where am I supposed to go? — — if only the concerts at least were over: it's impossible to describe all the kerfuffle and commotion: your brother's fortepiano has been taken from the house to the theatre or some other house at least 12 times since I've been here. he's had a big *forte piano pedal* made, which stands under the instrument and is about three spans longer and incredibly heavy, every friday it's taken to the mehlgrube, and it was also taken to Count Cziczi's and Prince Kaunitz's.[20]

Good Friday was 25 March, and thereafter Leopold had more time to collect music to take home for Nannerl, who was back in Salzburg for Easter. Leopold had now been absent eight weeks, though his leave of absence had been only six; but he was still not preparing to leave Vienna. The weather made it seem more like Christmas than Easter, and he did not want to travel until it was better. Salzburg too was still in the grip of winter; at Easter there was deep snow and bitter cold, and shortly afterwards, on 2 April, the bridge collapsed under the pressure of flood water, and eleven people were killed.[21] Leopold was using the time to supervise the copying of music for Nannerl, and told her that three sets of variations

---

[20] *MBA* 850/36–45 (*Letters* 525). Anderson translates 'where am I supposed to go?' ('wo soll ich hingehen?') as 'I feel rather out of it all'. Leopold did not necessarily mean that he felt excluded, however—he may simply have meant that it was hard to find a quiet place for writing letters or looking through music to have copied for Nannerl. His letters about the Lenten activities suggest that he was drawn into everything Wolfgang and Constanze did.

[21] See Martin, 'Die Salzburger Chronik', pt. 2, 66–7.

were currently being copied, and that he was also going to try to get cadenzas for her.[22] Which cadenzas he meant is not clear. There is no certainty that Nannerl at this point had the cadenzas to K. 449 and 453, despite the fact that she had had the actual concertos since May 1784, so Leopold could have been referring to these.[23] Alternatively or additionally he might have meant the cadenzas to K. 456 and 459; but there is no certainty that Nannerl had received by this date the bulk of the music to these concertos,[24] so it seems questionable whether Leopold would have mentioned only their cadenzas.[25]

In the same letter, Leopold referred to their old Salzburg friends the Amann family.[26] Basil and his wife had been living beyond their means since they married in 1772; they had bought an estate in Aigen just outside Salzburg and fitted out the house luxuriously. Basil's court salary as his father's assistant did not permit this level of expenditure, and the couple ran up huge debts. Becoming worried about these, Basil's father Franz Anton supported Basil's attempt to be allowed to take over the responsibility for handling the income of the brewery at Kaltenhausen in addition to the post he already had, and to be paid the previous (deceased) incumbent's salary in addition to his own. Colloredo, however, sniffing a saving, allowed Basil only an extra 60 fl. annually for the brewery work and placed the overall responsibility for it under the supervision

---

[22] Leopold to Nannerl, 25–6 Mar. 1785—*MBA* 854/12–15 (not in *Letters*).

[23] See Ch. 24, pp. 429–30 and Ch. 26, p. 465, for discussions about which cadenzas to the four concertos K. 449, 450, 451, and 453 Nannerl had probably already received before Leopold left for Vienna.

[24] The latest concerto known to have been received by Leopold and Nannerl in Salzburg by this date was K. 453.

[25] The *MBA* commentary (following the commentary in Deutsch and Paumgartner, *Leopold Mozarts Briefe an seine Tochter*, 513), suggests that the cadenzas in question were those to K. 466 and 467, but these seem the least likely candidates. Both concertos were brand new, only having been finished while Leopold was in Vienna, so it is highly unlikely that he would have mentioned their cadenzas to Nannerl (the parts of a concerto which she could most easily manage without until a performance was imminent) in this context before she had even glimpsed the rest of the music. Leopold was not able to take back with him to Salzburg in 1785 any material whatsoever for these two concertos, despite the note to *MBA* 860/79–80, which states (again following Deutsch and Paumgartner, *Leopold Mozarts Briefe an seine Tochter*, 516) that he intended to do so; he only received the scores from Wolfgang by mailcoach in Dec. 1785 after nagging him (*MBA* 906/9–12; *Letters* 534). Given the tendency of Wolfgang to delay offering his newest music to Leopold and Nannerl, and that of concerto cadenzas to lag behind the concertos they belonged to when Wolfgang was sending his music to Nannerl, it seems most likely that the cadenzas Leopold mentioned in *MBA* 854/13–14 were to concertos she already had (such as K. 449 and/or 453); that the two new concertos he promised on 8 Apr. 1785 (*MBA* 860/79–80; not in *Letters*) to bring back with him were K. 456 and 459; and that he had nothing to do with copying any part of K. 466 or 467 for her while he was in Vienna.

[26] See Ch. 11 for the background to this story, and Fig. 2 for a diagram of Amann/Berchtold/Polis relationships.

of Franz Anton, an upright and highly respected court official. Perhaps he did this partly because he did not trust Basil sufficiently to allow him total control over the substantial annual income from the brewery; but the result was that Basil was placed in 1778 in a position where his salary was not significantly higher than previously and he was simultaneously exposed to enormous temptation, as all this money passed through his hands. He started to embezzle the brewery funds, and by 1783 at latest the situation was catastrophic. The madness of Basil that Nannerl had noted in her diary in that year was generally held to be a direct consequence of his financial problems.[27] The fraud was discovered by his father Franz Anton, now in his seventies, and at the end of 1784, when Franz Anton was putting his affairs in order following an attack of illness, he made a clean breast of it to the authorities. In doing so, he declared himself willing to repay the sum of 5,765 fl. 4 kr. on behalf of his son, but asked for time to sell his Mühlberg estate in order to do so. Colloredo demanded immediate restitution, however, and Franz Anton went to his grave broken-hearted on 18 January 1785, just before Leopold left for Vienna, with everything still unresolved.[28] After his death, news of Basil's disgrace emerged, and steps were taken to recover the embezzled money (which proved to be a larger sum than Franz Anton had believed)—first by claiming from the old man's estate, and then, when this was not enough, by auctioning Basil's property. The auction of the goods at Aigen was to be quite a big affair, and while Leopold was in Vienna he was asked by Katherl Gilowsky's cousin Johann J. A. E. Gilowsky, on behalf of the Salzburg authorities, whether the large room in the Dancing-Master's House could be used for it. Payment was offered, but Leopold wrote declining it, and regretting that he could not offer the poor Amann family a more comforting service.[29] Just as Leopold was writing to tell Nannerl all this, however, Basil himself was dying, plunging his family into further misery. At the time of his death, his five children ranged in age from 12 down to 3.

Since Nannerl had returned to St Gilgen again after Easter, Leopold arranged for Katherl Gilowsky to help his servant Tresel clear out the large music room for the auction, and ensure that all the other doors in his apartment were locked. Katherl's brother Franz Xaver Wenzel (who was friendly with Wolfgang, and had been a witness at his wedding to

---

[27] See Ch. 23.

[28] Leopold had reported his death to Nannerl on 19–21 Jan. 1785—*MBA* 838/3–8 (not in *Letters*). Most of the information about the case is from Pirckmayer, 'Basil von Amann'.

[29] Leopold to Nannerl, 25–6 Mar. 1785—*MBA* 854/51–9 (not in *Letters*).

Constanze) was currently studying surgery in Vienna, so Katherl sent a message through him from her cousin to Leopold, to thank him for the offer of his room. Writing to Nannerl about this on 8 April 1785, Leopold took the opportunity to say something about Katherl's brother too:

The Gilowsky woman has written a few words to me in an enclosure to her brother, to say that the Hofrat thanks me for the room but declines it, since Fr: v amand has to go out to Eygen, where meanwhile everything in the house is being auctioned, — including everything of old Amand's—and that Balisili Amand died raving on Easter Monday. God comfort him. unhappy family! — — — Katherl's brother hasn't put in an appearance here. He sent me the letter again through your brother's old mother-in-law. They say not only that he's attached himself to a sweetheart here; but some people even reckon he's already secretly married. that would be an unfortunate prank! . . . the *admirably stupid letter* he once wrote me in connection with your brother's love affair is a sure sign to me that he's also capable of an act of tomfoolery, but a worse one, — because he isn't a hundredth in his profession what my [son] is in his: I'd pity the father and his sisters.[30]

Since Leopold's return was being hindered by the weather, he was able to see some plays and operas in Vienna before leaving, and he also had time to be initiated as a Freemason in the same lodge that Wolfgang had joined in December 1784, *Zur Wohltätigkeit* ('Beneficence').[31] A week after Easter, on 2 April, Leopold wrote to Nannerl to give her some idea when he might leave, and what route he would take home—he said that it would be about two weeks before his departure, and that he would go via Linz and possibly Gmunden, before returning Heinrich to Munich and travelling back alone to Salzburg. He had received a letter from Michael Haydn, who had been standing in for him in Salzburg, and he told Nannerl that he would have to reply to it at length.[32] The likelihood is that Haydn's letter was about court business, perhaps with a request to Leopold to seek musical personnel in Vienna. By now, Leopold's permitted

---

[30] *MBA* 860/29–49 (not in *Letters*). Leopold's reference to Katherl as 'die Gilowsky' did not necessarily have a pejorative connotation; this was a standard way of referring to women, and does not translate happily into English. The Hofrat was Katherl's cousin dealing with the auction, Johann J. A. E. Gilowsky.

[31] Unfortunately, though Freemasonry was of great importance to Wolfgang during his Viennese years, there is no adequate way of assessing what it might have meant to Leopold. The subject is hardly mentioned in the surviving correspondence of either man; and though in Wolfgang's case the topic can be approached through information about the structure and activities of the Viennese lodges, about the lodge meetings he attended and the Masonic friends he had, and above all of course through study of his music, these avenues of enquiry are not profitable for Leopold.

[32] *MBA* 858 (not in *Letters*).

six-week absence had been stretched to nine, but he apparently did not apply for any extension. His motive for this was probably fear that if he did so unsuccessfully he would have no excuse to stay; whereas by keeping quiet about it, the overstaying of his leave might go unremarked for longer. This was the way he had handled a similar situation in 1780–1, when Wolfgang had been in Munich to produce *Idomeneo*.[33]

In his next letter, written on 8 April, Leopold could still give Nannerl no firm departure date; but he told her that she should not write again unless it was urgent:

I can't expect any more letters from you, — and if there's something very important to write about, you can write, — in that case, your brother will send the letter after me to Linz or Munich, if I'm not here any more; in this way you can always write a letter, *which your brother can read too* . . .

He also assured Nannerl that he had been trying to find a new journeyman for Egedacher, but had had no success; and he responded to a rumour circulating in Salzburg that both Nannerl and Michael Haydn had mentioned to him, namely that the emperor had given Wolfgang 400 ducats (1,733 fl. 20 kr.); needless to say, there was nothing in it. Finally, he promised to bring Nannerl two new concertos, and some cadenzas and variations.[34]

By 16 April Leopold was able to give Nannerl his expected departure date:

At last we've decided to leave here on thursday the 21st in the company of Boudé and her husband, your brother and sister-in-law had firmly decided to make the journey with us: only now everything's limping again already, and presumably nothing will come of it, although they've each had six pairs of shoes made, which are already standing there. you should hear the outcome from Linz or Munich, where I can always find time to write.

Leopold spoke of the possibility of staying a few days in Linz, and the probability of a week in Munich, where he hoped to hear the Amateur Concert on Ascension Day.[35] In fact, he did not leave Vienna until 25 April (needless to say without Wolfgang and Constanze, though they accompanied him and Heinrich on their way for the first half-day, before turning back). After about a week in Linz, where he and Heinrich enjoyed the hospitality of the Thun family, he spent a further week in Munich, and left Heinrich there with his family. The weather was still appallingly cold,

---

[33] See Ch. 20, pp. 347–9.
[34] *MBA* 860 (not in *Letters*). On which concertos and cadenzas he meant, see p. 479 above.
[35] *MBA* 861/3–8 and 17–24 (not in *Letters*).

and he saw evidence everywhere of ruined crops. In Munich, he apparently received word that unless he was back in Salzburg by the middle of May, his salary would be stopped.[36] He arrived around 13 May, just in time to prevent this threat from being effected. Nannerl and Berchtold were staying in his house to greet him, and they seem to have remained with him for about ten days. This eased his return to the stagnant conditions in Salzburg, but when the Berchtolds left him again, his melancholy was severe:

I can't deny that time is passing very slowly for me, and it will only pass even more slowly when the players finish next week: because for about 4 months I had lots of people around me everywhere, and here I had the pleasure of having you; but now all I've got is the *agreeable* discourse with Tresel, in which I absolutely have to play the silent prince, except when I find it necessary to take a laxative, in which case I can save the 45 kr. for the dose. — and where am I supposed to go? — have I got anyone with whom I can have a sensible conversation? — I don't know if I'm too clever for many of them; or if many are too stupid for me! In short, I'm finding it a very sorry contrast with the company I had in Vienna, Lintz, and Munich.[37]

Why, since Leopold found Salzburg so dull, had he not stayed in Vienna with Wolfgang, which is what Wolfgang had suggested when Nannerl first married? Nannerl was now provided for, so the economic argument for continuing to work in Salzburg was no longer so strong. Nothing in the correspondence warrants a confident answer to this question, but plausible suggestions can be made. A combination of factors could have been involved, including a reluctance on Leopold's part to give up his independence to live as a guest in Wolfgang's household, disapproval of aspects of Wolfgang's life, and a feeling that he would not be able to regain the closeness to Wolfgang that he had once enjoyed. But by far the greatest consideration is likely to have been loyalty to Nannerl, and the desire to be near her to help her. Leopold had enjoyed magnificent food and drink, stimulating company, and rich musical experiences in Vienna, while Nannerl had endured a bitter village winter on much more frugal fare, with little company and an unusable fortepiano. It does not seem likely that he would happily have left her in this situation while he could be in Salzburg to ease it. The impression gained from the few confidential remarks about Wolfgang in Leopold's letters to Nannerl after her marriage is that father and daughter shared a number of beliefs about

---

[36] Leopold to Nannerl, 30 Apr. and 5 May 1785—*MBA* 863 and 864 (not in *Letters*). The court decrees threatening to withhold his salary are given in Deutsch, *Documents*, 245–6.

[37] Leopold to Nannerl, 27–8 May 1785—*MBA* 868/3–13 (not in *Letters*).

Wolfgang. One was that his words were not to be relied on (witness Leopold's ironic comment, quoted above, about the six pairs of shoes twice over, which were supposed to demonstrate Wolfgang's enthusiasm for returning to Salzburg with Leopold). Another was that he had been wrong to marry when he had (witness Leopold's comparison, quoted above, of Franz Xaver Wenzel Gilowsky's 'act of tomfoolery' with Wolfgang's). A third (despite Leopold's comment that Wolfgang's housekeeping was very frugal in terms of food and drink) may have been a fear that Wolfgang was spending money which it would be more prudent to save.[38] That Nannerl shared these beliefs and fears is suggested by the fact that Leopold thought it necessary to warn her, if she wrote to Vienna after he had left, to write a letter that her brother could read. The correspondence suggests that the two of them thought of each other as mutual comforts and supports, but that Wolfgang had distanced himself from them, and little was to be expected of him.

Despite Leopold's dissatisfaction on his return, there was one hopeful event approaching—Nannerl was in the seventh month of her pregnancy. As soon as she had returned to St Gilgen on 23 May, Leopold was hoping that she would decide to return to Salzburg for the confinement. His letter of 27–8 May suggests that he was trying to exert pressure on her to do this by mentioning all their acquaintances in Salzburg who were sure that she and Berchtold realized the good sense of this arrangement.[39] What Berchtold thought is unknown, but since his first two wives had died of problems connected with childbirth he probably felt that he could not resist even if he had wanted to. Leopold was therefore soon able to look forward to a long stretch of Nannerl's company. Her incoming journey, however, was dependent on someone accompanying her, and since Berchtold was not willing to travel in before he came to spend his name-day in Salzburg on 24 June, Leopold went out to St Gilgen to fetch Nannerl around 13 June. When writing to arrange this, he mentioned a letter he had received from Johann Evangelist Schmid, who had made Nannerl's fortepiano. Schmid was expressing willingness to give advice on how the instrument should be kept, if they would tell him exactly what was wrong with it. Leopold therefore intended to have a good look at it when he went out.[40]

---

[38] See p. 476 above for an explanation of my apparently wilful interpretation of Leopold's ostensible compliment about the housekeeping.

[39] *MBA* 868/26–48 (not in *Letters*).

[40] Leopold to Nannerl, 2–3 and 9–10 June 1785—*MBA* 869/67–80 and 871/64–86 (neither in *Letters*).

After this letter, the correspondence ceased while Nannerl was in Salzburg. Her baby, a son, was not born until 27 July, St Pantaleon's Day, five minutes before noon. He was christened Leopold Alois Pantaleon at five o'clock on the same day in the Church of St Andrä, very close to the Dancing-Master's House where he had been born. Leopold, as his god-father, took him to the church.[41] About five weeks later, around the time that Wolfgang was writing the Italian dedication for his six string quartets to Joseph Haydn, Nannerl was returning alone to St Gilgen. The baby, 'Leopoldl' ('little Leopold'), remained in Salzburg with his grandfather.

[41] Brno, MZA, Berchtold Family Archive, Family Chronicle, unpaginated, but p. 93 on my count.

28

Leopoldl

❧

I HOPE you got to Hof well before 1 o'clock, and found your husband and children in good health before 5 o'clock, and are well and happy. As sad as I found your departure, I spent the whole day happily (the only exception being from 12 till 1 o'clock) in the constant company of Leopoldl. I kiss my son-in-law heartily, and beg him to live completely free of worry about the Prince of Asturias, just as I hope that you too will have complete confidence in my care and watchfulness over him, since you both know how much I love the child. He was already much more friendly and cheerful again today than yesterday, — yesterday, as you know, none of us liked the look of him at all. But this afternoon he's got bright eyes again, and is sleeping completely softly and peacefully: in short, I'm quite calm again, and would like to have him until I could lead him by the hand to St. Gilgen, to do that, of course, I'd need to live about another 10 years, so that Leopoldl would have to lead me and not I him.[1]

Thus began Leopold's first letter to Nannerl after she had left Leopoldl with him in Salzburg. The day on which Nannerl made the journey was Friday, 2 September; she must have left early in the morning, and Leopold was writing later on the same day, by which time it was clear that Leopoldl was in better health and humour than he had been the day before. The baby had been visited by his father and perhaps his half-brothers and sister soon after his birth, but they had then returned to St Gilgen.[2]

It is evident from Leopold's letters that there had been at first an assumption that Leopoldl would live with his family in St Gilgen, but that the plan had been modified in stages mainly at Leopold's instigation. Though he made it clear that he would like to keep the child with him in the long term, he expressed willingness to return him when weather permitted the following spring if Berchtold and Nannerl so wanted, or if

---

[1] *MBA* 875/3–16 (not in *Letters*). The 'Prince of Asturias' was the title of the crown prince of Spain.

[2] Leopold's letter to Nannerl, 22–3 Sept. 1785 (*MBA* 881/80–7; not in *Letters*) gives greetings from the Salzburg servants to young Nannerl, suggesting that she had recently met them; and his letter to her of 9–10 Feb. 1786 (*MBA* 931/19–21; not in *Letters*) reveals that Berchtold had seen the baby soon after his birth.

necessary as early as Michaelmas. Michaelmas was again approaching, and servants were seeking new contracts; if Leopoldl was to be taken to St Gilgen then, it was the right time of year to ensure that Nannerl would have adequate help with him. In Salzburg, Leopold had his cook Tresel, and had hired a maid called Monica to help with the extra work caused by the confinement, and a nursemaid called Maria Anna Pietschner ('Nanndl') to look after Leopoldl. Nanndl was not, however, a wet-nurse— there is no evidence that Leopoldl was breast-fed at all, and he was eating thin gruels when he was only five weeks old.[3] In St Gilgen Nannerl was in need of a new cook and a new maid; one of her maids, Lena ('Lenerl'), was to stay on. While Nannerl had been in Salzburg, she had chosen a cook who was to join her at Michaelmas, and Monica was to join the St Gilgen household at the same time, to make up the full complement of servants. It is possible that under the original arrangement, Nanndl had also been engaged to go to St Gilgen at Michaelmas, to be Leopoldl's nurse there; alternatively Monica, who had been helping Nanndl care for Leopoldl in Salzburg, had perhaps been engaged to look after the children including Leopoldl: at any rate, when Nannerl returned to St Gilgen on 2 September, the servant arrangement made for Michaelmas ensured that Leopoldl could join his family then if necessary.

Leopold felt the need to write in persuasive terms to both Nannerl and Berchtold. He added a rare postscript to the letter quoted above, addressed specifically to Berchtold, and presented further arguments for keeping Leopoldl with him at least for the time being. His main motive seems to have been a longing to have the child with him, but the point on which his arguments rested was rather the question of how the baby would be cared for if he joined the rest of his family in St Gilgen. Since there were already five children to be looked after out there, and a newborn baby needed intensive care, Leopold pressed home the argument that he would keep Nanndl, and was therefore capable of looking after the child far better than would be the case in St Gilgen, especially since Berchtold's son Karl (now aged 3) needed very careful watching. He hinted at the dangerous early months of a new baby's life, and did not omit to mention that he would gladly pay all the costs of Leopoldl's upbringing.[4]

---

[3] In a letter to Leopold of 18 June 1783, Wolfgang mentioned the feeding of his first child Raimund Leopold. He claimed to be unhappy at the thought both of the baby's being breast-fed by Constanze (stating that he was afraid on her account of 'the milk fever'), and of his being wet-nursed; instead he wanted to have the child brought up 'on water, like my sister and myself . . .' See *MBA* 752/16–26 (*Letters* 492). He may have meant by water a type of gruel.

[4] *MBA* 875/25–57 (not in *Letters*).

If Nanndl as well as Monica had originally been destined for St Gilgen, this offer was probably welcome to Berchtold, because he would otherwise have had to pay her wages. What Nannerl thought of the arrangement is not recorded, though there are hints in the later correspondence that she did at times despair of bringing up children properly in St Gilgen, and was worried about how she would cope with Leopoldl if he had to live there with his siblings.[5]

Only four days after his allusion to the vulnerability of children in the first months of their lives, Leopoldl began to show signs of the illness which nearly killed him at two months. Leopold called it the *Mehlhund*, and it seems to have been a form of thrush—his mouth and tongue were completely white, he was in discomfort, and his sleep was disturbed. At first, Leopold thought there was no cause for alarm, and was confident that Nanndl and he could nurse the baby through it. He also mentioned that Dr Prex had visited them three times. Leopold first wrote about it on 9 September, three days after its onset, but most of his letter was taken up with other news. He had received a letter from Nannerl agreeing to the suggestion that Leopoldl should stay in Salzburg for the time being if Leopold really felt able to look after him; he answered the point by emphasizing the responsibility of good care for Karl, not only to keep him from danger, but also to develop good habits in him in the crucially important early years. It would be a pleasure for him to keep Leopoldl, to help them achieve this with Karl.[6]

When Leopold next wrote, five days later on 14–15 September, Leopoldl was no better, and the household was revolving around his care. The baby could drink but not eat, he had been feverish, and he could not sleep longer than an hour at a time. Dr Prex had been visiting regularly, Nanndl was tireless in her devotion to him, and was enduring willingly the broken nights; but everyone was telling Leopold that it would take time for the illness to work its way out of the baby.[7] Nannerl responded immediately, hoping that Leopoldl was now better, to which Leopold replied that she

---

[5] Rieger claims that Leopold was 'secretly' determined to keep Leopoldl, that he presented irresistible arguments to Berchtold to do so, and that he did not even consult Nannerl, but merely asserted his authority over her. To support her argument, she cites Leopold's letters to Nannerl from Munich in 1786 (by which time Leopoldl was six months old and the circumstances of the correspondence were quite different from those at the time of his birth). See Rieger, *Nannerl Mozart*, 206–7. Taken out of context, these quotations can be used to make Leopold seem dictatorial, but in context they assume rather the appearance of reassurance to the hard-pressed Nannerl, that whatever her problems with the stepchildren, she need never worry about Leopoldl while Leopold was capable of caring for him. See Ch. 29, pp. 508–10, for more detail.

[6] *MBA* 876/3–10 and 25–37 (not in *Letters*).   [7] *MBA* 878 (not in *Letters*).

clearly knew nothing about it if she could think it would be over so quickly—'nine days coming, nine days going' was the saying he quoted to her. He went on to say that Leopoldl was now suffering from excessive acidity in his urine and stools, as the sickness made its way out of the body, and that the baby's skin in the nappy area was consequently very sore.[8]

Though Leopold used every possible opportunity to send Nannerl news of her baby, it was not until the following Thursday and Friday, 22–3 September, that he could write again. By this time the situation had worsened further, and Leopoldl was fighting for his life. He now had the *Frais*—abdominal cramps thought to be caused by the acidic matter of the disease. There was a lump in his belly, and he was suffering periodic spasms which left him exhausted. The main concern was to neutralize the acidity by giving him marshmallow and camomile, and to continue to promote the evacuation of the harmful matter through the baby's stools and urine. In addition, spirit of hartshorn was applied to the soles of his feet, to draw the *Frais* downwards.[9] Following this account of the treatment, Leopold wrote:

We have not yet *in any way lost* hope of bringing Leopoldl through it; unless *God wills it so*, — then certainly the *Frais*, despite all our efforts and poor human help, may come so often and persistently that his feeble nature won't be able to hold out any more. we must wait on the outcome from the *goodness of God*, since I pray daily that God might preserve him *only for his salvation*; and *that not my will, but the will of God may be done.*
Do not believe that it's even worse with the child than I'm reporting. No! there's *more* hope of improvement; in that there are few people living who didn't have the *Frais* when they were children: only you have to regard a child as a borrowed blessing merely and constantly prepare yourself in advance for its loss, in that a child has very many dangers to overcome: birth is already half-way to death. so patience!—since then Dr Prex has been coming every day, morning and afternoon.[10]

It is not certain how soon after this alarming letter Leopold was able to get a message to Nannerl that the baby was still alive, because it is possible that a letter has been lost between that of 22–3 and that of 29–30 September;[11] but on this latter date he wrote to report Leopoldl's

---

[8] Leopold to Nannerl, 16–17 Sept. 1785—*MBA* 880/3–13 (not in *Letters*).
[9] There may have been a magical element in the hartshorn treatment—certainly ibex horn was used in popular medical practice to soothe cramps. See Bartelt, 'Anhänger und Amulette', 576–7.
[10] *MBA* 881/4–46 (not in *Letters*).
[11] In his letter of 29–30 Sept. (*MBA* 882/4–6; not in *Letters*), Leopold mentioned having written to Nannerl that Leopoldl was also teething. There is no surviving letter containing this information.

recovery. His letter reveals, however, that the baby had got worse before he had started to get better. Once the *Frais* spasms had started, he had suffered them every day except one for a week, and they had attacked him up to twelve times daily. His worst day had been 26 September, after Leopold had written the letter quoted above, and on this day they had attacked him uninterruptedly from midday until half past six in the evening. He could take nothing by mouth during this time, though by the evening he could drink again. Dr Prex had suggested to Leopold the cause of the *Frais*, as a result of which Leopold changed the diet they were attempting to feed him, omitting the milk gruel until the acidity in his body had lessened, and giving him only bread sops instead. Leopold attributed the baby's improvement from this time to the change in diet, and gave Nannerl a retrospective explanation: the *Mehlhund* had set up intestinal irritation through the excessive acidity of its matter; this irritation had caused the *Frais*; and the milk gruel had made things worse by becoming corrupted on contact with the putrid matter already present. He concluded, 'Here you have the complete explanation; and it's certain that with children there are *no half measures*. If you make a mistake, and don't find the cause of the illness, and consequently don't find the means to improve it either, they can be gone quickly. if you can help them, they quickly recover.'[12]

A comparison of Leopold's behaviour and attitude in the case of Leopoldl's illness with that when Nannerl had been ill in The Hague in 1765, and when his wife had died in Paris in 1778, suggests that his views of the relation of medicine to theology had not changed in the intervening period. When the situation became serious, and he was confronted with the pitiful sight of Leopoldl's suffering, and the possibility that he would die, he was forced (as he had been during Nannerl's dangerous illness in The Hague in 1765) to strive to find the key to the cure. In both cases, diet was thought crucially important to the outcome, not only or even chiefly because of its nourishing attributes, but also because the food eaten could interact with other matter in the body, becoming 'corrupted' and increasing the virulent properties of the disease (as in Leopoldl's case); or it could suppress the disease in one part of the body, only to drive it somewhere even more dangerous (as in Nannerl's case). In both cases, too, Leopold was tortured by his ignorance of God's design—when Nannerl had been ill, he had read the Gospel for clues to the outcome, and with Leopoldl he acknowledged that though they were

---

[12] *MBA* 882/3–33 (not in *Letters*).

coping with the spasms for the time being, God might choose to send them more often, in which case the baby would die. For this reason, the humility before God was essential—Leopold's motive in praying for the child's recovery may not be his own longing for the relief and joy such a recovery would bring. If Leopoldl had died, Leopold would perhaps have accounted for the death in the way he had when Maria Anna had died—God had caused the physician to mistake the diagnosis and hence the cure. Thus the basis of his beliefs was still the need to reconcile his duty to do his utmost to save the lives of sick members of his family with his conviction that the outcome was predetermined by God.[13]

Whatever the reasons for Leopoldl's recovery, the illness reveals aspects of Leopold's character entirely consistent with his past behaviour in similar situations. He did not shy away from the sickroom, but watched over the patient himself, observing symptoms, questioning doctors, checking that the correct diet and medicines were given, and nursing. Furthermore, he spared no expense, despite the fact that he still had to be careful to live within his means.[14] Yet he had willingly undertaken to bear the costs of having Leopoldl with him, which involved extra servants and sometimes (as during the previous three weeks) large medical bills.

By the time Leopoldl was better it was Michaelmas, and time for the servants to change over. The new cook appointed while Nannerl had been in Salzburg travelled out to St Gilgen to take up her duties, the old cook arrived in Salzburg bound for some other post, and Monica went out to St Gilgen to join Nannerl's household. The new cook had been six years in a convent before she had gone into domestic service, and she and Monica had then worked together in Salzburg service, and become friends. Leopold had never complained about Monica in his letters to Nannerl, and there was no indication of any trouble to come, as she and the cook moved to St Gilgen. But in Salzburg Leopold had difficulty in keeping Nanndl beyond Michaelmas. She had apparently promised her sister that she would attend her confinement when it took place in the autumn, and she tried to persuade Leopold to allow her temporary leave for this, and to fetch Monica into town again to look after Leopoldl. Leopold refused to agree, insisted that Nanndl's sister call on someone else, and threatened to complain to the town syndic (who had jurisdiction over servants' contracts) if Nanndl did not honour her agreement with

---

[13] See Ch. 7 for the account of Nannerl's illness, and Ch. 18 for that of Maria Anna.
[14] See pp. 496–7 below for more details about this.

him. The upshot was that Nanndl did stay with him, but at the cost of a rift with her sister.[15]

Meanwhile, things were going even worse for Nannerl, whose new cook gave trouble from the moment of her arrival. She apparently refused to do some of the work she had been engaged for, causing great annoyance to Nannerl. Lenerl, the maid who had been in St Gilgen since before Michaelmas, was good-natured enough to help Nannerl out by doing extra work herself, but Nannerl was seriously worried about how they would survive the next few months with a rebellious cook, little hope of replacing her, and a large household needing food several times a day. Leopold expressed amazement that anyone who had been in a convent for six years could be quite so bad as Nannerl described, and used the occasion to pour scorn on the usefulness of female religious orders in general, and to give thanks that Leopoldl, at any rate, was receiving excellent care in Salzburg. He advised Nannerl above all to keep calm for the sake of her health, and assured her that servants were the cross of the best marriages. He suggested that she try to improve the situation by kind treatment in the first instance, and that she enlist Monica as a persuasive influence on the cook. If there was no improvement, he suggested that Berchtold have the woman locked up in the cells on bread and water for a few days. Berchtold certainly had the power to do this, but responded through Nannerl that he would have difficulty getting future servants if he did so.[16]

The situation did not improve, and by late December Nannerl had decided to try after all to replace the woman. It was not until January 1786, however, that she was successful. The autumn of 1785 was thus a difficult time for her, the more so because on top of her worries about Leopoldl and her problems with the cook, her own health was troubling her. At the end of September, she had her first period following the birth, but satisfactory menstruation thereafter was not re-established, and she complained of pressure in the chest, of feeling flushed, and of an 'anxious' feeling on rising in the morning. Her symptoms were taken with the utmost seriousness both by herself and Leopold, and she described them to him several times in her letters, so that he could advise her. Sometimes he first consulted Dr Barisani or his physician son Joseph, both of whom lived close by.

---

[15] Leopold to Nannerl, 6–8 Oct. and 11–12 Nov. 1785—*MBA* 884/2–17 and 897/100–2 (not in *Letters*).

[16] Leopold to Nannerl, 14–15 and 20–2 Oct. 1785—*MBA* 885/56–100 and 887/67–9 (neither passage in *Letters*).

The case was naturally complicated by the possibility that she might be pregnant again, despite the fact that she was bleeding scantily at irregular intervals from the end of September until the end of December. But this possibility was not allowed to take precedence over the paramount need to treat the 'withheld blood'. According to the household medical manual used by the Mozarts, late or insufficient menstruation meant that the blood was 'blocked up'; it rose into the chest, causing breathlessness, dizziness, and symptoms similar to those of the 'falling sickness'. Women in this condition were prone to headaches, because the blood that should have made its exit below could rise even as far as the head. Consequently, it was dangerous not to be menstruating normally, and the period had to be induced. Detailed instructions for blood-letting were given—a specific vein in the right foot, and another in the left arm, were to be opened. The point of this was not primarily to drain the excess blood, but actually to promote menstruation, which should start within a week of the bloodletting. If it did not, further instructions involving medicaments and baths had to be followed.[17]

Leopold thought from the first that the discomfort in Nannerl's chest was caused by a problem in the womb, and eventually came to the conclusion that it all went back to insufficient evacuation of the womb following Leopoldl's birth. He sent medicines designed first to 'settle' a 'rising womb' (castor oil glands were an important ingredient of these, whether grated into drinks or tied in bandages and wrapped round the knees), and he urged her not to make the condition worse by allowing herself to become agitated about her servant problems. Nannerl seems to have been particularly worried about the hot flushes, in case they indicated the onset of a feverish illness; she also mentioned that her urine was pale, and questioned the 'heating' properties of the foods that Leopold was suggesting to her.[18] Leopold recognized the potential dangers of starting a feverish illness with too much blood circulating in the body (or perhaps one should rather say that he recognized that a sanguine body was susceptible to feverish illnesses); this, after all, was his view of what had happened to Maria Anna.[19] But he reassured her that her present symptoms were not those of such an illness. He passed on to her Barisani's advice

---

[17] See Eleonora Maria Rosalia, Duchess of Troppau and Jägerndorf, *Freywillig aufgesprungener Granat-Apffel des Christlichen Samariters* (Leipzig, 1709), 202 ff. Leopold indicated that he knew the book and that Nannerl had it in his letter of 26 Jan. 1787—*MBA* 1026/85–7 (not in *Letters*).

[18] Examination of urine was carried out to determine whether an infection was present; if it was, 'heating' foods had to be avoided.

[19] See Ch. 18 for details of Maria Anna's illness.

and prescriptions, which included womb-cleansing and gentle laxative medicines that Barisani claimed would be safe even if she were pregnant. The regime Nannerl had to follow was complicated and inconvenient—it involved observing her symptoms minutely and performing various tests of her own in order to determine the diagnosis, adjusting her diet as well as taking the medicines, co-ordinating the taking of the medicines with bloodletting (which in turn had to be co-ordinated with her menstrual cycle), and taking sufficient exercise at set times. Barisani also told her to send into town a sample of her early morning urine if she was hot and cold by turns. For his part, Leopold urged her to send him word by a specially hired messenger if she got any worse. He emphasized that he would pay the messenger.[20] Because Nannerl's symptoms may now seem somewhat nebulous or trivial, it is important to remember that Leopold believed that Maria Anna had acquired the feverish illness which proved fatal from neglecting to be bled in time, allowing herself to become 'heated', and not treating herself properly at an early stage.[21]

The correspondence about this phase of Nannerl's uncertain health petered out towards the end of 1785, but another major concern which had been discussed all through the autumn was still unresolved at the end of the year. This was the education of the Berchtold children. Whatever form it took, they apparently received only one hour's tuition per day, and the rest of the time were left to their own devices, supervised largely by servants.[22] Neither Berchtold nor Nannerl seems to have taught them formally, unless Nannerl's early attempts to instruct young Nannerl in keyboard playing are excepted. Not surprisingly, this caused problems. The children's concentration was poor, their level of achievement so low that it was impossible for them even to be entertained rationally, and their manners and behaviour not what they should have been. Both young Nannerl and young Wolfgang were old enough for their futures to be discussed, and both lacked the qualities that Leopold thought they would need in the class of adult life for which they were destined. In September,

---

[20] The information about Nannerl's health is from Leopold's letters to her from 29 Sept. to 22 Dec. 1785: *MBA* 882/63–5; 887/75–81; 892/94–8; 895/111–43; 897/71–100; 901/33–60; 904/69–72; 905/48–53; 906/104–15; 907/83–9; and 911/5–41. None of these passages is in *Letters*.

[21] See Ch. 18. It is because Nannerl's symptoms were of such concern to her and Leopold that they deserve to be taken seriously by commentators. In discussing this material, Rieger simply states that Leopold was concerned to control Nannerl's menstruation precisely, and that he believed her problems to be psychosomatic. See Rieger, *Nannerl Mozart*, 224–5. This is an inadequate interpretation of the evidence; the author does not appear to have read the letters carefully, her account is chronologically disorganized, and she does not show any interest in contemporary views of sickness in general or menstruation in particular.

[22] Leopold to Nannerl, 18–19 Nov. 1785—*MBA* 901/4–12 (not in *Letters*).

young Nannerl had written letters to Leopoldl's nursemaid Nanndl and to Nannerl Huber (a friend of the Mozarts who worked as a cap-maker), and Leopold had seen the letters. On 22 September, he wrote to send young Nannerl the return greetings of his servants:

Greetings from them all to your daughter as well. Nanndl and Hubernannerl thank her for the letters they received from her, they were quite amazed and astonished, and could hardly believe that a *Freu: von Sonnenburg,* who to cap it all is only *14 years* old, can already write so well, has such fine understanding, and has already grasped the art of spelling so splendidly that they could hardly read it, still less understand it. For example: *Lie Nantel* (Liebe etc.).[23]

The passage shows that young Nannerl could not even write the words 'Dear Nanndl' correctly. Whether or not in response to this blistering attack on her literacy, about three weeks later the Berchtolds were looking for a resident tutor for the children, and Leopold was asked if he knew of anyone suitable. He wrote to a man called Reitter, whom he evidently considered a possibility, but the answer was not encouraging. Reitter had some time to fill in before taking up a post in Salzburg, and was prepared to consider going to St Gilgen for this period, but the arrangement was far from what Leopold considered suitable. He wrote back to tell Reitter that the minimum time he should spend in St Gilgen would be a year; but to Nannerl and Berchtold, writing on 14–15 October, he expressed his doubt that Reitter would agree: 'my dear ones! It's going to be difficult to get a decent and reliable man out there; he's wasting his time, — and what's he got in the way of prospects? — —'[24] Nevertheless, the negotiations continued a little longer. On 20–2 October, Leopold told Nannerl that Reitter would hardly go to St Gilgen for less than 60 fl. annually, since he had received this in addition to his board and lodging at his last place, where he had had only one child to teach, in comparison with the Berchtolds' three.[25] Evidently nothing came of the idea, because on 18–19 November Leopold expressed in more detail his view of the unattractiveness of the situation:

Thank you for the chicken, and if it's as good as the duck, I'll recommend Nannerl, whom I greet, to the court hen-house as court hen and duck feeder. — it's absolutely right that the idleness of the children is a misfortune; and what can they be occupied with, since they can't do anything? — — and the little bit they do learn and achieve, they only do during the hour that the teacher's there, and apart from that *nothing.* Where will you get a preceptor who's prepared

---

[23] Leopold to Nannerl, 22–3 Sept. 1785—*MBA* 881/81–7 (not in *Letters*).
[24] *MBA* 885/113–15 (not in *Letters*).   [25] *MBA* 887/81–4 (not in *Letters*).

to be locked up like a prisoner *the whole day* with children who don't want to learn anything, — and on top of that who have so little talent that the teacher can't do himself any honour for all his drudgery? — it really will be difficult, though I've got it in mind all the time.[26]

A week later, on 24–6 November, he was renewing his attack on young Nannerl's upbringing:

I greet Nannerl in particular, and tell her that she might reflect a little on whether she can believe that a woman these days can please, if she's concerned to model herself only on the serving maids, and doesn't strive to distinguish herself through nobler manners. all the young people being appointed now, here as well as in Austria, are quite significantly different in morals, manners, behaviour and wit from former times and customs: such people come into positions, and look for an equally charming wife, — a wife who has respectability and a noble demeanour as well as housekeeping ability. times have changed, that's a fact that is indisputably evident. With a few 1000 florins and a kitchen rag round her waist, hen feed nicely smeared round her hands, she might certainly get a fusty 70-year-old husband, who like a bear slobbering with open chops will dance the bridal reel with her. But if she also has other qualities appropriate to *a lady*, then she can hope to get a charming, noble young man; otherwise definitely not![27]

The correspondence about these education problems gives some insight into how lucky the Mozart children had been. The level of Berchtold's education was broadly comparable with that of Leopold, yet how different was the situation of the children of both men. Children brought up in the country clearly laboured under a disadvantage compared with those in towns, because they lacked suitable company. But the Berchtold children had also been unlucky to have lost a mother and then a stepmother when they were very young, to have been thrown largely into the care of ignorant servants, and to have had a father who did nothing to compensate them for these disadvantages. The Mozart children, on the other hand, had been fortunate enough to keep both parents, and to have had a father who devoted enormous amounts of time to their education, and filled the house with stimulating company for them.

Leopold did not visit the theatre as much during the autumn of 1785 as he had in previous years. The reasons were mainly connected with Leopoldl. The visiting troupe was Waizhofer's, and the season began on

[26] *MBA* 901/2–12 (not in *Letters*). 'Nannerl' in this passage is young Nannerl, who had the care of the poultry.

[27] *MBA* 904/97–112 (not in *Letters*).

31 August,[28] just before Nannerl returned to St Gilgen following the birth. Early in September, when Leopold might have gone to the theatre, he stayed at home because of Leopoldl's illness; later in the autumn he went only once or twice a week (his previous practice had been to attend virtually every performance), for reasons of economy. Leopoldl's care had added to his household expenditure, the Marchands had left, he was very short of private pupils, and was apparently extremely liberal with the ones he did have. On 27–9 October, he revealed to Nannerl that he currently only had 'Sepperl' (Joseph Wölfl, son of the administrator of the hospital of St Johann in Mülln, just outside Salzburg). Not only were his charges extremely low, but he allowed the boy to cancel lessons at whim and to defer payment for as long as two years, by which time the record of lessons kept by Sepperl's father did not agree with Leopold's.[29]

Though Leopold missed many of the theatrical performances, however, Waizhofer's troupe seems to have afforded him a considerable amount of entertainment in the form of gossip about the sexual intrigues of its members. Later in the Salzburg theatrical season, it emerged that Maria Theresia Antonia von Amann was pregnant by one of the players. Antonia was the unmarried 21-year-old daughter of Franz Joseph von Amann, who in turn was elder brother to the recently deceased Basil. As in the case of Basil von Amann, Antonia's disgrace touched the Berchtold family too closely for comfort, because of their connection with the Amanns through Berchtold's first wife Maria Margarethe Polis.[30] Nannerl apparently therefore wrote to Leopold expressing the hope that the matter could be hushed up, but he replied that it was already too late for that, and used the occasion to berate Antonia's parents for not supervising her more closely.[31] When Nannerl mentioned the matter again in her next letter, Leopold launched into a vituperative attack on the sexual morals of virtually everyone in Waizhofer's troupe, reciting stories about prostitution and pregnancies with unprecedented coarseness.[32]

❧

The autumn of 1785 saw the problems of understaffing in the Salzburg court orchestra reach crisis level, as several key players left. Most keenly

[28] See Dahms, 'Das musikalische Repertoire', 346.
[29] See *MBA* 892/113–27 (not in *Letters*). See also Ch. 23, n. 3, for Leopold's charges.
[30] See Fig. 2 for a diagram of Amann/Berchtold/Polis relationships.
[31] Leopold to Nannerl, 28–9 Nov. 1785—*MBA* 905/53–65 (not in *Letters*).
[32] Leopold to Nannerl, 2–3 Dec. 1785—*MBA* 906/46–103 (not in *Letters*).

felt by Nannerl (and Leopold on her behalf) was the continued lack of an organ-builder to replace old Egedacher, who had already been too infirm to work at the end of 1784, and who had died on 14 June 1785, just as Nannerl was arriving in Salzburg to await her confinement. His son Rochus was still supposed to be filling in for him, but because of his other duties, it was just as hard for him to get out to St Gilgen as it had been the previous year. The correspondence suggests that the keys on Nannerl's fortepiano which had stuck while Leopold had been in Vienna had gradually been returning to normal during the summer of 1785, because on 16–17 September, Leopold wrote (apparently in response to some such statement of Nannerl's) to say that this was what he had expected, that the previous winter had been exceptionally cold, and that the room had been unheated while she had been in Salzburg—with proper temperature control, the fortepiano should survive the coming winter better.[33] In response, Nannerl must have written to ask for more advice about the temperature of the room and the positioning of the fortepiano, because on 22–3 September Leopold told her on no account to place it too near the stove. He also said that Egedacher would come out as soon as possible.[34] By late October, however, this had still not happened, and meanwhile relations between Egedacher and Colloredo had deteriorated over the question of a pension for Rochus's mother, old Egedacher's widow. On 20–2 October, Leopold told Nannerl that Egedacher was refusing to tune the keyboard instruments at court, because his mother still had no pension. It was almost a year after her husband's death before she received from the court 8 fl. per month.[35] Egedacher's defiance had the effect of spurring Colloredo on to find a new organ-builder and tuner, and he instructed Leopold to write to Johann Evangelist Schmid to ask if he was still interested in working for the Salzburg court. The passage reveals that Leopold had already tried to get Schmid appointed, and that Schmid had actually written to Colloredo to ask for the post, but that Colloredo had ignored his request until now, when the decision could be deferred no longer.[36]

Not until 24–6 November was Leopold able to tell Nannerl that Schmid had at last been appointed on the same terms as old Egedacher,[37] but this did not quickly solve Nannerl's problems. With winter approaching, her fortepiano was increasingly at the mercy of the climate by the lake, yet despite Leopold's protestations that Schmid was under an obligation

---

[33] *MBA* 880/14–20 (not in *Letters*).   [34] *MBA* 881/63–74 (not in *Letters*).
[35] See Hintermaier, 'Hofkapelle', 86–7.   [36] *MBA* 887/48–57 (not in *Letters*).
[37] *MBA* 904/56–60 (not in *Letters*).

to him for securing his appointment, and would therefore be happy to come out to service the instrument soon after his arrival in Salzburg, Schmid was far too busy to do any such thing. His wife was in advanced pregnancy, and he had to move himself and his family from Stühlingen (near Konstanz) to Salzburg, set up his business there (like Egedacher, he intended to carry on a private organ and keyboard instrument building business as well as perform his duties at court), and deal with the backlog of work that had built up since Egedacher's death. Naturally, the court demands had to come first, and he had still not been out to St Gilgen by February 1786.[38]

Despite Nannerl's frequent complaints about the keys, the strings, and the tuning of her fortepiano, she was as avid as ever for new music to play, and this meant, above all, Wolfgang's music. But Wolfgang was 'up to his eyes' in work on *The Marriage of Figaro*, and the autumn of 1785 slipped away with hardly any news from him. In mid-September he had written to Leopold promising him the 'Haydn' Quartets by the next mailcoach, but the promise was not kept. Leopold had hoped that Wolfgang might visit Salzburg during the autumn, but this hope was unfulfilled too.[39] Meanwhile, Leopold had been sending Nannerl all the music he could find. On 16–17 September he sent her concertos in which oboes were not essential, raising the possibility that she could gather together in St Gilgen, on occasions at least, other musicians for domestic performances of keyboard concertos.[40] On 20–2 October Leopold revealed that he had sent the keyboard part to Wolfgang's 'new concerto' out to St Gilgen with Nannerl's cousin Pertl,[41] but there can be no certainty about which concerto was meant. Wolfgang apparently did not write to Leopold between mid-September and mid-November, so it cannot have been a new one just sent by him from Vienna.[42]

---

[38] Leopold to Nannerl, 2–3 Dec. 1785 (*MBA* 906/140–8); 7–10 Dec. 1785 (*MBA* 907/105–14); 22–3 Dec. 1785 (*MBA* 911/43–8); 4–5 Jan. 1786 (*MBA* 916/15–17); 14 Jan. 1786 (*MBA* 920/11–18); 19–21 Jan. 1786 (*MBA* 923/4–26); 1–3 Feb. 1786 (*MBA* 929/120–2); and 9–10 Feb. 1786 (*MBA* 931/4–10). None of these passages is in *Letters*.

[39] Leopold to Nannerl, 16–17 Sept. 1785 (*MBA* 880/31–4 and 47–9; *Letters* 530); 3–5 Nov. 1785 (*MBA* 895/53–6; *Letters* 531); and 11–12 Nov. 1785 (*MBA* 897/4–18; *Letters* 532).

[40] *MBA* 880/23–5 (not in *Letters*).   [41] *MBA* 887/105–6 (not in *Letters*).

[42] The *MBA* commentary, following Deutsch and Paumgartner (*Leopold Mozarts Briefe an seine Tochter*, 526), asserts that the concerto was K. 467, but this does not seem likely. See Ch. 27, pp. 478–9, for my argument that Leopold had probably brought back K. 456 and 459 from Vienna, but not

Leopold's birthday was 14 November, and his name-day the following day. This year, for the first time, he was to share his name-day celebrations with Leopoldl. He had hoped and expected that Nannerl and Berchtold would visit him on the occasion, and see Leopoldl for the first time since Nannerl had returned home in early September, but they did not do so. Nor was there any word from Wolfgang, and Leopold and the baby thus celebrated their special day in the company only of servants, neighbours, and friends such as d'Ippold, who had taken a warm interest in Leopoldl from the beginning. Leopoldl was bedecked in new finery, and entertained the company with good-humoured crowing noises. Describing all this to Nannerl on 16–18 November, Leopold indicated that he had hoped for some word from Wolfgang, the more so since he had asked him for the two new keyboard concertos.[43] Not until after Leopold's name-day did Wolfgang write to congratulate him, and Leopold was quite displeased about it. On 24–6 November he wrote to Nannerl:

On the 16th your brother wrote to me again and asked my forgiveness for not having written to me for my name-day. but why did he think of it now? — — because I told him that he really might send me the quartets with the next mail-coach, and the scores of the two new keyboard concertos with them, which would be the nicest present for my name-day. so he promised that *his wife* (at my *suggestion NB*) would see to it by the next mailcoach.[44]

The passage suggests indignation that Wolfgang had had to be reminded about his father's name-day, and that even then Wolfgang did not intend to pack up the music himself, but was going to ask Constanze to do it.

At last, on 1 December, the long-awaited package arrived. It contained the six 'Haydn' Quartets, and the scores of the two keyboard concertos and of the Keyboard Quartet, K. 478. Leopold, who told Nannerl that he had been bored to death before the packet arrived, began to play through the quartets later the same day with his pupil Breymann. He also told her that he would get the copyist to start work, beginning with the keyboard parts; and he warned her that the concertos would require much practice.[45]

any part of K. 466 or 467; these latter two concertos only arrived in Salzburg by mailcoach on 1 Dec. 1785. The concerto Leopold called 'new' in the passage under discussion here could have been K. 456 or 459; if Leopold had brought them back from Vienna, both would still have been relatively new to Nannerl. Assuming that she played them while in Salzburg for her confinement, the keyboard part to one of them could have been left behind for some reason when she returned to St Gilgen.

43 *MBA* 900/27–76 (not in *Letters*).   44 *MBA* 904/82–8 (not in *Letters*).
45 Leopold to Nannerl, 2–3 Dec. 1785—*MBA* 906/9–24 (*Letters* 534).

On 4–5 January 1786 Leopold wrote sending the D minor Concerto, K. 466. He had not yet figured it, but since Nannerl was impatient for it he sent it anyway, telling her that when he had sent her the other new concerto (K. 467), she could send back K. 466 to be figured.[46] It is not clear when Leopold sent out K. 467, because the dispatch is not mentioned in any letter, but it must have reached Nannerl by 14 January, because on that date Leopold wrote to ask for it back. Nannerl had mentioned its difficulty, said that it did not sound right, and suggested that there might be copying mistakes, so Leopold wanted to check the parts against the score.[47] By early February, Leopold was sending more keyboard music of Wolfgang's to Nannerl;[48] there can be no certainty about what it was, but since he had promised her in mid-January a new keyboard sonata (probably the Fantasia and Sonata, K. 475 and 457), it may have been that.[49] Thus, though Nannerl's fortepiano still needed attention, and must have been a daily frustration to her, and though Wolfgang had disappointed Leopold by his neglect during the autumn, Nannerl and Leopold had none the less contrived to be sent a substantial quantity of masterpieces for their private enjoyment.

It was probably as well for Leopold that he was not fully informed about Wolfgang's activities that autumn, because the documents suggest that Wolfgang's financial position was precarious. At the end of Lent, on 19 March, Leopold had told Nannerl that Wolfgang ought to be able to bank 2,000 fl. if he had no debts; but on 20 November of the same year, Wolfgang was writing to Franz Anton Hoffmeister in Vienna to ask for money.[50] All the time that Leopold had been hoping for news, music, and a possible visit, therefore, Wolfgang must have been preoccupied with his finances as well as with the work on *The Marriage of Figaro*. Hoffmeister was the publisher of the Keyboard Quartet, K. 478, which Wolfgang was to send to Leopold in December, and the money Wolfgang was asking him for was perhaps therefore connected with his fee for the work.[51] Furthermore, Wolfgang had now written so much music in Vienna that he must have had a fair amount of work merely in negotiating with music-sellers about its marketing and checking up on their sharp practice —during the summer and autumn of 1785 the Viennese papers carried a

---

[46] *MBA* 916/69–76 (not in *Letters*).
[47] See Appendix 3, pp. 658–60, for an explanation of my reasons for identifying this concerto as K. 467.
[48] Leopold to Nannerl, 9–10 Feb. 1786—*MBA* 931/60–1 (not in *Letters*).
[49] Leopold to Nannerl, 13 Jan. 1786—*MBA* 918/22–9 (*Letters* 536).
[50] *MBA* 902 (*Letters* 533).
[51] See Eisen, *Documents*, 61, for more details about Wolfgang's arrangement with Hoffmeister.

number of advertisements by different firms for works by him, including the 'Haydn' Quartets, various keyboard concertos, and the Fantasia and Sonata, K. 475 and 457.[52] This administrative work had to be added to all his teaching, concert-giving, and composing. Wolfgang was also generous to anyone needing help, as numerous passages in the correspondence show. During this autumn, for example, he took in the Salzburg musicians Fiala and André, who were seeking new employment, and did what he could to help them. He also tried to arrange employment for Heinrich Marchand. Not surprisingly, he was not able to complete the keyboard arrangement he had begun of *Die Entführung*, and on 12 December an arrangement by Stark was advertised.[53] Stark thus robbed Wolfgang of the profit he could have made from the arrangement, and rendered Wolfgang's work a waste of precious time. Leopold announced the news resignedly to Nannerl on 16–17 December;[54] but if he had known in addition that all the money he had seen Wolfgang take in Lent only nine months previously (which ought to have allowed Wolfgang to live in comfort for more than a year, even without his more regular teaching income) had now disappeared, he would surely have been horrified and deeply dejected.

Colloredo's problems with Egedacher formed only a small part of the overall difficulties faced by the Salzburg court orchestra during the autumn and winter of 1785/6. On 9 September, Leopold reported the imminent departure of the oboist, violinist, and cellist Fiala, hinting that he had been treated shabbily by Colloredo.[55] Fiala had left a good post in Munich in 1778 because jobs there were so insecure following the merger of the Munich and Mannheim bands after the death of the elector Maximilian.[56] Leopold Mozart had introduced him to the Salzburg court as an oboist, and Fiala had become one of the regular visitors to the Mozart house. He succumbed to a 'chest defect', however, as a result of which Dr Barisani told him to stop playing the oboe. From 1783, therefore, Colloredo had to employ extra personnel to take over Fiala's oboe-playing duties, while Fiala continued to draw his salary but played the cello, violin, and gamba instead. By 1785 Colloredo had had enough of the situation, and gave Fiala what amounted to an ultimatum—either he would play the oboe again, or he would take a drop in salary. Fiala appealed, stating that he could not

[52] See Deutsch, *Documents*, 246–56.   [53] See Eisen, *Documents*, 65 and 67.
[54] *MBA* 909/17–24 (*Letters* 535).   [55] *MBA* 876/11–24 (not in *Letters*).
[56] See Ch. 19.

live on less, and asked either for the status quo to be preserved, or to be allowed to resign with one year's salary of 500 fl. Colloredo agreed to discharge him, but only gave him 300 fl.[57] Fiala had apparently been an excellent performer on all the instruments he played, and was going to be sadly missed. It was he who had played the cello part in the aria 'Martern aller Arten' in the performance of *Die Entführung* given by Schmidt's troupe in Salzburg in the winter of 1784/5.[58] From Salzburg Fiala sent his wife and children to his wife's parents in Munich, while he took with him his oboe pupil André and went to Vienna. It was while he and André were looking around for new employment that Wolfgang offered them temporary accommodation.[59]

Only four months after Fiala had left there was trouble with Ludwig Feiner, the second oboist. He had been engaged in 1778, initially on a trial contract, but when his position was made permanent it was only on condition that he also accept Kammerportier duties, which included waiting at table.[60] Feiner must have been nursing a grudge about this for some time, and was looking around for a more congenial post. In January 1786, according to Leopold, Feiner received a letter from his cousin in the Karlsruhe area. This letter made it clear that Feiner had complained to the cousin about his Kammerportier duties, and was worried about the long-term effect on his health of playing the oboe. The cousin suggested that Feiner ask for three months' leave (which was typically paid) and use the time to seek new employment around Karlsruhe. Feiner could stay with him indefinitely, so that even if he did not soon find a new job, he would gain three months' salary and be without expenses; if the request for leave were refused, however, he should resign and travel to his cousin anyway. For reasons best known to himself, Feiner showed the letter to Colloredo when submitting his petition for the leave. Leopold was full of scorn for this piece of crassness, and in no way surprised by the outcome; Feiner was dismissed as from the end of January.[61]

But it was the shortage of violinists that seems to have been particularly embarrassing during this period. The Italian Antonio Norman, engaged on a one-year trial contract after Hafeneder's death in 1784, had left in August 1785, and was not soon replaced.[62] His loss was compounded

[57] See Hintermaier, 'Hofkapelle', 112–16.
[58] Leopold to Nannerl, 19 Nov. 1784—*MBA* 825/28–37 (*Letters* 520).
[59] Leopold to Nannerl, 13 Jan. 1786—*MBA* 918/18–29 (*Letters* 536).
[60] See Hintermaier, 'Hofkapelle', 98–9.
[61] Leopold to Nannerl, 13 Jan. 1786—*MBA* 918/5–18 (not in *Letters*).
[62] Leopold to Nannerl, 27–8 Oct. 1785—*MBA* 892/98–108 (not in *Letters*); and Hintermaier, 'Hofkapelle', 300.

by Fiala's resignation the following month, and in December the old violinist Wenzel Sadlo suffered a stroke which rendered him unfit for duty. In reporting this to Nannerl, Leopold said that the two oldest choirboys from the Kapellhaus had been enlisted to play the violin in the cathedral. Colloredo seems to have intended that they should fill in until after Carnival, when he was expecting a new violinist from Italy, Giacomo Latouche. This did not please Leopold, who had been hoping even before Sadlo's illness that his pupil Breymann might be taken on as a junior member of the band, with a salary of little more than 100 fl. annually.[63] He sarcastically remarked to Nannerl that though nothing was yet known of Latouche's capabilities, he must be excellent because he was an Italian with, moreover, a French father.[64]

Leopold was also hoping to get Heinrich Marchand appointed as a violinist, though in a higher position than Breymann. On 20–2 October he claimed that Colloredo would be prepared to offer a salary of 200 fl. to a more able violinist, and that if he advanced to 300 fl., Leopold would recommend Heinrich to take the post.[65] Meanwhile, however, Wolfgang was trying to help Heinrich get a position in Vienna. Matters stuck like this for about three months, with Leopold deliberately doing nothing to help Colloredo out of his predicament. Then, following Feiner's departure, Colloredo instructed Leopold to write to Fiala's pupil André in Vienna and offer him a position as oboist in Salzburg.[66] Leopold wrote through Wolfgang, and the reply from André also came through Wolfgang. It was negative, and Wolfgang appeared to be taking satisfaction in emphasizing how much better off André was going to be outside Salzburg—he had just accepted a post with Count Erdödy in Hungary, and was being offered 200 fl. in Viennese currency, plus board and lodging, firewood, and candles; by contrast he would have earned 180 fl. with few other benefits in Salzburg, and the currency was worth less. Wolfgang's letter also mentioned that he was taking steps to establish Heinrich in Vienna. The letter was opened by Colloredo, and passed belatedly on to Leopold with an excuse about the broken seal; Leopold assumed that Colloredo had wanted to know what the Mozarts were saying about him.[67] It was in this way that Heinrich received an offer

[63] Leopold to Nannerl, 20–2 Oct. 1785—*MBA* 887/117–21 (not in *Letters*).
[64] Leopold to Nannerl, 16–17 Dec. 1785—*MBA* 909/43–54 (not in *Letters*).
[65] *MBA* 887/117–21 (not in *Letters*).
[66] Leopold to Nannerl, 13 Jan. 1786—*MBA* 918/18–22 (*Letters* 536).
[67] Leopold to Nannerl, 19–21 and 27 Jan. 1786—*MBA* 923/27–57 and 924/13–19 (not in *Letters*).

of employment from Colloredo—having seen from Wolfgang's letter that Heinrich might be about to slip out of his grasp as André had, he offered the 300 fl. that Leopold had been holding out for. Leopold recommended to the Marchands that Heinrich accept, and was then asked by them if he would go to Munich for part of Carnival, and accompany Heinrich back to Salzburg.[68] The Marchands had in any case wanted him to visit them for Carnival, had offered to pay his expenses, and had even invited Nannerl and Berchtold too. Leopold had hesitated while there was not a reason connected with duty; now he was inclined to accept the suggestion.

The main obstacle to the plan was the question of who would look after Leopoldl while he was away, and the solution that occurred most naturally to Leopold was that Berchtold and Nannerl would come into town to do so. He had hoped that they would visit him during Carnival in any case, since they had not seen the baby for months. But Berchtold raised objections and refused to come. The reasons he first supplied must have had something to do with money, and his fear of spending too much if they spent part of Carnival in Salzburg, because Leopold argued that it would not cost them much more to live in his house in Salzburg than it would to live at home. He also expressed surprise that the Berchtolds were not keener to see Leopoldl, and pressed home his arguments by making it clear that he could go to Munich with an easier mind if they were in Salzburg.[69] His words made little impression on Berchtold, however, and Nannerl's next letter claimed that they could not come because Berchtold had too much work in St Gilgen. At this, Leopold lost his patience, and wrote on 9–10 February:

That my son-in-law should make the excuse that he couldn't travel in *because of the sheer amount of work* is something I really couldn't tell anyone without going red myself, since everyone knows *the extent of the little Pfleg of St: Gilgen*, and can therefore deduce from that the terrible pile of work. I salute my son-in-law and ask him what he believes all reasonable people must think of a man who's capable of holding out for a whole 8 or 9 months, and perhaps even longer, without seeing his child, or maybe, which God forbid, ever seeing him again, when he's only 6 hours away from him? because he hasn't seen him for *5 months*, and I'll hardly be able to take him out in under *four months* because of the weather. — — what might and must reasonable people think? — — and then what are the outspoken scandalmongers saying? — *The former* see it as an acquired hard-heartedness, perhaps caused by exaggerated economy.

[68] Leopold to Nannerl, 1–3 Feb. 1786—*MBA* 929/59–68 (not in *Letters*).
[69] Leopold to Nannerl, 1–3 Feb. 1786—*MBA* 929/98–117 (not in *Letters*).

the latter say bluntly: Hah! the pennypincher! as long as he's got a wife; — to make the children good; he doesn't care anything for the rest! — — it's snowing quite appallingly now, it's going to be a big fall: — thanks be to God! though I'll get a wretched road to Munich: — at least my son-in-law will have a good sledge-run for his journey in, or if it doesn't settle — at any rate an honest excuse.

When he had written this far, Leopold received his usual weekly letter from Nannerl through the carrier. She must have expressed great anxiety at the thought of Leopoldl left for a lengthy period with only the servants, because Leopold continued his letter in a softer and more encouraging tone:

the carrier's brought your letter. I beg you, don't worry about anything. I'm travelling early tomorrow, and will go as far as Wasserburg, and Sunday with God's help in Munich by midday. the child is wonderfully provided for. Herr *v D'Ippold* will come every day while I'm away: he's incredibly concerned for the child, and I know for certain that there's no child in the whole town over whom more trouble is taken than Nanndl and Tresel take over the child. Mslle. janette and Mitzerl will always come, — and if need be, if it were absolutely necessary, we've got Dr: Joseph Barisani opposite us, whom we could call from the window. Do you really believe I'd go, if I had anything to worry about? — for all that, it's still very hard-hearted to be seen by the whole world with no other reason than a bit of business for not wanting to see one's child, because you may write what you like about a lot of work, it's ridiculous, — as if my colleagues here didn't know what work was etc: Enough! Nothing could provide an excuse except at a pinch, at the outside, a bad road making it impossible —: apart from that nothing! — apart from that nothing at all! — — —[70]

The Berchtolds did not come into town to stay with Leopoldl. What discussions took place between them on the subject, whether Berchtold read Leopold's unflattering opinion of him, and whether this issue caused trouble between husband and wife, is unknown; but as Leopold left for Munich on 11 February, the suspicion must be that the atmosphere in the Berchtold household was less than harmonious.

[70] *MBA* 931/11–30 and 37–52 (not in *Letters*).

29

The Return of Heinrich Marchand

Leopold had left Nanndl instructions to write to him each post day to let him know how Leopoldl was, and from her he learnt that the faithful d'Ippold was visiting daily to check up on the baby. In this way he gained the peace of mind he needed to enjoy his visit. His reunion with the Marchands was as warm as ever, and they had all manner of entertainments in mind for him. On Monday, 13 February he had the pleasure of seeing Gretl sing in the opera *La fiera di Venezia* by Salieri, and praised her highly.[1] Gretl was still trying to obtain a salaried position as a singer in Munich, and the part in this opera was a contribution to her goal, which was reached a few months later.[2] Leopold was also greatly impressed by Heinrich's keyboard playing, and selected his performance of Wolfgang's Fantasia and Sonata (K. 475 and 457) for special commendation.[3] His pride as a teacher was gratified by the accomplishments of these two talented young people, and he was already planning Heinrich's first public appearances in Salzburg.

Carnival progressed with more opera, masked academies, private music-making, and large dinner-parties. Leopold made special mention of a select concert in which Wolfgang's 'Haydn' Quartets were played to a small group of connoisseurs, after which eighteen people dined with Martin Lang. Leopold's original idea had been to stay until Ash Wednesday, which fell on 1 March, but he decided to extend his visit slightly in order to attend one of the Amateurs' Concerts on 2 March. He told Nannerl the programme of the concert he was to attend—it included a performance of Wolfgang's A major Keyboard Concerto, K. 414, by young Hanchen Brochard.[4] Leopold had already mentioned that Gretl would play Wolfgang's 'grand concerto in D' in one of the later Amateurs'

---

[1] Leopold to Nannerl after 14 Feb. 1786—*MBA* 932/10–11 (not in *Letters*).

[2] On 12 Apr. 1786, Leopold reported to Nannerl that Gretl had been given a three-year contract as court singer in Munich, at a salary of 500 fl. annually—*MBA* 948/39–55 (not in *Letters*).

[3] *MBA* 932/24–9 (*Letters* 537).

[4] Leopold to Nannerl, 1 Mar. 1786—*MBA* 936/4–19 (not in *Letters*).

Concerts. He intended Heinrich to play the same concerto in Salzburg on 14 March, the anniversary of Colloredo's election; so he asked Nannerl to send her copy into Salzburg with the glass-carrier to await his return, since Heinrich was going to leave his in Munich for Gretl.[5] The keyboard music traffic was to become more complicated now that Heinrich was about to return to Salzburg with Leopold, because copies of Wolfgang's music were sought by Nannerl in St Gilgen, Gretl in Munich, and Heinrich in Salzburg.

All the people Leopold met remembered Nannerl, asked if she was happy, and sent her warm greetings—most of them had last seen her when she had been in Munich in 1781 with Leopold and Wolfgang for the first performance of *Idomeneo*.[6] What she thought on reading all the Munich news (especially that of Gretl's burgeoning career), and the affectionate greetings of old friends, is not recorded. She had loved carnival events, music-making, and socializing, and had been invited with Leopold to this Carnival, but had not been able to accept the invitation. Gretl in particular was leading the kind of life that Nannerl might have led had events turned out differently; if Wolfgang had fulfilled Leopold's hopes, Nannerl would have had an outlet for her talent and would have been participating in events such as the Amateurs' Concerts, and enjoying all the other opportunities offered by a lively artistic centre.

Instead, she was struggling through her second winter in St Gilgen. During the previous one, she had had all the trouble with her fortepiano; this time there was a crisis caused by the children and the servants. She must have written all about it to Leopold, because he answered:

I will keep Leopoldl, you don't have to worry about this. — Monica is a slow coarse, and very touchy woman; I won't be at all sorry if she leaves. She's not healthy either; and I'm certainly not mistaken: *she loves brandy,* — she'll get dropsy; more-

---

[5] Leopold to Nannerl, 22–3 Feb. 1786—*MBA* 934/50–3 (not in *Letters*). There is some debate about whether he meant K. 451 in D major or K. 466 in D minor (Deutsch and Paumgartner, *Leopold Mozarts Briefe an seine Tochter*, 541, gives K. 466; the *MBA* commentary gives K. 451), but K. 451 seems more likely. First, Leopold had stated that Heinrich would play the same concerto in Salzburg on Election Day (14 Mar.). Just over a week after Election Day Heinrich played K. 466 at a public concert in Salzburg, and Leopold's description of this performance (letter to Nannerl of 23–4 Mar. 1786—*MBA* 943/4–12; *Letters* 538) suggests that it had not been given before in Salzburg. Secondly, if it had been K. 466 that had been left in Munich for Gretl to play at one of the Amateurs' Concerts, her parents would have heard it then; but they apparently did not know it before they visited Salzburg in Sept. 1786 (Leopold to Nannerl, 15–16 Sept. 1786—*MBA* 987/33–7; not in *Letters*).

[6] Leopold to Nannerl after 14 and on 22–3 Feb. 1786—*MBA* 932/34–5 and 934/31–44 (not in *Letters*).

over she's a muddler. Just see that you keep the *cook* and *Lenerl*, these two will get on quite well with each other. besides, one person is easily good enough for the children and the other housework, as long as she's hard-working. — How can it cross your mind that Nanndl would go out with Leopoldl among these troublesome evil-minded children? and the less so since she's got her own house and furniture here in town which she has to see to from time to time: she couldn't abandon it. as for the rest, I beg you not to get at all annoyed about the children, or as little as ever is possible. if anything happens between the children and Monica, say drily to your husband: *I've done everything I could, you're the father, they're your children, it's your responsibility.*—in short! let things go as they will: stick up for the cook and Lenerl, so that they like you, — send Monica away; and let him get whoever he likes for the children: stand firm on this, and leave him to take responsibility as father for the care of his children; *don't get angry about anything!* laugh! and go to your room. it's true that with three servants there's always going to be something to fight about: but I think that with the cook and Lenerl things will be peaceful. if a third one comes and doesn't fit in, you get a different one again: just so long as you keep the cook and Lenerl. as soon as ever it's possible, I'll come out. I kiss you heartily and remain eternally your honest father Mzt.

I greet Lenerl.

So that you know my complete way of thinking, I'm telling you *that I will keep Leopoldl with me as long as I live*; this is and was even from the beginning my intention. I'll bring him out for a little while in the summer with Nanndl; but then take him back with me again.[7]

What exactly had Nannerl complained about? Obviously the children were causing trouble, probably by refusing to co-operate with Monica, the maid who had helped Nanndl care for Leopoldl during his first few weeks, and had then gone out to St Gilgen at Michaelmas 1785.[8] Nannerl was clearly thinking that Monica would have to go, but was at a loss for someone to replace her, unless Nanndl would go out. The upset in the household was apparently bad enough to cause friction between Nannerl and Berchtold, and Leopold's advice on how to handle him suggests

---

[7] *MBA* 938 (not in *Letters*). The letter is not dated, but the paper suggests that it was written in Munich during Leopold's carnival visit in 1786—see Deutsch and Paumgartner, *Leopold Mozarts Briefe an seine Tochter*, 540. (This same commentary, however, simultaneously suggests a difficulty in assigning the letter to Leopold's Munich visit—it states that Monica had been replaced as cook before Leopold had gone to Munich. The difficulty is not a real one—the rebellious cook had certainly been replaced in Jan. 1786, but she was not Monica; Monica was a maid and had never been cook there). The letter begins so abruptly (it is quoted in full here) as to suggest that it is incomplete. The contents suggest that it precedes *MBA* 940 (cf. esp. 940/37–41; not in *Letters*), which was written on 17–18 Mar. 1786.

[8] See Ch. 28, pp. 486–7 and 491–2, for details of the St Gilgen servants following Leopoldl's birth.

that she had complained about his role in the trouble. It seems possible, since Leopold told her to make him choose the next maid, that Berchtold had blamed Nannerl for the choice of Monica. Nannerl had perhaps also expressed anxiety about Leopoldl, since Leopold mentioned him twice in extremely emphatic terms; but what had been her worry? Presumably it was fear that he might also have to suffer an unruly upbringing, since Leopold assured her that he would keep the child for as long as he lived. But why might she have feared otherwise? Was she worried that Leopold might not want to continue to care for Leopoldl, or had perhaps the suggestion that Nanndl take the baby and join the Berchtold family come from Berchtold himself? Whatever had caused Nannerl's anxiety, Leopold's expressed intentions about Leopoldl give the impression of solicitous reassurance.[9]

When Leopold and Heinrich left Munich on 3 March, Lent had begun. Heinrich had an audience with Colloredo and played in the court orchestra on 5 March, the day after his arrival in Salzburg, and he played quartets at court on 6 March, and a concerto on the following day;[10] but his real triumphs that Lent were in a series of public subscription concerts in the Town Hall. These had been arranged while Leopold and Heinrich had been in Munich, and were to take place on five Wednesdays, beginning on 8 March. They had been suggested by Colloredo who, according to Leopold, had got the idea from a similar series which had taken place in Lent 1781 while Colloredo himself had been absent in Vienna.[11] During that season, Wolfgang (who was with Colloredo in Vienna prior to his resignation) had written to ask if Nannerl had been asked to play at them, and to hope that she would demand a fee of two ducats (10 fl.) if she did;[12] but because of the loss of relevant letters, there is no record of whether she took part. Leopold threw himself with gusto into the organization of the 1786 series, and described the arrangements to Nannerl. Most of the orchestral players were paid 1 fl. per concert, but the more important members received 2 fl. Anyone playing a concerto received a ducat (5 fl.).[13] To cover the costs, subscriptions and

---

[9] This is the passage used by Rieger in her claim that Leopold behaved in an authoritarian way towards Nannerl in his attempt to keep Leopoldl. See Rieger, *Nannerl Mozart*, 206–7; and Ch. 28, pp. 487–8. Its context here, however, shows quite a different situation from that prevailing at the time of Leopoldl's birth. And assurance rather than authoritarianism is surely suggested by Leopold's words, '. . . you don't have to worry about this'.

[10] Leopold to Nannerl, 9–11 Mar. 1786—*MBA* 939/4–9 (not in *Letters*).

[11] Leopold to Nannerl, 9–11 Mar. 1786—*MBA* 939/9–14 (not in *Letters*).

[12] Wolfgang to Leopold, 24–8 Mar. 1781—*MBA* 585/90–5 (*Letters* 395).

[13] The ducat was still worth 5 fl. in Salzburg in 1786—see Leopold's own conversion in his letter to Nannerl of 18 Apr. 1786—*MBA* 950/21–3 (not in *Letters*).

single tickets were sold—for 1 ducat a subscriber could take the whole family to all five concerts. Single ticket prices were 36 kr., so that the series at single-ticket prices would cost 3 fl. per person; the subscription rate was thus very favourable to families of two or more people. There were over seventy subscribers, and gaming tables were provided, and refreshments served. As the series progressed, Leopold reported to Nannerl on the performances and the audience. When the first concert took place on 8 March, the town was full of merchants, and many of these attended the concert, giving an 'incredibly full' hall.[14] The second concert took place on the day following Election Day, when the town was again full, this time of people who had court business. Election Day was a court 'gala' day, with special celebrations (including music), and all the canons were given a present of 'election money' by Colloredo, in acknowledgement of the fact that they had chosen him. The second concert was thus also well attended, and since the canons tended to come from noble families, the cream of Salzburg society was there. But Leopold's letters make it clear that the audience covered a far broader spectrum of society than the court concerts did—in addition to the nobles there were university professors, clerics (even from outlying monasteries), court officials, town council officials, and merchants.[15]

At the first concert Heinrich played a violin concerto.[16] At the second (on 15 March, the day after Election Day) he played a keyboard concerto, which might have been K. 451.[17] At the third he played K. 466,[18] and at the fourth he played a violin concerto in E by Viotti.[19] The last concert before Easter, on 5 April, involved a concert performance of Gluck's *Orfeo*, organized and rehearsed by Leopold with parts borrowed from Munich.[20] By the time the second concert had been given, it was clear that the series promised to be a great success, and there was talk of extending it for three weeks beyond Easter.[21]

---

[14] *MBA* 939/14–29 (not in *Letters*).

[15] Leopold to Nannerl, 17–18 and 23–4 Mar. 1786—*MBA* 940/11–19 and 51–4, and 943/122–5 (none of these passages is in *Letters*).

[16] Leopold to Nannerl, 9–11 Mar. 1786—*MBA* 939/16–22 (not in *Letters*).

[17] K. 451 is tentatively suggested for the following reason. In *MBA* 939/21–2 (not in *Letters*), Leopold told Nannerl that Heinrich would play a keyboard concerto 'next Wednesday' (by which he meant the subscription concert on 15 March), and implied that he would play the same concerto at court on the day before this subscription concert. Since this would be Election Day, and the most likely candidate for the concerto Heinrich played on that occasion is K. 451 (cf. n. 5 above), he may well have played K. 451 at the second subscription concert too.

[18] Leopold to Nannerl, 23–4 Mar. 1786—*MBA* 943/4–19 (*Letters* 538).

[19] Leopold to Nannerl, 31 Mar.–1 Apr. 1786—*MBA* 947/27–30 (not in *Letters*).

[20] Leopold to Nannerl, 17–18 Mar. 1786—*MBA* 940/19–23 (not in *Letters*).

[21] *MBA* 940/49–51 (not in *Letters*).

Leopold's accounts of these Lenten concerts focus exclusively on the Mozart/Marchand element in them, although he was enclosing the programmes to give Nannerl a more complete picture than survives in his letters. Everything he wrote about them suggests that they were far more rewarding than any of the court music he was involved in, and that at the age of 66 he still had energy, ambition, and pride enough to make his part in them as excellent as possible. He seems to have relished the opportunity to display the fruits of his teaching through Heinrich's performances. He told Nannerl about all the congratulations he had received on Heinrich's playing at the second concert,[22] and he made Heinrich practise 'like an ox' for two days before playing the Viotti concerto at the fourth concert;[23] but the highlight of the season for Leopold was probably Heinrich's performance, on 22 March, of K. 466. Unfortunately, Leopold did not record any details about the orchestra at this first Salzburg performance. All he told Nannerl was that Heinrich had played from the score because the keyboard parts to all Wolfgang's concertos were out in St Gilgen, that Michael Haydn had turned the pages for Heinrich and thus appreciated all the more the difficulty and complexity of the work, that it had been rehearsed on the morning of the concert and the Rondo had received the most attention, that Colloredo had attended the concert, and that everything had been so fine that the emperor might have been there.[24]

When Heinrich had been appointed, Leopold had wanted his other pupil, Breymann, to be taken on too, but Colloredo had chosen instead the unknown Italian Latouche. Latouche had not yet arrived in Salzburg, but Leopold had begun the process of dooming the unfortunate man before he had even crossed the Alps, his pride as a teacher making him keen for Heinrich to establish himself as an outstanding performer before the arrival of the Italian. Following Heinrich's performance of a violin concerto in the first Lenten concert, he reported to Nannerl that the Italian musicians present had expressed pity for Latouche because of the inevitable comparisons that would be drawn between him and the 16-year-old German boy, Heinrich.[25]

Even before the end of the Lenten concert season, Leopold had been hoping that Nannerl would soon pay a visit to Salzburg. On 28 March he wrote returning a concerto (probably K. 451) with the glass-carrier, and

---

[22] *MBA* 940/16–19 (not in *Letters*).
[23] Leopold to Nannerl, 31 Mar.–1 Apr. 1786—*MBA* 947/27–30 (not in *Letters*).
[24] Leopold to Nannerl, 23–4 Mar. 1786—*MBA* 943/4–19 (*Letters* 538).
[25] Leopold to Nannerl, 9–11 Mar. 1786—*MBA* 939/16–21 (not in *Letters*).

told her to practise the new concertos (presumably K. 466 and 467), because she would both play and hear them in Salzburg.[26] But before Nannerl visited Salzburg, Leopold managed to steal a fleeting visit to St Gilgen. On 6 April, the day after the concert performance of Gluck's *Orfeo*, he went out with the organ-builder Schmid, and perhaps with Heinrich too. Nannerl had been giving Leopold no peace about the state of her fortepiano, which had still not been properly serviced since it had swollen up in February 1785. For the first time since Schmid's arrival in Salzburg, he could now make the time to get out and see to it, but they could not stay long, and were back in Salzburg on the afternoon of Sunday 9 April.[27] It does not seem likely that they took Leopoldl with them, because it was still too early in the year for the weather to be warm enough for him to travel, but Nannerl would almost certainly have been able to try over the new concertos with a miniature accompaniment.

Five days after Leopold's return to Salzburg, the new violinist Latouche arrived, and Leopold described him to Nannerl, apparently even before seeing him:

the new violinist arrived on Good Friday, but hasn't played a note of a solo yet, and as far as I can see, we'll hardly get to hear a concerto from him very soon either; something like a *quartet*, maybe, because the italians are saying: *the poor man, — he's a good professor, you've got to give him that, and he'll be good leading the second violins*: but he *hasn't been used* to playing concertos. *At most he can play a trio or quartet cleanly, and what's more he's timid.* Now it can't be held against him that he's timid either, because after all he's only *30 years* old. So the archbishop has once again been nicely diddled and with a salary of 500 fl. to boot, plus 40 ducats travel money here and back making 700 fl. good luck to him! — — on top of that the man isn't good-looking. he's of medium

---

[26] *MBA* 946/11–12 (not in *Letters*). The *MBA* commentary (following Deutsch and Paumgartner, *Leopold Mozarts Briefe an seine Tochter*, 544) identifies the concerto returned by Leopold as K. 466, but this does not seem the most likely candidate. I argued in n. 5 above that Leopold had probably asked Nannerl from Munich to send K. 451 for Heinrich to play on Election Day. On 23 Mar. he explained that Heinrich had played K. 466 at the subscription concert on 22 Mar. because Nannerl had the parts to all Wolfgang's other concertos, but Heinrich was able to play from the score of K. 466. It seems likely, therefore, that at the time of the concert on 22 Mar., the only concerto keyboard part that was in Salzburg was that to K. 451; when Leopold said that Nannerl had all the keyboard parts in St Gilgen, he was probably excepting K. 451 because Heinrich had already played it twice, and needed a new one for the concert on 22 Mar.

[27] Their intended departure date is known from Leopold's letter to Nannerl of 23–4 Mar. 1786—*MBA* 943/32–49 (not in *Letters*). In this passage, Leopold also told Nannerl that he would have to be back in Salzburg by 8 Apr. at the latest, but Leopold's letter of 12 Apr. 1786 (*MBA* 948/5–7; not in *Letters*) reveals that they actually returned on the day that Prince Waldburg-Zeil (bishop of Chiemsee) died, which was 9 Apr. See U. Salzmann, 'Der Salzburger Erzbischof Siegmund Christoph Graf von Schrattenbach (1753–1771) und sein Domkapitel', *MGSL* 124 (1984), 227–8.

build, has a pale rather puffed-up face, and yet has certain bony bits to it too, like a horse's head, hangs his head forward, and chews tobacco like the Zillerthal farmers; that's what the italians say. I pity the man, all the same it's a piece of Italian audacity to undertake something you're not capable of.[28]

Leopold was no less sarcastic when he heard Latouche play at court for the first time. He told Nannerl that his pupil Breymann could have played better the simple concerto chosen by Latouche, that Latouche's demeanour was that of a pupil repeating a lesson for the first time, and that with God's help and another twenty years' practice he might make a jaunty violinist by the time he was 50.[29] Leopold's words were cutting, but at 500 fl. annually Latouche was being paid more than Leopold the Vice-Kapellmeister; furthermore, Colloredo had initially wanted Heinrich for a mere 200 fl. annually, and Leopold had only managed to squeeze the offer up to 300 fl. through his wiliness.[30] Throughout Leopold's career, this salary-weighting in favour of Italians had occurred, and it seems to have been a major reason for some of the divisions in the court music.

Easter Sunday was 16 April, and the subscription concerts were supposed to continue for three weeks afterwards. At court, some of the rooms were being decorated, so that music-making there was restricted; and since Colloredo was expecting visitors from Vienna, Leopold thought there was all the more reason for the public concerts to continue.[31] However, only one was given after Easter, on 19 April. Heinrich and Leopold seem not to have played any part in it, but Leopold described part of it to Nannerl because their acquaintance Josepha Duschek sang in it. Duschek was related to the Weiser and Hagenauer families in Salzburg, and had come to claim an inheritance due to her. She had recently seen Wolfgang in Vienna, and was able to give Leopold some news of him. Leopold did not think much of her singing, and the concert she was involved in brought the series to a rather lame end, if Leopold's account is to be believed.[32]

After this event, concert life in Salzburg dried up for a while, and even at court there was not much going on. Colloredo was involved in a dispute with his courtiers which made him disinclined to socialize with them, and the thrice-weekly concerts shrank to once-weekly events, so that

---

[28] Leopold to Nannerl, 18–22 Apr. 1786—*MBA* 950/12–28 (not in *Letters*).
[29] Leopold to Nannerl, 28 Apr. 1786—*MBA* 952/29–37 (not in *Letters*).
[30] See Ch. 28, pp. 504–5.
[31] Leopold to Nannerl, 13 Apr. 1786—*MBA* 949/13–19 (not in *Letters*).
[32] Leopold to Nannerl, 18–22 Apr. 1786—*MBA* 950/41–59 (not in *Letters*).

by mid-May, when he had been in Salzburg nine weeks, Heinrich had played only two violin concertos and one keyboard concerto at court.[33] By this time, however, there was activity at the theatre. Part of Schikaneder's troupe had arrived in Salzburg on 30 April, and they gave about ten performances of opera and *Singspiel* between 3 May and 6 June, before moving on to Augsburg for the summer.[34] Schikaneder called on Leopold and offered Leopold and Heinrich free tickets to the performances; and Leopold, who was still trying to exert enough pressure on Nannerl and Berchtold to make them pay the visit he was hoping for, used Schikaneder's performances as a further inducement. One of the obstacles that apparently always made a visit from the Berchtolds doubtful was the cost of the journey. Writing on 5–6 May, therefore, Leopold urged them to travel in with Nannerl Huber (their friend the cap-maker, who was staying with them in St Gilgen) if she decided to return soon.[35]

Nannerl and Berchtold did visit while Schikaneder was there. They seem to have been in Salzburg from around 2 June for about ten days,[36] and this was the first time that they had seen Leopoldl since the first few weeks of his life some ten months previously. Leopold's letters had always catalogued his progress; they typically began with the sentence, 'Leopoldl is well'. After the early fright caused by his thrush, and another caused shortly afterwards by his almost choking to death from phlegm,[37] he had indeed been fairly well, and Leopold's letters in 1786 spoke of his bright eyes, his liveliness, his musical attention, and his intelligence. Heinrich was devoted to him from the moment he arrived back in Salzburg, carrying him round on his arm, eating his leftovers, and allowing himself to be bitten in the cause of the amusement of the rest of the household. As the weather got warmer, Leopold allowed the baby to be taken out to visit friends and neighbours, and fondly reported to Nannerl how everyone fell in love with his big blue eyes. He was still a great favourite with d'Ippold.

Just after Nannerl and Berchtold had returned home again it was Corpus Christi, one of the biggest festivals of the church year. Leopoldl was taken to Barbara Eberlin's to see the procession, and got very excited about

---

[33] Leopold to Nannerl, 12–13 May 1786—*MBA* 956/18–38 (not in *Letters*).
[34] See Dahms, 'Das musikalische Repertoire', 347.   [35] *MBA* 954/4–23 (not in *Letters*).
[36] Leopold to Nannerl, 26 May and 13–14 June 1786—*MBA* 960/19–24 and 962/3–4 (not in *Letters*).
[37] Leopold to Nannerl, 3–5 Nov. 1785—*MBA* 895/4–23 (not in *Letters*). On this occasion, Leopoldl had stopped breathing and turned blue. Leopold revived him by blowing into his mouth, but he also told Nannerl that his maid Tresel had been ready to blow into the baby's anus.

the horses.[38] Directly afterwards, on 16 June, Colloredo departed on political business which was to keep him absent until 9 September, so his Salzburg servants were relatively free for almost three months. Leopold fairly soon travelled out to St Gilgen, probably with Heinrich and Leopoldl, and stayed until about 20 July. It seems very likely that among the music they played through together out there was *The Marriage of Figaro*, which had received its première in Vienna on 1 May. Wolfgang had promised later in May to send Leopold the score, and Leopold mentioned that the glass-carrier had brought 'the opera' into Salzburg directly after his return from St Gilgen in July.[39] Since it was high summer during their visit, Heinrich presumably saw many of the sights round the Abersee. Young Karl, aged 4, was apparently interested in learning to play the violin, and Leopold was willing to encourage him. On 12–13 May he had promised, if he lived long enough, to take Karl as a pupil, and on 13–14 June he had sent him a violin.[40] Presumably, therefore, he spent some time fostering this interest of Karl's while he was out there. Yet he does not appear to have offered to teach young Wolfgang anything, although the boy would surely have benefited from Leopold's firm but patient dedication. Perhaps the offer was never made because Wolfgang was not musical and the education that Leopold could offer was best suited to a musical career. Or perhaps he thought that with Wolfgang it was already too late, in that the boy had reached the age of 12 without much proficiency at anything, and Leopold only liked pupils with whom he could see real progress.

No sooner was Leopold back in Salzburg than Nannerl's name-day and birthday were approaching. The name-day was of course shared by the two Nannerls, and Leopold wrote a greeting to each of them on 21–2 July. To his own daughter he wrote:

Now I really mustn't forget the main thing either and *wish you well for your name-day*: but you know how little we've all ever bothered about these things. *Deeds* and not *wishes* are the proofs of true friendship and tender fatherly love; I know you're convinced of this; and this pleases me. — I wish you sound health, and — you can wish all the rest for yourself.

To young Nannerl, however, he wrote, 'meanwhile I wish her plenty of application, and pleasure in *reading* and *keyboard playing*; and greater

---

[38] Leopold to Nannerl, 16 June 1786—*MBA* 963/31–4 (not in *Letters*).
[39] Leopold to Nannerl, 18–20 May and 21–2 July 1786—*MBA* 958/79–81 and 968/58–62 (not in *Letters*).
[40] *MBA* 956/40–2 and 962/45 (not in *Letters*).

desire to keep herself clean and clean her teeth, otherwise she won't get a husband: — and that would be terrible! if she comes in at Michaelmas, I'll observe straight away whether her breath smells.'[41]

On 28–9 July Leopold was sending Nannerl's birthday greeting. This time he stressed the importance of the education of young people, telling her that his only reason for wanting to live longer was to be of use to his children and his children's children—both the temporal and eternal well-being of children depended on their upbringing, and parents were required to account for this to God.[42] Whether or not Leopold intended to hint at the shortcomings of others in these greetings, the integrity of his avowals is striking; the care for others in deed as well as word, and the total dedication to the upbringing of children, is borne out by all the documented relations with his family over the previous twenty-five years.

By the summer of 1786 Leopold was very busy again with pupils, whereas the previous autumn he had had only the slow-to-pay Joseph Wölfl. On 21–2 July he indicated to Nannerl that he had begun to teach Nannerl Weiser and the daughters of Johannes Hagenauer.[43] He also still had his Kapellhaus teaching, though Heinrich sometimes did this for him. Heinrich was presumably paying Leopold something from his salary for board and lodging, so it seems odd that Leopold should have felt the need to saddle himself with extra pupils, especially since the Hagenauer girls were all less than 10 years old and must therefore have needed very basic and patient instruction. Leopold seems to have taught Nannerl Weiser six days a week, and the Hagenauer children three days,[44] so that with his other duties the days must have been full of interruptions. It is possible that he had again become a sought-after teacher following Heinrich's performances in the Lenten subscription concerts, and that he found it difficult to refuse to oblige people; at any rate, he was to add to his pupils further in 1787.

Very soon after Leopold returned from his visit to St Gilgen, a visit from the Marchands was mooted, and the Berchtolds also intended to come into town for young Nannerl to be confirmed. At first it looked as if these two events would be separate ones, but in the end the Marchands could not get away from Munich until Michaelmas, which was to be the time of the Berchtolds' visit. When Leopold realized that it might be possible to combine the two occasions, he was strongly in favour, since

---

[41] *MBA* 968/82–7 and 93–7 (not in *Letters*).   [42] *MBA* 969/37–45 (not in *Letters*).

[43] *MBA* 968/63–7 (not in *Letters*).

[44] Leopold to Nannerl, 12 Jan. 1787—*MBA* 1020/10–16 (not in *Letters*).

Nannerl would be able to enjoy a reunion with the family too, and the opportunities for music-making would be greater. He therefore urged the Berchtolds both to come at the right time and to stay long enough for the visit to be a real pleasure; but the problem, as usual, was Berchtold, whom Leopold suspected of not having the will to make the effort. On 6–9 September he wrote to spell out the attractions of a combined visit, saying that there would be 'nothing but music' going on, since with Gretl and the Marchands' cellist son Daniel there would be five people constantly available for ensemble playing. In addition, up to five local musicians would visit each afternoon to increase the scope of what could be attempted. He also stressed how much the Marchands would like to see both the Berchtolds, and went into minute detail about how the Berchtolds might organize their journey into town; the main difficulty seems to have been that though young Nannerl had to come into town to be confirmed, she could not long be spared from St Gilgen, perhaps because of her poultry tending or other duties there. Leopold was therefore worried that Berchtold might make young Nannerl's need to return early a reason for keeping the whole visit very short, and he spelt out various convoluted transport arrangements which would enable the girl to return economically whenever Berchtold chose, but without breaking up the main party. At the end of all this he wrote, 'amen! Really, how you have to rack your brains to bring people happily together when they want to see each other. After all, what have we after we're dead? — Shouldn't we use every moment to arrange a pleasurable gathering, since we're tormented enough by other malevolent people? — —'[45]

Leopold's efforts succeeded. The Berchtolds arrived during the week beginning Monday 18 September, and stayed well into October.[46] On 15–16 September Leopold told Nannerl what music to bring with her— he suggested the keyboard parts to all Wolfgang's new concertos to which Leopold had the other parts, and the new ones for which she had all the parts. Among these he picked out the D minor Concerto, K. 466, for special mention, and said that the Marchands had not yet heard it. On checking his music chest, however, he realized that he had most of the orchestral parts himself after all, so Nannerl needed to bring mainly keyboard parts, together with variations, and some of Berchtold's favourite sonatas, trios, and quartets.[47]

---

[45] *MBA* 984/49–73 and 82–96 (not in *Letters*).

[46] Leopold to Nannerl, 15–16 Sept. and 12 Oct. 1786—*MBA* 987/11–12 and 990 (not in *Letters*).

[47] *MBA* 987/33–42 (not in *Letters*).

There is no record of the programme of events during this visit, but it seems to have been a great success.[48] The D minor Concerto, which Heinrich had played in Lent and Nannerl must have tried over during the three occasions in the spring and summer when she was together with Leopold, was almost certainly played to the Marchands, and was presumably the grandest piece attempted. It is not known what forces were used, or whether Heinrich or Nannerl played the solo part; but although the numbers of people which Leopold could gather together were probably not large, the quality of their playing (at any rate of the core five —Leopold, Nannerl, Heinrich, Gretl, and Daniel) must have been high. Moreover, the groupings were versatile, and it is quite likely that, in addition to all the chamber music, parts of *The Marriage of Figaro* were performed, since Gretl was an accomplished singer. Leopold's emotions as he heard this feast of Wolfgang's latest music played by family, pupils, and friends can only be guessed. What is certain is that Heinrich's return had brought him a busy and fruitful time, and eased his loneliness. Through Heinrich he had had the means since Lent to recover the pride in his teaching and hear Wolfgang's music whenever he wanted to, and through Heinrich too he had attracted his old friends the Marchands back to Salzburg for the last dazzling reunion he was to enjoy in full health.

Leopold's pride in Heinrich's achievements was presumably all the more consoling because of his disillusionment with his court career. His feelings about this towards the end of his life can be inferred from a story he told Nannerl in his letter of 3–4 August 1786:

H: *Pergman*, who's now administrator in the Abtenau, was with me before his departure. There happened to be various people with me. It was really very moving to hear his speech, in which he thanked me with great emotion for all the good things I'd done for him in word and deed since his student years, and he didn't forget the slightest thing, how I got him into the choir at St: Peter's, and then got him a position as court music *access*, afterwards a salary too, — advised him to become an *access* in the St: Peter's Chancellery, and on the archbishop's entrance into government, using all my persuasion, prevented him from leaving St: Peter's and staying at court as a horn player with a supplement, as they wanted him to. I told him all the advancements he can make at St: Peter's, which have all come to pass too, whereas at court he could have blown the soul out of his body to his dying day for about *18 or 20 fl.* a month. in fact he became *Mitterschreiber*, — then *Oberschreiber*, and enjoyed *12 fl. a month from the court as a horn*

---

[48] Leopold told the Berchtolds on 12 Oct. 1786 of the Marchands' enormous pleasure in the visit—*MBA* 990/7–11 (not in *Letters*).

player, for which he went to court for an hour and a half in the *evening* when there was music: He particularly gave me his most obedient greetings for St Gilgen.[49]

The position of *Access* mentioned by Leopold was a post-in-waiting, in which someone performed a job without salary until a paid position became vacant, but without any guarantee of obtaining it. The posts of Mitterschreiber and Oberschreiber referred to by Leopold were administrative posts within St Peter's, which owned a lot of land—a Mitterschreiber was a middle-ranking clerk, and an Oberschreiber a more important clerk. Assuming that Leopold was remembering accurately and reporting truthfully, this means that by 1772, on Colloredo's election, he had been completely disenchanted with the court music.[50] In 1772 he himself had been receiving 25 fl. a month for a full-time job. Bergmann could have hoped for 20 fl., also for full-time court work, whereas (thanks to Leopold's advice) he drew 12 fl. just for appearing on three evenings a week, and was completely free to take full salaried employment from St Peter's as well. Leopold's wide-ranging intelligence and ability to organize would have fitted him well for an administrative career such as the one he had recommended to Bergmann, but he was 53 in 1772, and it was too late. His salary had risen from 1746 to 1756, but had then stuck until 1778. The period of stagnation had been precisely the period of Nannerl's and Wolfgang's formative years, when the excitement of having such special talents to nurture gave him a reason for continuing to serve the court music despite the fact that it offered him personally little satisfaction. If the situation had been like this, it would help explain why Leopold had such high hopes that Wolfgang would provide the means for him to leave Salzburg, and why in his disappointment that this had not happened he talked of having sacrificed his best years.

❧

Meanwhile Wolfgang still had no salaried appointment in Vienna, and was still working frantically to earn money and keep the goodwill of the Viennese public. Between March and September 1786 he entered into the thematic catalogue of his works the Keyboard Concertos K. 488 and K. 491, two extra pieces (K. 489 and 490) for a performance of *Idomeneo* in Prince Auersperg's theatre, *The Marriage of Figaro*, the Keyboard Quartet K. 493, a keyboard Rondo K. 494, the Horn Concerto K. 495, the Keyboard

---

[49] *MBA* 971/37–52 (not in *Letters*).
[50] This attitude is borne out by his letters from that date.

Trio K. 496 and the Trio for keyboard, clarinet, and viola K. 498, the four-hand Keyboard Sonata K. 497, the String Quartet K. 499, and the Keyboard Variations K. 500.[51] There is little documentation about the Viennese Lenten concerts in 1786, and no indication of how successful they were for him financially. He received a fee of 50 ducats (225 fl.) for the composition and performance of *Der Schauspieldirektor* at the imperial palace of Schönbrunn on 7 February, and was presumably paid by Prince Auersperg for the performance of *Idomeneo* on 13 March.[52] He was probably also recompensed for accompanying Josepha Duschek when she sang at court in the second half of March, and was paid 450 fl. for *The Marriage of Figaro*.[53] Together with income from teaching and sundry other sources (in August and September he was selling music to Prince Fürstenberg of Donaueschingen),[54] 1786 ought not to have been a very lean year for him.[55] Yet by November at the latest (to anticipate events which will be discussed in the next chapter) he was thinking of going to England. Since this was an expensive and risky undertaking, the most likely explanation for the idea is that he was not satisfied with his position in Vienna. When Josepha Duschek had met Leopold in Salzburg in April, she had told him that Wolfgang intended to go to Prague.[56] Leopold had not given his opinion on this to Nannerl, but it is unlikely to have worried him, since Prague had close connections with Vienna and involved a relatively easy journey. When he was told about the English plans, however, he was to become plunged into misgiving and melancholy, because it was brought home to him first that Wolfgang still had no imperial appointment to keep him in Vienna, second that his chances of obtaining one would be reduced by a long absence, and third that his freelance income was probably not sufficient for his needs.

⁓✴︎⁓

Leopold had often noted the deaths of other people in terms of a lesson to the living, but in 1786 his description of the death of Count

---

[51] *MBA* 937, 944, 953, 961, 965, 972, 970, 978, and 985.

[52] Deutsch, *Documents*, 263 and 267. From the beginning of Feb. 1786, the imperial ducat was worth $4\frac{1}{2}$ fl.—see Edge, 'Mozart's Fee for *Così fan tutte*', 218.

[53] Deutsch, *Documents*, 271–2 and 274.

[54] Wolfgang to Sebastian Winter, 8 Aug. and 30 Sept. 1786—*MBA* 974 and 988 (*Letters* 540 and 541).

[55] After Wolfgang's death, a loan of 300 fl. from him to Franz Gilowsky was noted as having been made on 23 Aug. 1786. This loan was written off as irrecoverable. See Deutsch, *Documents*, 585.

[56] Leopold to Nannerl, 13 Apr. 1786—*MBA* 949/19–24 (not in *Letters*).

Waldburg-Zeil, bishop of Chiemsee and Colloredo's long-standing enemy,[57] suggests that this particular death brought the prospect of his own very close to him. On 12 April, three days after having arrived back from St Gilgen with the keyboard instruments tuner Schmid, he told Nannerl that Zeil had died on the day of his return, 9 April. Leopold explained that Zeil had had a 'heated catarrh' for a fortnight, but that his doctor, Ernst Anton von Helmreichen, had made nothing of it. At the Lenten subscription academy on Wednesday, 5 April, the one at which Gluck's *Orfeo* was performed, Barisani was called away to see Zeil without Helmreichen's knowledge. Barisani discovered the bishop with a swollen abdomen, considered the situation very serious, and advised him on the Friday to put his affairs in order. On Saturday he warned him that he was not likely to survive the weekend. Though Zeil was at first reluctant to believe Barisani, he made his confession and had the last rites administered to him. On Sunday morning he received extreme unction, and then summoned all his staff to his room. According to Leopold, he said to them:

thank you for your good service etcetc: nothing pains me more than the fact that I can't reward you, I can give you nothing but my blessing. (which he proceeded to give) *and pray to God for you — I have paid many of my debts, and if God had prolonged my life another two years, everything would be paid. H: doctor* (he said to Helmreich) *I also commend to you the people I leave behind, you have reason to provide for them at every opportunity that arises.* that was spoken clearly. — he sent a note by the dean to the archbishop, in which he took leave of him and in the presence of the Spirit asked pardon for past differences, so that the archbishop laid the note on the table and burst into tears, together with the dean. at 2 o' clock everything was still all right, — then he suddenly got the *Freys* and died at quarter to 3. he was about 7 or 8 months older than I, born in *the year 1719*, so he was in the 67th year of his age.[58]

Leopold's account of Zeil's end cannot be accepted unreservedly as accurate. Another contemporary account had Zeil actually present and eating ices at the concert on 5 May, while according to Leopold he was then sick at home; and Colloredo's tears on reading Zeil's note are not mentioned.[59] The chief significance of the passage, however, is Leopold's presentation of it to Nannerl. In his view Zeil, who had won Leopold's trust and sympathy both because he had tried to help the Mozarts in earlier days, and had himself suffered through Colloredo's succession, had died a dignified death. While blaming Helmreichen for his incompetence,

---

[57] See Ch. 11 for the origins of this enmity.   [58] *MBA* 948/3–38 (not in *Letters*).
[59] F. Martin, 'Die Salzburger Chronik des Felix Adauktus Haslberger', pt. 3, *MGSL* 69 (1929), 100.

Zeil had not complained of this on his own account, but had used the accusation to do what he still could for his servants, who would soon be unemployed. He had made peace with his enemy Colloredo. And he had prepared himself to meet God. In all this can be seen the process of dying as a learnt experience; it was necessary to die well.[60] Leopold's letters at the height of his worries about Wolfgang in 1778 and 1779 had stressed the fact that he wanted to use his last years to prepare peacefully for death, rather than to spend them worrying about leaving debts and an unsettled son. Now in 1786, with the death of a man his own age, he seems to have been brought very close to his own mortality.

On 1–2 September, just a few days before he started to plan in earnest the visit from the Marchands and the Berchtolds, Leopold reported to Nannerl that he had been suffering all week with bad pains in his chest. He consulted the doctor (not Helmreichen but Barisani!), who prescribed medicine which brought some improvement,[61] and did not mention his chest again to Nannerl before she visited in the second half of September. But from this time on he was to complain increasingly about his health; and as it declined, so he was to become more melancholy and pessimistic about all the less than perfect situations he knew he would leave behind him.

[60] There is much detail on preparing for death in McManners, *Death and the Enlightenment*, esp. ch. 7.

[61] *MBA* 982/99–102 (not in *Letters*).

❧ 30 ❧

Towards Death: Leopold's Declining Months

❧❧

WHILE Nannerl and Berchtold had been in Salzburg at Michaelmas 1786 for young Nannerl's confirmation and to see the Marchands, it had been decided that Wolfgang Berchtold should go to school in town. It was Leopold who was left to make all the arrangements once the Berchtolds had returned home just before 12 October; the correspondence suggests that Berchtold was disinclined to spend time or money on his son's education, and that the initiative had come from Leopold and Nannerl.[1] On 12 October Leopold wrote to tell them about a possible school. It was run by a man called Abele, whose sister organized the boarding side of the establishment. Only four boys were taken as boarders, and there was currently one vacancy. Leopold was impressed by the cleanliness of the place, and described the large room shared by the boys, who each had a bed and a desk, and who said prayers several times a day at an altar in Abele's own interconnecting room. Each boy paid 2 fl. 15 kr. weekly for boarding and 6 kr. weekly for the actual education; if a special instructor were needed for remedial work, a fee of 1 fl. 30 kr. per month was paid directly to him. A laundry service could be provided as an extra, or the clothes could be sent home and returned by the carrier. The boys attending the school were from respectable families, and included the sons of other Pfleger. It seems to have been generally accepted that young Wolfgang was academically poor for his age, but Leopold reassured the Berchtolds that Abele was confident he would make progress.[2]

Leopold's figures show that the education itself was very cheap, but that the boarding was expensive. If the school were open every week of the year,[3] the fees for education alone would only be 23 fl. 12 kr. annually even if the extra instructor were needed, whereas the sum for boarding (excluding washing) would come to 117 fl. annually. If Leopold had

---

[1] See p. 539 below.   [2] *MBA* 990/14–61 (not in *Letters*).
[3] In fact, there tended to be a long vacation in the autumn, occupying part of September and all of October, as several entries in the Family Chronicle show (Brno, MZA, Berchtold Family Archive).

offered to allow Wolfgang to live with him, he could have saved Berchtold a good deal of money, but this idea was apparently not discussed. Perhaps Leopold could not afford to make the offer, but it is also possible that he thought that Berchtold should be made to take full responsibility for his son's education. Whatever may have been the thoughts of both men, Berchtold agreed to the arrangement, and it was decided that he would himself bring Wolfgang into Salzburg around All Saints' Day (1 November) for the beginning of the new school session.[4] Nannerl did not accompany them to Salzburg, but Leopold was hoping to visit her in St Gilgen once Colloredo had departed on a trip he was intending to make to Vienna. Leopold's hope was not to be fulfilled, however, and he never saw St Gilgen again.

The state of the court music was still extremely unsatisfactory, and the orchestra lurched from one crisis to the next. The violinist Brunetti was taken ill in October 1786 and could no longer play at court. Leopold thought he would not recover, and he was proved right. Meanwhile the new violinist Latouche, who had only arrived at Easter six months previously, had made an excuse to Colloredo about his health and departed for Italy, leaving 'something' (a pregnant girl) behind him.[5] Moreover the Italian oboist Pietro de Simoni had run up debts of 1,000 fl., and had asked Colloredo for travel leave so that he could earn money to repay them. Colloredo's response was negative, and his counter-suggestion (presumably designed to prevent de Simoni's flight from his creditors) was that de Simoni should be locked up in the fortress, should be accompanied by soldiers to each session of the court music, and should repay his debts from the 6 kr. daily that Colloredo would allow him during this arrangement. What with all this and a quarrel between the castrato Ceccarelli and the tenor Tomaselli, Leopold claimed ironically that the Italians were doing honour to Colloredo's protection, but that Colloredo at least could not complain of boredom.[6] The archbishop had to take with him to Vienna on 3 November a shopping list of musicians to engage.

Colloredo was absent until 21 December, so there were some seven weeks in which Leopold could have been in St Gilgen. But it was not so straightforward. In the first place, he was not well when Colloredo went. On 18 October he had been bled, had seen that the blood was unhealthy, and had sent it to Barisani for a diagnosis. Barisani had reported that the blood was 'full of heat', and had recommended that more

---

[4] Leopold to Nannerl, 20 Oct. 1786—*MBA* 992/67–70 (not in *Letters*).
[5] Leopold to Nannerl, 20 Oct. 1786—*MBA* 992/22–30 (not in *Letters*).
[6] Leopold to Nannerl, 27 Oct. 1786—*MBA* 994/22–44 (not in *Letters*).

be let, and a diet and medication regime be followed.[7] Leopold told Nannerl that his chest was not troubling him, and that he was free from pain, but that he had a pounding in his ears. This worried him because he did not know whether it came from wind, his stomach, a weakness of the nerves, or 'moisture'.[8] He wanted to follow precisely the course prescribed by Barisani, which involved drinking chocolate at seven in the morning, taking a preparation of whey at eight, and a tincture made of rhubarb water and alcohol at nine. At half past four and half past five respectively the whey and rhubarb preparations had to be repeated, and again at ten and eleven in the evening. He was also required to eat meat on Fridays and Saturdays, something he preferred to avoid. Leopold obviously thought that he could follow his regime more easily in Salzburg than in Nannerl's house, and he perhaps thought too that it would be best to stay near Barisani in case there was no improvement.

By the time his name-day was approaching, in mid-November, there had not been enough improvement in his health for him to accept an invitation from Nannerl to spend some time in St Gilgen. The roads were in any case poor because of the weather, and he was still following his diet, so he spent the name-day in Salzburg brooding over his health and the request he had just received from Wolfgang to take in his two children.[9]

Wolfgang's third child, a son called Johann Thomas Leopold, had been born on 18 October, and Wolfgang had asked Leopold to look after him and the 2-year-old Carl while he and Constanze went through Germany to England during the next Carnival. Wolfgang had apparently thought of asking this favour of Leopold because he had just learnt from a mutual acquaintance that Leopold was looking after Leopoldl, a fact that Leopold had never yet mentioned to him. Obviously Wolfgang hoped that what Leopold was prepared to do for Nannerl's child he would also do for Wolfgang's two. But Leopold was quite indignant at the mere thought, and wrote to Nannerl on 17 November:

Leopoldl is well!
And I? — — also rather better, since I sh– – out my 67th year with a laxative on my birthday; and I was still extremely tempted to drive to St: Gilgen on the 15th, who knows what often cures people. I really have to divert myself so that I don't fall into melancholy. Today I had to answer a letter from your brother *which cost me a lot of writing*, so I can write very little to you, — it's late, and I want

---

[7] Leopold to Nannerl, 20 and 27 Oct. 1786—*MBA* 992/4–18 and 994/46–55 (not in *Letters*).
[8] Leopold to Nannerl, 2–3 Nov. 1786—*MBA* 995/43–9 (not in *Letters*).
[9] Leopold to Nannerl, 7, 9, and 20 Nov., and 8 Dec. 1786—*MBA* 997/19–20, 999/3–7, 1004/51–4, and 1010/10–17 (none in *Letters*).

to go to the theatre today too, since I can now go *free*, and I've only just got to the end of the Viennese letter too. You'll readily understand that I had to write a very *emphatic letter*, because he made no lesser suggestion than that I should take *his 2 children* into my care, since he would like to make a journey through Germany to England half way through Carnival etc: — but I've written in detail, and promised to send him the continuation of my letter with the next post. The good honest silhouette maker H: Miller had sung *Leopoldl*'s praises to your brother, so he found out that the child is with me, which I'd never told him: so this was how the good idea occurred to him or perhaps his wife. that would certainly not be bad, — They could travel in peace, — could die, — — could stay in England, — — then I could run after them with the children etc: as for the payment he's offering me for the children, for servants and the children etc: — Basta! my excuse is forceful and instructive, if he cares to profit from it. —[10]

Leopold wrote further on 24 November, 'you can easily imagine that I haven't told your brother the circumstances of the child's being with me: but it would take too long to explain what and how I wrote to him, and I'll have to tell you in person sometime. addio!'[11]

These are mysterious passages. What is clear is that Wolfgang had not been told about Leopoldl because Leopold could give him no satisfactory reason for having him. He evidently felt that Wolfgang must not be told the real reason. But why not? One plausible hypothesis is that there was something about Nannerl's marriage which Leopold and Nannerl did not want Wolfgang to know. It could have been merely the practical nuisances of village life, which made it difficult to bring up children well, or it could have been that Berchtold himself was thought by Leopold and Nannerl to be very inadequate as a father. But a dislike that Wolfgang should know anything of this kind suggests that the marriage had originally been presented to him as a good match, perhaps as a more prudent one than his own, and that Leopold and Nannerl would suffer from wounded pride if they now had to acknowledge its shortcomings to Wolfgang.

As for the question of why Leopold refused the care of Wolfgang's children (in fact, the new baby had died of *Stickfrais* or 'suffocating spasms' on 15 November, just before Leopold wrote to tell Nannerl of the request),[12] there seem to be some reasons between the lines in addition to the practical difficulties he mentioned; Leopold's hint about the payment Wolfgang had offered suggests either that he thought it too little and he was being taken for granted, or that he was sceptical about whether it would really be made. Since he seems to have felt habitually neglected

---

[10] *MBA* 1002/3–24 (*Letters* 542, but not quite complete).
[11] *MBA* 1005/61–4 (not in *Letters*).   [12] Deutsch, *Documents*, 280.

by Wolfgang, and since he was himself ailing and would presumably have welcomed more support and comfort from his son, Wolfgang's suggestion might well have struck him as extremely self-centred.[13]

It is also possible that Leopold believed that both his own son and Berchtold were too apt to shy away from their paternal responsibilities, and that the request from Wolfgang, coming as it did at a time when Leopold was disenchanted with Berchtold's attitude to his children, exacerbated feelings of disapproval that the young in both families were in danger of neglect from their fathers. Since Nannerl's ability to change the situation into a better one for Leopoldl would have been very limited without Leopold's help, it is likely that this consideration had prompted him to do more for Nannerl than he was prepared to do for Wolfgang; and certainly it would not have been easy to explain this to Wolfgang.

But the melancholy Leopold claimed to be striving to avoid was probably also partly caused by his assumption that Wolfgang's wish to go to England stemmed from the fact that he was not happy with his position in Vienna. Furthermore, Leopold believed that the timing of the English plan betrayed hot-headedness on the part of Wolfgang, since if he left Vienna during Carnival he would not only miss the Viennese Lenten season (normally the most lucrative period of the year), but would earn little money on the way, and would arrive in England just as the season was ending, so that he would have to live through the summer there with hardly any income. These thoughts were certainly enough to worry Leopold, who had experienced for himself all the things that could go wrong on undertakings of this kind. He appears to have done what he had told Nannerl he would do, and followed up the letter refusing to accept care of the children with another pointing out the risks of Wolfgang's plan and encouraging him to sit tight in Vienna unless he had ample sound funding for such an ambitious journey; at any rate, he reported to Nannerl on 8 December that his letter had 'calmed' Wolfgang, which suggests that Wolfgang had acknowledged the force of something Leopold had

---

[13] Rieger sees it as ironic that while Leopold had taken Leopoldl from Nannerl 'against her will', he would not look after Wolfgang's children at his request; Leopold wanted to decide whom he would bring up, and his 'satisfaction' in refusing to help Wolfgang stemmed from a desire for revenge for past offences. See Rieger, *Nannerl Mozart*, 207–8. Solomon proposes an eccentric interpretation of the evidence: Wolfgang's suggestion was not a request for practical help, but the offer of a gift to Leopold, to match Nannerl's gift to him of Leopoldl. The offer was an act of 'utter abasement' on Wolfgang's part, while Leopold perversely suspected that something was wanted of him rather than being offered him; in refusing to agree to Wolfgang's suggestion Leopold was rejecting Wolfgang's children, just as he had already rejected Constanze; his 'master plan' was to bring up Leopoldl as a Wolfgang substitute, and his 'extravagant speculations' about death and emigration show how morbid his thoughts were. See Solomon, *Mozart*, 394–8.

written to him. The refusal to take in the children, therefore, was not the result simply of pique, but merely one part of a critique of the plan as a whole. Viewed in this light, it is possible to see even in Leopold's uncooperative behaviour continuing concern for Wolfgang's welfare.[14]

By the time Leopold's health had improved slightly it was mid-December. He might have thought of going out now to St Gilgen, but he did not want to be out of town when Colloredo returned, and the foremost violinist Brunetti was close to death; Leopold expected orders to sort out the music in Brunetti's care after this event. It was also rumoured that Colloredo was bringing back with him a number of new recruits to the court music, and though Leopold expressed scepticism about the reality of these people, he needed to be in town to supervise their settling-in period if they should arrive. Finally, he had been postponing his church duties, perhaps because of his poor health, so that they were now all piling up, and he had to make sure that Heinrich carried out his properly too. He therefore told Nannerl he would not be able to come, and suggested instead that she and Berchtold come into town for the Christmas period.[15]

Thus the autumn of 1786 passed without much pleasure for Leopold after the Marchands and Berchtolds had dispersed in October. He was visiting the theatre once a week,[16] but otherwise seems to have had little to cheer him. In addition to all his usual weekly shopping commissions for Nannerl, he was now expected to check up on young Wolfgang's progress, and this appears to have given him scant satisfaction. Wolfgang had apparently settled in happily initially, and when he visited Leopold to offer name-day greetings in November had described enthusiastically the Martinmas feast they had had at school;[17] but soon afterwards Leopold was reporting back to the Berchtolds what the teacher thought of his new pupil. On 24 November, after telling a story illustrating Wolfgang's coarse manners, he wrote:

the teacher also said to me: *I realize that one has to have sympathy and patience with the feeble talent of the boy. It will be all right in the end; I think he's come too late: because it's too difficult and unfamiliar for him to get a grip on his memory and concentration, since they previously had their heads full of nothing but childish nonsense.*[18]

---

[14] MBA 1010/41–4 (not in *Letters*). See also Leopold to Nannerl, 1–2 Mar. 1787 (*MBA* 1036/22–60; *Letters* 545), which outlines the considerations Leopold claimed to have encouraged Wolfgang to take seriously in the autumn of 1786. The passage is quoted below on p. 537.

[15] Leopold to Nannerl, 8 and 22 Dec. 1786—*MBA* 1010/37–41 and 1013/4–20 and 31–3 (not in *Letters*).

[16] Leopold to Nannerl, 27 Oct. 1786—*MBA* 994/68–73 (not in *Letters*).

[17] Leopold to Nannerl, 17–18 Nov. 1786—*MBA* 1002/35–8 (not in *Letters*).

[18] *MBA* 1005/19–36 (not in *Letters*).

Though Leopold wrote as though he were quoting the words of the teacher, the reference to the other children in St Gilgen suggests that the opinion of Wolfgang was his own. Perhaps Leopold enjoyed humbling Berchtold by these plain words about his son and heir—it could have been a form of revenge for his annoyance that Berchtold's irresponsibility made things more difficult for Nannerl.

Berchtold was apparently suspicious about whether he was getting value for his money at Abele's school. On 29 November Leopold was ridiculing Berchtold's complaint that the family in St Gilgen had received a letter from Wolfgang which did not contain the formal greeting that should have been there; Berchtold seems to have thought that Abele should not have let the letter be sent uncorrected.[19] There was also trouble about Wolfgang's washing. The Berchtolds had decided that rather than pay Abele's sister extra to do it, the carrier would take it back and forth each week so that it could be done in St Gilgen. But the carrier charged by weight, and Leopold was apparently slow to realize that this would be a potential source of friction with Berchtold. Leopold arranged for a waterproof bag to be made for the washing to travel in, since the carrier travelled in all weather without adequate protection, but when the bag was finished not only was it expensive in itself, but the complaint came back from St Gilgen that it was very heavy even when empty, and that the weekly carrier's fee would be too high. On 8 December Leopold wrote mocking this charge, and launching a counter-lament to the effect that he had never imagined he would have to get caught up in the business of the washing; if the carrier's charges were dearer than the Salzburg laundry costs, it was quite simple to ask Abele's sister to wash the clothes.[20]

Colloredo returned on 21 December, bringing with him only one new musician, a bass singer, instead of the half-dozen or so that he had wanted. This did not surprise Leopold, who had seen similar situations countless times.[21] Four days later, on Christmas Day, Brunetti finally died, and Heinrich was present at his end. The Mozarts had despised Brunetti for his coarseness and poor morals, but after his marriage in 1778 to Maria Judith Lipp, Leopold's view of him seems to have become more sympathetic. He claimed that when the couple had married, Brunetti had had debts of 1,300 fl., but that by the time of his death, thanks to his wife, he only owed 400 fl.[22] As Brunetti lay with wrecked lungs all through the autumn of 1786, Leopold prayed for him to be spared for the sake of his

[19] *MBA* 1006/14–24 (not in *Letters*).   [20] *MBA* 1010/45–56 (not in *Letters*).
[21] Leopold to Nannerl, 19 Dec. 1786—*MBA* 1012/4–8 (not in *Letters*).
[22] Leopold to Nannerl, 2 Feb. 1787—*MBA* 1027/45–50 (not in *Letters*).

wife and two small children.[23] On 29 December, however, he had to report the death to Nannerl:

On Christmas Day H: Brunetti passed into eternity between 5 and 6 in the evening. The service is at 9 o'clock today in St: Peter's. Heinrich, who had never in his life seen anyone die, went there at 4 o'clock, just after Vespers, and heard that the doctor and priest had been sent for, stayed there, because Dr: Barisani said, *he won't last much longer*, and so he looked on at *everything, everything* with inquisitive attention, the way you know he does. the curiosity was soon transformed into awed reflection and mature contemplation, and so he came home quite speechless and petrified, because this treatment has more effect than 10 sermons. it was really salutary for him! and he said: *My God! so Brunetti had to be the first person I saw die.* He looked better after his death than he had in life, except that he looked thinner. He no longer had the strength to bring up the abscess matter, which he'd been coughing up in quantities all this time, presumably because his lungs were by now almost completely putrid, — so that was his end.[24]

When Leopold had earlier suggested that the Berchtolds visit him for Christmas, he believed that his invitation should seem all the more attractive to them because they were being plagued by the embarrassing Maria Franziska von Amann in St Gilgen. Since the death of her husband, Basil, and father-in-law, Franz Anton, early in 1785, things had been going from bad to worse for the Amann family; the shattered finances were still in complete chaos, because the debts could not be paid until certain pieces of property were sold. This did not happen quickly, and in fact it was to be 1792 before all the accounts were wound up. The situation was complicated by the inheritance claims of other family members on the estate of Franz Anton von Amann; the court officials were determined to plunder this estate to recover the embezzled money, but because it should have been able to provide inheritances for Franz Anton's other children and grandchildren, guardians and legal advisers had to be involved in all the negotiations. One loser was Genofeve, future wife of Berchtold's brother Franz Anton Maximilian; she and her sister Therese were granddaughters of Franz Anton von Amann, but lost virtually the whole of their inheritance from him and his wife.[25] Meanwhile Basil's widow (who according to all sources had loomed large in his

---

[23] Leopold to Nannerl, 1–2 Dec. 1786—*MBA* 1007/31–9 (not in *Letters*).

[24] *MBA* 1015/6–19 (not in *Letters*).

[25] On 3 Oct. 1789 Franz Anton Maximilian von Berchtold wrote to tell his sister-in-law Therese that the whole of Franz Anton von Amann's estate had been swallowed up by the court, but that with great difficulty a small sum had been salvaged from the estate of Franz Anton's wife; Therese and her sister Genofeve were therefore each to receive 70 fl. See Eibl, 'Zur Familiengeschichte', 16–17.

problems because of her spendthrift nature) had been awarded a pension from the court of 10 fl. per month, and had been busily contracting new debts ever since, despite the fact that a guardian had been appointed to her as well as to her children. By 1786 Colloredo was heartily sick of her, but this was still not the worst. Some time during that year she became pregnant by one Petrazani, and was apparently keeping out of the way in Strobl, presumably in an attempt to avoid the further displeasure of the court. Leopold's letters suggest that she was from time to time actually staying with the Berchtolds, and he thought that they should travel to Salzburg for Christmas to escape her, since her condition was a disgrace to their house. The Berchtolds did not come, though Nannerl felt keenly the shame of being connected to such an improper woman, and hoped continually that the matter could be hushed up.[26] In 1787 the Amanns continued to crop up as topics of conversation in Leopold's letters to Nannerl, because the five Amann children were being cared for by relations in Salzburg while their mother hid in the country. Though Leopold was sure that the court would try to prevent her remaining with the children, on account of her bad influence, she was reputedly trying to secrete some of them out to join her.[27] In 1788 the children were effectively to lose their mother for ever, because Maria Franziska saw the chance of marrying again, and eventually obtained permission to leave Salzburg with her new husband Kraus, a merchant from Trient, on condition that she never return or seek any benefit from the Salzburg court. She left all the children behind, and they were then brought up by relations under the supervision of guardians. The most devoted of these was Rochus Alterdinger; he and his wife managed magnificently for the abandoned children whose case had seemed so hopeless. They educated them for lives of service, and husbanded what few family resources remained so that each child somehow received an inheritance of sorts on coming of age.[28]

❧

[26] Leopold to Nannerl, 22 Dec. 1786—*MBA* 1013/33–49 (not in *Letters*).
[27] Leopold to Nannerl, 12 Jan. 1787—*MBA* 1020/59–72 (not in *Letters*).
[28] See Pirckmayer, 'Basil von Amann', 45–59. There is confusion over the relationship between the Alterdingers, the Zezis, and the Amanns: some sources state that Rochus Alterdinger's wife had been a Polis, a sister to Maria Franziska von Amann and Maria Margarethe von Berchtold; others state that Maria Anna Zezi, who like the Alterdingers also had the care of some of the children for a while, was such a sister. Though it is possible that both were, I have not discovered reliable information to this effect. See Fig. 2 for a diagram of the better-known Amann/Berchtold/Polis relationships.

Though Leopold's health seems to have improved slightly towards Christmas 1786, after he had been bled and followed Barisani's prescribed regimen, there were still problems. He complained that his left arm was always colder than his right since the bloodletting, and that the pain in his chest was again troublesome. Because he thought it was caused by wind, he treated it through his diet, which he disliked having to do because it involved eating meat on fast days.[29] He was also harassed by all his work. In early December 1786 he had told Nannerl that he was probably going to be asked to teach two noble ladies from the Lodron family. One was the 25-year-old Aloysia ('Louise') Lodron, whom Leopold had taught when she had been younger, who had moved from Salzburg on the death of her mother to be looked after by other relations, and who had now returned to live with her brother Hieronymus ('Momolo').[30] The other was Momolo's young bride Maria Cäcilia. Since the death in 1780 of the music-loving countess Maria Antonia Lodron, the mother of Louise and Momolo, music had dried up in the Lodron palace. The family had been broken up and the keyboard instruments dispersed. Now it seemed as though life was returning, and that Leopold was again to be involved in it.[31] So by January 1787, despite his indifferent health, his routine was extremely hectic. On 12 January he outlined his timetable for Nannerl, by way of explaining why he could not forever be going to Abele to check up on young Wolfgang, or collect his socks so that new ones the right size could be ordered. On Monday, Wednesday, and Friday he gave lessons at the Lodron palace to the two countesses at ten and eleven, then went at twelve to the Kapellhaus on the other side of the river. At two he went to Weiser's, and then on to the Hagenauer children. On Tuesday, Thursday, and Saturday he again taught the countesses at ten and eleven, and Joseph Wölfl came to him for a lesson after one, following which he went to Weiser. At the end of the afternoon he made a flying visit home to take sago before going to the theatre—the sago was supposed to build up his strength, and was typically taken only by invalids.[32] Friday was a particularly difficult day for him, because as well as all the teaching he received Nannerl's letter and always had to do shopping for her. By the time he had returned home

---

[29] Leopold to Nannerl, 29 Dec. 1786 and 4 Jan. 1787—*MBA* 1015/46–9 and 1017/38–46 (not in *Letters*).

[30] See Ch. 20 for the story of the countess's death, the breakup of the family, and the unsuccessful attempt to marry the then 19-year-old Aloysia to a 61-year-old groom.

[31] Leopold to Nannerl, 1–2 Dec. 1786—*MBA* 1007/69–74 (not in *Letters*).

[32] *MBA* 1020/4–16 (not in *Letters*).

from his lessons the shops were close to shutting because it was Ave Maria time (half past four), so there was a great rush to get the things Nannerl wanted for the carrier to take back to St Gilgen on the Saturday. If the glass-carrier brought Nannerl's letter it was even worse, because she tended to deliver it and return to St Gilgen within the hour. Leopold's letters during this period were therefore peppered with complaints that he never knew when the glass-carrier might appear, that he had to race back from his teaching to catch the shops before they shut, and that there was simply not enough time to buy the goods Nannerl wanted.[33]

Despite his poor health and new teaching commitments Leopold was keen to go to Munich with Heinrich for part of Carnival if possible, and though he accepted that Barisani must have the last word about whether his health would stand up to the strain of a winter journey, the main problem was as always obtaining permission from Colloredo. On 29 December, after announcing Brunetti's death, Leopold expressed doubt about whether Heinrich could be spared, because the shortage of good violinists was so severe.[34] By 12 January there was talk of engaging the violinist Antonio Strinasacchi, the brother of Regina Strinasacchi. He had arrived in Salzburg and played to Colloredo, and though Leopold listed his faults and claimed that he was nowhere near as good as his sister, he expected him to be taken on because at 23 he was young enough to improve. Leopold was also still trying to get a court post for his pupil Breymann.[35] Strinasacchi was engaged on a temporary contract, and the next question was whether he would be placed above or below Heinrich. On 26 January Leopold was able to report that Heinrich was above Strinasacchi, but that Colloredo was still hunting for someone to replace Brunetti (who had been superior to Heinrich).[36] On 2 February Leopold told Nannerl that Colloredo had refused permission for them to go, because Strinasacchi lacked the experience to stand in for Heinrich;[37] but only a week later, on 9 February, Colloredo reversed his decision and allowed them leave after all. The news was given to Leopold by another new candidate for a post as violinist, Joseph Vanschenz, and Leopold decided to travel with Heinrich on the following day.[38] He was not completely easy about his health, but hoped that if he travelled in a glazed coach with hay, felt shoes, footsacks, plenty of clothes, and a fur, everything would be all right.[39]

[33] Leopold to Nannerl, 20 Nov. and 14–16 Dec. 1786, and 18 Jan., 5 Feb., and 13 Mar. 1787—*MBA* 1004/4–7 and 42–4, 1011/90–3, 1023/6–15, 1028/4–7, and 1040/5–7 (none in *Letters*).
[34] *MBA* 1015/37–40 (not in *Letters*).   [35] *MBA* 1020/39–47 (not in *Letters*).
[36] *MBA* 1026/11–15 (not in *Letters*).   [37] *MBA* 1027/4–23 (not in *Letters*).
[38] *MBA* 1032/4–13 (not in *Letters*).
[39] Leopold to Nannerl, 26 Jan. 1787—*MBA* 1026/24–31 (not in *Letters*).

Leopold's sudden departure took Colloredo by surprise, since he had not expected Leopold to leave before Sunday 11 February. On Saturday the 10th therefore, when Leopold and Heinrich were in the coach, Colloredo sent to Leopold to tell him to bring Vanschenz to play at the evening court concert. Leopold probably received news of this demand in Munich, and decided that he must not risk incurring Colloredo's further displeasure by overstaying his leave.[40] He therefore limited their stay in Munich to less than a fortnight. While he was away d'Ippold again looked in daily to check up on Leopoldl. He was very attached to the baby, who was by now displaying all the mischievousness of a toddler, and was trying to talk. Leopold's letters to Nannerl since October had described him playing with his toy horses and skittles, pretending to read books aloud and to sing from music, 'praying' when he heard the bell for Ave Maria in the afternoon, kissing the hands of visitors, and having his hand guided to write a greeting for d'Ippold on his name-day. He was developing a will of his own, and had to be cajoled into doing what Leopold wanted— Leopold's stratagem for persuading him to go to bed was to pretend to climb into Leopoldl's bed, whereupon Leopoldl would gleefully try to push him away and get in himself. To Leopold's surprise he was dry at night, and was also able to indicate by day when he wanted to urinate. D'Ippold called frequently to play with him, and Nanndl occasionally took Leopoldl to return the visits, so the two were thoroughly used to each other.[41] This was presumably a comfort to Nannerl, who must have seen d'Ippold together with Leopoldl while she had been in town for the Marchands' visit and young Nannerl's confirmation.

Though Leopold survived the arduous journeys to and from Munich quite well, it is clear from his letters to Nannerl that he felt the decline in his health. On 13 February he wrote to her from Munich, 'I'm no worse for this journey, rather I hope that the change of air and the movement will be better for me; because on the whole the end of my 67th year and the beginning of my 68th have brought about a big reversal and change in my old body: quite naturally! old people won't be young again! — — —'[42] Despite Leopold's hopes, he was able to do far less in Munich than he had in previous years. He saw Gretl sing twice in the opera *Castore e Polluce* by Vogler, and he went twice to German performances

---

[40] Leopold to Nannerl, 24 Feb. 1787—*MBA* 1034/5–13 (not in *Letters*).

[41] Leopold's letters to Nannerl between 20 Oct. 1786 and 9 Feb. 1787—*MBA* 992/64–5, 1004/70, 1010/5–9, 1011/3–4 and 37–9, 1017/75–81, 1020/77–82, 1026/4–10 and 89–91, and 1032/36–45 (none in *Letters*).

[42] *MBA* 1033/7–11 (not in *Letters*).

in the theatre—Paisiello's *Il barbiere di Siviglia* in a German translation, and the play *Der politische Kanngiesser* by Detharding. Otherwise he hardly went out—he attended no balls nor even a masked academy. He met all his old Munich friends (who again had hoped to see Nannerl there), but they probably visited him at Marchand's; certainly he mentioned that their old friend Bullinger was visiting him daily. He did not mention any domestic music-making.[43]

Leopold and Heinrich arrived home in the early evening of Friday 23 February, to find a bitterly cold house, the only heated room being Leopoldl's. Tresel should have been expecting them, but she was evidently not good at taking the initiative, and had not bothered to light any other stoves.[44] This cheerless welcome was mitigated slightly by a letter from Nannerl, who expressed concern about his health and asked for more details. On 24 February he wrote:

You're always wanting me to write to you about my *perfect* health. You don't realize the difference between an old man and a young one. I haven't got time to write much, suffice it to say that there can no longer be any question of *perfect* health in an old man, since there's always something wrong and an old man declines as a young one thrives. in short, you've got to patch yourself up as long as you can. At the moment I can reasonably place hope in the better warmer weather which is gradually approaching. for the rest, you're quite obviously going to find me very thin, which however doesn't make any difference to the main state of affairs. Now addio! don't worry! I kiss you all heartily, greet the children, and remain your old honest father Mozart.
Leopold is charming!
I found him fresh and well, and as there was no light in the room when I arrived, he clutched my face all over, because he recognized my voice.[45]

Three days after his return, on the evening of Monday, 26 February, Leopold received a note telling him that English friends of Wolfgang's were in Salzburg. Wolfgang had been in Prague for about a month in January and February, to see *The Marriage of Figaro* and give concerts. Leopold had known about the trip, but had had no news from Wolfgang about how it had gone, or when he had returned. In fact Wolfgang had arrived back in Vienna at around the time Leopold was arriving in Munich, in mid-February. Wolfgang's friend Nancy Storace then gave her last Viennese concert on 23 February, and subsequently packed up for

---

[43] Leopold to Nannerl, 13 and 24 Feb. 1787—*MBA* 1033/12–22 and 1034/18–31 (not in *Letters*).
[44] Leopold to Nannerl, 24 Feb. 1787—*MBA* 1034/3–13 (not in *Letters*).
[45] *MBA* 1034/32–45 (not in *Letters*).

her return to England.[46] The journey took her through Salzburg, and her travelling companions were her mother, her brother Stephen, the tenor Michael Kelly, Wolfgang's pupil Thomas Attwood, and an unknown man whom Leopold described as probable *cicisbeo* either of the mother or the daughter. Wolfgang had left a letter at Attwood's lodgings in Vienna for the party to deliver to Leopold in Salzburg, but old Mrs Storace, who had taken receipt of it, had mislaid it. Leopold therefore had to write to Wolfgang to ask for the news again. He 'galloped' round Salzburg on Tuesday, 27 February showing them the sights, and gave them lunch. Nancy Storace sang at court the same evening, and then they left at midnight in two coaches with eight horses, an outrider to go on ahead to order the next change of horses, and mountains of luggage. They brought Leopold news of Wolfgang which clarified Wolfgang's English plans:

With regard to your brother, I've discovered that he's back in Vienna, because I'd had no answer since I wrote to him in Prague; that he earned 1000 fl. in Prague (according to them); that his latest boy Leopoldl has died; and that, as I told you, he wants to go to England, only his pupil is supposed to be arranging something definite for him in London in advance, that is a contract to write an opera, or a subscription concert etcetc: Mdme. Storace and the whole company will also have made his mouth water about this, and these people and his pupil will also have prompted his initial idea of going with them to England. But after I wrote paternally to him that he'd earn nothing on the journey in summer, would also arrive in England at the wrong time, — that he would have to have *at least 2000 fl.* in his purse to undertake this journey, and finally that he would have to be prepared to suffer certain want at least in the beginning, however clever he was, unless he'd already got some definite engagement in London; — he'll have lost heart, because obviously the singer's brother will write an opera for this season.[47]

On 28 February, the first Wednesday after Leopold's return, Salzburg's first Lenten subscription concert took place, the new violinist Vanschenz playing a violin concerto but failing to impress Leopold.[48] As in 1786 there were to be five such events on successive Wednesdays. Then Leopold had itched to show off Heinrich's talents; now he seems to have been too weary to make quite the same effort. In the first place his health was less robust, and secondly he became seriously displeased with Heinrich soon after his return. Vanschenz had been engaged by Colloredo, and had been placed above Heinrich, who still had a year of his temporary

[46] Deutsch, *Documents*, 284–5.
[47] Leopold to Nannerl, 1–2 Mar. 1787—*MBA* 1036/22–60 (*Letters* 545).
[48] Leopold to Nannerl, 1–2 Mar. 1787—*MBA* 1036/6–13 (not in *Letters*).

contract (which was probation without any guarantee of future work) to serve. Nannerl had expected Heinrich to be disappointed about his position relative to Vanschenz, because he had been filling the breach admirably for a year, while Latouche had proved no use and Brunetti had sickened and died; but Leopold told her that the boy was actually quite pleased. This was apparently because he did not want to be too indispensable in Salzburg—he wanted to feel free to leave when his contract expired. Leopold was disgusted with his attitude, despite the fact that his own opinion of Salzburg employment was so low. After contrasting Heinrich's puerility and 'indescribable idleness' with Gretl's infinitely more mature behaviour, and expressing pity for the Marchand parents, who had been so proud to see their young son doing well in his first post, Leopold told Nannerl that all he could do about Heinrich was to report the situation to his parents; his health was too frail to take issue vigorously with Heinrich himself.[49]

In the second subscription concert, on 7 March, Leopold's pupil Breymann played a violin concerto by Giarnovichi. Breymann was still hoping to get a court appointment, and Leopold was keen for Colloredo to hear him. Leopold, despite his failing health, gave Breymann extra tuition so that he would appear to advantage, and was pleased with his playing and reception.[50] At the third concert, on 14 March (which was also Election Day), a *Singspiel* by Michael Haydn was given, and the venue was therefore changed from the Town Hall to the theatre opposite Leopold's house. The work was Michael Haydn's *Andromeda e Perseo*, which Leopold criticized for its lack of dramatic effectiveness. Heinrich was to play a violin concerto at the fourth concert, and Strinasacchi one at the fifth, when Heinrich would play a keyboard concerto, but Leopold did not write news of these last two concerts to Nannerl.[51] Probably he did not even attend them, because there was apparently a sudden and marked deterioration in his health just after 16 March, and Nannerl came into town to look after him. There was thus a gap in the correspondence of eight weeks, which suggests that he must have been very ill. Perhaps it was because of the deterioration in his health that there was virtually no mention in the correspondence after October 1786 of domestic music-making by Leopold or Nannerl, or of nagging Wolfgang to send more keyboard music. Until the visit of the Marchands at Michaelmas 1786 Nannerl

[49] Leopold to Nannerl, 9–11 Mar. 1787—*MBA* 1038/6–26 (not in *Letters*).

[50] *MBA* 1038/33–47 (not in *Letters*).

[51] Leopold to Nannerl, 9–11, 13, and 16 Mar. 1787—*MBA* 1038/124–7, 1040/18–29, and 1041/41–4 (none in *Letters*).

seems to have had plenty to occupy her with the Concertos, K. 466 and 467, but Wolfgang had long since written the later ones, K. 482, 488, 491, and 503, and there is no indication either of his sending them to Salzburg or of Leopold and Nannerl asking for them. Both liked to receive music from him for their name-days, but there is no record that they did so in 1786.

Not only had the supervision of Heinrich begun to be too much for Leopold, but also his dealings with young Wolfgang Berchtold. In the New Year, before Leopold's Munich trip, young Wolfgang had visited him and expressed his gratitude to Nannerl for arranging his schooling. Leopold had been pleased by this acknowledgement of how much better off he was at Abele's than he had been in St Gilgen, and had chaffed the boy about the discipline at school.[52] But when Wolfgang visited him again after his return from Munich, Leopold was less pleased. He had heard that Wolfgang was in trouble at school for having opened a parcel from St Gilgen containing money and a letter to the instructor (this was probably Abele's assistant, who gave remedial instruction), and that he had been boasting that he had thoroughly harassed his 'second mother', and spun lie after lie for her. Leopold wanted to get to the bottom of both sets of allegations, but could not face the prospect of climbing three steep flights of stairs to see Abele.[53] A week later, however, on 16 March, Leopold reported that Berchtold's brother Franz Anton Maximilian had also had complaints from Abele: 'The brother from Deissendorf was with Wolfgangerl, — he told me that among other things the teacher had said to him that he'd once asked Wolfgang if he hadn't been punished at home for his lies and naughtiness? — his answer was: *Papa always put the blame on the servants and on Mamma, and told them off.*'[54] Leopold did not follow up this account with a sermon, however, as he formerly might have done—he seems no longer to have felt up to the business of exhorting anyone to greater efforts towards moral behaviour—but contented himself with noting in this way Berchtold's faults as a husband and father.

Little is known of what passed while Nannerl was in Salzburg looking after Leopold from the middle of March, but Wolfgang was apparently not notified immediately about the state of affairs. On 4 April he was writing a chatty letter to Leopold from Vienna to give him some of the news that had been contained in the letter lost by old Mrs Storace. Half-way

---

[52] Leopold to Nannerl, 4 Jan. 1787—*MBA* 1017/59–69 (not in *Letters*).
[53] Leopold to Nannerl, 9–11 Mar. 1787—*MBA* 1038/113–23 (not in *Letters*). The 'second mother' was, strictly speaking, Nannerl's predecessor Jeanette.
[54] *MBA* 1041/78–82 (not in *Letters*).

through, he broke off his amusing description of the oboe playing of Johann Fischer to express concern about Leopold's health, about which he had just been informed (perhaps in a letter from Nannerl). He comforted Leopold with reflections on death as a friend, as the final purpose of man's life, and as the key to true bliss, and stated that he never lay down at night without reflecting that he might die before the morning. Nevertheless, he hoped for Leopold's recovery and begged him to let him know if this did not occur, so that he could go to Salzburg to be with his father.[55]

It would probably have been very difficult for Wolfgang to visit Leopold, and it is likely that this was the reason why he did not simply leave for Salzburg on receipt of the news. For one thing he was almost certainly short of money, and may not have been able to afford the journey; later the same month he was to move to new lodgings in the Landstrasse suburb, probably for reasons of economy.[56] He would have earned no money if he had gone to Salzburg, and a break from work was a luxury he could not afford without a salary. Furthermore he had brought back from Prague the commission for *Don Giovanni*, which he was composing for performance there later the same year. He was thus as usual extremely busy. These circumstances made it understandable that he should prefer to wait to see if there was any improvement in Leopold's condition. Nevertheless the situation could be seen as poignant vindication of Leopold's long-held belief that the security of a salary coupled with sensible management of money was essential to the living of a responsible life, for since leaving Salzburg service in 1781 Wolfgang had been able to do virtually nothing for his father and sister, despite all his loving words.

At some time before 10 May Nannerl returned to St Gilgen, though Leopold was still quite ill. She had apparently been away almost two months, and although still anxious about her father, presumably hoped that he could manage without her for the time being. On 10–11 May he wrote the last surviving letter to her, and it reveals further family worries. Young Wolfgang Berchtold was now also ill at school, and had been visited by the doctor. The only symptoms Leopold mentioned were that he was much wasted, and had 'another' swelling on his hand, which he could not flex. He was declared constitutionally unhealthy, and the doctor's advice was that he should return to the fresh air of St Gilgen

---

[55] *MBA* 1044 (*Letters* 546).

[56] Deutsch, *Documents*, 291. And see Ch. 31 for further contributory evidence to the suggestion that Wolfgang had financial problems in 1787.

and abandon his studies for the rest of the year. Leopold explained to the doctor the difficulty of the unsuitable company out there, but was unable to form an opinion on what should be done about him, and gave up the problem as one he had not the strength to tackle. During this period Heinrich visited Wolfgang for Leopold. As for Leopold's own illness, he had swollen feet and a pulsation under his stomach. One element in his treatment was the application of a plaster, and he was still waiting to see how effective this would be. He claimed he had open bowels and a reasonable appetite, hoped for some improvement with the warmer weather, expressed pleasure that Nannerl could rest now that she was not 'plagued' by him all day long, and told her not to worry about him. But he was obviously very unwell, and had not even the strength to count some money brought to him by an acquaintance for onward transmission to Berchtold. A different servant, Lisel, had been assigned to Leopoldl so that Nanndl could look after Leopold; and d'Ippold was visiting him daily. Leopold was also slightly concerned about money, because his medicines and doctors' bills were costing so much and he had no con-venient way of paying Mitzerl the half-year's rent he owed her of 45 fl. Berchtold had offered to lend him some money until Leopold could get access to his own funds, and Leopold gratefully accepted. Right at the end of the letter, just before he signed off, he mentioned Wolfgang's change of address: 'Your brother is now living in the Landstrasse *No. 224*. But he doesn't give me any reason for it. none at all! unfortunately I can guess it.'[57]

At some point in the spring of 1787 Leopold asked Heinrich to write home to tell his father that Leopold hardly expected to survive the sum-mer. Leopold presumably wanted to warn Marchand that other arrange-ments for Heinrich might have to be made, but Marchand's concern was of course first with Leopold himself. On 29 May he wrote a sympathetic letter in which he revealed that Leopold's previous letters to him had suggested that Leopold was being treated for blockage of the spleen. Marchand therefore sent a cure for this condition which he claimed had worked wonders for two other people of his acquaintance earlier in the year. Marchand seems to have offered this to Leopold because all Leopold's letters until his most recent message through Heinrich had spoken of his hope of recovery, and Marchand was not therefore suf-ficiently prepared for the possibility of death. It seems, however, that Leopold's attitude had changed, and that at some point after 11 May he

---

[57] *MBA* 1048 (not in *Letters*, though p. 908 n. 5 conveys the news of Wolfgang's move).

had started to put his affairs in order and prepare himself to leave the world. Marchand's letter also mentioned Bullinger, who was apparently in Salzburg and visiting Leopold. It had been Bullinger who had tried to console him after the death of Maria Anna; evidently he was involved at Leopold's too.[58]

The end came at six in the morning on Whit Monday, 28 May, the day before Marchand wrote his letter. Though Leopold had been ill for a long time,[59] the death itself was so sudden that Nannerl was apparently not with him, and he may not even have been able to receive the sacraments. Both circumstances must surely have added immensely to Nannerl's grief.[60] It is not known how well Wolfgang was kept informed of the situation during April and May, but he was afterwards to claim that he had not been expecting his father to die.[61]

On the day of Leopold's death the old family friend Kajetan Hagenauer, who had become a monk at St Peter's while the Mozarts had been on their grand European tour from 1763 to 1766, had taken the name Pater Dominikus, and had been warmly supported by Leopold in 1786 in his successful candidacy to become abbot of that institution, wrote an appraisal of Leopold in his diary. He mentioned Leopold's wit, wisdom, and manifold talents, which would have fitted him for careers other than music, and claimed that he had always been persecuted in Salzburg.[62]

Leopold's death was recorded as follows in the Berchtold Family Chronicle:

On the *28th May 1787* in *Salzburg* death tore from him his above-mentioned father-in-law *Leopold Mozart*, who died suddenly at *6 o'clock* in the morning in the *68th year of his life* of hardenings in the lower abdomen, and in the end of a stroke, leaving a fortune of almost 3000 fl. in Convention coins, imperial currency. He was famous as a talented musician, especially on the violin, also as a composer, and the author of the widely esteemed Violinschule, held the *Bavarian*

---

[58] *MBA* 1052 (not in *Letters*).

[59] Marchand had mentioned *MilzVerstoppung* ('blockage of the spleen'); the *Salzburger Intelligenzblatt* of 2 June 1787 gave a diagnosis of *Auszehr* ('consumption')—cf. Deutsch, *Documents*, 293; and the Family Chronicle stated that he had suffered from *Erhärtungen im Unterleib* ('hardenings in the lower abdomen'), followed by a stroke—cf. Brno, MZA, Berchtold Family Archive, Family Chronicle, unpaginated, but pp. 42–3 on my count.

[60] Ibid. 42–3 on my count. The entry on Leopold's death (Plate 17, transcription below, and n. 63) is made from the point of view of Berchtold, in a section devoted to his biography, and it does not explicitly indicate what Nannerl's involvement was. However, it seems to suggest that Berchtold *and* Nannerl missed the burial on 29 May, but travelled in from St Gilgen for the service on the 31st. If this is so, Nannerl cannot have been present at the end.

[61] See Ch. 31, p. 547. [62] Deutsch, *Documents*, 293.

Order for learned men and artists, and had the happiness of being the father of that most immortal *Wolfgang, Amadeus Mozart*. At his burial, which took place after the hour of prayer in the evening of *the 29th* of the same month, and on which occasion *Mozart's* exanimate body was committed to earth in an ordinary grave of *St: Sebastian's* churchyard, Herr *Johann Baptist the elder* was not present, but he did travel from *St: Gilgen* to *Salzburg* with his wife, the actual daughter of the deceased, for the service for his soul, which was solemnly celebrated at 9 o'clock in the morning on *the 31st May* of the above-mentioned year in *St: Sebastian's Church.*

After noon on the same day he was also present at the publication of the will of the afore-mentioned *Mozart* in the then *Salzburg* princely-archiepiscopal Hofrat chancellery, and on the following day, *the 1st June*, at the requisite inventory, at which Herr *Johann Hofer*, then *Salzburg* princely-archiepiscopal secretary to the Hofrat, was present as appointed commissioner, and Herr *Johan Michael Ludwig*, at that time *Salzburg* princely-archiepiscopal Hofrat chancellery associate, was present as actuary.[63]

Leopold was dead, but life went on for Nannerl. She had to deal with the authorities, see that Wolfgang was informed, come to an agreement with him about the inheritance, organize the sale of the household effects once the official procedures had been completed, and take charge of Leopoldl. At the same time the household in St Gilgen still had to be run, and young Wolfgang's health was worsening alarmingly. In all these tasks Nannerl must have had plenty of help from her husband and friends, one of whom was certainly d'Ippold. As the Family Chronicle entry

[63] See Plate 17: '*den 28sten May 1787* entrieß ihm der Tod zu *Salzburg* seinen obbesagten Schwiegervater, *Leopold Mozart*, welcher am obigen Tage, Morgens um *6 Uhr*, an Erhärtungen im Unterleib, und zuletzt am Schlag mit Hinterlassung eines Vermögens von beinahe 3000f in Conventions-Münze, Reichs-Währung, unversehens in seinem *68sten Lebens-Jahre* starb. Er war als ein geschickter Musickus, besonders auf der Violine bekannt, auch Compositeur, und Herausgeber der allgemein geschätzten Violinschule, hatte von *Baiern* den, für Gelehrte und Künstler bestimten Orden, und hatte das Glück, Vater jenes so unsterblichen *Wolfgang, Amadeus Mozart* zu seyn. Bey dessen Begräbnis, welche den *29sten* des selben Monats Abends nach der Gebethstunde erfolgte, und zu welcher Zeit *Mozarts* entseelter Leichnam in den Comungruft des *St: Sebastians*-Freydhofes zu Erde gesenkt wurde, war Herr *Johann Baptist, der Aeltere*, nicht zugegen, wohl aber reißte er mit seiner Gattin, des verbleichenen leibliche Tochter, von *St: Gilgen* nach *Salzburg*, zu dessen Seelen-Gottes-Dienst, der *den 31sten Mai* obigen Jahres in der *St: Sebastians Kirche* vor Mittag um *9 Uhr* feyerlichst abgehalten wurde. *Am selben Tage nach Mittag* wohnte er auch der Publication des Testaments des besagten *Mozarts* auf der damaligen fürsterzbischöflich *Salzburgischen* Hofraths-Kanzlei bei, und den darauffolgenden Tag, als *den 1sten Junius*, der diesfälligen Inventar, wozu sich Herr *Johann Hofer*, damals fürsterzbischöflich-*Salzburgischer* Hofraths-Secretaire, als abgeordneter Comissair, und Herr *Johan Michael Ludwig*, zu jener Zeit fürsterzbischöflich-*Salzburgischer* Hofraths-Kanzlei-Verwandter, als Actuar einfand' (Brno, MZA, Berchtold Family Archive, Family Chronicle, unpaginated, but pp. 42–3 on my count). The German word 'unversehens' can mean both 'unexpectedly' and 'without the sacraments'; this is why it is not certain whether or not a priest was present at Leopold's death, though clearly if he died unexpectedly, it is unlikely that a priest could have been there.

shows, the burial took place at St Sebastian's in the evening of 29 May, and a larger service was held at the same church at nine in the morning on 31 May. The same afternoon, Leopold's will was read out in the court chancellery, and on 1 June two court officials started to prepare the inventory of his household goods.[64]

There is every reason to believe that Leopold's death was devastating to Nannerl.[65] Since her marriage almost three years previously she had depended on him for all kinds of practical help, from shopping to the engagement of servants, and even more for moral support in the difficulties caused by the situation in St Gilgen. He had relayed news from Salzburg, Munich, and Vienna to divert her; done his best to organize the maintainance of her fortepiano; paid for Wolfgang's music to be copied and arranged for her to receive it; collected musicians together when she had visited him so that she could play it with most of the parts; undertaken the care of Leopoldl at his own expense; tried to look after her health; and encouraged her to stand up to her husband when he was being unreasonable. Perhaps most important of all, he had shown countless times by precept and example his method of tackling problems—mature consideration and the ability to take one step at a time, trusting patiently in God. Now that she was without him, this was perhaps to prove his greatest gift to her. The letters to Nannerl after her marriage demonstrate nothing so forcefully as the absolute sincerity of his often-repeated claim that he would strive for his children to his dying day; with respect to Nannerl, the pledge had been almost literally fulfilled.

[64] Brno, MZA, Berchtold Family Archive, Family Chronicle, unpaginated, but pp. 42–3 on my count. The records of the Greater Marian Congregation in Salzburg state that the funeral took place on the day of the death (Deutsch, *Documents*, 605), but this information is contradicted by the entry in the Family Chronicle.

[65] See Ch. 31, p. 554, for suggestions that Nannerl succumbed to a prostrating illness directly after Leopold's death.

31

After the Funeral (I):
The Settlement of Leopold's Estate

⌇⌇

'ONLY death costs nothing, and not even that', Maria Anna had written to Leopold from Mannheim on 7 December 1777.[1] When someone died in Salzburg, the authorities moved promptly into action. The point of their procedures was to ensure that all outstanding debts of the deceased were settled from the estate, and death duties paid, before the family could profit from it. It follows that the deceased's possessions had to be frozen while enquiries were made about monies owed to and by the estate, any will that may have been made, the number and where-abouts of beneficiaries, and the value of the property. As soon as prac-ticable after the death (often on the next day) the will was read, and the *Sperr-Commission* (the committee which dealt with inheritances) sent offi-cials to the home of the deceased to ensure that nothing improper took place. A standard document, the *Sperr-relation*, was drawn up. It gave, in question and answer form, the kind of information mentioned above, and included a valuation of the deceased's effects based on an inventory which was made immediately. This inventory could show which items were destined to go to beneficiaries named in the will.[2] After the *Sperr-relation*, the most urgent task, had been completed, there might be a delay while all the claims on the estate were processed. The debts and taxes were paid, and the remaining fortune divided among the beneficiaries according to the will and any other relevant deeds. If it had been agreed that an auction of the effects would take place, a further document, the *Licitations-Protocoll*, was produced. This was an inventory of the goods to be auctioned, and a record of what they fetched. Thus two different

---

[1] *MBA* 386/57 (*Letters* 256a).

[2] For example, the *Sperr-relation* drawn up after Nannerl's death showed that some items on the inventory were designated for her maid Franziska Dietl, to accord with the instructions left in her will. See R. Angermüller, 'Testament, Kodizill, Nachtrag und Sperrelation der Freifrau Maria Anna von Berchtold zu Sonnenburg, geb. Mozart (1751–1829)', *MJb* (1986), 97–132, esp. pp. 119 and 123.

inventories might be produced—the first showing everything owned by the deceased, and a later one showing only items to be sold at auction.

Leopold Mozart's estate is not well understood, because the documentation is incomplete. The will, the *Sperr-relation*, and some of the correspondence between Wolfgang and Nannerl is missing, and although the *Licitations-Protocoll* has recently been brought to general attention, twenty of its seventy-five pages are lacking. The situation is complicated by the fact that the *Licitations-Protocoll* was for a long time thought to have been lost; a small amount of information from it was published in 1891, and this was used repeatedly to convey what was thought to be the estimated and the actual value of Leopold's estate until the *Licitations-Protocoll* again became accessible. Some of the information published in 1891 can now be shown to be misleading, but it has been so often used that a thorough reappraisal of the situation is desirable. I propose here to review the sources of information pertaining to Leopold's estate, paying particular attention to the *Licitations-Protocoll*. Large and difficult questions remain unanswered, but I do suggest a possible different evaluation of what Nannerl and Wolfgang each expected to gain and actually did gain from Leopold's estate, and of the meaning of the correspondence between them, from that which has previously been given. Since frequent reference has to be made to the documents involved, I reproduce them here, apart from the *Licitations-Protocoll*, which is too long, but which I describe.[3]

Wolfgang to Nannerl, 2 June 1787

Dearest Sister!
You can easily imagine how painful the sad news of the sudden death of our dearest father was to me, since the loss is the same for us both. — — Since I can't possibly leave Vienna at the moment (which I would do more for the pleasure of embracing you) and it would hardly be worth the trouble for the inheritance of our departed father, I must confess to you that I too am quite of your opinion with respect to a public sale; I'm just waiting for the inventory of it first, so that I can make a selection; — but if, as H. von d'Yppold writes, there's a dispositio paterna inter liberos, I'll need to know what this dispositio is first, so that I can make further arrangements; — — so I'm just waiting for an exact copy of it, and when I've looked it over briefly I'll give you my opinion straight away. — — Please pass on the enclosed letter to our true good friend H. von

---

[3] The *Licitations-Protocoll* is given in R. Angermüller, 'Leopold Mozarts Verlassenschaft', *MM* 41 (1993), 1–32.

d'Yppold; — — as he's already shown himself on so many occasions a friend of our house, I hope he'll also extend his friendship to me and represent *me* where necessary. — — Farewell, dearest sister! I remain eternally your faithful brother W. A. Mozart.

P:S: My wife asks to be remembered to you and your husband, as I do too. — —[4]

Wolfgang to Nannerl, 16 June 1787

Dearest, best of sisters!

I wasn't at all surprised that you didn't report the sad and to me completely unexpected death of our dear father yourself, since I could easily guess the reason. — May God take him unto himself! — Rest assured, my love, that if you want a good brother to love and protect you, you will certainly find one in me on every occasion. — My dearest, best of sisters! if you were still unprovided for, there would be no need for all this. I would leave everything to you with real pleasure, as I've thought and said a thousand times already; but since it's now no use to you, so to speak, but on the other hand advantageous to me, I count it my duty to think of my wife and child.[5]

Wolfgang to Nannerl, 1 August 1787

dearest, best of sisters!

At the moment I'm only writing to answer your letter — Not a lot, and that in haste, because I've simply got too much to do. — since both your husband, my dear brother-in-law (whom I ask you to kiss a thousand times for me) and I want to make an end of the whole business as soon as possible, I'm accepting his suggestion. But with the single stipulation that the 1000 florins be paid not in imperial but in Viennese currency, and moreover by exchange. — next post day I'll send your husband the draft of an agreement or rather a contract between us, and then two originals will follow, one signed by me, the other to be signed by him. — as soon as possible I'll send you new things by me for the keyboard. I beg you not to forget my *scores*. — a thousand farewells. I must close. — My wife and Carl ask to be remembered to your husband and you a thousand times, and I remain eternally your sincere loving brother W. A. Mozart.[6]

[4] *MBA* 1055 (*Letters* 547). The 'dispositio paterna inter liberos' was the will.

[5] *MBA* 1058 (*Letters* 548). The problematic nature of this letter, which is known only from Nissen's biography, is discussed on p. 555 below.

[6] *MBA* 1061 (*Letters* 549). See p. 555 below and Glossary for the significance of the specification of Viennese currency.

Court Council records of 21 August 1787

The heirs in tail of Leopold Motzart present to this exalted office, *sub dato et prae-sentato* 20 August *anni curr.* their humble petition for gracious authorization of a legally valid auction of effects during the first week of the coming Michaelmas Fair.

The auction is to be permitted in the requested term, with the proviso that no disadvantage shall thereby accrue to the *hochfürstl. Versatzamt.*[7]

Advertisement placed in the Salzburger Intelligenzblatt, 15 September 1787

Auction. It is herewith made known to all and sundry that on the 25th inst. and on the days following, from 9 to 11 in the forenoon, and also from 2 to 5 in the afternoon, at the so-called Tanzmeisterhaus, beyond the bridge, will be sold by public auction and assigned to the highest bidders, various valuables, fancy goods and silver ware, personal and other linen, men's clothing, pewter, brass, porcelain and domestic utensils, together with some books and musical instruments. Among the goods to be sold are: *Firstly* a composite microscope with all appurtenances, made by Dollond of London, still in prime condition and deficient in no particular. *Secondly* an excellent solar microscope with all appurtenances, likewise made by Dollond. *Thirdly* an achromatic *tubus* of *three* feet in length with double objective glass made by the same *Dollond* and in first-rate condition: as also *fourthly* a harpsichord by the celebrated *Friderizi* of *Gera* with two manuals of ebony and ivory throughout five whole octaves, with moreover a special cornett and lute stop. *Salzburg,* 14 September 1787. The Chancellery of His Serene Highness's Council.[8]

Court Council records of 21 September 1787

Herr Josef Ernst von Gilowsky, Princely Councillor, here resident, as representative of Wolfgang Amade Mozart in Vienna, and Herr Johann Bapt. Berchtold von Sonnenburg, Princely Councillor and Prefect of St. Gilgen, here supplicate *sub praes.* 21 *huius,* for most gracious ratification, according to its full contents, of the submitted agreement arrived at by Herr von Sonnenburg with Wolfgang Mozart, and with respect to the latter's assignment with Herr von Gilowsky, Princely Councillor, as representative, concerning one half of the paternal inheritance apportioned to him under date of the 18th inst, which agreement is to the effect that Mozart is to resign to his brother-in-law Herr von Sonnenburg the

---

[7] Deutsch, *Documents,* 296. This is the translation given, but leaving *Versatzamt* untranslated, because the translation given in Deutsch ('Princely Pledge Office') does not indicate the function of the office any better than the German term does. The *Versatzamt* was the official court pawn office.

[8] Deutsch, *Documents,* 296–7.

goods specified in the inventory as his legitimate property against payment of a purchase sum of 1,000 fl., Viennese currency, in consideration of which the purchaser promises

a) to have the purchase sum paid at once by a bill of exchange on Vienna;

b) to discharge all legal and other expenses, howsoever named and so far as they would have fallen upon the vendor; and

c) to pay the duty money on the 1,000 fl. going abroad to the Government of the Province.

Conclusum: fiat decretum to Herr von Gilowsky, Princely Councillor, as Wolfgang Mozart's representative and Herr von Sonnenburg as assignee of Wolfgang Mozart's share in the paternal heritage, that the submitted purchase contract is to be ratified by proper authority, and that Herr von Sonnenburg and his spouse shall with the assistance of a third party so formulate their guarantee that they will be and shall be fully responsible and liable in case sooner or later claims should be made on Leopold Mozart's heritage.

Concerning the minute, however, from Herr Hofer, secretary to the *Sperr-commission*, that at the making of the inventory of Mozart's goods for probate a few ducats and silver pieces amounting to some 30 fl. were found, and since Herr von Sonnenburg makes a claim thereto because he took over everything, Herr von Gilowsky, Princely Councillor, is to be informed of this, more especially because this sum of money is not included in the inventory to which this contract refers.[9]

Wolfgang to Berchtold, 29 September 1787

dearest brother in law!—

In all haste; — I'm very pleased with our fine agreement; — when you make over the exchange to me, I beg you *to address it to Hr: Michael Puchberg. in Count Walsegg's house, on the Hohe Markt*, because he has orders to take receipt of the

---

[9] Ibid. 297–8. The translation is that given in Deutsch, except for two details. First, I do not translate Hofer's title, which Deutsch renders as 'Hereditary Commissioner of Foreclosure'; since I do not elsewhere translate the terms concerning the *Sperre*, it would have been confusing to do so here. Secondly, in the final paragraph the translation of Deutsch has, '...since Herr von Sonnenburg, having taken over everything, makes a claim thereto...'; I prefer the stronger indication that Berchtold's claim was made *because* he had taken over everything—the German is '... H[err] v[on] Sonnenburg hierauf, weil er alles übernommen habe, einen Anspruch mache...'. At one point Deutsch's text differs from that given for the same document by Senn. Senn's rendering runs: '.... which agreement is to the effect that Mozart is to resign to his brother-in-law Herr von Sonnenburg that half of the paternal inheritance belonging to him as well as the goods specified in the inventory as his legitimate property...'. See W. Senn, 'Zur Erbteilung nach Leopold Mozart', *Zeitschrift des historischen Vereins für Schwaben* (also known as *NAMB*) 62/3 (1962), 383–95; here at 393. Senn's rendering is correct, as a comparison with the original shows (SLA, Hofratsprotokoll in Justiz, Civil und Jurisdictionssachen, fos. 731ᵛ–733ᵛ (21 Sept. 1787). I am grateful to Frau Christiane Gärtner for sending me a copy of this document. More details about Senn's interpretation of Leopold's estate documents are given below.

money, since I'm travelling to Prague first thing on Monday. — farewell; kiss our dear sister for us both a thousand times, and rest assured that I will always be your sincerest brother W. A. Mozart.[10]

Tax decree of the Government of the Province of Salzburg, 10 October 1787

Intimation to the Provincial Government of this place.
The Princely Councillor and Prefect of St. Gilgen, Herr Johann von Sonnen-burg, and Wolfgang Motzart in Vienna, have come to an agreement in respect of the heritage of Leopold Motzart, late Princely Vice Kapellmeister here, by the terms of which the latter has assigned to the former his share in the paternal heritage against payment of 1,000 fl., Viennese currency.

Since on the occasion of this payment the *Sperrs-Commission* has duly taken into consideration the usual export duty of 10 fl. per cent., this amount of 120 fl. shall without fail be handed over against the proper receipt.

Enacted at Salzburg in the Princely Council this 10 Oct. 1787.
Pres. 20 Oct. 1787
In re dues from Leopold Mozart's estate.
Franz Thad[dä] v. Kleinmayrn m.p. Joh. Martin Sauter m.p.
Actum St[eue]r [Tax]: Stuben, 12 Nov. 1787.
To be filed after payment of 120 fl. duty.[11]

Johann Ev. Engl's note of 1891 on the Licitations-Protocoll which subsequently disappeared

Leopold Mozart's *Licitations-Protokolle* of 23., 26., 27., and 28. September 1787 (drawn up by Joh. Nep. Hofer, secretary to the Princely Council as commissioner) — 579 items entered, valued at 999 fl. 42 kr., of which 314 items (55.5%) gave a yield of 1507 fl. 56 kr., in which Marianne and Wolfgang shared, shows a mod-erately good standard of living for the time, from several sets of valuable court clothes, hunting equipment, linen, kitchen and domestic utensils, jewellery, musical instruments, among them the 'large harpsichord' valued at 100 fl.[12]

Nannerl to Breitkopf & Härtel, 4 August 1799

I sent all my brother's scores which were still in the hands of our father straight to my brother in Vienna after the death of our father in 1787, but I regret

---

[10] *MBA* 1067 (*Letters* 549). I translate 'liebster H: Bruder' as 'dearest brother-in-law' in order to try to convey the element of formality in Wolfgang's address.

[11] Deutsch, *Documents*, 299. The translation follows Deutsch except for my non-translation of *Sperrs-Commission*.

[12] J. E. Engl, 'Fünf Ländler von W. A. Mozart', *Jahresbericht der Internationalen Stiftung Mozarteum in Salzburg* 11 (1891), note on p. 76. Engl's note is reproduced by Senn, 'Erbteilung', 395. 'Marianne' is Nannerl.

myself that I didn't hold back some of his earlier compositions, they would certainly have been well preserved with me, whereas I've discovered from a reliable source and an eye witness that with him his scores always just lay around under the keyboard, and the copyists could just take from them what they wanted, and I could believe this all the more easily, because it was well known to me that my brother tolerated his older works less and less the stronger he grew in composition, so I don't doubt that many of his earlier works will have been lost.[13]

Until recently the documents cited above were the main sources of information about Leopold's estate, and they were used in 1962 by Walter Senn to write the most thorough account to date of the aftermath of Leopold's death.[14] But since then two other important documents have resurfaced—the *Licitations-Protocoll*, and the Family Chronicle recording events in the Berchtold family. The *Licitations-Protocoll* in particular allows Senn's conclusions to be modified.[15]

The main Family Chronicle entry on Leopold's death confirms what had always been believed but for which until now there was no unequivocal testimony—that Leopold *did* leave a will.[16] The same entry is also the only known source of information about the value of Leopold's savings at the time of his death—it states that he left almost 3,000 fl. in *Conventions-Münze, Reichs-Währung* (imperial currency). The entry does not state how the sum was bequeathed, and since the will is lost, this question is one of the big unknowns.[17] But what is clear is that Leopold's estate

---

[13] *MBA* 1250/11–21 (not in *Letters*).   [14] See n. 9 above for the citation.

[15] These documents, together with others pertaining to the Berchtold family (including other branches), are in the MZA in Brno. In 1967 an inventory of the collection was compiled—see V. Bräuner and A. Hamerníková, *Inventáře a Katalogy Fondů Státního Archivu v Brně c. 24: Rodinný Archiv Berchtoldů (1202–1494–1945) Inventář* (Brno, 1967). The documents relating to Johann Baptist von Berchtold zu Sonnenburg and his family are inventoried on pp. 67–8 under the item numbers 188–200. But it was not until 1991, when one of the authors gave a presentation about the collection at the Internationaler Mozart-Kongress in Salzburg, that wider interest was aroused—see A. Hamerníková, ' "Licitations-Protocoll über die Leopold Mozartische Verlassenschaft" im Familienarchiv Berchtold', *MJb* 1991 (*Bericht über den Internationalen Mozart-Kongress 1991*), vol. i, pp. 122–5.

[16] Despite Senn's caution with regard to d'Ippold's apparent mention of Leopold's will (Wolfgang's letter to Nannerl of 2 June 1787)—caution caused by the fact that the sentence could be read as conditional, as a hypothetical suggestion of d'Ippold's—he points out that the court council document of 21 Sept. 1787 suggests that Leopold had left instructions about how the estate was to be shared. See Senn, 'Erbteilung', 385. See Ch. 30 for a summary of the main events after Leopold's death, derived from the Family Chronicle in the Brno MZA, Berchtold Family Archive.

[17] For *Conventions-Münze, Reichs-Währung*, see Glossary. For the Chronicle entry on Leopold's death, see Brno, MZA, Berchtold Family Archive, Family Chronicle, unpaginated, but pp. 42–3 on my count. The Family Chronicle contains brief biographies of various Berchtold family members, including notes about their relations. Hence information about one person is sometimes given in several different places. The largest entry about Leopold's death occurs in the section about

fell into two parts—the sum of money mentioned by the Chronicle, and his possessions in the Dancing-Master's House, some of which he had explicitly bequeathed to one child or the other. In all further discussion of the auction in this chapter, it is to be understood that unless I specifically state otherwise, references to Leopold's estate mean only that part of it made up of the possessions.

The *Licitations-Protocoll* is a list of everything offered for sale at the auction on 25, 26, 27, and 28 September, and gives, among other things, useful information about Leopold's possessions and hence his life-style. Unfortunately, however, the *Licitations-Protocoll* does not survive complete, and care has to be taken in analysing what can be learnt from it.

It is a bundle which originally consisted of seventy-five numbered pages containing information about the 579 items which were offered for sale at the Michaelmas auction. For each numbered item an *Ausrufpreis*, a selling price, the name of the buyer, and notes on payment were given. The *Ausrufpreis* was the auction starting price, and it has been claimed by Senn that this figure also served as the valuation of each item prior to the auction.[18] At the end of each page the selling price total (but not the *Ausrufpreis* total) for that page was entered. Pages 47–66 inclusive are missing, but page 67 continues with the listings, which finish on page 69. Pages 70–5 draw together the essential information in the following way—pages 70–3 list the selling-price totals (but again not the *Ausrufpreis* totals) for each page and add them together to give a grand total, and pages 73–4 list the coins produced for payment, convert them into florins, and add them up. But before this counting and addition took place, sums of money must have been paid out from the auction income to people who had a claim on the estate: pages 74–5 list eight outgoing sums, some of which were for taxes, and some in settlement of bills; and the sum of the

---

Nannerl's husband. It should be noted here that Solomon's comments about Leopold's estate are unreliable. He speculates (unaware of the evidence of the Family Chronicle) that Leopold left at least 6,000 and possibly substantially more than 10,000 fl. to Nannerl, and states that Wolfgang was disinherited. His remarks about Nannerl's finances after her husband's death are based on inadequate knowledge of the documentation (see Ch. 35, pp. 615–18, for more details), and there is (as yet) no evidence for Wolfgang's having been disinherited. On the contrary, Leopold evidently bequeathed him at the very least some specified possessions, and it seems to have been understood that brother and sister were to share equally in any gain from the sale; these facts weaken all suggestions that Nannerl was favoured above Wolfgang. Solomon appears to be relying for the assertion that Wolfgang was disinherited mainly on Senn's essay, which he seems not fully to understand—he mistranslates part of it, and places faith in Senn's suggestion (itself speculation, and framed as a question; furthermore, not convincing) that Wolfgang was not satisfied with what he had been left. See Solomon, *Mozart*, 410–13 (p. 411 for the comments derived from Senn); and Senn, 'Erbteilung', 385.

18 See ibid. 386.

coins counted and the cash paid out for these claims equals the grand total of all the selling prices.[19]

The fact that the final summarizing pages survive means that a certain amount can be deduced about the missing pages 47–66. By the end of page 46, the last surviving page before the interruption in the sequence, 391 items had been offered for sale but only 289 of them sold. The *Ausrufpreis* totals for the items sold had reached 482 fl. 59 kr., the *Ausrufpreis* totals for the items unsold had reached 558 fl. 46 kr., and the selling price totals 739 fl. 7 kr. If one then adds on to these figures the few remaining *Ausrufpreis* figures from pages 67–9, after the interruption, the total surviving *Ausrufpreis* figure for the items sold is 489 fl. 11 kr., and for the items unsold 573 fl. 13 kr.; unless the missing pages are ever recovered, the complete *Ausrufpreis* totals will never be known. But for the selling-price figures it is possible to go further, because after similarly adding on the few remaining selling-price figures from pages 67–9 (16 fl. 29 kr., giving 755 fl. 36 kr. as a total for the surviving pages), there is still the summary of the selling-price figures on pages 70–3. The sum of selling prices for the missing pages 47–66 is here shown to be 752 fl. 20 kr., and when this figure is added to the 755 fl. 36 kr. the total income from the auction is revealed as 1507 fl. 56 kr. By this stage, of course, all 579 items had been offered for sale. But there is no way of knowing how many items were actually sold. Pages 67–9 show 21 items sold (of 40 offered), which when added to the 289 sold from pages 1–46 gives a total of 310; but further items were clearly sold from the missing pages 47–66. Table 2 summarizes these data.[20]

---

[19] Yet the claims on the estate listed at the end of the *Licitations-Protocoll* were probably not the only ones, for it was common for burial expenses, alms, and the cost of Masses for the soul of the deceased to be deducted too. How these expenses were met remains unknown.

[20] There are one or two minor problems with the information in the *Licitations-Protocoll*. The addition on some pages is inaccurate; two items (87 and 102) listed with an *Ausrufpreis* were apparently sold before the auction and the selling price (though given) was not included in the auction total; and occasionally an *Ausrufpreis* is not given. However, these problems do not affect the figures to any significant extent. One point not consistently commented on by Angermüller in his rendering of the document is that the original contains occasional pencilled notes in a different hand from that of the main body of information, which is written in ink. This happens on p. 72 of the *Licitations-Protocoll*, where the marginal comment 'fehlen im Betrage v[on] 752. 20 kr. 149 Gegenstände auf 17 Seiten', although printed by Angermüller as though it were part of the original document, is written in pencil; furthermore, a pencilled bracket round items 47–63 on this page is not reproduced by Angermüller. It also happens on p. 73, where the figure of 752 fl. 20 kr. (being subtracted from the selling prices total of 1,507 fl. 56 kr.), and that of 755 fl. 36 kr. (the result of the sum), are written in pencil. And it happens on p. 75, where the words 'davon Gebühr 240 [fl.] 05 [kr.] 16%' are in pencil. These notes may represent later attempts to analyse the information in the document.

TABLE 2. Summary of the data of the *Licitations-Protocoll* (prices in florins and kreuzer)

Pages	Number of items offered	Number of items sold	Number of items unsold	*Ausrufpreis* of items sold	*Ausrufpreis* of items unsold	*Ausrufpreis* of items sold and unsold	Selling price
1–46	391	289	102	482.59	558.46	1041.45	739.07
47–66 (missing)	148 (deduced)	?	?	?	?	?	752.20
67–69	40	21	19	6.12	14.27	20.39	16.29
Totals for all pages	579	? (but more than 310)	? (but more than 121)	? (but more than 489.11)	? (but more than 573.13)	? (but more than 1062.24)	1507.56

At first sight it seems that when Engl wrote his note about the *Licitations-Protocoll* in 1891 he saw the same incomplete document that survives today; for he mentions 579 items, and says that 314 of them were sold and that the yield was 1,507 fl. 56 kr. His figure of 314 items sold corresponds more or less (the discrepancy is trivial) to the 310 items listed as sold in the pages that today survive, and he too could have taken the yield figure (which is correct to the last kreuzer) from pages 70–5, where the sale information is summarized. But there are problems here. If he had seen the document in its present state, it should have been obvious from pages 70–3 that many more than 310 (or 314, to use his figure) items had been sold. Furthermore his valuation figure for the whole sale of 999 fl. 42 kr. cannot have been derived from the *Licitations-Protocoll*. It was certainly not the *Ausrufpreis* total, for though this cannot be calculated, it is clear that it was 1,062 fl. 24 kr. for the items on pages 1–46 and 67–9 alone. It is possible that he saw the *Sperr-relation* or other documentation, but until more information comes to light there is no way of knowing where he got his valuation figure from, or what the significance of the valuation figure was and how it related to the *Ausrufpreis* figure.[21]

Turning now to the sequence of events after Leopold's death, it is clear that d'Ippold wrote to inform Wolfgang, probably because Nannerl was prostrated with grief.[22] Through him she had mentioned the possibility

---

[21] This relationship is discussed further below.

[22] Solomon takes Wolfgang's words in his letter of 16 June ('I wasn't at all surprised that you didn't report the sad and to me completely unexpected death of our dear father yourself, since I could easily guess the reason') as an expression of anger and hurt that Nannerl had not cared to

of an auction, to which Wolfgang agreed, but asked for the inventory and a copy of the will. He indicated his intention to make a selection from the inventory. What happened next is unclear. Nannerl evidently wrote herself to explain why the initial letter had come from d'Ippold rather than from her, and must have mentioned the question of the auction, but Wolfgang's reply of 16 June is enigmatic, almost certainly because it is not complete. The original of the letter is missing, and it is known only from Nissen's biography.[23] It seems highly likely that Wolfgang outlined his own wishes about the estate between his declaration that Nannerl would always find in him a protective and loving brother and his announcement that if she were still unprovided for, 'all this' would not be necessary; and that the words 'all this' referred to the wishes he had just expressed, but which Nissen probably omitted.

No further correspondence survives until Wolfgang's letter of 1 August. By this time it is clear that Berchtold had made him an offer of 1,000 fl., and the court council records of 21 September show that in return Wolfgang was to renounce his half-share in Leopold's estate to Berchtold. But Wolfgang's stipulation in this letter of Viennese currency was effectively a demand for an increase of 200 fl., since 1,000 Viennese fl. equalled 1,200 imperial ones. In addition, as the court council records for 21 September and 10 October show, Berchtold was responsible for paying the export tax of 10 per cent on this sum, and for discharging all the debts and other expenses from the estate. Wolfgang was represented not by d'Ippold (of whom he had asked this favour on 2 June) but by Johann J. A. E. von Gilowsky—it has always been assumed that d'Ippold, as a close friend of Nannerl's, declined to act in a way that set him legally against her. Gilowsky was the same cousin of Nannerl's friend Katherl who had been involved in the official procedures following the death of Basil von Amann in 1785—it had been he who had asked Leopold for the use of the Dancing-Master's House for an auction of Basil's effects while Leopold had been in Vienna visiting Wolfgang.[24]

inform him herself, and states that she was asking him through a third person to waive his claim to the proceeds of the sale. See Solomon, *Mozart*, 412. Though the words could theoretically bear an interpretation that Wolfgang was angry, the context in the correspondence as a whole suggests rather that he was expressing sympathetic understanding of circumstances beyond her control which had prevented her writing in person. Furthermore, there is no evidence that Nannerl was asking Wolfgang to waive his claim; the subject matter of this letter is mysterious.

[23] See von Nissen, *Biographie*, 525–6. Comparisons of letters whose originals are known with their renderings in Nissen's biography show that he omitted much, and rephrased frequently; see Ch. 35, pp. 624–6, for more details.

[24] See Ch. 27.

The interval of six weeks between Wolfgang's letters of 16 June and 1 August has elicited questions about what was going on during this time, and the question of why Berchtold offered to buy out Wolfgang's share has also been raised. After Wolfgang's letter of 1 August a further seven weeks elapsed before he and Berchtold reached agreement on 18 September. On 21 September the court council ratified this agreement, the auction took place at Michaelmas (when the town was full of people for the fair), and by mid-October it was all wound up. Thus, though it is clear what Wolfgang gained financially from Leopold's death, there are several unanswered questions about how and why this agreement was struck, about Nannerl's role in the matter, and about whether the negotiations affected the relationship between Wolfgang and Nannerl.

When Senn tried to explain the details of how Leopold's estate was settled, he had knowledge of all the documents mentioned above except the will, the *Licitations-Protocoll*, and the Family Chronicle.[25] He used Engl's valuation figure of 999 fl. 42 kr., and by way of answering the question why Berchtold offered Wolfgang 1,000 fl. as his share, claimed that the valuation figure corresponded to the *Ausrufpreis*, which in auctions of this period would itself have been less than half the market value. He implied, in other words, that Berchtold himself also expected to realize 1,000 fl. (or possibly more) by the arrangement. He gave no clue as to where he derived his claim about the relationship of the valuation, the *Ausrufpreis*, and the actual yield of auctions during this period. He answered the question of the long delay in applying for an auction by suggesting that Wolfgang and Nannerl were arguing about details such as the choices from the inventory, and claimed that Nannerl must have been persistent in her demands. He detected impatience in Wolfgang's letter of 1 August, and thought that Berchtold had agreed to buy out Wolfgang's share in order to prevent him from making further demands. The conclusion of his article was that the business had caused deep estrangement between brother and sister, to the extent that Nannerl subsequently gave away music by Leopold and Wolfgang to the monastery of Heilig Kreuz in Augsburg rather than offer it to Wolfgang.[26]

Even allowing for the fact that the *Licitations-Protocoll* was not available to Senn, his case is open to question. If Berchtold had been interested in realizing the same amount of cash as Wolfgang was to receive, why did he not simply wait for the sale to take place? The claims on the estate could have been settled, and the remaining profit shared equally. By the time

---

[25] Senn, 'Erbteilung'.   [26] See pp. 561–2 below.

they reached their agreement the auction was in any case almost upon them. Furthermore, Berchtold had been able to agree to Wolfgang's demand for the extra 200 fl., and knew that he would have to pay 120 fl. in export tax as well as settling other claims; so that even if Senn was right that the sale could be expected to yield twice the 999 fl. 42 kr. valuation figure, Berchtold would have been undergoing a significant risk of realizing much less than Wolfgang.

One necessary consequence of a putative desire of Berchtold's to realize as much cash as possible, and certainly at least as much as Wolfgang, would have been that everything of Leopold's would have been required to go into the sale, for the documentation shows that Wolfgang was determined to get his half of the inheritance in cash. But although it is clear from the court council records of 21 September that Wolfgang was ultimately only interested in cash, and that he even made over to Berchtold the articles that had been specified as his (presumably by Leopold's will), it is well-nigh impossible to believe that Nannerl would not have wanted to keep some articles for herself. In her own will she was to draw attention to six objects which had come down to her from a great-grandmother on the Mozart side of the family—she left them to her son Leopold for his lifetime, but specified that they should then pass to Wolfgang's children, who she hoped would value them, as she always had, because of their provenance.[27] This clause of her will is a strong indication that she attached sentimental value to family possessions, and in particular of course it strongly suggests that the items were not included in the auction of Leopold's effects. Nannerl also owned in later life a number of other possessions which had come from Leopold—among them the family portrait and Leopold's clavichord.[28] These too had surely been withheld from the auction. It is equally hard to believe that Nannerl could have kept belongings of Leopold's any way other than officially, through having their valuation taken into account by the authorities and Wolfgang's representative Gilowsky. For the official side of the settlement seems to have been conducted with scrupulous exactitude, and the court council records of 21 September show that the *Sperr-Commissarius* Hofer had even reported the late finding of loose coins amounting to about 30 fl. (to which Berchtold laid a claim), and had insisted that Gilowsky be informed of their existence.

If Senn's case is now examined from the perspective gained by the finding of the *Licitations-Protocoll*, it becomes even clearer that the docu-

---

[27] See Angermüller, 'Testament', 107.
[28] See V. and M. Novello, *A Mozart Pilgrimage*, 89–90.

mentation as a whole raises more questions than it answers. In particular, his claim that the valuation corresponded to the *Ausrufpreis*, and that this represented rather less than half what the sale could be expected to realize, is not borne out by the evidence of the *Licitations-Protocoll*. Not only does the valuation figure noted by Engl bear no relation to the *Ausrufpreis* total of the *Licitations-Protocoll*, but in addition the *Ausrufpreis* totals for the surviving pages show a vastly different relationship to the selling-price totals from that suggested by Senn. The evidence of pages 1–46, for example, for which both *Ausrufpreis* and selling-price figures survive, shows that the *Ausrufpreis* total of all the items offered for sale was 1,041 fl. 45 kr., and the selling price 739 fl. 7 kr. One hundred and two of the items had failed to sell, of course; nevertheless, Senn's claim that the *Ausrufpreis* represented slightly less than half the selling price was made to imply that Berchtold, before the sale and hence before anyone could have known how many items would remain unsold, could have expected the yield to be at least twice the *Ausrufpreis*. He did not explain how unsold items might affect the equation. And even if a comparison is made between the selling price and the *Ausrufpreis* only for the items sold, Senn's figure still does not correspond, for in this case the *Ausrufpreis* total was 482 fl. 59 kr. and the selling price 739 fl. 7 kr. Although it is of course possible that there was something anomalous about the relation between the *Ausrufpreis* and the selling price in this particular auction, it seems to me unwise to continue to accept Senn's claim until other contemporary auction figures have been compared with Leopold's.

It is possible to work out from the knowledge of what Berchtold agreed to pay Wolfgang and from the figures given in the *Licitations-Protocoll* what Berchtold realized from the sale. The total income was 1,507 fl. 56 kr. Wolfgang had to receive 1,200 fl. of this, the export tax on the sum was 120 fl., and pages 74–5 reveal that the settlement of other duties and claims on the estate accounted for 240 fl. 5 kr. The sum of these figures is 1,560 fl. 5 kr.[29] Thus not only did Berchtold himself realize nothing, but he was out of pocket by 52 fl. 9 kr.[30] The question which naturally arises from this realization is how, if he had hoped to do at least as well as Wolfgang, he could have got it so wrong. Rieger pointed to his tendency to be over-optimistic about the value of goods he was

---

[29] Or 1,484 fl. 23 kr.; it is not clear whether the sums of 69 fl. to Franz Aniser and of 6 fl. 42 kr. to Berchtold (shown on p. 75 of the *Licitations-Protocoll*) should be counted as claims on the estate which were paid out from the auction proceeds.

[30] Or he realized a small profit of 23 fl. 33 kr. if the two sums mentioned in the immediately preceding note were not claims on the estate.

trying to sell—in 1784 he had tried to sell some jewellery that had belonged to his first wife, and the discrepancy between what he thought it was worth and the official valuation was enormous—and claimed that he similarly mismanaged the auction of Leopold's estate.[31] But in view of such a gross incongruity between the cash sum realized by Wolfgang and the (possibly negative) one realized by Berchtold, and especially in view of the fact that Berchtold would have had the *Sperr-relation* valuation to guide him before reaching his agreement with Wolfgang, other possibilities have to be considered. I suggest below that it is possible that Berchtold may not have expected or wanted any cash from the sale himself, and that the auction (in the form that it eventually took) may have been arranged almost solely for Wolfgang's benefit.

If the documentation about the case is now re-examined in the attempt to suggest a more plausible reason for the nature of Berchtold's offer to Wolfgang, it seems from Wolfgang's letter to Nannerl of 2 June that his initial idea had been to choose some items from Leopold's estate as keepsakes before the rest were sold at auction. Had he done so, it is conceivable that Nannerl would have chosen articles to an equivalent value and that the goods of less sentimental value could have been sold and the profit divided. But at some point Wolfgang evidently changed his mind and opted for cash only, eventually making over to Berchtold even items which had been specifically marked as his (presumably by Leopold's will). It is quite possible that it was this decision which complicated the arrangement. For whereas in the former scenario both he and Nannerl would have been choosing items of equal valuation from the inventory and then selling the rest and sharing the profit (which would have made it easy to compare the gain of each with the like gain of the other), what was Nannerl supposed to do once Wolfgang had decided to take his half in cash if she still wanted goods to keep? The valuation figure was not the same as an auction yield, so that her gain would not be so obviously a like gain to his; how could Wolfgang be given precisely his half-share in cash unless everything was first sold? It is possible that this was the problem responsible for Berchtold's offer to buy out Wolfgang's share. If so, Nannerl must have chosen some goods from the *Sperr-relation* inventory and removed them, and a calculation must have been done about what the rest might fetch, how this figure related to the value of the goods Nannerl had chosen, and how the balance between

[31] See Rieger, *Nannerl Mozart*, 229–31. The passage about the jewellery is Leopold's letter to Nannerl of 3 Dec. 1784—*MBA* 827/76–88 (not in *Letters*).

the gain of sister and brother might be affected by items which did not sell at the auction. If Nannerl was more interested in goods than cash, the main thing from the point of view of her and Berchtold was presumably that they should not be out of pocket as a result of the arrangement with Wolfgang. The offer of 1,000 fl. was therefore perhaps thought to be well within the bounds of safety (taking into account all the other demands which Berchtold must surely have known would be made on the estate), and this was why he agreed to increase it by 200 fl. at Wolfgang's demand. It is also possible that the difficulty of comparing valuation figures with possible auction yield figures contributed to Wolfgang's increasing hard-headedness—his letter of 1 August, in particular, suggests that he had taken legal advice. In the event, although Berchtold might have been out of pocket by 52 fl. 9 kr., this may not have seemed so galling if Nannerl had already taken what she wanted, and considering that the Berchtolds were now entitled to take possession of all the unsold goods—some of which, as the *Licitations-Protocoll* shows, were valuable.

Berchtold's reputation as a pennypincher need not be allowed to stand in the way of this suggestion; he was not necessarily determined to realize as much cash as possible from the sale, understandable though this suspicion might be. The marriage contract between him and Nannerl had stipulated that gifts bestowed on either of the parties did not become the property of both.[32] In managing the settlement, therefore, he might well simply have been carrying out Nannerl's wishes.[33]

The scenario I set out above is speculative. In particular the question of how Berchtold arrived at his offer to Wolfgang of 1,000 fl., and how he was able to increase it on demand to 1,200 fl., is something on which light still needs to be shed. In the continuing absence of the rest of the documentation about Leopold's estate, some further progress might be possible from a study of other people's *Sperr-relation* and *Licitations-Protocoll* documents, but at present the data simply are not readily available to

---

[32] Clause 5 reads: '*Fifthly*: But anything that the bride or bridegroom receives either during the betrothal or the marriage vel per actum inter vivos vel mortis causa [as a deed between living persons or as a result of death], such thing should be regarded as a separate and not a common good, so that ownership and the free disposition of it belongs to each party' ('Was aber ſtens die Jungfer Braut, oder der Herr Bräutigam entweder in Brautständen, oder während der Ehe vel per actum inter vivos; vel mortis causa überkomt, dasselbe soll als ein separirtes, und nicht gemeinschaftliches Gut angesehen werden, sohin jedem Theile das Eigenthum, und die freye Disposition hierüber gebühren.') See SLA, 'Marriage Contract'; and Ch. 24 for more details about the contract. I am grateful to Professor Manfred Heim for transcribing the contract.

[33] Rieger asserts the opposite, that Berchtold took control of everything, and that he had the legal right to do so. Though she cites secondary literature in support of her claim, the evidence of Nannerl's marriage contract is a powerful counter-argument. See Rieger, *Nannerl Mozart*, 229.

make confident pronouncements. The conclusions that can be drawn from Leopold's *Licitations-Protocoll* are largely negative, in that they challenge previous assumptions about how the estate was settled without allowing an obvious alternative to replace them. But it does seem very plausible that Nannerl was interested more in goods, and Wolfgang only in cash. And if this was so, a different light would be cast on some details of the whole business—in particular on the effect the settlement had on the relationship between Nannerl and Wolfgang.

In the first place it would help explain why there was such a long delay before they applied on 20 August to hold an auction. Senn suggested that this delay might have been caused by the fact that they each wanted the same items from the inventory.[34] In fact there were reasons unconnected with Leopold's estate why the Berchtolds might have held things up for a while at this stage, for young Wolfgang lay dying during the early part of this period. He was removed from school in Salzburg and returned with Leopoldl to St Gilgen on 6 June, and he died at home on 6 July 1787, aged 13.[35] The Berchtolds therefore had a desperately sick child to nurse just when they were trying to settle Leopold's estate. This, coupled with the difficulties of balancing Nannerl's gain in goods with Wolfgang's in cash, could amply account for the delay without introducing Senn's scenario of brother and sister bickering over individual articles.

Next, there is the question of the music sent by Nannerl to the Heilig Kreuz Monastery in Augsburg. This was performance material of church music by Leopold and Wolfgang, which Senn suggests was offered for sale in the auction but not sold.[36] Senn, in asking the question how Nannerl could have given it to Heilig Kreuz rather than offer it to Wolfgang, assumed that it was because the whole business had caused a deep estrangement between them, and he followed up this claim by the (irrelevant)

---

[34] See Senn, 'Erbteilung', 387–8.

[35] Documentation about the death of Wolfgang Berchtold von Sonnenburg is preserved in SLA, Verlassakt Stadtgericht Salzburg Nr. 1. 713/1822, Johann Baptist von Sonnenburg (Inventarium Wolfgang Berchtold von Sonnenburg); and Brno, MZA, Berchtold Family Archive, 'Family Chronicle', unpaginated, but pp. 32, 43, and 94 on my count. These documents state that Wolfgang died at ten in the evening, 'in the 14th year of his promising age' ('im 14ten Jahre seines hoffnungsvollen Alters'); on 1 July he had received the sacraments, and on 9 July he was buried at eight in the morning in the tomb of the Schmauss family (the owners of the glassworks) in St Gilgen. The inheritance of 4,864 fl. 45 kr. which he would have received from his mother's estate had he lived to maturity was shared (together with some smaller amounts of money) among his heirs, who were his father and his siblings from his father's first marriage; his half-brothers Karl and Leopoldl were not named as heirs.

[36] For more detail about the Heilig Kreuz bequest, and Senn's reasons for suggesting that the music was first offered for sale in the auction, see W. Senn, 'Die Mozart-Überlieferung im Stift Heilig Kreuz zu Augsburg', *NAMB*, 333–68.

assertion that Nannerl was still irreconcilably opposed to Wolfgang's marriage.[37] In view of the fact that everything had been so carefully inventoried, however, it is highly improbable that Wolfgang did not know about the music at an earlier stage, and it must surely have been part of what he specifically rejected in assigning his half of the inheritance to Berchtold. Why, then, should Nannerl have offered to him after the sale music in which he had previously shown no interest? The only music he did ask for in the surviving letters was his scores (which probably did not in any case form part of Leopold's estate). Although Nannerl may not at the time have had in mind the best means of preserving the music, it is probably the case that it was better cared for by Heilig Kreuz than it would have been by Wolfgang. At any rate, Nannerl's letter to Breitkopf & Härtel of 4 August 1799 regretted that she had not kept with her more of Wolfgang's earlier works, and claimed that they would have been safer with her because he was so cavalier about his older music.

There is no unequivocal evidence for any degree of positive estrangement between the two in the documentation that survives about Leopold's estate. What can perhaps be seen is Wolfgang's apparent unconcern with the worry, work, and grief the settlement might have been to Nannerl. In his first letter of 2 June, in explaining that he could not leave Vienna, he said that if he were to do so it would be for the pleasure of seeing her—it was not worth his while on account of the estate. It appears not to have occurred to him that he might have taken some of the responsibility from her, or at any rate that he might express regret that he could not do so. It is also quite possible that Nannerl was dismayed by Wolfgang's demand for cash because she had assumed and hoped that everything of sentimental value would be shared between them and thus stay in the family. To give Wolfgang his share in cash could easily have meant difficult choices for her, as she tried to decide which articles she least wanted to see sold to strangers. All this notwithstanding, there was nothing very new in Wolfgang's thoughtless treatment of Nannerl during this period, and the two were on friendly enough terms when he wrote to her on 1 August for him to promise her new keyboard music as soon as possible.

A brief look at some of the objects sold at the auction may serve as a coda to this examination of the settlement of Leopold's estate. It should be borne

---

[37] See Senn, 'Erbteilung', 390–1.

in mind, of course, that if Nannerl did take her inheritance in goods the *Licitations-Protocoll* (even if it were complete) would not have itemized all Leopold's belongings at the time of his death. Listed on the pages that survive are clothes, including expensive suits which did not sell, with an *Ausrufpreis* of up to 60 fl. each; personal and household linen; beds and mattresses, bedclothes and curtains; crockery and cutlery, china and glass; lamps, writing equipment, and scales for weighing money; kitchen equipment, a medicinal pestle and mortar, and blood-letting bowls; shaving and hairdressing materials; pictures, several with religious themes; airguns for recreational shooting; a good deal of jewellery, snuff and other boxes, toothpicks, watches and chains, and buckles; minerals; a globe; and musical instruments and books. The musical instruments included a large harpsichord (presumably the one by Friederici mentioned in the advertisement in the *Salzburger Intelligenzblatt* of 15 September) with an *Ausrufpreis* of 100 fl., and a Cremonese violin with an *Ausrufpreis* of 25 fl., both of which remained unsold. There were several other violins, a cello, a keyboard instrument, and a viola, most of which did sell. The lowest *Ausrufpreis* in the instruments category was 45 kr. for a violin; this was bought by a violin maker for 51 kr.

Some items are conspicuous by their absence, but the meaning of the absence is in some cases unfortunately obscured by the fact of the missing pages. The newspaper advertisement for the auction, for example, picks out as being of especial interest the English-made optical instruments, so that although these do not appear in what survives of the *Licitations-Protocoll* the assumption can safely be made that they were entered on some of the missing pages; but should it also be assumed that these pages listed other items notably missing from the surviving ones (for example, furniture other than beds), or had Nannerl perhaps chosen some of these things for herself?

When the sequence of pages in the *Licitations-Protocoll* is interrupted, pages 67 and 68 (the first pages following the interruption) list books, including both a French and a Dutch translation of Leopold's *Violinschule*. None of the books on these two pages sold, and the summary of selling-price totals on pages 70–3 shows that none of the items on the preceding (missing) pages 64–6 sold either. This might suggest that pages 64–6 also contained books, and perhaps the music that was subsequently sent to Heilig Kreuz. From the summary of selling-price totals can also be seen that three of the missing pages listed particularly valuable items—page 50 had a selling-price total of 124 fl. 1 kr., page 53 of 100 fl. 48 kr., and page 55 of 125 fl. 21 kr. Perhaps the English optical equipment was listed on these pages, but if so there were probably other valuable goods too, because the advertisement in the *Salzburger Intelligenzblatt* picked out only three such items, while any one page of the *Licitations-Protocoll* typically contained more than six items.

～✳～

When everything was over, Wolfgang had his 1,200 fl., paid over to the merchant Puchberg while he himself was in Prague for the production of *Don Giovanni*. Nannerl was left with goods—the unsold ones from the auction and any she might have chosen previously—and music and letters. It had evidently been agreed between them that she would return Wolfgang's scores to him, but she kept for herself the copies of parts which had been made for her use. She also kept the family letters, which were to remain with her until the 1820s, when they passed to Constanze.[38] Leopold had indicated in his last surviving letter to Nannerl of 10–11 May that he had a shrewd idea that Wolfgang was in financial trouble, but even he would probably have been shocked that Wolfgang had not kept a single thing from his father's estate, even though the profit was a complete windfall which he could not have had built into his financial calculations at the time. As for Nannerl, she must surely have wondered what was going on in Wolfgang's household to account for such a strong attachment to cash. Perhaps this is indicative of financial desperation on Wolfgang's part; the suggestion of greed either of Constanze or of Wolfgang cannot adequately explain his having decided to keep nothing at all, not even the articles which Leopold had specifically allocated to him. If it is true that he had pressing debts during this period, there are implications for his failure to visit Leopold during his last illness and to visit Nannerl to comfort and help her after Leopold's death.

[38] See Ch. 35, p. 620, for more detail about this.

PART VI

The Biographical Legacy
(1787–1858)

32

After the Funeral (II):
The Mozarts and the Berchtolds

THAT so much primary documentation about Mozart's life exists is chiefly Leopold's doing, for he had written not only regularly but methodically and at length whenever any member of the family was not with him. He had also expected his letters to be answered (though Wolfgang increasingly did not reply regularly), and for many years he had ensured that much of the correspondence was kept. So it is not surprising that knowledge both of Wolfgang's and of Nannerl's family becomes far more sporadic after Leopold's death; the link between brother and sister weakened, since they had tended to pass news to each other through the medium of Leopold's letters, and never established a pattern between themselves of regular letter-writing.[1]

When Wolfgang received from Berchtold his share of Leopold's estate, he was bound for Prague for the première of *Don Giovanni*. Gluck died on 15 November, just around the time that Wolfgang was returning to Vienna, and this event provided Wolfgang's long-awaited breakthrough; after more than six years of freelance work in Vienna, he was given a court appointment. His title was Imperial and Royal Chamber Composer, and the annual salary was 800 fl.; the post began on 1 December 1787.[2] Though Gluck's salary had been 2,000 fl., Wolfgang could consider himself fortunate to have been appointed at all. His duties were exceptionally light, and later documentation suggests that the court offered

---

[1] Notwithstanding this lack of surviving regular family correspondence, there is an enormous quantity of documentation covering the years between Leopold's death in 1787 and the deaths of Mozart's wife and sons in the mid-19th c. Important topics such as Mozart's finances during the last few years of his life, his illnesses and death, the composition of the Requiem, the growth of legends about him after his death, the reception of his music, the life events of other members of his family, and the handing down of source material such as scores, performance parts, letters, diaries, and objects, all warrant (and in many cases have received) specialist studies of their own. In what remains of this book, I propose to focus mainly on the use and fate of the biographical source material, in which Nannerl and Constanze were heavily involved.

[2] Deutsch, *Documents*, 305–7.

him the post more for the sake of avoiding the shame of forcing such a talented man to earn his living in a different country than because there was an urgent need for his services. This fact was to be significant after his death to the question of whether Constanze was to be granted a pension; since it was not thought necessary to fill his position, the salary of 800 fl. reverted to the court, which could still realize a saving even after Constanze's modest pension had been allowed for.[3]

On 19 December 1787 Wolfgang wrote to Nannerl to tell her his good news, to ask again for his scores, and to assure her that he would continue to send her keyboard music if she would let him know what she already had. He mentioned that Constanze was about to give birth (this was their fourth child, who also died in infancy), and asked her to write to him frequently, even though he would probably be too busy to reply.[4]

Thus the news which would have delighted Leopold so greatly came just after his death. Wolfgang's move out to the Landstrasse suburb, which Leopold had guessed had been made because of financial difficulties, was followed in December by a return to the city centre. However, the acquisition of a regular source of income was not the turning-point in Wolfgang's financial fortunes that might be expected, and during the next few years he seems to have lived continually in a state where the quarterly instalments of his salary were largely committed to tradesmen and other creditors before he had received them. He then had to borrow in order to live until the next instalment was due. Leopold's hope when he saw Wolfgang's Viennese Lenten earnings in 1785 that his son would be able to bank 2,000 fl. had surely formed part of a belief that in cases where income was uncertain it was essential to have a fund of capital which could be drawn on in hard times. Wolfgang, however, did not consistently keep such a sum in reserve, and though he scraped by through borrowing against the security of his salary (as well as against occasional fees for operas and so forth), it took very little in the way of unwelcome contingencies to plunge the family into misery. One of his earliest known letters to Michael Puchberg, the Freemason friend whom Wolfgang used as a banker and creditor, asked for a substantial interest-attracting loan of between one and two thousand fl. over one or two years, precisely because Wolfgang wanted to extricate himself from this position.[5] Puchberg,

---

[3] Constanze's pension application is discussed briefly on pp. 576–7 below.

[4] *MBA* 1074 (*Letters* 552).

[5] Wolfgang to Puchberg shortly before 17 June 1788—*MBA* 1077 (*Letters* 554). The dates of the letters to Puchberg are not always known exactly, and the autographs of most of them are lost; see Ch. 36 for a brief account of the way in which the texts have been handed down despite this. In this case, the dating rests on Puchberg's remark at the end of the letter: '17th June 1788 sent f 200'.

however, seems never to have agreed to this, and instead only lent much more modest sums ranging from ten to three hundred fl. (but apparently without interest), the minimum required to rescue Wolfgang from the latest crisis.[6] Hence the succession of begging letters to Puchberg, which robbed Wolfgang of his dignity and which even now are so embarrassing to read. Although it seems fairly certain what Leopold's view of this situation would have been if he had known it (after all, he had also had extensive experience of the uncertainty of freelance income and the expenses of sickness, but had apparently always seen to it that he had sufficient cash or honourable credit behind him to cope with the problems), there is debate about whether Wolfgang's financial management should be judged according to Leopold's standards; it has been argued that Wolfgang might have led the life-style he did clear-sightedly, that he might not have wanted to be a 'super-Leopold' with bourgeois values, and that if he had been he might not have been the composer he was.[7]

Yet on the specific point that it would have been sensible to have a substantial capital sum in reserve, Wolfgang himself several times agreed. The unsuccessful attempts to borrow such a sum from Puchberg in 1788, the successful taking out of a large consolidation loan (1,000 fl. over two years, at interest of 20 per cent) from the merchant Lackenbacher in 1790,[8] and his avowals to Constanze in letters of 28 and 30 September 1790 that once this loan was arranged he would ensure that they never again got into such desperate circumstances,[9] provide a strong counter-argument to the one that he handled his financial affairs in Vienna purposefully and rationally.

The heaviest blows to the fragile financial situation in the Mozart household seem to have begun in 1789, when Constanze became seriously

---

[6] For a summary of the amounts lent by Puchberg, see the commentary to *MBA* 1076.

[7] See Stafford, *Mozart's Death*, 116–17. According to Stafford, the 'super-Leopold' tag derives from J. and B. Massin, *Wolfgang Amadeus Mozart* (Paris, 1959), 223. Braunbehrens, in his book *Mozart in Vienna*, also puts forward the view that Mozart's high standard of living in Vienna was policy rather than foolishness. The discussion in this chapter of Wolfgang's financial difficulties is intended only as an overview; see Ch. 23, n. 2, for refs. to more detailed works on this topic.

[8] Stafford (*Mozart's Death*, 258) gives the interest figure at 5 per cent, but if the agreement reached corresponded with the one discussed by Wolfgang and Constanze in their letters of the same period, it was 5 per cent for each six months of the two-year loan, adding up to 20 per cent altogether. Cf. Deutsch, *Documents*, 371–2, and Wolfgang to Constanze on 8 Oct. 1790—*MBA* 1139 (*Letters* 587). Though Wolfgang's letter to Constanze makes it clear that he wanted to borrow 2,000 fl. in order to clear debts of 1,000 fl. and still have money in hand after the interest of 400 fl. had been allowed for, the amount loaned was only 1,000 fl. Wolfgang did not expect to have to repay the capital; it seems that he was trying to make some arrangement with his friend and publisher Hoffmeister whereby he would write music for Hoffmeister, who would then settle the repayment for him.

[9] *MBA* 1135 and 1136 (*Letters* 584 and 585).

ill with a leg or foot ulcer and had to undergo a cure in the spa town of Baden, just outside Vienna. She was to go to Baden again from time to time from this date until Wolfgang's death in December 1791. In April 1789, before her illness began, Wolfgang set off for Berlin via Prague, Dresden, and Leipzig, in order to try to earn extra money. His travelling companion on the first stage of the journey was Prince Karl Lichnowsky. The nature of the relationship between them on this journey is unknown, but in November 1791 Lichnowsky was to file a formal complaint against Wolfgang for the repayment of 1,435 fl. 32 kr., so he must at some point have become another of Wolfgang's creditors.[10] It is not possible to say what profit, if any, Wolfgang brought back from the trip to Berlin, but only a month after his return to Vienna, in July 1789, Constanze's health problems began and the situation soon became desperate. At first her life was apparently in danger, and since she was pregnant there must also have been concern for the life of the child. In November, after she had been in Baden for part of the recuperation period, the birth took place, but the child died later the same day.[11] The extra expenses of this long-drawn-out period of trial are unknown, but Wolfgang claimed to have been robbed of the peace of mind which was essential to his ability to compose and thus to improve their financial situation, and begged Puchberg for help. Small wonder that in the autumn of 1790, when he finally managed to arrange the consolidation loan with Lackenbacher, so that a number of pressing debts could be settled at one fell swoop and all he had to do was work, he gave expression to his relief and optimism in the letter to Constanze of 28 September mentioned above. By this time, when he was 34 and Constanze still only 28 years old, they had been married eight years, and had seen the births of five children, only one of whom was still alive. Constanze had survived a life-threatening illness, and their financial situation had apparently never been stable. Though Wolfgang's letters to Constanze throughout this period are exceptionally tender, there are occasional hints at possible tension between them caused by the financial difficulties.[12] Constanze appears, at least on occasions, to have

---

[10] See W. Brauneis, '"... wegen schuldigen 1435 32 xr": Neuer Archivfund zur Finanzmisere Mozarts im November 1791', *MM* 39 (1991), 159–63. Brauneis notes that further possible documentation about the case would have been lost in a fire in Vienna in 1927 and in the total destruction of the Lichnowsky archive at Schloss Hradec in 1945.

[11] Deutsch, *Documents*, 357.

[12] See e.g. Wolfgang's letter to Constanze of 8 Oct. 1790 from Frankfurt, in which he urged her to arrange the terms of the loan with Hoffmeister if she really wanted her husband to return— *MBA* 1139 (*Letters* 587).

thought that he ought to earn more than in fact he did.[13] Puchberg, too, appears to have thought along the same lines, and at one stage he urged Wolfgang to take on more pupils.[14] After Wolfgang's death, the picture of their marriage disseminated by Constanze was to be that of mutual loving fondness movingly surviving all the blows dealt them by life, but with hints that she also had much to forgive. This picture is reconcilable with the small amount of evidence surviving about their marriage, so that although many of the stories which were later to circulate about Wolfgang's life with Constanze's blessing were inventions, this was not necessarily one of them.

In the spring of 1791 hope of further stability came to the Mozarts when Wolfgang's petition for the post of unpaid assistant to the ageing Kapellmeister at St Stephen's Cathedral was successful. This gave him extra work, but with the promise of the salaried post once the incumbent, Leopold Hofmann, became too infirm or died.[15] Thus when their sixth child (Franz Xaver Wolfgang, who with Carl was to survive into adulthood) was born on 26 July, Wolfgang and Constanze may have begun to believe that there was light at the end of the tunnel. Nevertheless there were still debts and large expenses. Constanze was in Baden before the birth, and Carl was now attending a boarding school. Wolfgang and Constanze went together to Prague in August for the first performance of *La clemenza di Tito*, and when they returned Constanze continued the cure in Baden. Wolfgang's letters to her there in the summer of 1791 had mentioned new efforts to borrow money, though it is possible that income from *La clemenza di Tito* and *The Magic Flute* helped repay some of the debts. The Lichnowsky case cropped up in November, but there is no surviving correspondence mentioning it. It is thus not possible to gauge how hard Wolfgang was hit by this. Since financial credit and honour were inextricably linked, it is quite possible that the Lichnowsky affair was a mighty body blow, perhaps even affecting Wolfgang's ability to recover from the illness which struck him down in November. Yet when he died on 5 December 1791, the *Sperr-relation* showed only tradesmen's debts amounting to 918 fl. 16 kr. No mention was made of debts to loan creditors.[16]

---

[13] Wolfgang to Constanze, 23 May 1789 and 30 Sept. 1790—*MBA* 1102/37–52 and 1136/8–10 (*Letters* 565 and 585).

[14] Wolfgang to Puchberg in early May 1790—*MBA* 1123/5–9 (*Letters* 578).

[15] See Wolfgang's petition of late Apr. 1791—*MBA* 1151 (*Letters* 594); and the replies of the city council of 28 Apr. and 9 May 1791—Deutsch, *Documents*, 394–5.

[16] The *Sperr-relation*, together with other documents relating to Wolfgang's death, is given in full in Deutsch, *Documents*, 583–604.

It therefore remains an open question whether Lichnowsky had somehow been paid before Wolfgang's death, or whether he renounced his claim. Nissen's biography of Mozart mentioned that Puchberg did not at the time of the settlement of the estate press his claim to 1,000 fl. owed him by Mozart, but that he asked for it later and Constanze repaid it.[17]

When Wolfgang died, Constanze was left with two sons aged respectively 7 years and 4 months. She had no right to a court pension, because Wolfgang had been employed less than ten years. Neither was she entitled to anything from the Tonkünstlersozietät, because Wolfgang had not joined it.[18] There was no will, and the only documentation showing her entitlement to a share in the estate was the marriage contract. In view of this lack of formal provision for her and the children, Wolfgang's letter to Leopold of 4 April 1787, in which he had claimed never to lie down at night without thinking of death,[19] seems, on the face of it, hollow— another example of fine-sounding sentiments not backed up by deeds. However, notwithstanding the fairly commonplace nature of deaths among young men, financial forethought may still have been more a feature of the outlook of older men; it would be interesting to know how many married contemporaries of Mozart (whether or not they died young) had made any sort of provision for their families by the age of 35.

Meanwhile, life went on for the Berchtolds in St Gilgen too. When Nannerl and Berchtold had taken Leopoldl and the sick young Wolfgang back to St Gilgen with them on 6 June 1787 after dealing with the immediate aftermath of Leopold's death, young Nannerl assumed the greatest part of Leopoldl's care. As a result of this a close bond was formed between them, and when this half-sister married in 1807, Leopoldl was to be the only relative on her side present at the wedding.[20] The autumn of 1787 must have been a trying time for the Berchtolds. On 24 September 1787, some two months after the death of young Wolfgang, the day before the auction of Leopold's effects in the Dancing-Master's House began, and as Wolfgang Mozart was preparing to go to Prague for *Don Giovanni*, smallpox announced itself in the St Gilgen house. First

---

[17] See von Nissen, *Biographie*, 686. [18] See Ch. 27 for further details about this.
[19] See Ch. 30, p. 540.
[20] See Brno, MZA, Berchtold Family Archive, Family Chronicle, unpaginated, but pp. 31 and 95 on my count.

to fall ill was the 7-year-old Johann Baptist; he was followed by 2-year-old Leopoldl on 12 October and 5-year-old Karl on 14 October.[21] The older children, Nannerl and Joseph, were apparently spared, and young Nannerl must have helped nurse the others to recovery. The Berchtold children had evidently not been inoculated against the terrifying disease, and though no one died, the next child to be born into the family, Johanna, was to be vaccinated a few months before her first communion, fifteen years later in 1802. By this date, a vigorous vaccination campaign was being waged in Salzburg.[22]

At midnight between 22 and 23 March 1789 this next child was born. Young Nannerl, now aged 17, took her to be christened, and she received the name Johanna, the choice of her father. She was apparently always called Jeanette within the family, however.[23] Later that spring, on 11 May, Berchtold's brother Franz Anton Maximilian married Genofeve Greissing, who as a granddaughter of Franz Anton von Amann strengthened the links between the Berchtold and the Amann families.[24] Nannerl and Berchtold maintained close links with Franz Anton Maximilian's family, as they also did with the family of Berchtold's other brother Joseph Sigismund at Strobl.

On 27 November 1790, at seven in the evening, another daughter was born, Maria Babette. Again young Nannerl took the baby to be christened, but this child did not live long; she died of *Frais* at four in the morning on 24 April of the following year, and was buried (like her half-brother Wolfgang) in the Schmauss family tomb in St Gilgen.[25]

On 2 November 1791, just before Wolfgang Mozart succumbed to the illness which killed him in December, the three oldest Berchtold boys, Joseph, Johann Baptist, and Karl, were sent to school in Salzburg. One of the entries in the Family Chronicle suggests that the initiative might have come from Nannerl, as it apparently had when young Wolfgang's schooling had been arranged. The new pattern of life must have eased the situation in St Gilgen every way except financially, because the only small children left there were now Leopoldl and Jeanette; young

[21] See ibid. 54, 80, and 95 on my count.

[22] See Ch. 35 for more details about this campaign.

[23] See Brno, MZA, Berchtold Family Archive, Family Chronicle, unpaginated, but p. 105 on my count.

[24] See ibid. 71 on my count. See also Fig. 2 for the relevant Amann/Berchtold/Polis relationships.

[25] See Brno, MZA, Berchtold Family Archive, Family Chronicle, unpaginated, but pp. 44–5 and 107 on my count. See also Ch. 3, p. 40, for evidence from the Family Chronicle about the effects of the deaths of children on their parents.

Nannerl was grown up, and had apparently long been an asset to the household.[26]

During the period between the deaths of Leopold and Wolfgang Mozart, there is scant record of contact between Nannerl and Wolfgang. In 1788 Wolfgang wrote to Nannerl for her name-day and sent some keyboard music, including a trio and a quartet. He also wanted her to invite Michael Haydn out to hear the new music, partly because he hoped that Haydn would then be induced to send Wolfgang some of his own church music. Nannerl had asked a question about Wolfgang's new status in imperial employment, and Wolfgang replied giving the salary and hinting that it would not be inappropriate to call him Kapellmeister. As usual he apologized for not having written more often, but begged her nevertheless to write frequently to him.[27] This is the last surviving record of communication between them. Nannerl was to claim, several years after Wolfgang's death, that she had not known of her brother's sad situation until she read the biography by Niemetschek in 1800, and that the knowledge had distressed her deeply.[28] Wolfgang apparently never approached her for money, but if he had, she might have been able to help him in 1790, for on 1 February of that year, during a period when he was asking Puchberg for money, she deposited 1,000 fl. as savings.[29] She was to add to her savings fairly regularly after Berchtold's death in 1801, but the sum saved in 1790 was the only one documented as being deposited before his death. It is possible that the money had come from Leopold's estate, but hard information is lacking; if it had, it remains unknown what she was doing with it between 1787 and 1790.

Wolfgang's death was noted in four separate places in the Berchtold Family Chronicle—in the biography first of Nannerl's husband Johann Baptist, and then of his children Johann Baptist, Karl, and Jeanette. The details in each entry were broadly similar—he had died in his 36th year

---

[26] See Brno, MZA, Berchtold Family Archive, Family Chronicle, unpaginated, but pp. 34, 45, 55, and 81 on my count. The entry on p. 45 states that Berchtold, 'through his wife Marianne' ('durch seine Gattin Marianne'), sent the boys to school. This might suggest that Nannerl had influenced the decision, but since two of the other entries state that she accompanied them into Salzburg it might simply mean that she, rather than Berchtold, delivered them there.

[27] *MBA* 1082 (*Letters* 557). The letter is undated, but the reference to *Don Giovanni* and the fact that Nannerl had apparently only recently asked for further information about Wolfgang's appointment suggests 1788 as the likeliest year. It was written shortly after her name-day, which was 26 July. The *MBA* commentary assigns to it the precise date of 2 Aug. 1788, but without explaining why; perhaps the letter is mentioned, with this date, in some later piece of documentation, but I have not been able to determine this.

[28] Nannerl to Breitkopf & Härtel, 8 Feb. 1800—*MBA* 1280/31–7 (not in *Letters*). See Ch. 34 for further details about Niemetschek's biography.

[29] See Angermüller, 'Testament', 111.

at 12.55 a.m. on 5 December 1791 of *Friessl-Ausschlag*, he had been Imperial and Royal Austrian court Kapellmeister; had held the papal Order of the Golden Spur; had been a member of the academic societies of Bologna and Verona; and was famous for his extraordinary talent in composition. The entry in Karl's biography stated explicitly that he had been the most famous composer of his time.[30]

❧

When Wolfgang died the authorities, just as they had on Leopold's death, moved into action. The *Sperr-relation* was drawn up, so that nothing could be done with the estate until all creditors had been paid and arrangements had been made for the welfare of the children.[31] This document included an inventory of all Wolfgang's belongings—cash, his personal clothing and effects, and all the furniture in the apartment. Even the household linen, crockery and cutlery, and kitchen utensils were included, and everything was assigned a value. The only exceptions were the matrimonial bed and a child's bed, which were listed in the inventory but not valued. The total value of the assets was given as 592 fl. 9 kr.[32] From the estate all claims had to be met, and any balance would belong to Constanze. Since the outstanding tradesmen's bills alone came to 918

---

[30] See Brno, MZA, Berchtold Family Archive, Family Chronicle, unpaginated, but pp. 46, 55, 81, and 107 on my count. The Family Chronicle gives biographical information (including births, marriages, and deaths of relations, and career details) about various members of the Berchtold family; this is why the same event is sometimes reported more than once. Wolfgang's death is not reported in the entry on Leopoldl because there is a break in this entry from 27 Nov. 1790 to 15 Oct. 1795 (pp. 96–7 on my count). *Friessl-Ausschlag* is the *hitziges Frieselfieber* of the death register, and is usually translated as 'heated miliary fever' (see Deutsch, *Documents*, 415). An enormous quantity of literature has debated Mozart's illnesses, death, and burial. On the diagnosis of the fatal illness, which seems to have involved among other things fever and a characteristic rash, some authors believe the term *hitziges Frieselfieber* to have been non-specific and all-embracing; others quite the reverse. For an overview of the sceptical viewpoints followed by a case for taking the diagnosis seriously, see R. Fuhrmann, ' "Frieselfieber und Aderlass" im Spiegel der medizinischen Literatur zur Zeit Mozarts', *MM* 37 (1989), 83–136; this work cites much other literature. For a summary of later diagnostic suggestions, see R. Ludewig, 'Zum derzeitigen Stand der Forschung über die Ursachen des Todes von Mozart', *MJb* (1991) (*Bericht über den Internationalen Mozart-Kongress 1991*), i. 132–44. For Stafford's remark about the relationship of primary evidence to secondary literature in the case of Mozart's death, see the Introduction to this book, p. xxvii.

[31] The following discussion of Mozart's estate is based mainly on the documents reproduced in Deutsch, *Documents*, 583–604.

[32] It has been claimed that estates of people who died leaving indigent families were valued as low as possible for charitable reasons, since the valuation was relevant to the calculation of estate duty—see Deutsch, *Documents*, 600. Some idea of the expense of sickness can be obtained from the fact that 214 fl. 23 kr. of the total figure for debts to tradesmen was owed to apothecaries. Moore has pointed out the oddities in Mozart's estate, including as it did little cash and large debts, but yet also luxury items—see Moore, 'Mozart in the Market-Place', 37.

fl. 16 kr. there was clearly not going to be any official balance (though it must be remembered that if the estate had been sold to pay the debts, it would probably have fetched much more than the valuation in the *Sperr-relation*).

The next stage was to call a meeting in March 1792 at which any other creditors could lodge their claims. When this took place no other creditors appeared, but Constanze made a claim of her own for the money to which she should have been entitled by a clause in the marriage contract.[33] But there were technical difficulties with Constanze's claim, apparently arising because she could not prove ever having paid the 500 fl. which was said by the contract to have been the sum she brought to the marriage. In the end she was allowed to list this dowry of 500 fl. as a liability for the purposes of death duties; together with the figure for debts to tradesmen, and a further sum of 55 fl. which was exempt from estate duty, the total liability figure was 1,473 fl. 16 kr. Since this figure considerably exceeded that of the assets, so that Constanze could not even inherit the sum stipulated by the marriage contract, she was not required to pay duty on the 1,000 fl. provided by Wolfgang on the marriage.

Somehow Constanze was able to pay the tradesmen's bills of 918 fl. 16 kr., and the estate was therefore eventually released to her instead of being sold. But the matter dragged on until August 1793, and she first paid into court 200 fl. for each of her sons. Since Wolfgang had left no will they were technically unprovided for, and the guardian appointed to them, Dr Niklas Ramor, had a duty to secure what he could for them. The sum of 200 fl. each thus represented their paternal inheritance, but it had been secured by the efforts of their mother. Where Constanze obtained the money to pay these expenses is unknown, but she had her family and friends, and was also helped by the income of concerts arranged for her benefit by well-wishers. In addition, she was almost certainly given presents of money by some of Wolfgang's private patrons immediately after his death.[34]

Constanze was obviously keen to secure a court pension if possible, and pressed her claim less than a week after Wolfgang's death.[35] In her petition she acknowledged that she had no entitlement to one because Wolfgang had not served the court for ten years, so she relied on the court's charity. She claimed that Wolfgang had never been fortunate enough in

[33] Deutsch, *Documents*, 203–4.
[34] See Deutsch, *Documents*, 430–1. These reports are from newspapers and may not be accurate; however, Constanze was surely given generous alms by some at least of Wolfgang's patrons.
[35] Deutsch, *Documents*, 421–3.

Vienna to gain an appointment that would have enabled him to provide an inheritance for his family, and that he could have earned more and left her better provided for if he had left Vienna, but that he had preferred to serve the Viennese court. She also claimed that his youth and talent had led him to expect that he would be able to provide for his family before dying, and this was also the reason why he had not joined the Tonkünstlersozietät. His prospects had been about to improve at the moment that he died, in that he had just secured the reversion of the post at St Stephen's Cathedral, and had arranged a composition contract of 1,000 fl. annually with a group of nobles in Hungary, and something similar with patrons in Amsterdam. Finally she stressed the vulnerability of her two children. Her appeal had the desired effect, partly because Wolfgang's appointment was not to be filled, and she was granted a pension of 266 fl. 40 kr. (a third of his salary) annually from 1 January 1792.[36]

With the pension secured, Constanze now had to find ways of building on it to lift herself and the boys above the breadline. Benefit concerts, arranged both by herself and by others, seem to have provided her with occasional welcome sums, and she devoted considerable energy to tapping the resources of her 'treasure'—the autograph scores left behind by Wolfgang. The most immediate project of this kind was to arrange for the Requiem to be finished, so that she was entitled to the fee for it; Wolfgang had been working on it when he succumbed to his final illness. The confusion resulting from her actions and subsequent claims about the work (which were all designed to maximize her profit from it while she sustained her public image of a dignified widow) has caused much ink to be spilt on the subject of which parts were written by whom, and on the provenance of the vivid stories which circulated about its composition and Wolfgang's death; suffice it here to note that Constanze did apparently receive the fee, and also had copies made for sale elsewhere.[37] In a similar manner she also tried to sell copies of other recently composed Mozartian works which had not yet been widely disseminated— for example *La clemenza di Tito* and *The Magic Flute*.[38] In all her dealings

---

[36] Ibid. 429–30, 435, and 441–7.

[37] It is impossible here to discuss, or give even a moderately comprehensive bibliography on, this important and complex sub-topic of Mozart studies. For a recent critical examination of the corpus of evidence, see C. Wolff, *Mozart's Requiem: Historical and Analytical Studies, Documents, Score*, trans. M. Whittall (Oxford, 1994).

[38] As early as 28 Dec. 1791 Constanze was negotiating with Luigi Simonetti (who as an employee of Archduke Maximilian, the elector of Cologne, was presumably acting for this former patron of Wolfgang's) about the sale of these two operas for 100 ducats (450 fl.) each—see *MBA* 1206 (not in *Letters*). And in Feb. 1792 Constanze seems to have sold eight works to the king of Prussia, also at 100 ducats apiece—see Deutsch, *Documents*, 440–1.

with possible purchasers, as well as in announcements for the concerts she arranged, she seldom neglected to mention her bereft sons, and made the most of her status as widow and mother. She seems to have placed great reliance on the high visibility of herself and the children, making concert tours on which she herself sang, and even getting the 6-year-old Franz Xaver Wolfgang to sing in a concert in Prague on 15 November 1797.[39]

As far as the education of the children was concerned, she received help from a number of people. Carl was sent to live and study in Prague for several years with the schoolmaster, music critic, and Mozart lover Niemetschek, and young Wolfgang also lived with the Niemetscheks while Constanze was making one of her concert tours. Niemetschek was later to claim that van Swieten had offered to pay the costs but had never in fact done so, so that Niemetschek himself had had to bear them.[40] When it became clear that Carl was not suitable for grooming as a professional musician, this role was transferred to young Wolfgang, who was provided with a series of prestigious teachers in Vienna, including Hummel, Albrechtsberger, and Salieri.[41] However all this was paid for, the boys do not seem to have lacked a good education. After his time in Prague, Carl attended school for a while in Vienna, and was then apprenticed to a merchant in Livorno (Leghorn) around 1799 at the age of about 15.[42] By this time at latest it seems that the financial affairs of the family were healthier than they had ever been while Mozart had been alive, for on 22 November 1797 Constanze lent the singer Josepha Duschek 3,500 fl. at 6 per cent.[43] There has been much discussion about how it was that Constanze, on what ought to have been a far smaller income than the family had received while Mozart had been alive, was able to manage the finances so much better than they had been managed during his lifetime. No doubt charitable actions by friends and patrons played their part in the early years following the death, and perhaps the cessation of pregnancies and confinements meant that medical expenses dropped sharply. There is no certainty about whether it was easier to run the household economically once Wolfgang was not part of it, but this must be a strong

[39] Deutsch, *Documents*, 484–5.

[40] Niemetschek to Breitkopf & Härtel, 21 Mar. 1800—see W. Hitzig, 'Die Briefe Franz Xaver Niemetscheks und der Marianne Mozart an Breitkopf und Härtel', *Der Bär* (1928), 101–16, here at 109–10.

[41] Constanze to Carl, 30 Jan. 1807—*MBA* 1375/16–23 (not in *Letters*).

[42] See W. Goldinger, 'Archivalisch-genealogische Notizen zum Mozartjahr', *NAMB* (Augsburg, 1962), 77–96; here at 79–80.

[43] Deutsch, *Documents*, 485.

suspicion; for even if the argument that he spent money foolishly and uncontrollably is not accepted, Constanze's status as a widow must have been in marked contrast to her former status as the wife of a composer striving to be fashionable in order to command the respect of his patrons. One element in her success was undoubtedly the fact that Mozart's music became extremely sought-after; the processes by which this happened are still debated, and Constanze herself probably played no small part through her own efforts to arouse interest both in the music and the life. What does seem clear is that she was energetic in pursuing every possibility that might bring in money (including more and less dignified forms of begging), and that she was good at saving. These qualities have earned her the opprobrium of many Mozartian biographers, some of whom seem to have resented on Wolfgang's behalf the fact that she did not take decisive control of the financial situation while he was alive. A common viewpoint is that she allowed herself to be pampered by, for example, the cures at Baden (and some versions of this story even insist that there was never anything wrong with her), increasing Wolfgang's worries and hastening his death, when all the time, as her later actions proved, she could have been supporting him by managing their affairs better.[44]

By 1797, when Constanze's affairs no longer seemed by any means so hopeless as they once had, she had also met the Danish diplomat Georg Nikolaus Nissen.[45] He then started to help her with her business affairs, gradually assuming more and more of the work. He was also willing to take responsibility for many aspects of the upbringing of the boys (though Carl was by this time already launched on his educational path). In 1809 he and Constanze were to marry, and the later correspondence shows that he played the role of a caring father within the family. It was with Nissen's help that Constanze pursued her correspondence with the publishers

---

[44] The most gratuitously virulent attacks on Constanze occur in A. Schurig, *Wolfgang Amadeus Mozart: sein Leben, seine Persönlichkeit, sein Werk*, 2 vols. (Leipzig, 1923); id., *Konstanze Mozart: Briefe, Aufzeichnungen, Dokumente 1782–1842* (Dresden, 1922); A. Einstein, *Mozart: His Character, his Work*, English trans. A. Mendel and N. Broder (New York, 1945; London, 1946); and W. Hildesheimer, *Mozart* (Frankfurt am Main, 1977; English trans. M. Faber, London, 1985). It would be tempting to label all these works misogynist, but the scorn and bitterness they contain seem rather a manifestation of possessiveness on the part of the biographers in question; Schurig's biography, for example, is withering about Leopold's character as well as Nannerl's and Constanze's, suggesting that Schurig believed no one good enough to be close to his subject. Prejudiced outlooks such as these have not served Mozartian biography well.

[45] See Nissen's letter to Franz Xaver Wolfgang Mozart (Mozart's youngest son) of 5 Mar. 1826, in which Nissen gave the date when he had first met Constanze—*MBA* 1410/12–18 (not in *Letters*).

Breitkopf & Härtel from 1798, and with André from 1799/1800; these letters are of outstanding importance for the contribution they make to knowledge about the dissemination of Mozart's music, the ways in which music publishers operated, and the development of some of the Mozartian myths.[46]

[46] See Ch. 34 for more details about aspects of this correspondence.

33

The Women and the Publishers (I):
Schlichtegroll's *Nekrolog*

〜❧〜

WOLFGANG had not long been dead before there was interest in the story of his life. Obituary notices of course appeared immediately, but the fascination of the story of the Requiem triggered a virtually insatiable demand for other anecdotes about his life, illness, and death.[1] The obituaries were not on the whole very accurate in terms of key dates in his life, or of remuneration for his work, but in the spring of 1792 Friedrich Schlichtegroll started to write the first biography of Mozart, and his work (termed a *Nekrolog*) was published in 1793.[2] Schlichtegroll approached Albert von Mölk, the old Mozart family friend from Salzburg, for help with the work.[3] He began by sending a list of eleven questions,[4] which Mölk apparently forwarded to Nannerl in St Gilgen for more accurate answers. These concerned the date of Wolfgang's birth; the biographies of his parents; the date of his first public appearance; information

---

[1] As early as 7 Jan. 1792 the tale that Mozart had become convinced that he was writing the Requiem for himself appeared in the *Salzburger Intelligenzblatt*—see Eisen, *Documents*, 119. I am very grateful to Bruce Cooper Clarke for his careful reading of this chapter, and his several suggestions for its improvement. His article on the same topic is cited in n. 2, and though my views do not always coincide exactly with his, his treatment of the subject is the fullest and clearest to date.

[2] F. Schlichtegroll, 'Johannes Chrysostomus Wolfgang Gottlieb Mozart', *Nekrolog auf das Jahr 1791* (Gotha, 1793), ed. L. Landshoff (Munich, 1924); as *Mozarts Leben* (Graz, 1794)—facsimile reprint ed. J. H. Eibl (Kassel etc., 1974). The 1974 reprint of the Graz edn. is cited hereafter. For further details of Schlichtegroll's authorial activities (the essay on Mozart formed one of a series of essays on interesting recently deceased people), see R. Angermüller, 'Friedrich Schlichtegrolls Nekrolog auf Ignaz von Born, *MM* 35 (1987), 42–55; and B. Cooper Clarke, 'Albert von Mölk: Mozart Myth-Maker?', *MJb* (1995), 155–91.

[3] Mölk's involvement is mentioned by Deutsch (*Documents*, 462–3) without any indication of the evidence on which his identification is made. In fact, the connection between the two men is made by a letter from Schlichtegroll to Mölk of 25 May 1792, which forms one document in a collection of material about Mozart made by Nissen when he was preparing to write his biography of Mozart in the 1820s. The collection is usually called 'Nissens Kollektaneen', and a summary of its contents is given in R. Angermüller, 'Nissens Kollektaneen für seine Mozartbiographie', *MJb* (1971–2), 217–26. The letter from Schlichtegroll to Mölk is reproduced on pp. 221–2. An English translation of the letter appears in Cooper Clarke, 'Albert von Mölk', 156–7.

[4] *MBA* 1211; not in Deutsch, *Documents*, though Nannerl's answers are.

about his travels; the date and the circumstances of his leaving Salzburg service and the details of his subsequent career; facts about his marriage; information about his children, final illness, and death; the names of his greatest pieces; whether his greatness was the result solely of his genius and Leopold's teaching; whether Leopold and Maria Anna had had any children other than Wolfgang and Nannerl; whether Wolfgang had ever received an offer from another great court; and whether his talents and interests had been confined to music.

Nannerl's reply amounted to an essay, in which she took one question at a time. It was the first account of Wolfgang's life to be based on primary written evidence, and the first (but not last) to gloss over his failures and faults. In writing it, Nannerl divided the page into two columns, writing her first thoughts in one and afterthoughts in the other.[5] Among the points of significance in what she wrote is her specific statement that Leopold had given violin tuition and had composed and written on music theory during his early career, but that he had later given up these activities to devote all the time left after his court duties to the education of his children, since only two of them survived infancy.[6] The longest section of her work concerned the childhood tours, and she used the letters to list the public engagements undertaken on these and to recount some anecdotes about Wolfgang's triumphs. Yet some of the stories and details about the tours written by Nannerl are not documented by the surviving letters; thus, for example, she gave further information about how Wolfgang had 'stolen' Allegri's *Miserere* in Rome, and she told the story of superstition in Naples, when an audience of Wolfgang's had believed that his musical powers resided in the ring he was wearing—when he took it off the onlookers were astounded.[7] Perhaps there were once other letters, now lost, or perhaps Nannerl was relying on memory—either her own memories of the events themselves, or her memories of oral reports of events she had not witnessed. She glossed over the frustrating failure of *La finta semplice* to be performed in Vienna in 1768 (stating only the bare fact, and saying how highly it had been praised by Hasse and

---

[5] This was a common practice; the Family Chronicle in Brno (MZA, Berchtold Family Archive) also follows it. It allowed space for corrections and second thoughts, and (in the case of the Chronicle) for later biographical information to be added to an entry begun on the birth of a child.

[6] *MBA* 1212/15–22; Deutsch, *Documents*, 454. The reference to Leopold having given up violin tuition may have been to his private tuition only; he was obliged to teach the violin in the Kapellhaus during Nannerl's and Wolfgang's childhood (see Hintermaier, 'Hofkapelle', 290), though it is also possible that he passed on the extra remuneration for this duty to someone deputizing for him.

[7] *MBA* 1212/260–8 and 273–5; Deutsch, *Documents*, 459.

Metastasio), she accounted for Wolfgang's return from Paris in 1778–9 only by his antipathy to French taste, and she did not give any details whatsoever about his leaving Salzburg service.[8] Neither did she breathe so much as a hint of the disagreements with Leopold. She ignored the question about his marriage (referring Schlichtegroll to Viennese sources for all details of Wolfgang's later life), and misunderstood (whether wilfully or not is unclear) the one which asked whether Mozart had ever been approached by another great court—her answer referred to other invitations to appear before European courts as a child on tour, rather than (as Schlichtegroll more probably meant) as an adult seeking permanent employment.[9]

The essay finished, she sent it to Mölk, though she considered it a draft which needed to be written up in a fair copy; perhaps she first wanted Mölk's opinion as to its overall suitability. Mölk, however, did not return it to be copied, nor did he have it copied himself. Instead he made a few pedantic corrections and additions, added a significant postscript of his own, and sent the whole thing direct to Schlichtegroll.[10] His postscript praised Nannerl's virtues as wife and mother and as a teacher of keyboard instruments, and commented favourably on the physical appearance of Leopold, Maria Anna, and Nannerl, but criticized Wolfgang for a lack of physical prepossession. Most damaging of all, however, Wolfgang was described as a child in everything but music—he had always needed a keeper, he could not manage money, and he had married an unsuitable wife against Leopold's wishes. From these faults had stemmed the domestic chaos at and after his death.[11]

Thus by the time Schlichtegroll received the essay it contained damaging criticisms both of Wolfgang and Constanze, despite the fact that Nannerl had taken care to avoid any hint of a negative aspect to Wolfgang's life.

---

[8] *MBA* 1212/205–10, 342–6, and 354–6; Deutsch, *Documents*, 458 and 461.

[9] *MBA* 1212/384–5 and 390–4; Deutsch, *Documents*, 462.

[10] See Nannerl's draft letter to Mölk on a date unknown in 1792—*MBA* 1213/70–5 (not in *Letters*). The order in which the documents concerning Schlichtegroll's *Nekrolog* are placed in the relevant text vol. of *MBA* is incorrect, a fact which was realized by the time the commentary vol. was published; see *MBA* 1208–13 (text and commentary) for most of the documents and an improved (but not final) explanation of the sequence of events involving Schlichtegroll, Mölk, Nannerl, and Schachtner (which last-named also became concerned in the affair). See also the additional commentary to *MBA* 1213 in the Appendix to *MBA* vol. vii; this mentions Schlichtegroll's letter to Mölk of 25 May 1792 (details in n. 3 above), which is an important piece of the jigsaw. The best exposition of the sequence of events (including a reappraisal of the dates of all the relevant documents) is given in Cooper Clarke, 'Albert von Mölk', 183–91.

[11] *MBA* 1212/395–417; Deutsch, *Documents*, 462–3.

What happened next is that Schlichtegroll wrote back to Mölk with more questions for Nannerl, having been delighted and surprised to have been put in contact with someone who could give him so much detailed information. He now wanted to know what Mozart's favourite childhood games had been; how he had behaved as a child when his talent was admired by great people; what scholarly subjects he had liked best; which language he had most enjoyed; what kind of daily routine he had followed, what had been his maxims, and what his character had been like. In forwarding this new set of questions to Nannerl, it seems more than likely that Mölk added a significant extra one of his own, which asked for an account of Wolfgang's faults.[12] Some of these questions Nannerl did not feel competent to answer, so she wrote to the old family friend, the court musician Johann Andreas Schachtner, who had been very close to the Mozarts while Nannerl and Wolfgang had been small children. Schachtner supplied the desired information, including several childhood anecdotes which have been found particularly touching. But perhaps the most interesting aspect of Schachtner's reminiscences is his remark that Wolfgang was 'full of fire' and extremely impressionable, so that had it not been for the excellent education he had received from Leopold, he might have become 'the most dastardly villain'.[13]

Although Nannerl had forwarded these questions to Schachtner, she also tried to answer them herself. The reply that she sent to Schlichtegroll via Mölk is lost, but a draft of her letter to Mölk has survived.[14] From

[12] The second group of questions is slightly problematic. With the exception of the one asking about faults, those given above are reconstructed from Schachtner's letter to Nannerl of 24 Apr. 1792, which is also an important clue to the order of events in the correspondence between Schlichtegroll, Mölk, Nannerl, and Schachtner; and from the draft letter from Nannerl to Mölk mentioned in n. 10 above. See *MBA* 1210 (Deutsch, *Documents*, 451–4; not in *Letters*) and 1213 (not in *Letters* or Deutsch, *Documents*). But though they seem to have been the questions to which these documents were responding, and though they seem at first sight to have originated with Schlichtegroll, Schlichtegroll's letter to Mölk of 25 May 1792 does not pose quite the same ones in every detail. Schlichtegroll did *not* explicitly ask for information about faults, even though the answers both of Schachtner and of Nannerl suggest that he had; he did, however, ask why Maria Anna had accompanied Wolfgang to Paris on his last visit there. See Angermüller, 'Nissens Kollektaneen', 221–2. My suggestion that all the initiative for describing the faults came from Mölk rests on the additional fact that Nannerl's draft letter to Mölk specifically alluded to Mölk's request for an account of Wolfgang's weak side (*MBA* 1213/77–9); the most obvious explanation of this state of affairs is that Mölk did not transmit to Nannerl Schlichtegroll's questions with scrupulous exactitude, but made suggestions of his own as to what was required of her reply.

[13] *MBA* 1210/43–9; Deutsch, *Documents*, 452. It must be remembered that the initiative for this comment did not originate with Schachtner; he was responding to Nannerl's request for his view of Wolfgang's propensities both for good and for evil (see *MBA* 1210/43–9), while she in turn was apparently relaying Mölk's request for this information.

[14] *MBA* 1213; not in *Letters* or Deutsch, *Documents*. This is the draft which has already been mentioned in nn. 10 and 12 above.

this can be seen that she was pleased with Schlichtegroll's satisfaction with her first set of answers, but annoyed with Mölk for having forwarded them in their raw state. She also asked Mölk to return her manuscript, which presumably means that at this point she had not seen Mölk's post-script. And though she had apparently wanted to avoid any discussion of Wolfgang's faults, she now addressed the question rather defensively in three different parts of her draft letter (which contains repetitions). In one place she stated that the only fault she could think of was that Wolfgang had had too good a heart and could not manage money; anyone who flattered him could wheedle it from him. While he had lived in Salzburg, Leopold had protected him from this weakness, and Maria Anna had accompanied him to Paris on its account. In another place she repeated much of this, but added that his head had always been full of music and other cerebral pursuits. And in a third she tried to explain the trait by stating that it was not to be expected that such a great genius should be able to cope with everyday affairs, and indeed that it would have been degrading in him to strive for a superfluous income. She suggested, how-ever, that others were probably better qualified than she to comment on his faults, and that he might have changed since living in Vienna; and she referred Schlichtegroll to Viennese sources for more information on this possibility.[15]

Schlichtegroll edited all the information he had received, and wrote his *Nekrolog*. He included very little material from Wolfgang's ten Viennese years. In referring him to Viennese sources for information about this period, Nannerl had claimed that she herself possessed no documenta-tion that would allow her to write anything thorough;[16] but from the dearth of data about Vienna in his work it would seem that he got little or nothing from Constanze. Why this should have been so is unknown, as are also the sources of the small amount of Viennese material that his *Nekrolog* does contain.[17] He made extensive use of the material supplied

---

[15] *MBA* 1213/56–64, 102–14, 16–23, and 80–5; not in *Letters* or Deutsch, *Documents*.

[16] *MBA* 1212/358–60; Deutsch, *Documents*, 461. Nannerl's claim seems to have been made from a feeling that her documented information about the Viennese years was thin compared with that for the Salzburg period, and that Viennese sources must have much fuller knowledge of Wolfgang's life from 1781. She did not entirely lack documentation for the Viennese period, how-ever; it is assumed that she did in fact have Wolfgang's letters to Leopold from 1781 to 1784, and Leopold's letters to her from 1784 to 1787 (which often, especially those written from Vienna in 1785, gave news of Wolfgang). See Ch. 36 for information on what is known about which letters were in whose possession when.

[17] It is not known if Schlichtegroll even tried to contact Constanze. Schlichtegroll's letter to Mölk of 25 May 1792 mentions a 'Herr von Retzer' in Vienna, whom Schlichtegroll had approached for information—see Angermüller, 'Nissens Kollektaneen', 221–2. Cooper Clarke gives some

by Nannerl and Schachtner, but modified Mölk's postscript to Nannerl's first essay significantly; he took over from Mölk the praise for Leopold, Maria Anna, and Nannerl, and included the criticism of Wolfgang to the effect that he was a child in all but music, could not manage money, and always needed a minder. But instead of including Mölk's criticism of Constanze, Schlichtegroll praised her. He called her a good wife and mother, who had tried to save Mozart from many acts of foolishness and dissipation. He claimed nevertheless that it had been Wolfgang's sensual nature and domestic disorder that were responsible for his having left his family with nothing but the fame of his name.[18] The source for this first written report of sensuality and dissipation is unknown, but it did not come from Nannerl, nor apparently from Mölk, and may well have been Viennese.

Thus the depiction in the first biography of the dark side of Mozart's character comes from a number of sources. The story that he was unable to manage money came from Mölk in Salzburg, and was confirmed by Nannerl, though she had not initially mentioned any faults.[19] (It is possible that the way in which Leopold's estate had been settled contributed to a Salzburg view of Wolfgang's finances, for a good many people at court must have known that he had taken his entire paternal inheritance in cash.) The claims about Mozart's sensuality and dissipation were perhaps Viennese, and Schlichtegroll presumably received contradictory reports about Constanze, since he turned Mölk's adverse criticism of her on its head.

Despite the fact that Schlichtegroll was not unkind in print to Constanze she disapproved fairly strongly of the *Nekrolog*, even to the extent

---

biographical details about Retzer, but it is not clear exactly what Retzer's involvement in Viennese sources for the *Nekrolog* was—cf. Cooper Clarke, 'Albert von Mölk', 160–2, for the little that is known about Retzer.

[18] Schlichtegroll, *Mozarts Leben*, 5, 6, and 30–1.

[19] Rieger claims that Mölk's postscript to Nannerl's essay has been responsible for the negative view of Nannerl held by many biographers—Nannerl was wrongly believed to have written the critical remarks about Wolfgang and Constanze, and was attacked for her views. In Rieger's opinion this is quite unjust, for the offending passage was not written by Nannerl at all. See Rieger, *Nannerl Mozart*, 240–2. Though her remarks on the treatment of Nannerl by biographers are generally perceptive, Rieger is in error in denying completely Nannerl's connection with the offending passage; for she did confirm, in her draft letter to Mölk (*MBA* 1213), some of the views expressed in the postscript about Wolfgang, and hence *can* be said to have claimed that he could not, for example, manage money. Indeed, Nannerl's confirmation of this alleged trait of Wolfgang's character is the most compelling piece of evidence about Wolfgang's faults in all the early biographies, for it seems clear that Nannerl had not wanted to publicize the idea that he was incapable of practical affairs, and had only admitted it in response to the pressure from Mölk to provide information about the darker side of her brother's character.

of claiming in 1799 that she had bought up all six hundred copies of the Graz reprint of 1794, in order to destroy them.[20] Why should she have felt so strongly about it? The only plausible reason seems to be that she feared that the picture of Wolfgang as a high earner but a reckless spender with tendencies to dissipation might damage her chances of public sympathy and charity—her claims for support were based on a picture of Wolfgang as unlucky in his finances, and in no way to be censured for the plight in which he had left his family.[21] Certainly she seems later to have been very concerned with her own public image as a dignified widow doing her utmost both for the support of her sons and for the posthumous reputation of her husband.

As for the later fate of Nannerl's original essay (with its Mölkian postscript), it seems that it eventually found its way into Constanze's (or at any rate into Nissen's) hands, and that the offensive remark about Constanze which had been kept from her knowledge in 1792 through Schlichtegroll's tact probably became known to her from the essay in the 1820s.[22] What seems to have happened is that in 1799 Breitkopf & Härtel wrote to Nannerl in search of biographical information about Mozart. She expressed surprise at their enquiry, because Schlichtegroll had used her material fairly comprehensively, and she would have expected them to extract what they wanted from the *Nekrolog*. However, she offered them her essay and sundry loose items such as praise of Mozart in verse if they were interested.[23] They were, and she sent the material she had originally sent to Schlichtegroll, and which had subsequently been returned to her.[24] It was the practice of Breitkopf & Härtel to copy into notebooks items sent by their correspondents if the correspondent wanted them to be returned. This is apparently what happened to Nannerl's essay—Breitkopf & Härtel kept a copy and returned the original to her.[25] It seems likely that Nissen was then given or lent the essay by Nannerl in the 1820s, when he was working on his biography of Mozart; and it

[20] Constanze to Breitkopf & Härtel, 13 Aug. 1799—*MBA* 1253/2–13 (not in *Letters*).
[21] There are hints in the documentation covering Constanze's life after Wolfgang's death, however, that Constanze might have felt that Wolfgang had in some respects wronged her, and certainly her second husband Nissen seems to have disapproved of some of Wolfgang's character traits which were revealed to him. See Ch. 35, pp. 620–3, for more details about Nissen's view of Wolfgang, indicated in part by a letter to Carl suggesting criticism of Wolfgang for the plight in which Constanze had been left on his death.
[22] Though it is not impossible that Constanze learnt of this remark earlier, despite the fact that Schlichtegroll did not print it.
[23] Nannerl to Breitkopf & Härtel, 4 Aug. 1799—*MBA* 1250/25–36 (not in *Letters*).
[24] Nannerl to Breitkopf & Härtel, 24 Nov. 1799—*MBA* 1268/3–9 (not in *Letters*).
[25] See G. Nottebohm, *Mozartiana* (Leipzig, 1880; repr. 1972), pp. v–xix.

is assumed that it was he who was responsible for making illegible the derogatory remark about Constanze (but leaving the criticisms of Wolfgang untouched). The deletion was so thorough that the lines to the effect that she was an unsuitable wife can no longer be deciphered, and would not be known today were it not for the copy which had been made by Breitkopf & Härtel. For in 1880 Gustav Nottebohm used copies of various documents in the Breitkopf & Härtel archive when writing his book *Mozartiana*. In this work he reproduced from the archival copy Nannerl's essay with the complete postscript, and it is from his book that the full text is taken today, even though Nannerl's original essay also survives.[26]

It has often been claimed that relations between Nannerl and Constanze were very poor, that this is shown by the offending passage in Nannerl's essay, and that this very passage also made things worse when Constanze discovered it. But though there is a small amount of evidence for strained relationships between Nannerl and Constanze at certain times, the story of Nannerl's essay does not necessarily contribute to it. First, Nannerl did not write the passage about Constanze, so it cannot be said to be known that she thought her sister-in-law an unsuitable wife, and secondly Constanze and Nissen should have been able to see this when the manuscript came to them, even if Nannerl did not explain to them what had happened. When Nottebohm's book was published, however, the printing of Nannerl's essay with the complete postscript (in which, because Nottebohm was working from a copy, there was no way of knowing that two different hands had been involved) gave wide acceptance to the idea that Nannerl had written it all. With this idea as a foundation, stories of poor relations between Nannerl and Constanze proliferated with manifold decorations from the end of the nineteenth century. More disturbing is the fact that even recent works on Mozart continue to make

---

[26] I have not examined the autograph of Nannerl's essay for Schlichtegroll, and this account of the deleted passage about Constanze is based on the description of it in the commentary to *MBA* 1212/415–17, on Nottebohm's text in *Mozartiana*, 111, and on my inspection of a copy of the autograph. Many deleted passages in the Mozart correspondence have now been deciphered by John Arthur, who in a private communication of 12 Apr. 1996 kindly informed me that the style of deletion strokes is not the same in all the letters containing deletions; this suggests that more than one person was involved in the obliteration attempts. It is possible, therefore, that examination of the autograph of Nannerl's essay might yield further clues about the interference with the passage relating to Constanze. In a further private communication of 21 June 1996, Dr Arthur informs me that his cursory examination of the autograph of *MBA* 1212 suggests that the deleted words do match the *MBA* text derived from Nottebohm; however, the darkness of the cancelling strokes makes it difficult to be certain. (See Plate 18.) For Arthur's successful decipherment of some deleted passages in Mozart's late correspondence, and for illustrations of Nissen's cancelling technique, see J. Arthur, 'N. N. Revisited', *MT*, Early Music Issue (Sept., 1995), 475–80. For more detail on the later fate of the Mozart material in the Breitkopf & Härtel archive, see Ch. 36.

false claims about what Nannerl's essay and Schlichtegroll's biography reveal about relations between Nannerl and Constanze, although the extent of Nannerl's contribution to Schlichtegroll has long been known in its essential outlines. Thus Gruber attributed the whole of the postscript to Nannerl, invented 'reasons' why Nannerl should have written such an unpleasant passage (she was wounded, first that she had not been able to follow her brother artistically, and second that she had lost contact with him personally), and asserted that Constanze knew that Nannerl was responsible for the unflattering description of Wolfgang.[27] Gärtner claimed that Schlichtegroll's biography contributed to the complete deterioration of relations between Nannerl and Constanze, because although the critical description of Constanze (which he implied Nannerl had written) was omitted from the first edition, the Graz edition of 1794 reproduced it.[28] (This is not true—it did not.) Solomon asserted that the postscript to Nannerl's essay was written by her, so that the claim in Schlichtegroll's *Nekrolog* that Mozart was a child in all but music emanated from her.[29] (In fact Nannerl never made this claim, not even in her draft letter to Mölk—the most she said was that Wolfgang's head had always been filled with music.)[30] On the other hand, at least one work which is careful to point out that the postscript was not Nannerl's goes too far the other way by failing to take account of the fact that the draft of her letter to Mölk confirms some at least of the criticism contained in the postscript.[31] Nevertheless, the damage to biographical truth arising from the confusion of attribution of sources in Schlichtegroll's *Nekrolog* pales into insignificance by comparison with the labyrinthine complexity of the question of sources in later early biographies of Mozart.

[27] See G. Gruber, *Mozart and Posterity*, trans. from the German by R. S. Furness (London, 1991), 20–1.

[28] H. Gärtner, *Constanze Mozart: After the Requiem*, trans. from the German by R. G. Pauly (Portland, Ore., 1991), 105.

[29] M. Solomon, 'The Rochlitz Anecdotes: Issues of Authenticity in Early Mozart Biography', in C. Eisen (ed.), *Mozart Studies* (Oxford, 1991), 24.

[30] *MBA* 1213/102–9; not in *Letters* or Deutsch, *Documents*. Cooper Clarke compiles some more samples of misguided comments by biographers on the postscript to Nannerl's essay—see Cooper Clarke, 'Albert von Mölk', 179–82.

[31] See Rieger, *Nannerl Mozart*, 240–2. The passage is discussed in n. 19 above.

❧ 34 ❧

The Women and the Publishers (II):
The Breitkopf & Härtel Affair

❧❧

I N 1798 the second biography of Mozart appeared, this one more to Constanze's liking. It was written by Niemetschek, the Bohemian music-lover who had known Mozart from the visits to Prague, and had educated Carl after Mozart's death. Niemetschek used Schlichtegroll's work for Mozart's early years, and was sent material (including, as he claimed, letters) by Constanze for the Viennese ones. Adding pieces of information from others who had known Mozart, as well as from first-hand data, he made a whole.[1] He too glossed over Mozart's faults, admitting that he could have handled his financial affairs better and was not a good judge of human nature,[2] but laying most emphasis on the fact that he had been extremely unlucky. For years he had struggled along in Vienna with no fixed income, so that when his wife had been ill they had nearly starved. Only when he had been about to leave for England was he granted his court appointment.[3] The envy of Italian musicians in Vienna had contributed to his lack of worldly success there, while on the other hand Bohemians had always shown their appreciation of him.[4] When he died his situation had just been about to improve, with his appointment as Kapellmeister at St Stephen's Cathedral (Niemetschek did not mention that this post was to be unpaid until Hofmann died), and commissions in hand from Hungary and Amsterdam.[5] His debts had amounted to 3,000 fl. rather than the rumoured 30,000, and Constanze had cleared them with the proceeds of a concert.[6] She had been a model wife and they had been very happy; she had been able to moderate his hasty decisions, and he had confided in her, even confessing his petty sins

---

[1] F. X. Niemetschek, *Leben des k.k. Kapellmeisters Wolfgang Gottlieb Mozart nach Originalquellen beschrieben* (Prague, 1798, enlarged 2nd edn. 1808). English trans. (as *Life of Mozart*) by H. Mautner, with an intro. by A. H. King (London, 1956). The English trans. is cited here.

[2] F. X. Niemetschek, *Life of Mozart*, 50 and 68.   [3] Ibid. 33 and 39.   [4] Ibid. 32–5.

[5] Ibid. 45.   [6] Ibid. 48–9.

(which she forgave). Niemetschek added that Constanze was now dedicating her life to her children, and that she was managing to live on her pension of 260 fl. and a small income from the money left by Mozart.[7] Niemetschek also mentioned the nobility of people who supported Constanze through concerts for her benefit.[8] His book contained a number of anecdotes in addition to those taken over from Schlichtegroll. The most dramatic was the story of the commissioning of the Requiem, complete with cloaked stranger and Mozart's conviction that he was being poisoned.[9]

The picture of Mozart and Constanze given by Niemetschek presumably pleased Constanze, uniting as it did Mozart's extraordinary talent, his love for her, his persecution and misfortune in Vienna, her dignified demeanour as widow and mother, and her continuing need for public support, complete with hints as to what form this might take. Yet it was not a long book, and she still possessed letters and other papers which probably made her realize that the biographical potential was by no means exhausted. If Niemetschek had indeed used letters supplied by Constanze, there is little sign of them in his biography, except perhaps very generally as the source for his statement about Mozart's love for his wife.

In the same year that Niemetschek's book appeared, Breitkopf & Härtel announced their intention of publishing the complete works of Mozart. They had a powerful publicity machine in the form of their house journal, the *Allgemeine musikalische Zeitung*. Their intentions were to reprint those works of Mozart which had already been printed, to advertise through the *AmZ* for works in private hands which had never been printed, and to publish a biography to accompany the project. The edition would proceed volume by volume in genres, each being released as it was completed, and there was to be a favourable subscription price as well as a higher price for those customers wanting to buy only odd volumes. Within the subscription scheme there were various options—it was possible, for example, to subscribe only to the volumes containing solo keyboard music. Music-lovers could also choose more expensive, higher-quality volumes or cheaper versions of the same pieces. The *AmZ* was to be used to keep interest alive by giving progress reports, to ask the public for information and material, to advertise the purchasing options, and so forth.

The background paperwork alone was a substantial undertaking. Thematic catalogues had to be compiled of the pieces that were offered by individuals as Mozart's work, so that they could be checked against

---

[7] Ibid. 72.   [8] Ibid. 47–8.   [9] Ibid. 41–4.

existing catalogues of printed music in order to verify the authenticity of what was being offered. Negotiations about payment for the music Breitkopf & Härtel were offered had to be conducted. Strangers had to be approached for information if the firm suspected that they might have something of interest. Pieces that were sent in had to be copied so that the originals could be returned. Incoming letters were filed for future reference, and a copy was made in a notebook of the gist of every outgoing letter, so that a complete record of all the negotiations was preserved.[10] The sums paid out for information received had to be sent through whatever channel was most convenient to the recipient, merchants usually acting as bankers. To help with the gathering of information, the firm tried to find dependable correspondents in strategic towns, effectively to act as its agents. Niemetschek was one such correspondent, and Nannerl was later to undertake a modest amount of this kind of work in Salzburg.

The relationship between Constanze and Breitkopf & Härtel suffered a mighty blow right at the beginning (one might even say before it had begun) and never recovered from it. Mutual suspicion and distrust existed between them from the start. For the firm advertised its intention of producing the edition, and asked members of the public to send in details of any Mozart works in their possession, before it had contacted Constanze to enlist her support. Writing in embarrassment and apology to Constanze about this on 15 May 1798, Breitkopf & Härtel explained that they had long had their project in mind, but had been forced to rush into its announcement by the knowledge that another publishing firm, Spehr of Brunswick, had just broadcast the intention of producing its own edition of Mozart's works. Their letter explained that they felt quite justified in reprinting those works already published, because they understood that most publishers had no right to them, having received them through third parties rather than from Mozart himself in return for a fee. They were sure that their edition would be finer and more successful than Spehr's, and they pleaded for her co-operation. Moving on to the question of obtaining works which had never been printed, they said that many people had offered them music in this category. Some wanted no reward, while others specified a fee; but Breitkopf & Härtel assured Constanze that at this stage they were only asking the public for the themes of any such pieces, since in cases where they were going to have to pay they wanted to buy from her wherever possible. Finally they

---

[10] For further information about these letter 'copy books', see Hitzig, 'Die Briefe Franz Xaver Niemetscheks', 112–3; and R. Elvers, 'Breitkopf und Härtels Verlagsarchiv', *Fontes Artis Musicae*, 17 (1970), 24–8, here at 26.

mentioned the biography that they also intended to produce, and asked if she had any material that could be used in it.[11]

Constanze had already had dealings with Breitkopf & Härtel, because she had herself arranged the publication of some of Mozart's works with them. She was nursing a grievance about the way in which they had handled the publication of the *Bandl-Terzett* (K. 441), believing that they had been guilty of sharp practice. Now she enlisted Nissen's help in replying on 26 May to their overture. He in fact wrote the letter and she signed it. This was to be the pattern in her subsequent correspondence both with Breitkopf & Härtel and with the publisher André, making it impossible to know for sure how far she was responsible for the contents of the letters; nevertheless, it seems to me preferable to continue to name her as the author.[12] The conciliatory tone of the letter from Breitkopf & Härtel does not seem to have impressed Constanze, and it is quite likely that she simply did not believe their claim that they wanted to buy unprinted works from her wherever possible; for the skulduggery of publishers was well known. Her reply made it clear how displeased she was, pointing out the impossibility of their proceeding without her because of the amount of music of which she was the sole owner. She admitted that it might be profitable for them to unite in partnership, but warned that she was going to arm herself with caution because of what had happened over the *Bandl-Terzett*. She said that she would compile a thematic catalogue, but that it would be for her sole use and would remain in her possession until the edition was complete. Among the warnings in the letter was one to the effect that she might bring out her own edition of those Mozart works which had never been printed—if she were to do so their edition, consisting as it would only of reprints of known works, would be sure to fail.[13]

Business proceeded, but Constanze was determined to wrest from them a price she considered fair, and they were determined to avoid paying if possible. Thus the two parties pirouetted around each other, the firm trying (by fair means and foul) to discover what she had, and seeking material elsewhere for a lower price; she obstructing their knowledge of the extent

---

[11] *MBA* 1223 (not in *Letters*).

[12] On 5 March 1826, when he thought (correctly) that his death might be approaching, Nissen wrote to Constanze's younger son Franz Xaver Wolfgang, and gave him a solemn declaration that he alone had handled Constanze's business from shortly after the end of 1797, that she had rarely seen the letters except to sign them, and that he took full responsibility for them. But his motive for the declaration (which was evidently a matter of great importance to him) is obscure. *MBA* 1410, inc. the text in the commentary vol. (not in *Letters*).

[13] *MBA* 1224 (not in *Letters*).

of her possessions, and trying to give the impression that she owned a treasure-trove of limitless depth. The full details of their relationship cannot be recounted here, but the following is a summary of the types of problem which caused most trouble between them.

First, there was little agreement about the rights to Mozart's works. The only point about which there was no argument was that neither Mozart nor his heirs were entitled to further remuneration for works which had already been published in return for a fee. Breitkopf & Härtel maintained that only the composer (from which term they seem to have excluded his heirs) could demand a fee for the publication of unprinted works, and then only if he had not already sold them or otherwise brought them to the hearing of the public. Constanze, on the other hand, insisted that she, as one of Mozart's heirs, represented the composer, and thus had the right to profit from anything that had not already been published, and that nothing else could be published without her permission. If, therefore, Breitkopf & Härtel came into possession of a work which had not been printed, such possession was not sufficient to allow them to publish it. Furthermore, she insisted that she was entitled to a fee so long only as the work had not already been sold—if it had merely been 'given' to 'a few friends' (this formulation seems to have been a euphemism for the situation where a work had been sold to private patrons in a manuscript copy), her rights did not lapse.[14]

Secondly, as would be expected, there was a significant discrepancy between what Constanze demanded for a work and what Breitkopf & Härtel were prepared to pay. They thought, for example, that 5 ducats (22 fl. 30 kr.) was reasonable for a keyboard concerto, while she initially suggested 36 ducats (162 fl.), and later demanded 24 ducats (108 fl.).[15] She asked 12 ducats (54 fl.) for the Quintet for Glass Harmonica K. 617, while they tried to beat her down to 6 ducats (27 fl.) and eventually paid 7 ducats (31 fl. 30 kr.).[16] It seems that Constanze already had a reputation for hardheadedness, untruthfulness, and possibly even sharp practice before the negotiations about the edition had begun in earnest, so that Breitkopf & Härtel may well have been forewarned that they would get no bargains from her.[17]

[14] Constanze to Breitkopf & Härtel, 15 June 1799—*MBA* 1245/71–100 (not in *Letters*).
[15] Constanze to Breitkopf & Härtel, 28 May and 15 June 1799—*MBA* 1244/23–41 and 1245/52–5 and 84–7 (not in *Letters*). In 1799 an imperial ducat was still worth 4 fl. 30 kr. See Constanze's letter to Breitkopf & Härtel of 8 July 1799—*MBA* 1246/10 (not in *Letters*).
[16] Constanze to Breitkopf & Härtel, 13 Feb. and 8 July 1799—*MBA* 1234/12–18 and 1246/11 and 49–50 (not in *Letters*).
[17] See Hitzig, 'Die Briefe Franz Xaver Niemetscheks', 106–7 and 110; and Gärtner, *After the Requiem*, 83–4.

But the negotiations over prices became much more complicated than this. At the heart of the problem was the mutual distrust between the two parties. Breitkopf & Härtel knew that Constanze owned Mozart's autograph scores and the thematic catalogue of every work he had written since 1784, but they had at first no reliable information of their own about the contents of her collection.[18] When she sent them a work for sale, they did not trust her word as to its authenticity or the date of composition, and were frightened of paying good money for a work which might be spurious or have been written in Mozart's youth. Ideally they would have liked the thematic catalogue, but since they could not persuade her to part with it, they carried out checks of their own on her truthfulness, and while they were about it they tried to locate copies of the works she was trying to sell to them, in order to obtain them more cheaply. This in turn was the main reason for Constanze's mistrust of them. Since manuscript copies of Mozart's works were in circulation, she feared that Breitkopf & Härtel would buy these rather than pay her, so that she would be left with no financial gain at all from some of the works.

By March 1799 they were discussing a rudimentary agreement. Constanze expected them to buy from her wherever possible, and in return she would sell only to them if they would pay her reasonably. In cases where she did not possess the original, she would try to alert them to people who could supply the work in question. Constanze's refusal to part with a catalogue of works in her possession stemmed from her fear that they would use the information to locate and buy copies from others (though she denied that she thought them capable of this, and said simply that it might accidentally fall into the wrong hands). Instead she suggested that they send her a catalogue of works they already had, so that she did not duplicate items in their possession.[19]

Breitkopf & Härtel appear to have been quite shameless in ignoring Constanze's stipulation that they should buy only from her. The prices she asked were high, and as well as driving a hard bargain with her they sought actively elsewhere; one of their main spies seems to have been Niemetschek. From time to time Niemetschek certainly sent them

---

[18] In a letter to Breitkopf & Härtel of 21 Mar. 1800 Niemetschek announced that he would send them his own copy of Mozart's thematic catalogue; presumably Constanze had lent him this with other material when he had been writing his biography. See Hitzig, 'Die Briefe Franz Xaver Niemetscheks', 109–10. All the time that Breitkopf & Härtel were negotiating with Constanze, therefore, they ought to have been able to obtain accurate information from Niemetschek about Mozart's works after 1784; but this letter suggests that they did not have their own copy of the catalogue until after Constanze had broken off her agreement with them.

[19] Constanze to Breitkopf & Härtel, 2 Mar. 1799—*MBA* 1237 (not in *Letters*).

extracts from a thematic catalogue; if, as seems likely, these were from his copy of Mozart's own catalogue, he was giving Breitkopf & Härtel the necessary knowledge not only to check the authenticity and dates of the works Constanze was offering, but also to search elsewhere for copies of these works.[20]

When Constanze discovered that a work she was trying to sell them was already in their possession, she knew that she was in danger of making nothing from it. She therefore devised a system whereby she offered to lend Breitkopf & Härtel the autograph score of the work in question, so that they could check their copy and obtain a more accurate text. Naturally she wanted a fee for this loan, in addition to the carriage expenses. Equally naturally, the fee was considerably less than the sum she could command when selling them a work that had not been printed. Thus when she sold them a keyboard concerto that they did not already possess in any form, she asked (modifying her original thought that 36 ducats or 162 fl. was fair) 24 ducats (108 fl.); but if they already had the concerto and merely wanted to check their copy against her autograph, she asked 5 ducats (22 fl. 30 kr.).[21] This system enabled her to retrieve something from a situation which otherwise would have yielded her nothing.

Gradually, and often painfully, the two sides edged towards a mutual recognition that the value of a work depended on how well known it already was. Constanze accepted that she could demand most for a work that was hardly known, less for one that was known to a limited degree, and less still for one that was already printed.[22] But the necessity to specify unambiguously in the correspondence the category of rarity in which a work belonged, coupled with the huge discrepancy that in any case existed between what each of the two sides thought was a reasonable offer, meant that there was still ample scope for misunderstanding and ill

[20] See Hitzig, 'Die Briefe Franz Xaver Niemetscheks', 106–8. This article gives more evidence about the underhand way in which Breitkopf & Härtel negotiated with Constanze. Hitzig was the first archivist of the firm, and had access in the 1920s to all the correspondence surviving at that date (considerably more than is now preserved; see Ch. 36). He wrote (on pp. 103–4) of the negotiations over the complete edition of Mozart's works, 'When the full context of the story of the origin of the "Œuvres complettes" is surveyed, as it is portrayed by our archival material, the description "fantastic and fabulous" springs spontaneously to mind. Above all it was about the procuring of the right documents, where possible the original manuscripts of the master. From the letters in the archive the picture emerges of a well-nigh incredible confusion, an inconceivable muddle, a sometimes deliberate obfuscation, the picture of the most wicked deception and professional falsification in all the questions pertaining to the artistic estate of Mozart.'

[21] Constanze to Breitkopf & Härtel, 28 May and 15 June 1799—*MBA* 1244/23–41 and 1245/84–7 (not in *Letters*).

[22] Constanze to Breitkopf & Härtel, 28 May 1799—*MBA* 1244/23–53 (not in *Letters*).

will. Thus on one occasion when Breitkopf & Härtel offered Constanze
5 ducats (22 fl. 30 kr.) for a concerto, she assumed it was merely for the
loan of the score to check the text that they already had from another
source, and was highly indignant when she later discovered that they
had not possessed the work at all. But when she challenged them on this
point, they claimed that they had considered 5 ducats to be a fair price
for a concerto in the rarest category, that of unprinted works.[23]

Constanze had no way of knowing whether or not they were being
truthful when they told her that they possessed a work and wanted to borrow the score merely to check its accuracy—she feared she might send
the score for the lowest category of fee, when they might not have possessed it at all. The dispute over the categories came to a head in negotiations about the Requiem, and it was complicated by the fact that (as
Constanze claimed) under the terms of the original commission it could
not be published without permission from the commissioner, Count
Walsegg-Stuppach. Constanze, however, hoped that she would be able
to obtain this permission. On 11 March 1799 Breitkopf & Härtel wrote
sending her a thematic excerpt from it and asking if it corresponded
with the music in her possession. Because of the complicated way in
which the work had been passed round to be completed after Mozart's
death, Constanze herself did not possess the autograph score, but only a
copy; however, she tried to make the firm believe that their excerpt was
different from (and hence less authentic than) the music she had.[24] She
presumably hoped that since the work had been unfinished on Mozart's
death, its circulation would have been limited. She was therefore dismayed to be told by Breitkopf & Härtel that they had two copies of it
and intended to publish it, and that they were only interested in her music
as a means of checking the accuracy of theirs. For this they offered 20
fl. Constanze responded by demanding 50 ducats (225 fl.), trying to exert
moral pressure on them to buy it from her rather than merely borrowing her copy.[25] When they remained immovable, however, she settled for
25 fl. and ten free copies, and sent them the music.[26] Breitkopf & Härtel
then publicized the imminent appearance of the Requiem, claiming in the
AmZ that their edition was to be based on music supplied by Constanze.[27]

---

[23] Constanze to Breitkopf & Härtel, 28 May, 15 June, and 13 Aug. 1799—*MBA* 1244/23–53,
1245/44–55, and 1253/37–77 (not in *Letters*).
[24] Constanze to Breitkopf & Härtel, 27 Mar. 1799—*MBA* 1240/18–20 (not in *Letters*).
[25] Constanze to Breitkopf & Härtel, 25 May 1799—*MBA* 1243/70–87 (not in *Letters*).
[26] Constanze to Breitkopf & Härtel, 15 June 1799—*MBA* 1245/56–71 (not in *Letters*).
[27] See *Intelligenzblatt* of the *AmZ*, Sept. 1799; reproduced in Gärtner, *After the Requiem*, 94–5.

To her, however, they wrote that her copy contained mistakes and that their own copies were preferable. These mistakes, which they apparently listed, were the justification for their paying her the lower fee.[28]

To all this Constanze objected that they had no right to compromise her in the eyes of the commissioner of the work by advertising that their source for the edition was the music she had sent them, since she had understood all along that they intended to publish the work in any case; but that if they had indeed used her copy as the basis for their edition, they should have paid her more. Her annoyance increased when the edition appeared and she thought it proved that they *had* used her copy as its basis; for although they had previously claimed that her music contained a number of mistakes (Constanze claimed they were merely minor copying errors), their edition reproduced a few different ones, all of which were contained in her copy.[29]

By the summer of 1799 Breitkopf & Härtel had got round to a volume of Mozart songs suitable for amateurs to sing, and the idea was discussed of including the simpler songs from the operas out of context. The way in which negotiations about this proceeded is indicative of how poor relations between the two parties had become. Breitkopf & Härtel wanted her to send the scores of the operas in question, so that they could choose the items they wanted and have them copied under their own supervision. She refused, ostensibly because the carriage charges would be too high (this seems an implausible argument, because Breitkopf & Härtel had always paid all her postage costs), but more probably because she did not want them to have the chance of using anything else from the scores without her knowledge or permission. She was also concerned that they might be too choosy, and she wanted them to agree in advance that they would take everything she sent. She first suggested that the firm should pay for the pieces to be copied at her house from the autograph scores,[30] but they would not agree to this. To break the deadlock, Constanze therefore temporarily mutilated the scores, removing the relevant numbers, sending them to Breitkopf & Härtel to be copied, and replacing them when they were returned.[31] (The risk to the long-term preservation of Mozart's autograph scores can be imagined.)

---

[28] Constanze to Breitkopf & Härtel, 6 Aug. 1800—*MBA* 1304/11–17 (not in *Letters*).

[29] Constanze to Breitkopf & Härtel, 28 Oct. 1799—*MBA* 1261/7–24 (not in *Letters*), and 6 Aug. 1800—*MBA* 1304/3–17 (not in *Letters*).

[30] Constanze to Breitkopf & Härtel, 9 and 28 Aug. 1799—*MBA* 1252/3–30 and 1256/30–4 (not in *Letters*).

[31] Constanze to Breitkopf & Härtel, 28 Aug. 1799—*MBA* 1256/2–35 (not in *Letters*).

By this time both she and Breitkopf & Härtel were heartily sick of the trouble the negotiations were causing. The firm complained that she was always making difficulties; she replied that she was merely protecting the inheritance of her sons. She objected to the fact that she frequently went to the trouble of looking out a work and sending it to them, only to have it returned because they did not want it after all. The arguments about categories of remuneration involved time-consuming rereading of the older correspondence, and the small-scale thematic catalogues they sent her were written on separate pieces of paper from that on which the accompanying letter was written, so that there was a constant risk that the two items would become separated in storage, making back-reference difficult. The correspondence had filled an enormous quantity of paper in its first year, and Constanze had had to bring in an assistant (Abbé Maximilian Stadler) to help sort and catalogue the music she had. Material had to be posted off regularly, and she had to note what had been sent and make sure it was returned safely. The accounts had to be kept up, and even the postage was reckoned up to the last kreuzer. The firm had no entirely reliable representative in Vienna who could have discussed matters with Constanze verbally, or supervised copying at her house, both of which procedures would have saved time and trouble. It is hardly surprising, therefore, that by the autumn of 1799 Constanze (or perhaps her letter-writer, Nissen) had had the idea of selling all the scores at one fell swoop, to net a large sum of money and be rid of the burden.[32]

⤳✦⤲

What is the connection between Constanze's dealings with Breitkopf & Härtel about Mozart's works, and Mozartian biography? Summed up most crudely and succinctly the answer is marketing. For side by side with the work on the edition the firm mounted a vigorous campaign, through its organ the *AmZ*, to arouse the interest of the music-loving public in subscribing to the volumes. A major way in which this was done was by publishing anecdotes about Mozart in instalments, and it seems that the demand was difficult to satisfy. Constanze was repeatedly asked for them, some were lifted from Niemetschek's biography and recycled, Nannerl was approached for more, and Friedrich Rochlitz, the editor of the *AmZ*, wrote some of his own. Between October 1798 and May 1801 there

---

[32] Constanze to Breitkopf & Härtel, 29 Sept. 1799—*MBA* 1258/22–41 (not in *Letters*).

appeared three by Niemetschek, ten by Constanze, four by Nannerl, and twenty-seven by Rochlitz (who claimed to have known Mozart personally in Leipzig in 1789, and vouched for the accuracy of his tales).[33] All passed through the hands of Rochlitz on their way into print. Nannerl and Constanze sent their versions of these oral accounts of Mozart, and both women also sent batches of primary written documentation intended for use in the biography which the firm intended to publish. Among the non-anecdotal material sent by Constanze were books from Mozart's library, some of Mozart's letters to her, the Italian letter to Aloisia Weber,[34] and Mozart's letters to his cousin Maria Anna Thekla, the *Bäsle*, which Constanze had presumably requested back from the original recipient.[35] She also sent Mozart's begging letters to Puchberg.[36] From these items Rochlitz was given the opportunity to see, as Constanze put it, Mozart's range of culture, his tender love for his wife, his good humour, his recreations, his love of arithmetic and algebra, his sometimes Shakespearian mood, and the ways in which he and she had been honoured by others. She warned that the letters to the *Bäsle* were in poor taste and must not be reproduced without her agreement (they included scatological passages), but sent them because they were indicative of his wit.[37]

From all this it is clear that Rochlitz had in his hands pieces of evidence of two markedly different types—the anecdotes deriving from oral tradition (albeit in part from sources extremely close to Mozart), and some of Mozart's own letters; his use of the material shows that he preferred the stories deriving from oral tradition. For he did not use any of the information from these letters in his *AmZ* pieces, except for one allusion in Anecdote 26 to a 'naughty' but witty echo letter.[38] However

---

[33] See Solomon, 'The Rochlitz Anecdotes', 7 n. 19.

[34] Dated 30 July 1778—*MBA* 470 (*Letters* 318).

[35] Constanze to Breitkopf & Härtel, 25 May, 15 June, 28 Aug., and 10 Oct. 1799—*MBA* 1243/63–5, 1245/11–13, 1256/49–63, and 1259/36–7 (none in *Letters*).

[36] When Breitkopf & Härtel wrote to Nannerl on 28 Feb. 1800 (*MBA* 1286; not in *Letters*), they mentioned that the material sent them by Constanze showed how unfortunate Mozart had been in many of his undertakings, and how his spirit had struggled to rise above hindrances. They may have been referring to the letters to Puchberg, which were used by Nottebohm in 1880 for his book *Mozartiana*; Nottebohm saw copies of these letters in the Breitkopf & Härtel archive. See G. Nottebohm, *Mozartiana*, pp. v–vi and Contents page, in which places Nottebohm specifically stated both that the material sent by Constanze was placed as an entity in one book (separately from the material sent by Nannerl, which was in a book of its own), and that the Puchberg letters were in this collection.

[37] Constanze to Breitkopf & Härtel, 28 Aug. 1799—*MBA* 1256/49–63 (not in *Letters*).

[38] This was probably the letter to the *Bäsle* of 5 Nov. 1777—*MBA* 364 (*Letters* 236). See Solomon, 'The Rochlitz Anecdotes', 39–40, for a reproduction of the anecdote. The numbering of the anecdotes in this discussion follows Solomon's; this section of the chapter is heavily indebted to his work.

problematic it might be to derive an accurate picture of Mozart's character from his letters (especially from so few as these), however necessary it is to guard against the naïvety of supposing that the picture of
himself he wanted others to see from his letters was truthful, the letters
do at least come from his pen, and were an attempt to relate emotionally to the recipients; whereas the anecdotes are removed another stage
from him by being recounted by others, any of whom might have had
private reasons for being careless with the truth. There is in fact good
reason to believe that most of the anecdotes as recounted in the *AmZ*
were products of the grossest cynical indifference to veracity. If this is
right they can tell us nothing about Mozart; for whereas letters can be
compared with others and examined critically for such markers as tensions between Mozart's portrayal of himself and the view of him held by
others, and inconsistencies between words and deeds, anecdotes (especially when edited by one person with a dubious agenda) are far more
slippery. Rochlitz, for example, deliberately avoided mentioning places,
names, and dates in the stories he told about Mozart.[39]

The twenty-seven anecdotes written by Rochlitz himself have been
accorded close scrutiny by Maynard Solomon, who reproduced them all
in English and tested their accuracy where possible.[40] The view of Mozart
put across by Rochlitz was that of a composer unappreciated by Vienna
and the emperor, who gave him too small a salary too late. Mozart also
suffered from the jealous rivalry of others, especially Italians, and from
unscrupulous publishers and theatrical impresarios. To all these unfavourable circumstances the 'excellent, dear, estimable' man responded like a
saint. Out of loyalty to his emperor he agreed to stay in Vienna despite
his lack of remuneration, turning down a lucrative offer from the king of
Prussia (who according to Rochlitz was a patron the polar opposite of the
stingy Emperor Joseph); he scorned to respond to his enemies with like
wiliness, and was above vengeful acts; he was always ready to encourage
young talent, and was generous to a fault, refusing payment for his
services in a good cause, and handing out money (of which he had little
enough) right, left, and centre to those even less fortunate than himself.
During his last year, when nothing was getting any easier, and he was
constantly ill, he retreated into his art and wrote the Requiem.

---

[39] Rochlitz's determination to present the view of Mozart that he wanted the *AmZ* readers to
see, regardless of its accuracy, is shown by the fact that when Niemetschek pointed out errors in
some of Rochlitz's anecdotes, his corrections never found their way into the *AmZ*. See Solomon,
'The Rochlitz Anecdotes', 45–6.
[40] Ibid.

Solomon shows convincingly that Rochlitz's method of writing the anecdotes was fictional; for he traces many of them back to an earlier source, and proves that in cases where Rochlitz departed from that source he usually introduced elements easily shown to be factually inaccurate. Thus, for example, Rochlitz connected Mozart's courtship of Constanze (the description of which he had lifted from Niemetschek's biography) with the writing of *Idomeneo* instead of, as Niemetschek correctly had it, with *Die Entführung*. A host of other examples belies Rochlitz's claim that all the anecdotes had been certified as accurate by Constanze and others who had known Mozart well.[41]

Very few of Rochlitz's anecdotes betrayed so much as a hint of disapproval of Mozart's character. In Anecdote 9 he alluded to the criticism that Mozart was careless with money, but glossed over the fault by relating examples (which he claimed to have witnessed in Leipzig) of his exceptional generosity to people around him.[42] Solomon notes, however, that Rochlitz privately despised Mozart's free spending, and judged that he should have provided more security for his own family before trying to help others (the very criticism of Mozart made by Leopold in 1778, when Mozart had wanted to help the Weber family by establishing Aloisia as a singer).[43] If this is true it shows a cynical disregard for truth of overwhelming proportions on the part of Rochlitz. His integrity suffers a further blow when it is considered that he probably forged the infamous letter to the anonymous baron, purportedly written by Mozart in 1789, about Mozart's creative processes.[44]

Yet the temptation to believe the anecdotes was for a long time overwhelming. At the time that they were published the primary documentary evidence was not generally available. It was not until 1828 that the biography by Nissen reproduced excerpts from the letters, and even then the texts were heavily and misleadingly expurgated. Not only therefore were the anecdotes the only way by which the hunger of the public for information about Mozart's life was satisfied, but there was little material publicly available from which any of them could be challenged. By the time they were first subjected to sceptical scrutiny (by Otto Jahn in the 1850s) it was too late, because they had found their way into several

---

[41] Cf. the commentary to Eisen, *Documents* 121 (p. 80), for a case where Rochlitz published an anecdote as deriving authentically from Constanze, and then reprinted it some years later stating that it derived from a Parisian source and was apocryphal.

[42] Solomon, 'The Rochlitz Anecdotes', 17–18. There was also a non-specific allusion to vulgarity, disorder, and foolishness in Anecdote 26.

[43] Ibid. 48 n. 147.   [44] For evidence and bibliography about this view, see ibid. 3–7.

other biographies and were too well established to be unwritten.[45] On the contrary, they continued to acquire further accretions and decorations in still later biographies, so that the popular impression of Mozart is now distressingly confused.

A great deal of weight has always been placed (beginning with Rochlitz himself) on the extent to which Constanze did or did not vouch for the accuracy of the anecdotes, as though her seal of approval was significant merely because she had been in a position to know Mozart better than anyone. Thus, although Breitkopf & Härtel's correspondent Griesinger stated that Constanze would not vouch for the truth of Rochlitz's anecdotes,[46] it has been suggested that the inclusion of many of them in the biography written by Constanze's second husband Nissen enhances their status.[47] In contesting this point, Solomon notes the chaotic way in which Nissen's work was patched together. Not only did Nissen die before it was finished, but probably almost even before it was started—an extreme example of authorial haplessness. The lack of any editorial stamp, the number of different people involved in its completion, and the number of errors and contradictions contained in it means that it is impossible to say how much Constanze contributed to it, or how much she cared about its accuracy. She had motives of her own for seeing Mozart portrayed in a particular way, and she was untruthful on several known occasions about details of his life, so any information deriving only from her is extremely suspect.[48]

Thus the anecdotes published in the *AmZ* were all part of the Breitkopf & Härtel publicity machine, which drew attention to the firm's edition of Mozart's works, and at times even challenged the integrity of other publishers and mocked their attempts to print Mozart's works.[49] The vested interest being so strong, and the disregard for biographical truth so blatant, it may seem surprising that any credence whatsoever is still given to them. Yet even Solomon, despite the sober and sceptical way in which he examines them, does not reject them completely. Instead he divides the ones by Rochlitz into three categories—those deriving from Niemetschek's biography, those containing gross errors of fact, and those

[45] On Jahn's view of them, see ibid. 5–6. [46] Ibid. 5.

[47] See H. C. Robbins Landon, *1791: Mozart's Last Year*, 74.

[48] See Solomon, 'The Rochlitz Anecdotes', 49–55. More details about Nissen's biography are given in Ch. 35.

[49] See Anecdote 10, which had Mozart being cheated by rogue publishers, and Anecdote 13, which openly advertised a set of variations published in the 2nd vol. of Breitkopf & Härtel's edn. of Mozart's works. Solomon also relates Breitkopf & Härtel's scorn, expressed in the *AmZ*, for André's publishing house. See Solomon, 'The Rochlitz Anecdotes', 56–7.

possibly based on Rochlitz's own observations of Mozart in Leipzig in 1789. He suggests that in the first category it is preferable to return to Niemetschek's text, since Rochlitz added his own decorations which make the anecdotes depart unnecessarily from their first versions; and that the anecdotes in the second category should be entirely discarded, because the errors suggest that they might have been fabricated. But he countenances the idea that there may be some vestiges of truth in those in the third category (because Rochlitz was in a position to know Mozart in Leipzig), and suggests that these might continue to be used with caution.[50] It is difficult to see, however, what this means in practice. In deciding how much credence to give to any biographical information it is necessary to consider not only what the disseminator of the information was in a position to know, but also whether there was any motive for distorting the picture, and whether there is any evidence that such distortion in fact took place. Thus, for example, while Nannerl and Constanze were both in a position to know a great deal about Mozart, both not only had reasons for wanting to gloss over his faults and failures, but can also be shown to have done so. It may be wiser, therefore, only to use biographical information coming from either of these sources (and their later derivatives, beginning with Schlichtegroll, Niemetschek, and Nissen) or from Rochlitz (together with *his* derivatives) when it can be checked against more reliable documentary information. The alternative would seem to be to continue to give their accounts book space while warning that they are suspect; this does not seem a particularly useful procedure.

On 2 July 1799, at a time when relations between Constanze and Breitkopf & Härtel were deteriorating rapidly, the firm wrote to Nannerl in St Gilgen to ask if she knew the whereabouts of any of Mozart's scores or other source material, and to request information about his life. Nannerl had already heard from Constanze that the firm was producing an edition of Mozart's works, but she had no idea what progress had been made. On 4 August she replied, explaining that she no longer had any scores, but sending the catalogue (which had been compiled by Leopold in Vienna in 1768) of everything he had written up to the age of 12. Nannerl thought that Constanze ought to have the scores for all the works in the catalogue, but warned that Mozart had been very careless

[50] Solomon, 'The Rochlitz Anecdotes', 48–9.

with his scores, especially those of youthful works. It was in this letter, too, that she offered all the material that she had previously made available to Schlichtegroll. Breitkopf & Härtel had obviously mentioned Niemetschek's biography to Nannerl, but this was the first she had heard of it. She was equally ignorant of all the notices about Mozart that had been appearing in the *AmZ*. In response to their request for information about songs composed before 1784, she stated that she could not remember him writing songs before that date, only Italian arias. She did, however, have one French aria and copies of a few songs, but was not sure whether they had been written before or after 1784. She sent the French aria and the opening bars of the songs in her possession, and expressed her heartfelt willingness to be of further use to them.[51]

Nannerl's life was of course even more isolated in her St Gilgen 'wilderness' after Leopold's death, and her letter shows that she was out of touch with developments in the musical world. Breitkopf & Härtel's Mozart project was therefore exceptionally welcome to her. When they replied expressing interest in all the things she had offered them, she sent them willingly on 24 November 1799—the material she had lent to Schlichtegroll, and four new anecdotes about Mozart's childhood. She thought it possible that she might find more of his music in Salzburg, and asked them for a catalogue of works they already had. Her letter indicated that she had kept and treasured all the odds and ends relating to Wolfgang which had been in her possession, even minuets written during his childhood, and stated how pleased she would be to receive from them the volumes of their edition which had already appeared.[52]

Nannerl apparently had a tendency to hoard family possessions for sentimental reasons, and attached great importance to everything that could remind her of her parents, her brother, and her childhood. Initially, therefore, it was child's play for Breitkopf & Härtel to please her. When they sent her five volumes of their edition early in 1800, she was absolutely delighted, and wrote back on 8 February 1800 promising all the help of which she was capable. This included sending anything (mainly keyboard music) in her possession, obtaining copies of any works at the Salzburg court in which the firm expressed interest, and collecting subscribers in and around Salzburg for both the Mozart and the Haydn edition.[53]

Breitkopf & Härtel were presumably highly satisfied to have found a correspondent so eager to help them, and apparently desirous of no

---

[51] *MBA* 1250 (not in *Letters*).   [52] *MBA* 1268 (not in *Letters*).
[53] *MBA* 1280 (not in *Letters*).

fee for the work she was prepared to do and the material she was prepared to send.[54] Her early letters to them are extremely, some would say embarrassingly, deferential, and she seems to have adopted the attitude that the nobility of their undertaking called not only for her unpaid help, but for her humble gratitude to boot.[55] Later she was to lose her initial naïvety, but Mozartian biography has continued to contrast her demeanour with Constanze's nevertheless. The basis of this contrast is found in the correspondence of Breitkopf & Härtel.

❧

For just as Nannerl was beginning her relationship with the firm, Constanze was to a large extent breaking hers off. The difficulties described above had made her decide to sell all Mozart's autograph scores and be free of the work they had brought her. On 29 September 1799 she wrote to Breitkopf & Härtel to suggest that they bought them all. She reasoned that if she died before their edition was complete, they would have trouble concluding it, and she suggested that once the scores had been used as the basis for the edition they could be sold on, to a library in England or elsewhere. She suggested they visit Vienna during Carnival to discuss the question with her.[56] A month later she had had no reply,[57] and had opened negotiations with the rival publisher Johann Anton André. On 8 November 1799 she signed a contract with André for the sale of the scores. Most of these were sealed in fifteen packets, but a list was made of others (it included keyboard concertos, quartets, and quintets). The contract specified that the works in this list, called Appendix A, were to be sold by Constanze immediately for 600 fl. She was allowed a period of two months, however, to decide whether she definitely wanted to sell the rest of the works. If she did, they were to be handed over to André by 9 January 1800, for 2,550 fl., making 3,150 fl. in all.[58] In the event that Constanze should choose to sell only the works in Appendix A, André would keep them for his own use only until 1 September 1800, and would then return them to her. If he failed to do so he would be obliged to pay her another 600 fl.[59]

---

[54] See p. 609 below for evidence that Nannerl did not want money from the firm.
[55] Though Nannerl received a copy of each vol. published, Constanze was paid in money as well.
[56] *MBA* 1258/22–41 (not in *Letters*).
[57] Constanze to Breitkopf & Härtel, 28 Oct. 1799—*MBA* 1261/45–6 (not in *Letters*).
[58] This sum was equivalent to almost eight years' worth of Leopold Mozart's salary in Salzburg at the time of his death, and almost four years' worth of Wolfgang Mozart's salary in Vienna.
[59] *MBA* 1262; Deutsch, *Documents*, 490–2.

The day after signing this contract, Constanze wrote to Breitkopf & Härtel. Having obtained the offer from André she now again invited Breitkopf & Härtel to bid for the scores themselves. She indicated that she had been offered 700 imperial ducats (3,150 fl.), but stated that she would like 1,000 ducats (4,500 fl.), and that if they agreed by the New Year she would reduce the price by 100 ducats (to 4,050 fl.). If they refused, their edition would have to continue, as it had begun, without her help, although she would still be prepared to support the biography project. She made it clear that she did not intend to waste time haggling.[60]

Breitkopf & Härtel appear, however, to have thought she was bluffing when she said that she had a good offer. On 16 November they replied, apparently rejecting her terms completely. She did not immediately give up the attempt to wrest a better offer from them, but wrote on 27 November and again on 14 December to offer them 'one last chance'.[61] When they failed to take it, she wrote to André on 8 January 1800 to accept his offer in full.[62]

Only slowly does it seem to have dawned on Breitkopf & Härtel that the scores had actually passed irrecoverably to a rival publisher. On 4 February 1800 they wrote to Constanze ostensibly regretting that the scores must now be in the hands of a third person, but it seems likely that they still hoped that Constanze's decision could be reversed, for the tone of their letter was friendly; they seem to have tried to explain away the failure to answer adequately her previous letters by reference to Christoph Gottlob Breitkopf's ill health, and they may even have promised more advantageous terms in return for the continuation of their previous arrangement. At any rate Constanze stated in her reply of 15 February that if they had written in such an amicable way earlier she might not have sold the scores to André. It was in this letter that she first named him as the buyer, and she made it clear that the sale was concluded and that Breitkopf & Härtel had nothing more to expect from her, since if anything else were to turn up it was promised to André.[63]

This was the letter which convinced Breitkopf & Härtel that they really had lost the scores, and they were mortified. On 20 February they replied, indicating that they were going to make a public announcement that they had been let down by her, but that what André had bought was nevertheless only leftovers. They wanted her to add her signature to the declaration. They also spelt out the terms they claimed to have been

---

[60] *MBA* 1263 (not in *Letters*).   [61] *MBA* 1269 and 1271 (not in *Letters*).
[62] *MBA* 1273 (not in *Letters*).   [63] *MBA* 1283 (not in *Letters*).

about to suggest to Constanze if she had continued to sell Mozart's works to them, stating that they had intended to offer her 4–5 thaler (6–7½ fl.) per *Bogen* (bifolium), and to promise to bring out fourteen volumes annually. From this Constanze was able to calculate that even if each volume had contained only twenty *Bogen*, and reckoning the *Bogen* rate at 4½ thaler (6 fl. 45 kr.), she would have received 1,260 thaler (1,890 fl.) in the first year alone, and by the end of the second year would have earned the entire sum she had asked from them, while keeping possession of the scores.[64] Naturally she was chagrined by the thought that she could have profited to this extent, and when she replied on 5 March she asked them with some acerbity why they had left their best offer until it was too late. She also not only refused to sign the declaration they intended to print, but threatened to publish her own counter-declaration complaining about their treatment of her.[65]

Gradually the affair simmered down, but not before Breitkopf & Härtel had written to Nannerl on 28 February 1800 to complain about Constanze's behaviour. In thanking Nannerl for her help both with the edition and the biography they contrasted her attitude with Constanze's, suggesting that Mozart's widow cared more about her immediate advantage than about Mozart's honour (this was presumably a reference to the fact that André had a reputation for the poor quality of his editions).[66] They must have stated that Constanze had broken her promise to them, because Nannerl alluded to this when she replied on 23 March. At this point Nannerl had only recently received, some six weeks previously, the first five volumes of the Breitkopf & Härtel edition which had so delighted her, and was probably still filled with grateful enthusiasm for their project. At any rate she seems to have felt very disappointed at the prospect that their edition was now at risk, and this feeling, together with the flattering contrast they had drawn between her behaviour and that of

---

[64] See Constanze to Breitkopf & Härtel, 5 Mar. 1800—*MBA* 1289/89–105 (not in *Letters*). I am grateful to Cliff Eisen for advice on the meaning of *Bogen* in this context. The thaler/florin conversion given here is tentative: it rests on the announcement by Breitkopf & Härtel in the *Intelligenzblatt* of the *AmZ* of Sept. 1799, which offered for sale the score of Mozart's Requiem for 3 thaler (Saxon currency) or one ducat. See Gärtner, *After The Requiem*, 94–5. If there were 3 thaler to the ducat (which itself was worth 4½ fl.), each thaler was worth 1½ fl. The conversion is only valid if Constanze, in her letter to Breitkopf & Härtel of 5 Mar. 1800, understood a thaler to mean one of the same type mentioned in the *AmZ* announcement; but her calculation of how the rate offered by their new proposal (2,520 thaler after two years) would compare with the lump sum of 4,050 fl. she had asked from them shows that she must have had a conversion of this order in mind.

[65] *MBA* 1289 (not in *Letters*).

[66] *MBA* 1286 (not in *Letters*). *MBA* gives the letter incomplete because it is known only from the excerpt printed by Nottebohm in *Mozartiana*. See Nottebohm, *Mozartiana*, 139; and Ch. 36 for further information about the letters in the Breitkopf & Härtel archive.

Constanze, and of course the fact that she had only been told one side of the story, may have been responsible for her condemnation of her sister-in-law. She described Constanze's behaviour as ungrateful and ignoble, and made it clear that she believed Mozart's honour would be far better served if all his works appeared with Breitkopf & Härtel. She hoped that their edition would be able to continue with the use of copies, and promised her continued help.[67]

By the summer of 1800 Nannerl was acting as agent to Breitkopf & Härtel in Salzburg. She was collecting subscribers to their edition of Haydn's *Creation*, and was trying to find out what music by Mozart (and later by both Joseph and Michael Haydn) was kept at the Salzburg court. She then notified the firm of her discoveries, and tried to arrange for copies to be made of the works in which they expressed interest. They offered her a fee for everything she sent which had not already been printed, and a further one if they were able to use the works she sent. They also promised to safeguard everything carefully and return it promptly, and it was understood that they would pay all the copying expenses.[68] However, it is not clear that Nannerl did receive any fee from them, or even that she wanted one. Breitkopf & Härtel transmitted funds to Mayr's bookshop in Salzburg, and Nannerl drew on these to pay copyists' bills, but there is no record in the surviving letters of her taking or demanding money for herself.[69]

At first it was not at all convenient for Nannerl to arrange for copies to be made from music held by the court, because apart from the fact that she was not on the spot, it was a clandestine operation which must not come to the notice of the archbishop, the nominal owner of the music. She therefore had to work through a third person who had access to the music and was prepared to take the risk of secreting it out to be copied. It is not known who this intermediary was, but Nannerl was completely dependent on him for everything she tried to procure for Breitkopf & Härtel. Furthermore, from June 1801 at the latest he was in turn dependent on the goodwill of the Kapellmeister Gatti, who had overall charge of the court music. And whereas Gatti was initially either ignorant of the arrangement or happy to allow it, he began to put obstacles

---

[67] *MBA* 1293 (not in *Letters*).

[68] The documentation showing that the firm initially offered Nannerl a fee is Nannerl's letter of 30 Apr. 1807—*MBA* 1377/31–40 (not in *Letters*).

[69] Nannerl's letters to Breitkopf & Härtel of 18 June 1801 and 4 Jan. 1804 listed the incoming and outgoing sums of money on her account with the firm. Each of the two reckonings covered a period of approximately a year, and neither showed any sum designated for Nannerl herself—see *MBA* 1336/48–74 and 1364/61–82 (not in *Letters*).

in Nannerl's path from this time, saying that music she had previously understood to be available could no longer be found. Nannerl suspected Gatti of fishing for a fee in return for producing the music, so she asked Breitkopf & Härtel for authorization to offer one, which they did. Then the copying continued with Gatti's blessing, until he eventually started to deal with the firm direct.[70]

During the early stages of Nannerl's work for Breitkopf & Härtel, great upheavals were taking place in her environment. French soldiers were occupying Salzburg, and plundering and terrorizing the Abersee area as elsewhere.[71] In the midst of this confusion, on 26 February 1801, Berchtold died; and on 27 May Nannerl told Breitkopf & Härtel, by way of explaining why she had not answered their letters written in February, how she had become gravely ill after the loss of her 'most dearly beloved husband'.[72] At Michaelmas of the same year Nannerl moved back to Salzburg, where she had close supervision only over her own children Leopoldl and Jeanette, now aged 16 and 12 respectively.[73]

Once Nannerl was back in Salzburg, she was much better placed to fulfil the commissions of Breitkopf & Härtel. The copying continued with Gatti's co-operation, and works by Mozart and by both Haydn brothers were supplied to Leipzig. Michael Haydn was still working in Salzburg until he died in 1806, but Breitkopf & Härtel preferred to obtain his music through Gatti, Nannerl, and secret copies, rather than entering into negotiations with the composer himself; and Nannerl was willing to help them do this. On 20 September 1802 she wrote to explain that the Salzburg court possessed only copies of parts, not scores, of Michael Haydn's works, and that it would be more expensive to prepare a score from parts than from a score. The only way to copy more cheaply (from score to score) was through Michael Haydn himself, but Nannerl feared that he would ask too large a fee, whereas this fee could be avoided if the copies of the court parts were used.[74]

It seems clear from this that Breitkopf & Härtel cheated Michael Haydn out of fees he could reasonably have asked, for the sake of their

[70] Nannerl to Breitkopf & Härtel, 29 Oct. 1800, and 18 June and 27 Aug. 1801—*MBA* 1317, 1336, and 1337 (not in *Letters*). The relevance of this correspondence to particular aspects of authenticity in Mozart's music is discussed in C. Eisen, 'Problems of Authenticity Among Mozart's Early Symphonies: The Examples of K. Anh. 220 (16a) and 76 (42a)', *Music and Letters*, 70 (1989), 505–16.

[71] See Ziller, *Geschichte St. Gilgens*, ii. 9–10.   [72] *MBA* 1335/4–7 (not in *Letters*).

[73] Further information about the aftermath of Berchtold's death, and the further lives of the children, is given in Ch. 35.

[74] *MBA* 1354/16–26 (not in *Letters*).

own edition and profit. Gatti was party to their deception, for they paid him a 'sweetener' through Nannerl simply for making the parts available, and Nannerl also connived at it. If this was indeed the way the firm had also tried to avoid paying Constanze for the Mozartian works in their edition, her hard bargaining may be seen in a more sympathetic light. More generally, it seems that the whole of the musical profession was riddled with corruption in this respect, that Kapellmeisters far and wide were able and willing to cheat their own underlings for the sake of their private purse, and that even the relations of court musicians (who must have been aware of the effect of such deception on the robbed composers) could be without conscience in the matter.

Gradually Nannerl became extremely disenchanted with Breitkopf & Härtel. They did not acknowledge receipt of material she sent, or answer her letters. They failed to send the music ordered by the subscribers she had collected, or to return things she had lent them. And when she had made a provisional arrangement with her intermediary to have certain works copied, they delayed in confirming that the works in question were actually wanted, so that Nannerl was constantly having to fend off enquiries from her contact. She also had to nag them repeatedly to allay her worries that valuable, irreplaceable material had not been lost in transit. Her irritation reached a peak in 1807, by which time she felt that they were a plague to her. On 30 April she wrote to express her grievances. Michael Haydn had died in 1806 and his widow Maria Magdalena had disposed of most of his scores. According to Nannerl only two works remained with her—a Requiem and a Mass—and she had offers for these too. Nannerl complained that if Breitkopf & Härtel had kept in regular contact with her, she could have obtained much more of Haydn's music from his widow. She continued by quoting their early letter to her in which they had made all manner of fine promises, and by listing all the ways in which they had fallen short of them. She stressed the time and care she had devoted to her work for them, and upbraided them bitterly for their ingratitude. Finally she criticized aspects of their Mozart edition, accusing them of printing spurious works without attempting to check their authenticity.[75]

The tone of Nannerl's later letters to Breitkopf & Härtel is markedly more blunt than that of her earlier ones. She seems to have lost a good deal of her innocence about the goodwill of publishers, and it is quite possible that she would not have criticized Constanze in 1807 in the same

---

[75] *MBA* 1377 (not in *Letters*).

terms she had used in 1800. Nevertheless, Mozartian biographers have fastened on the remarks she made about Constanze in her letter to Breitkopf & Härtel of 23 March 1800, as if they represented her immutable opinion of her sister-in-law, and have used them, in conjunction with equally unsatisfactory evidence, to support the commonly held view that the two women were on very poor terms. Nannerl's co-operation in the matter of Nissen's biography of Mozart is one factor which suggests that this was not the case.

The Women and the Publishers (III):
Nissen's Biography of Mozart

ॐॐ

Aᴌʟ the time that Constanze and Nannerl had been involved with the dissemination of Mozart's music, and the story of his life, their own families were growing up and the children had to be settled in life. Carl Mozart, despite the fact that he had been apprenticed to a merchant, hankered after a musical career. In 1806 he left Leghorn and moved to Milan to study music with Bonifazio Asioli, to whom he had been recommended by Joseph Haydn. After four years he decided after all to pursue his interest in music solely as an amateur, and entered the civil service in Milan. Constanze and Nissen were concerned at his changes of direction, but he settled down in Milan and apparently worked steadily there until his retirement.[1]

Constanze's younger son, Franz Xaver Wolfgang, accepted his first appointment in 1808, at the age of 17—he became music teacher in a household living in Podkamien, east of Lemberg (now Lvov in the Ukraine). The situation was rural, and he soon disliked the isolation. He moved to Lemberg and began a freelance life, but his career seems to have been blighted by the twin facts that he was a rather ordinary musician and that his father had been Mozart. He was apparently easily discouraged by the perception that he was under pressure to be something special; when Carl had announced to Constanze in 1806 that he wanted to try to forge a musical career, she had warned him that no son of Mozart might be musically mediocre.[2] Wolfgang undertook a number of journeys, including a long concert tour from 1819 to 1821, but was tied to Lemberg by his love for Josepha Baroni-Cavalcabò, a married woman still living with her husband, in whose household Wolfgang gave music lessons. Both

---

[1] See W. Goldinger, 'Archivalisch-genealogische Notizen zum Mozartjahr', 77–83. Constanze's personal letters to her sons are not given complete in *MBA*, but a much fuller collection is contained in Schurig, *Konstanze Mozart*.

[2] Constanze to Carl, 5 Mar. 1806—*MBA* 1370/2–9 (not in *Letters*).

his career and his personal life were to remain causes of concern to Constanze.[3]

In 1792 Berchtold and his brother Johann Nepomuk Martin had been raised to the nobility, together with their descendants. From this time the members of Nannerl's family were barons and baronesses, and were called 'von Berchtold zu Sonnenburg'.[4] They continued to maintain close relations with other members of Berchtold's family, especially with the families of his brothers Joseph Sigismund in Strobl and Franz Anton Maximilian in Lofer. Births, marriages, and deaths of people in these families were recorded in the biographies of the children of Berchtold and Nannerl, and the 9-year-old Leopoldl even went to stay for more than a year in Lofer with his uncle's family, from 16 September 1794 (three months after the birth and immediate death of their only son Ubald August Kaspar) until 15 October 1795.[5] In the year of his return his older half-brother Johann Baptist, aged almost 16, started to work alongside his father in the chancellery of the Pfleggericht, Karl was sent to Augsburg to continue his education, and his younger sister Jeanette, aged 6, began to learn to play the keyboard with Nannerl.[6] Karl did not stay long in Augsburg, however; his father judged it too dangerous when the French began to threaten the city, and he returned home in 1796 and went to school in Salzburg again, joined for the first time by Leopoldl.[7] Young Nannerl was apparently living away from home from 1797, or perhaps even earlier,[8] so that for the last few years of Berchtold's life the only children living there on a daily basis were Johann Baptist the younger and Jeanette.

Berchtold died at half past nine in the evening of 26 February 1801, during a period when French soldiers were billeted on the family in

---

[3] The standard work on Mozart's sons is W. Hummel, *W. A. Mozarts Söhne* (Kassel, 1956). Basic biographical information about them is available in English in Gärtner, *After the Requiem*, 135–54. The diary written by Wolfgang on his concert tour from 1819 to 1821 is published—see F. X. W. Mozart, *Reisetagebuch 1819–1821*, ed. R. Angermüller (Bad Honnef, 1994).

[4] The baronetcy diploma is reproduced in R. Angermüller, 'Das Diploma Baronatus für die Gebrüder Johann Baptist und Johann Nepomuk Martin Berchtold zu Sonnenburg aus dem Jahre 1792', *MM* 19 (1971), 13–24.

[5] Brno, MZA, Berchtold Family Archive, Family Chronicle, unpaginated, but pp. 49 and 73 on my count. See Ch. 3 for Franz Anton Maximilian's lament on the death of Ubald August Kaspar.

[6] Brno, MZA, Berchtold Family Archive, Family Chronicle, unpaginated, but pp. 59, 85, and 110 on my count.

[7] Ibid. 60, 97–8, 100, and 102–3 on my count.

[8] Ibid. 60 on my count. Though this entry does not state how young Nannerl was living, and merely remarks that she paid a visit to her father in St Gilgen, it is possible that she was living in Mondsee. Berchtold's sister Marie Catherine Francisce had lived there until her death in 1784 (ibid. 54 and 78 on my count), and there may still have been family connections there in the 1790s. I have not been able to discover evidence for this, but young Nannerl certainly settled in Mondsee after Berchtold's death until her marriage.

St Gilgen. The cause of death was given as 'the consequences of *Brand*'; this word literally means 'fire', and in the context of illness designated a severe inflammation, by which the body was totally consumed. At eight in the morning of 2 March the burial took place, and on three separate occasions afterwards Masses were said for Berchtold's soul. Johann Baptist the younger organized the erection of a monument to his father in the village church of St Ägidius—it was ordered from Salzburg at a cost of 342 fl., displayed praise of the deceased in verse, and can still be seen there today.[9]

After Berchtold's death, an inventory of all his assets and liabilities was compiled, and the process of settling his estate began. Though it was complicated by the facts that the children had three different mothers (and hence differing maternal inheritances, which interacted in various intricate ways with their paternal inheritance) and that Berchtold wanted to provide an annual allowance for Nannerl from the capital bequeathed to his children, the survival of the most important of his estate documents, together with earlier and later relevant documentation, enables the procedures of settlement to be broadly understood. First the heirs were named; they were all the children, ordered according to which marriage each had issued from, and boys ahead of girls (Berchtold's wife Nannerl was not an heir, though provision was made for her and she received a named bequest). Then a list was given of relevant documentation—this consisted mainly of Berchtold's baronetcy diploma, the contract of his marriage to Nannerl, and his will of 25 September 1798. Next the listing of the assets began; savings and cash were counted first, and then every piece of Berchtold's property was named and valued. Berchtold had made a particular bequest to Nannerl and to each child of a small number of named items, and these were valued too. After the assets came the liabilities; these were debts, costs, the total of the named bequests, the money that had to pass to Nannerl to fulfil the terms of the marriage settlement, and some miscellaneous items. The capital sum specified in the marriage contract was 2,000 fl., made up of the 500 fl. brought by Nannerl, the 1,000 fl. provided by Berchtold, and the extra 500 fl. promised by him as *Morgengabe*. Berchtold's estate inventory makes it clear that Nannerl had never yet received any of this capital, but had instead been paid interest on the relevant elements during the course of the marriage. Since the

---

[9] Ibid. 88–9 and 114–15 on my count. The billeting of the soldiers was mentioned in a letter from Nannerl to Breitkopf & Härtel on 9 Feb. 1801—*MBA* 1327/7–12 (not in *Letters*); and also in the inventory compiled after Berchtold's death—Brno, MZA, Berchtold Family Archive, Appendix to the Will and Inventory of Johann Baptist.

interest payments were several years in arrears at the time of Berchtold's death, Nannerl now had to receive a total of 2,134 fl. 14 kr. for the marriage contract specifications alone.

When everything had been accounted for and all the obligations had been fulfilled, Berchtold's estate amounted to 27,144 fl. 44 kr. 1 pf., a sum which had to be divided equally among his six surviving children.[10] But they could not inherit it immediately, because he had stipulated that until she died Nannerl should receive 300 fl. annually from the interest on the sum, in return for her loyalty, love, tenderness, and good housekeeping.[11] This clause in Berchtold's will proved problematic for the children on account of Nannerl's longevity, and in 1808 the survivors (by that date both Joseph and Jeanette had died) were to be allowed to inherit their portions of their father's estate in return for a guarantee that they would each pay Nannerl a fair share towards her annual entitlement, which had by that time grown to 336 fl.[12] Nannerl may also have received a widow's pension of 300 fl. from the Salzburg court,[13] so that she would have had a comfortable income had there not been rampant inflation during the Napoleonic upheavals.

Nannerl returned to Salzburg at Michaelmas 1801, but it is not clear that any of the stepchildren went with her. Young Nannerl, aged 29, went to live in Mondsee, and took with her the sickly 23-year-old Joseph.[14] Though Joseph shared equally with his siblings in the main part of Berchtold's estate, he was not accorded the same treatment with respect to the particular named bequests. He was merely invited to choose three snuff-boxes from his father's collection, whereas Berchtold himself had chosen the articles for the other children and for his wife.[15] In the inventory Joseph's snuff-boxes were valued at 5 fl. 30 kr., while the lowest value of Berchtold's legacies to his other children was 76 fl.[16] Joseph continued to be relatively helpless. In 1805 his guardian reported that he could never be released from guardianship because of his condition,[17] suggesting that his mental state was poor. He died young in 1806.

---

[10] The information in this paragraph and the preceding one is from ibid. Inventory of Johann Baptist.

[11] Ibid., Will of Johann Baptist, clause 2—see Ch. 24, n. 47, for a translation of part of this clause.

[12] SLA, Verlassakt Stadtgericht Salzburg Nr. 1. 713/1822, document dated 21 Mar. 1808. I have not been able to determine why the sum of 300 fl. stipulated by Berchtold had grown to 336 fl. by this date. The documents about the Berchtold inheritances both in Brno and in Salzburg show complex interlinkings, and it would be useful if they could all be published and thoroughly studied.

[13] Brno, MZA, Berchtold Family Archive, Pension Document dated 7 May 1806.

[14] SLA, Verlassakt Stadtgericht Salzburg Nr. 1. 713/1822, Guardianship Report of 22 Jan. 1805.

[15] Brno, MZA, Berchtold Family Archive, Will of Johann Baptist.

[16] Ibid., Inventory of Johann Baptist, pp. 20–3.

[17] SLA, Guardianship Report of 22 Jan. 1805.

Johann Baptist the younger was aged 21 on his father's death. He moved from the St Gilgen Pfleger's chancellery to a post in the Landschaft in Salzburg, under the old mutual friend of the Mozarts and the Berchtolds, J. B. J. Joachim Ferdinand von Schiedenhofen. Karl first became a cadet with the Tyrolese *Jäger* regiment in 1805, and later served in the police force in Linz. He was 18 when his father died. It is possible that Johann Baptist and Karl first lodged with Nannerl in Salzburg when she moved back in the autumn of 1801, but by January 1805 she was caring only for her own children, Leopold and Jeanette.[18]

Leopold's schooling at the St Peter's Gymnasium continued after Nannerl's move, the only difference being that he could now lodge at home instead of being boarded out.[19] On completion of his education he first entered an infantry regiment based in St Pölten, but left it again in 1807. He then joined the Salzburg army, and in 1809 was taken prisoner by the French and incarcerated in Vienna. Later he became a customs official, and continued to occupy administrative positions, eventually settling in Innsbruck.[20]

The youngest surviving child, Jeanette, was only 11 when her father died. She stayed with Nannerl after the move to Salzburg, continuing with her musical studies, and in addition learning housekeeping from her mother.[21] Jeanette was evidently a singer as well as a keyboard player, for a number of opera arias bearing her name survive. She had not been born when the Berchtold household had been struck by smallpox in the autumn of 1787, and was immunized against it in Salzburg on 20 April 1802, one of the many patients so treated in Dr Doutrepont's campaign.[22] The background to this was that following an epidemic of smallpox in Vienna in 1800, Jenner's new method of vaccination was introduced there. Doutrepont learned the technique under the doctors Carro and Ferro, and therefore had the necessary expertise when he went to work in Salzburg. Popular resistance was fierce, and in 1802 a vigorous campaign was waged to try to persuade people to have their children immunized. Whereas formerly the Church had opposed the procedure and made parents fearful of challenging God's omnipotence, Church and State now

---

[18] Ibid. [19] Ibid.

[20] See Goldinger, 'Archivalisch-genealogische Notizen zum Mozartjahr', 92–4.

[21] SLA, Guardianship Report of 22 Jan. 1805.

[22] Brno, MZA, Berchtold Family Archive, Family Chronicle. This piece of information is not contained in the chronicle proper, however, but rather on one of three scraps of paper residing unattached between two of its pages. They contain what seem to be jottings for the chronicle, and note among other things what appears to have been Jeanette's confirmation on 18 Sept. 1802. (Vaccination and confirmation may have been linked.)

worked together, and sermons were preached on the duty of having children protected.[23] People of status, such as Pfleger, were urged to have their children publicly vaccinated, priests put pressure on parents to have their children treated before they were confirmed, and poor people receiving alms were required to produce vaccination certificates for their children before they were helped. Of all the sanctions employed, however, the one that hit parents hardest was the refusal to allow a child who had died unvaccinated of smallpox to be accompanied at the burial; in addition, the parents' names were read from the pulpit.[24]

Despite the vaccination, Jeanette was destined to die young. She sickened of 'nerve fever' in 1805, died aged 16 on 1 September in the Blasius Hospital, one of Salzburg's hospitals, and was buried with Leopold, the grandfather she had never known, in St Sebastian's churchyard.[25] She left an estate of 5,283 fl. 36 kr. 2 pf. after deductions; it was to be shared between her mother Nannerl and her brother Leopold.[26]

It was Jeanette's name on the above-mentioned opera arias that was later to help link the set of performance parts of many of Mozart's keyboard concertos (preserved in St Peter's in Salzburg) with Nannerl. For

[23] There was nevertheless still a conservative movement within the clergy, and each immunization calamity eroded the fragile trust of parents; one such case was provided by the deaths around the turn of the century of children in one family who had recently been immunized by Dr Johann Jakob Hartenkeil, one of Colloredo's most trusted reformers. Hartenkeil's progressive medical ideas were viciously attacked by the clergyman Felix Adauctus Haslberger who, with reference to Hartenkeil's midwifery reforms, claimed on 20 Nov. 1801 that no midwife in Salzburg had yet managed, as Hartenkeil had, to rip the head off a child in the womb during delivery, so that the mother died too. See S. Falk and A. S. Weiss, ' "Hier sind die Blattern" ', 166; and F. Martin, 'Die Salzburger Chronik des Felix Adauktus Haslberger (Nachtrag)', *MGSL* 74 (1934), 159–68 (here at 168).

[24] See S. Falk and A. S. Weiss, ' "Hier sind die Blattern" ', 163–86.

[25] Salzburg, Erzbischöfliches Konsistorialarchiv, St Blasius, Sterbebuch 1, p. 117 (details kindly communicated by Dr Ernst Hintermaier). One of the three scraps of paper slipped into the Family Chronicle in Brno (see n. 22 above) gives a series of dates without explanation—3 Aug., and 1, 3, and 4 Sept. 1805. Since 1 Sept. was the date of Jeanette's death, the date in August may have marked something significant about her illness, and the two later dates in Sept. may have marked her burial date and the date of a service for her soul.

[26] Brno, MZA, Berchtold Family Archive, Inventory of Johanna von Sonnenburg. Nannerl's inheritance from Jeanette needs to be taken into account when considering the provenance of the sum she left on her own death in 1829. Solomon's discussion of Nannerl's finances, whose purpose is to estimate the sum she might have inherited from Leopold, is not based on the most recently rediscovered Berchtold papers, of which Jeanette's inventory is one; see Solomon, *Mozart*, 413. The reason why a more detailed discussion of Nannerl's family is given than of Constanze's is that most of the primary documents relating to the Berchtolds have not yet been published and are hardly known. The two main biographies of Nannerl (W. Hummel, *Nannerl. Wolfgang Amadeus Mozarts Schwester* (Zurich, 1952); and Rieger, *Nannerl Mozart*) were written before the collection in Brno was brought to general attention and do not use them, and since the documents in this collection allow much information which has found its way into secondary literature to be confirmed, corrected, and supplemented, they deserve to be more widely known.

a long time the provenance of these parts was unknown. When they were examined for the purpose of publishing the works in the *Neue Mozart Ausgabe*, however, it became clear that the handwriting of Leopold, Wolfgang, and Nannerl Mozart was present. Jeanette's name on the arias stored with the keyboard music confirmed beyond reasonable doubt that these parts had been Nannerl Mozart's own performance material for her brother's concertos, a discovery of outstanding importance to questions of performance practice in Mozart's concertos.[27]

Soon after their marriage in 1809 Constanze and Nissen were preparing to leave Vienna for Copenhagen, where Nissen took up a post as censor after leaving his diplomatic career. Prior to their departure in 1810 Constanze arranged for a number of valuable items from her Mozartian possessions to pass to her sons. Carl was sent Mozart's fortepiano, and urged never to part with it; Wolfgang received a different keyboard instrument which had belonged to his father. The Nissens also tied up various financial arrangements concerning the boys before their departure.[28] From 1810 until 1820 the family was fairly widely scattered. Nannerl and the Berchtolds were all still based close to Salzburg, but Constanze was in Copenhagen, young Wolfgang in Lemberg, and Carl in Milan. And Breitkopf & Härtel's plans for a new biography of Mozart were still slumbering.

In 1820, however, Nissen retired, and he and Constanze moved to Salzburg. By 1823 he had decided that he would write the long-planned biography of Mozart, and he set to work gathering material for it. He used two assistants, Anton Jähndl and Maximilian Keller. Together they wrote to people who might have information to communicate about Mozart, interviewed people in Salzburg who had known him, and tracked down as much of the printed material about him as possible.[29] The eventual list of printed items collected numbered more than fifty, although some were histories of music containing only short articles on Mozart, and many were biographical works deriving ultimately from the biographies of Schlichtegroll and Niemetschek. The Rochlitz anecdotes were also among the items collected.[30]

---

[27] See M. H. Schmid, 'Nannerl Mozart und ihr musikalischer Nachlass'; and id., 'Musikalien des Mozartschen Familienarchivs', 173–4.

[28] See the correspondence for 1809 and 1810 given in Schurig, *Konstanze Mozart*.

[29] See von Nissen, *Biographie*, Foreword (by R. Angermüller), pp. v–xiii.

[30] See ibid., Appendix, pp. 212–17.

But by far the most valuable material communicated to Nissen was a collection of some four hundred family letters which Nannerl gave him for the purpose. By 1820 her sight was failing, and she perhaps felt that she had no more use for them. These letters had apparently never until now left Nannerl's possession and had certainly not been used in any work about Mozart, so that they alone would have provided the basis for a substantial biography of Mozart, at least until 1784. Leopold's letters to Wolfgang from 1781 and Wolfgang's to Leopold from 1784 were apparently no longer in existence by 1823; but Nannerl also let Nissen see at least some of Leopold's letters to her following her marriage in 1784, some of which gave news of Wolfgang. Nissen was well aware of the value of these primary documents, but in his attempts to fill in gaps of knowledge about Mozart he continued to pursue all the other leads he could think of.[31] The result was a huge mass of material which would need considerable editorial skill if it was to be used coherently.[32] Checking anecdotal reports against primary evidence (bearing in mind that the letters were of course still in manuscript) and tracing claims about Mozart in printed biographies to their source would alone have been a considerable task.

What Nissen himself would have done with all this material will never be known, because he died while it was still being collected, on 24 March 1826. The only part of the work definitely written by him was the incomplete introduction, or Author's Preface. From this, however, it is clear that he had read the letters given him by Nannerl, that he was keenly interested in them, and that they had caused him to question what kind of biography of Mozart he could legitimately write. For while he developed from them a profound respect for the character of Leopold Mozart (whom he resembled in terms of a strong sense of paternal responsibility), he disapproved of many traits of Wolfgang's character which were

---

[31] Constanze to Benedikt Schack, 16 Feb. 1826—*MBA* 1407 (not in *Letters*). This letter (at ll. 82–92) seems at first sight to suggest that the material supplied by Nannerl only reached the year 1781. Since Nissen's biography quoted from the family correspondence after that date, however, this was clearly not the case. The context of the passage is Constanze's explanation to Schack of Nissen's desire to render Leopold Mozart's character as well as Wolfgang's, so perhaps the reference to 1781 meant simply that Leopold's letters to Wolfgang had not survived beyond that date.

[32] The collection of material is what is now known as Nissen's *Kollektaneen*, and is preserved in the archive of the Mozarteum in Salzburg. It contains, in addition to printed works, and manuscripts sent to Nissen by people who had information about Mozart to communicate, Nissen's own copies of some of the documents he was sent; some of these copies are extracts only. Not everything in the *Kollektaneen* found its way into the biography. For further information about the contents of the *Kollektaneen*, see R. Lewicki, 'Aus Nissens Kollektaneen', *MM* 2 (1919), 28–30; and R. Angermüller, 'Nissens Kollektaneen'. These two works complement each other; Angermüller's is an overview of the whole collection, while Levicki's discusses individual items, often pointing out differences between the material in the *Kollektaneen* and its use in the biography.

shown up by the letters, and was perplexed by the problem of how much he might reveal.

Nissen began his introduction by explaining that Leopold Mozart had intended to write his son's biography, and that this was the chief reason for the survival of so many family letters. He continued by sorting the letters into categories, explaining what had occasioned the writing of each set, what kind of material they contained, and how far they still existed. About the letters to Hagenauer, for example, he commented that they would have been more interesting had they been written to a musician or an educated man—a clear indication that Nissen believed Leopold to have tailored his travel reports to the outlook of his recipient, who was inferior to him in intellect. The letters written home to Maria Anna and Nannerl from the three Italian journeys and from Vienna in 1773 and Munich in 1775 Nissen found more interesting, but not surprisingly his greatest enthusiasm was for the 'man to man' correspondence between Leopold and Wolfgang. He accordingly picked out the letters from 1777 to 1779 (when Wolfgang had travelled to Paris and back without Leopold) and from 1780 to 1784 (when Wolfgang had gone to Munich for *Idomeneo*, and on to Vienna, where he stayed) as being of special interest. In this latter group, Nissen noted the loss of Leopold's letters to Wolfgang after March 1781, suggesting that Wolfgang had been too independent of Leopold and also too distracted to preserve them (or indeed to write much in return).

Nissen commented, in mentioning the letters written from Italy, that Wolfgang's youthful letters to Nannerl posed a problem, since they contained so much tasteless wit, childish vulgarity, and a far-reaching boisterousness. He indicated that they would have to be heavily edited if they were to offer the public an attractive and characteristic view of Mozart which would not damage his reputation. Later in his introduction, with regard to the biography as a whole, he returned to this point, summing up his dilemma under the twin tags of: '*De mortuis nil, nisi bene!*'; '*De mortuis nil, nisi vere!*' ('Speak nothing but good of the dead!'; 'Speak nothing but truth of the dead!'), and adding in brackets 'Concealment is a form of untruth'.[33] He acknowledged the claim on biographers to show their subjects as they really were, but mentioned the many limitations hemming them in, and suggested that an accurate picture of a recently deceased person was probably impossible. The limitations he meant were the familiar ones. He questioned the right of the biographer to disseminate material from letters which the subject had not written for publication and would

---

[33] 'Verschweigung ist schon Unwahrheit'.

probably not have wanted to be published. He also pointed out that the subject's moral weaknesses, revealed by his letters, might later have been corrected, but that it might not always be possible to show this. He mentioned the difficulty of understanding the letters according to the accepted norms of the society in which they had been written (for more than thirty years had elapsed since Mozart's death, and many more since his childhood). And he pointed out the difficulties caused by giving possible offence to people mentioned in the letters, some of whom were still alive.[34]

Behind all these reservations about what he should and should not reveal was probably chiefly Nissen's concern for the feelings of Constanze and Nannerl. It is difficult to believe that Constanze would not have felt it grossly disloyal to her first husband to allow his more embarrassing letters to be printed. On the other hand, Nissen's sympathies as far as character was concerned were not really with Wolfgang—Leopold, rather, was the man he admired. He called Leopold a 'pattern of order', said that his letters were more interesting than Wolfgang's, and praised his intellect and morals, and the education he had given his son. By contrast, he seems to have thought that Wolfgang's frivolity had been carried too far. Nissen's disapproval of traits in Mozart's character which he obviously thought immature probably owed something to his observance of the way in which Constanze had had to pick up the pieces of her life after Mozart's death, since no provision had been made for her. In his and Constanze's letters to Carl and young Wolfgang can be discerned a view (admittedly slightly veiled, perhaps out of consideration for the boys' feelings about their father) that she should not have been left in a position where she had had to pay Mozart's debts, provide an inheritance for her sons, and try to feed, clothe, and educate them, all by her own efforts. Nissen himself had gradually taken over responsibility for the financial welfare of the whole family, and the correspondence suggests that he had done so with admirable patience and generosity. As the boys had grown up and moved away from Vienna to work, he had continued to write to them with practical and moral advice and support, and had thus shared to some extent the experience of Leopold when he had tried to set his son on what he considered the right path.[35]

---

[34] The material in this paragraph and the preceding one is from von Nissen, *Biographie*, Author's Preface, pp. xiii–xxiv.

[35] See e.g. Nissen and Constanze to Carl, 13 June 1810—Schurig, *Konstanze Mozart*, 66–70; extract only in *MBA* 1388 (not in *Letters*). This letter even exhorts Carl to jot down notes for his letters, so that they would not omit anything of interest or importance—just as Leopold had often exhorted his son to follow this methodical practice.

Although Nissen had mixed feelings about what he should reveal of Mozart, he decided that it was impossible, for all the above reasons, to allow Mozart's letters simply to speak for themselves. He stated specifically that he would omit many of Mozart's more childish postscripts to the letters home written on the journey to Paris, so it seems clear that he intended to edit out some at least of the material that he felt would have damaged Mozart's reputation.

Nissen's introduction broke off during a discussion of Mozart's letters to Constanze. It is not clear what happened first about the biography after his death, but Constanze for some reason eventually entrusted its completion not to Nissen's assistants Jähndl and Keller, but to a Mozart enthusiast in Pirna, the medical doctor Johann Heinrich Feuerstein. She continued to send Feuerstein material and suggestions for inclusion, so that the biography would conform, at least in some respects, to her wishes. But her main concern (as it had been with the Requiem after Mozart's death) seems to have been at all costs to get the work finished. To the end of her life she was actively saving in order to swell the inheritance of her sons, of which the proceeds of Nissen's biography were to form a part; and the subscribers had to be satisfied too. Furthermore the work was a monument to both her husbands, and as such meant a good deal to her. Whether she could not face the prospect of checking its contents carefully, whether she placed too much trust in Feuerstein, or whether she simply did not care much about it so long as it portrayed the 'right' picture of her marriage with Mozart, is not clear. At any rate, the book was cobbled together in a haphazard fashion from the raw material, and the result was disastrous in terms of quality. Repetitions were rife, sources were frequently not given, and anecdotal material was reproduced without comment even when contradicted by primary evidence also given in the book.[36] Nissen would probably have

---

[36] For a more detailed critique of the editorial practice in Nissen's biography, see Solomon, 'The Rochlitz Anecdotes', 49–55. Solomon rightly points out that the confusion in the work is so great that a critical edition is needed, in order that the stories told in it about Mozart can be traced back to their sources. It is surely also the case, given that the biography is essentially a heap of material, that the contents of the *Kollektaneen* should become more widely known, because in many cases they give the unexpurgated details. As long ago as 1919, Levicki noted that the biography toned down some of the material in the *Kollektaneen*. One example is the story of Mozart's attempt at bravado after Aloisia Weber had rejected him in Munich at the end of 1778; in the biography he was described singing the words, 'I'll gladly leave the girl who doesn't want me' ('Ich lass das Mädel gern, das mich nicht will'); in the *Kollektaneen* the words were, 'The slut who doesn't want me can lick my a– – –' ('Leck mir das Mensch im A– – – –, das mich nicht will'). Cf. von Nissen, *Biographie*, 414–15; and Lewicki, 'Aus Nissens Kollektaneen', 29. Aloisia was still alive when the biography was published—she did not die until 1839.

been horrified if he had known that his name would forever be linked with the work.[37]

The most exciting new material for the biography came from the family letters to 1787, and the biography relied heavily on them to tell the story of Mozart's life, merely providing link passages between groups of letters where they were necessary to a coherent account. The question of biographical truth in Nissen therefore hangs to a large extent on the selection from the letters. Where material was omitted, paraphrases were often resorted to in order that the letter would still make sense. The paraphrases in themselves were often harmless, but the omissions show with tremendous force the truth of Nissen's own phrase, 'Concealment is a form of untruth', and it cannot be too heavily stressed that the text of a letter rendered in Nissen can only be accepted as reliable if a comparison with the original shows it to be so. The importance of this point will shortly become apparent.

In the early section of the biography, up to 1777, the omissions are perhaps not too damaging, although the immature aspects of Wolfgang's character were suppressed, and Leopold's preoccupation with and difficulty in obtaining a good post for Wolfgang was obscured. The letters home from Vienna in 1773, for example, were stripped of the material hinting at the purpose of the trip, and Nissen, commenting on Mozart's prospects as he set off on the journey that was to take him to Paris in 1777, suggested that he could take his pick of Europe's great cities.[38] This claim obscures the fact that the foremost purpose of the journey was to obtain a court appointment, Leopold already having tried and failed to gain one for his son in Italy, Vienna, and Munich. Thus even by this stage of the biography, early failures documented by the letters had been edited out.

But it is in the part of the biography covering the journey of 1777–9 that the grossest misrepresentations occurred. In the first place, Leopold's reasons for not accompanying Wolfgang were distorted. Nissen claimed that Leopold felt that the travel expenses for four people would be too heavy, and that his post would be jeopardized by a long absence.[39] Given that Nissen had letters showing that Leopold had already come within a whisker of losing his job before Wolfgang set out,[40] it is clear that he did not want to reveal how poor the relations between the Mozarts and the

---

[37] Despite the fact that the book can hardly be said to have been 'written' by Nissen, I refer to him as the author in the following discussion, simply to avoid awkwardness of reference.

[38] Von Nissen, *Biographie*, 275–80 and 292–3.   [39] Ibid. 293–4.

[40] Cf. e.g. Leopold to Wolfgang, 28–9 Sept. 1777—*MBA* 337 (*Letters* 211).

Salzburg court had become. What is perhaps less excusable is that he suggested that the correspondence from the journey to Paris and back was given complete. This was by no means true, and the claim was the more reprehensible because he had already pointed out that it was in these letters that Wolfgang had effectively started to write his autobiography.[41]

In fact, almost every passage revealing negative aspects of Wolfgang's character was omitted from the letters of this period. The account of the interview with the elector in Munich, showing Wolfgang's youthful impatience and arrogance, was pruned to blandness,[42] and the big bones of contention between Wolfgang and Leopold occasioned by Wolfgang's behaviour in Mannheim were cut completely. Thus Wolfgang's frivolity with Schmalz and his credit notes was omitted, as were his scatological flippancy with Marie Elisabeth Cannabich, his squandering of money at Kirchheimbolanden, his attempts to help Aloisia and the Webers while still unable to keep out of debt himself or do anything for his family, and the most tactless part of his expressed disdain for teaching, which was so insulting to Leopold. And this is to say nothing of Leopold's complaints that he did not write his letters methodically, keep his father abreast of his plans, or report the financial situation accurately, all of which were likewise omitted.[43] Furthermore, the story of the child Wolfgang saying that he would put Leopold in a glass case to keep him safe with him for ever was recounted out of context as a touching anecdote in that part of Nissen's biography covering Wolfgang's childhood; whereas its context was a letter written by Leopold to Wolfgang on 11–12 February 1778 (when Wolfgang was in Mannheim), in which Leopold bitterly upbraided Wolfgang for neglecting his family, and tried to put moral pressure on him by reminding him of his childhood expressions of love for his father.[44] The passages referring to the mounting of debt on the way home from Paris did not appear, nor Leopold's attempt to pin some of the blame for Maria Anna's death on to Wolfgang.[45] When it is considered how loving Wolfgang's letters could be, and how it is at times of conflict (especially with Leopold) that this professed love can best be put to the test, it becomes clear how significant the omissions in Nissen are.

---

[41] Von Nissen, *Biographie*, 293–4.   [42] Ibid. 302–3.   [43] Ibid. 320–57.

[44] The story occurs in ibid. 35. In context it is at *MBA* 422/27–32 (*Letters* 285). Though Nissen's rendering of this story is derived partly from an anecdote offered on 24 Nov. 1799 to Breitkopf & Härtel by Nannerl (and published in the *AmZ* on 22 Jan. 1800—cf. *MBA* 1268/18–26; Deutsch, *Documents*, 493–4), Nannerl's anecdote does not include the 'glass case' part of the story, whose sole source is Leopold's letter to Wolfgang in Mannheim.

[45] Von Nissen, *Biographie*, 380–413.

Later conflicts were glossed over by Nissen in the same way. Leopold's fury at Wolfgang's resignation was entirely ignored, and in fact Nissen claimed that Wolfgang's statement that he could be more use to Leopold in Vienna than in Salzburg was borne out by the fact that he was from time to time able to send Leopold gifts of money, ranging from 10 to 30 ducats (45–135 fl.).[46] This claim must be treated with extreme scepticism. There is only one recorded instance of Leopold actually receiving money from Wolfgang during Wolfgang's Viennese years,[47] and although the loss of much of the correspondence means that there can be no certainty that there were not other occasions, which Nissen might have known about from Constanze, Wolfgang's record of unfulfilled promises and financial embarrassments does not inspire confidence. Yet it would be easy to gain the impression from this passage in Nissen's work that Leopold was contented with Wolfgang's decision to live in Vienna. Similarly, the deep disagreement about Wolfgang's marriage was ignored by Nissen,[48] and the last disagreement of all, when Leopold refused to take charge of Wolfgang's two children in 1786, was obscured by cutting and paraphrasing the two relevant letters. Instead of indicating Leopold's dissatisfaction with the money he was being offered and with the whole arrangement, the impression given by Nissen was simply that Wolfgang had offered to pay for the children's care, and that Leopold's sole doubts concerned the financial viability of the proposed trip to England.[49]

These enormous faults in Nissen's biography can be understood when the context in which it was written is considered. It joins the work of Schlichtegroll and Niemetschek (albeit on a larger scale) in the category of biographies which were hampered by having been written while too many people closely connected with Mozart were still alive and in control of the source material. Now that all this primary evidence is published, it may be asked why it matters that Nissen's work was so badly flawed. The reasons are first that claims once made in an influential work are very difficult to uproot, and secondly that the inclusion of material such as Rochlitz's anecdotes has enabled the argument to be put forward that this constituted an endorsement of them on Constanze's part.[50] These considerations mean that the circumstances of the writing of Nissen's biography need to become much more familiar. But the most important reason is that some of the source material has disappeared since it was in Nissen's hands, and there are seven letters and a postscript that are known

---

[46] Von Nissen, *Biographie*, 446.
[47] In Apr. 1783—*MBA* 736/11–15 and 739/44–5 (*Letters* 485 and 486).
[48] Von Nissen, *Biographie*, 445–67.   [49] Ibid. 523.   [50] Cf. Ch. 34, p. 603.

only from their rendering in Nissen's biography. And because when Nissen's letter texts can be checked against the originals they are frequently found deliberately to have distorted the truth (even if 'only' by omissions), those letters which are known only from Nissen have to be used with great caution. The letters in question are:

1. Wolfgang to Nannerl from Bologna, 24 March 1770—*MBA* 168 (*Letters* 84*a*).
2. Part of Wolfgang's postscript (to a letter of Leopold's) to Nannerl from Rome, 21 April 1770—*MBA* 177/71–4 (*Letters* 88*a*, 2nd paragraph).[51]
3. Leopold to Maria Anna from Milan, 13 September 1771—*MBA* 245 (*Letters* 143).
4. Wolfgang to Leopold from Munich, 29 November 1780—*MBA* 545 (*Letters* 365).[52]
5. Leopold to Wolfgang from Salzburg, 25 December 1780—*MBA* 569 (*Letters* 380).
6. Wolfgang to Leopold from Vienna, 24 April 1784—*MBA* 786 (*Letters* 510).
7. Leopold to Nannerl, 19 March 1785—*MBA* 852 (*Letters* p. 889 n. 1).[53]
8. Wolfgang to Nannerl from Vienna, 16 June 1787—*MBA* 1058 (*Letters* 548).

With most of these letters, there is no way of knowing what might be missing from them in Nissen's rendering.[54] In two, however, he can be suspected of having omitted material of importance. One of these cases is *MBA* 852, in which Leopold had said that if Wolfgang had no debts to pay he ought to be able to bank 2,000 fl., and that the housekeeping

[51] Though the original of the whole postscript is lost, a draft survives in Nissen's *Kollektaneen*; everything in the postscript as rendered in Nissen's biography is in the draft, except for the paragraph specified here. I have relied here on the commentary to *MBA* 177, but its attempt to explain exactly which parts of the postscript (draft or corrected versions, in Mozart's hand or Nissen's copy) survive in the *Kollektaneen* is not lucid.

[52] The original of this letter was apparently sold at auction by Puttick & Simpson, and the catalogue—dated 20 Dec. 1848—mentioned a postscript in which Wolfgang urged Leopold to write frequently, but during the day and wearing spectacles. This postscript is not given by Nissen. See commentary to *MBA* 545.

[53] The commentary to this letter in Deutsch and Paumgartner, *Leopold Mozarts Briefe an seine Tochter* (p. 511) states that the letter was known to Otto Jahn, but that he also only reproduced in his biography the one sentence known today; neither does any more of it survive in the Nissen *Kollektaneen*. But the English edn. of Jahn's biography, at any rate, does not show or even suggest that the whole letter was known to Jahn—his remarks about Leopold's visit to Vienna in 1785 could have been derived from the extract of the letter in Nissen's *Kollektaneen*. Cf. Jahn, *Life of Mozart*, ii. 320.

[54] The exception is *MBA* 545, some at least of whose contents were summarized in the auction catalogue mentioned in n. 52 above.

of Wolfgang and Constanze, as far as food and drink was concerned, was extremely economical; there are strong grounds for believing that Leopold actually had grave reservations about the domestic economy of Wolfgang and Constanze.[55] The other case is *MBA* 1058, the letter in which Wolfgang explained to Nannerl after Leopold's death that if it were not his duty to consider his wife and child he would gladly leave everything to his sister.[56] This is one of the most regrettable single losses (together with Nannerl's letter to which it is an answer) in the whole of the Mozart correspondence, for it probably shed more light on the way in which Leopold had disposed of his estate; if Nissen's renderings had been more reliable the loss of the original would not matter so much.

In the case of *MBA* 1058, what has been printed in Nissen's biography is at least so puzzling that it should not lead to the drawing of false inferences, but *MBA* 852 is susceptible to misuse as evidence that even the prudent and thrifty Leopold could find no fault with the housekeeping of Wolfgang and Constanze. In the light of Nissen's practice of concealment, this inference cannot safely be made, and it would be helpful if loud, clear, and repeated warnings were attached to the few remaining letters known only from his biography.

[55] See Ch. 27, p. 476, for an explanation of these grounds.
[56] It is discussed in Ch. 31, p. 555.

❧ 36 ❧

Handing on the Source Material

~✦~

WHEN Leopold Mozart's grave in St Sebastian's churchyard had been opened in 1805 for Jeanette's burial, it was not for the first time; in 1798 Genoveva Weber, an aunt by marriage of Constanze's, and mother of the composer Carl Maria von Weber, had also been buried there. And when Nissen died in 1826, the grave was opened yet again for him. Next year, Nannerl added a codicil to the will she had made in 1823; whereas she had then requested to be buried in her father's grave, she now changed the stipulation and instead asked to be interred in St Peter's churchyard.[1] Nannerl's biographer Walter Hummel states that by having had Nissen buried in Leopold's grave Constanze had avoided paying for the use of it; that when she had a headstone made for the grave it gave only Nissen's name, and not those of the other three inhabitants; and that Nannerl was so indignant at the behaviour of the sister-in-law to whom she had never in any case been close, that she altered her will in order not to have anything more to do with Constanze, even after her death.[2] This has become the standard view on the subject, and the evidence of the codicil certainly lends plausibility to the estrangement theory. However, Hummel does not adduce any evidence for his claim that the grave 'belonged' to the Mozarts; nor does he state under what circumstances Genoveva Weber was buried in it (long before Constanze went to live in Salzburg and seven years before Jeanette's death), address broader questions of contemporary burial practice (including grave-sharing), or state whether Constanze had removed a headstone containing the names of Leopold and Jeanette in order to put up Nissen's.[3] Without knowing

---

[1] See Angermüller, 'Testament', 102 and 106.   [2] See Hummel, *Nannerl*, 83–4.
[3] Hummel also appears to misdate Genoveva Weber's death—he states that when Nissen died she had been buried 18 years. This would have been in 1808, but all the other literature I have consulted gives 1798 as the date of her death. I have not studied burial practice in Salzburg, and do not challenge Hummel's views from a position of knowledge; but the picture he gives is incomplete, and he does not divulge the sources of most of his information. Considering how often his position has been cited in subsequent biographies, caution is surely not unreasonable.

more about these arrangements, it seems to me unwise to draw such confident inferences about the precise state of Nannerl's mind when she added her codicil; there may have been other factors (including silent ones bearing on cultural assumptions about the value of long-buried bodies) not illuminated by the surviving documentation. Taken as a whole, the evidence for poor relations between the two women is extremely unconvincing; minute in quantity and doubtful in quality, it has been worked to death while there is at least as much (which is to say, also hardly any) to suggest that they were on good terms. This is one of those areas where biographers can only admit that the state of the evidence makes it impossible to pronounce judgement.

In the summer of 1829 the English Mozart enthusiasts Vincent Novello and his wife Mary visited Salzburg to hunt up both Nannerl and Constanze. Vincent was organist and choirmaster at the chapel of the Portuguese Embassy in London, and far more besides. His passion was that musical taste in England should be improved by greater exposure of audiences to 'sterling' music (especially Purcell, Bach, Handel, Haydn, and Mozart). All his activities—teaching, editing, collecting and copying, publishing, concert-giving, and acting as programme adviser to the nineteenth-century music festivals—were informed by the pursuit of this quest. Temperamentally, he and Mary were evidently both ideally suited to the job; they cultivated friendships warmly and assiduously, adored their family of eleven children (seven of whom lived to be adults), involved them completely in their incessant musical socializing, and spared no pains to encourage them in their chosen careers. The house was always open, so that the potential for infecting others with Vincent's own enthusiasm for the music of the great masters was considerable.

The journey to Europe in 1829, when Vincent was 48 and Mary 40 years old, was made for three main purposes. First they wanted to take their 11-year-old daughter Clara for voice trials for a singer's education in Paris; secondly they wanted to present Nannerl with a sum of money which had been collected by a number of Mozart enthusiasts in England on hearing that Nannerl was impoverished and in poor health; and thirdly Vincent had it in mind to write a biographical sketch of Mozart, and was in search of information to supplement that contained in Nissen's biography, which had appeared the previous year. Both husband and wife kept a diary of the tour.[4]

---

[4] See V. and M. Novello, *A Mozart Pilgrimage*. The information in this paragraph and the preceding one is from the Introduction, pp. xxi–xxx.

During their time in Salzburg, the Novellos saw Nannerl briefly and Constanze a good deal. Nannerl was not in fact impoverished, though she may have been living very frugally, but she was blind and virtually bed-ridden; so feeble was she that the Novellos were told she could no longer depress the keys of her keyboard with her left hand. They came away feeling sure that she was not long for this world. However, they had a little conversation with her, described some of the artefacts in her rooms, and commented on the affection between her and Constanze's younger son Wolfgang, who happened to be paying his mother a visit while the Novellos were there, and conducted the English couple to his aunt Nannerl.

From Constanze the Novellos got more information, but though they seemed highly satisfied with it, it was only the oral accounts of Constanze and her widowed younger sister Sophie Haibel, who lived with her. As mementos Constanze gave them bits of a hairbrush and some hair, the cover of a letter from Mozart to Leopold, and two modest pieces of music, but did not offer access to letters or other biographical documents. The Novellos were probably not the people to make searching biograph-ical enquiries in any case; the list of questions they had prepared to ask Constanze was bland, and they were immediately satisfied with her answers.[5] Their itinerary gave them two visits to Salzburg with an excur-sion between the two to Vienna. While in Vienna they met Maria Anna ('Nanette') Streicher and her husband; Nanette was the daughter of Johann Andreas Stein, the Augsburg keyboard instrument maker who had been friendly with the Mozarts since Leopold's youth, and she and her hus-band were still in the instrument-making business. The Streichers hinted that they could tell stories to Constanze's detriment, but Vincent liked to believe himself too much of a gentleman to press for anything that smacked of gossip. Even when the Streichers told the Novellos amus-ing tales about some of Beethoven's outlandish behaviour to the people around him, Vincent merely commented in his diary that Beethoven had had 'no kind Lady to take care of him'.[6] During their second stay in Salzburg, they noted a visit by Constanze to Nannerl,[7] and wrote noth-ing to suggest that relations between Constanze and Nannerl were not cordial; but the guiding spirit of the Novellos' tour was worship rather than persistent enquiry, and the book describing it is aptly called a pil-grimage. Their diaries offer only limited and problematic evidence for the characters of the two women who had been so close to Mozart.

---

[5] The information about the Novellos' activities in Salzburg is from ibid. 66–118.
[6] Ibid. 184–90. [7] Ibid. 213–14.

The Novellos left Salzburg in early August 1829; on 29 October of the same year Nannerl died, aged 78. Her son Leopold was her sole heir and inherited the net estate of 7,837 fl. 40½ kr., though Nannerl first made a number of named bequests to her step-grandchildren and her maid Franziska Dietl. She also stipulated that a small number of her possessions (chiefly jewellery and a clock), which had come down to her from her Mozart forebears, should remain with Leopold only until his death, and should then return to the Mozart family. Leopold, however, handed them over immediately to Constanze.[8]

Nannerl clearly believed that Constanze's family, rather than her own, had chief claim on the material in her Mozart archive; after her death, a group of letters written by her father Leopold passed to Constanze.[9] Since Nannerl had earlier given to Nissen all the other family letters in her possession, Constanze now had almost all the correspondence Nannerl had preserved; almost, but not quite, because a small amount had already been given away. From this point on, the history of the handing down of the biographical source material was to become steadily more labyrinthine, and for the sake of greater clarity and convenience in the following discussion of the subject, a recapitulation is first given of the known fate, before Nannerl's death, of particular bodies of letters.

The story begins with Leopold Mozart who, because he intended to write his son's biography,[10] ensured that the letters he considered most important were kept. All the travel reports written to the Hagenauers during the childhood of Wolfgang and Nannerl had been copied at his instigation, and the copies kept within the Mozart family; almost all the originals (which were presumably kept for a while by the Hagenauers), and the replies of the Hagenauers, are now lost without trace. At some point, probably when the Dancing-Master's House was being cleared out after Leopold's death, the copies of the letters to the Hagenauers passed to Nannerl (with many other family letters), who gave them to Nissen for his biography in the early 1820s.[11] Nissen then copied parts of the copies into a notebook which he called an *Einband*,[12] so that much of the

---

[8] See Angermüller, 'Testament', 100–1 and 107.

[9] See Constanze's diary entry of 9 Feb. 1830—*MBA* 1442. These were probably the letters written to Nannerl between Nannerl's marriage in 1784 and Leopold's death in 1787. There is no documentation recording an express wish of Nannerl's that the letters to which this diary entry refers should be given to Constanze; it is possible that her son and heir Leopold took the initiative and gave them to her.

[10] Leopold to Hagenauer, 10 Nov. 1767—*MBA* 121/101–4 (*Letters* 51). Cf. also Leopold's 'Preliminary Notice' to the 2nd edn. of his *Violinschule*, published in 1769, in which he also alluded to writing Wolfgang's biography—Deutsch, *Documents*, 91–2.

[11] See Ch. 35, p. 620. [12] See commentary to *MBA* 32.

material from these letters existed in two forms (or three if the originals are also counted) before Nissen's death. Had Leopold not arranged for the copies to be made, these remarkable documents would today be unknown.

Unfortunately, most of the letters written by Maria Anna and Nannerl to Leopold and Wolfgang, at times when Leopold and Wolfgang were away from home without the women, are lost. Since the letters home of Leopold and Wolfgang for these periods are still in existence, and since there is surviving two-way correspondence from periods when Wolfgang and Leopold were separated, it seems likely that Leopold only thought it worth while keeping letters which bore directly on Wolfgang's development and his own paternal role in this, and that the women's letters may have been destroyed very early on; however, there are no explicit references explaining when they ceased to exist, or why they were not kept. The periods when the letters in both directions survive are September 1777 to January 1779, when Wolfgang went to Paris without Leopold, and from November 1780 to January 1781, when Wolfgang went to Munich ahead of Leopold and Nannerl for *Idomeneo*, immediately prior to his permanent move to Vienna. If the above-mentioned hypothesis about the reasons why some letters were kept while others were not is correct, it follows that only because Maria Anna went to Paris with Wolfgang as second-best chaperone, and wrote some of the news from that journey, have any of her letters been preserved at all. And only because Leopold was unable to go have both sides of the correspondence been kept, which better than anything else permits to be seen the testing of Wolfgang's character and the essentials of what Leopold expected him to do for his family.

Although Wolfgang and Leopold continued to correspond until Leopold's death in 1787, Leopold's letters to Wolfgang have not survived beyond January 1781. Though there is no hard evidence explaining what happened to these, it seems probable that Wolfgang did not bother to keep them. Since this was the year in which he wrenched himself permanently away from Salzburg, he might have felt that he was no longer to be so accountable to Leopold. Alternatively, he might simply have been careless with them.[13] Leopold, however, continued to keep

---

[13] It has often been suggested that Constanze destroyed these letters of Leopold's, but there is no evidence for the claim, which rests rather on the presumption that they contained unflattering allegations about her and that she therefore had a motive for annihilating them. Set against this hypothesis, however, is the fact that no letters from other people (including Constanze) to Mozart survive from this period either. Though it is a theoretical possibility that Constanze destroyed all Mozart's incoming post after his death, it seems more likely that he simply ceased to keep his letters.

Wolfgang's letters until Nannerl's marriage in the summer of 1784. After that date only one letter from Wolfgang to Leopold survives.[14] Except for this one, the letters in this group (Wolfgang to Leopold between 1784 and 1787) were already all lost when Nissen was collecting material for his biography, and Nannerl apparently told him that Leopold had destroyed them because they alluded to Freemasonry.[15] Whether Nannerl gave this reason from positive knowledge or was merely hazarding a guess is not clear. Nannerl's letters to Leopold after her marriage are also lost, and though there are no references to indicate what might have happened to them after Leopold had received them, one possibility (if Nannerl's allusion to Freemasonry was only a theory) is that Leopold simply decided at this time that there was no need to continue to keep the letters of either of his children. Certainly the idea of writing his son's biography had apparently been by this date completely abandoned. Nannerl, however, saved all Leopold's letters to her after her marriage, and also took over all the correspondence that Leopold had kept, probably after his death. In ensuring that everything she possessed passed to Nissen and Constanze she played a great part in its survival.

Once all this material was in the hands of the Nissens, however, the situation changed. For while Nannerl appears to have led a fairly retired life, even after her return to Salzburg in 1801, Constanze and Nissen had effectively been operating a Mozart industry. They had husbanded the documentary resources which had been left to Constanze after Mozart's death: in part by preserving them, in part by adding to them through enquiries of people who also had material to communicate (this was how they had acquired, in the 1820s, all the documents kept by Nannerl), and in part by disseminating them, either through loans or sales. The active use of all their source material inevitably led to situations which sometimes put its long-term preservation at risk. One such had arisen as early as 1799 with some of the letters already in Constanze's possession on Mozart's death. In this year, Constanze had sent several batches of letters to Breitkopf & Härtel during their search for biographical information about Mozart. On 25 May 1799 she mentioned enclosing three letters written to her by Mozart about his visit to Potsdam in 1789.[16] Although the firm's usual practice was to copy letters sent to them for this type of purpose, so that the originals could be returned to the owners, these letters apparently escaped the copyist, and the originals

---

[14] That of 4 Apr. 1787—*MBA* 1044 (*Letters* 546).
[15] See von Nissen, *Biographie*, Author's Preface, p. xvi.
[16] *MBA* 1243/63–5 (not in *Letters*).

have also been lost; today there is no knowledge of the information they contained.[17]

Nissen's labours in preparing his biography of Mozart had chiefly taken the form of collecting—he had spent countless hours writing to people who had known Mozart, and hoarding and filing the material they sent him. Much of it he had laboriously copied out, either complete or in extract form, and Constanze had commented on one occasion that he could hardly be seen in his study for the pile of papers and books surrounding him.[18] Although it is probable that the one group of letters by Leopold which Nannerl did *not* intend the Nissens to keep while she was still alive was the one containing Leopold's letters to her from 1784 to 1787,[19] she must have lent them to Nissen so that the material about Mozart could be extracted from them.[20] They were presumably then returned to her, but not before five had been given to Feuerstein, the man who helped Constanze finish the biography after Nissen's death.[21] This situation, where biographical material slowly leached from the collection so carefully preserved by Nannerl, was to crop up again and again until Mozart's sons made their chief bequests to the Dommusikverein und Mozarteum in the 1840s and 1850s; anyone who performed a kindness for Nissen or Constanze (and later for Carl and Wolfgang) might be given a relic of some kind, and pilgrims seeking mementos were also often rewarded if Constanze took a liking to them. The mutilation and dispersal of Nannerl's diary came about in this way.[22]

Much of the correspondence available to Nissen he considered unfit not only to be printed at the time but presumably even to be seen at any time in the future. For in addition to excluding from his biography everything that might give the 'wrong' idea of Mozart, or cause embarrassment or offence to people still living, he obliterated certain passages, sentences, words, and names in the documents themselves. Intimate

---

[17] *MBA*, Foreword to vol. vii, p. xvi. The statement that these three letters escaped the Breitkopf & Härtel copyist is based on Nottebohm's declaration (*Mozartiana*, Foreword, pp. viii–ix) that, though he knew from Constanze's letters to the firm that these Mozart letters ought to have been in Breitkopf & Härtel's archive, he presumed them to be lost. Further, since his book *Mozartiana* was based on material sent to the firm by Constanze and Nannerl and copied into two separate books (one relating to each woman) which he found in the archive, and since he did not reproduce the three letters about Potsdam, they cannot have been in the book containing copies of documents sent by Constanze.

[18] Constanze to Carl, 22 Jan. 1826—*MBA* 1405/2–12 (not in *Letters*).

[19] See n. 9 above.   [20] Material from these letters was included in Nissen's biography.

[21] See commentary to *MBA* 844, 848, 869 (in the appendix to the index vol., vol. vii), 932, and 1033. The letters were sent to Feuerstein on 20 Feb. 1826, only a few weeks before Nissen's death.

[22] See Ch. 14 and Appendix 1 for further details about this.

sexual passages written to Constanze were among these, though most have now been deciphered. (The other main body of letters containing sexual and scatological passages, those from Mozart to the *Bäsle*, Maria Anna Thekla Mozart, were also to prove embarrassing to the people through whose hands they passed, and were at times at great risk of destruction.)

After Nannerl's death in 1829, and then Constanze's in 1842, the story of the preservation of the letters becomes steadily more complicated. For although the Dommusikverein und Mozarteum had been founded in Salzburg in 1841, providing an appropriate repository for Mozartiana, the letters were not bequeathed to this institution on Constanze's death, but shared between her sons Carl and Wolfgang.[23] This meant that the possibility of further losses from the collection through gifts and loans continued. The later fate of all these documents is bewilderingly involved, and will probably never now be disentangled with complete satisfaction. Each time an individual letter was parted from its fellows, it embarked on a transmission history of its own, meandering down the years, perhaps being lent, copied or printed (in whole or in part), given away again, sold (privately or at auction), forgotten, lost, or deposited in a library. The search for accurate information about these events therefore necessitates investigations into the correspondence of anyone who might have handled the letters in question, the statements of biographers and editors who used and sometimes printed them, the auction catalogues of dealers who sold them, library acquisition catalogues and notes, secondary literature dating back into the nineteenth century, and so forth. Comparisons of printed versions with originals and copies is also necessary, in order to try to check which source was used for which purpose. Collating and analysing all this information is a perplexing task, especially since the number of missing links makes it exceedingly difficult to reconcile the contradictions in much of the evidence.[24] Though individual studies have been made of the

---

[23] The reason they were not given to the Dommusikverein und Mozarteum at this point, however, may have been that they had been given to Carl and Wolfgang *before* Constanze died, so that the heirs were not confronted by the decision of what to do with the material in the immediate aftermath of her death. Certainly some at least of the *Bäsle* letters were apparently in Carl's hands in 1818, as explained below, p. 637.

[24] One example of difficulties in the evidence is Otto Jahn's statement that in 1852, after Wolfgang's death but before Carl's, he saw in the Mozarteum in Salzburg all the correspondence bequeathed to it by Wolfgang, covering the years 1777–1784. See Jahn, *Life of Mozart*, pp. xiv–xvi. In the English edn., the Introduction also states that Carl had the letters from 1762 to 1775—cf. p. xvi. But the situation cannot have been as simple as these two statements suggest. For Carl had some of the *Bäsle* letters, none of which had been written before 1777, and also at least one letter to Puchberg, written in 1791 (*MBA* 1147; *Letters* 592: cf. *MBA*, vol. vii, Foreword, pp. xvii–xviii);

transmission of particular parts of the correspondence, a detailed examination dedicated to the entire corpus is a desideratum; all that can be
offered here is an overview of the types of situation which had a bearing on it.[25]

The case of the handing on of the *Bäsle* letters offers examples of
some of the convoluted ways in which originals and copies were passed
around. Nine of these letters survive today, though there were once
others. In the first place they must have been returned, either to Mozart
but more likely to Constanze, by Maria Anna Thekla herself. Constanze
then sent seven of them to Breitkopf & Härtel in 1799, but warned them
not to print anything without her permission.[26] The firm had these seven
copied into the book containing other biographical material sent by
Constanze, and returned the originals to her. Even before Constanze's death
some at least of the originals passed to her sons—it is difficult to say with
exactitude who had which ones when, but Carl apparently had at least five
and Wolfgang at least one. In 1818 Carl was visited in Milan by the
musician Wilhelm Speyer. Carl gave Speyer a letter written by Mozart and
also let him see other letters, among them the *Bäsle* ones in his possession. Speyer claimed that Carl hardly knew what to do with these letters
on account of their contents, and talked of destroying them; however, at
Speyer's earnest representations, he allowed Speyer to make copies of them
on condition that nothing should be published. Later Wilhelm Speyer's
son Edward claimed that Wilhelm had allowed Jahn access to these
copies in 1854. From the letters he saw, Jahn published the more harmless extracts in the first edition of his biography.[27] Before Carl Mozart
died in 1858, he disposed of the letters in his possession. Most were sent
to the Dommusikverein und Mozarteum,[28] but at least four (and almost
certainly more) of the *Bäsle* letters were apparently given to Andreas
Wagner, the executor of his will. From Wagner these passed to his son,

and it is thought that Wolfgang may have had Leopold's letters to the Hagenauers, all of which
had been written before 1777. For the transmission history of the *Bäsle* letters, cf. J. H. Eibl, 'Zur
Überlieferungsgeschichte der Bäsle-Briefe', *MM* 27 (1979), 9–17; for that of the Hagenauer letters,
cf. commentary to *MBA* 32.

[25] A brief account of what happened to the Mozart correspondence after it was first written is
given in the Foreword to vol. vii of *MBA*, pp. ix–xx (although a short essay on the later fate of
the letters to Hagenauer is also given in the commentary to *MBA* 32). The chief purpose of these
explanations, however, is to state the sources for the letters printed in *MBA*; details not relevant
to this aim are rarely given, and in addition the account sometimes lacks clarity.

[26] Constanze to Breitkopf & Härtel, 28 Aug. 1799—*MBA* 1256/60–3 (not in *Letters*).

[27] See Eibl, 'Zur Überlieferungsgeschichte der Bäsle-Briefe', 9–12.

[28] See W. Senn, 'Das Vermächtnis der Brüder Mozart an "Dommusikverein und Mozarteum"
in Salzburg', *MJb* (1967), 57.

who apparently lent them to Rudolph Genée at the end of the nineteenth century. Genée claimed he copied them accurately before returning them to their owner; he then wrote an article on them in 1904.[29] Meanwhile the copies in the Breitkopf & Härtel archives had been discovered in the 1870s and published with other material from the same collection by Nottebohm in his book *Mozartiana* in 1880. Although these copies were unexpurgated, Nottebohm omitted the most salacious passages from his edition, but added them back in manuscript to his own copy of the book, which later found its way to the library of the Gesellschaft der Musikfreunde in Vienna. This annotated copy of Nottebohm's book is regarded as the most reliable surviving source for one (*MBA* 384; *Letters* 254) of the three *Bäsle* letters whose originals are now lost (the Breitkopf & Härtel copies on which Nottebohm's book was based are also presumed lost).[30] Apart from these three, however, the originals of the nine whose texts are known today have fortunately survived; one is privately owned, one eventually came to rest in the Pierpont Morgan Library in New York, and four passed (through their most recent former owner Stefan Zweig) to the British Library in London.[31] Clearly, in the case of the *Bäsle* letters, the contents put them at greater risk of loss than was the case with letters in other categories; for not only were the originals not bequeathed to the obvious public institution, the Dommusikverein und Mozarteum, by members of Mozart's family, but the complete texts were not considered suitable for fixing in print either; as late as 1914, in Ludwig Schiedermair's edition of the Mozart correspondence, they were still being rendered in extract form only, and the first edition to give them unexpurgated was Emily Anderson's in 1938.

Complex enough though all this might seem for a mere nine letters, the account given above is only a sketch of some aspects of the story —many details are omitted, and other copies were almost certainly also made, in addition to those mentioned here.[32] The other groups of letters went through similarly tangled procedures before reaching their present-day locations (in most cases, a library). Carl and Wolfgang Mozart shared all the other letters which had been in Constanze's possession, with the exception of the few that she or Nissen had already given away to others

---

[29] See Eibl, 'Zur Überlieferungsgeschichte der Bäsle-Briefe', 12–14.

[30] Ibid. 10–11 and 15. The fate of the Breitkopf & Härtel archive copies is briefly discussed below, pp. 640–1.

[31] See Eibl, 'Zur Überlieferungsgeschichte der Bäsle-Briefe', 10.

[32] Constanze apparently allowed Nissen's assistant Anton Jähndl to borrow at least one of the *Bäsle* letters before she gave them to Carl, and Jähndl made a copy of it. See ibid. 14.

or that had been lost. At some point Wolfgang became friendly with Aloys Fuchs, a music-loving official in Viennese court service and a keen collector of Mozartiana. Though the course of their friendship is not documented in detail, Fuchs apparently knew a good deal of the Mozart material in Wolfgang's possession, and even had the Mozart family's copies of Leopold's letters to the Hagenauers. Fuchs later sold these letters to the collector Friedrich August Grasnick, and from him they eventually found their way into the Prussian state library in Berlin.[33] Before Wolfgang died in 1844, he named his companion Josepha Baroni-Cavalcabò as his heir, and left instructions for the remaining letters in his possession, together with a number of other items of Mozartian interest, to be given to the Dommusikverein und Mozarteum in Salzburg. Aloys Fuchs helped Josepha to inventory and pack everything, and the collection was in Salzburg and catalogued by January 1845.[34]

Shortly after this occurred, the classical philologist and amateur musician Otto Jahn was embarking on the research for his biography of Mozart. Motivated by dissatisfaction with Nissen's work, and by the realization that Rochlitz's anecdotes about Mozart were suspect, he decided to try to trace for himself the sources used by Nissen, in order to do a better job. In 1852 he arrived in Vienna to hunt up people who could be of use to him, and came across Aloys Fuchs. Fuchs placed his considerable collection of Mozartiana at Jahn's disposal, but died the following year before Jahn had assessed everything in it. Jahn did, however, learn from him that all the surviving Mozart letters had been given to the Mozarteum. (This was not quite true, because Carl was still in possession of his share, and Fuchs himself had possessed the copies of the letters to the Hagenauers, but Jahn apparently set off for Salzburg without knowing this.) There, to his excitement, he found a good deal of the material as it had been used by Nissen, and set about reading it. It was not long before he recognized the enormity of Nissen's concealments, and sat day and night for three weeks copying for himself all the correspondence preserved there. Then he hunted for people in Salzburg who might have more to communicate, either of an oral or a written nature. To his bitter disappointment, although Constanze and her sister Sophie Haibel had only died within the last decade, there seemed nothing about Mozart left to be discovered—'all was as completely forgotten', he noted, 'as irrecoverably lost as his grave'.[35]

---

[33] See commentary to *MBA* 32.
[34] See Senn, 'Das Vermächtnis der Brüder Mozart', 52–6.
[35] Jahn, *Life of Mozart*, Introduction, pp. ii–xvi.

The first edition of Jahn's work began to appear (it was in four volumes) in 1856, the year after Carl Mozart had decided to give to the Mozarteum items from his Mozart collection, including those family letters which he still possessed. These arrived in Salzburg in 1856, and Jahn was able to consult them before the second edition of his work appeared in 1867.[36] It was more than a hundred years after Mozart's birth, therefore, before justice began to be done, through this first critical biography of Mozart, to the letters chronicling his life. By this date, however, the bulk of the collection had at least reached a library which would preserve it from further dispersal.

Despite the tortuous ways in which the letters were passed around, despite the many occasions when their chances of preservation must have hung by a thread, dependent on someone's whim or on sheer chance, most of those which were once in the possession of Nannerl and then Constanze have survived in the original. The main exceptions, in terms of discrete categories, are Leopold's letters to Hagenauer (whose printed texts, as described above, are based on copies made under the supervision of the Mozarts) and Mozart's begging letters to Puchberg. The Puchberg letters were sent by Constanze to Breitkopf & Härtel with other biographical material, and were copied into the book kept in the firm's archive. Presumably the originals were returned to Constanze, but most are now lost. In 1880 Nottebohm published them in his book *Mozartiana*, using the Breitkopf & Härtel copies.[37] Needless to say, the Mozart-related documents were not the only important pieces of musical source material in the Breitkopf & Härtel archive; by the 1920s the archive held, in correspondence alone, some thirty thousand letters written by composers who had published music with the firm. Some items had, however, already left the collection before this period through Hermann Härtel, co-proprietor of the firm with his brother Raymund from 1835. He had removed material from the archive to swell his own private collection, which was eventually deposited in the Prussian state library in Berlin in 1969, almost a hundred years after his death. But these losses pale into insignificance compared with the devastation that was wrought during the Second World War. A very few of the letters, including some from Niemetschek which showed how the firm had used him to strengthen its position against Constanze Mozart in the late 1790s, had

---

[36] See Senn, 'Das Vermächtnis der Brüder Mozart', 57–8, and Jahn, *Life of Mozart*, Introduction to the Second Edition, p. xxvi.

[37] See *MBA*, vol. vii, Foreword, pp. xvii–xviii. This essay does not, however, attempt to explain how the Breitkopf & Härtel copies of Mozart's letters to Puchberg were later lost.

been published in the firm's journal, *Der Bär*, between 1924 and 1930,[38] but the vast majority were still awaiting publication when the building where the archive was kept suffered bomb damage during an air raid on Leipzig in the night of 3/4 December 1943. Much material is presumed to have perished, although it subsequently emerged that some of it was rescued from the building, was later designated for sale at auction, and found its way into the Landes- und Hochschulbibliothek in Darmstadt. After the war the firm of Breitkopf & Härtel effectively split into two branches, one remaining in Leipzig while the other started afresh in Wiesbaden. What had been a single rich collection, therefore, was split up and dispersed in distressing and confusing circumstances, so that a search for much of the original archival material would theoretically have to be made in these four places at least.[39] But though there are many gaps in the knowledge of the sequence of all these events, it seems that the books containing the biographical material on Mozart sent by Constanze and Nannerl are lost, so that the contents of most of the Puchberg letters would today be unknown if it were not for Nottebohm's book.

Similarly involved situations have affected the transmission of Mozart's music, despite the fact that the majority of his autograph scores were in the hands of one person (Johann Anton André), who recognized their value as an entity, as early as 1800. During 1840 and 1841 André repeatedly offered the collection for sale to the Prussian government, but it was declined, despite the vigorous protestations of many eminent people, including Mendelssohn. In 1842, therefore, when Johann Anton died, the manuscripts became the property of his five surviving sons, who continued to try to dispose of them to libraries in Berlin, Vienna, and London. When these attempts failed too, they divided them among themselves and each disposed of his share according to his own wishes; three of the sons began to sell items individually and in small groups.[40] When Jahn visited two of the brothers, Carl and Julius André, in Frankfurt during the summer of 1853, while undertaking research for his biography of Mozart, he was hospitably received and given access to their collections, which had remained intact. Realizing from the material he saw what a treasure the total collection had been, Jahn gave expression to his despair that Germany's idea of honouring Mozart was to erect statues.[41] Slowly,

[38] See e.g. Hitzig, 'Die Briefe Franz Xaver Niemetscheks, 101–16.
[39] See Elvers, 'Breitkopf & Härtels Verlagsarchiv', 24–8.
[40] See K.-H. Köhler, 'Die Erwerbungen der Mozart-Autographe der Berliner Staatsbibliothek —ein Beitrag zur Geschichte des Nachlasses', *MJb* (1962–3), 55–6.
[41] See Jahn, *Life of Mozart*, Introduction, pp. xvii–xviii.

painstakingly, and thanks to the passionate dedication of a small number of individuals, about a third of these manuscripts had been acquired for the state library in Berlin by the time the Second World War broke out —some hundred years after the total collection had first been offered it.[42] During the war, however, the Berlin collections had to be sent away for safe keeping. Some of the Mozart material found its way to libraries in the Eastern bloc, rendering it inaccessible for many years after peace had returned, and hampering the production of some volumes of the *Neue Mozart Ausgabe*, the second and the most ambitious complete critical edition of Mozart's works. Virtually all these scores were, however, recovered, and are now in Poland.

These stories about the transmission of source material show how quickly, easily, and casually a culturally priceless collection can be placed at risk, and how difficult it can be to redeem the situation later. Given the circumstances outlined above, however, it is surely miraculous that the losses have not been more extensive. Two hundred years after Mozart's lifetime this great correspondence, which does so much more than chronicle the events of that one life, at last received a critical edition worthy of it, and one which complements those both of the music and of the biographical documents other than the letters. These major published collections of source material, to which will soon be added the new edition of Köchel's thematic catalogue of Mozart's works, lay the foundations on which the further endeavours of Mozart studies will be built in the next century.

---

[42] See Köhler, 'Die Erwerbungen der Mozart-Autographe', 55–68.

APPENDIX I

The Date of the Mozart/Böhm
Schlackademie in Lent 1780

IT has long been thought that the concert presented by the Mozarts and members of Böhm's theatrical troupe in Salzburg in Lent 1780, for which Mozart wrote a humorous programme in Nannerl's diary,[1] was given on Saturday, 18 March, probably in the Dancing-Master's House. The date is based on the detective work of Walter Hummel, who published Nannerl's diary with a commentary in 1958.[2] Because Wolfgang sometimes wrote entries in it, the diary was mutilated by Wolfgang's widow Constanze when she had possession of it after Nannerl's death. Constanze occasionally removed sheets on which Wolfgang had written, and gave them away to pilgrims seeking samples of his writing. Other sheets no doubt became lost in different ways. Some of the missing sheets have gradually come to light, but because so many are still lost, the surviving ones have often been difficult to date. When Hummel was preparing his edition, he used clues contained in the entries to try to assign dates to the problematic cases. In the case of the sheet containing the concert programme, neither year, month, nor day of the week was indicated, and all he had to go on were four entries 'dated' respectively 'the 18th', 'the 21st', 'the 27th', and 'the 28th'. Supplementing these indications by information in the entries, he decided that the month was March, and the year 1780.[3]

When these entries were made, the concert programme in Wolfgang's hand occupied one side of the sheet (the recto), and was dated 'the 18th'. On the other side of the same sheet (the verso), Nannerl wrote a number of entries which chronicled chiefly the departure of the members of Böhm's troupe of travelling players from Salzburg for their next destination, Augsburg. When Constanze removed it, she also cut it in half latitudinally, so that the concert programme was now in two parts, and so, of course, was Nannerl's writing on the verso. She then gave the top half of the sheet to one person, and the bottom half to another. The owner of the bottom half pasted it into an album, thereby making it impossible for a long time to read Nannerl's entries.[4] Figs. 5*a* and 5*b* illustrate

---

[1] *MBA* 529; the date of the entry is the subject under question.
[2] W. Hummel, *Nannerl Mozarts Tagebuchblätter, mit Eintragungen ihres Bruders Wolfgang Amadeus* (Salzburg, 1958).
[3] Ibid. 68.   [4] Commentary to *MBA* 529.

Line number in MBA	1c – MBA 530 Nannerl's hand, verso, upper
2	*den 21 ten auf 6 uhr auf die nacht ein feierwerk in der Sommer Reitschuble*
3	*den 27 ten wägen fortgefahren: in ersten wagen br und fr müller, br und fr*
4	*stierle, 2 kinder von der Madame Müller. und die dienstmägd. den 2 ten*
5	*wagen br und Madame smitt, die mutter von Ma: stierle, br und fr kerscher,*
6	*ein kind von Ma: smitt, und die dienstmagd von Madame smitt.*
7	*den 28 ten um 7 uhr mr: et ma: böhm ihre 3 kinder und bilau in einem*
8	*wagen ....*) und schwester*

Line number in MBA	1d – MBA 529a Nannerl's hand, verso, lower
2	*br und fr: zimerl ... und br Murschbausser in 2 waagen und in einem schlitten*
3	*die 2 Dienstmägde von Böhm von hier auf augspurg gerreist.*
4	*Das Monat Merz*
5	*den 3t wieder ein feuerwerk in der Sommer Reitschuhl.*
6	*den 6t der first von berchtolsgarn gestorben:*
7	*den 7t die geweste bauerfeind Stanzel ...*

Line number in MBA	1a – MBA 529 Mozart's hand, recto, upper
2	*den 18:ten die zweyte schlackademie –*
3	*1:t Eine sinfonie /: nemlich die haffner Musique /*
4	*2:t Eine italienische welsche aria getrillert von Mad:me schmitt*
5	*3:t: Ein dreystimmiges Terzett von b: Salieri. gesungen von Mad:me Böhm,*
6	*b: kammerl, und b:Weichsler*
7	*4:t Ein fiala auf einen Concert, verfertigt und gespiellt vom b: violoncello*
8	*5:t Eine aria vom b: gretri mit 1 oboe und barfe solo, gesungen von b: fiala,*
9	*die oboe von Mad:me Böhm und der Murschbausner von der Mad:me barfe.*

Line number in MBA	1b – MBA 529 continued Mozart's hand, recto, lower
10	*6:t die aria von trompetten, paucke, flöten, oboe: bratschen, fagotte und Bässe*
11	*von mir.*
12	*7:t das Erste finale vom Anfoßi aus der Perseguita incognitata.*
13	*8:t aus lauter betteln haben wir den Ceccarelli singen lassen. ein Runderl.*
14	*9:t zum schluss haben wir die ganze stadt Mayland aufgeführt NB:*
15	*mit trommeten und Maucken.*

FIG 5a. Reconstruction of Nannerl Mozart's mutilated diary pages for February and March 1780, German

Line number in MBA	1a – MBA 529 Mozart's hand, recto, upper
2	On the 18th the second schmonzert –
3	1st: a symphony (namely, the haffner music).
4	2nd: an Italian Wop aria trilled by Madlle schmitt
5	3rd: a three-voice trio by b: Salieri, sung by Madme Boihm,
6	b: kammerl, and b:Weichsler
7	4th: a fiala on a concerto, composed and performed by b: violoncello
8	5th: an aria by b: gretri with one oboe and harp solo, sung by b: fiala,
9	the oboe by Madme Boihm, and the Murschhaussner by Madme harp.

Line number in MBA	1b – MBA 529 continued Mozart's hand, recto, lower
10	6th: the aria with trumpets, kettledrums, flutes, oboes, violas, bassoons and bass-instruments
11	by me.
12	7th: the first finale from Anfossi's Perseguita incognitata.
13	8th: after sheer begging we allowed Ceccarelli to sing: a little round-dance.
14	9th: to close we performed the entire City of Milan NB:
15	with strumpets and metaldrums.

Line number in MBA	1c – MBA 530 Nannerl's hand, verso, upper
2	on the 21st at 6 o'clock at night, fireworks in the Summer Riding School.
3	on the 27th carriages departed: in the first carriage br and fr müller, br and fr
4	stierle, 2 of Madame Müller's children. and the maid. The 2nd
5	carriage br and Madame smitt, Mo: stierle's mother, br and fr kerscber,
6	a child of Mo: smitt, and Madame smitt's maid.
7	on the 28th at 7 o'clock mr: and md: böihm their 3 children and bilau in a
8	carriage ....*) and sister

Line number in MBA	1d – MBA 529a Nannerl's hand, verso, lower
2	br and fr: zimerl … and br Murschhausser in 2 carriages and in a sledge
3	Böhm's 2 maids set off from here for augspurg
4	The month of March
5	on the 3rd fireworks in the Summer Riding School again.
6	on the 6th the prince of berchtolsgarn died:
7	on the 7th the former bauerfeind Stanzel …

FIG 5b. Reconstruction of Nannerl Mozart's mutilated diary pages for February and March 1780, English

Explanatory Notes to Fig. 5

Zaslaw's introductory biographies of the concert performers

Madame Schmitt, soprano, a member of Johann Böhm's visiting theatrical troupe, who sang first romantic lead in operettas and acted second lead in plays.

Marianne Böhm née Jacobs, soprano, wife of the director of the troupe, who acted young maids in plays and sang character roles in operetta.

Zimmerl (= Kammerl; both words mean 'small room'), baritone, first lead in operetta and second in plays.

Kerscher (= Weichsler; a 'Weichsel' is a sour-tasting type of 'Kirsche', which is a cherry), sang older men, fathers, and servants.

Joseph Fiala, friend of the Mozarts, oboist, flautist, and composer, Salzburg court musician 1778–85; also active in Wallerstein, Vienna, Saint Petersburg, Prague, Regensburg, Munich, Donaueschingen; mentioned in Chapter 1.

Johann Georg Murschhauser, romantic lead in plays, tenor in bravura arias in operetta.

Francesco Ceccarelli, castrato, friend of the Mozarts, Salzburg court musician 1778–88.

Zaslaw's decoded version of the concert programme

A Lenten Concert
At the Dancing Master's House in the Hannibalplatz
Friday 18 February 1780
Programme

Symphony in D major, K. 250	W. A. Mozart
An Italian aria Mme Schmitt, soprano	[unknown]
A Trio Mme Böhm, Herr Zimmerl, Herr Kerscher	Antonio Salieri
Concerto for violoncello Herr Fiala, violoncello	Joseph Fiala
'Du dieu d'amour en bravant la puissance' from *L'amitié à l'épreuve* Mme Böhm, soprano, Herr Fiala, oboe, Mme Murschhauser, harp	A. E. M. Grétry
'Dentro il mio petto' from *La finta giardiniera*, K. 196 Herr Murschhauser, tenor	Mozart
'Dove vado, tremo tutta' from *L'incognita perseguitata* four sopranos, tenor, and two basses	Pasquale Anfossi
'Ombre felice—Io ti lascio', K. 255 Signor Ceccarelli, castrato	Mozart
'The entire city of Milan with trumpets and kettledrums'	[Mozart?]

the imaginary reconstruction of the sheet: the top half of the recto is labelled 1*a*, is in Wolfgang's hand, and contains the entries in *MBA* 529/2–9; the bottom half of the recto is called 1*b*, is also in Wolfgang's hand, and contains the entries in *MBA* 529/10–15; the top half of the verso is called 1*c*, is in Nannerl's hand, and contains the entries in *MBA* 530; and the bottom half of the verso is called 1*d*, is also in Nannerl's hand, and contains the entries in *MBA* 529*a* (the ones which for a long time were illegible). The latitudinal dotted line represents the place where the sheet was cut. The figure is given twice, once with the entries in the original German, and once with their English translations. The concert programme written by Wolfgang on the recto of the sheet was full of puns and other pieces of word-play, all of which have been translated and interpreted by Neal Zaslaw in his book on Mozart's symphonies: Zaslaw introduces the characters who took part in the concert, and gives an apt translation of the programme with all its word-play, followed by a decoded list of the pieces and the performers. The English translation of the figure is Zaslaw's in all essentials, and his introduction of the performers and the decoded programme are also included here.[5]

What Hummel had to work on was the top half of the sheet only, so that he had 1*a* and 1*c*—the first half of the concert programme, and entries by Nannerl about the departure of the troupe dated 'the 21st', 'the 27th', and 'the 28th'. Because Böhm's schedule of places and dates could be reconstructed from other sources, it was clear that the year was 1780; and because it was known that in 1780 Böhm went to Augsburg from Salzburg, and that his first performance in Augsburg took place on 28 March, Hummel decided that all these entries were made in March. He explained away the problem that Nannerl had the troupe still leaving Salzburg on 'the 28th' by suggesting that she had misdated some of her entries by a few days. This seemed plausible to him because she normally made an entry for every day, but on this sheet she entered nothing between 'the 21st' and 'the 27th'.[6]

Only after Hummel's work had been published did the bottom part of the sheet come to light, and it was not until 1967 that it was successfully removed from the album and Nannerl's writing on the verso (1*d*) could be read.[7] It began in mid-entry, and when this entry was completed, it was followed by the words 'Das Monat Merz' ('The month of March'), under which were three more entries for 'the 3rd', 'the 6th', and 'the 7th'. Instead of using this information to reappraise Hummel's dating of the entries on 1*a* and 1*c*, however, the editors of *MBA*

[5] The items are found in Zaslaw, *Mozart's Symphonies*, 340–3. I am grateful to Professor Zaslaw for his kind consent to my use of his material, and to the slight changes I proposed. The only one of any substance is the date of the concert in his formal rendering of the programme.

[6] Hummel, *Tagebuchblätter*, 68.

[7] Commentary to *MBA* 529. Hummel became aware of this discovery, but not of the contents of its verso, although he speculated (correctly) that the verso might contain further clues to the dating. See W. Hummel, 'Nannerl Mozarts Tagebuchblätter: Neue Funde—Neue Fragen', *MM* 7 (1958), 7–9.

TABLE 3. Calendar for February and March 1780

	February					March				
Monday		7	14	21	28ᶜ		6	13	20	27
Tuesday	1	8	15	22	29		7	14	21	28ᵉ
Wednesday	2	9ᵃ	16	23		1	8	15	22	29
Thursday	3	10	17	24		2	9	16	23	30
Friday	4	11	18ᵇ	25		3	10	17	24	31
Saturday	5	12	19	26		4	11	18	25	
Sunday	6	13	20	27ᶜ		5	12	19	26ᵈ	

ᵃ Ash Wednesday
ᵇ Date of Mozart/Böhm Lenten Concert
ᶜ Dates of departure of Böhm's troupe for Augsburg
ᵈ Easter Sunday
ᵉ Date of first Augsburg performance by Böhm's troupe

continued to assign to these entries the dates suggested by Hummel. In fact, as the diagram of the imaginary physical reconstruction of the diary shows, it is clear that the entries on 1*a*, 1*b*, 1*c*, and 1*d* should follow one another to be chronologically correct. This means that it makes much better sense if all the entries Hummel placed in March are placed in February. The concert would then have taken place on Friday, 18 February (it would still have been a Lenten concert, because Ash Wednesday fell on 9 February in 1780), and Böhm's players would have departed on 27 and 28 February. In this way, they could be comfortably in Augsburg for their first performance on 28 March, and a mistake on Nannerl's part does not have to be assumed.

This suggestion also clears away another problem. Because the *MBA* editors continued to believe that all Hummel's original dates were correct, they had difficulty in explaining the information on 1*d*. The first such information concerns the departure of 'hr und fr: zimerl', 'hr Murschhausser', and two of Böhm's maids for Augsburg by carriage and sledge. Because this entry is followed directly by the words 'The month of March', it is clear that these people were departing at the end of February. But because the *MBA* editors still wanted to believe that the troupe had departed at the end of March, they suggested that some members went at the end of February and others at the end of March.[8] Yet if 'zimerl' had departed at the end of February, and the concert took place on 18 March, how could he have taken part in it, as Wolfgang's entry shows he did?[9] This problem is circumvented if all the entries up to the words 'The month of March' were made in February. If my arguments are correct, the proper order of these entries in *MBA* should be 529, 530, and 529*a*.

[8] Commentary to *MBA* 529*a*.
[9] As Zaslaw's introductory biographies of the performers show, 'zimerl' was the name of Zimmerl, called 'kammerl' as a pun by Wolfgang in the concert programme (*MBA* 529/6).

List of Surviving and Missing Letters
between Wolfgang and Leopold Mozart
from 17 March to 9 May 1781

MBA 583 (surviving), Wolfgang to Leopold, 17 March 1781 (*Letters* 393).

MBA 583*a* (lost), Leopold to Wolfgang, 20 March 1781. Unnumbered by *Letters*. Explicitly mentioned in *MBA* 585/2 (*Letters* 395).

MBA 584 (surviving), Wolfgang to Leopold, before 24 March 1781 (*Letters* 394).

MBA 584*a* (lost), Leopold to Wolfgang, 24 March 1781. Unnumbered by *Letters*. Explicitly mentioned in *MBA* 585/133 (*Letters* 395).

MBA 585 (surviving), Wolfgang to Leopold, 24–8 March 1781 (*Letters* 395).

Unnumbered by *MBA* and *Letters* (lost), Leopold to Wolfgang, before 4 April 1781. Answered by *MBA* 586/4–6 (*Letters* 396).

MBA 586 (surviving), Wolfgang to Leopold, 4 April 1781 (*Letters* 396).

Unnumbered by *MBA* and *Letters* (lost), a probable letter from Leopold to Wolfgang, before 8 April 1781. Answered by *MBA* 587/31–2 (*Letters* 397).

MBA 587 (surviving), Wolfgang to Leopold, 8 April 1781 (*Letters* 397).

Unnumbered by *MBA* and *Letters* (lost), Leopold to Wolfgang, before 11 April 1781. Answered by *MBA* 588/9–10, 27–45, and 60 (*Letters* 398).

MBA 588 (surviving), Wolfgang to Leopold, 11 April 1781 (*Letters* 398).

MBA 589 (lost), Leopold to Wolfgang, before 18 April 1781. Unnumbered by *Letters*. Explicitly mentioned in *MBA* 590/5 (*Letters* 399).[1]

MBA 590 (surviving), Wolfgang to Leopold, 18 April 1781 (*Letters* 399).

MBA 590*a* (lost), Leopold to Wolfgang, before 28 April 1781. Unnumbered by *Letters*. Answered by *MBA* 591/3 (*Letters* 400).

MBA 591 (surviving), Wolfgang to Leopold, 28 April 1781 (*Letters* 400).

Unnumbered by *MBA* and *Letters* (lost), Leopold to Wolfgang, before 9 May 1781. Answered by *MBA* 592/59–61 (*Letters* 401).

MBA 592 (surviving), Wolfgang to Leopold, 9 May 1781 (*Letters* 401).

---

[1] The *MBA* commentary to this lost letter notes the loss of more letters from Leopold to Wolfgang during this period, and states that their original existence can be deduced from passages in Wolfgang's letters. Yet, as is clear from the list here, the assignment of *MBA* numbers to them is not carried out systematically, which makes the situation confusing and misleading.

Since the progression of the dispute between Wolfgang and Leopold about Wolfgang's final break with Colloredo is central to discussions about the relationship between father and son, it is essential to base these discussions on accurate information about the letters that were written, their contents, and the letters to which they were responding. Clearly this is difficult when one side of the correspondence is missing, but any future edition of the letters must tackle this question as systematically as possible; it is almost impossible to discuss family altercations clearly and succinctly without the assignation of letter numbers. And although it is natural to place the letters chronologically according to the date on which they were written, it would also be useful to indicate the order in which they were received and responded to. For because of the travelling time of mail, any given letter frequently did not answer the one immediately preceding it according to the date written, but an earlier one in the sequence: in the list above, Wolfgang's letter to Leopold of 4 April 1781 (*MBA* 586) was answered, I believe, not by Leopold's lost letter written before 8 April, but by the one written before 11 April (both are unnumbered by *MBA*).[2]

[2] See Ch. 21, esp. n. 20, for a more detailed account of my arguments about which letters answered which in the correspondence of this period.

Communication Channels between Salzburg and St Gilgen: Their Occasional Relevance to the Dating of Undated Letters and to the Identification of Mozart's Keyboard Concertos

✥

DETAILED knowledge of the communication channels between Leopold and Nannerl after her move to St Gilgen in August 1784 is helpful on several counts: it contributes to the elucidation of puzzling passages in the letters; helps the reconstruction of sequences of events involving Wolfgang in Vienna, Leopold in Salzburg, and Nannerl in St Gilgen; plays a part in the accurate identification of Mozartian works (especially for the keyboard) being sent to Nannerl; and facilitates the attempt to date more precisely some of the undated letters from this period. Two undated letters which can profitably be considered in the context of the Salzburg–St Gilgen communications arrangements are those numbered 813 and 820 by *MBA*, both written by Leopold to Nannerl. *MBA* 813 has no date at all, while *MBA* 820 is marked 'November 1784', leaving a blank space for the precise date. The *MBA* commentary is vague in assigning dates to these letters: 813 is given as 'after 9 October 1784' (on the grounds that it follows Wolfgang's letter to Leopold of 9 October); while 820 is given as 'before 12 November 1784' (on the grounds that it pre-dates Leopold's letter to Nannerl of 12 November). Precise dates for both letters can, however, be suggested with a fair degree of confidence from internal evidence.

The St Gilgen carrier took official court documents and packets to Salzburg once a week.[1] In addition, he undertook private commissions, carrying goods as well as letters. For these, he charged according to their weight.[2] Calling at the Pfleger's house very early on Friday morning of each week, he would pack everything into his *Krachse* or backpack and set off for Salzburg. Typically he would arrive around midday, put up at the Blue Pike in the Linzergasse (not far from Leopold's house), deliver his letters and goods, and collect others to take back

---

[1] See Ch. 25, p. 453, for more general information about the carrier and the roads. Here, as there, I translate the German *Both* (= *Gerichtsbote*) as 'carrier'; other messengers are distinguished from him by additional designations.

[2] See Leopold to Nannerl, 14–16 Dec. 1786—*MBA* 1011/136–40 (not in *Letters*).

to St Gilgen. He would leave Salzburg again very early on Saturday morning. Occasionally he would change his day; sometimes because an important church festival occurred on a Friday, and sometimes no doubt for reasons of his own such as illness: but by and large Leopold relied on being able to send a weekly letter to Nannerl by him, as well as the shopping, music, books, and keyboard strings requested by her. Among the candles, clothes, caps, lard, and other groceries in his pack was quite often Wolfgang's latest keyboard music, rolled up for protection. In almost three years it hardly ever happened both that Leopold failed to write on a Friday/Saturday and that the reason was not his absence from Salzburg or the carrier's change of day. One of these occasions is to be discussed here.

In addition to the St Gilgen carrier, Leopold and Nannerl could communicate through the Graz carrier (who operated a similar service to that of the St Gilgen one, and travelled from Graz to Salzburg via St Gilgen, but on a different day); travelling salespeople such as the salt-carrier or a woman selling wooden bowls; or the glass-carrier. The glass-carrier was the most important paid messenger after the St Gilgen carrier. She too walked into Salzburg with her wares on her back, and took private commissions as well as the glass from Aich. But her movements were not as regular as those of the carrier, and therefore she could only be used as a supplementary messenger. Leopold and Nannerl, however, tried to give custom to both the carrier and the glass-carrier, even if both happened to be travelling in to Salzburg on the same day. The reason for this was that they wanted as many communications options as possible, because they could never tell when they might want to send an urgent message one to the other; consequently they wanted to keep the goodwill of both carriers.[3] This consideration became even more important after the birth of Nannerl's son Leopoldl, because since Leopold kept the baby with him in Salzburg, he had to be able to report to Nannerl on Leopoldl's health as often as possible. Of considerable importance to the arrangement between Leopold and Nannerl was that she should catch each carrier before (s)he left St Gilgen, and give each something to take; for otherwise the carrier in question would not call on Leopold, and he might be deprived of the opportunity to send an urgent message. This did not matter quite so much with the regular carrier, because Leopold knew his routine and could send a message round to the Blue Pike;[4] but he never knew when the glass-carrier was in town unless she brought something to him.

The carrier and the glass-carrier were Nannerl's and Leopold's chief paid messengers, and were loaded up with all kinds of goods—soap, candles, lemons, shoes, sago, mustard, lard, fish, game, rice, vegetables, books, music, and so on;

---

[3] See Leopold to Nannerl, 14 Jan. and 7–10 Dec. 1785—*MBA* 836/14–17 and 907/83–4 (neither passage is in *Letters*). The commentary to *MBA* 803/16 states that Leopold and Nannerl later communicated mostly through the glass-carrier, but this is not true; they never ceased using the carrier as their main line of communication.

[4] See Leopold to Nannerl, 27–8 Jan. 1786—*MBA* 925/41–2 (not in *Letters*).

TABLE 4. Calendar for September–November 1784

	September	October					November	
Monday	27		4	11	18	25	1	8
Tuesday	28		5	12	19	26	2	9
Wednesday	29		6	13	20	27	3	12
Thursday	30		7	14	21	28	4	11
Friday	24	1	8	15	22	29	5	12
Saturday	25	2	9	16	23	30	6	13
Sunday	26	3	10	17	24	31	7	14

but father and daughter also used unpaid messengers when the opportunity arose. These were acquaintances who lived in the Abersee region and had business in Salzburg—Berchtold's brother in Strobl, or one of his assistants in St Gilgen. These people who took messages (and occasionally light articles) purely from goodwill were never burdened with the type of goods carried by the paid messengers—indeed, Leopold was scrupulous not to do this, for fear that the 'goodwill-messengers' might avoid him on future occasions, and he might thereby miss the chance of sending an important message to Nannerl.[5]

Moving now to the events of the two letters in question, Nannerl almost certainly arrived in Salzburg to visit Leopold on Tuesday 28 September 1784.[6] Leopold then visited her in St Gilgen; and though neither his departure from nor his return to Salzburg can be dated with certainty, he obviously left just before a letter from Wolfgang dated Saturday 9 October reached Salzburg.[7] Leopold had mentioned to Nannerl that he thought of staying a week in St Gilgen,[8] so he probably left Salzburg between, say, Monday, 11 October and Wednesday, 13 October (the post from Vienna usually took three or four days to reach Salzburg), and probably returned the following week, between, say, Monday, 18 October and Wednesday, 20 October. Wolfgang's letter had contained the request that Leopold should send him his keyboard concerto in G and that in D (though it is possible that the only material he wanted for the concerto in D was the cadenzas). The requested material was with Nannerl in St Gilgen, and from the urgency of Leopold's tone to her,[9] it is clear that he thought there was only just time to get it to Wolfgang for the required occasion. Leopold therefore had to write to Nannerl as soon as possible after, say, Wednesday 20 October, and

---

[5] See Leopold to Nannerl, 9 Sept. 1785—*MBA* 876/73–9 (not in *Letters*). The other observations about messengers in this paragraph and the preceding two are gleaned from numerous passages in the correspondence between Leopold and Nannerl from 1784 to 1787.

[6] Leopold to Nannerl, 24 Sept. 1784—*MBA* 810/2–3 (not in *Letters*).

[7] Leopold to Nannerl on the earlier of the dates being discussed—*MBA* 813/2–4 (not in *Letters*).

[8] Leopold to Nannerl, 24 Sept. 1784—*MBA* 810/23–4 (not in *Letters*).

[9] *MBA* 813/5–6 (not in *Letters*).

she had to respond with equal promptness, in order that the G major concerto could be copied in Salzburg and dispatched to Vienna in time. Letter *MBA* 813 is Leopold's attempt to set all this in motion, and is given here—first in German, with the *MBA* line numbers, and then in English.

> Als ich nach Hauß kamm *um 6 uhr*, gieng ich noch in die Comoedie.—die tresel war der Esel und schickte mir den brief von meinem Sohn nicht, der schon den 9ᵗᵉⁿ geschrieben und gleich nach meiner hinausreise ankamm.
>
> 5 Schicke mir also bey der allerersten Gelegenheit das Concert *ex G*, damit es geschwind kann abschreiben lassen.
>
> unterdessen schreibe dir die *Cadenzen zum Concert ex D* selbst ab, und schicke mirs durch den Bothen: du magst nun deine Schrift alsdann behalten, oder deines Bruders, das ist eins.
>
> 10 Herr Haselberger schickte nur 100 f, ließ mir dabey sagen, er hätte vom Syndicat einen anderen Befehl befehl bekommen. ich ließ ihm melden, er möchte es nur an H: Pfleger selbst berichten.
>
> Hier sind die 2 Thaler zurück.
>
> folgt dann auch *die Seifen*, und die *Kerzen. die 7 Th:* des Carl Grandison.
>
> 15 die *4 Th: Schoberths Sonaten. die Phantasien. 6 grosse Limonien* à 5x. anders waren sie nicht zu bekommen. die *Hausenblater à 8 Xʳ.* und *der Spiegl.* H: Pertl wird ihn leimen. Die Hausenblater liegt im Spiegl. Ich danke dem H: Sohn auf das verbindlichste für alle empfangene Höflichkeiten küsse beyde von Herzen und bin der alte redliche Vatter
>
> 20   Mozart
>
> Küsse die Kinder alle! in Eyle.

When I got home *at 6 o'clock*, I still went to the theatre.—tresel was an ass and didn't send me the letter from my son, which was written as long ago as the 9th and arrived just after my journey out. So send me the concerto *in G* at the first possible opportunity, so that I can have it copied quickly.

meanwhile copy the *cadenzas to the concerto in D* for yourself, and send it to me with the carrier: then you can keep your own copy or your brother's, it's all the same.

Herr Haselberger only sent 100 f, and sent me a message with it that he'd received different orders orders from the syndic. I sent him a message that he could just report it to the H: Pfleger himself.

Here are the 2 Thaler back.

then follows *the soap* too, and the *candles. the 7 pts:* of Charles Grandison. *the 4 pts: of Schoberth's sonatas. the fantasies; 6 large lemons* at 5 kr. they were the only ones to be had. the *isinglass at 8 kr.* and *the mirror.* H: Pertl will glue it. The isinglass is in the mirror. A thousand thanks to my son-in-law for all the attentions I received I kiss you both heartily and am the old honest father
Mozart

I kiss all the children! in haste.

The goods Leopold mentioned were of the type he sent regularly with his paid messengers, the carrier and the glass-carrier (and which he would hesitate to send with anyone taking a message to Nannerl from goodwill, because they were burdensome). Since it happened only very seldom that the carrier did not travel in from St Gilgen on a Friday and return on a Saturday, since Leopold hardly ever missed the opportunity of writing to Nannerl with the carrier (even when he had written via the glass-carrier on or around the same date), and since there is no letter explicitly dated Friday 22 October/Saturday 23 October 1784, *MBA* 813 may well be this letter. If so, Leopold's instructions to Nannerl meant that she must if possible find some way of getting the G major concerto in to Salzburg before the following Friday (which would, according to my argument, be 29 October), to leave time for it to be copied. The fact that he seemed happy for the cadenzas to travel in with the carrier (on Friday 29 October) suggests that he knew he could still dispatch all the requested material so as to arrive in Vienna in time.

Proceeding now to letter *MBA* 820, this was almost certainly written on Friday 5 November/Saturday 6 November 1784: from the evidence of the contents it post-dates *MBA* 813 and pre-dates *MBA* 824 (written on Friday, 12 November); it was written in November; and it was sent with the St Gilgen carrier,[10] whose delivery days were Friday into Salzburg and Saturday out. The relevant parts of it are reproduced here—first in German with the *MBA* line numbers, and then in English.

Salzb: den Nov: 1784

Am *donnerstage* der vorigen Woche um halbe 1 uhr, als ich am Mittagessen sass brachte die Tresel die Rolle, das *Concert*, herein und sagte, es hätte solche ein Weibsperson gebracht, — ich schickte nach Tische gleich hinauf um mich
5   erkundigen zu lassen, wenn der Both wieder abgehet: allein die Antwort war, der Both wäre schon den vorigen Tag am Mittwoche gekommen, und wäre heut schon wieder nach 12 uhr mittags weg und hätte diese Rolle zurückgelassen, daß man mir solche überbringen solle. Diese ist also die Ursache warum ich nicht hab schreiben können; denn da die Glastragerin die Stifel
10   brachte, so dacht' ich mit dem Bothen zu schreiben; dieser schickte mir aber das aufgegebne Concert nachdem er schon weg war, und ich von seinem Hierseyn nichts wusste. Nach Wienn habe schon vorhinein auch in euerm Nahmen gratuliert; unterdessen aber auch von ihm ein in 8 Zeilen bestehenden Lamentations Brief erhalten, weil er so lange von mir kein schreiben
15   erhalten, indem |:ganz natürlich:| unter der Zeit, da ich draussen war, ein Brief von ihm vom 9ten schon hier lag. H: von D'Ippold hat einen schönen Annanas, und dann eine Schachtl mit kostbaren Birn geschickt. den Annanas soll ich euch nebst seiner Empfehlung schicken, und ich werde sehen, daß der Both die Birn auch mitnehmen kann. — die Schachtl ist zimmlich schwer:

---

[10] Leopold to Nannerl on the later of the dates in question—*MBA* 820/17–20 (not in *Letters*).

20   muß halt sehen was der Both sagt.

Da alle Tage um 1 uhr bis halbe 3 uhr spazieren gehe, so finde itzt, da zu hause komme deinen Brief und erfahre, daß der Grazer both das Paquet gebracht hat. wäre der Both nur einen Augenblick zu mir gekommen, so würde alle diese Verwirrung nicht gewesen seyn. um halbe 5 uhr wird der
25   Both wieder herkommen, dann muß erst sehen was er mitnehmen kann: denn es sind 2 Hauben in einer Schachtl, die Ohrringl und die Schue auch da.

On *Thursday* of last week at half past twelve, as I was sitting at lunch, Tresel brought in the roll, the *concerto*, and said a woman had brought it,—after the meal I sent up there straight away to find out when the carrier was leaving again: but the answer was, the carrier had already come the previous day on Wednesday, and had gone again already after midday today and left this roll behind for someone to bring round to me. So this is the reason why I couldn't write; because as the glass-carrier had brought the boots, I thought I'd write with the carrier; but he sent me the concerto he'd been given after he'd already gone, and I knew nothing of his presence here. I've already sent congratulations to Vienna in your names too; but meanwhile I've also had an eight-line letter of lamentation from him, because he's received no letter from me for so long, since (quite naturally) all the time that I was out there a letter from him dated the 9th was lying here. H: von D'Ippold has sent a beautiful pineapple, and also a bag containing luscious pears. I've to send you the pineapple with his compliments, and I'll see if the carrier can take the pears with him too. — the bag is quite heavy: just have to see what the carrier says.

Since I go out walking every day at one o' clock till half past two, I've just got your letter on my return home, and have realized that the Graz carrier brought the packet. if the carrier had only spent a moment coming to me all this confusion wouldn't have happened. at half past four the carrier's coming back here, then I'll just have to see what he can take with him: because there are two caps in a bag, the earrings and the shoes as well.

If this letter was indeed written on Friday 5/Saturday 6 November 1784, Leopold's reference to 'Thursday' of last week', with the emphasis on Thursday (*MBA* 820/2), would therefore mean Thursday, 28 October (not, as the *MBA* commentary suggests, Thursday, 4 November). *MBA* 820/2–24 enables the way in which Nannerl had carried out Leopold's instructions with regard to the concerto and cadenzas to be pieced together. On receiving his letter (*MBA* 813), probably on Saturday 23 October, she almost certainly (see below) copied out the cadenzas to the D major concerto and sent them, together with the G major concerto, to Salzburg with the Graz carrier on Wednesday 27 October. The Graz carrier, however, not being in the routine of carrying things regularly for Leopold and

Nannerl, did not deliver the music to Leopold in person, but left it behind for a woman to take to Leopold's house after he himself had left Salzburg again on Thursday, 28 October. Meanwhile, and before Leopold had received the music and learnt that this carrier had been in town, he had had a visit from the glass-carrier (who must presumably have left St Gilgen after the Graz carrier, otherwise Nannerl would have sent the music with her). On this occasion the glass-carrier had been charged with some commission concerning boots, but had not been given a letter to take from Leopold to Nannerl; he had decided to send his letter with the carrier, in accordance with his desire, mentioned above, to give business to each of them. By the time he realized that the carrier had left town without calling on him, the glass-carrier had also gone and so he could send no letter to Nannerl. It is important to note that at this stage (i.e. in *MBA* 820/2–20) Leopold apparently believed that the carrier who had brought the music was the St Gilgen carrier, despite the fact that Wednesday and Thursday were not his usual days. On Friday, 29 October the St Gilgen carrier, if he operated according to his usual routine, would have come into Salzburg again; so it might be asked why Leopold did not realize his error then and write a letter for him to take to Nannerl. This question can be answered by assuming that Nannerl, having sent the music midweek with the Graz carrier and, almost certainly, other goods and/or a letter with the glass-carrier, had nothing left to send to her father or to write to him about on 29 October. (It is this assumption which requires us to believe that she had sent both the concerto and the cadenzas earlier in the week, instead of following Leopold's suggestion (*MBA* 813/7–9) of sending the cadenzas with the (St Gilgen) carrier). The St Gilgen carrier, therefore, did not call on Leopold on 29 October and Leopold, under the mistaken impression that he had missed him for that week, did not send to the Blue Pike to ask him to take anything.

The argument outlined in the preceding paragraph helps explain why Leopold emphasized the word 'Thursday' (*MBA* 820/2) as if it were something unusual (as indeed it would have been as an operational day for the St Gilgen carrier). Only by *MBA* 820/21–4, on receipt of Nannerl's letter (of Friday, 5 November, according to my argument), had he realized that the bearer of the music had been the *Graz* carrier. One result of the confusion was that he was not able to write his usual weekly letter to Nannerl on Friday 29/Saturday 30 October; and this is what he was explaining in *MBA* 820/8–9. *MBA* 813, therefore, can very plausibly be assigned the date Friday 22/Saturday 23 October 1784; no letter was written on Friday 29/Saturday 30 October 1784; and *MBA* 820 was almost certainly written on Friday 5/Saturday 6 November 1784. This hypothesis allows the letters *MBA* 813, the 'would-be' one of 29/30 October, and *MBA* 820 to fit neatly into the usual pattern followed by Leopold of writing each Friday/Saturday to Nannerl with the carrier.

Sometimes the details of the ways in which Leopold and Nannerl communicated after her marriage become relevant to other questions thrown up by the correspondence. One such case is Leopold's letter to Nannerl of 14 January 1786, in which the identity of one of the keyboard concertos is to be established. The scores of two new concertos had arrived in Salzburg from Wolfgang on 1 December 1785, and Leopold started to have them copied for Nannerl.[11] On 4/5 January 1786 he sent her some at least of the material for K. 466,[12] but her keyboard part was not yet figured, and he told her that she could send it back for this purpose after he had sent her the other concerto.[13] No correspondence survives to tell what happened next, but on 14 January Leopold asked Nannerl to return a concerto:

Send me the *concerto in C* the new one from Vienna with all the parts by the glass carrier, together with its cadenzas, I must have it,—I'll send it back again straight away. The new concerto is certainly incredibly difficult. but I doubt if there's something wrong, because the copyist has looked through it. many passages may not sound right if you don't hear the complete instrumental harmony:—but at the same time it's not impossible that the copyist maybe read a ♮ for a ♭ in the score or something of the kind, in which case it certainly won't be right. It will soon be clear when I see it.[14]

My interpretation of this passage is that the concerto mentioned was K. 467, which Leopold had somehow (see below) sent out to Nannerl between 4/5 January and 14 January. Nannerl had tried to play it, but thought it did not sound right, and had suggested that the copyist had made mistakes. Leopold therefore wanted the parts back to check them against the score, though he doubted whether there was anything wrong with them, and suggested that her problems arose partly because of the work's difficulty (by which he may have meant difficulty in comprehension as well as execution) and partly because she had not yet heard all the parts together. Other commentators, however, take different views. The *MBA* commentary identifies the concerto mentioned first (*MBA* 920/21) as K. 467, but the one mentioned second (*MBA* 920/24) as K. 482. The *NMA* editor Heussner suggests that *MBA* 920/21 refers to the earlier C major Concerto, K. 415 (which in its printed form had reached Nannerl in St Gilgen in the autumn of 1785), and *MBA* 920/24 to K. 467.[15] Anderson does not comment on the concerto in *MBA* 920/21, because she does not translate the first part of the passage, and she identifies the concerto in *MBA* 920/24 as K. 467. Her translation, however, is inaccurate; Leopold's German runs:

---

[11] Leopold to Nannerl, 2–3 Dec. 1785—*MBA* 906/9–24 (*Letters* 534).
[12] The identification can be made with confidence from *MBA* 916/69–76 (not in *Letters*), because Leopold referred to the Adagio as a Romance and mentioned the triplets in it.
[13] See Ch. 28, pp. 499–501, for the broader context of this correspondence.
[14] *MBA* 920/21–9; partially rendered in *Letters*, p. 894, n. 4, but with an inaccurate translation which obscures the meaning.
[15] Cf. H. Heussner, *Kritischer Bericht* to *NMA* V/15/6 (Kassel, 1986), f8–f10.

Schicke mir das *Concert ex C* das neue von Wienn mit allen Stimmen durch die glastragerin herein, sammt den Cadenzen dazu, ich muß es haben,—werde es gleich wieder zurük schicken.
Das neue Concert ist freylich erstaunlich schwer. ich zweifle aber ob etwas gefehlt ist, denn der Copist hat es durchgesehen. manche Passagen mögen nicht recht stimmen, wenn man nicht die ganze Harmonie der Instrumenten hört:—doch ists auch nicht unmöglich, daß der Copist etwa ein ♮ für ein ♭ in der Spart angesehen oder so was dergleichen, denn kanns freilich nicht gehen. Es wird sich schon zeigen, wenn ich es sehe.

Anderson's partial translation of the passage is:

Indeed the new concerto is astonishingly difficult. But I very much doubt whether there are any mistakes, as the copyist has checked it. Several passages may not harmonise unless one hears all the instruments playing together. But of course it is quite possible that the copyist may have read a ♯ for ♭ in the score or something of the kind, for if so it cannot be right. I shall get to the bottom of it all when I see the original score.

By inventing the two words 'original score' as a translation of 'es', Anderson obscures the possibility of a connection between the work whose copying Leopold wanted to check and the work he had asked Nannerl to return. Yet the passage suggests that Leopold meant the same concerto throughout—first he asked for it back, and then he said that he would know if it contained copyist's mistakes when he had seen it. The question of this connection is also the main difficulty with the positions of *MBA* and *NMA*—if the same concerto was not meant throughout, what could have been the meaning of Leopold's words 'Es wird sich schon zeigen, wenn ich es sehe'?
The *MBA* commentary's identification of the concerto in *MBA* 920/24 as K. 482 appears to rest merely on the fact that this was the latest concerto to have been composed. But though Wolfgang had entered K. 482 in his thematic catalogue on 16 December 1785,[16] it does not seem to have found its way to Salzburg so soon—on 13 January 1786 Leopold mentioned it to Nannerl as though it was the first he had heard about it.[17] Heussner's rejection of K. 467 as an identification of the concerto in *MBA* 920/21 is founded on the awkwardness of timing—on 2/3 December 1785 Leopold told Nannerl that he was having the concertos K. 466 and K. 467 copied for her, and that he would have the keyboard parts copied first; on 4/5 January 1786 he sent her K. 466; but on 14 January 1786 he asked for all the parts to the new concerto in C to be returned to him, which would have to mean that all its parts had been copied, sent, and commented upon by Nannerl within nine days. Yet it is by no means impossible that K. 467 with all its parts could have reached St Gilgen before 14 January. And though there is no surviving letter of Leopold's mentioning the

[16] *MBA* 910.   [17] *MBA* 918/22–9 (*Letters* 536).

dispatch of K. 467, it may be that one of Nannerl's St Gilgen acquaintances (such as her cousin Pertl) called on Leopold between 4/5 January (when he sent her K. 466) and 14 January (when he asked for the C major concerto), and was given K. 467 to take, but without a letter. There would be nothing inherently surprising about this, since if Pertl called on Leopold unexpectedly there may not have been time for Leopold to write an accompanying letter. Because Nannerl's letters to Leopold have not survived, no acknowledgement by her of the receipt of the concerto can be expected to have come to light; but it could have been contained in a letter to which Leopold was replying in his of 14 January.[18]

[18] *MBA* 887/105–6 offers a case which supports this hypothesis. On this occasion, Leopold had sent Nannerl a concerto with Pertl, and there is no surviving letter in which the dispatch is mentioned. Only (presumably) because Nannerl did not acknowledge receipt of it did Leopold ask her (on 20/2 Oct. 1785) if Pertl had brought it to her—otherwise no information about the matter would have survived. The passage is not in *Letters*.

GLOSSARY

꧁꧂

Akademie (and some variant spellings) common term for concert in 18th-c. Germany

Access, Accessist person with an unpaid post, undertaking it in the hope of obtaining a future paid one, but without any absolute promise of this

Affekt 'affection', emotion, or passion, the arousing of which was widely held in the 17th and early 18th c. to be the chief purpose of music. In his *Violinschule* of 1756, Leopold Mozart made it clear that he subscribed to the belief that a movement (or at least a major and clearly defined part of it) should display a unity of affections; if the composer had written it 'properly', the performer (by studying sensitively the clues offered by mode, time signature, rhythm, tempo, phrasing, dynamics, modulations, and so forth) ought to be able to arouse in his listeners the *Affekt* intended

Amtmann Pfleger's assistant in disciplinary matters; duties included overseeing prisoners

Amtshaus house and offices of **Amtmann**

Anwartschaft 'expectancy'; the unpaid post occupied by an **Access** or **Accessist**

Ausrufpreis the starting price at an auction; the price first called out, and not usually undercut

Auszehr wasting, consumptive disease

Bäsle 'little cousin'; diminutive of *die Base*, a female cousin or aunt

Bestgeber, Bestgeberin (feminine ending) the provider of target, prizes, and sometimes refreshments at a **Bölzlschiessen** contest (see Ch. 16 for a description of **Bölzlschiessen** proceedings)

'Black powders' (*pulvis epilepticus niger*) a fever-reducing preparation, a staple of the Mozarts' medicine chest, and always the first-tried medicine in the early stages of any febrile illness

Bölzlschiessen informal shooting contest among friends, often indoors, using air-guns (see Ch. 16 for a description of the proceedings)

Bogen in music manuscripts circulating among the Mozarts and their acquaintances, a bifolium

Both, Bote see **Gerichtsbote**

Brand literally, 'fire' or 'conflagration'. Used medically of an inflammatory sickness; much dreaded as the often fatal consequence of neglected or intractable fevers

Brandeln (vb) to play a round of a **Brandlspiel**

Brandlspiel name of a card game popular in the Mozarts' circle

Contredanse in origin, an English country dance; a fast dance in duple metre, in which major tonality predominated. Very popular in the late 18th c.; **contredanse** gatherings were organized by the people in the Mozarts' Salzburg circle and probably often took place in the Dancing-Master's House during the Mozarts' tenancy. One such occasion, attended by almost twenty guests, was noted by Nannerl in her diary on 18 Oct. 1783—see Table 1

Conventionsmünze a coin whose value was determined by inter-state agreements about the 'foot' or standard. In 18th-c. Salzburg two main sets of standards affected financial affairs. One was set by Austria in 1750 and was later commonly known as Wiener Währung: according to this, 20 fl. was fixed as the value of coins to be minted from one Mark of fine silver, and the relationship of gold to silver was also laid down. The other was set by Bavaria in 1754 (immediately after Bavaria had abandoned the standard set by Austria), and was later commonly called Reichs Währung: according to this, coins to the value of 24 fl. were minted from one Mark of fine silver. Salzburg adopted the Austrian standard in 1753, but under pressure from Bavaria went over to the Bavarian one in 1755. When the Berchtold Family Chronicle (Brno, MZA, Berchtold Family Archive) described the value of Leopold Mozart's fortune at the time of his death as 'nearly 3000 fl. in *Conventions-münze, Reichs-Währung*', it meant that he left coins whose total value was nearly 3,000 fl. according to the Bavarian standard. And when Mozart insisted on having the 1,000 fl. Johann Baptist Berchtold von Sonnenburg had offered him (in return for Mozart's share of Leopold's estate) paid to him in Wiener Währung rather than Reichs Währung, it meant that he was effectively demanding another 200 fl., since 1,000 fl. in Wiener Währung were the equivalent of 1,200 fl. in Reichs Währung

Edelknaben 'noble boys'; boys from noble families educated at court. They undertook page duties, had their own establishment and tutors, and learned fencing, riding, dancing, and the other accomplishments necessary to nobles

Eingang short introductory flourish or 'lead-in' by the soloist in a concerto movement. Often has an improvisatory quality, and was typically not written out by Mozart unless someone else (e.g., Nannerl) was to play the work. Bars 74–9 in the first movement of Mozart's Keyboard Concerto in C, K. 467, are an example of a keyboard **Eingang**

Erhärtungen im Unterleib 'hardenings in the lower abdomen'; non-specific diagnosis, perhaps involving growths. According to the Berchtold Family Chronicle (Brno, MZA, Berchtold Family Archive), this was what had ailed Leopold Mozart before he finally died from a stroke

Fallsucht literally, 'tendency to fall'; neurological condition where swoons or fits were common. Usually identified with epilepsy

Finalmusik work organized and performed by university students in Salzburg at the end of the academic year in summer, to honour their professors. Local composers were commissioned to write the music. A **Finalmusik** could contain up to eight movements and sometimes included a whole instrumental concerto. It was performed outdoors and partly on the move; hence it began and ended with a march. See Ch. 14, pp. 219–20, for a fuller description of the evening's routine when a **Finalmusik** was being performed

Fischmeister the court official responsible for the supply of fish for the court tables, and for regulating the industry as a whole

Frais, Freys (and other variant spellings) illness involving spasms or cramps; much dreaded because it was often fatal, especially in babies. Though it manifested itself in very different types of condition (for example, Johann Baptist Berchtold von Sonnenburg's second wife died of **Frais** following childbirth, while Nannerl's baby Leopoldl suffered from **Frais** when he was ill with something like thrush), it seems to have been considered a sufficient, self-contained diagnosis

Fraiskette a chain or necklace hung with charms to ward off **Frais**. Pagan objects were used as well as Christian ones

Frieselfieber (hitziges) 'heated miliary fever'; the diagnosis of Mozart's final illness, as given by the death register of St Stephen's Cathedral in Vienna. There has been much debate about the nature of this illness

Friessl-Ausschlag the rash or 'outbreak' of **Frieselfieber**. In the Berchtold Family Chronicle (Brno, MZA, Berchtold Family Archive), the cause of Mozart's death was recorded as **Friessl-Ausschlag** rather than as **Frieselfieber**

Galanterie a piece of music in *galant* style; that is, elegant, light, and 'pleasing' (though detractors of the style would term it superficial). Mozart used the term to Nannerl during a period when she was practising the more learned aspects of keyboard playing, such as improvisation, figured bass, and other skills associated with accompaniment at sight; he urged her not to neglect her *galanterie* playing in her zeal for 'score-bashing'

General-Einnehmer superior and highly responsible court position in one of the several finance departments. Franz Anton von Amann, the father of Basil von Amann, was **General-Einnehmer** at the time of his death and Basil's disgrace

Gerichtsbote messenger employed to deliver documents and packages from a Pfleger to the court, and vice versa. Took private commissions as well. Leopold Mozart called him the **Both**; translated in this book as 'carrier'

Gerichtsdiener see **Amtmann**

Gliedersucht 'limb or joint sickness'; the cause of death of Nannerl's stepson Wolfgang Berchtold von Sonnenburg. The boy was ill with painful, swollen joints for weeks before his death

Gymnasium academic school for boys, in which Latin and Greek formed part of the curriculum

Harmonie wind band

Harmoniemusik music written for a wind band

Hitziges Frieselfieber see **Frieselfieber**

Hofkriegsrat court war councillor

Hofrat court councillor. The designation *Rat* was a title for occasional duties rather than a full-time post; Nannerl's husband Johann Baptist Berchtold von Sonnenburg, for example, was a Salzburg Hofrat as well as Pfleger of St Gilgen

Hoftafel 'court table'; dining rights of court employees, much prized as a special perk not offered to most

Kämmerer treasurer

Kammerportier valet or other servant with menial duties; even during Mozart's time in Salzburg, some musicians still had **Kammerportier** duties

Kanzlei chancellery

Kapellhaus choir school, where boys were trained for the cathedral choir

Kapellmeister head of a court musical establishment

Konzertmeister court musician required to lead in concerts. Usually a violinist, though Mozart occupied the post as a keyboard player from Jan. 1779 until he left Salzburg in 1781. The **Konzertmeister** was expected to be able to play concertos, and to have a deportment which would do the court honour

Krachse (also **Kragse, Kraxe**, and other variant forms) backpack used by the **Gerichtsbote** or carrier, and anyone else walking long distances with goods to sell. Mozart's keyboard music often travelled in one between Salzburg and St Gilgen

Land see **Salzburg Land**

Landschaft one class or element in the political structure of Salzburg; it possessed revenue-raising powers and was linked to other aspects of the political structure by a complicated network of duties and privileges

Licitations-Protocoll document showing details of goods sold at auction

Masked 'redoubt' masked ball, especially popular during Carnival

Mehlhund infant ailment, apparently akin to thrush. In Nannerl's baby Leopoldl it began as a white coating in the mouth, spread to his genital area, and was followed by **Frais**; he nearly died

Milzverstoppung congestion or blockage of the spleen; the ailment, according to Leopold Mozart's report to Theobald Marchand, from which Leopold was suffering immediately before his death. It is possible that *Milz* then comprised more than simply the organ today called the spleen

Mitterschreiber middle-ranking clerk

Morgengabe gift from husband to wife after the wedding night, if the bride proved to have been a virgin. Nannerl Mozart received a **Morgengabe** from her husband of 500 fl.

Oberbereiter senior court official closely concerned with the stables and riding school. Eleonore von Weyrother, whose dramatic collapse and death was described by Leopold Mozart, was the wife of the Oberbereiter Gottlieb von Weyrother

Oberschreiber senior clerk; a post often occupied directly before promotion to a position such as **Pfleger**

Obersthofmeister one of the most senior court posts; the man (a high-ranking noble) with overall responsibility for the running of the archbishop's domestic arrangements. In Salzburg, the musicians were directly under his jurisdiction

Oberstkämmerer chief treasurer; another very senior post

Oberstlandmarschall literally 'Senior Province Marshal'—high-ranking court title held by a member of the top nobility

Obristjägermeister the man with overall responsibility for the court hunting department

Pfleg administrative area under the supervision of one man, who might have the assistance of several clerks if the workload was heavy. Hallein was the busiest **Pfleg** in Salzburg **Land**—it was the centre of the salt industry, and its **Pfleger** had sixteen assistants, including many clerks

Pflegeamtsmitverwalter co-administrator of a **Pfleg**

Pfleger literally, 'carer' or 'tender'; the man responsible for the smooth running of a **Pfleg**. Duties encompassed tax collection, administration of justice in simple cases, and reporting all the **Pfleg**'s business regularly to the central authorities in Salzburg

Pfleggericht that element of a **Pfleg** which dealt with the administration of justice

Pflegsverwalter administrator of a **Pfleg**; the term was sometimes used instead of **Pfleger**

Primogenitur-Majorat a foundation for the benefit of the first-born son. Sometimes a Secundogenitur-Majorat was also set up for the second-born son

Primiz the first Mass celebrated by a newly ordained priest

Pulvis epilepticus niger see '**black powders**'

'**Redoubt**' ball, sometimes masked; one of the most glittering attractions of Carnival

Residenz the palace or 'residence' of the archbishop (or other ruler)

Salzburg Land the state of Salzburg, as distinct from the city (see Map 2)

Schatulle the archbishop's privy purse, expenditure from which did not have to be justified to anyone

Schatullegelder money from the **Schatulle**

Schreiber clerk

Sedisvacanz interregnum; period between the death of one archbishop and the election of the next. The Chapter ruled the archbishopric during such a period

Seege fishing net of specified and regulated dimensions; the right to set up a **Seege** carried an entitlement to fish for a specified quota and the duty to pay a specified fish tax

Singspiel musico-dramatic work with a German text in which spoken dialogue alternates with the musical numbers. The characters are usually less exalted than those in serious opera. Mozart's *Die Entführung aus dem Serail* and *The Magic Flute* are famous examples of the genre

Sperr-Commission the commission set up to investigate the estates of deceased people

Sperr-Commissarius an official working for a **Sperr-Commission**

Sperre literally, 'bar'; a process whereby the estate of a deceased person was frozen while the **Sperr-Commission** investigated the assets and liabilities. Only after any outstanding debts and taxes had been paid, and satisfactory provision made for children of minor years, was the estate released to the family

Sperr-relation document produced by the **Sperr-Commission** as soon as possible after death. It detailed such things as the cause of death, the age of the deceased, the whereabouts of any will, and the beneficiaries. It was also accompanied by an inventory of all the deceased's assets and personal belongings

Stickfrais a variation of **Frais**; 'suffocating spasms'

Stubenmädl chambermaid

Tarock name of a card game popular in the Mozarts' circle

Tresette name of a card game popular in the Mozarts' circle

Turnergesellen watchman's assistants; duties included blowing musical signals on trombones at set times from the tower of the Town Hall. The men usually played other instruments too, and were leased out to play at country weddings and on other occasions requiring their musical services. In addition they played the trombone for the court whenever necessary

Turnermeister the chief watchman, appointed by the city council rather than by the court; however, he was usually also a court violinist

Untermensch serving maid in the humblest category

Versatzamt official court pawnbroking service, designed to assist the poor through the low interest rates

Verwalter 'administrator'; often the director of an institution such as a hospital

Vorhaus entrance hall of a house

Wilder Adel minor aristocracy

BIBLIOGRAPHY

MANUSCRIPTS

Austria, Salzburg, Landesarchiv (SLA)

Domkapitel Protokoll (Sedisvacanz), 27 Feb. 1753, fos. 636–7: judgement on a dispute involving Leopold Mozart.

Hochfürstlichen Salzburgischen Kirchen- und Hofkalender, Historische Bibliothek, B00192.

Verlassakt Nr. 1.713/1801/17, Johann Baptist von Sonnenburg: Marriage Contract relating to his marriage to Nannerl Mozart.

Verlassakt Stadtgericht Salzburg Nr. 1.713/1822, Johann Baptist von Sonnenburg: Will of Johann Baptist von Berchtold zu Sonnenburg; Inventory of Wolfgang Berchtold von Sonnenburg; Guardianship Report of 22 Jan. 1805; document dated 21 Mar. 1808 concerning the allowance paid from the estate of Johann Baptist von Berchtold zu Sonnenburg to his widow Nannerl.

Austria, Salzburg, Erzbischöfliches Konsistorialarchiv

St Blasius, death register 1, p. 117: records the death of Jeanette von Berchtold zu Sonnenburg.

The Czech Republic, Brno, Moravský Zemský Archiv (*Moravian Provincial Archives*, MZA)

Rodinný archiv Berchtoldů (Berchtold Family Archive): Family Chronicle; Inventory of Maria Margarethe von Berchtold, née Polis; *Licitations-Protocoll* relating to Leopold Mozart; Will and Inventory of Johann Baptist von Berchtold zu Sonnenburg; Inventory of Jeanette von Berchtold zu Sonnenburg; Pension Document relating to Nannerl von Berchtold zu Sonnenburg (née Mozart).

PUBLISHED WORKS

ANGERMÜLLER, R., 'Das Diploma Baronatus für die Gebrüder Johann Baptist und Johann Nepomuk Martin Berchtold zu Sonnenburg aus dem Jahre 1792', *MM* 19 (1971), 13–24.

—— 'Nissens Kollektaneen für seine Mozartbiographie', *MJb* (1971–2), 217–26.

—— 'Der Tanzmeistersaal in Mozarts Wohnhaus, Salzburg, Makartplatz 8', *MM* 29 (1981), 1–13.

ANGERMÜLLER, R. (with W. Hess), *'Auf Ehre und Credit': die Finanzen des W. A. Mozart*, catalogue of exhibition promoted by the Internationale Stiftung Mozarteum in Salzburg, the Staatliche Münzsammlung in Munich, and the Bayerische Vereinsbank in Munich (Munich, 1983).

—— 'Testament, Kodizill, Nachtrag und Sperrelation der Freifrau Maria Anna von Berchtold zu Sonnenburg, geb. Mozart (1751–1829)', *MJb* (1986), 97–132.

—— 'Friedrich Schlichtegrolls Nekrolog auf Ignaz von Born, *MM* 35 (1987), 42–55.

—— 'Ein ungedruckter Brief Constanze Mozarts an ihren Schwiegervater Leopold', *MM* 39 (1991), 45–6.

—— 'Leopold Mozarts Verlassenschaft', *MM* 41 (1993), 1–32.

—— '"Können Sie denn noch ein paar Zimmer anbauen lassen?": Zur Geschichte des Mozart-Wohnhauses', *MM* 44 (1996), 1–83.

—— and KASERER, H. P., 'St Gilgen und die Mozarts', *MM* 32 (1984), 1–15.

—— and RAMSAUER, G., '"du wirst, wenn uns Gott gesund zurückkommen läst, schöne Sachen sehen": Veduten aus dem Nachlass Leopold Mozarts in der Graphiksammlung des Salzburger Museums Carolino Augusteum', *MM* 42 (1994), 1–48.

ARTHUR, J., 'N. N. Revisited', *MT*, Early Music Issue (Sept., 1995), 475–80.

BACH, C. P. E., *Versuch über die wahre Art das Clavier zu Spielen* (Berlin, 1753–62); English trans. W. J. Mitchell as *Essay on the True Art of Playing Keyboard Instruments* (London, 1949, 2nd edn. 1951). Cited from the 2nd English edn.

BÄR, C., *Mozart: Krankheit, Tod, Begräbnis* (Salzburg, 1972).

—— 'Er war...kein guter Wirth. Eine Studie über Mozarts Verhältnis zum Geld', *AM* 25 (1978), 30–53.

BARTELT, J., 'Anhänger und Amulette in Volksglauben und Volksmedizin', *MGSL* 100 (1960), 569–77.

BARTH, G., 'Die Hagenauers. Ein Salzburger Bürgergeschlecht aus Ainring: Die Einbindung einer Handelsfamilie in Wirtschaft, Politik und Kultur Salzburgs im späten 17. und 18. Jahrhundert', in *Ainring: Ein Heimatbuch* (Ainring, 1990).

BAUER, G. G., 'Bölzschiessen, Brandeln und Tresette: Anmerkungen zum spielenden Menschen Mozart', *MM* 39 (1991), 21–40.

BAUMOL, W. J. and H., 'On the Economics of Musical Composition in Mozart's Vienna', in J. M. Morris (ed.), *On Mozart* (Cambridge, 1994), 72–101.

BEALES, D., *Joseph II*, vol. i: *In the Shadow of Maria Theresa* (Cambridge, 1987).

BIRSAK, K., 'Salzburg, Mozart und die Klarinette', *MM* 33 (1985), 40–7.

BLANNING, T. C. W., *Joseph II and Enlightened Despotism* (London, 1970).

BRANSCOMBE, P., *W. A. Mozart: Die Zauberflöte*, Cambridge Opera Handbooks (Cambridge, 1991).

BRAUNBEHRENS, V., *Mozart in Vienna 1781–1791*, trans. T. Bell (New York, 1990).

BRAUNEIS, W., '"...wegen schuldigen 1435 32 xr": Neuer Archivfund zur Finanzmisere Mozarts im November 1791', *MM* 39 (1991), 159–63.

BRÄUNER, V. and HAMERNÍKOVÁ, A., *Inventáře a Katalogy Fondů Státního Archivu v Brně č. 24: Rodinný Archiv Berchtoldů (1202–1494–1945) Inventář* (Brno, 1967).

BREITINGER, F., 'Mozart Nannerls unglücklicher Verehrer', *Salzburger Volksblatt* (9–10 Aug. 1958), 5.

BURNEY, C., *Music, Men and Manners in France and Italy 1770*, ed. H. Edmund Poole (London, 1969).

CARLSON, D. M., 'The Vocal Music of Leopold Mozart (1719–1787): Authenticity, Chronology and Thematic Catalogue' (Ph. D. diss., University of Michigan, 1976).

CARTWRIGHT, F. F., *A Social History of Medicine* (London, 1977).

COOPER CLARKE, B., 'Albert von Mölk: Mozart Myth-Maker?', *MJb* (1995), 155–91.

CROLL, G., and VÖSSING, K., *Johann Michael Haydn: sein Leben, sein Schaffen, seine Zeit* (Salzburg, 1987).

CUVAY, M., 'Beiträge zur Lebensgeschichte des Salzburger Hofkapellmeisters Johann Ernst Eberlin', *MGSL* 95 (1955), 179–88.

DAHMS, S., 'Das musikalische Repertoire des Salzburger fürsterzbischöflichen Hoftheaters (1775–1803)', *ÖMz* 31 (1976), 340–55.

DALCHOW, J., *Drei Rezepte für Nannerl Mozart* (Berlin, 1952).

—— 'Leopold Mozarts Haus- und Reiseapotheke', *AM* 25 (1955), 3–6.

DEUTSCH, O. E., 'Aus Schiedenhofens Tagebuch', *MJb* (1957), 15–24.

—— and PAUMGARTNER, B. (eds.), *Leopold Mozarts Briefe an seine Tochter* (Salzburg/Leipzig, 1936).

DOPSCH, H., and SPATZENEGGER, H. (eds.), *Geschichte Salzburgs: Stadt und Land* (8 vols.), vol. ii, pt. 1 (Salzburg, 1988).

EDGE, D., 'Mozart's Fee for *Così fan tutte*', *JRMA* 116/2 (1991), 211–35.

—— Review Article of M. S. Morrow, *Concert Life in Haydn's Vienna*, *The Haydn Yearbook*, 17 (1992), 108–66.

Eibl, J. H., 'Der "Herr Sohn"', *MM* 14 (1966), 1–9.

—— 'Zur Familiengeschichte der Berchtold zu Sonnenburg und der Amann', *MM* 19 (1971), 12–17.

—— *Wolfgang Amadeus Mozart: Chronik eines Lebens* (2nd paperback edn., Kassel, 1977).

—— 'Zur Überlieferungsgeschichte der Bäsle-Briefe', *MM* 27 (1979), 9–17.

EINSTEIN, A., *Mozart: His Character, his Work*, Eng. trans. A. Mendel and N. Broder (New York, 1945; London, 1946/paperback edn. 1971); cited from the 1971 edn.

EISEN, C., 'The Symphonies of Leopold Mozart and their Relationship to the Early Symphonies of Wolfgang Amadeus Mozart: A Bibliographical and Stylistic Study' (Ph. D. diss., Cornell University, 1986).

—— 'Leopold Mozart Discoveries', *MM* 35 (1987), 1–10.

—— 'The Symphonies of Leopold Mozart: Their Chronology, Style and Importance for the Study of Mozart's Early Symphonies', *MJb* (1987–8), 181–93.

—— 'Problems of Authenticity Among Mozart's Early Symphonies: The Examples of K. Anh. 220 (16a) and 76 (42a)', *Music and Letters*, 70 (1989), 505–16.

EISEN, C., 'Salzburg under Church Rule', in N. Zaslaw (ed.), *The Classical Era: From the 1740s to the end of the 18th Century* (Basingstoke, 1989), 166–87.

—— 'The Mozarts' Salzburg Copyists: Aspects of Attribution, Chronology, Text, Style, and Performance Practice', in C. Eisen (ed.), *Mozart Studies* (Oxford, 1991), 253–307.

—— 'Mozart's Salzburg Orchestras', *Early Music* (Feb. 1992), 89–103.

—— 'The Scoring of the Orchestral Bass Part in Mozart's Salzburg Keyboard Concertos: The Evidence of the Authentic Copies', in N. Zaslaw (ed.), *Mozart's Piano Concertos: Text, Context, Interpretation* (Ann Arbor, Mich.: University of Michigan Press, 1996), 411–25.

ELEONORA MARIA ROSALIA, Duchess of Troppau and Jägerndorf, *Freywillig aufgesprungener Granat-Apffel des Christlichen Samariters* (Leipzig, 1709).

ELVERS, R., 'Breitkopf und Härtels Verlagsarchiv', *Fontes Artis Musicae*, 17 (1970), 24–8.

FALK, S. and WEISS, A. S., '"Hier sind die Blattern": Der Kampf von Staat und Kirche für die Durchsetzung der (Kinder-) Schutzpockenimpfung in Stadt und Land Salzburg (Ende des 18. Jahrhunderts bis ca. 1820)', *MGSL* 131 (1991), 163–86.

FUHRMANN, R., '"Frieselfieber und Aderlass" im Spiegel der medizinischen Literatur zur Zeit Mozarts', *MM* 37 (1989), 83–136.

GÄRTNER, H., *Mozarts Requiem und die Geschäfte der Constanze Mozart* (Munich, 1986): English trans. R. G. Pauly as *Constanze Mozart: After the Requiem* (Portland, Ore., 1991).

GOETHE, J. W., *Italienische Reise*, ed. H. von Einem (Munich, 1985); English trans.: *Italian Journey*, trans. and ed. W. H. Auden and E. Mayer (Harmondsworth, 1970).

GOLDINGER, W., 'Archivalisch-genealogische Notizen zum Mozartjahr', *NAMB* (Augsburg, 1962), 77–96.

GRUBER, G., *Mozart and Posterity*, trans. from the German by R. S. Furness (London, 1991).

HAMERNÍKOVÁ, A., '"Licitations-Protocoll über die Leopold Mozartische Verlassenschaft" im Familienarchiv Berchtold', *MJb* 1991 (*Bericht über den Internationalen Mozart-Kongress 1991*), vol. i, 122–5.

HAMMERMAYER, L., 'Die Aufklärung in Salzburg (ca. 1715–1803)', in H. Dopsch and H. Spatzenegger (eds.), *Geschichte Salzburgs: Stadt und Land*, vol. ii, pt. 1 (Salzburg, 1988), 375–452.

HEARTZ, D., 'Mozart, his Father and *Idomeneo*', *MT* 119 (1978), 228–31.

HEIM, M., *Bischof und Archidiakon: Geistliche Kompetenzen im Bistum Chiemsee (1215–1817)* (St Ottilien, 1992).

HESS, W., 'Münzsorten und Geldsysteme zu Mozarts Zeiten' in R. Angermüller and W. Hess, *'Auf Ehre und Credit': Die Finanzen des W. A. Mozart*, catalogue of exhibition promoted in 1983 by the Internationale Stiftung Mozarteum in Salzburg, the Staatliche Münzsammlung in Munich, and the Bayerische Vereinsbank in Munich (Munich, 1983).

HEUSSNER, H. (ed.), *NMA Kritischer Bericht* V/15/6 (Kassel, 1986).

HILDESHEIMER, W., *Mozart* (Frankfurt am Main, 1977; English trans. M. Faber, London, 1985).

HINTERMAIER, E., 'Die Salzburger Hofkapelle von 1700 bis 1806. Organisation und Personal' (Ph.D. diss., University of Salzburg, 1972).

——— 'Das fürsterzbischöfliche Hoftheater zu Salzburg (1775–1803)', *ÖMz* 30 (1975), 351–63.

HITZIG, W., 'Die Briefe Franz Xaver Niemetscheks und der Marianne Mozart an Breitkopf und Härtel', *Der Bär* (1928), 101–16.

HUMMEL, W., *Nannerl. Wolfgang Amadeus Mozarts Schwester* (Zurich, 1952).

——— *W. A. Mozarts Söhne* (Kassel, 1956).

——— 'Tagebuchblätter von Nannerl und Wolfgang Mozart', *MJb* (1957), 207–11.

——— *Nannerl Mozarts Tagebuchblätter, mit Eintragungen ihres Bruders Wolfgang Amadeus* (Salzburg, 1958).

——— 'Nannerl Mozarts Tagebuchblätter: Neue Funde—Neue Fragen', *MM* 7 (1958), 7–9.

HUTTER, E., 'Abwehrzauber und Gottvertrauen. Kleinodien Salzburger Volksfrömmigkeit', *Jahresschriften Salzburger Museum Carolino Augusteum*, 31 (Salzburg, 1985), 198–359.

JAHN, O., *W. A. Mozart*, 4 vols. (Leipzig, 1856, 2nd edn. 1867); English trans. P. D. Townsend, as *Life of Mozart*, 3 vols. (London, 1891).

KARMI, G., 'The Colonization of Traditional Arabic Medicine', in R. Porter (ed.), *Patients and Practitioners: Lay Perceptions of Medicine in Pre-Industrial Society* (Cambridge, 1985).

KEYSSLER, J. G., *Neueste Reisen durch Teutschland, Böhmen, Ungarn, die Schweiz, Italien und Lothringen*, 3 vols. (Hanover, 1751; 2nd edn. by G. Schütze, 1752).

KLEIN, H., 'Ein unbekanntes Gesuch Leopold Mozarts von 1759', *Neues MJb* (1943), 95–101.

——— 'Unbekannte Mozartiana von 1766–67', *MJb* (1957), 168–85.

——— 'Zur Herkunft Franz Armand d'Ippolds', *MM* 7 (1958), 2–3.

——— 'Nachrichten zum Musikleben Salzburgs in den Jahren 1764–1766', *Festschrift Alfred Orel zum 70. Geburtstag 1959* (Vienna, 1960), 93–101.

——— 'Salzburg zur Zeit Mozarts', *MJb* (1964), 55–61.

——— 'Autobiographisches und Musikalisches aus dem Jugendtagebuch des späteren Abtes P. Dominikus Hagenauer', *ÖMz* (Sonderheft) (1967), 22–30.

KÖHLER, K.-H., 'Die Erwerbungen der Mozart-Autographe der Berliner Staatsbibliothek—ein Beitrag zur Geschichte des Nachlasses', *MJb* (1962–3), 55–67.

KRAEMER, U., 'Wer hat Mozart verhungern lassen?', *Musica*, 30 (1976), 203–11.

Landon, H. C. Robbins, *1791—Mozart's Last Year* (London, 1988).

——— *Mozart: The Golden Years* (London, 1989).

——— *Mozart and Vienna* (London, 1991).

LEESON, D. N., and WHITWELL, D., 'Mozart's Thematic Catalogue', *MT* 114 (Aug. 1973), 781–3.

LEWICKI, R., 'Aus Nissens Kollektaneen', *MM* 2 (1919), 28–30.

LUDEWIG, R. 'Zum derzeitigen Stand der Forschung über die Ursachen des Todes von Mozart', *MJb* (1991) (*Bericht über den Internationalen Mozart-Kongress 1991*) vol. i. 132–44.

McMANNERS, J., *Death and the Enlightenment: Changing Attitudes to Death among Christians and Unbelievers in Eighteenth-Century France* (Oxford, 1981; paperback edn. 1985).

McVEIGH, S., *Concert Life in London from Mozart to Haydn* (Cambridge, 1993).

MANČAL, J., 'Vom "Orden der geflickten hosen": Leopold Mozarts Heirat und Bürgerrecht', in Mozartgemeinde Augsburg (ed.), *Leopold Mozart und Augsburg* (Augsburg, 1987), 31–54.

—— 'Leopold Mozart (1719–1787): Zum 200. Todestag eines Augsburgers', in W. Baer (ed.), *Leopold Mozart zum 200. Todestag* (Augsburg exhibition catalogue, 1987), 1–23.

—— '". . . durch beyhülff hoher Recommandation": Neues zu Leopold Mozarts beruflichem Anfang', in J. Mančal and W. Plath (eds.), *Leopold Mozart: Auf dem Weg zu einem Verständnis*, Beiträge zur Leopold-Mozart-Forschung I (Augsburg, 1994), 157–69.

MARTIN, F., 'Die Salzburger Chronik des Felix Adauktus Haslberger', pt. 2, *MGSL* 68 (1928), 51–68.

—— 'Die Salzburger Chronik des Felix Adauktus Haslberger', pt. 3, *MGSL* 69 (1929), 97–119.

—— 'Die Salzburger Chronik des Felix Adauktus Haslberger (Nachtrag)', *MGSL* 74 (1934), 159–68.

—— 'Vom Salzburger Fürstenhof um die Mitte des 18. Jahrhunderts', *MGSL* 77 (1937), 1–48.

—— 'Vom Salzburger Fürstenhof um die Mitte des 18. Jahrhunderts', *MGSL* 80 (1940), 145–204.

—— 'Beiträge zur Salzburger Familiengeschichte', *MGSL* 82 (1942), 70–2.

MASSIN, J. and B., *Wolfgang Amadeus Mozart* (Paris, 1959).

MAUNDER, R., *Mozart's Requiem: On Preparing a New Edition* (Oxford, 1988).

MOORE, J., 'Mozart in the Market-Place', *JRMA* 114 (1989), 18–42.

MORRIS, J. M. (ed.), *On Mozart* (Cambridge, 1994).

MORROW, M. S., *Concert Life in Haydn's Vienna: Aspects of a Developing Musical and Social Institution* (New York, 1988).

MOŸ, J. Graf von, 'Die Hintergründe der Fürstungen im Salzburger Domkapitel: ein Beitrag zur Verfassungsgeschichte des Erzstiftes im 18. Jahrhundert', *MGSL* 119 (1979), 231–59.

MOZART, F. X. W., *Reisetagebuch 1819–1821*, ed. R. Angermüller (Bad Honnef, 1994).

MOZART, L., *Versuch einer gründlichen Violinschule* (Augsburg, 1756). For an edn. with introduction and commentary, cf. that by H. R. Jung (Wiesbaden, 1983).

English trans.: E. Knocker, as *A Treatise on the Fundamental Principles of Violin Playing* (Oxford, 1948, 2nd edn. 1951).

[MOZART, L.], 'Nachricht von dem gegenwärtigen Zustande der Musik Sr. Hochfürstl. Gnaden des Erzbischoffs zu Salzburg im Jahr 1757', in F. W. Marpurg (ed.), *Historisch-Kritische Beyträge zur Aufnahme der Musik* (Berlin, 1757), iii. 183–98. The report is translated into English and included as Appendix C in N. Zaslaw, *Mozart's Symphonies: Context, Performance Practice, Reception* (Oxford, 1989), 550–7.

[MOZART, W. A.], *Mozart: Eigenhändiges Werkverzeichnis Faksimile* (British Library Stefan Zweig MS 63). Einführung und Übertragung von A. Rosenthal und A. Tyson; Lizenzausgabe mit Genehmigung der British Library. Serie X Supplement to *NMA* (Kassel, 1991).

NIEMETSCHEK, F. X., *Leben des k. k. Kapellmeisters Wolfgang Gottlieb Mozart nach Originalquellen beschrieben* (Prague, 1798, enlarged 2nd edn. 1808). English trans. (*Life of Mozart*) H. Mautner, with an introduction by A. H. King (London, 1956).

NISSEN, G. N. von, *Biographie W. A. Mozarts* (Leipzig, 1828); cited here from the unaltered reprint by Georg Olms Verlag (Hildesheim, 1991).

NOTTEBOHM, G., *Mozartiana* (Leipzig, 1880; repr. 1972).

NOVELLO, V. and M., *A Mozart Pilgrimage: Being the Travel Diaries of Vincent and Mary Novello in the Year 1829*, ed. N. Medici di Marignano and R. Hughes (London, 1955 and 1975; here cited from the 1975 edn.).

OREL, A., 'Zu Mozarts Sommerreise nach Wien im Jahre 1773', *MJb* (1951), 34–49.

PETROBELLI, P., 'La cultura di Leopold Mozart e la sua "Violinschule"', *MJb* (1989–90), 9–16.

PIRCKMAYER, F., 'Basil von Amann: Ein Kulturbild aus der letzten Zeit des geistlichen Kleinstaates', *MGSL* 48 (1908), 45–59.

PLATH, W., 'Beiträge zur Mozart-Autographie I. Die Handschrift Leopold Mozarts', *MJb* (1960–1), 82–117.

—— 'Zur Echtheitsfrage bei Mozart', *MJb* (1971–2), 19–36.

—— 'Beiträge zur Mozart-Autographie II: Schriftchronologie 1770–1780', *MJb* (1976–7), 131–73.

—— 'Leopold Mozart und Nannerl: Lehrer und Schülerin', in W. Plath, *Mozart-Schriften: Ausgewählte Aufsätze*, ed. M. Danckwardt (Schriftenreihe der Internationalen Stiftung Mozarteum Salzburg, 9; Kassel etc., 1991), 375–8.

PORTER, R., 'The Patient's View: Doing Medical History from Below', *Theory and Society*, 14/2 (Mar. 1985), 175–98.

—— (ed.), *Patients and Practitioners: Lay Perceptions of Medicine in Pre-Industrial Society* (Cambridge, 1985).

RAINER, W., 'Anton Cajetan Adlgasser: Ein biographischer Beitrag zur Musikgeschichte Salzburgs um die Mitte des 18. Jahrhunderts', *MGSL* 105 (1965), 205–37.

RIEGER, E., *Nannerl Mozart: Leben einer Künstlerin im 18. Jahrhundert* (Frankfurt am Main, 2nd edn. 1991).

SADIE, S., *The New Grove Mozart* (London, 1980).

SALZMANN, U., 'Der Salzburger Erzbischof Siegmund Christoph Graf von Schrattenbach (1753–1771) und sein Domkapitel', *MGSL* 124 (1984), 9–240.

SCHENK, E., *Mozart: Eine Biographie* (Vienna, 1955; 2nd edn. 1975; citations from Goldmann Sachbuch paperback edn., no place or date).

SCHLICHTEGROLL, F., 'Johannes Chrysostomus Wolfgang Gottlieb Mozart', *Nekrolog auf das Jahr 1791* (Gotha, 1793); ed. L. Landshoff (Munich, 1924) as *Mozarts Leben* (Graz, 1794; repr. ed. J. H. Eibl, Kassel, 1974).

SCHMID, E. F., 'Der Mozartfreund Joseph Bullinger', *MJb* (1952), 17–23.

SCHMID, M. H., *Die Musiksammlung der Erzabtei St. Peter in Salzburg. Katalog. Erster Teil. Leopold und Wolfgang Amadeus Mozart. Joseph und Michael Haydn. Mit einer Einführung in die Geschichte der Sammlung* (Schriftenreihe der Internationalen Stiftung Mozarteum 3/4; Salzburg, 1970).

—— *Mozart und die Salzburger Tradition* (Tutzing, 1976).

—— 'Nannerl Mozart und ihr musikalischer Nachlass: Zu den Klavierkonzerten im Archiv St. Peter in Salzburg', *MJb* (1980–3), 140–7.

—— 'Zu den Klaviersonaten von Leopold Mozart', *MJb* (1989–90), 23–30.

—— 'Musikalien des Mozartschen Familienarchivs im Stift St. Peter', in P. Eder and G. Walterskirchen (eds.), *Das Benediktinerstift St. Peter in Salzburg zur Zeit Mozarts* (Salzburg, 1991), 173–85.

—— 'Zur Mitwirkung des Solisten am Orchester-Tutti bei Mozarts Konzerten', *Basler Jahrbuch für Historische Musikpraxis*, 17 (1993), 89–112.

SCHULER, H., 'Mozarts Grossvater Pertl in St. Gilgen', *MM* 23 (1975), 27–36.

—— 'Nannerl Mozarts Stiefkinder', *AM* 23 (1976), 30–5.

—— 'Dr. med. Franz Joseph Niderl, Hausarzt der Familie Mozart: ein Beitrag zu seiner Familiengeschichte', *MM* 26 (1978), 4–11.

—— 'Die Hochzeit der Eltern Mozarts. Eine Quellenstudie', *AM* 28 (1981), 3–11.

—— 'Mozart und Mailand: Archivalisch-genealogische Notizen zu den Mailänder Mozartbriefen, zugleich ein Beitrag zur Trogerforschung', *Genealogisches Jahrbuch*, 22 (Neustadt a. d. Aisch, 1982), 7–119.

—— 'Mozart und das hochgräfliche Haus Lodron: eine genealogische Quellenstudie', *MM* 31 (1983), 1–17.

—— 'Die Herren und Grafen von Arco und ihre Beziehungen zu den Mozarts: Anmerkungen zu Mozart-Briefen', *MM* 32 (1984), 19–34.

—— 'Zur Dedikationsträgerin von Mozarts "Lützow-Konzert" KV 246', *MM* 33 (1985), 1–10.

—— '"Nun kömt eine merkwürdige Reise!": Mozarts herbstliche Rhein-Fahrt des Jahres 1763 in zeitgenössischen Schilderungen', *MM* 42 (1994), 49–77.

SCHUMANN, K., 'Ein Genie der Rechtschaffenheit: Leopold Mozarts Weg durch das 18. Jahrhundert', in W. Baer (ed.), *Leopold Mozart zum 200. Todestag* (Augsburg exhibition catalogue, 1987), 1–13.

SCHURIG, A., *Wolfgang Amadeus Mozart: sein Leben, seine Persönlichkeit, sein Werk*, 2 vols. (Leipzig, 1913; 2nd edn. 1923).

—— *Konstanze Mozart: Briefe, Aufzeichnungen, Dokumente 1782–1842* (Dresden, 1922).

SENN, W., 'Zur Erbteilung nach Leopold Mozart', *Zeitschrift des historischen Vereins für Schwaben*, also known as *NAMB* 62/3 (1962), 383–95.

—— 'Die Mozart-Überlieferung im Stift Heilig Kreuz zu Augsburg', *NAMB* 333–68.

—— 'Das Vermächtnis der Brüder Mozart an "Dommusikverein und Mozarteum" in Salzburg', *MJb* (1967), 52–61.

SOLOMON, M., 'The Rochlitz Anecdotes: Issues of Authenticity in Early Mozart Biography', in C. Eisen (ed.), *Mozart Studies* (Oxford, 1991), 1–59.

—— *Mozart: A Life* (London, 1995).

STAFFORD, W., *Mozart's Death: A Corrective Survey of the Legends* (London, 1991).

STEEGMULLER, F., *A Woman, a Man, and Two Kingdoms: The Story of Madame d'Épinay and the Abbé Galiani* (London, 1992).

STEPTOE, A., 'Mozart and Poverty: A Re-Examination of the Evidence', *MT* 125 (1984), 196–201.

—— *The Mozart–Da Ponte Operas* (Oxford, 1988).

TYSON, A., 'Mozart's Truthfulness', *MT* 119 (1978), 938–9.

—— *Mozart: Studies of the Autograph Scores* (Cambridge, Mass., 1987).

—— 'Proposed New Dates for Many Works and Fragments Written by Mozart from March 1781 to December 1791', in C. Eisen (ed.), *Mozart Studies* (Oxford, 1991), 213–26.

VALENTIN, E., 'Das Testament der Constanze Mozart-Nissen. Mit biographischen Notizen über Constanze und Georg Nikolaus Nissen', *Neues MJb*, 2 (1942), 128–75.

VOLEK, T., and BITTNER, I., *The Mozartiana of Czech and Moravian Archives* (Prague: Archives Department of the Czech Ministry of the Interior, 1991).

WAGNER, H., 'Das Salzburger Reisetagebuch des Grafen Karl von Zinzendorf vom 31. März bis zum 6. April 1764', *MGSL* 102 (1962), 167–90.

—— 'Die Aufklärung im Erzstift Salzburg', in *Salzburg und Österreich: Aufsätze und Vorträge von Hans Wagner* (ed. *MGSL* as *Festschrift für Hans Wagner zum 60. Geburtstag*), (Salzburg 1982), 99–115.

WANDRUSZKA, A., *Österreich und Italien im 18. Jahrhundert* (Vienna, 1963).

WOLFF, C., *Mozart's Requiem: Historical and Analytical Studies, Documents, Score*, trans. M. Whittall (Oxford, 1994).

H. Z. (initials only given), 'Mozarts Mutter, Gattin und Freunde als Gasteiner Kurgäste', in *Bad Gasteiner Badeblatt*, 16/22, 15 July 1956.

ZASLAW, N. (ed.), *The Classical Era: from the 1740s to the end of the 18th century* (Basingstoke, 1989).

ZASLAW, N. *Mozart's Symphonies: Context, Performance Practice, Reception* (Oxford, 1989).

—— 'Mozart as a Working Stiff', in J. M. Morris (ed.), *On Mozart* (Cambridge, 1994), 102–12.

—— (ed.), *Mozart's Piano Concertos: Text, Context, Interpretation* (Ann Arbor, Mich.: University of Michigan Press, 1996).

ZILLER, L., *300 Jahre Schule St. Gilgen: Geschichte einer Salzburger Dorfschule* (St. Gilgen, 1965).

——*Vom Fischerdorf zum Fremdenverkehrsort: Geschichte St. Gilgens und des Aberseelandes* (3 vols., St Gilgen, 1988–90).

INDEX

❧❧

677

Blue Pike inn, Linzergasse 651, 652, 657; *see also* Map 1
burial practice 629–30
cathedral: disposition of musical forces 275, 277–8, *see also* Fig. 4 and Plate 5; miscellaneous references 12, 17, 220, 258, 275, 299–300, 313, 315, 339, 469, 504, 529, *see also* Table 1 *and* Map 1
cathedral Dean and Chapter 12, 14, 16–17, 166, 173–4, 177–8, 208, 442
church festivals 21–2, 339, 403, 406, 515–16
communication channels with St Gilgen, *see reciprocal entry under* St Gilgen
court: advantages and disadvantages of service 14, 46, 302, 313–14, 316, 326, 330, 341, 519–20; calendars 21–2, 214; career progressions (including emoluments and duties) xxix, 16–17, 38, 41, 72–3, 92–3, 109–11, 143, 164–70 *passim*, 177–9, 186, 191–2, 213–14, 215–27 *passim*, 257–9, 275, 278, 282, 288, 298–302 *passim*, 312–17 *passim*, 326–7, 333, 354–64 *passim*, 365–6, 384, 427–8, 435, 450, 498–9, 502–5, 512, 513–14, 519–20, 525, 534, 537–8, 582; castrati (*qua* castrati) 110, 259, 405 n. 60, for individual castrati, *see* Michelangelo Bologna *and* Francesco Ceccarelli; celebrations on feast days 21–2, 119, 141, 185, 203, 217–18, 511; composition of 12–15, 203; discontentment within band xxix, 73, 93, 109–15, 129–31, 133–4, 144, 164–70 *passim*, 178–9, 191–2, 194–7, 206–9, 211–14 *passim*, 215–27 *passim*, 248, 256–9 *passim*, 269, 275, 277, 288, 298–302, 315–17, 321–4, 328, 329–32, 337–8, 340–1, 347–9, 352–64 *passim*, 384, 386–8, 427–8, 467, 483, 498–9, 502–5, 512, 513–14, 519–20, 525, 537–8, 624–5; *Edelknaben* 15, 203, 662 (Glossary); Election Day (*Wahltag*) 14, 27, 185, 508, 511, 513 n. 26, 538; expressions of displeasure with employees (includes employees' fears of sanctions) 14, 120, 129–30, 133–6 *passim*, 225–6, 255–6, 257, 277, 299, 360, 362, 363, 386–7, 400–1, 483, 502–3, 525, 532, 624–5; favouritism towards Italians 73, 178–9, 222, 223–4, 259, 504, 513–14; *Hoftafel* 664 (Glossary), *see also* [Salzburg Court]: career progressions (including emoluments and duties); intrusions into employees' private lives (includes their fears of such intrusion) 14, 145–6,

183–5, 255–6, 299, 348 n. 32, 359, 504, 525; lack of consistent employment principles for musicians xxix, 41, 73, 109–14, 164–70 *passim*, 178–9, 221–6 *passim*, 259, 333, 384, 513–14; leave for musicians (probably salaried unless otherwise indicated) xxi, 46, 72–3, 110–11, 114, 119, 120, 127, 129–30, 133–6 *passim*, 143, 148, 149, 166, 168, 173–4, 181–2, 194, 223–6, 340–1, 343, 347–9, 468, 478, 481–2, 483, 503, 525, 534–5; music library 605, 609–11 *passim*; musicians' routines 21–2, 338, 354–6 *passim*; pensions 7–8, 14, 17, 83, 168, 169, 179, 279, 286, 437, 498, 531–2, 616; salaries, *see* [Salzburg Court]: career progressions (including emoluments and duties); *Schatulle* 46 nn. 1 and 3, 73, 110, 111, 120 n. 9, 143, 167, 168, 665 (Glossary); *Sedisvacanz* situations 16–17, 166, 173–4, 665 (Glossary); social position of musicians 15, 16, 17, 119, 250, 253–4, 297–8, 337, 342, 347, 354–6, 437, 503, 519–20; staffing problems 250, 256–8, 275–9, 288–9, 298–302, 312–16, 351–64 *passim*, 427–8, 467, 474, 482, 497–9, 502–5, 513–14, 525, 529, 530–1, 534, 537–8; *Wahltag, see under* [Salzburg Court]: Election Day
Dancing-Master's House (Mozart family home from 1773–1787) xix, 12, 93, 190, 202–3, 213, 220, 224, 251, 252, 273, 297, 330, 340, 352 n. 5, 378, 380, 402–5 *passim*, 432, 433, 465, 473 n. 6, 480, 481, 485, 536, 541, 548, 552, 555, 572, 632, 643 (Appendix 1); *see also* Map 1 *and* Plates 6 and 7
Dommusikverein und Mozarteum 635–40 *passim*
Eizenberger inn, *see* Table 1
Enlightenment 70, 215, 447, 452, 617–18
Erzbischöfliches Konsistorialarchiv (St Blasius' death register) 618 n. 25
Finalmusik 662–3 (Glossary); *see also under* [Salzburg]: music-making not primarily connected with court
fortress (Mönchsberg) 12, 278, 525; *see also* Map 1
Gnigl 296–7, 453; *see also* Table 1 *and* Map 3
Greater Marian Congregation 544 n. 64
Hagenauer house and shop (Mozart family home from 1747–1773, and birthplace of Nannerl and Wolfgang Mozart) 12, 107–9, 202; *see also* Map 1